An Ong Reader
Challenges for Further Inquiry

Walter J. Ong
Saint Louis University

edited by

Thomas J. Farrell
University of Minnesota
at Duluth

Paul A. Soukup
Santa Clara University

HAMPTON PRESS, INC.
CRESSKILL, NEW JERSEY

Printed in the United States of America.

Library of Congress Cataloging-in-Publication Data

Ong, Walter J.
   [Selections. 2002]
   An Ong reader : challenges for further inquiry / Walter J. Ong ; edited by Thomas J. Farrell and Paul A. Soukup.
      p. cm. -- (The Hampton Press communication series. Media ecology)
Includes bibliographical references and index.
ISBN 1-57273-444-2 -- ISBN 1-57273-445-0
   1. Communication. 2. Philology. I. Farrell, Thomas J. II. Soukup, Paul A. III. Title. IV. Series.

P90 .O532 2002
302.2--dc21

Hampton Press, Inc.
23 Broadway
Cresskill, NJ   07626

This book is to be returned on
or before the date stamped below

The Hampton Press Communication Series
Media Ecology

Lance Strate, supervisory editor

Online Connections: Internet Interpersonal Relationships
Sue Barnes

Walter Ong's Contribution to Cultural Studies:
The Phenomenology of the Word and I-Thou Communication
Thomas J. Farrell

The Power of Metaphor in the Age of Electronic Media
Raymond Gozzi, Jr.

An Ong Reader: Challenges for Further Inquiry
Walter J. Ong
Thomas J. Farrell and Paul A. Soukup, editors

No Safety in Numbers: How the Computer Quantified Everything
and Made People Risk Aversive
Henry J. Perkinson

forthcoming

The Technology of Song
Robert Albrecht

Bookends: The Changing Media Environment
of the American Classroom
Margaret Cassidy

Constructing the Heartland: Television and Natural Disaster News
Katherine Fry

Understanding Media Ecology
Lance Strate

Walter J. Ong, S.J.

Contents

Foreword

Lance Strate

Walter Jackson Ong, S.J., is a consummate scholar, a scholar's scholar. Anyone undertaking an inventory of the diverse fields and disciplines to which he has contributed would have to include rhetoric, communication, education, media studies, English, literary criticism, classics, biblical studies, theology, philosophy, psychology, anthropology, cultural studies, history, medieval studies, Renaissance studies, American studies, gender studies, biology, and computer science. The list could be extended indefinitely, but however long we make it, it would not do justice to the totality of Ong's learning. It would perhaps be better simply to say that he is an expert in the liberal arts in their entirety. To be still more precise, Walter Ong is a master of noetics, of knowledge and our ways of knowing. Whereas contemporary academics seek the confines of ever more specialized niches from which to claim expertise, Dr. Ong is a free-ranging polymath whose expertise encompasses expertise itself.

Walter Ong is arguably one of the most significant intellectuals of the twentieth century. Of course, judgment regarding his place in intellectual history can only be authoritatively rendered when we are well into this new millennium, only a few months old as of this writing. No doubt, it will take a twenty-first-century mind, a mind born and educated in this new century, to appreciate in full his scholarly accomplishments. Contemporary intellectuals certainly acknowledge and respect Ong's contributions, and incorporate his insights into their own work. Still, at present, he might best be characterized as quietly influential, his ideas subject to gradual but steady diffusion within the scholarly community. Novitiates in Ongian noetics can be found with increasing frequency across the intellectual landscape, suggesting that we are moving towards a critical mass in appreciation of his work.

Walter Ong's writings are especially appreciated in the emerging discipline of media ecology, the study of media environments, and it is altogether fitting that this collection is published in a book series devoted to the media ecology perspective. As the supervisory editor of this series, I am doubly honored to be able to see this book through to publication, and to have been asked to write this foreword. Ong is rightly considered one of media ecology's foundational scholars. Put another way, *media ecology* is a term used to refer to the kind of perspective associated with Ong, his former teacher Marshall McLuhan, and orality-literacy scholars such as Eric Havelock, Dorothy Lee, and Jack Goody. Media ecology also incorporates the work of language-oriented critics such as Susanne Langer and Neil Postman, technology theorists such as Lewis Mumford and Jacques Ellul, and media researchers such as Harold Innis, Joshua Meyrowitz, and Jay David Bolter. Media ecology is not a term that Ong himself has used until recent years, it should be noted, although lately he has been using it more and more. More importantly, however, he has had much to say about the many modes of communication that human beings employ, which are also the means and methods through which we gain knowledge. Ong's own brand of noetic ecology suggests that our ways of knowing about the world have much to do with the kind of world that we find ourselves living in.

Ong has established with great rigor and clarity how differences in our methods of communication make a difference, psychologically, socially, and culturally. He has studied the dialectics between numerous polarities, such as the acoustic and the visual, orality and literacy, memory and the written record, tradition and documentation, alphabetic and nonalphabetic writing systems, chirography and typography, rhetoric and Romanticism, as well as the electronic media and all previous means of communication. Above all, he has been concerned with the word as the fundamental form of human communication, and the foundation of human knowledge. Three of his book titles make specific reference to "the word": *Presence of the Word*, *Interfaces of the Word*, and *Orality and Literacy: The Technologizing of the Word*. To Ong, the study of the word is the most essential form of humanistic study, for it is the word that makes us human; it is language that defines and distinguishes our species.

Ong and many of his fellow media ecology scholars have argued that the ongoing technologizing of the word has been one of the most fundamental sources of social and psychological change in human history. As we have moved from sole reliance on the spoken word to subsequent additions of the written word, the printed word, and the electronically recorded and transmitted word, we have done more than transform our modes of communication—we have altered our forms of culture and consciousness as well. Whereas some media ecology scholars have presented this process as a series of dramatic upheavals, Ong shows us that media revolutions are often the product of a more gradual evolution. His measured and precise analysis of media environments reveal them to be true ecologies, systems that seek homeostasis and stability. They can be undermined and destabilized by the sudden introduction of a new medium, of course, but they can also adapt and modify themselves by integrating new technologies into the system. For example, what Ong refers to as residual orality represents a form of continuity between the original world of primary orality and newer media environments marked by literacy.

Ong focuses on four main types (one might even say archetypes) of media environment, the oral, chirographic, typographic, and electronic, and on the kinds of cultures that emerge within them. We today are products of several layers of media-cultural metamorphoses, and therefore extremely distanced from the original human condition of primary orality, of speech without writing, printing, or electronic gadgetry. Consequently, it is extraordinarily difficult for us to imagine the oral mindset, the ways of knowing that prevailed over tens of thousands of years, the vast majority of human existence. Ong has the unique ability to explain that lifeworld that we find so alien, to convey not only the logos of our predecessors' thought and procedures, nor merely the pathos that they experience and express, but also the ethos of their lives and relationships. One of Ong's greatest gifts is his empathy, which he shares through his writing, thereby helping us to know the world as it was known in other times, within other cultures, and through other media environments.

In this way, Ong provides us with a baseline from which we can survey the subsequent mutations of media environment, culture, and mindset. Simply put, as speech makes us human, writing sets the stage for civilization as it has traditionally been understood, that is, for the type of culture first associated with the early cities of Egypt, Mesopotamia, India, and China (to this day, the words literate and urbane are synonymous). Alphabetic writing in particular is associated with the two ancient legs on which Western culture stands: Hebraic culture with its emphasis on monotheism, history, and law; and Hellenic culture with its innovations in democracy, philosophy, and rhetoric. The written word reorders our senses by appealing to vision rather than hearing, changes our sense of time by making permanent what once was ephemeral, and distances and objectifies the word that otherwise could only exist through immediate human presence. And as Ong puts it in *Orality and Literacy*, "writing restructures consciousness" (78), giving rise to a literate mindset characterized by highly abstract and analytical thinking, introspection and objectivity, and ultimately, explosive, accelerating growth in accumulated knowledge.

Printing, in turn, lays the groundwork for modernity, and the electronic media have moved us into our present postmodern condition. Ong can be understood as a postmodernist himself, in that he posits a major break with modernity occurring over the course of the twentieth century. Unlike others who are more typically associated with postmodernism, Ong has a theory that explains the postmodern as a product of a changing media environment, one characterized by secondary orality, the electronically amplified and reproduced word. And unlike so many other postmodernists, poststructuralists, and cultural theorists, Ong does not fall victim to obscurantism, mystification, and "critspeak." Rather, he exemplifies the Jesuit ideal of *eloquentia perfecta*, of communicating in a lucid, accessible, and aesthetically pleasing manner. And his writing reflects the Jesuit order's firm commitment to education—his scholarship is marked not only by great learning, but also by great teaching. Ong's writing has a pedagogical flavor, not pedantic, but rather enlightening as are lectures delivered by a master teacher. He writes not just to increase our knowledge, but also to impart in us new ways of looking at the world, and to open up new territories for scholarly exploration, the latter being especially true of the pieces collected in this volume.

Perhaps a word about religion would be appropriate at this juncture. Walter Ong is a Roman Catholic priest and a member of the Jesuit order, more properly known as the Society of Jesus (hence Walter Ong, S.J.). He has produced books on religion, such as *Frontiers in American Catholicism, American Catholic Crossroads,* and *Darwin's Vision and Christian Perspectives.* His literary analysis, *Hopkins, the Self, and God,* is devoted to the Jesuit poet Gerard Manley Hopkins. And explicitly Christian references can be found in many of his other works. Ong speaks from a position that is centered in his faith, and because I speak from a position centered in a different faith, Judaism, I can attest that you do not have to be Catholic to appreciate Ong's writings. Nor does his faith affect the validity of his scholarship from a purely secular perspective.

I also speak with some understanding of Ong's order, having spent twelve years (as of this writing) on the faculty at Fordham University, one of the twenty-eight Jesuit colleges and universities in the United States. The Jesuits possess an admirable devotion to humanistic scholarship, liberal education, and the life of the mind. I would therefore like to take a page from Thomas Cahill, and characterize Ong as one of the "gifts of the Jesuits." That is to say that his mission is not exclusive to his order, his Church, or Christianity. Although he does address concerns specific to these institutions in some instances, for the most part he speaks to humanity as a whole, as a fellow human being, about what it means to be human.

Ong's own ethical and spiritual center belies the charge of technological determinism sometimes leveled against media ecology scholars.
From Ong's point of view, individuals always have alternatives and must
take personal responsibility for the choices that they make. This is consistent with the philosophy of personalism that Ong is identified with (as
is Martin Buber). It is a philosophy of the human person, which makes it
a philosophy of human relationships, and human relationships in turn
form our social and cultural environments, our symbolic and technological environments, our human and media ecologies.

My own relationship to Ong has been largely that of reader to writer.
I therefore write this foreword to *An Ong Reader* as an Ong reader
myself. I began reading Ong as a graduate student in 1979 and found the
experience to be enormously rewarding—since then, I have tried to be an
Ong reader as often as is humanly possible. I would go so far as to say
that no writer has had a greater impact on my own development as a
scholar than Professor Ong. *Orality and Literacy*, Ong's most widely
known book, has been a source of great inspiration and excitement; a
milestone in communication and cultural studies, as well as media ecology scholarship, it firmly establishes orality-literacy studies as a field in its
own right, and suggests innumerable opportunities for further study. It
also is an excellent follow up to *The Presence of the Word*, which many
consider to be his finest book, providing us with his most comprehensive
comparison of the media environments dominated by primary orality,
writing, printing, and the electronic media.

There is also much to be said for Ong's more specialized book-length
studies, *Fighting for Life*, an examination of masculinity; *Hopkins, the
Self, and God*, a literary psychoanalysis; and his Harvard University doctoral dissertation on the sixteenth-century scholastic Peter Ramus, published as *Ramus, Method, and the Decay of Dialogue*. The latter is an
excellent model of research in cultural history that should be required
reading for anyone undertaking serious study in media ecology or cultural studies. Numerous articles focusing on various aspects of communication, consciousness, and culture were published by Ong in four collections: *The Barbarian Within*; *In the Human Grain*; *Rhetoric, Romance,
and Technology*; and *Interfaces of the Word*. Also of interest in this
respect is the anthology he edited and contributed to (with a chapter by
Marshall McLuhan), *Knowledge and the Future of Man* (complete references for all works cited in this foreword can be found in the Works Cited
section at the end of Farrell's introduction).

What is truly extraordinary about this present volume, *An Ong Reader:
Challenges for Further Inquiry*, is that it represents the great range of Ong's

scholarship, bringing together publications that span fifty-seven years. As such, it represents a remarkable collection of Walter Ong's work, from his early research on Hopkins and Ramus, to his most recent articles on computer-mediated communication, which have yet to receive wide distribution. Among the twenty-eight selections are many of Ong's best known essays, such as "The Jinnee in the Well-Wrought Urn," "Oral Residue in Tudor Prose Style," "The Writer's Audience is Always a Fiction," and "Literacy and Orality in Our Times." Also included in its entirety is *Why Talk?*, an interview with Ong originally published as a pamphlet.

Scholars throughout the liberal arts owe a great debt of gratitude to the editors of this book, Thomas J. Farrell and Paul A. Soukup. Farrell, an associate professor in the Department of Composition at the University of Minnesota at Duluth, is the author of the first comprehensive analysis of Ong's work, *Walter Ong's Contribution to Cultural Studies: The Phenomenology of the Word and I-Thou Communication*, which was also published through Hampton Press' Media Ecology Series. Soukup, an associate professor in the Department of Communication at Santa Clara University and recently a visiting professor at the Gregorian University in Rome, is one of Ong's fellow Jesuits. Together, Farrell and Soukup have also edited four volumes of Ong's more religious work under the title of *Faith and Contexts*, and in collaboration with Bruce E. Gronbeck they have co-edited an anthology of essays about Ong's work, *Media, Consciousness, and Culture: Explorations of Walter Ong's Thought*. Farrell and Soukup have labored long and hard to deliver *An Ong Reader*, and it is with pride and appreciation that I include it in the Media Ecology Series.

I am confident that their anthology will prove satisfying to many different types of Ong readers. For those new to Ong, the range of selections and their accessibility will serve as a superb introduction to Ong's body of work. Those already familiar with Ong's major publications such as *Orality and Literacy* and *The Presence of the Word* will find much in here to supplement and enrich their understanding, and direct their future reading. And even the Ong expert may find a few surprises here, and will no doubt delight in the collection itself. Those who teach Ong will appreciate the representative character of Farrell and Soukup's selections, and their heuristic value. And students and scholars alike will find here a model for excellence in scholarship, and a wealth of possibilities for further research. Ong readers of any background will truly find in Farrell and Soukup's collection a call to arms to pursue further inquiry, a challenge to undertake an intellectual quest, a summons to scholarship.

Acknowledgments

Walter J. Ong and the editors gratefully acknowledge permission to reprint the selections in the present collection.

Chapter 1, Ong's review of *The Interior Landscape: The Literary Criticism of Marshall McLuhan, 1943-1962*, was originally published in *Criticism: A Quarterly for Literature and the Arts* 12 (1970): 244-51. Reprinted by permission of Wayne State University Press.

Chapter 2, "An Interview with Walter J. Ong Conducted by George Riemer," is reprinted from *The New Jesuits*, ed. George Riemer (Boston: Little, Brown, 1971: 147-86). Copyright ©1971 by George Riemer. By permission of Little, Brown and Company, Inc.

Chapter 3, "Hopkins' Sprung Rhythm and the Life of English Poetry," was originally published in the collection edited by Norman Weyand, *Immortal Diamond: Studies in Gerard Manley Hopkins* (New York: Sheed & Ward, 1949: 93-174). Reprinted with the permission of Sheed & Ward.

Chapter 4, "The Province of Rhetoric and Poetic," was originally published in the *Modern Schoolman* 19.2 (1942): 24-27. Reprinted with the permission of the *Modern Schoolman*.

Chapter 5, "Historical Backgrounds of Elizabethan and Jacobean Punctuation Theory," was originally published in *PMLA: Publications of the Modern Language Association of America* 59 (1944): 349-60. Reprinted by permission of the Modern Language Association of America from *PMLA*. Copyright ©1944.

Chapter 6, "The Jinnee in the Well-Wrought Urn," was originally published in *Essays in Criticism* (Oxford) 4 (1954): 309-20. Reprinted by permission of Oxford University Press.

Chapter 7, "Ramus: Rhetoric and the Pre-Newtonian Mind," is reprinted from *English Institute Essays 1952*, ed. Alan S. Downer (New York: Columbia UP, 1954: 138-70). ©1954 Columbia University Press. Reprinted by permission of the publisher.

Chapter 8, "Ramus and the Transit to the Modern Mind," was originally published in the *Modern Schoolman* 32.4 (1955): 301-11. Reprinted with the permission of the *Modern Schoolman*.

Chapter 9, "Metaphor and the Twinned Vision: *The Phoenix and the Turtle*," was first published in the *Sewanee Review*, vol. 63, no. 2, Spring 1955: 193-201. Copyright 1955 by the University of the South. Reprinted with the permission of the editor.

Chapter 10, "Grammar in the Twentieth Century," was originally published with a slightly different title in *Problems of Communication in a Pluralistic Society*, ed. Reynolds C. Seitz (Milwaukee: Marquette UP, 1956: 23-40). Reprinted by permission of Marquette University Press.

Chapter 11, "Voice as a Summons for Belief: Literature, Faith, and the Divided Self," was originally published in *Thought: A Review of Culture and Idea* 33 (1958): 43-61. Reprinted with permission of Fordham University Press.

Chapter 12, "The Barbarian Within: Outsiders Inside Society Today," is reprinted from *The Barbarian Within: And Other Fugitive Essays and Studies* by Walter J. Ong, S.J. (New York: Macmillan, 1962: 260-85). Copyright ©1954, 1955, 1956, 1958, 1960, 1961, 1962 by Macmillan Publishing Company, copyright renewed 1982, 1983 by Walter J. Ong. Reprinted with the permission of Scribner, a Division of Simon & Schuster, Inc.

Chapter 13, Ong's review of Albert B. Lord's *The Singer of Tales*, was originally published in *Criticism: A Quarterly for Literature and the Arts* 4 (1961-1962): 74-78. Reprinted by permission of Wayne State University Press.

Chapter 14, Ong's review of Marshall McLuhan's *The Gutenberg Galaxy*, was originally published in *America* 107 (1962): 743, 747. Reprinted with permission of America Press, Inc. Copyright ©1962. All rights reserved.

Chapter 15, Ong's review of Eric A. Havelock's *Preface to Plato*, was originally published in *Manuscripta* 8 (1964): 179-81. Reprinted with the permission of *Manuscripta*.

Chapter 16, "Oral Residue in Tudor Prose Style," was originally published in *PMLA: Publications of the Modern Language Association of America* 80 (1965): 145-54. Reprinted by permission of the Modern Language Association of America from *PMLA*. Copyright ©1965.

Chapter 17, "Written Transmission of Literature," was originally published with the title "Literature, Written Transmission of" in *The New Catholic Encyclopedia*, ed. William J. McDonald (New York: McGraw-Hill, 1967: Vol. 8, 833-38). Copyright © 1967 by The Catholic University of America, Washington, D.C. Reprinted by permission of the Gale Group, www.galegroup.com.

Chapter 18, Ong's preface to Hugo Rahner's *Man at Play*, was originally published in the English translation of Rahner's *Man at Play* (Trans. Brian Battershaw and Edward Quinn; New York: Herder & Herder, 1967: ix-xiv). Reprinted by permission of the author.

Chapter 19, Ong's review of Brian Vickers' *Classical Rhetoric in English Poetry*, was originally published in *College English* 33 (1971-1972): 612-16. Reprinted with the permission of the National Council of Teachers of English.

Chapter 20, Ong's review of Wilbur Samuel Howell's *Eighteenth Century British Logic and Rhetoric*, was originally published in *William and Mary Quarterly* 29 (1972): 637-43. Reprinted by the permission of the Omohundro Institute of Early American History and Culture.

Chapter 21, "Why Talk? A Conversation about Language with Walter J. Ong Conducted by Wayne Altree," was originally published in the National Humanities Faculty Why Series as a short paperback book entitled *Why Talk? A Conversation about Language with Walter J. Ong Conducted by Wayne Altree* (San Francisco: Chandler & Sharp, 1973: 1-40). Reprinted with the permission of The National Faculty.

Chapter 22, "The Writer's Audience Is Always a Fiction," was originally published in *PMLA: Publications of the Modern Language Association of America* 90 (1975): 9-21. Reprinted by permission of the Modern Language Association from *PMLA*. Copyright ©1975.

Chapter 23, "Typographic Rhapsody: Ravisius Textor, Zwinger, and Shakespeare," was originally published with a slightly different title in *Classical Influences on European Culture, A.D. 1500-1700*, ed. Robert R. Bolgar (Cambridge, UK: Cambridge UP, 1976: 91-126). Reprinted with the permission of Cambridge University Press.

Chapter 24, "Literacy and Orality in Our Times," was originally published in the *ADE Bulletin*, Serial No. 58 (1978): 1-7. [ADE = Association of Departments of English, part of the Modern Language Association of America.] Reprinted by permission of the Modern Language Association of America from the *Ade Bulletin*. Copyright ©1978.

Chapter 25, "The Agonistic Base of Scientifically Abstract Thought: Issues in *Fighting for Life: Contest, Sexuality, and Consciousness*," was originally published in the *Proceedings of the American Catholic Philosophical Association* 56 (1982): 109-124. Reprinted with permission of the American Catholic Philosophical Association.

Chapter 26, "Technological Development and Writer-Subject-Reader Immediacies," was originally published in *Oral and Written*

Communication: Historical Approaches, ed. Richard Leo Enos (Newbury Park, CA: Sage, 1990: 206-15). Copyright ©1990 by Sage Publications. Reprinted by permission of Sage Publications.

Chapter 27, "Information and/or Communication: Interactions," was originally published in *Communication Research Trends* 16.3 (1996): 3-17. Reprinted with permission of the Centre for the Study of Communication and Culture.

Chapter 28, "Digitization Ancient and Modern: Beginnings of Writing and Today's Computers," was originally published in *Communication Research Trends* 18.2 (1998): 3-21. Reprinted with permission of the Centre for the Study of Communication and Culture.

The editors have standardized the documentation system so that parenthetical citations are incorporated in the text, with complete bibliographic information in the Works Cited at the end of the selection. We have usually incorporated discussion notes in the text. Shorter notes have been incorporated parenthetically; longer ones, either as additional sentences or as a new paragraph, depending on their length. Occasionally, translations of Latin passages have been supplied parenthetically by Paul A. Soukup, S.J., and Alfred G. Playoust, S.J. The editors have not altered generic masculine terms when they have appeared in the earlier essays reprinted in the present collection, because altering them would require extensive rewriting of sentences.

For the institutional support that our home universities have provided us while we were working on the present collection, we thank the University of Minnesota at Duluth and Santa Clara University and Michelle Wangler at Santa Clara. We are grateful to Lance Strate, supervisory editor of the Media Ecology Series, and to Barbara Bernstein, president of Hampton Press, for their interest in and commitment to publishing this collection. Finally, we wish to thank Walter J. Ong, S.J., for writing the selections reprinted in this collection and so many other well-informed, incisive works. In the foreword to this collection, Lance Strate has taken a page from Thomas Cahill and referred to Walter Ong as one of the gifts of the Jesuits. We can only hope that the gifts that Ong has given the scholarly world are not only understood, admired, and celebrated by others, but also put to work and advanced further by others. Northrop Frye has described Walter Ong as a seminal thinker. Because the term "seminal" refers to seeds, we hope that the seeds of his thought bear further fruit.

Thomas J. Farrell
University of Minnesota, Duluth
Paul A. Soukup, S.J.
Santa Clara University

Introduction: Walter J. Ong's Work and Western Culture

Thomas J. Farrell

An Ong Reader: Challenges for Further Inquiry is needed because Walter J. Ong's deeply original thought still invites further and further examination and greater follow up. In many ways Ong has been ahead of his time. As a result, his many-faceted work still holds great potential for further development by other scholars. In my book *Walter Ong's Contributions to Cultural Studies: The Phenomenology of the Word and I-Thou Communication*, I have suggested that his many-faceted work has implications for literary, communication, religious, and cultural studies (2).

But far be it from me to try to capture here the interest of certain readers by enumerating more specific studies in which Ong's work might have further impact—as graduate faculty members might suggest possible topics for dissertations to graduate students. Beyond saying that his many-faceted thought holds implications for further development in literary, communication, religious, and cultural studies, I would prefer not to try to delimit here the possibilities of further studies. To be sure, I will from time to time point out certain broad possibilities, but my suggestions are not as sharply focused as topics for a dissertation should be. In sum, I see Ong's work as a rich resource that could still be fruitfully mined and put to further use by other scholars. Despite thousands of citations of individual works by Ong, however, only a relatively few studies could be characterized as distinctively Ongian in their use and extension of his thought.

In *Orality and Literacy: The Technologizing of the Word* (18-28, 58-61), which is Ong's most widely known book, he has highlighted the approach to studying oral tradition that Milman Parry and Albert B. Lord

1

pioneered. Parry was a classicist at Harvard University who undertook field studies of Yugoslavian singers of tales in the 1930s. Lord was a graduate student who worked with Parry and later wrote his doctoral dissertation on the findings of their field studies. Lord's revised dissertation was subsequently published in 1960 as *The Singer of Tales*, a landmark study. Parry and Lord identified certain compositional patterns as formulas and formulaic elements. In addition, Lord identified a compositional pattern that involved a certain theme and an expected way to develop the set theme (e.g., the arming of the hero).

In *Oral-Formulaic Theory and Research: An Introduction and Annotated Bibliography*, John Miles Foley has provided annotations of some 1,800 books and articles involving ninety different language areas. The Parry/Lord approach has been a fruitful line of inquiry; no doubt it will continue to be. Since 1986, Foley has edited the journal *Oral Tradition*, and in 1998 the Modern Language Association published a 500-page collection of essays that he edited on *Teaching Oral Tradition*. Even if we give Ong a certain amount of credit for calling attention to the work of Parry and Lord, and for calling attention more generally to oral tradition, we should allow that the line of inquiry that they pioneered would probably have been carried forward by scholars even if Ong had not called attention to it.

However, we should also note that Ong himself has appropriated certain points from Parry and Lord, and extended those points in distinctively Ongian directions. In my estimate the distinctively Ongian directions could still be developed further by scholars in a great variety of fields of study—for example, by classicists, by medievalists, by Renaissance specialists. In the new *Encyclopedia of Rhetoric*, however, Gregory Nagy has surveyed the Parry/Lord approach to studying oral tradition, but without even mentioning Ong's appropriations and extensions of their approach for the purposes of studying commonplaces in the Western rhetorical and literary tradition (see Ong's *The Presence of the Word: Some Prolegomena for Cultural and Religious History* [see the index and esp. 79-87], *Rhetoric Romance, and Technology: Studies in the Interaction of Expression and Culture* [see the index], and *Interfaces of the Word: Studies in the Evolution of Consciousness and Culture* [see the index and esp. 147-88]).

One point of *An Ong Reader: Challenges for Further Inquiry* is to show that his work in literary and communication studies can be seen as in effect a manifesto calling on others to carry forward certain orientations through further research studies of their own. The task of developing the great potential of Ong's hermeneutic of orality is enormous. But this task has recently been advanced considerably by Jeffrey Walker in his new book on *Rhetoric and Poetics in Antiquity*, where he makes the invaluable point that in antiquity both rhetoric and poetry were expected to sound good. As several of the selections in the present collection should help clarify, Ong has long been calling attention to the sound dimension of both rhetoric and poetry. Perhaps the time has come when more scholars are ready to come to terms with Ong's major claims about orality as fully as Walker has.

To come to terms with Ong's hermeneutic of orality requires that we first of all understand his thought. This in itself is no easy task. For example, we need to recognize that the single term "orality" is not a univocal term in Ong's writings, nor is the term "literacy." He has used these two terms together in the title of his best-selling book *Orality and Literacy*, but he has been using them for decades, along with variant terms such as oral-aural, primarily oral, primary orality, secondary orality, and others. The selections in *An Ong Reader: Challenges for Further Inquiry* are generally accessible, and so studying them should enable many people to understand the themes in Ong's work in literary and communication studies that are here represented. But certain selections here represent challenges that Ong has issued to scholars in general in an effort to draw their scholarly attention to studying further matters that in his estimate they have not yet taken into account sufficiently.

Ong has reported that Hannah Arendt once told him that he has a dialectical mind. At the time when she made this comment, they both were Fellows at the Center for Advanced Studies at Wesleyan University in 1961-1962. In light of her own background in phenomenology, Ong took her statement as a profound compliment (see Weeks and Hoogestraat 11). I take her statement to be an apt characterization of Ong: he truly does have a dialectical mind, and he positively glories in working with contrasts, such as the orality-literacy contrasts that he is most widely known for. In addition, he is very well informed, and he usually writes with extreme precision. However, in my estimate this dialectical quality of his mind seems to elude his various detractors, some of whom seem to tend toward either/or thinking. People with strong tendencies toward either/or thinking will probably never understand Ong. Other carefully nuanced distinctions that he makes also appear to have eluded certain critics, as we will see below. To understand Ong, people may need to have a certain quality of mind that could be styled dialectical. In addition, they will have to read him carefully because his thought is so precise and nuanced.

I happen to consider Ong to be a truly great thinker. I would be happy to have others join me in making this judgment of him. But rather than just taking my word for it, they will have to reach the judgment on their own after studying his thought in detail. However, it is not the goal of *An Ong Reader: Challenges for Further Inquiry* to convince people of his greatness; only by reading his five book-length studies and other collections of his essays besides this one could people form this judgment intelligently and reasonably on their own.

Today much work still remains to be done to carry forward Ong's suggestions for studying the history of rhetoric and literary history in Western culture. Other scholars who wish to join Walker in studying aspects of Ong's suggestions will need to study the selections in this reader carefully and then study some of his other works as well. Because Ong is so well informed, most of his publications still repay careful consideration. For those of us who today stand within the Western cultural tradition, Ong's many-faceted work can help us better understand this cultural tradition. But his work can also help us lay the groundwork for understanding non-Western cultural traditions, provided that we proceed with the same caution and restraint that he does in approaching non-Western cultural traditions.

Broadly speaking, two major facets of Ong's many-faceted work are represented in the present collection: (1) his manifold study of rhetoric in Western culture and (2) his pioneering work in orality-literacy studies. These two major facets within his large corpus of work at times intersect, as do other aspects of his work that are less fully represented in the present collection (e.g., his interest in agonistic tendencies). But certain other themes in his large corpus of work are not represented in the present collection, such as his interest in religious faith (concerning which see the four volumes of his essays entitled *Faith and Contexts*). Moreover, all of the essays in the present collection were selected because they are generally accessible.

An Ong Reader: Challenges for Further Inquiry contains no selections from Ong's five book-length studies, even though themes treated in the present collection are interconnected with themes in those five books. The coeditors of the present collection have had the honor of coediting now four volumes of Ong's essays that have been published under the general title of *Faith and Contexts*. Because those volumes are still available, we have attempted to keep overlap with them to a minimum. In addition, we have attempted to keep overlap to a minimum with Ong's 1971 collection *Rhetoric, Romance, and Technology* and with his 1977 collection *Interfaces of the Word*, both of which Global Publications has recently arranged to reprint in new paperback editions. Thus many of the selections in the present collection have not appeared in other collections of Ong's writings. The selections included here show a certain consistency and interconnectedness of themes in Ong's work over several decades.

For Ong's more specialized studies, interested readers should consult his five book-length studies and the various other collections of his essays. Because only two of his five book-length studies have been mentioned thus far, it would be in order to list all five here, including the year of original publication: (1) *Ramus, Method, and the Decay of Dialogue: From the Art of Discourse to the Art of Reason* (1958), (2) *The Presence of the Word: Some Prolegomena for Cultural and Religious History* (1967), (3) *Fighting for Life: Contest, Sexuality, and Consciousness* (1981), (4) *Orality and Literacy: The Technologizing of the Word* (1982), and (5) *Hopkins, the Self, and God* (1986). Besides the four recent collections published under the title *Faith and Contexts*, mentioned above, Ong's six earlier collections are (1) *Frontiers in American Catholicism: Essays on Ideology and Culture* (1957), (2) *American Catholic Crossroads: Religious-Secular Encounters in the Modern World* (1959), (3) *The Barbarian Within: And Other Fugitive Essays and Studies* (1962), (4) *In the Human Grain: Further Explorations of Contemporary Culture* (1967), (5) *Rhetoric, Romance, and Technology: Studies in the Interaction of Expression and Culture* (1971), and (6) *Interfaces of the Word: Studies in the Evolution of Consciousness and Culture* (1977). In addition, Ong has edited and contributed to two collections by diverse hands: *Darwin's Vision and Christian Perspectives* (1960) and *Knowledge and the Future of Man* (1968).

For a bibliography of Ong's publications, including information about reprintings, interested readers should access Betty R. Youngkin's bibliography of his publications on the Internet (search engines such as Alta Vista or Yahoo can be used by entering Ong, Walter). The Department of English at Saint Louis University has designed a website that will include a bibliographic listing and synopsis of the substance of well over one thousand citations of Ong's works by various scholars, which will be updated periodically. In addition, three collections of essays about Ong's thought have been published (see Foley, 1987; Gronbeck, Farrell, and Soukup, 1991; and Weeks and Hoogestraat, 1998).

In *Walter Ong's Contributions to Cultural Studies*, I have surveyed Ong's life and eleven of his books and selected articles, and I have responded there to certain criticisms of his work. In the brief account of his life that follows, I will draw on points from my book. However, when I turn from recounting his life here to discussing his thought, I will be covering certain aspects of his thought that I did not dwell on in detail in my book. Even though I will clearly state what I consider to be strengths of Ong's thought and even celebrate them, I do not wish to prompt uncritical adulation of the man or his work. Thus I will also note limitations at various points here, as I have done in my book. Put differently, this introduction is not intended primarily to celebrate Ong's accomplishments, but to provide a balanced introduction to those lines of thought in his work that I think still hold out considerable potential for further development by others. In addition, I will defend him and his thought in response to certain critics: Beth Daniell (1999), Wilbur Samuel Howell (1960), Frank Kermode (1968), and Brian Vickers (1988).

This introduction will unfold in the following manner: (1) an introduction of Walter Ong; (2) background information concerning Ong and Ramism; (3) information concerning selections in *An Ong Reader: Challenges for Further Inquiry*, contextualizing them; (4) further consideration of Ong and Marshall McLuhan; (5) a concluding consideration of various contexts in which Ong's thought has a bearing and could presumably be developed further. Readers who are familiar with my book about Ong's work may want to skip the first two subsections here and proceed directly to the third subsection for the preview of the present collection. Because McLuhan is not everybody's cup of tea, the fourth subsection may not be everybody's cup of tea. But in a retrospective assessment of Ong, we do need to reconsider his far more famous and controversial friend and former teacher, whose reputation among academics in the United States needs to be restored. The concluding paragraphs in the fourth subsection concern recent studies of print culture, and so they lead naturally enough into the final subsection concerning additional contexts in which Ong's insights might be extended. Throughout the essay I will provide references to related scholarly literature; interested readers should also consult the extensive bibliography in my book.

Who Is Walter Ong?

This brings me to introducing Walter Ong himself. Born on November 30, 1912, in Kansas City, Missouri, Walter Jackson Ong, Jr., and his younger brother Richard were raised as Roman Catholics, which was their mother's religion. Their father was an Episcopalian (who was received into the Roman Catholic Church shortly before his death). (The family name is English; in much earlier centuries it was spelled Onge.) The Ong boys attended a Catholic grade school and then attended the Jesuit high school and then the Jesuit college in Kansas City, Rockhurst College. After Walter Jr. graduated from college in 1933, he worked full-time for two years. (Concerning these and other points regarding Ong's education and life, see Farrell 33-53.)

After careful deliberation and prayer, Ong entered the Jesuit order in the fall of 1935. Jesuit training requires a number of years to complete, most of which are devoted to studies. During his years of Jesuit training, Ong earned three formal degrees, all from Saint Louis University: a master's in English (1941), a licentiate degree in philosophy (1941), and a licentiate degree in theology (1948). (Each licentiate is roughly equivalent to a master's degree.) For his master's degree in English, Ong wrote a lengthy thesis on sprung rhythm in the poetry of the Victorian Jesuit Gerard Manley Hopkins (1844-1889), whose poetry had been introduced at Saint Louis University by a young Canadian fresh from Cambridge University named Marshall McLuhan (1911-1980).

Having been ordained a priest in 1946, Ong proceeded in the fall of 1948 to Harvard University to take up doctoral studies in English. He passed his oral comprehensives on December 8, 1949. When Ong's superlative master's thesis on Hopkins' sprung rhythm was published in 1949, perhaps he (Ong) passed out reprints of it to his Harvard professors. In any event, Clarence Miller, who was himself a graduate student at Harvard at the time when Ong was there, has recently recounted how "my *Doctorvater* at Harvard, Hyder Rollins, said to me one day that Father Ong was going to be a star" (13). As Miller notes, Rollins here was a true prophet. However, it would be fair to say that Ong rose as a star about the same time that McLuhan did; because of certain connections between Ong's *Ramus, Method, and the Decay of Dialogue* and McLuhan's *The Gutenberg Galaxy*, many people still connect the two men with one another—for the good reason that this book by Ong inspired McLuhan to write this book of his (see Marchand 59, 155). McLuhan had been working on his 1943 Cambridge University doctoral dissertation during the years when he taught Ong and others at Saint Louis University (1937-1944). As a matter of fact, McLuhan called Ong's attention to Perry Miller's discussion of Peter Ramus (1515-1572) and his followers in Miller's *The New England Mind* (1939). Ong subsequently went on to do his doctoral dissertation on Ramus and Ramism under Perry Miller at Harvard, the published version of which then inspired McLuhan to write one of his finest books, *The Gutenberg Galaxy*.

With the assistance of Guggenheim Fellowships in 1949-1950 and in 1951-1952, Ong was able to travel abroad to research Peter Ramus and his followers. Counting those in the British Isles, Ong worked in well over one hundred libraries (often several in one locale). From March to November 1950, Ong lived in England, first in London and then later in Cambridge. Then for three years (November 17, 1950 to November 16,

1953), he lived at the Jesuit residence in Paris at which Pierre Teilhard de Chardin also lived.

During those years Ong first read a good deal of Teilhard's work in manuscript. Despite others' statements to the contrary, Teilhard had not been forbidden by his superiors in the Jesuit order to publish his work in his lifetime. His book published posthumously in English translation as *The Phenomenon of Man* was not passed by censors in Rome (who were not Jesuits) and for this reason was not published in his lifetime. Ong was one of the first Americans to call attention to Teilhard's thought: see Ong's collections of essays, *Frontiers in American Catholicism* (1, 37, 92), *American Catholic Crossroads* (22, 110-11), *The Barbarian Within* (49, 239-40), and *In the Human Grain* (50, 75, 99, 113, 126, 144-45). I once asked Ong if Teilhard had influenced his thought. Ong said no, explaining that he himself had been thinking along parallel lines and did not think that Teilhard had started for him any new lines of thought. Even so, Ong found it encouraging and exhilarating to read Teilhard's work.

In his 1952 review-essay about McLuhan's *The Mechanical Bride* (1951), Ong also devotes a substantial paragraph to setting forth Teilhard's thought concerning the history of the earth in terms of spheres: the cosmosphere, the biosphere, and the noosphere:

> In a third stage, slowly, man, with human intelligence, has made his way over the surface of the earth into all its parts, and now in our day—with the whole world alerted simultaneously every day to goings-on in Washington, Paris, London, Rio de Janeiro, Rome, and (with reservations) Moscow—human consciousness has succeeded in enveloping the entire globe in a third and still more perfect [i.e., more fully developed] kind of sphere, the sphere of intelligence, the "noosphere," as it is has been styled by Father Pierre Teilhard de Chardin, S.J. (84)

It is important to note that Ong was writing about the noosphere as early as 1952, before he had completed his doctoral dissertation on Ramus and Ramism (which he completed late in the summer of 1954). As we will discuss at length later, Daniell objects to Ong's thought as grand theory, but I seriously doubt if she understands how Ong can align his account of Western cultural developments with Teilhard's account of the noosphere. I also seriously doubt if she understands Ong's various writings about cosmology, the basic outlines of which Ong claims to have been developing before he read Teilhard's work. In his early classes at Saint Louis University, Ong told the students that Roman Catholicism had no cosmology. When we read Ong's "Where Are We Now? Some Elemental

Cosmological Considerations" (2000), we need to remember that cosmological considerations have been a lifelong preoccupation of Ong's.

Ong's initial major and still chief claim to scholarly fame is his massively researched 1954 Harvard doctoral dissertation, which was published in two volumes by Harvard University Press in 1958: *Ramus, Method, and the Decay of Dialogue* and *Ramus and Talon Inventory*. The former is a extraordinarily detailed study in the history of logic, dialectic, and rhetoric, centering on Peter Ramus (Pierre de la Ramée) and his followers. In it Ong first adumbrated the implications of his insights about orality and visualism.

At the time when Ong undertook to study Ramus and the antecedents to his work, Ramus had become a forgotten figure, despite his tens of thousands of earlier followers through Germany and the British Isles, as well as France and much of Western Europe. As a result, it was and still is a tremendous service to the scholarly world for Ong to track down all the editions he accounts for in his *Ramus and Talon Inventory*. This volume alone is massively researched in a spectacular way. To track down the data here accumulated, Ong worked in over one hundred libraries, mostly European; at the time there was no Internet or email to facilitate checking the holdings of far-flung libraries.

A careful reading of *Ramus, Method, and the Decay of Dialogue* shows massive research and carefully targeted references to specific points in an impressive concatenation of works—by Plato, Aristotle, Cicero, Boethius, Peter of Spain, Rudolph Agricola, Philip Melanchthon, Ramus, and numerous other writers. Despite Ong's occasional impatience with Ramus, this is exemplary research of a magnitude and depth that few scholars have equaled. (In 1972, 1987, and 2000, Peter Sharratt published reviews of subsequent studies of Ramus and Ramism; also see Joseph S. Freedman's recent collection of essays; and the translation of John Milton's Ramist *Logic* that Ong and Charles J. Ermatinger prepared, as well as Ong's magnificent introduction to it.)

When I say that Ong's two volumes on Ramus and Ramism together still constitute Ong's chief claim to scholarly fame, I mean that anyone who wants to set forth a carefully considered judgment of Ong's work cannot skip over these two substantial books and pass judgment on only selected other subsequent books and/or articles. By chief claim, I mean that these two books represent the font and origin, the most substantial and detailed work, the point of departure for his subsequent work. Ignore these two books, and you will most likely consider his other books as sketchy at best, as sweeping generalizations made by somebody who has not done his homework and therefore has not established his credentials for making any sweeping statements that we should pay attention to and take seriously. But few scholars have undertaken to carry out studies with the scope and depth of what Ong has done in these two books. Subtract these two books from your consideration of Ong and you might understandably conclude that his other work represents nothing but grand theory, as Daniell has claimed.

In recognition of the competence evident in these two volumes and in his published articles, Ong was invited to serve the *Quarterly Journal of Speech* as the advisory editor for classical rhetoric, a position he held from 1960 to 1977. For his two volumes and related articles on Ramus and Ramism, the French government in 1963 dubbed Ong a knight, *Chevalier dans l'Ordre des Palmes Académiques*, an accolade that is rarely bestowed on people who are not French citizens. On the strength of these two volumes and other works, Ong had established his scholarly credentials sufficiently enough to be invited to deliver the Terry Lectures at Yale University in April 1964. Yale University Press published these lectures in expanded form in 1967 as *The Presence of the Word: Some Prolegomena for Cultural and Religious History*.

Ong's scholarly standing grew from this time on. In 1972, he was elected to the American Academy of Arts and Sciences. In commemoration of the twenty-fifth anniversary of the Fulbright Act, the United States Board of Foreign Scholarships selected about a dozen scholars and writers to serve as Lincoln Lecturers over a period of three years, and Ong was selected to be one of them. On his Fulbright Lecture tour in April and May of 1974, Ong delivered twenty-six presentations in Central and West Africa: in Cameroon, Zaire, and Senegal in French; and in Nigeria in English. In 1978, he served as elected president of the Modern Language Association, which, with some 30,000 members, made up the largest professional association of scholars ever known in the world. In 1979, he delivered the Messenger Lectures at Cornell University, which were published in expanded form in 1982 by Cornell University Press as *Fighting for Life: Contest Sexuality, and Consciousness*. In 1981, Ong presented the Alexander Lectures at the University of Toronto, which the University of Toronto Press published in 1986 as *Hopkins, the Self, and God*. The most widely known of Ong's books is his 1982 hardbound and paperback book *Orality and Literacy*, which Ong reports has been translated into twelve different languages.

Ong and Ramism

It is fashionable today in certain academic circles to speak of archive fever, following the example of Jacques Derrida in *Archive Fever*. In some other academic circles today, it is fashionable to refer to historical-mindedness, following the example of Bernard Lonergan (also see McPartland). Ong himself has pointed out the contribution of Renaissance humanists in the development of our sense of historical-mindedness ("Humanism" 221, 224). Ong has a strong sense of historical-mindedness, which is exemplified in *Ramus, Method, and the Decay of Dialogue*.

Ong undertook his massive study of Ramus and Ramism because of points that had surfaced in various works of scholarship earlier. As we have noted above, Ong credits McLuhan with calling his attention to Perry Miller's account of the influence of Ramus in Miller's *The New England Mind: The Seventeenth Century* (1939). (McLuhan does mention Ramism in his 1943 Cambridge University doctoral dissertation on Thomas Nashe.) The influence of Ramus had also surfaced in Samuel Eliot Morison's history of Harvard College. At the time when Ong undertook his study, literally nobody knew what to make of the material about Ramus and his influence that had surfaced in Miller's and Morison's books (1935, 1936). Consequently, the territory was unexplored. Ong undertook to explore it.

By the time when Ong had proceeded to graduate studies in English at Harvard University in the fall of 1948, he had acquired certain competencies that equipped him well for this undertaking. He knew Latin and French well enough to undertake the kind of study that was needed, and he also knew enough about the history of rhetoric and philosophy and theology. He knew something about the history of rhetoric at least in part from McLuhan, whose doctoral dissertation was a study of the history of the trivium (grammar, rhetoric, and dialectic). Ong knew about the history of philosophy from his study of philosophy as part of his Jesuit training; as we have noted above, he holds a licentiate degree in philosophy from Saint Louis University (1941). He knew about the history of theology because he had studied theology for four years as part of his Jesuit preparation for ordination to the priesthood and for many years afterwards as part of his study of intellectual and cultural history. As we have also noted above, he holds a licentiate degree in theology from Saint Louis University (1948).

Prior to entering the Jesuit order in the fall of 1935, Ong had majored in Latin at Rockhurst College (now Rockhurst University) in Kansas City, Missouri (class of 1933). After he entered the Jesuit order, the courses he took in both philosophy and theology were taught in Latin. All examinations for these courses were in Latin and were oral (thus preserving the pristine oral tradition of all university education). As part of his training in the Jesuit order, he taught at Regis College in Denver (now Regis University) from the fall of 1941 to the spring of 1943, where he taught English and French. Thus he was well equipped to undertake a thorough study of the heretofore unexplored territory surrounding Ramus and Ramism.

We might consider what kinds of expectations or presuppositions Ong would have brought to this undertaking, even though this will be somewhat conjectural. Three points seem worth mentioning in this connection. First, he certainly had listened to McLuhan talk at length about the history of rhetoric in Western culture, as had Maurice B. McNamee. McNamee and Ong were among the Jesuit graduate students who had studied under McLuhan at Saint Louis University. Ong today credits McLuhan with being aware of just how extensive training in rhetoric had been in Western culture, when he (McLuhan) was teaching at Saint Louis University. McLuhan's doctoral dissertation is a century-by-century survey of the trivium (of grammar, rhetoric, and dialectic or logic) from approximately the time of Cicero to the time of Nashe. In the culminating chapter, then, McLuhan brings the various insights he has gleaned to bear on understanding certain features of controversies in which Nashe was involved. Briefly, Nashe favored the rhetoricians. The last chapter is too cryptic and underdeveloped to suit my tastes, and I surely would have recommended other revisions in McLuhan's earlier chapters. But the range and depth of his chapters are impressive. To be sure, McLuhan does not bring to those chapters the range of knowledge and acumen that we find in Ong's *Ramus, Method, and the Decay of Dialogue*. Then again, McLuhan turned thirty-two in 1943, the year in which he completed his dissertation, whereas Ong turned forty-two in 1954, the year in which he completed his dissertation. But McLuhan has done yeoman work in his dissertation, which is a formidable achievement. Once we see the historical sweep of his dissertation, we can see that the historical sweep of Ong's *Ramus, Method, and the Decay of Dialogue* roughly parallels that of McLuhan's dissertation, which could account in part for why McLuhan seems to have been prompted by Ong's book to write *The Gutenberg Galaxy*.

Second, McNamee was evidently impressed with McLuhan's research. McNamee himself went on to write his doctoral dissertation on the tradition of learning as reflected in the writings of Francis Bacon. After he had completed his dissertation in 1945, McNamee published a lengthy article in 1950 in the *Saint Louis University Studies* about Francis Bacon and the history of grammar and rhetoric, which Ong most likely would have seen about the time when he himself was undertaking his massive study of Peter Ramus. (For a recent consideration of Bacon and the art of discourse, see Jardine.)

Third, we can also read Ong's own lengthy 1946 article in *Theological Studies* on "Newman's *Essay on Development* in Its Intellectual Milieu." Newman's *Essay* is about John Henry Newman's sense of tradition, specifically with reference to the development of Christian doctrine. It seems reasonable to assume that Ong would have a parallel sense of tradition with respect to the development of Christian doctrine that would also give him a certain set of expectations concerning other intellectual developments in Western culture.

As an appendix to a recent collection of Marshall McLuhan's non-secular writings entitled *The Medium and the Light: Reflections on Religion* (214-19), Eric McLuhan, Marshall McLuhan's eldest son, has arrayed parallel passages from Newman's *Essay on Development* and T. S. Eliot's essay on "Tradition and the Individual Talent." By noting certain parallels in these sets of passages, we can gain insight into McLuhan's mind; from at least the time of his 1943 Cambridge University dissertation onward, he had a strong sense of how tradition was at work in Western culture in various ways. But Ong also mentions Eliot's essay often in his publications in the 1950s. As a result, we might take a hint from Eric McLuhan's appendix and connect Eliot's and Newman's fluid senses of tradition with Ong's general expectations as he undertook to explore the unexplored territory surrounding Ramus: Ong probably did expect to find that Ramus was working out of some identifiable intellectual tradition or traditions.

Although this much is a conjecture about Ong's expectations, he did indeed situate Ramus within the larger context of an intellectual tradition that grew out of antecedents in the work of Peter of Spain and Rudolph Agricola. So far as I know, nobody has since challenged Ong's account of Peter of Spain and Rudolph Agricola as being the historical antecedents of Ramus' work. These points amount to considering Ramus as an individual talent, as it were, within a larger tradition, to paraphrase Eliot's title. In addition, Ong claims that Ramus was not an original thinker, in the sense that he (Ramus) did not make an original contribution to the study of dialectic, logic, or rhetoric. Subsequent studies have often confirmed Ong's evaluation here (see, for example, Ashworth). However, these are not the only points that Ong makes in his overall account of Ramus' work and influence.

When Ong submitted his dissertation in the summer of 1954, Howell's *Logic and Rhetoric in England, 1500-1700* had not yet been published. It was published in 1956, and Ong was able to incorporate specific references to it when he revised his dissertation for publication—in two volumes in 1958. In the fall of 1954, Ong took up a teaching position at Saint Louis University. There he later directed John G. Rechtien's 1975 doctoral dissertation on developments in Ramist circles. Rechtien has since published several articles touching on Ramism and various Ramists (one of Rechtien's articles is mentioned below). But so far as I know, nobody in American studies has undertaken to revisit the original nexus of material that turned up in Morison and Miller in light of Ong's far more thorough account of Ramus and Ramism.

According to Perry Miller, practically everybody at Harvard College considered themselves to be Ramists. Does it follow from this that our American educational heritage stands in some way in the Ramist tradition? If it does, does it make any difference that it does? Ong aligns the centuries-old tradition of teaching the verbal arts with dialogue—or pro and con debate of the sort that Thomas O. Sloane celebrates and champions. Ong sees Ramist method as manifesting on the contrary a monologic tendency, a tendency to concentrate on setting forth only one's own line of thought.

Evidently the most controversial claim that Ong makes concerns the arrays of branching dichotomies that Ramus in time came to favor and that his hundreds of followers also favored. Ong correctly notes that such arrays of branching dichotomies can be found in manuscripts that were composed before the movable printing press was invented. However, because the printing press expanded the possibility of exact duplication of such branching dichotomies, Ong connects their popularization by Ramus and his followers with the development of the printing press. In his recent collection of essays, Freedman devotes nine pages (24-32) to reproducing examples of such arrays of dichotomies from eighteen authors, with more than one example from a few authors. Rechtien has also reproduced several examples of arrays of dichotomies from the Ramist Puritan minister John Udall.

Because Vickers has contributed significantly to making scholars aware of the influence of rhetoric in Western literary culture, we should consider his criticism of Ong's interpretation of Ramus and Ramism. In his 1988 book *Defense of Rhetoric*, Vickers has singled out certain aspects of Ong's account of Ramus and Ramism for comment:

> One of Ong's main interpretive claims was that Ramus' preference for bracketed tables of contents, where a topic was divided into two headings, most often, each of those into a further two, until he had dealt with the whole subject he was treating—that this lay-out in printed books led to a "spatializing of consciousness" in the Renaissance mind, and was somehow bound up with the influence of print. (One detects the influence of Marshall McLuhan on this theo-

ry: Ong has always claimed that the debt was the other way around.) Several scholars have voiced doubts about this thesis, and anyone familiar with the textbook tradition knows that bracketed tables exists aplenty in manuscripts long before printing, and in printed books before, or independently of Ramus. (475-76)

In the comments set off in parentheses, Vickers correctly notes that Ong has always claimed that he had developed his own line of thought about the influence of print in *Ramus, Method, and the Decay of Dialogue* (1958) before McLuhan had developed his particular line of thought regarding print in *The Gutenberg Galaxy* (1962). In that book McLuhan quotes Ong in several places; but nowhere does Ong quote McLuhan to a comparable extent, not even in places where he does refer favorably to McLuhan's work. However that may be, in *Ramus, Method, and the Decay of Dialogue* (79), Ong himself has acknowledged bracketed arrays of dichotomies can be found in manuscripts long before printing was developed, so this objection by Vickers does not reflect very careful reading of Ong.

In addition, Vickers to the contrary notwithstanding, Ong does not deny that such bracketed arrays were also developed independently of Ramus and in printed books before Ramus. Ramus' books that featured arrays of dichotomies were indeed printed books, not hand-copied manuscript duplicates, and his printed books did indeed go through remarkably numerous editions and printings (see Ong's *Ramus and Talon Inventory* for works not only by Ramus but also by others as well). Moreover, Ramus' followers also produced arrays of dichotomies of all sorts of concepts in their printed books. In consequence, it is not farfetched for Ong to suggest that the power of print to reproduce exact duplicates of such arrays of dichotomies contributed to their increased popularity.

Of course, whether such arrays were produced by hand in manuscripts or by print in printed books, they did represent something visual in space, to spell out the obvious. Would Vickers have us believe that the visual representation of such arrays had no impact on the psyches of the hundreds of writers who produced them or on the thousands of readers who studied them carefully? If he wishes to claim that the visual representation of the written word has no impact whatsoever on either the writers or the readers who study the texts, then he stands squarely opposed to the *ur*-thesis that Ong had adumbrated in *Ramus, Method, and the Decay of Dialogue* (1958) and that Eric A. Havelock has developed independently of Ong in *Preface to Plato* (1963). This is the heart of the matter, the crux of the debate.

Because Vickers also mentions spatialization in the above quotation, this point from Ong's work needs to be clarified. Ong does indeed refer to the spatialization of thought in various places throughout *Ramus, Method, and the Decay of Dialogue*, where he connects spatialization of thought with the quantification of thought in logic. Indeed, the fourth chapter is entitled "The Distant Background: Scholasticism and the Quantification of Thought" (53-91; also see 184, 262, 263). In one discussion note he tells us that "[q]uantification is explained in Willard Van Orman Quine, *Mathematical Logic* . . . and in [Joseph T.] Clark, *Conventional Logic and Modern Logic*" (334). Ong clearly considers quantification of thought in logic to have begun to develop in centuries prior to the Renaissance and the invention of the printing press. In an article originally published in 1956 in the *Bibliothèque d'Humanisme et Renaissance* and then reprinted in Ong's 1962 collection *The Barbarian Within*, he explains how medieval scholastic logic, out of which Ramist logic emerges, is best understood as a prelude to modern mathematics and mathematical physics and modern science:

> In this historical perspective, medieval scholastic logic appears as a kind of premathematics, a subtle and unwitting preparation for the large-scale operations in quantitative modes of thinking that will characterize the modern world. In assessing the meaning of [medieval] scholasticism, one must keep in mind an important and astounding fact: In the whole history of the human mind, mathematics and mathematical physics come into their own, in a way that has changed the face of the earth and promises or threatens to change it even more, at only one place and time, that is, in Western Europe immediately after the scholastic experience. Elsewhere, no matter how advanced the culture on other scores, and even along mathematical lines, as in the case of the Babylonian, nothing like a real mathematical transformation of thinking takes place—not among the ancient Egyptians or Assyrians or Greeks or Romans, not among the peoples of India nor the Chinese nor the Japanese, not among the Aztecs or Mayas, not in Islam despite promising beginnings there, any more than among the Tartars or the Avars or the Turks. These people can all now share the same common scientific knowledge, but the scientific tradition itself that they share is not a merging of various parallel discoveries made by their various civilizations. It represents a new state of mind. However great contributions other civilizations may hereafter make to the tradition, our scientific world traces its origins back always to seventeenth- and sixteenth-century Europe, to the place where for some three centuries and more the arts course taught in universities and parauniversity schools had pounded into the heads of youth a study program consisting almost exclusively of highly quantified logic and companion physics, both taught

on a scale and with an enthusiasm never approximated or even dreamt of in the ancient academies. (72)

Even though Ong understandably centers his attention on thought developed in logic, it should be noted here that Alfred W. Crosby has recently documented certain parallel developments in *The Measure of Reality: Quantification and Western Society, 1250-1600*. Further parallel developments have been detailed by Michael E. Hobart and Zachary S. Schiffman in *Information Ages: Literacy, Numeracy, and the Computer Revolution*. (Concerning the critique of Ong and Havelock set forth by Hobart and Schiffman, see Farrell 16-26, 200-04.)

In the preface to the 1983 paperback edition of *Ramus, Method, and the Decay of Dialogue*, Ong has called attention to how Ramus' dichotomized charts resemble digital computer programs:

One connection that would have to be brought out [in a revised edition] would be the resemblance of Ramus' binary dichotomized charts (see pages 202 and 317, and cf. pages 200-01) to digital computer programs. Like computer programs, the Ramist dichotomies were designed to be heuristic: they belong to the part of logic known as "invention," that is, finding. The quantifying drives inherited from medieval logic were producing computer programs in Ramus' active mind some four hundred years before the computer itself came into being. Perhaps nothing shows more strikingly the subterranean connections between much that was going on in the sixteenth-century consciousness and what is going on in the modern world. When this book was written, computers were not present enough to our own consciousness to have made this now obvious comparison compelling. (viii)

It should be noted here that Philip Leith, who is himself a computer scientist, has drawn extensively on Ong's work on Ramus to suggest that Ramus can be seen as a forerunner of today's computer scientists.

Because many people have found Ong's book daunting to read, we should allow that *Ramus, Method, and the Decay of Dialogue* could have been made more reader friendly through a few small additions: (1) an early chapter-by-chapter preview and explanation of the structure of the book as a whole; (2) a few well-placed internal summaries of the parts that have been covered, with a brief preview of what is to come next and how it is connected with the previous part(s); (3) a review at the end of key points in the overall argument that has been developed in the book as a whole. However, Ong was probably just too close to all of the material he had gathered to use such small distancing techniques as these. In short, he was not deliberately trying to make the book as daunting to read as it is—out of some kind of misdirected agonistic spirit to challenge the readers. Instead, he did his best to make it as readable as he could at the time, and it still repays careful reading. Indeed, the insights in his book about orality and visualism are like a spectacular Fourth-of-July fireworks display designed to light up the sky. Since writing this book, Ong has devoted much of his scholarly writing to further elucidating insights that he had adumbrated in kernel form at least in it. One reason for reading the selections in *An Ong Reader: Challenges for Further Inquiry* is that they should help interested readers undertake the daunting task of reading Ong's big book on Ramus and Ramism.

Ong's account of the heightened visualism that printing contributed to has been further delineated in Richard Yeo's *Encyclopaedic Visions: Scientific Dictionaries and Enlightenment Culture* (for a study of related interest see Leigh Eric Schmidt's *Hearing Things: Religion, Illusion, and the American Enlightenment;* also see Cuddihy; Habermas).

In *Paul and the Stoics*, Troels Engberg-Pedersen repeatedly calls attention to St. Paul's language about participation (for page references, see the index for this term). Engberg-Pedersen points out that people today would probably consider themselves quite removed from the possibility of experiencing such participation in depth. I would agree with that much. However, I would use the author's observation to make two points based on Ong's account of the human sensorium and the impact of heightened visualism associated with print culture: (1) St. Paul was closer to the oral-aural orientation of the human sensorium in antiquity (as were Plato and Aristotle, despite their pronounced literate orientation); and (2) we today have been strongly conditioned by the heightened visualism of print culture, the result of which is to distance us from the more participatory sense of life that St. Paul refers to and that Ong associates with the world-as-event sense of life in antiquity.

To consider the larger import of Ong's account of Ramism and visualism in Western cultural history, we should reflect further on Eliot's title "Tradition and the Individual Talent." Even if we do not consider ourselves to have a talent for poetry, we may need to consider ourselves as part of the Western cultural tradition, even though we may also critique this tradition. For better or worse, we in the United States today are the heirs and beneficiaries of the Western cultural tradition.

As we have noted, Daniell likes to sneer at Ong's work by referring to it deprecatingly as grand theory. Ong himself strongly dislikes the word theory; he prefers to characterize his thought as phenomenological (or descriptive) in cast. However, he does allow that he is working with a thesis that he himself has characterized as sweeping in scope. As we consider Daniell's sneer about grand theory, we should note how carefully Ong has framed his own thesis about cultural developments in the preface to *Interfaces of the Word* (1977):

> The thesis of these two earlier works [*The Presence of the Word* (1967) and *Rhetoric, Romance, and Technology* (1971)] is sweeping, but it is not reductionist, as reviewers and commentators, so far as I know, have all generously recognized: the works do not maintain that the evolution from primary orality through writing and print to an electronic culture, which produces secondary orality, causes or explains everything in human culture and consciousness. Rather, the thesis is relationist: major developments, and very likely even all major developments, in culture and consciousness are related, often in unexpected intimacy, to the evolution of the word from primary orality to its present state. But the relationships are varied and complex, with cause and effect often difficult to distinguish. (9-10)

Later in the preface to *Interfaces of the Word*, Ong notes that his book has its own history in his earlier studies. "From the time of my studies of Peter Ramus and Ramism, my work has grown into its own kind of phenomenological history of culture and consciousness, . . . elaborated in terms of noetic operations . . ." (10-11).

Before we consider Daniell's general objection to Ong's thesis, we need to clarify the implications of the thesis itself. Does Ong's thesis, as quoted above, imply that he is a media determinist, or a technological determinist? No, not quite. He characterizes his own position as relationist, not as determinist. His relationist position leaves a lot of room for human freedom and ingenuity in response to shifts in communication media or in technology. As we will discuss later in the subsection on Ong and McLuhan, Ong in 1952 published a rousing review-essay about McLuhan's *The Mechanical Bride* (1951). If Ong is a technological determinist, then why would he in that piece urge his fellow Catholics to christen (his word—in the subtitle) technological culture? A true technological determinist would not write about transforming technological culture in accord with certain Christian values, because such an undertaking would be pointless from the standpoint of a technological determinist. But Ong does urge his coreligionists to undertake such a transformation of technological culture, and so he thereby acknowledges human freedom and ingenuity. Of course, he also acknowledges that human freedom is exercised and enacted in highly specified contexts. Four volumes of his essays have now been published under the title of *Faith and Contexts*, which title he himself selected. This title advertises that he is aware that human freedom is contextualized, not in some sense absolute. Indeed, we always exercises our human freedom in determinate contexts, certain of which are influenced in significant ways by shifts in communication media and in technology.

But let us now return to Daniell's general objection. Both Ong's word "sweeping" and Daniell's word "grand" are intended to characterize the scope of his thought. Both Ong and Daniell seem to agree that the scope of his thought is rather broad. Because the word theory has been used so frequently over the last two decades, it seems to be somewhat elastic and even protean. Nevertheless, Daniell's word theory still strikes me as suggesting something that is far more fully elaborated than Ong's word thesis suggests. He has elaborated and supported his basic contentions sufficiently enough to say that he is developing a thesis.

Because any thesis can be argued against, we should expect that some people would argue against Ong's thesis by adding the word "no" to it and thus formulating the direct antithesis of it: "No major developments in culture and consciousness are related to the evolution of the word from primary orality through writing and print to electronic orality today." No doubt there are some people who hold this skeptical position.

However, if this skeptical position were true, then we could call off all efforts in formal education to teach reading and writing. In addition, we could tell Paulo Freire and his followers to call off their literacy programs. But no organized movement today is working for the abolition of all efforts to teach reading and writing. On a common-sense level most people agree that it is worthwhile to continue the effort to teach people to read and write. If absolutely no major developments in culture and consciousness are related to learning how to read and write, then we collectively are surely wasting an enormous amount of time and energy and money to promote reading and writing. It is counterintuitive to say that nothing depends on learning to read and write. Even so, it may be very difficult to identify and specify precisely what all does depend on learning to read and write, especially when we are referring to young people.

When Ong himself moves to specifying certain historical developments as associated with literacy, he usually refers to certain aspects of Plato's thought or Aristotle's thought. The aspects of their thought that Ong calls attention to were carried forward in subsequent philosophic thought and also in Christian theological thought. When Ong moves to specifying certain historical developments associated with print, he often refers to Ramus and his followers. But nowhere does Ong claim to have said all that can be said in support of his above-quoted thesis. Thus other scholars can explore still further ramifications of his sweeping thesis. In this respect, his thesis could be styled a hypothesis, or even a heuristic orientation.

To be sure, because Ong's thought is truly sweeping in scope, it is in a certain sense grand—he gives us the big picture. Daniell may be surprised to see that more and more books are coming out today that purport to set forth sweeping accounts of Western culture, along lines that often parallel the developments that Ong has traced. In *Information Ages: Literacy, Numeracy, and the Computer Revolution*, for example, Hobart and Schiffman set forth a sweeping survey of Western culture. Similarly, in *Holding on to Reality: The Nature of Information at the Turn of the Millennium*, Albert Borgmann surveys a wide range of material. But in my estimate the order of intellect at work in Ong's thought surpasses what we find in these two books and other recent surveys. In light of these later efforts not only Ong's *Ramus, Method, and the Decay of Dialogue* but also Ong's *The Presence of the Word: Some Prolegomena for Cultural and Religious History* are pioneering efforts to which these subsequent efforts can be related as detail work completing the larger panorama sketched by Ong.

As we have noted, Ong himself likes to say that we need both closeness and distance to understand something. If there is some truth to this observation, then his work can provide us with the distance we need to understand certain developments in Western culture. After all, there may be a certain truth to the saying about not being able to see the forest for the trees. It might be helpful at times to be able to see the forest. Through our own further study, we will then have to supply the closeness component. However invaluable the big picture that Ong's work provides may be to us, though, certain other parts of his thought, such as his ideas about oral residue in written and printed texts, hold out the greatest promise for further development by other scholars.

But to understand Ong's attention to the big picture, we should consider his own remarks in his review of McLuhan's *The Gutenberg Galaxy* (reprinted here as Chapter 14):

> If the human community is to retain meaningful possession of the knowledge it is accumulating, breakthroughs to syntheses of a new order are absolutely essential. McLuhan aids one such breakthrough into a new interiority, which will have to include studies of communication not merely as an adjunct or sequel to human knowledge, but as this knowledge's form and condition.

No doubt Ong would also see his own work as aiding the breakthrough that McLuhan's *The Gutenberg Galaxy* aids. In addition, Ong would doubtless see Teilhard as aiding another such breakthrough into a new

interiority in *The Phenomenon of Man* and elsewhere, which Ong would
see his own work as also aiding (for a critique of Teilhard, see Dodson).

But let us examine more carefully the exact wording of Ong's statement here. "If the human community is to retain meaningful possession of
the knowledge it is accumulating" clearly implies that the human community has previously attained meaningful possession of the knowledge it has
accumulated. This is the import of the word "retain" here. In the closing
statement of his 1967 encyclopedia article on "Humanism," Ong has in
effect summed up the overall humanist achievement in terms of the human
community's meaningful possession of the knowledge it has accumulated:

> The typical humanist devotion to written texts and to stored knowl-
> edge came about because of the growing weight of knowledge avail-
> able in writing. In these perspectives humanism was a stage in man's
> growing self-possession achieved through improved penetration of
> the world around him and of his own history. (224)

We should not forget that Ramus and his numerous followers were part
of this overall humanist achievement, even though they were more like
the supporting cast than they were like the stars of the show. Ramus was
no Erasmus. Even so, we should allow that the Ramist love for arraying
terms in unfolding dichotomies can be understood as part of the overall
trend that Ong here describes as a stage in the human community's growing self-possession of the knowledge it has accumulated. For each
dichotomized array of key terms can be seen as representing in effect an
encyclopedic vision (to borrow the title of Richard Yeo's book), or at least
the vision for a lengthy encyclopedia article.

As we have also noted above, Lonergan has urged us to develop a
strong sense of historical-mindedness, which Ong has done in an exemplary way, and Derrida has urged us to develop archive fever, which Ong
has also done to an exemplary degree. Ong's work does invite us to consider Western culture from antiquity to the present time. Daniell to the
contrary notwithstanding, we may need Ong's sweeping hypothesis about
cultural evolution to work with in cultural studies today. After all, where
would biology be today if it did not have Darwin's sweeping hypothesis
about evolution to work with? In any event, people need to rise above
Daniell's small-mindedness, because we can still profit from studying
Ong's work carefully.

Concerning *An Ong Reader: Challenges for Further Inquiry*

As we have noted above, the central themes that Ong develops in the various selections in *An Ong Reader: Challenges for Further Inquiry* still

hold considerable potential for further development, which is exactly why they have been chosen. Moreover, if this reader works as an introduction to Ong's thought, then it should serve as a springboard for reading his other works. For only by reading a good sample of his works can readers equip themselves properly to develop further certain lines of thought found in this reader and in his other writings.

Except for the first two selections, most of the selections in *An Ong Reader: Challenges for Further Inquiry* have been arranged chronologically, based on their year of original publication (except for the third chapter). The first two selections have been placed at the beginning because of biographical information they contain concerning the development of Ong's thought. The third selection is Ong's 1941 master's thesis; it was published in 1949, but it is placed here to reflect its original completion date of 1941. The title of the present collection, *An Ong Reader: Challenges for Further Inquiry*, contains the indefinite article "an" as a way to acknowledge that other selections could have been chosen to represent a sample of Ong's thought.

The selections here are generally accessible, and many of them call attention to matters that could be explored further by other scholars. Indeed, some of the selections are so accessible as to require virtually no introduction, which is why they are not dealt with in detail here. In a few instances I have provided parenthetical references to related literature for interested readers, as I have done above. The discussions here are not meant to summarize the selections, but to contextualize the ideas in them.

In the review-essay published here as Chapter 1, Ong has outlined certain matters that he and McLuhan and others had been discussing during McLuhan's years at Saint Louis University (1937-1944). Some of these matters are echoed in both Ong's *Ramus, Method, and the Decay of Dialogue* and McLuhan's *The Gutenberg Galaxy*. From those discussions at Saint Louis University, each of them proceeded to develop his own thought. Because of the different studies with which they grew, the trajectories of McLuhan's and Ong's thought diverged considerably, but continued along roughly parallel or somewhat interactive lines.

Some background information about McLuhan is in order. Born on July 21, 1911, in Edmonton, Herbert Marshall McLuhan died in his sleep in his home in Toronto in the early hours of January 1, 1980 (for complete biographies of McLuhan, see Gordon, 1997; Marchand, 1989). McLuhan had completed a bachelor's and a master's degree in English at the University of Manitoba in 1933 and 1934, respectively. He then proceeded to further studies at Cambridge University (1934 to 1936), where he studied under I. A. Richards and F. R. Leavis, among others. In 1936-

1937, McLuhan held a teaching position at the University of Wisconsin. During this academic year he was formally received into the Roman Catholic Church, a conversion that he had been moving toward during his years at Cambridge. As we have noted above, McLuhan's teaching at Saint Louis University extended from 1937 to 1944, with a year's leave of absence in 1939-1940 during which he returned to Cambridge University to work on his doctoral dissertation.

On August 4, 1939, McLuhan had married Corinne Lewis of Fort Worth, Texas, and so their trip to Cambridge was something of a honeymoon trip. After they returned to St. Louis, their first child, Eric McLuhan, was born there, whereas the subsequent McLuhan children were born in Canada. In 1943 McLuhan's doctoral dissertation on Thomas Nashe was accepted at Cambridge University. McLuhan's widow has recently signed a contract with Gingko Press for the publication of his dissertation (for which Ong has written the introduction), but no date for its publication has been announced yet. In my estimate it is still worth publishing. It is truly a shame that McLuhan did not get it published in his own lifetime, because its publication would have strengthened his scholarly credentials.

Chapter 2 is George Riemer's 1971 interview with Ong. Ong's remarks about his work on Ramism are particularly noteworthy here, as is Ong's clarification of what he means by agonistic structures, which is a topic discussed at length in Chapter 25 in the present collection. This interview appeared in Riemer's book entitled *The New Jesuits*, in which each chapter featured Riemer's interview with a different Jesuit in the following order: Daniel Berrigan, John Padberg, John Walsh, John Culkin, Ong, George Shoup, Paul J. Weber, Theodore Cunningham, Barthelemy A. Rousseve, R. James Arenz, Ken Feit. The rationale for this order is not spelled out in the book. (Culkin was instrumental in working out the arrangements that enabled McLuhan to become visiting professor at Fordham University in 1967-1968.)

Riemer had entered the Jesuit order in 1940 at the age of twenty and withdrew from it seven years later (3). He entered the same Jesuit novitiate at Florissant, Missouri, that Ong had entered in the fall of 1935. In 1971, the year in which his book of interviews with Jesuits was published, Riemer married Margaret Flanagan. He died of cancer in New York City on March 31, 1973. He clearly had an insider's sense of Jesuit life, as parts of his discussion with Ong show.

Between the times when each of them entered the Jesuit novitiate at Florissant and the time of the interview, the Jesuit order had experienced a dramatic downturn in its membership, as had many other Roman

Catholic religious orders. This downturn also contributed to the questions that Riemer raises concerning Jesuit community.

At a certain juncture in their wide-ranging conversation, Riemer asks Ong to explain what he means by irenic structures, a term Ong uses to contrast with polemic structures He also uses the term "polemic" predominantly in *The Presence of the Word* (192-207), but in *Fighting for Life: Contest, Sexuality, and Consciousness*, he tends to favor the term "agonistic" over the term polemic. In any event, Riemer frames his question about irenic structures by asking if they are forces that work toward peace. Ong then answers that by irenic structures he means something a little less positive than peace. What he means is that irenic forces simply mute polemic. Put differently, they do not accentuate struggle or antagonism. Among other things, he discusses educational practices in the past that tended to institutionalize antagonisms and a certain kind of competitiveness. He declares that he wouldn't want to go back to the older educational practices.

Although Ong explicitly adverts in passing to cooperation, he does not explore in detail how teachers might structure educational experiences for students to foster cooperation in learning—and perhaps simultaneously to foster learning cooperation. However, the topic of cooperative learning has been explored in detail by David W. Johnson and Roger T. Johnson and by others. In *Cooperation and Competition: Theory and Research*, the Johnsons have explained the well-developed theory behind cooperative learning and reviewed the research studies that have been conducted to examine its effectiveness. The theory identifies three different kinds of learning—individualistic, competitive, and cooperative—each of which is recognized as having a certain validity for certain kinds of learning. The Johnsons also explore the ways in which teachers must structure units and must instruct students in the various roles they will need to play for cooperative learning to become a successful undertaking. (Also see their textbooks for teachers-in-training: *Learning Together and Alone* and *Circles of Learning*.) However, as long as we are discussing the prolific Johnsons' writings about cooperative learning, we should also note that these same authors have written a whole book advocating that teachers should structure classroom experiences around controversies (polemics) so that students will have to learn the pros and cons of the issues under discussion (see *Creative Controversy: Intellectual Challenge in the Classroom*). We will consider this book of theirs further in the last subsection of this introduction.

Chapter 3 is "Hopkins' Sprung Rhythm and the Life of English Poetry," which is Ong's 1941 master's thesis that was published originally in 1949. As we noted above, Philip Marchand (48) credits McLuhan with introducing Hopkins to his students at Saint Louis University, based on Leavis' championing of Hopkins' poetry in *New Bearings in English Poetry* (1932, 159-93). McLuhan was the director of Ong's thesis. It is hard to imagine that anyone will ever undertake to study Hopkins' sprung rhythm more thoroughly than Ong has. Hopkins writes poetry as though he owns the English language. Indeed, at the risk of trivializing his achievement, his poetry could be described as providing an owner's manual to the use of the English language. To be sure, English is his mother tongue. Even so, few poets have capitalized on the sound and stress of ordinary spoken English to the degree that he has in his use of sprung rhythm. Rhythm is established through stress, which is patently a sound effect implemented by the sound of one's voice in speaking the language aloud. Sprung rhythm is the particular stress pattern that Hopkins has discovered in the English language.

In the introduction to his fine new verse translation of *Beowulf*, Seamus Heaney acknowledges that "the poet who had first formed my ear was Gerard Manley Hopkins" (xxiii). Heaney also acknowledges that the earliest lines he published were "as much pastiche Anglo-Saxon as they were pastiche Hopkins," and he then gives some examples of his "Hopkins ventriloquism," as he styles it, and likens his Hopkins ventriloquism to the speech patterns of Ulster. In addition, he characterizes Hopkins as "a chip off the Old English block." There is a point to this characterization. (Concerning Hopkins, also see Heaney, "Feeling" 44-45; "The Drag" 14-15.)

However, in *Hopkins, the Self, and God*, Ong has called attention to Hopkins' fascination with particularity. As Ong points out, this fascination with particularity distinguishes Hopkins from the tendency toward the typical or the generalized that characterizes oral poetry, such as the poetry that Lord studies in *The Singer of Tales*, and early written poetry close to oral tradition, such as *Beowulf*. Hopkins' fascination with the particular is a culmination of the pervasive movement of human thought over the centuries from engagement less and less with stylized generalities and more and more with particulars.

Hopkins' fascination with the particular can also be connected with his understanding of the Christian doctrine of the Incarnation. Hopkins strongly favored the interpretation of the Incarnation suggested by the theologian John Duns Scotus (c.1266-1308). In the more common interpretation of the Incarnation set forth in earlier (and in later) theologies, the Son, the Second Person of the Divine Trinity (as much God, in Christian teaching, as is the Father and the Holy Spirit), became a human being to counter the effects of so-called original sin. The story of the Fall of Adam and Eve is probably best understood as a reflection on the human condition, especially on human suffering, but Paul the Apostle and Augustine of Hippo interpreted it as a story of original sin. Many other theologians, then, interpreted the Christian doctrine of the Incarnation in terms of atonement for this alleged original sin. But Duns Scotus side-stepped this line of reasoning by suggesting that the Incarnation was the first thing in God's intention. It was not a Plan B brought about by Adam and Eve, when Plan A (a sinless Adam and Eve) failed. For Duns Scotus, God's first basic intention in creation was to become himself a human being. To make this possible, God created human beings, and to make that possible God created the universe in which human beings were eventually generated. The way that Duns Scotus interpreted the Incarnation appealed enormously to Hopkins and doubtless connected with his fascination with particulars. (Duns Scotus' interpretation of the Incarnation also appeals enormously to Ong.)

Hopkins' mysticism strongly resembles what today is known in Roman Catholic circles as creation spirituality (see, for example, Matthew Fox, esp. 36-37). In any event, most new readers of Hopkins today will probably require the assistance of a good commentary to follow the sense of many of his poems (see Mariani; for a brief but fascinating study of Hopkins' style, see Vender; also see Ward). But Ong's essay on Hopkins' sprung rhythm is still the best guide available to Hopkins' sense of prosody. When Geoffrey H. Hartman's *Hopkins: A Collection of Critical Essays* appeared in the Twentieth Century Views series in 1966, it included a nine-page selection from Ong's essay on Hopkins' sprung rhythm.

Chapter 4 is Ong's 1942 article "The Province of Rhetoric and Poetic." Ong today credits McLuhan with being aware of the pervasiveness of rhetoric in Western culture since Greek antiquity, when he (McLuhan) was teaching at Saint Louis University from 1937 to 1944. During those years McLuhan was working on his 1943 Cambridge University doctoral dissertation on the history of the trivium (of grammar, rhetoric, and dialectic). We can readily see some of McLuhan's influence on Ong in the very choice of topics in this early article of his. In a certain sense Walker's *Rhetoric and Poetics in Antiquity* now provides extensive background information for understanding the issues that Ong treats in this early essay—as does the passage quoted from C. S. Lewis in the last subsection of the present essay.

Chapter 5 is Ong's 1944 *PMLA* article "Historical Backgrounds of Elizabethan and Jacobean Punctuation Theory." Once we remember how closely Ong had to attend to sound and stress patterns in his master's thesis on Hopkins' sprung rhythm, we can readily understand how he might move from that undertaking to study the oral background of Elizabethan and Jacobean punctuation theory. In *Space Between Words: The Origins of Silent Reading*, Paul Saenger reminds us that punctuation was relatively underdeveloped in hand-copied manuscripts (71-77). Because oral reading was so common for centuries, it would seem to follow that punctuation theory would connect punctuation with oral patterns of speech. (For other recent works of related interest, see M. B. Parkes' *Pause and Effect: An Introduction to the History of Punctuation in the West* and A. Graham-White's *Punctuation and Its Dramatic Value in Shakespearean Drama*.)

Chapter 6 is "The Jinnee in the Well-Wrought Urn," which was published originally in 1954. In his interview with Riemer, Ong recounted how after he had amassed material about Ramus and Ramism, he had a breakthrough insight that enabled him to align certain tendencies in Western culture. He aligned certain tendencies with sound and others with sight. He reports to Riemer that he was quite excited by this breakthrough and that he published some articles related to it. This is one of them. William K. Wimsatt, Jr., is on record as praising it as "the only sensible response that has ever been written to that essay of ours" ("The Critic"), by which he means the essay that he wrote with Monroe Beardsley entitled "The Intentional Fallacy" (1954). This article by Ong contains the *ur*-point that Ong likes to make about spoken language being primarily sound. Sound as such cannot be seen, but writing as such can be seen. As a result of being able to be seen and returned to, writing enables people to reflect on thought and expression. Ong makes this twofold point in a number of other selections reprinted in the present collection (e.g., Chapters 10, 11, 27). This twofold point holds the keys to accounting for numerous cultural constructs. However, apart from the pioneering efforts of Ong, McLuhan, Havelock, and a few other scholars, the vast potential of this twofold point has not been widely understood.

Chapter 12, "The Barbarian Within: Outsiders Inside Society Today," is the title essay first published as the culminating essay in Ong's 1962 collection *The Barbarian Within*. This essay is somewhat different from many of the other essays reprinted in the present collection. On the one hand, Ong's attention to patterns of thinking in terms of outsiders versus insiders can be connected with his discussion of agonistic tendencies in *Fighting for Life: Contest, Sexuality, and Consciousness* and with his distillation of that book in Chapter 25 in the present collection (concerning the Greek invention of the barbarian, see Hall; concerning the theme of outsiders versus insiders in Christian tradition, see Pagels). On the other hand, Ong's consideration of outsiders and insiders can be connected with the theme of saying "we" and "us" to various works of literature that he announces in the title of an introduction he wrote for a collection of essays: "Introduction: On Saying We and Us to Literature" (1982). For Ong, saying "we" and "us" to various works of literature is a way to enrich our sense of ourselves, because our sense of the other is connected with our sense of ourselves.

> As he composes his thoughts in words, a speaker or writer hears these words echoing within himself and thereby follows his own thoughts, as though he were another person. Conversely, a hearer or reader repeats within himself the words he hears and thereby understands them, as though he were himself two individuals. (*Barbarian* 51)

Later, Ong will draw on various sources to elaborate this basic insight further in "The Writer's Audience Is Always a Fiction" (1975), which is Chapter 22 in the present collection.

Chapter 13 is Ong's review of Lord's *The Singer of Tales*. Lord's book has prompted hundreds of studies of oral tradition. It probably would have done so without any promotion from Ong. But Lord's book stands as one of the most frequently cited works in Ong's entire body of work. His enthusiasm for Lord's book is almost unsurpassed. (If Ong was familiar with Parry's work before the publication of Lord's book, I can find no evidence of this in Ong's publications prior to 1960.)

Chapter 14 is Ong's review of McLuhan's *The Gutenberg Galaxy*. *The Gutenberg Galaxy: The Making of Typographic Man* is McLuhan at his best. In a course I took from Ong at Saint Louis University in the spring of 1966, he assigned us to look at this book, but he cautioned us to take it with a grain of salt. That is a good caution; McLuhan at times overstates certain points. In the bibliography of his 1967 encyclopedia article on "Written Transmission of Literature" (Chapter 17 in the present collection), Ong has characterized this book as "a racy survey, indifferent to some scholarly detail, but uniquely valuable in suggesting the sweep and depth of the cultural and psychological changes entailed in the passage from illiteracy to print and beyond." Indeed, this is a book that still repays careful reading. It deserves to be widely read by English majors and graduate students today, provided that they abide by Ong's caution. In the next subsection of the present essay, I will explain why people should take certain language with which McLuhan works with a grain of salt.

Chapter 15 is Ong's review of Havelock's *Preface to Plato*. Havelock's book has been in print continuously since it was first published, and Ong surely deserves some credit for this. He has cited this book frequently; it would be hard to say whether he has cited Lord's *The Singer of Tales* more often than he has cited Havelock's *Preface to Plato*. I recently reread *Preface to Plato*. It is a gem. According to a report made by Richards in 1947 (reprinted 1976, 204), Havelock had by then already formulated the basic thesis that he develops so convincingly in this 1963 book. (For some studies of related interest, see Goody.)

Chapter 16 is Ong's 1965 *PMLA* article "Oral Residue in Tudor Prose Style," which is reprinted in his 1971 collection *Rhetoric, Romance, and Technology: Studies in the Interaction of Expression and Culture.* Had Ong made this chapter one of a book devoted chapter by chapter to studies of oral residue in Tudor prose style, it would have been a wonderful book, and we would all be immensely indebted to him for it. Even so, I cannot think of any other article by Ong that still holds out as much potential for prompting further research as this one does. But the research need not be restricted to Tudor prose style, because oral residue can be found in earlier writing in English and numerous other languages. However, it should be considered in connection with Chapter 23 in the present collection on commonplaces.

Better than a decade after the publication of Ong's essay on oral residue, John Webster published "Oral Form and Written Craft in Spenser's *Fairie Queene*" (1976). Webster demonstrated that Spenser uses certain forms that resemble oral forms studied by Lord. In *Interfaces of the Word* (195-99), Ong discusses Webster's work in some detail and even points out one way in which his overall argument about oral form could be further strengthened. Because the *Fairie Queene* is poetry, it makes good sense for Webster and Ong to consider it in light of Lord's study of oral formulas and formulaic elements. However, because Ong himself has suggested expanding Lord's findings about oral formulas and formulaic elements to include formulary expressions such as proverbs and sententiae, we could reconsider studies such as Bartlett Jere Whiting's *Chaucer's Use of Proverbs* (1934), Charles G. Smith's *Spenser's Proverb Lore* (1970), Smith's *Shakespeare's Proverb Lore* (1963), and Whiting's *Proverbs in the Earlier English Drama* (1938) as providing further evidence of the kind of oral orientation that Ong refers to as oral residue.

As a matter of fact, John R. Cavanaugh (1970) did his doctoral dissertation under Ong on proverbs and sententiae in Thomas More's prose. Naturally, such an expanded sense of oral residue would add considerably to the points made by C. S. Lewis about the oral-aural appeal of rhetoric (quoted in the last subsection of the present essay). As Ong himself notes in his extensive discussion of commonplaces in Chapter 23 in the present collection, T. W. Baldwin has studied commonplace collections in use by schoolboys and adults in Shakespeare's day; Ong contends that the use of commonplaces in composition can be considered to be deeply rooted in oral tradition and also a sign of oral residue. Whiting (1977) has also compiled a rather extensive collection of early American proverbs and proverbial expressions. Because he culled these from printed sources, they strengthen Ong's overall contention about the carryover of oral residue in written prose and poetry. (Also see the collections compiled by Taylor and Whiting, 1967; and Whiting and Whiting, 1968.)

Chapter 18 is Ong's preface to Hugo Rahner's *Man at Play*. Hugo Rahner was a Jesuit priest and theologian and the brother of the famous Jesuit theologian Karl Rahner. In *Man at Play* Hugo Rahner draws on his classical and patristic learning to refresh our understanding of the concept of *eutrapelia*, the grave merriness that both Aristotle and Thomas Aquinas associate with the ethical person. We have noted above that Hannah Arendt once told Ong that he has a dialectical mind. This short selection nicely illustrates his dialectical mind at work.

Ong's preface to *Man at Play* was reproduced in its entirety in *Moreana*. The editor, Germain Marc'hadour, preceded it with a full-page note entitled "Toward a Theology of Merriment," in which he makes the following points:

> One of the most characteristic features of the humanism of St. Thomas More and his circle is its spirit of play. In his *Encomium Moriae*, Erasmus linked the concept of grave merriment or merry seriousness for all time to the name of More himself, and More responded with a work about *Nowhere* or *Utopia*. Erasmus and More were working in a long-standing tradition of rhetorical *topoi* when they presented these works as jesting trifles (*nugae*), in which what is normally serious is taken as play because what is play is serious. With other Christian humanists, they were bringing to a new intensity of focus the ancient idea of the grave-merry man, the man who is serious and playful at the same time. (327)

In his 1967 encyclopedia article "Humanism," Ong points out that the Latin title *Encomium Moriae* is "a pun on More's name meaning simultaneously 'The Praise of Folly' and 'The Praise of More-ishness'" (222).

In any event, Marc'hadour has elsewhere reminded us that Ong served on the editorial advisory board for Yale's *Complete Works of St. Thomas More* from the inception to the completion of the project ("Editor's Postscript" 15). Ong's considered judgments about More and Erasmus appear in his fine article entitled "Humanism" that was published originally in volume seven of the 1967 *New Catholic Encyclopedia* and has been reprinted in volume four of the selection of Ong's essays published under the general title of *Faith and Contexts* (for a fascinating study of Erasmus in terms of the then emerging print culture, see Jardine).

The chief reason for reprinting this short selection here is that it nicely connects with the themes in *Fighting for Life* and therefore with "The Agonistic Base of Scientifically Abstract Thought: Issues in *Fighting for Life: Contest, Sexuality, and Consciousness*" (Chapter 25 in the present collection). Suffice it to say that Ong had been reflecting on the matters he writes about in this preface to *Man at Play* long before the publisher of the English translation of Hugo Rahner's originally German work provided him (Ong) with the opportunity to write this piece.

Even so, we may wonder about the value of sorting out the matters that Ong sets himself to sort out in this relatively short piece. Can it be worthwhile for us to get clear about what is work and what is play? Work appears to be here to stay. But the nature of work seems to be changing. Work usually helps give us the sense that we are making a certain contribution to our personal and to the overall social good. In short, we are making a contribution to society. This is no mean achievement. But does our work also help us become more authentically human? This question in turn raises the question of just what it might mean to be authentically human.

When we turn our attention from work to play, we can raise the same basic questions: (1) Does our play help us become more authentically human? (2) What are our expectations concerning authentic humanity? Ong does not undertake to give us guidelines for assessing when we are becoming more authentically human. But he does intimate in this selection that both work and play are authentically human. Naturally this twofold claim does not exhaust the subject of what it might mean to be authentically human. For example, he would undoubtedly hold out for counting love of God and of other persons as part of becoming authentically human, just as he would count I-thou communication as part of becoming authentically human. Even so, the import of this short selection is to establish that both work and play are authentically human, and to distinguish them from one another inasmuch as this is possible to do.

As Marc'hadour's comments above indicate, the contrast between work and play with which Ong works and plays in this piece can be connected with the spirit of witty play found in Erasmus' *Praise of Folly* and More's *Utopia.* For a discussion that can be connected with the theme of play that Ong here develops, see Harold Bloom's discussion in *Shakespeare: The Invention of the Human* of the Fool in Shakespeare's *King Lear* (476-515). In his rather ambitious survey of Shakespeare's plays, Bloom also elaborates his theory of Shakespeare's agonism or spirit of contesting with other contemporary playwrights. This aspect of

Bloom's 1998 book on Shakespeare carries forward the central theme of Bloom's earlier book entitled *Agon: Towards a Theory of Revisionism* (1982). In neither of these books does Bloom give evidence of being familiar with Ong's *Fighting for Life: Contest, Sexuality, and Consciousness* (1981). However far apart Ong and Bloom may be with regard to their own personal theism or atheism, there are certain noteworthy parallels in the discussions of contesting behavior and even in their respective brief discussions of the spirit of play. The theme of male agonism could probably be studied more extensively than Bloom and Ong have studied it thus far. The connection between the contesting spirit and the spirit of play could probably also be explored further.

The preceding has been a somewhat lengthy discussion of one selection, and we must now turn our attention to other selections. In the next two selections Ong calls attention to his own thought and suggests that it holds out certain potential for further inquiry by other scholars. Chapter 19 is Ong's review of Vickers' *Classical Rhetoric in English Poetry*. There is a certain value to Vickers' book, as Ong allows. But he suggests that Vickers and others need to develop a richer sense of orality to work out a rounder account of both classical rhetoric and English poetry. Ong advances this same suggestion in the next selection as well.

Chapter 20 is Ong's review of Howell's *Eighteenth Century British Logic and Rhetoric*. In 1960, Howell had reviewed Ong's two big books on Ramus and Ramism in the *Quarterly Journal of Speech*. Even though Howell found much to praise in Ong's books, he also expressed reservations about certain points in *Ramus, Method, and the Decay of Dialogue*. For example, Howell repeatedly refers to oral delivery, even though Ong does not single out oral delivery as part of his concern about the shift from an oral to a visual paradigm of thought, both of which can culminate in oral delivery. Referring to the whole elocutionary movement of the eighteenth century, Howell declares that "[i]t is hard to see how Ramist rhetoric could have caused oral delivery to perish of neglect, if even before the end of the Ramist era oral delivery suddenly begins to have more importance than it had ever enjoyed in the great classical rhetorics of Greece and Rome" (91). But Ong has not said that oral delivery perished of neglect. Clearly Howell does not understand what Ong is saying. Ong answers Howell's concerns in this review-essay.

Chapter 21 reprints the 1973 book *Why Talk? A Conversation about Language with Walter Ong Conducted by Wayne Altree*. Their conversation is wide ranging and accessible enough to need no introduction. However, Ong does remark in passing that a certain confidence accompanies learning. We might want to apply this point to Ong himself. For example, throughout *Ramus, Method, and the Decay of Dialogue*, he usually sounds quite confident. I would attribute his confidence to the fact that he knows what he is talking about, not to some kind of false confidence that might more aptly be styled bravado or grandiosity. In saying that Ong's confidence comes from his being well informed, I do not wish to imply that his judgments are always correct or beyond dispute. But they are based on study of pertinent material. Perhaps some of them occasionally need to be corrected because of oversights on his part or updated because of subsequent advances in scholarship. But even so, he is not given to opining about matters that he has not studied. When he expresses judgments about certain matters, he does so because he can justifiably claim a certain competence in the matters in question. In short, his confidence comes from his competence.

Even though many of Ong's comments in this discussion with Wayne Altree can be connected with various selections in the present collection, Ong's comments about print culture deserve to be singled out for special attention here. He points out that print eventually moved writers away from the abundant (or copious) use of sayings and moved them toward a greater stress on "facts" (or particularized details). (For a recent study of how Ramism contributed to the emergence of fact-oriented technical writing, see Tebeaux; also see Ong's "Ramist Method and the Commercial Mind" [reprinted in *Rhetoric* 165-89].)

Chapter 22 is Ong's 1975 *PMLA* article "The Writer's Audience Is Always a Fiction," which is perhaps Ong's most frequently cited article. In it he does not discuss how teachers might help students learn how to fictionalize an audience, but he himself suggested a way to do this in the course I took from him at Saint Louis University in the fall semester of 1964, Practical Criticism: Poetry. In addition to reading the two required textbooks, we were expected to read certain books or parts of books that he had placed on reserve in the library, and we were then tested on the assigned readings. After he had tested us on T. S. Eliot's *On Poetry and Poets*, Ong assigned a short paper. The paper had no explicit connection with Eliot. But Ong suggested that we try to imagine ourselves as writing the paper for Eliot to read; he suggested that we try to tell Eliot something that he did not already know. Well, I decided to try this. As a result of applying the standard of telling him something that he did not already know, I discarded my entire first draft. I also discarded my entire second draft. But I was definitely catching on to how to fictionalize an audience.

In any event, Ong himself is a past master at fictionalizing different audiences. As his numerous articles over the decades in the Jesuit magazine *America* show, he is quite capable of writing for a semipopular audience. At the same time he is able to write for more specialized scholarly audiences, and oftentimes he sets out to tell them something that they do not already know. This aspect of his work is most pronounced in his books that were originally published by university presses. Then again, he is also able to write more routine works in which he summarizes scholarly work, such as encyclopedia articles and his own widely translated book *Orality and Literacy: The Technologizing of the Word*.

Chapter 23 is "Typographic Rhapsody: Ravisius Textor, Zwinger, and Shakespeare," which was originally published in 1976. In "Rhetoric and Intertextuality" Heinrich F. Plett has recently discussed the commonplace tradition in connection with the current interest in literary studies in intertextuality, so it is timely to reprint this fine essay by Ong treating the commonplace tradition. Ong's approach to studying the commonplace tradition was strengthened by Lord's study of the composition patterns of oral singers of tales. He identified how they composed their works by remembering basic patterns and working variations on them. These patterns included not only small units (in effect, lines) but also sequences for larger units (such as the arming of the hero). Ong then recognized that orators for centuries had learned similar composition techniques involving commonplaces. As the title of this selection indicates, Ong suggests that people trained in rhetoric learned how to work with and stitch together (rhapsodize) commonplaces.

Because Ong considers the commonplace tradition to be deeply rooted in oral tradition, the use of commonplaces in composition can also be considered to be a sign of oral residue, as Ong has delineated this idea in Chapter 16. (Concerning the commonplace tradition, see Sister Joan Marie Lechner's 1962 study of Renaissance commonplaces, which she did originally as a doctoral dissertation under Ong's direction; for a more recent study, see Moss, which includes an extensive bibliography of scholarly literature; also see Baldwin; Rechtien; Yeo.)

Chapter 25 is Ong's 1982 plenary address to the American Catholic Philosophical Association, "The Agonistic Base of Scientifically Abstract Thought: Issues in *Fighting for Life: Contest, Sexuality, and Consciousness*." This piece is actually a fine distillation of certain points in Ong's book.

However, if we are going to take a hint from Ong and try to recognize the agonistic base of certain kinds of thought and expression, we should turn our attention to the anti-Jewish material in the Christian New Testament. Pontius Pilate crucified Jesus of Nazareth. Earlier the local authorities of the Roman empire had executed John the Baptist, but without executing any of his followers. After John's death, Jesus' death was

predictable, unless of course he stopped his public activities. He did not
stop, and as a result he too was executed. But once again there was no
immediate attempt to execute the followers.

So far as we can tell, the anti-Jewish material in various places New
Testament was composed at different times and in different locales by
writers who were themselves Jews. They were Jews engaged in fierce
polemics with their fellow Jews. Christians today need to recognize the
agonistic base of that material. Simply stated, it amounts to name calling
by people whose views were being strongly rejected by their fellow Jews.
No doubt those Jews who were rejecting the new (Christian) views contributed their fair share to the name calling. But the time has come for
Christians around the world to recognize the name-calling features of the
New Testament and to put an end to Christian supersessionism. Christian
supersessionism is undeniably agonistic. The agonistic drive can at times
lead to fruitful developments, but in this instance it surely has not (for a
recent history of the church and the Jews, see Carroll; for related scrip-
ture studies, see Crossan; Fredriksen; Gager; Pagels).

This is a tragic example of agonism gone awry. No doubt readers can
think of other examples. But we need to note that the agonistic spirit is
integral to human life, as Ong reminds us. It is central to the development
of any work that we might conceivably admire. It is the only game in
town. By definition, a totally nonagonistic approach to life would be tantamount to a catatonic state. Thus the real challenge facing all of us is to
learn how to direct our agonistic spirit toward forms of human striving
that are truly worthwhile. The basic psychological dynamism underlying
the agonistic spirit was referred to by Plato and Aristotle as *thumos*,
which is usually translated as the "spirited" part of the psyche or soul (the
other parts being the rational part and the desiring part). (Concerning *thumos* in Plato's writings, see Hobbs; concerning *thumos* in Aristotle's
thought, see Koziak; for a discussion of the agonistic spirit in the form of
mimetic desire, see Girard; for a discussion of certain excesses in Greek
agonistic spirit, see Burckhardt.)

Because Ong has written with such great lucidity about agonistic
behavior, we might wonder about his own agonism. This address to the
American Catholic Philosophical Association, I would suggest, reveals a
certain degree of agonism with certain unnamed people who have used
sociobiology "to generate some quite indefensible, and indeed, naive,
philosophical speculation." He immediately goes on to allow that "this
does not mean that the details sociobiology deals with are irrelevant to
philosophy, which, I believe, should be concerned in its own way with
everything." Indeed, we could see Ong's own efforts in *Fighting for Life:*

Contest, Sexuality, and Consciousness as agonistic because he clearly sets out to use data from sociobiology to set forth his own philosophical speculations from a nonmaterialist philosophical position (for recent critiques of the exaggerated materialist position known as scientism, see Postman's *Technopoly* [esp. 144-63]; and Huston Smith's *Why Religion Matters*).

Chapter 26 is Ong's 1990 essay "Technological Development and Writer-Subject-Reader Immediacies." In this selection Ong once again returns to considering Hopkins, but this time Ong turns his attention to reports Hopkins received through newspaper accounts that it turn were based on information transmitted via telegraph. (For studies concerning the telegraph, see McLuhan's *Understanding Media* [246-57]; Postman's *Amusing Ourselves to Death* [65-71]; Carey's "Technology and Ideology: The Case of the Telegraph.")

Ong focuses on the sense of immediacy that the reports Hopkins read gave him, and we can connect Ong's discussion of immediacy here with his earlier discussions of presence in *American Catholic Crossroads* (149-51), *The Barbarian Within* (58-59), and *The Presence of the Word* (see the index). We should note here that Ong has drawn on Martin Buber's idea of personal presence in I-thou communication, not on Martin Heidegger's rather different use of the term "presence" to refer to conceptualizations. However, when Jacques Derrida writes about presence, he is indeed drawing on Heidegger's use of the term, as Alan Bass has explained in his "Translator's Introduction" to the collection of Derrida's essays entitled *Writing and Difference* (x-xi). Even though Ong has written about presence in a few essays, he has not developed the matter further. But his earlier discussions of presence can be connected with his treatment of writer-subject-reader immediacies in this selection about Hopkins. Thus we can see the discussion of immediacies as a way to open up and expand the discussion of presence. To spell out the obvious, face-to-face presence entails sensing immediacies; it is through sensing immediacies that we experience the presence of one another in face-to-face communication. In this selection Ong turns his attention to describing Hopkins' highly responsive reception of newspaper reports about a shipwreck. Hopkins was moved by these newspaper reports. Through them he was able to enter into the experience that was being reported. This kind of responsiveness involves a sense of presence of the person, but without the person being actually present. Poetry can also evoke at times a similar sense of immediacy and presence.

Even though newspaper accounts of the wreck of the *Deutschland* were able to evoke such empathy and identification from Hopkins, we need to note that they were based largely on words. In comparison, television news coverage today often includes on-the-spot photographs and sometimes even interviews, both of which can add to the reporter's words to enhance the sense of immediacy. When we turn our attention to email and Internet communication today, we note that they can also communicate words with a lively sense of immediacy, which at times can be similar to the sense of immediacy in face-to-face communication. However, as we note these various points concerning experiences of immediacy, we also should note that not all experiences of immediacy move us as deeply as Hopkins was evidently moved by the reports he was reading.

Even though Hopkins was not engaged in face-to-face communication with the German nun on the sinking *Deutschland* who was crying out to Jesus Christ, we might say that his deep response to those reports represents something like the I-thou communication that Buber writes about. Hopkins was moved at the nun's reported words. In any event, he was responding to more than just information. To be sure, responding to information is often a key element involved in ordinary communication. If we allow that I-thou communication is somewhat special, then we would also allow that it usually involves something more than information exchange, even of highly meaningful information. Ong himself explores this distinction in detail in the next selection in the present collection. Chapter 27 is Ong's 1996 article "Information and/or Communication: Interactions." In this invaluable essay Ong distinguishes I-thou communication from information transmission.

Chapter 28 is Ong's 1998 article "Digitization Ancient and Modern: Beginnings of Writing and Today's Computers." On June 16, 2000, the Media Ecology Association conferred its Walter Benjamin Award on Walter Ong for this article. In a certain sense this essay represents *ur-*Ong. The *ur-*point that Ong has made so many times is that spoken language involves sound primarily, not sight, even though sight can obviously supplement the sound. When after tens of thousands of years or more with only oral verbalization some few human beings first developed visualizable writing systems, they thereby formed ways to use sight in coded written (and later, printed) patterns to cue in sound. In time their innovation would lead to the forming of philosophic and scientific conceptualizations, as Havelock has in effect suggested in *Preface to Plato*. Because Denise Schmandt-Besserat has done more than anyone else to advance our understanding of the ancient development of writing systems, Ong devotes a substantial part of this essay to praising and celebrating her work. But then he also connects his observations concerning the beginnings of writing with computers today. In addition to considering the development of the alphabet, he also considers the development of numeracy. This aspect of this essay can be connected with his attention to the quantification of thought in logic, as he styles it in *Ramus, Method, and the Decay of Dialogue*. This aspect of this essay can also be connected with Hobart and Schiffman's *Information Ages: Literacy, Numeracy, and the Computer Revolution*, despite their explicit criticisms of certain other aspects of Ong's thought.

A final word is in order about Ong's humanism, as we may style it. His humanism is a theistic humanism, as distinct from an atheistic humanism. Because Ong is a Roman Catholic priest, it will come as a surprise to no one to learn that he tends to favor strongly christocentric views. Like Hopkins, Ong is deeply impressed with the Christian doctrine of the Incarnation, and like Hopkins, Ong is deeply impressed with Duns Scotus' theological interpretation that the intention of the Incarnation was a first intention in the mind of God; in short, it did not arise as a result of something that Adam and Eve did. With respect to creation, Ong is not a biblical literalist, but he does explicitly favor a position that we can style mild creationism—that God does create each individual human soul. In his 1967 collection of essays entitled *In the Human Grain*, Ong has stated that "the creation of the human soul is always a special act of [God], since the soul in its spirituality transcends the merely material" (78). This is a comparatively mild form of creationism. However, the clear implication of this position is that God's creation is ongoing.

When we move from the domain of theological considerations to the domain of philosophic considerations, we find that Ong values quality human communication: I-thou communication. At least to a certain degree, he also values the spirit of agonism (contesting behavior) and the spirit of play. As he states in his interview with Riemer, struggle at some level is here to stay. However, he is not uncritical of agonism; he recognizes that agonism can lead at times to very foolish behavior and at other times to deadly violence, neither of which he condones. On balance, he tends to downplay the agonistic spirit in favor of a more cooperative spirit. But he does not investigate what factors contribute to and what other factors detract from developing a cooperative spirit, which, after all, can be seen as a practical orientation of the agonistic spirit. (Concerning positive factors that can contribute to cooperation in learning, see the Johnsons.)

With regard to what today is referred to as multiculturalism, we find that Ong is committed to saying "we" and "us" to literary works from various cultural traditions. Indeed, he sees orality-literacy studies as potentially all-inclusive in scope, because it includes both oral traditions and written traditions. But he does not see orality-literacy studies as the only way to proceed; this approach can be supplemented by related studies, including some of Ong's own related studies in the history of rhetoric and his studies of agonistic tendencies. In his discussion of "The Barbarian Within," he notes the basic human deficiency in setting up an overly strong sense of an in-group that in effect demonizes the out-group(s). When this kind of overly strong polarization occurs, it can be seen as the agonistic spirit gone awry. But he is not uncritical here either; he is not condoning all groups or all group behavior uncritically. Ong is not a moral relativist. But he probably would subscribe to the standard Christian teaching to distinguish between the sin, on the one hand, and the sinner, on the other.

Ong and McLuhan

Let me state my basic contention plainly at the outset of this section: Should we decide to cultivate historical-mindedness, as Lonergan has urged us to do, and should we decide to cultivate archive fever, as Derrida has urged us to do, then we should be reading Teilhard's posthumously published *The Phenomenon of Man* (1959), Ong's *Ramus, Method, and the Decay of Dialogue* (1958), McLuhan's *The Gutenberg Galaxy* (1962), McLuhan's *Understanding Media* (1964), and Ong's *The Presence of the Word* (1967), as well as numerous other related works. I have noted above Ong's claim that we need both closeness and distance for understanding. These five books can go a long way in providing us with some needed distance in order to understand Western culture today. To be sure, we should read other pertinent books as well. But these five books are arguably unsurpassed for giving us a sense of the big picture, and thus the kind of distance we need to have to help us study any number of cultural developments in Western culture.

In the minds of many people, Ong's name is linked with McLuhan's. The link is surely understandable. However, McLuhan's scholarly standing has fallen under the shadow of an overreaction in the United States, which has been so strong that it now needs to be questioned and challenged. The overreactors have thrown out the baby with the bath water. Because the overreaction to McLuhan was so successful in eclipsing his scholarly standing, Daniell and others have more recently tried using similar smear tactics against Ong, Havelock, and me. Even though my efforts alone will not be able to turn the tide of opinion in McLuhan's favor, I surely want to set forth my views of his work here. As we consider Ong's work and the potential for further developments by others of lines of inquiry he has developed to a certain degree, we need to consider why more follow-up work has not yet been undertaken. At least part of the hesitancy derives from the enormous overreaction to McLuhan's work in the United States. Thus we may need to get clear about McLuhan's work in order to clear the way for further developments of Ong's thought. Hence this subsection is needed because of its importance in my overall project of introducing and elucidating and defending Ong's thought.

In a word, McLuhan has been demonized among academics in the United States. The publicity that he received in the United States was in my estimate wildly out of proportion. But the overreaction to him and his work in the United States has, I think, also been wildly out of proportion. His best books—*The Mechanical Bride: Folklore of Industrial Man* (1951), *The Gutenberg Galaxy: The Making of Typographic Man* (1962), and *Understanding Media: The Extensions of Man* (1964)—still repay careful reading and should be read by scholars and graduate students, provided that they take them with a grain of salt, as Ong has advised. I believe there is a more capacious mind at work in these three books than there is many other books I have read by a good number of other scholars. McLuhan at his best is very good—not perfect, but very, very good.

In addition to these three early books, McLuhan later published a number of other books that are clearly aimed at a popular audience, which means that they should not be judged by the same standards as we would apply to these three books in which his erudition is clearly aimed at a scholarly audience. When we find McLuhan in the 1960s and 1970s cultivating public attention beyond academia through his various books aimed at a popular audience, we should remember that as a young man McLuhan greatly admired G. K. Chesterton (1874-1936), who was not only a public intellectual and author of books but also a prolific journalist and commentator in his day. As a public intellectual and commentator, McLuhan became more widely known in his day than Chesterton had been in his.

Because Chesterton is not quite so well known today as he was in his own day, a word is in order here about him. He was well known for his witty paradoxes. He uses paradoxes so extensively that Hugh Kenner has written a short book entitled *Paradox in Chesterton* (1947), which includes a twelve-page introduction by McLuhan. Chesterton was a prolific author, writing newspaper columns, detective novels, literary criticism, religious reflections, and biographies, including still notable biographies of Thomas Aquinas and Francis of Assisi (for a recent biography of Chesterton, see Pearce, 1996). Chesterton also became a convert to Roman Catholicism (on July 30, 1922), a step that McLuhan himself would later take (on March 30, 1937), when he had completed his course work at Cambridge University and was teaching at the University of Wisconsin in 1936-1937.

McLuhan's first article was "G. K. Chesterton: A Practical Mystic" (1936), and I want to suggest that the subtitle can also be applied to McLuhan. Even though McLuhan wrote relatively little about religious matters compared to what Chesterton wrote, McLuhan does cultivate something comparable to a mystic viewpoint, or at least a religious detachment from the passing things of this world. When we read McLuhan's preface to *The Mechanical Bride* (1951), we should read this preface in light of his earlier characterization of Chesterton as a practical mystic. If McLuhan aimed at something like a Christian mystic's detachment from the passing things of this world, then the well-known imagery that he borrows in this preface from Edgar Allan Poe's "A Descent into the Maelstrom" to characterize his own undertakings seems playful and witty—a put on of something that "comes to mind," as he says. Regardless of how well or poorly Poe's sailor serves as an analogy, McLuhan characterizes his own undertaking as involving a certain rational detachment as a spectator of his own situation. I would liken such detachment to that of a Christian mystic, as he himself has seen Chesterton as a practical mystic. McLuhan explicitly characterizes his undertaking in this book as an amusement, which calls to mind the grave-merry theme that we considered above in connection with Erasmus' *Praise of Folly* and More's *Utopia*.

In this preface McLuhan explicitly states that the present situation in industrial society "is full not only of destructiveness, but also of promises of rich new developments to which moral indignation is a very poor guide" (v). Thus we have him eschewing moral indignation, but not a moral standpoint, because he acknowledges the destructiveness of some developments while calling attention to the positive potential of other new developments—and proffering his reflections on the current situation as an amusement. Expressions of moral indignation presumably aim to arouse moral indignation in others. But what does an amusement aim to do—to delight? Could we hear in this a cagey echo of Cicero's observation that a good speech should teach, delight, and move? Is McLuhan trying to delight us into thinking along lines that he sets forth in this admittedly novel book, or at least start us thinking about them?

In 1952, when Ong was living in Paris, he published a highly favorable review-essay about McLuhan's *The Mechanical Bride* in *Social Order*, which at the time was a new periodical published out of Saint Louis University. Seven pages in length, Ong's "The Mechanical Bride: Christen the Folklore of Industrial Man" is doubtless the lengthiest and most substantial review of McLuhan's book at that time. However, we should note that the notion of christening is Ong's way of providing a larger Christian context in which readers can situate McLuhan's ambitious undertaking. In an effort to urge Catholics to transpose and transform elements of industrial culture around them, Ong highlights certain past examples of such transformation. For example, he correctly notes that "Catholics once transformed—not without change, to be sure—a whole family of pagan 'virtues' which they found . . . in the pagan Aristotle" (83). For a fascinating account of just how this kind of transformation worked out, see McNamee's 1960 study of Aristotle's conceptualization of magnanimity and of later Christian understandings of it (for a study of another Christian transformation of the sort Ong mentions, see C. Stephen Jaeger's *The Origins of Courtliness: Civilizing Trends and the Formation of Courtly Ideals, 939-1210*; also see the selections by Christopher Dawson gathered together in *Christianity and European Culture* and Marcia L. Colish's *Medieval Foundations of the Western Intellectual Tradition*).

However, Ong explicitly states that "Professor McLuhan does not treat explicitly of dogmatic or liturgical implications, but he leaves open a hundred doors here into every area of Catholic life" (83). And so does Ong; he does not delineate any specific suggestions. Thus this review-essay sounds like a rousing call to action, or at least to consider undertaking transformative action, but I have no idea of what actions he would expect Catholics to undertake as a result of reading either his essay or McLuhan's book—or both. But Ong's basic point seems to be to urge Catholics to use elements of industrial culture for positive religious purposes. Rather than what? Rather than express moral indignation, to borrow McLuhan's term?

McLuhan began teaching in 1946 at the University of Toronto (at St. Michael's College). After *The Mechanical Bride* was published in 1951, he was impressed to learn that Harold Innis (1894-1952, Ph.D. in economics from the University of Chicago) had placed it on his course reading list. By the time that McLuhan joined the University of Toronto, Innis was already established as an intellectual titan there. After hearing that Innis had placed his book on his course reading list, McLuhan read Innis' *Empire and Communication* (1950) and *The Bias of Communication* (1951), both of which McLuhan then wrote about in his 1953 article "The Later Innis." There can be little doubt that McLuhan learned a lot from Innis' later books.

McLuhan's thought was also influenced by a number of other people with whom he came in contact at the University of Toronto, perhaps most notably by the anthropologist Edmund S. Carpenter. With the aid of a grant from the Ford Foundation, Carpenter and McLuhan and some of their colleagues began seminars on culture and communication. In addition, they undertook the publication of the journal *Explorations: Studies in Culture and Communication*, nine issues of which appeared between 1953 and 1959. According to Carpenter (240), the anthropologist Dorothy Lee contributed six essays to *Explorations* and also met occasionally with Carpenter, McLuhan, and others to discuss issues of interest. McLuhan was an omnivorous learner, and he had learned much more between the time when he had completed his own doctoral dissertation in 1943 and the time when he read Ong's published doctoral dissertation (for a fuller account of the people with whom McLuhan came in contact in Toronto, see Theall; also see Carpenter's appendix about McLuhan in Theall's book).

The pump of McLuhan's thought had been primed by his reading of Innis and by other intellectual endeavors he had engaged in at the University of Toronto. When Ong's report of the trajectory of his own thought was published in book form as *Ramus, Method, and the Decay of Dialogue*, bingo! In relatively short order, McLuhan wrote his masterpiece, *The Gutenberg Galaxy* (see Marchand 59, 155). McLuhan had previously completed a draft of another book; after he had completed the manuscript of *The Gutenberg Galaxy*, he then reworked the other book manuscript, which then became *Understanding Media* (see Marchand 167). And we heirs and beneficiaries of this explosion in creative thought are still trying to digest all that he has bestowed on us in these two seminal books. As we have noted above, Ong has said that Teilhard started no new lines of thought for him. McLuhan might say this of Ong's book, even though he does quote Ong in *The Gutenberg Galaxy*. Even so, Ong's book served as a catalyst for McLuhan to set forth his own line of thought.

After the publication of *The Gutenberg Galaxy* in 1962 and of *Understanding Media* in 1964, Marshall McLuhan was easily the most publicized English professor in North America. He was a celebrity. *Newsweek* magazine ran a cover story about McLuhan. *Playboy* magazine published an interview with him. He even made a cameo appearance, playing the role of himself, in Woody Allen's movie *Annie Hall*. In 1967 McLuhan's book *The Medium Is the Massage* was published. This title is an interesting variant of his much-quoted dictum, "The medium is the message," which he never used as a title. According to Ong, McLuhan tended to regard puns as often more truth-providing than more direct statement. In any event, this book is reported to have sold nearly one million copies worldwide (Marchand 193).

The publicity McLuhan received over a period of years spanning two decades was phenomenal. Before McLuhan came along, intellectuals had long been discussing technology and the influence it has. But McLuhan's particular blend of ideas concerning technology seemed to electrify people. The phenomenal publicity that this Canadian academic received in the United States spanned two decades that included highly publicized events such as the black civil-rights movement, the assassination of President John Kennedy, the escalation of American involvement in Vietnam and protests about it, the assassination of the Reverend Martin Luther King, Jr., and the assassination of Senator Robert Kennedy. In the years since McLuhan's death in 1980, various living scholars have been lionized and/or had best-selling books: Stanley Fish, Jacques Derrida, Richard Rorty, and Harold Bloom, for example. But no other academic has received publicity remotely comparable to the amount that McLuhan received.

However, in my estimate the amount of publicity McLuhan received was out of proportion. In a way, it was unbelievable. In a certain sense I understand the overreaction that set in among academics in the United States. The amount of attention that McLuhan received would predictably generate a counterreaction. Oh my, did it! But had any other academic received comparable publicity, it would have predictably generated a counterreaction, because of the ingrained sense that most academics have that no academic truly deserves such publicity. In other words, such phenomenal publicity will understandably bring on the naysayers. (In 1975 McLuhan published a bibliography of writings by and about him and his work; the number of items that he lists about his work is extensive.)

Understandable as the overreaction in the United States may have been, we should note that Canadian authors have now produced two biographies of McLuhan (Gordon; Marchand) and a number of worthwhile studies of his thought (see, for example, Genosko; Theall; Wilmott). However, even though a number of Canadian authors have managed to write reasonably sensible books about him and his thought, it is almost impossible to discuss him and his work in certain circles in the United States.

McLuhan's *The Gutenberg Galaxy* (1962) can be seen as a friendly response to and an amplication of certain themes in Ong's *Ramus, Method, and the Decay of Dialogue* (1958). In this respect McLuhan's book can be seen as a friendly example of the kind of male contesting behavior that Ong delineates in *Fighting for Life: Contest, Sexuality, and Consciousness* (1981). Of course, McLuhan in his 1962 book refers to Lord's *The Singer of Tales* (1960), which both McLuhan and Ong repeatedly referred to after its publication. Ong's 1964 Terry Lectures at Yale University can in turn be seen as a friendly response to and an amplication of certain themes not only in McLuhan's 1962 book, but also in his own 1958 groundbreaking book, strengthened of course by Lord's 1960 book and Havelock's 1963 book *Preface to Plato*. As we have noted in passing above, Ong's Terry Lectures were published in expanded form by Yale University Press as *The Presence of the Word* in 1967, and so was Ong's collection *In the Human Grain*. In 1966-1967, Ong was the Berg Visiting Professor of English at New York University, and in 1968-1969, Ong was the Willett Visiting Professor in the Humanities at the University of Chicago. Thus Ong's star in the scholarly firmament was rising about the same time that McLuhan's was, which is part of the reason why their names are frequently linked.

McLuhan was visiting professor at Fordham University in 1967-1968, a year in which he received great publicity but also suffered serious health problems. He underwent delicate brain surgery. McLuhan responded to the overall publicity he was receiving by publishing a number of short books, some of which I think could have been left unpublished. For example, McLuhan published a short book about war for a popular audience, *War and Peace in the Global Village* (1968). However, to the disappointment of many of his fans, he failed to condemn the United States' involvement in Vietnam. But to his credit, he did not publicly endorse American involvement either. (Ong also failed to condemn publicly American involvement in Vietnam, but of course he did not have the temerity to publish a short book on war at the height of the Vietnam War.)

But when all is said about McLuhan, he may have been the victim of overexposure. The saying has it that familiarity breeds contempt, and McLuhan was certainly the recipient of more than his fair share of contempt. He attracted many detractors; probably no other twentieth-century professor has attracted as many detractors as McLuhan did, not even Derrida. At his best, McLuhan is one of the more capacious minds of the twentieth century, regardless of whatever shortcomings he may have.

The American space program was able to provide us with a photograph of the earth as a planet in space that was wonderful and powerful to behold, and so was—and so is—the global sweep of *The Gutenberg Galaxy*. Despite whatever imperfections it may have, it is a brilliant work. For those who were willing to learn from it, it helped us to think on a global scale about world cultures. No, we should not take every statement that McLuhan makes in this landmark book as though it were an inerrant revelation from God. McLuhan got some things wrong in this book. In addition, he oversimplified certain matters and he overstated some points. Ong's brief assessment of it that was quoted above from his 1967 encyclopedia article "Written Transmission of Literature" strikes me still as a fair and balanced assessment.

In *The Gutenberg Galaxy* McLuhan works with the verbal sequence of tribalization, detribalization, and retribalization, which in my estimate is too simplistic and alarmist. We should also recognize the sheer sensationalism of McLuhan's three terms. By contrast with them, David Riesman's terms outer-directed (tradition-directed), inner-directed, and other-directed sound far more neutral. Because Riesman's *The Lonely Crowd* had been published in 1950, which McLuhan surely would have known about, these more neutral terms were available for McLuhan to use. With regard to tribalization, we should note the humanity of all peoples. Tribal peoples are human too. We could note other shortcomings in McLuhan. But we should not be distracted by them to the point where we fail to draw fruit from his best work. When he is wrong, he is wrong; let us note it and move on. However, several of McLuhan's later books are written for a popular audience, including the one on war. They are less significant. But most are noteworthy enough to read, provided that we recognize them as popular works and do not judge them by standards that would be more appropriate for scholarly works.

If McLuhan's term "retribalization" refers to a return to cultural conditions as they were prior to the development of phonetic alphabetic literacy in antiquity, then we do not appear to be in danger of such a massive cultural regression. Literacy appears to be here to stay. In the United States taxpayers could save an enormous amount of money if all forms of formal education in reading and writing were abolished so that we could return to some pristine oral culture, but nobody is seriously promoting such a scheme. Even if somebody were to talk it up, how many adults would take it seriously?

In *Illiterate America* Jonathan Kozol unequivocally endorses functional literacy for all. In *Pedagogy of the Oppressed* Paulo Freire also strongly endorses functional literacy. There simply are no books arguing against the spread of literacy. Similarly, there are no organized political movements with the announced goal of closing down schools, the organizations through which reading and writing are taught. Instead of outright opposition to literacy, we find today and earlier a wide spectrum of discontent about shortcomings in producing functionally literate students. In other words, there is a broad consensus in the United States about the goal of functional literacy. Despite all-too-real shortcomings in attaining the goal, literacy appears to be here to stay in the sense that there is no organized effort to abolish it.

In addition to literacy, modern science also appears to be here to stay. Because of the practical uses of the physical and life sciences, mathematics, and even the social sciences, they will almost certainly continue to receive social, financial, and institutional support, The future of these forms of learning appears to be far more assured than does the future of philosophy, history, and literary studies, for example. But in the age of television, such human creations as philosophy, history, and literary studies may go the way of classics, because television vaunts lowbrow culture, not learned culture. However, even though McLuhan overstated the danger posed by the advent of television when he imagined some kind of retribalization, television does nevertheless still pose some sorts of dangers, as he clearly sensed.

We do not find the likes of Aeschylus or Sophocles or Shakespeare writing for television or for Hollywood movies. As it has emerged thus far in the United States, television represents an enormous trivialization—indeed, an infantilization—as do most movies. Moreover, watching television and movies can become addictive. Therein lies the danger. To borrow an expression from Karl Marx, watching television and movies is the opium of the people. The danger posed by such enormously popular opiates is that most people will be satisfied with being amused in their leisure time, when they could be using this time for more substantial intellectual and social endeavors (see Postman's *Amusing Ourselves to Death*). This could lead many children to self-select out of becoming scientists, for example, as well as to self-select out of studying philosophy, literature, history, and anything else that requires disciplined effort to learn.

In an article that was published originally in 1957 and was then reprinted in his 1962 collection *The Barbarian Within*, Ong makes some pertinent observations about how popular media can condition people's thinking in ways that they will have to overcome in order to cultivate serious intellectual development:

> [I]t may well be that until we can make students break through the press-movie-radio-television barrier in their own lives, they cannot react intelligently to language at all. Until they can replace the undiscriminating hypnotic response to these media in which they have been trained from infancy, with a discriminating response, they remain impervious to any communication or thinking other than the crudest sort. My own experience has been that persons undiscriminating in their reaction to these mass media are undiscriminating in their thinking and speaking, and that a person unaware of the way in which advertisements and Hollywood movies work is incapable of responding to a good contemporary poem or to any first-rate literature. (162)

McLuhan's *The Mechanical Bride* is a concerted attempt to prompt readers to reflect critically on an array of media appeals from contemporary culture. The kind of analysis and commentary that McLuhan undertakes in this book can be styled rhetorical analysis, because he largely under-takes to analyze persuasive appeals. In *The Image Industries* William F. Lynch sets forth a fine critique of movies and television, which Ong assigned us to read in the course in Practical Criticism: Prose that I took from him at Saint Louis University in the spring of 1966. In that course he brought in Walker Gibson's then new book *Tough, Sweet, and Stuffy* and read portions of it to us and commented on them. Like McLuhan's and Lynch's books, Gibson's book can be seen as a kind of rhetorical analysis of persuasive appeals that impinge upon us in our contemporary culture. (For more recent views of television, see Edwards; Silverstone.)

Even though McLuhan received substantially more publicity than did either Ong or Havelock, we should note here certain developments in their lives. Havelock's *Preface to Plato* was originally published in 1963, and it has been in print continuously since then. In it he develops in careful detail a thesis that he had formulated by 1947 (see Farrell 17). As McLuhan him-self recognized and acknowledged, Havelock's book provides strong sup-port for certain basic claims that McLuhan had made in a more sweeping fashion in *The Gutenberg Galaxy* (1962). Because Havelock had come to his own conclusions independently of McLuhan, Havelock's book was like a godsend for McLuhan (as it also was for Ong).

Because McLuhan manages at times to sound sensationalistic and even alarmist, we should note that Ong at times manages to sound hope-ful about the advent of communication media that accentuate sound. The hopeful note is perhaps strongest toward the end of *The Presence of the Word*. In shorter works his basically hopeful note can sound like he is announcing the advent of something like Joachim of Fiore's age of the Holy Spirit. (In a variation of Christian supersessionism, this age project-ed by Joachim was supposed to supersede the earlier age of the Father introduced in the Old Testament and the subsequent age of the Son ush-ered in with the New Testament.) See, for example, Ong's "Worship at the End of the Age of Literacy," which was published originally in 1969 in the periodical *Worship*. As we have noted above, literacy appears to be here to stay. However, because communication media that accentuate sound play such a strong role in contemporary life in Western culture, perhaps in a sense the age of literacy can be said to have come to an end.

In fairness to Ong, we should also explain the sense in which his ref-erence to the end of the age of literacy may have come to an end. He has repeatedly called attention to the need for both closeness (proximity) and distance in order to understand something well. From his standpoint, the impact of the communication media that accentuate sound now enable us to establish sufficient distance in order to understand the influence of literacy and of print. Scholars ranging from Jürgen Habermas to Richard Yeo have been delineating the influence of print culture in shaping our modern sense of ourselves (numerous studies of print culture are mentioned below). Other scholars such as Hobart and Schiffman are now constructing sweeping accounts of literacy and numeracy in Western cultural history. Even though the straightforward cataloguing of books is well established, the more recent accounts formulated by Habermas, Yeo, Hobart and Schiffman, and many others carry forward the early and still most incisive studies of literacy that Ong, McLuhan, and Havelock pioneered. These various studies of literacy and of print culture do not signal the end of literacy, which appears to be here to stay. Ong himself has repeatedly noted that new communication media do not wipe out old communication media, but the new may transform the old in some way(s). But these studies do signal a new reflectiveness about the role of literacy and of print culture. When Ong refers to the end of the age of literacy, he means something like the end of the age of unreflective literacy, not the end of literacy as such.

Even so, it remains to be seen whether or not Ong's hopefulness about the communication media that accentuate sound is well founded. If a new age of spiritual renewal is to emerge, we will have to forge something new in the smithies of our souls, to borrow an expression from James Joyce. Naturally we may wonder if we collectively are ready to forge something new in the smithies of our souls. We in Western culture today surely need to work against the centuries-old anti-semitism that led to the Shoah. We in the United States also need to recognize that the United States hit bottom morally in dropping atomic bombs on Hiroshima and Nagasaki, because those bombs killed noncombatants indiscriminately. As these examples show, there is ample room for us collectively to work on questioning old attitudes and to work toward forging new ones.

The hope for the present and the future that Ong expresses toward the end of *The Presence of the Word* is surely to be preferred over a defeatist attitude. With a defeatist attitude, we would probably not set out to right any wrongs or to fight for worthy causes. In general, I would prefer to be optimistic about the future, rather than pessimistic. After all, even the people who are pessimistic about the future would probably prefer to be optimistic about it. Thus almost everybody would prefer to see Ong's hope emerge as being well founded.

However, since the publication of *The Presence of the Word* in 1967, we have seen a sharp decline in the United States in the number of undergraduate majors in English, foreign languages, history, and philosophy. I, for one, find these trends disheartening to see. When we look beyond higher education, we find Kozol writing book after book trying to alert us to the shortcomings of our American schools in failing to produce functionally literate students (e.g., his *Illiterate America*). Even though there is a broad consensus that American schools should help children learn to read and write well, we collectively should not be complacent about our American schools.

Next, we should examine the question that Kermode raises in his 1968 review of Ong's *The Presence of the Word* in the *New York Review of Books*: What is Ong's account of Western cultural history for? Because Ong has used the word "for" in the subtitle of this book ("Some Prolegomena for Cultural and Religious History"), he has in effect suggested an answer: He is setting forth some prefatory considerations for undertaking cultural studies, as we today would style it. There is even a certain modesty in his subtitle: He claims only to be setting forth some prolegomena, not all. Even so, the words "cultural and religious history" are admittedly sweeping in scope, as he himself has said in the above-quoted passage from the preface to *Interfaces of the Word*.

Because the word "for" in the subtitle seems to promise that something further will follow this work, we should note that his collections *Rhetoric, Romance, and Technology* (1971) and *Interfaces of the Word* (1977) do follow up and further develop themes in *The Presence of the Word*. In addition, *Fighting for Life: Contest, Sexuality, and Conscious* (1981) directly follows up the discussion of polemic structures in *The Presence of the Word* (195-222, 236-55, 262-86). Within the parameters of the series in literary studies for which it was commissioned, *Orality and Literacy* (1982) summarizes and to a certain extent elaborates themes related to *The Presence of the Word* and the two major collections that followed it. Ong also carries forward certain themes from these earlier books in *Hopkins, the Self, and God* (1986), which can be seen as a follow up to the part of his subtitle that refers to religious history. Of course, religious history has long been a central theme in Ong's writings, as can be seen in the two short collections *Frontiers in American Catholicism* (1957) and *American Catholic Crossroads* (1959).

When we look for the ways in which Ong's various works are connected, we can see that the connections are there. Thus he has amply fulfilled the promise announced in the subtitle of *The Presence of the Word*. But he himself has not exhausted all possible amplifications or developments of his own thought. Indeed, certain aspects of his work still stand as challenges to the rest of us to carry out further inquiries on our own. In a certain sense then, we can respond to Kermode by saying that Ong's account of cultural history in *The Presence of the Word* sketches a research agenda for him to follow up, as he has, and for others to follow up, as certain others have already. But he has set forth a research agenda that is so sweeping in scope that much more follow-up work can be done.

In any event, after a protracted period of poor health, McLuhan died in his sleep in the early hours of January 1, 1980. For a commemorative issue of the *Journal of Communication* devoted to pieces about McLuhan, Ong wrote "McLuhan as Teacher: The Future Is a Thing of the Past," which may be the most positive assessment of McLuhan that has yet been published. As the title indicates, Ong considers McLuhan as a teacher, but he does not mean by this simply his own experiences as a graduate student in McLuhan's courses at Saint Louis University. Instead, he invites everybody who has read McLuhan's books to consider him as a teacher. It turns out that Ong thinks that a really superb teacher is somebody who can stimulate others to think. By this measure, even McLuhan's critics would have to allow that he stimulated them to think, or else what are they writing about? However, even McLuhan at his best is not everybody's cup of tea. Moreover, even McLuhan at his best should be read with a grain of salt, as Ong has advised and I have previously stated.

Ong in *Ramus, Method, and the Decay of Dialogue* and McLuhan in *The Gutenberg Galaxy* pioneered referring to print culture, as part of what today would be called a cultural studies approach to studying the human lifeworld. Other early studies of print culture included Richard Daniel Altick's *The English Common Reader: A Social History of the Mass Reading Public, 1800-1900* (original 1957; 2nd ed. 1998), Lucien Febvre and Henri-Jean Martin's *The Coming of the Book: The Impact of Printing, 1450-1800* (original 1958; English translation 1997), and Jürgen Habermas' *The Structural Transformation of the Public Sphere* (original 1962; English translation 1989). Subsequently, referring to a rather different level of reference than either Ong or McLuhan, Elizabeth L. Eisenstein published a two-volume study of *The Printing Press as an Agent of Change* (1979).

More recently, we find Adrian Johns' *The Nature of the Book: Print and Knowledge in the Making*, Peter Harrison's *The Bible, Protestantism, and the Rise of Natural Science*, Lisa Jardine's *Ingenious Pursuits: Building the Scientific Revolution*, Daniel R. Headrick's *When Information Came of Age: Technologies of Knowledge in the Age of Reason and Revolution, 1700-1850*, and Neil Rhodes and Jonathan Sawday's collection *The Renaissance Computer: Knowledge Technology in the First Age of Print*.

Concerning religion and print culture, we have Cecile M. Jagodzinski's *Privacy and Print: Reading and Writing in Seventeenth-*

Century England and now Ian Green's *Print and Protestantism in Early Modern England*. In *In the Beginning: The Story of the King James Bible and How It Changed a Nation, a Language and a Culture*, Alister McGrath has delineated a broad range of influences that he attributes to the English translation of the Bible that print made readily available. In *Wide as the Waters: The Story of the English Bible and the Revolution It Inspired*, Benson Bobrick has suggested even broader influences to the English translation of the Bible that print made so readily available (concerning Tyndale, also see the essays edited by Day, Lund, and O'Donnell).

Concerning various literary developments in print culture, we have Adrian Armstrong's *Technique and Technology: Script, Print, and Poetics in France 1470-1550*, Julie Stone Peters' *Theatre of the Book 1480-1880: Print, Text and Performance in Europe*, Adam Fox's *Oral and Literate Culture in England, 1500-1700*, Arthur F. Marotti's *Manuscript, Print, and the English Renaissance Lyric*, Marotti and Michael D. Bristol's collection *Print, Manuscript, and Performance: The Changing Relationships of the Media in Early Modern England*, Carla Mazzio and Douglas Trevor's collection *Historicism, Psychoanalysis, and Early Modern Culture*, and Patricia Crain's *The Story of A: The Alphabetization of America from* The New England Primer *to* The Scarlet Letter. On a more specialized note, we also find Daniel Woolf's *Reading History in Early Modern England*. But the recent works in English that I have mentioned here are but a sampling of the studies of print culture that have been undertaken since Ong and McLuhan published their pioneering studies of print culture. No doubt further studies of print culture will be undertaken.

Indeed, there is now a professional organization of scholars devoted to studying various aspects of print culture, the Society for the History of Authorship, Reading, and Publishing. Furthermore, the University of Massachusetts Press has begun publishing a series of Studies in Print Culture and the History of the Book, and Pennsylavania State University Press has its own series in the History of the Book. No doubt many more aspects of print culture remain to be explored by other scholars (for guidebooks on book history, see Howard-Hill; Greetham; Zboray and Zboray; various resources are also available on the Internet, including some extensive bibliographies).

Further Contexts for Considering Ong's Thought

We should also note other scholarly studies to which various themes in Ong's many-faceted work can be connected. Concerning orality in public speaking, or at least the portrayal of public speaking, we should consider the speeches in the Homeric epics. If we allow that Homer was considered to be the educator of ancient Greece, then we should also allow that the speeches in the Homeric epics exemplified public speaking or rhetoric, as Andrew J. Karp has suggested. As is well known, the Homeric epics became standard fare for imitation in ancient formal education. Recently Dennis R. MacDonald has noted that even the anonymous author of the Gospel of Mark has imitated certain features of the Homeric epics. Because of the prominence of the Homeric epics in ancient Greek education, we probably should consider Homer as a major source of the Western tradition of rhetoric, prior to and for centuries after the ancient Greek Sophists, Isocrates, Socrates, Plato, and Aristotle.

In his 1954 book *English Literature in the Sixteenth Century, Excluding Drama*, which is volume three of *The Oxford History of English Literature*, C. S. Lewis makes the following sweeping statement about rhetoric and a certain feature of rhetoric that I would refer to as orality:

> Rhetoric is the greatest barrier between us and our ancestors. If the Middle Ages had erred in their devotion to that art, the *renascentia*, far from curing, confirmed the error. In rhetoric, more than in anything else, the continuity of the old European tradition was embodied. Older than the Church, older than Roman Law, older than all Latin literature, it descends from the age of the Greek Sophists. Like the Church and the law it survives the fall of empire, rides the *renascentia* and the Reformation like waves, and penetrates far into the eighteenth century; through all these ages not the tyrant, but the darling of humanity, *soavissima*, as Dante says, "the sweetest of all the other sciences." Nearly all our older poetry was written and read by men to whom the distinction between poetry and rhetoric, in its modern form, would have been meaningless. The "beauties" which they chiefly regard in every composition were those which we either dislike or simply do not notice. This change of taste makes an invisible wall between us and them. Probably all our literary histories, certainly that on which I am engaged, are vitiated by our lack of sympathy on this point. (61)

Lewis is to be commended not only for the candor with which he has expressed his distaste, but also for the basic truth about rhetoric that he has encompassed in only one paragraph. By the standards of the time and place, rhetoric was supposed to sound good, and so was poetry. Because Lewis mentions Dante here, we should note that David Robey has elaborated a careful account of sound in *Sound and Structure in the Divine Comedy*. (For a study of medieval rhetoric of related interest, see Enders; see also Mostert for a bibliography.)

On the opening pages of his collection *Rhetoric, Romance, and Technology: Studies in the Interaction of Expression and Culture*, Ong refers to this passage by Lewis and basically allows that there is a truth in each point Lewis makes here (1-2, 89). Ong agrees that the Western rhetorical tradition did extend from antiquity to well into the eighteenth century and even beyond. He also agrees that a certain kind of sensibility was associated with this well-developed tradition of orality, even though he does not usually refer to it in its later days as a sensibility. Instead, he refers to oral residue. By oral residue, he means features of thought and expression, even in written discourse, that are designed to help expression sound impressive and memorable.

In *Motives of Eloquence: Literary Rhetoric in the Renaissance* (33-34), Richard Lanham also quotes and then accepts the essential accuracy of Lewis' characterizations of rhetoric. I know of no one who challenges the essential correctness of Lewis' claims about rhetoric in this passage. As this paragraph intimates, books could still be written by scholars who want to take into account this change of taste, as Lewis puts it. We might wonder if the time has come to rewrite not only our Western literary histories but also our histories of Western rhetoric to take into account the beauties of orality (or oral residue), as I would style the features that Lewis refers to in this passage.

In this connection I would point out that Walker has recently undertaken to do something along these lines in *Rhetoric and Poetics in Antiquity*. In *Electric Rhetoric: Classical Rhetoric, Oralism, and a New Literacy*, Kathleen E. Welch has recently detailed the dominance of the study of rhetoric over all other verbal arts in the lengthy Western intellectual tradition—an early awareness that Ong credits McLuhan with having when he (McLuhan) was teaching at Saint Louis University.

When Michael Eric Dyson refers to Martin Luther King's brilliant uses of black orality (179), he is referring to the features of expression that Ong refers to as oral residue. As Dyson indicates, many of these residual, but strongly evident oral features can be found today in black hip-hop culture. When Ong and Lewis refer to these residually oral features of rhetoric and poetry, they are referring to a well-developed living tradition of orality that still throve and was carried forward for centuries in a culture with a well-developed tradition of writing. Literacy did not and could not force these oral features of thought and expression to disappear overnight.

We should also note that Ong aligns the entirety of biblical literature, to varying degrees, with the kind of thought and expression he associates with primary orality. In "Where Are We Now? Some Elemental

Cosmological Considerations" (2000), Ong has described and elucidated his own position concerning the changing relationships of the Bible and human knowledge now that it is commonly known, as it was known to no one at all until quite recently, that the universe that Christians and other biblical religions believe God created is some twelve to fourteen billion years old and of an immensity not yet fully surveyed.

Concerning the varying degrees of oral thought and expression that can be found in the Bible, I myself would suggest that the Word in the prologue to the Gospel of John may be an exception; the conceptualization of the Word there may have been very radically influenced by Greek philosophic thought, which is to say by the kind of thought that Ong identifies as distinctively literate thought. Regardless of how we may adjudicate this one example, Ong sees the Bible as a major collection of examples of primary oral thought and expression. He does not deny that the various texts show signs of what Julia Kristeva (66) and other literary scholars today refer to as intertextuality—in short, later texts amply reveal influences of thought and expression found in earlier texts. Ong would consider this kind of intertextuality to be an echoing of traditional material that characterizes oral tradition (concerning intertextuality and rhetoric, see Plett). Moreover, Ong would see this kind of intertextuality in the Bible as falling short of the distinctively literate thought that he sees emerging in Plato's Ideas (or Forms) and in Aristotle's development of the formal study of logic.

From the various considerations outlined thus far, we can begin to construct a continuum of writing (representing literacy) that is close to primary orality and writing that moves toward distinctively literate thought. In antiquity the Bible, Homer, and Hesiod would be very close to primary orality. In *Orality and Literacy* Ong has suggested that the tight plotting of action rising toward the climax in Sophocles' *Oedipus the King* may show the influence of writing on drama (142-48; see also Wise). But apart from such plotting, ancient Greek drama remains close to primary oral thought and expression, as Havelock has suggested in *The Literate Revolution in Greece and Its Cultural Consequences* (261-313). Had there been no writing and hence no reflection of the written word in ancient Greece, it is hard to imagine that the Greek Sophists would have appeared; thus I would see them and their thought and expression as the byproduct of literacy in ancient Greece. However, as Lewis intimates in the above-quoted passage, the Greek Sophists remain close in certain respects to orality, especially a figure such as Gorgias of Leontini. Welch (29-74) has painstakingly suggested that Isocrates remains close to primary orality, as compared to Plato.

In Plato and Aristotle, both Ong and Havelock see distinctively liter-ate thought emerging. In *Redirecting Philosophy: Reflections on the Nature of Knowledge from Plato to Lonergan*, Hugo A. Meynell has sug-gested that all subsequent philosophic and scientific thought in Western culture derive from the kind of philosophic and scientific conceptualiza-tion pioneered by Plato and Aristotle. Surely the tradition of thought known as dialectic and logic that Ong has traced in *Ramus, Method, and the Decay of Dialogue* derives directly from the thought of Plato and Aristotle, as Ong himself shows. But Ong also notes that dialectic and logic were taught alongside rhetoric for centuries, and rhetoric was deeply oriented toward the sound effects of orality, as was poetry (see Walker).

In *Body, Text, and Science: The Literacy of Investigative Practices and the Phenomenology of Edith Stein*, Marianne Sawicki uses the tantalizing expression "The Literacy of Investigative Practices" in the subtitle and then entitles her sixth chapter "Science as Literacy." However, she does not draw on Ong's work or Havelock's. Their work could be used to stengthen her claims about science being a distinctively literate mode of thought.

For Aristotle, both dialectic and rhetoric entail being able to argue both sides of an issue. For him, dialectic entailed considering theoretical issues; by contrast, the issues in rhetoric were about practical matters. But for him, the educated person was to be able to debate both sides well. Sloane has shown that Renaissance educational practices inculcated stu-dents in this orientation toward debate, and he sees this as an education-al practice that should be resurrected. In *Creative Controversy: Intellectual Challenge in the Classroom*, mentioned above, the Johnsons, who give no evidence of knowing about the educational tradition of debate that Sloane writes about, have set forth an educational program that in effect would do much to resurrect this still valuable tradition.

What ever happened to the educational practices that Sloane has described? In large measure, they were abandoned by Ramus and his fol-lowers, whose recipes marked much of the thought for subsequent cen-turies. Simply stated, Ramism favors setting forth one's own line of thought. To be sure, skilled debaters need to know how to do this much. But people trained in Ramist dialectic and rhetoric are not going to prac-tice arguing both sides of issues. Instead, they are simply going to prac-tice setting forth their own line of thought. For all practical purposes, the Ramist tradition is carried forward today in college composition courses, where all students are asked to do is to set forth their own line of thought. Sloane is well aware of this sorry state of affairs, and this is what prompts him to suggest that college composition courses should resurrect the tra-dition of teaching pro and con debate. Evidently without knowing about the extensive educational tradition of teaching pro and con debate, the Johnsons are in effect urging that it be resurrected on the secondary level of education.

In summary, Walter Ong is a deeply original thinker. In many ways he has been ahead of his time. Much remains to be done by other scholars to put his seminal thought about orality to work. Even though Walker does not happen to advert to the quotation given above from Lewis, Walker has shown just how much more we have yet to learn about the orality of ancient rhetoric and poetry. When we start to follow up Ong's work by taking account of orality, as Walker has undertaken to do, we will rewrite the history of rhetoric and literary history in Western culture. No doubt such an enormous undertaking must unfold gradually as individual scholars study oral residue in particular works in detail. After enough individual works have been duly studied for oral residue, then we will see the larger patterns in our cultural past more fully.

However that may be, the present collection makes for delightful reading. The selections are accessible, and the interconnections abound. Seamus Heaney may learn more here about Hopkins' sprung rhythm than he (Heaney) ever really wanted to know, and so will most other people. Most people will probably also learn more here about Ramus and Ramism than they ever wanted to know. But to borrow a well-known expression, the keys to the kingdom of understanding Ong's work overall are reading his *Ramus, Method, and the Decay of Dialogue* and at least carefully looking over his 550-page *Ramus and Talon Inventory*. Perhaps the time is coming when more people will take the trouble to study these key works carefully.

Works Cited

Altick, Richard Daniel. *The English Common Reader: A Social History of the Mass Reading Public, 1800-1900*. 2nd ed. Columbus: Ohio State UP, 1998.

Armstrong, Adrian. *Technique and Technology: Script, Print, and Poetics in France 1470-1550*. New York: Oxford UP, 2000.

Ashworth, E. J. "Some Notes on Syllogistic in the Sixteenth and Seventeenth Centuries." *Notre Dame Journal of Formal Logic* 11 (1970): 17-33.

Baldwin, T. W. *William Shakspere's Small Latine and Lesse Greeke*. 2 vols. Urbana: U of Illinois P, 1944.

Bass, Alan. Translator's Introduction. *Writing and Difference*. By Jacques Derrida. Trans. Alan Bass. Chicago: U of Chicago P, 1978. ix-xx.

Bloom, Harold. *Agon: Towards a Theory of Revisionism*. New York: Oxford UP, 1982.

—. *Shakespeare: The Invention of the Human*. New York: Riverhead/Penguin Putnam, 1998.

Bobrick, Benson. *Wide as the Waters: The Story of the English Bible and the Revolution It Inspired.* New York: Simon & Schuster, 2001.

Borgmann, Albert. *Holding on to Reality: The Nature of Information at the Turn of the Millennium.* Chicago: U of Chicago P, 1999.

Buber, Martin. *I and Thou.* Trans. Walter Kaufmann. New York: Charles Scribner's Sons, 1970.

Burckhardt, Jacob. *The Greeks and Greek Civilization.* Trans. Sheila Stern. Ed. Oswyn Murray. New York: St. Martin's P, 1998.

Carey, James W. "Technology and Ideology: The Case of the Telegraph." *Communication as Culture: Essays on the Media and Society.* Boston: Unwin Hyman, 1989. 201-30.

Carpenter, Edmund. "That Not-So-Silent Sea." *The Virtual Marshall McLuhan.* By Donald F. Theall. Montreal: McGill-Queen's UP, 2001. 236-61.

Carroll, James. *Constantine's Sword: The Church and the Jews: A History.* Boston: Houghton Mifflin, 2001.

Cavanaugh, John R. *The Use of Proverbs and Sententiae for Rhetorical Amplification in the Writings of Thomas More.* Diss. Saint Louis U, 1969. Ann Arbor: UMI, 1970.

Clark, Joseph T. *Conventional Logic and Modern Logic: A Prelude to Transition.* Washington, DC: Woodstock College P for the American Catholic Philosophical Association, 1952.

Colish, Marcia L. *Medieval Foundations of the Western Intellectual Tradition.* New Haven: Yale UP, 1998.

Crain, Patricia A. *The Story of A: The Alphabetization of America from* The New England Primer *to* The Scarlet Letter. Stanford: Stanford UP, 2000.

Crosby, Alfred W. *The Measure of Reality: Quantification and Western Society, 1250-1600.* Cambridge, UK: Cambridge UP, 1997.

Crossan, John Dominic. *Who Killed Jesus? Exposing the Roots of Anti-Semitism in the Gospel Story of the Death of Jesus.* San Francisco: Harper Collins, 1995.

Cuddihy, John Murray. *The Ordeal of Civility: Freud, Marx, Lévi-Strauss, and the Jewish Struggle with Modernity.* 2nd ed. Boston: Beacon P, 1987.

Daniell, Beth. "Narratives of Literacy: Connecting Composition to Culture." *College Composition and Communication* 50 (1999): 393-410.

Dawson, Christopher. *Christianity and European Culture: Selections from the Work of Christopher Dawson.* Ed. Gerald J. Russello. Washington, DC: Catholic U of America P, 1998.

Day, John T., Eric Lund and Anne M. O'Donnell, Eds. *Word, Church, and State: Tyndale Quincentary Essays.* Washington, DC: Catholic U of America P, 1998.

Derrida, Jacques. *Archive Fever: A Freudian Impression.* Trans. Eric Prenowitz. Chicago: U of Chicago P, 1996.

Dodson, Edward O. *The Phenomenon of Man Revisited: A Biological Viewpoint on Teilhard de Chardin.* New York: Columbia UP, 1984.

Dyson, Michael Eric. *I May Not Get There with You: The True Martin Luther King, Jr.* New York: Free Press, 2000.

Edwards, Lee. *Mediapolitik: How the Mass Media Have Transformed World Politics.* Washington, DC: Catholic U of America P, 2001.

Eisenstein, Elizabeth L. *The Printing Press as an Agent of Change.* 2 vols. Cambridge, UK: Cambridge UP, 1979.

Eliot, T. S. "Tradition and the Individual Talent." *Selected Prose of T. S. Eliot.* Ed. F. Kermode. New York: Harcourt Brace Jovanovich, 1975. 37-44.

Enders, Jody. *Rhetoric and the Origins of Medieval Drama.* Ithaca, NY: Cornell UP, 1992.

Engberg-Pedersen, Troels. *Paul and the Stoics.* Louisville: Westminster John Knox P, 2000.

Farrell, Thomas J. *Walter Ong's Contributions to Cultural Studies: The Phenomenology of the Word and I-Thou Communication.* Cresskill, NJ: Hampton, 2000.

Febvre, Lucien and Henri-Jean Martin. *The Coming of the Book: The Impact of Printing, 1450-1800.* Trans. David Gerard. Ed. Geoffrey Nowell-Smith and David Wootton. London: Verso, 1997.

Foley, John Miles, ed. A Festschrift for Walter J. Ong. *Oral Tradition* 2.1 (1987): 7-382.

—. *Oral-Formulaic Theory and Research: An Introduction and Annotated Bibliography.* New York: Garland, 1985.

—, ed. *Teaching Oral Traditions.* New York: Modern Language Association, 1998.

Fox, Adam. *Oral and Literate Culture in England, 1500-1700.* New York: Oxford UP, 2000.

Fox, Matthew. *Sheer Joy: Conversations with Thomas Aquinas on Creation Spirituality.* San Francisco: Harper Collins, 1992.

Fredriksen, Paula. *Jesus of Nazareth, King of the Jews: A Jewish Life and the Emergence of Christianity.* New York: Random House, 1999.

Freedman, Joseph S. "The Diffusion of the Writings of Petrus Ramus in Central Europe, c.1570-c.1630." *Renaissance Quarterly* 46 (1993): 98-152.

—. *Philosophy and the Arts in Central Europe, 1500-1700: Teaching and Texts in Schools and Universities.* Aldershot, UK: Ashgate, 1999.

Freire, Paulo. *Pedagogy of the Oppressed.* 30th anniversary ed. Trans. M. B. Ramos. New York: Continuum, 2000.

Gager, John G. *Reinventing Paul.* New York: Oxford UP, 2000.

Genosko, Gary. *McLuhan and Baudrillard: The Masters of Implosion.* London: Routledge, 1999.

Gibson, Walker. *Tough, Sweet, and Stuffy: An Essay on Modern American Prose Style.* Bloomington: Indiana UP, 1966.

Girard, René. *A Theater of Envy: William Shakespeare.* New York: Oxford UP, 1991.

Goody, Jack. *The Power of the Written Word.* Washington, DC: Smithsonian Institution P, 2000.

Gordon, W. Terrence. *Marshall McLuhan: Escape into Understanding: A Biography.* New York: Basic Books, 1997.

Graham-White, Anthony. *Punctuation and Its Dramatic Value in Shakespearean Drama.* Cranbury, NJ: U of Delaware P, 1995.

Green, Ian. *Print and Protestantism in Early Modern England.* New York: Oxford UP, 2001.

Greetham, D. C. *Textual Scholarship: An Introduction.* New York: Garland, 1992. Includes extensive bibliography.

Gronbeck, Bruce E., Thomas J. Farrell, and Paul A. Soukup, eds. *Media, Consciousness, and Culture: Explorations of Walter Ong's Thought.* Newbury Park, CA: Sage, 1991.

Habermas, Jürgen. *The Structural Transformation of the Public Sphere.* Trans. Thomas Burger and Frederick Lawrence. Cambridge, MA: Massachusetts Institute of Technology P, 1989.

Hall, Edith. *Inventing the Barbarian: Greek Self-Definition Through Tragedy.* New York: Oxford UP, 1989.

Harrison, Peter. *The Bible, Protestantism, and the Rise of Natural Science.* Cambridge, UK: Cambridge UP, 1998.

Hartman, Geoffrey H., ed. *Hopkins: A Collection of Critical Essays.* Englewood Cliffs, NJ: Prentice Hall, 1966.

Havelock, Eric A. *Preface to Plato.* Cambridge, MA: Belknap P of Harvard UP, 1963.

—. *The Literate Revolution in Ancient Greece and Its Cultural Consequences.* Princeton: Princeton UP, 1982.

Headrick, Daniel R. *When Information Came of Age: Technologies of Knowledge in the Age of Reason and Revolution, 1700-1850.* New York: Oxford UP, 2000.

Heaney, Seamus. "The Drag of the Golden Chain." *TLS: [London] Times Literary Supplement* No. 5041 (November 12, 1999): 14-16.

—. "Feeling into Words." *Preoccupations: Selected Prose, 1968-1978.* New York: Farrar, Straus & Giroux, 1980. 41-60.

—. "Introduction." *Beowulf: A New Verse Translation* (Trans. Seamus Heaney). New York: Farrar, Straus & Giroux, 2000. ix-xxx.

Hobart, Michael E. and Zachary S. Schiffman. *Information Ages: Literacy, Numeracy, and the Computer Revolution.* Baltimore: Johns Hopkins UP, 1998.

Hobbs, Angela. *Plato and the Hero: Courage, Manliness and the Impersonal Good.* Cambridge, UK: Cambridge UP, 2000.

Howard-Hill, T. H. *British Literary Bibliography and Textual Criticism, 1890-1969.* Volume 6 of and index to *British Literary Bibliography.* Oxford: Clarendon P of Oxford UP, 1980.

Howell, Wilbur Samuel. *Eighteenth Century British Logic and Rhetoric.* Princeton: Princeton UP, 1971.

—. *Logic and Rhetoric in England, 1500-1700.* Princeton: Princeton UP, 1956.

—. "Ramus and the Decay of Dialogue [Review of Ong's *Ramus, Method, and the Decay of Dialogue* and Ong's *Ramus and Talon Inventory*]." *Quarterly Journal of Speech* 46 (1960): 86-92.

Innis, Harold. *The Bias of Communication*. Oxford: Clarendon P, 1951.

—. *Empire and Communication*. Toronto: U of Toronto P, 1950.

Jaeger, C. Stephen. *The Origins of Courtliness: Civilizing Trends and the Formation of Courtly Ideals, 939-1210*. Philadelphia: U of Pennsylvania P, 1985.

Jagodzinski, Cecile M. *Privacy and Print: Reading and Writing in Seventeenth-Century England*. Charlottesville: UP of Virginia, 1999.

Jardine, Lisa. *Erasmus, Man of Letters: The Construction of Charisma in Print*. Princeton: Princeton UP, 1993.

—. *Francis Bacon: Discovery and the Art of Discourse*. London, UK: Cambridge UP, 1974.

—. *Ingenious Pursuits: Building the Scientific Revolution*. New York: Nan A. Talese, 1999.

Johns, Adrian. *The Nature of the Book: Print and Knowledge in the Making*. Chicago: U of Chicago P, 1998.

Johnson, David W. and Roger T. Johnson. *Cooperation and Competition: Theory and Research*. Edina, MN: Interaction Book Company, 1989.

—. *Creative Controversy: Intellectual Challenge in the Classroom*. Edina, MN: Interaction Book Company, 1992.

—. *Learning Together and Alone: Cooperative, Competitive, and Individualistic Learning*. 4th ed. Boston: Allyn & Bacon, 1994.

Johnson, David W., Roger T. Johnson and Edythe Johnson Holubec. *Circles of Learning: Cooperation in the Classroom*. 4th ed. Edina, MN: Interaction Book Company, 1993.

Karp, Andrew J. "Homeric Origins of Ancient Rhetoric." *Arethusa* 10 (1977): 237-58.

Kenner, Hugh. *Paradox in Chesterton*. Introduction by Marshall McLuhan. New York: Sheed & Ward, 1947.

Kermode, Frank. "Free Fall [Review of Ong's *The Presence of the Word*]." *New York Review of Books* (14 March 1968): 22-26.

Kozol, Jonathan. *Illiterate America*. Garden City, NY: Anchor Books/ Doubleday, 1985.

Koziak, Barbara. *Retrieving Political Emotion: Thumos, Aristotle, and Gender*. University Park: Pennsylvania UP, 2000.

Kristeva, Julia. *Desire in Language: A Semiotic Approach to Literature and Art*. Ed. Leon S. Roudiez. Trans. Thomas Gora, Alice Jardine, and Leon S. Roudiez. New York: Columbia UP, 1980.

Lanham, Richard A. *The Motives of Eloquence: Literary Rhetoric in the Renaissance*. New Haven: Yale UP, 1976.

Leavis, F. R. *New Bearings in English Poetry*. London: Chatto & Windus, 1932.

Lechner, Sister Joan Marie, O.S.U. *Renaissance Concepts of the Commonplaces: An Historical Investigation of the General and Universal Ideas Used in All Argumentation and Persuasion with Special Emphasis on the Educational and Literary Tradition of the Sixteenth and Seventeenth Centuries*. New York: Pageant, 1962.

Lee, Dorothy. *Freedom and Culture*. Prospect Heights, IL: Waveland P, 1987.

—. *Valuing the Self: What We Can Learn from Other Cultures*. Prospect Heights, IL: Waveland P, 1986.

Leith, Philip. "Postmedieval Information Processing and Contemporary Computer Science." *Media, Consciousness, and Culture: Explorations of Walter Ong's Thought*. Ed. Bruce E. Gronbeck, Thomas J. Farrell, and Paul A. Soukup. Newbury Park, CA: Sage, 1991. 160-76.

Lewis, C. S. *English Literature in the Sixteenth Century, Excluding Drama. The Oxford History of English Literature: Volume 3*. Ed. F. P. Wilson and Bonamy Dobrée. Oxford: Clarendon P of Oxford UP, 1954.

Lonergan, Bernard. "The Transition from a Classicist World-View to Historical-Mindedness." *A Second Collection*. Ed. William F. J. Ryan and Bernard J. Tyrrell. Philadelphia: Westminster, 1974. 1-9.

Lord, Albert B. *The Singer of Tales*. Cambridge, MA: Harvard UP, 1960.

Lynch, William F. *The Image Industries*. New York: Sheed & Ward, 1959.

MacDonald, Dennis R. *The Homeric Epics and the Gospel of Mark*. New Haven: Yale UP, 2000.

Marc'hadour, Germain P. "Editor's Postscript [To Clarence H. Miller's brief article about Ong]." *Thomas More Gazette* (1996): 14-15.

—. "Toward a Theology of Merriment." *Moreana* 15 (Nov. 1967): 326.

Marchand, Philip. *Marshall McLuhan: The Medium and the Messenger*. New York: Ticknor & Fields, 1989.

Mariani, Paul L. *A Commentary on the Complete Poems of Gerard Manley Hopkins*. Ithaca, NY: Cornell UP, 1970.

Marotti, Arthur F. *Manuscript, Print, and the English Renaissance Lyric*. Ithaca, NY: Cornell UP, 1995.

Marotti, Arthur F. and Michael D. Bristol, Eds. *Print, Manuscript, and Performance: The Changing Relationships of the Media in Early Modern England*. Columbus: Ohio State UP, 2000.

Mazzio, Carla and Douglas Trevor, Eds. *Historicism, Psychoanalysis, and Early Modern Culture*. New York: Routledge, 2000.

McGrath, Alister. *In the Beginning: The Story of the King James Bible and How It Changed a Nation, a Language and a Culture*. New York: Doubleday, 2001.

McLuhan, Marshall. "G. K. Chesterton: A Practical Mystic." *Dalhousie Review* 15 (1936): 455-64.

—. *The Gutenberg Galaxy: The Making of Typographic Man*. Toronto: U of Toronto P, 1962.

—. "The Later Innis." *Queen's Quarterly* 60 (1953): 385-94.

—. *The Mechanical Bride: Folklore of Industrial Man*. New York: Vanguard, 1951.

—. *The Medium and the Light: Reflections on Religion* (Ed. Eric McLuhan and Jacek Szklarek). Toronto: Stoddart, 1999.

—. *Understanding Media: The Extensions of Man.* New York: McGraw-Hill, 1964.

—. *The Writings of Marshall McLuhan: Listed in Chronological Order from 1934 to 1975, with an Appended List of Reviews and Articles about Him and His Work.* Fort Lauderdale, FL: Wake-Brook House, 1975.

McLuhan, Marshall with Quentin Fiore and Jerome Agel. *The Medium Is the Massage: An Inventory of Effects.* New York: Bantam, 1967.

—. *War and Peace in the Global Village.* New York: Bantam, 1968.

McNamee, Maurice B. *Honor and the Epic Hero: A Study of the Shifting Concept of Magnanimity in Philosophy and Epic Poetry.* New York: Holt, Rinehart and Winston, 1960.

McPartland, Thomas J. *Lonergan and the Philosophy of Historical Existence.* Columbia: U of Missouri P, 2001.

Meynell, Hugo A. *Redirecting Philosophy: Reflections on the Nature of Knowledge from Plato to Lonergan.* Toronto: U of Toronto P, 1998.

Miller, Clarence. "To Walter J. Ong, S.J., on the Occasion of His 84th Birthday (30 November 1996): Congratulations and Felicitations." *Thomas More Newsletter* (1996): 13-14.

Miller, Perry. *The New England Mind: The Seventeenth Century.* Cambridge, MA: Harvard UP, 1939.

Milton, John. *A Fuller Course in the Art of Logic Conformed to the Method of Peter Ramus.* Ed. and Trans. Walter J. Ong and Charles J. Ermatinger. *Complete Prose Works of John Milton: Volume 8.* Ed. Maurice Kelley. New Haven: Yale UP, 1982. 206-407.

Morison, Samuel Eliot. *The Founding of Harvard College.* Cambridge, MA: Harvard UP, 1935.

—. *Harvard College in the Seventeenth Century.* 2 vols. Cambridge, MA: Harvard UP, 1936.

Moss, Ann. *Printed Commonplace Books and the Structuring of Renaissance Thought.* Oxford Clarendon P of Oxford UP, 1996.

Mostert, Marco. "A Bibliography of Works on Medieval Communication." *New Approaches to Medieval Communication.* Ed. Marco Mostert. Turnhout: Brepols, 1999. 193-318. [Utrecht Studies in Medieval Literacy, 1]

Nagy, Gregory. "Orality and Literacy." *Encyclopedia of Rhetoric.* Ed. Thomas O. Sloane. New York: Oxford UP, 2001. 533-38.

Newman, John Henry. *An Essay on the Development of Christian Doctrine.* 6th ed. Notre Dame, IN: Notre Dame UP, 1989. (Original work published 1845)

Ong, Walter J. *American Catholic Crossroads: Religious-Secular Encounters in the Modern World.* New York: Macmillan, 1959.

—. *The Barbarian Within: And Other Fugitive Essays and Studies.* New York: Macmillan, 1962.

—, ed. *Darwin's Vision and Christian Perspectives.* New York: Macmillan, 1960.

—. "Educationists and the Tradition of Learning." *Bulletin of the Ontario Secondary School Teachers Federation* 37 (1957): 341-44, 375-77. Reprinted in *The Barbarian Within* (149-63).

—. *Faith and Contexts.* 4 vols. Ed. Thomas J. Farrell and Paul A. Soukup. Atlanta: Scholars P, 1992a, 1992b, 1995, 1999; now distributed by Rowman & Littlefield.

—. *Fighting for Life: Contest, Sexuality, and Consciousness.* Ithaca, NY: Cornell UP, 1981.

—. *Frontiers in American Catholicism: Essays on Ideology and Culture.* New York: Macmillan, 1957.

—. *Hopkins, the Self, and God.* Toronto: U of Toronto P, 1986.

—. "Humanism." *The New Catholic Encyclopedia.* Ed. William J. McDonald. 15 vols. New York: McGraw-Hill, 1967. Reprinted in *Faith and Contexts: Volume 4* (69-91).

—. *In the Human Grain: Further Explorations of Contemporary Culture.* New York: Macmillan, 1967.

—. *Interfaces of the Word: Studies in the Evolution of Consciousness and Culture.* Ithaca, NY: Cornell UP, 1977.

—. Introduction. *A Fuller Course in the Art of Logic Conformed to the Method of Peter Ramus.* By John Milton. Ed. and Trans. Ong and Charles J. Ermatinger. *Complete Prose Works of John Milton: Volume 8.* Ed. Maurice Kelley. New Haven: Yale UP, 1982. 139-205. Ong's Introduction, slightly abbreviated, is reprinted in *Faith and Contexts: Volume 4* (111-41)

—. "Introduction: On Saying We and Us to Literature." *Three American Literatures: Essays in Chicano, Native American, and Asian-American Literature for Teachers of American Literature.* Ed. Houston A. Baker, Jr. New York: Modern Language Association of America, 1982. 3-7.

—. ed. *Knowledge and the Future of Man.* New York: Holt, Rinehart and Winston, 1968.

—. "Literature, Written Transmission of." *The New Catholic Encyclopedia.* Ed. William J. McDonald. 15 vols. New York: McGraw-Hill, 1967. Reprinted in *An Ong Reader.*

—. "McLuhan as Teacher: The Future Is a Thing of the Past." *Journal of Communication* 31 (1981): 129-35. Reprinted in *Faith and Contexts: Volume 1* (11-18).

—. "The Mechanical Bride: Christen the Folklore of Industrial Man." *Social Order* 2.2 (1952): 79-85.

—. "Newman's *Essay on Development* in Its Intellectual Milieu." *Theolgical Studies* 7 (1946): 3-45.

—. *Orality and Literacy: The Technologizing of the Word.* London: Methuen, 1982.

—. Preface [To the 1983 Paperback Edition]. *Ramus, Method, and the Decay of Dialogue: From the Art of Discourse to the Art of Reason.* By Ong. Cambridge, MA: Harvard UP, 1983. vii-viii.

—. *The Presence of the Word: Some Prolegomena for Cultural and Religious History.* New Haven: Yale UP, 1967.

—. *Ramus, Method, and the Decay of Dialogue: From the Art of Discourse to the Art of Reason.* Cambridge, MA: Harvard UP, 1958.

—. *Ramus and Talon Inventory: A Short-Title Inventory of the Published Works of Peter Ramus (1515-1572) and of Omer Talon (ca. 1510-1562) in Their Original and in Their Variously Altered Forms, with Related Material: 1. The Ramist Controversies: A Descriptive Catalogue; 2. Agricola Check List: A Short-Title Inventory of Some Printed Editions and Printed Compendia of Rudolph Agricola's Dialectical Invention* (De Inventione Dialectica). Cambridge, MA: Harvard UP, 1958.

—. Review of Wilbur Samuel Howell's *Eighteenth Century British Logic and Rhetoric*. *William and Mary Quarterly* 29 (1972): 637-43. Reprinted in *An Ong Reader*.

—. Review of Brian Vickers' *Classical Rhetoric in English Poetry*. *College English* 33 (1971-1972): 612-16. Reprinted in *An Ong Reader*.

—. *Rhetoric, Romance, and Technology: Studies in the Interaction of Expression and Culture*. Ithaca, NY: Cornell UP, 1971.

—. "System, Space, and Intellect in Renaissance Symbolism." *Bibliotheque d'Humanisme et Renaissance* 18 (1956): 222-39. Reprinted in *The Barbarian Within* (68-87) and in *Faith and Contexts: Volume 3* (9-27).

—. "Where Are We Now? Some Elemental Cosmological Considerations." *Christianity and Literature* 50 (2000): 7-13.

—. "Worship at the End of the Age of Literacy." *Worship* 44 (1969): 474-87. Reprinted in *Faith and Contexts: Volume 1* (175-88).

—. "Written Transmission of Literature." See entry above on "Literature, Written Transmission of."

Pagels, Elaine. *The Origin of Satan*. New York: Random House, 1995.

Parkes, M. B. *Pause and Effect: An Introduction to the History of Punctuation in the West*. Berkeley and Los Angeles: U of California P, 1993.

Parry, Milman. *The Making of Homeric Verse: The Collected Papers of Milman Parry*. Ed. Adam Parry. Oxford: Oxford UP, 1971.

Pearce, Joseph. *Wisdom and Innocence: A Life of G. K. Chesterton*. San Francisco: Ignatius P, 1996.

Peters, Julie Stone. *Theatre of the Book 1480-1880: Print, Text and Performance in Europe*. New York: Oxford UP, 2000.

Plett, Heinrich F. "Rhetoric and Intertextuality." *Rhetorica: A Journal of the History of Rhetoric* 17 (1999): 313-29.

Postman, Neil. *Amusing Ourselves to Death: Public Discourse in the Age of Show Business*. New York: Viking Penguin, 1985.

—. *Technopoly: The Surrender of Culture to Technology*. New York: Knopf, 1992.

Quine, Willard Van Orman. *Mathematical Logic*. Cambridge, MA: Harvard UP, 1951.

Rahner, Hugo. *Man at Play*. Trans. Brian Battershaw and Edward Quinn. New York: Herder and Herder, 1967.

Rechtien, John G. "The Ramist Style of John Udall: Audience and Pictorial Logic in Puritan Sermon and Controversy." *Oral Tradition* 2.1 (1987): 188-213.

—. *Thought Patterns: The Commonplace Book as Literary Form in Theological Controversy during the English Renaissance*. Diss. Saint Louis U, 1975. Ann Arbor: UMI, 1975.

Rhodes, Neil and Jonathan Sawday, ed. *The Renaissance Computer: Knowledge Technology in the First Age of Print*. London: Routledge, 2000.

Richards, I. A. "Literature, Oral-Aural and Optical." *Complementarities: Uncollected Essays*. Ed. John Paul Russo. Cambridge, MA: Harvard UP, 1976. 201-08.

Riemer, George. *The New Jesuits*. Boston: Little, Brown, 1971.

Riesman, David with Rueul Denny and Nathan Glazer. *The Lonely Crowd: A Study of the Changing American Character*. New Haven: Yale UP, 1950.

Robey, David. *Sound and Structure in the* Divine Comedy. New York: Oxford UP, 2001.

Saenger, Paul. *Space Between Words: The Origins of Silent Reading*. Stanford: Stanford UP, 1997.

Sawicki, Marianne. *Body, Text, and Science: The Literacy of Investigative Practices and the Phenomenology of Edith Stein*. Dordecht, Netherlands: Kluwer Academic Publishing, 1997.

Schmandt-Besserat, Denise. *Before Writing*. 2 vols. Austin: U of Texas P, 1992.

Schmidt, Leigh Eric. *Hearing Things: Religion, Illusion, and the American Enlightenment*. Cambridge, MA: Harvard UP, 2000.

Sharratt, Peter. "The Present State of Studies on Ramus." *Studi francesi* 47-48 (1972): 201-13.

—. "Ramus 2000." *Rhetorica: A Journal of the History of Rhetoric* 18 (2000): 399-455.

—. "Recent Work on Peter Ramus (1970-1986)." *Rhetorica: A Journal of the History of Rhetoric* 5 (1987): 7-58.

Silverstone, Roger. *Why Study the Media?* London: Sage, 1999.

Sloane, Thomas O. *On the Contrary: The Protocol of Traditional Rhetoric*. Washington, DC: Catholic U of America P, 1997.

Smith, Charles G. *Shakespeare's Proverb Lore: His Use of the* Sententiae *of Leonard Culman and Publius Syrus*. Cambridge, MA: Harvard UP, 1963.

—. *Spenser's Proverb Lore: With Special Reference to His Use of the* Sententiae *of Leonard Culman and Publius Syrus*. Cambridge, MA: Harvard UP, 1970.

Smith, Huston. *Why Religion Matters: The Fate of the Human Spirit in an Age of Disbelief*. San Francisco: Harper Collins, 2001.

Taylor, Archer and Bartlett Jere Whiting. *A Dictionary of American Proverbs and Proverbial Phrases, 1820-1880*. Cambridge, MA: Belknap P of Harvard UP, 1967.

Tebeaux, Elizabeth. *The Emergence of a Tradition of Technical Writing in the English Renaissance, 1475-1640*. Amityville, NY: Baywood Publishing, 1997.

Teilhard de Chardin, Pierre. *The Phenomenon of Man*. Trans. Bernard Wall. New York: Harper & Row, 1959.

Theall, Donald F. *The Virtual Marshall McLuhan*. Montreal: McGill-Queens UP, 2001.

Vendler, Helen. *The Breaking of Style: Hopkins, Heaney, Graham*. Cambridge, MA: Harvard UP, 1995.

Vickers, Brian. *Classical Rhetoric in English Poetry*. New York: St. Martin's P, 1970.

—. *In Defense of Rhetoric*. Oxford: Clarendon P of Oxford UP, 1988.

Walker, Jeffrey. *Rhetoric and Poetics in Antiquity*. New York: Oxford UP, 2000.

Ward, Bernadette Waterman. *World as Word: Philosophical Theology in Gerard Manley Hopkins*. Washington, DC: Catholic U of America P, 2001.

Webster, John. "Oral Form and Written Craft in Spenser's *Faerie Queene*." *Studies in English Literature* 16 (1976): 75-93.

Weeks, Dennis L. and Jane Hoogestraat. Introduction. *Time, Memory, and the Verbal Arts: Essays on Walter Ong's Thought*. Ed. Dennis L. Weeks and Jane Hoogestraat. Cranbury, NJ: Susquehanna UP/Associated U Presses, 1998. 9-22.

Welch, Kathleen A. *Electric Rhetoric: Classical Rhetoric, Oralism, and a New Literacy*. Cambridge, MA: Massachusetts Institute of Technology P, 1999.

Whiting, Bartlett Jere. *Chaucer's Use of Proverbs*. Cambridge, MA: Harvard UP, 1934.

—. *Early American Proverbs and Proverbial Phrases* [Up to approximately 1820]. Cambridge, MA: Belknap P of Harvard UP, 1977.

—. *Proverbs in the Earlier English Drama: With Illustrations from Contemporary French Plays*. Cambridge, MA: Harvard UP, 1938.

Whiting, Bartlett Jere and Helen Wescott Whiting. *Proverbs, Sentences, and Proverbial Phrases from English Writings Mainly Before 1500*. Cambridge, MA: Belknap P of Harvard UP, 1968.

Wilmott, Glenn. *McLuhan, or Modernism in Reverse*. Toronto: U of Toronto P, 1996.

Wimsatt, William K., Jr., and Monroe Beardsley. "The Intentional Fallacy." *The Verbal Icon: Studies in the Meaning of Poetry*. Lexington: U of Kentucky P, 1954. 2-18.

Wimsatt, William K., Jr., with Walter J. Ong and Sheila Hough. "The Critic and the Arts." *Yale Reports* [Transcript], WTIC-Hartford [Radio station] (May 24, 1964).

Wise, Jennifer. *Dionysius Writes: The Invention of Theater in Ancient Greece*. Ithaca, NY: Cornell UP, 1998.

Woolf, Daniel. *Reading History in Early Modern England*. Cambridge, UK: Cambridge UP, 2000.

Yeo, Richard. *Encyclopaedic Visions: Scientific Dictionaries and Enlightenment Culture*. Cambridge, UK: Cambridge UP, 2001. Includes commonplace books.

Zboray, Ronald J. and Mary Saracino Zboray. *A Handbook for the Study of Book History in the United States*. Washington, DC: Center for the Book, Library of Congress, 2000; available from Oak Knoll Books. Includes extensive bibliography.

1

Review of *The Interior Landscape*
(1970)

McLuhan, Marshall. *The Interior Landscape: The Literary Criticism of Marshall McLuhan 1943-1962.* Ed. Eugene McNamara. New York: McGraw-Hill, 1969. Pp. xvi + 239.

Marshall McLuhan frequently provides the most direct explanations of his own work. He has long insisted quite explicitly that many of his germinal insights trace to Harold Innis, and in the December 1969 *Atlantic Monthly* (93-98), elaborates on his relationship to Wyndham Lewis. In the Foreword to the present collection McLuhan adds further self-explanation, stating forthrightly that his study of the media "began and remains rooted" in the work of I. A. Richards, F. R. Leavis, Eliot, Pound, and Joyce, as well as in Thomas Nashe, who was the subject of his doctoral dissertation at Cambridge University.

Those who have known McLuhan since he was completing this dissertation in the later 1930's have been aware of these roots of his all along. For he has never made a secret of what he reports here, the shock he received at Cambridge after his earlier "conventional and devoted initiation to poetry as a Romantic rebellion against mechanical industry and bureaucratic stupidity." Cambridge University of the 1930's showed him, largely through the work of those just named, how poetry was not a rebellious escape but rather a mode of organizing sensibility and of adjusting to the contemporary world. "These fragments I have shored against my ruins." To lay claim to his present field of interest, McLuhan had only to extend the purlieus of "poetry" and its adjacent rhetoric to include all the media of communication—not a difficult feat for anyone who knows Aristotle.

Those who denounce McLuhan today for not being sufficiently condemnatory are sometimes only reviving the Romantic censoriousness he was shocked out of. His critics often seem to feel that whoever does not stand off from technology and bureaucracy far enough to throw stones at

69

them is betraying the cause of humanity. McLuhan is aware that there is no way to stand off from technology and bureaucracy. They need criticism, but the criticism has to come from within them. The Cambridge tradition in the 1930's was itself not always aware of this: at times it could react with blind hostility to the nonliterary—technology, bureaucracy, and all the rest, including commercialism—as phenomena that were "out there," to be taken care of by amputation. But the tradition contained its own cure for this hostility in its conviction that literature was one of the modes whereby society dealt with its problems—a way of understanding society and culture, and thus technology, bureaucracy, and commerce, too, and even, ultimately, politics. This conviction, articulated or inarticulated, was one of the strengths of the Cambridge branch of the New Criticism at its best.

The New Criticism was the first mature academic criticism of English vernacular literature. At Cambridge and elsewhere it came into being in academic circles shortly after English was fully established in the 1920's as a higher academic subject for the first time in the history of the world. There was no competing Old Criticism for it to supplant, as I attempted to show some time ago in a study now part of *The Barbarian Within* (177-205). Earlier academic criticism had dealt almost entirely with classical Latin, Greek, or Hebrew—and not only in the English-speaking world, but everywhere in Western Europe. Vernacular literature was treated extra-academically, which meant largely in genteel, if not always gentlemanly periodicals, after hours. The implication was that vernacular literature was not quite serious. No one made his living teaching or studying it. Latin and Greek literature was serious but basically on other than purely literary grounds: it was politically or sociologically or, in the large sense, ethically serious, for Latin and Greek literature awakened young males to the great public issues of the *polis* and trained them in the ritual polemic of a rhetorical and dialectical education that produced statesmen and nourished Empire.

When vernacular literature moved into the universities, it changed the situation far more radically than most were or are aware. With the vernacular came women (Latin had been a sex-linked language, spoken for 1200 years or more only by males, with exceptions so few as to be quite negligible) and, with women, came an irenic mode of teaching. The ritual male polemic of the dialectical and rhetorical method that had completely controlled formal education in all subjects from language through physics, theology, and medicine for some 2500 years was simply no part of a woman's world. In the old dialectical and rhetorical world, Latin (inculcated normally with physical punishment), epic poetry, parliamentary debate, and war formed one ideological continuum. The new vernacular world by contrast was the world of the mother tongue (mothers had not used Latin since it ceased to be a vernacular in the sixth through the eighth centuries). This was a close-in world, where ritual challenge and response languished in the classroom. But it was a very live world, where a great many other things were going on. When classical scholars, the only persons available at the beginning to teach the vernaculars, brought to the study of the mother tongue the full panoply of academic skills developed for the classics, a host of new issues made themselves felt.

The nonliterary classical world had been for the literary scholar essentially "background," something distant. The nonliterary vernacular world was hardly such. It was foreground and even more: it was milieu, something around you and in you, which became particularly immediate as academic attention worked its way from the remote English past to include the literature of the contemporary world and as the social sciences dealing with this world invaded academia. I. A. Richards came to literary criticism from behaviorist psychology: for him, words are rats in a maze, they "behave." And of course there was Freud. The result of the new immediacy was a two-way interaction between literature and everything else more intense than had ever before been known.

Here is the context for McLuhan because it is the context for Leavis, who in so many ways was at the very center of the New Criticism. Thus Leavis' insistence on the seriousness of literature and on its immediate social and complex moral implications (not to be confused with direct moralizing), his antipathy for the bridge generation of English teachers, such as Quiller-Couch, who were neither classicists nor really in the new vernacular world but unthinking and dangerous noncritics who took literature to be no more than fun.

The newly urgent insistence that literature was not an escape from experience but a way of organizing it was not totally a Cambridge product. Its roots can be found in classical antiquity, in the association of poetry with rhetoric. But in the 1930's Cambridge was the locale where the approach was being worked on with more concentration than anywhere else. The approach has since become known all through the English-speaking world today and beyond—though outside the English-speaking world to a far less degree than one might suppose. It accounts for many courses in freshman English in the United States and for some courses in American studies. In England it shows itself in the perceptive and fecund work of Raymond Williams (Leavis-cum-Labor Party, but with significant transformations of both) and, with further significant transformations, in the Centre for Contemporary Studies at the University of Birmingham, where a breakthrough has been made into a serious cultural analysis of commercial advertising, a major field of expression largely scorned (inconsistently) and hence neglected by early New Criticism. The world of McLuhan grows out from here, too. In this context McLuhan's work is seen to be the same, in many basic ways, as that of Richard Hoggart at the Birmingham Centre, and, be it said, as that of Benjamin DeMott, who has worked and taught at Birmingham. This is why DeMott at times so excruciatingly disagrees with, or seems to disagree with, McLuhan. We are all in the same room and treading on one another's toes.

A close look at McLuhan's sensitive criticism collected in the present volume reveals its connection with this earlier New Critical world as well as the continuity of McLuhan's later thought with his earlier interests and stands here. The individual authors treated in the present essays include Joyce, Mallarmé, Dos Passos, Hopkins, Pound, Wyndham Lewis, Keats, Coleridge, Tennyson, Pope, and Poe and the themes focusing McLuhan's discussion run from the medieval *artes sermocinales* (grammar, rhetoric, and dialectic), through analogy (in the philosophical sense), the picturesque and other uses of landscape, to the aesthetic moment and the difference between the New England and the Southern cultural heritage. The individual studies here had appeared originally in publications such as the *Sewanee Review*, the *University of Toronto Quarterly*, the *Kenyon Review*, the *Classical Journal*, *Essays in Criticism*, *Thought*, and *English Institute Essays: 1951*, with the one on Pope's *Dunciad*, the only one from after 1953, excerpted from *The Gutenberg Galaxy* (1962).

Most of these studies in one way or another turn on the seriousness of literature as a means of organizing experience. For Lewis, art is patterned energy, the opposite of the death swoon. Keats' odes are not escapes from conflict but active resolutions of conflict, effected by aesthetic means and at the aesthetic level. Coleridge moves from "linear" rhetorical statement to symbolic ritual and analogical perceptions, which allow of fuller organization of experience. (The term "linear," subsequently a McLuhan favorite, is here—on page 117—credited to Joseph Barrell.) In-depth analogies are the substance of Hopkins' poems, each of which is both utterly individual and inclusive of all the rest through analogues running from external nature to God. Hopkins' thought moves within the economy of the Incarnation, which both reinforces analogical thinking and transcends it. Like Cervantes and Byron, Poe was the aristocratic rebel whose art fought against indiscriminate appetite, chaos. Joyce's sensibility turns from the spatially organized world of Newtonian science to speech, action, and a timeless present. His "trivial and quadrivial" puns connect him with the rhetorical heritage at the center of Western culture and enable him to perceive through language "the paradoxical exuberance of being." Dos Passos had at his disposal Joyce's techniques, but his sensibility was not up to Joyce's. Pound's critical prose is not impressionist effusion but compares and contrasts specific qualities with "decisive discrimination"—"discrimination" was a highly approbatory term in Leavis' Cambridge.

McLuhan treats landscape in connection with cubism. Tennyson had the eye of a movie cameraman but lacked cubist techniques. The symbolists turned to interior landscapes, which they composed as a page in a modern newspaper, juxtaposing items that have no assignable relationship to one another except that they have occurred at the same time. The "same time" for the symbolists was the aesthetic moment, which organized on a field in the interior consciousness items otherwise unrelated. The connection with cubist dismantling and rearrangement of structure is patent, as is also the connection with McLuhan's own later "mosaic" presentation of material, already practiced in *The Mechanical Bride* (1951) and both practiced and labeled in *The Gutenberg Galaxy* (1962).

In one of the latest essays here (1953), on "Joyce, Mallarmé, and the Press," McLuhan elaborates on the press as effecting a reorganization of sensibility. At this point the connections between the author's present concern with the media and Leavis' Cambridge become perhaps most clear. But his judgment of the popular press is more from the inside, more benign, and ultimately more fecund than that of Q. D. Leavis in *Fiction and the Reading Public* (1932).

In three or four or more of the essays here it is also quite apparent how McLuhan's concern with the media of communication today grew out of his preoccupation with the arts of communication in classical antiquity, the Middle Ages, and the Renaissance—grammar, rhetoric, and dialectic or logic. He finds the difference between the South and New England to parallel the difference between rhetoric and logic, between the Sophists' practical rhetoric (the South) on the one hand and the Socratic-Platonic-Aristotelian "philosophy" on the other (New England), between patristic and scholastic thought, between Renaissance humanism and scholasticism, between the Hutchins-Adler great books programs (for the activist encyclopedic understanding of the practical rhetorician engaged in the affairs of the *polis*) and the "scientific" education that prepared "liberals" for abstract, less activist thinking. Details of its application may be disputable, but the dyad being worked with here is an old one—ultimately that of the active versus the contemplative life—and it can be used to polarize much of the human lifeworld.

McLuhan's interest in rhetoric and to a lesser extent in dialectic that these essays make plain connects more with the United States than with Cambridge or any other place in Europe or perhaps even in Canada. To this day most of the work on the history of rhetoric is still done by Americans, who in their extreme commitment to literacy have been far enough removed from the old rhetorical or oratorical culture underlying European education to find its phenomena intriguing. With some few distinguished exceptions, Continental scholars have remained innocent of this American scholarship, and those British scholars who have become aware of it have often reacted negatively and defensively. In a well-known 1949 *Kenyon Review* article on "The Places and the Figures" I. A. Richards undertook to dismiss the history of rhetoric in the name of psychological theory, and the late C. S. Lewis in his *English Literature in the Sixteenth Century, Excluding Drama* (1954), after a dythyrambic avowal of the utterly dominant importance of the rhetorical tradition not only in literature but in the whole of Western culture, states that he nevertheless cannot treat the subject in his history and drops it there, with little indication that he even knew what recent scholarship in the field had done (61).

To a significant extent this scholarship concerning the history of rhetoric and dialectic has been not only an American but even more particularly a Midwestern specialty, with centers at the Universities of Chicago (where Perry Miller came from to Harvard), Illinois, Wisconsin, Michigan, and Saint Louis University, and considerable reinforcement from the University of Toronto. McLuhan taught at Saint Louis University from 1937 to 1944, before and after he completed his dissertation and received his Ph.D. at Cambridge. It was an interesting era at the oldest university west of the Mississippi, which McLuhan himself reflects on in his recent *Atlantic* article on Wyndham Lewis. Concern with rhetoric and dialectic in particular was fortified by a keen philosophical concern with problems of knowledge, noetic and sensory.

One of the active intellectual influences at the University was Bernard J. Muller-Thym, who with McLuhan is included by Richard Kostelanetz in his recent *Master Minds*. After receiving his bachelor's degree from Rockhurst College, Muller-Thym had done his M. A. in philosophy at Saint Louis University, writing his master's thesis there in Latin just for kicks. (Although he was a layman, he took the courses in philosophy given for the Jesuit scholastics, with textbooks and lectures and disputations and examinations in Latin.) His University of Toronto doctoral dissertation on *The Establishment of the University of Being in the Doctrine of Meister Eckhart of Hochheim* was immediately published in 1939 in the Monograph Series of the Institute of Mediaeval Studies, with a preface by Etienne Gilson. After serving in the Navy in World War II, Muller-Thym became and has remained a management consultant, lecturing on management at Columbia University and M. I. T. and being celebrated in *Esquire* and other places equally unlikely for his highly original work in this field.

In the strongly anti-Cartesian climate where an existentialist "St. Louis Thomism" was winning over old-fashioned Suarezianism even on the faculty, interest in the problem of knowledge entailed a large-scale and sophisticated attention to sensory perception, although I do not recall anyone's using the specific term "sensorium" as such. Muller-Thym in particular was concerned with philosophical and psychological interpretation of sensory activity. The *Fleur de Lis*, the University literary magazine, in which he regularly did sophisticated music reviews, in November, 1938, published an article of his undertaking to show that in listening to music the object of specifically intellectual aesthetic contemplation was the movement in one's own senses, which he likened to discourse. The article became such a *cause célèbre* that the *Fleur de Lis* republished it in May, 1940. (Muller-Thym himself was a first-rate violinist, and his wife Mary a first-rate pianist, the daughter of a symphony conductor.) His 1942 *Modern Schoolman* article, "Of History as a Calculus Whose Term Is Science," equally celebrated, advertised his concern with problems of knowledge on another front. So did his vigorous attack on Mortimer Adler in the *Fleur de Lis*. Muller-Thym accused Adler of treating philosophy at the University of Chicago too abstractly and independently of history and of philosophizing about the movies in *Art and Prudence* in a way that was both *a priori* and exterior to the medium.

The study of the ways and conditions of knowing, sensory and intellectual, had of course been particularly urgent in philosophy since Kant or, if one wishes, Descartes. In the Saint Louis University milieu it was rendered more acute by a long-standing quarrel of neoscholastics with Descartes and Kant, sharpened by Gilson's historico-philosophical work in Paris and Toronto and by other Continental European philosophy and given body by the large number of students in the philosophy courses, which, unlike the theology courses, were required even of non-Catholic undergraduates as central to liberal education even apart from religious commitment. In a variety of ways this interest in problems of knowledge reveals itself in the since published work of a large number of students and faculty members besides Muller-Thym at Saint Louis University around McLuhan's incumbency there, such as Robert Henle, President of Georgetown University [from 1969-1976], whose central philosophic interests have been largely epistemology, William Van Roo, later Professor of Theology at the Gregorian University in Rome, Charles Leo Sweeney, now Professor of Philosophy at the Creighton University, and in my own work, as I suppose.

Against this background McLuhan's thought and style of teaching stood out in high but congenial relief. He was an omnivorous reader and vigorous interactor, then as now, and one of his principal assumptions in his teaching was the relevance of everything to everything, an assumption that helps account for his interest in James Joyce and that was abetted by the Cambridge insistence on literature as quintessential relevance. The assumption included of course a strong sense of the relevance of past to present and of present to past. McLuhan's own doctoral dissertation subject, Thomas Nashe, had led him directly into the Renaissance, but his contact with the past was strengthened permanently at Saint Louis University. A certain first-hand knowledge of classical, medieval, and Renaissance texts was taken for granted in this University milieu, being made possible in great part through the massive, communal command of Latin possessed by the hundreds of Jesuit students and several score Jesuit faculty members who formed a small but distinctive part of the Saint Louis University world. The more than twelve million pages of Vatican Library manuscripts now at Saint Louis University came there in the early 1950's, but the milieu was ready for them and the medieval historian who conceived the idea of this collection, Lowrie J. Daly, was a graduate student at the University in McLuhan's time. In this situation it was impossible for McLuhan not to improve his grasp of history and philosophy and theology simultaneously. No wonder that in this present collection of essays he can, for example, drop a reference (12) to *materia signata* without batting an eye.

McLuhan himself was contributing massively and permanently to the University's ongoing work, most of all in making known a teaching style that saw literature as continuous with everything else. The influence of Cambridge that is so evident in the present essays was obvious here in St. Louis. In the *Fleur de Lis* McLuhan published an article on "The Cambridge English School" and related pieces. He propelled others toward Cambridge, notably (Eugene) Marius Bewley, who had begun his undergraduate work at Rockhurst College, too, and had come to Saint Louis University to finish it, and who was already publishing in the *Fleur de Lis* poetry and articles that included a judicious reappraisal of Tennyson à la Richards and Leavis. Bewley went on to Cambridge University for his doctorate.

The Department of English at Saint Louis University was in fact quite a Cambridge stronghold, so that it was far less than an accident that McLuhan came there. Father Francis J. Yealy, the historian of the oldest permanent Missouri settlement, his home town of St. Genevieve, and now Professor Emeritus of English at the University, had earned one of the first Ph.D.'s in English ever awarded at Cambridge, where, curiously enough, one of the readers for his dissertation had been a fellow Missourian but non-Cantabrigian, T. S. Eliot. The late William Hugh McCabe, subsequently President of Rockhurst College but until 1940 Chairman of the Saint Louis University Department of English, was also a Cambridge Ph.D. in English (Renaissance) with first-hand familiarity with Richards' and Leavis' work. Father McCabe was the one who had brought McLuhan from Cambridge to St. Louis. In the Department of Classical Languages the late Francis A. Preuss was a Cambridge man, of earlier vintage.

The Cambridge tradition that McLuhan is at pains to avow in his Foreword emerges in these essays as Cambridge true enough, all the more because it is continuous in McLuhan's own total milieu and mind with much else, not all of which by any means has been accounted for in this present account of mine. It is a tribute to Cambridge that McLuhan carne away from Cambridge with more than Cambridge had to give. When you read back over the criticism of the 1940's and 1950's, you find his to be some of the most rewarding. It is both more widely knowledgeable and more immediate than what you are likely to find elsewhere.

Works Cited

Adler, Mortimer. *Art and Prudence*. In *Poetry and politics*. Pittsburg: Duquesne UP, 1965.

Kostelanetz, Richard. *Master Minds: Portraits of Contemporary American Artists and Intellectuals*. New York: Macmillan, 1969.

Leavis, Q. D. *Fiction and the Reading Public*. London: Chatto & Windus, 1932.

Lewis, C. S. *English Literature in the Sixteenth Century Excluding Drama*. Oxford: Clarendon P of Oxford UP, 1954.

McLuhan, Marshall. *The Gutenberg Galaxy: The Making of Typographic Man*. New York: New American Library, 1962.

—. *The Mechanical Bride: The Folklore of Industrial Man*. New York: Vanguard P, 1951.

Muller-Thym, Bernard J. *The Establishment of the University of Being in the Doctrine of Meister Eckhart of Hochheim*. New York: Sheed and Ward, 1939.

—. "Of History as a Calculus Whose Term is Science." *Modern Schoolman* 19 (1942): 41-47.

Ong, Walter J. *The Barbarian Within and Other Fugitive Essays*. New York: Macmillan, 1962.

Richards, I. A. "The Places and the Figures." *Kenyan Review* 11 (1949): 17-30.

2

An Interview with Walter J. Ong
Conducted by George Riemer (1971)

ONG: I've never checked this, but my dissertation on Peter Ramus, the sixteenth-century French philosopher and educator, may be the longest dissertation that was ever handed in at Harvard—over seventeen hundred pages.

I worked in over a hundred different European libraries—I didn't realize that until I tallied them up afterward. I started in 1950, finished in 1953, turned in the dissertation in 1954. Two books from it were published by Harvard University Press in 1958. They were *Ramus, Method and the Decay of Dialogue* and *Ramus and Talon Inventory*.

One way of looking at these two Ramus books is to take them as studies in the history of the human mind. In a sense, that's what a history of education is because education is the transmission of knowledge from one generation to the next. The way you hand down what you know varies from culture to culture. If you can find out what's going on when people are being educated at any particular time, you can find out what it means at that time to be a human being.

RIEMER: How did you get started on Ramus?

ONG: I dedicated one of these two Ramus books this way: "For Herbert Marshall McLuhan who started all this." By "this" I meant he had first called my attention to Perry Miller's work on Ramus' influence in early New England. Miller was a far-ranging and profound historian of American thought. His work got mine started. Marshall and I were both at Saint Louis University in the late thirties and early forties. There was a milieu in St. Louis at that time that nurtured noetic problems, problems of knowledge. Marshall lived over on McPherson Street, where some other young Saint Louis University faculty lived, too. Slightly dotty neighborhood. Marshall likes to tell how one of the faculty used to grouse

79

about the noise the bicycles made wheeling down the street. Another was known to meet his classes by coming through the window.

Marshall's first book, *The Mechanical Bride*, was published by Vanguard Press. I am pretty certain that only two people in the world reviewed it and I was one of them. Vanguard Press had just changed hands. The new owners didn't think much of the old owners' list and never advertised the book at all. Never gave it a chance. Marshall bought up a load of the remaindered books and stored them near Columbia University in New York City in the home of Bernard Muller-Thym, a former colleague of Marshall's on the Saint Louis University faculty. Ultimately they became collector's items. I'm sure they're all gone by now, because after *The Gutenberg Galaxy* there was a big demand for his old books.

RIEMER: Do you and McLuhan keep in touch?

ONG: Since those days Marshall and I have pretty much gone our separate ways, although the ways have often intersected. We had both been interested in medieval and Renaissance rhetoric, but I've become rather more of a specialist in that. We are good friends, and I see his things regularly. But I haven't read everything of his by a longways. Because our interests do intersect, it may sound strange, but I don't keep up with absolutely everything Marshall writes. Still, we're well tuned to one another.

RIEMER: What makes Ramus important?

ONG: I knew Ramus was some kind of bridge between the early Middle Ages and the modern world. I couldn't figure out exactly how. I had accumulated a tremendous mass of material and had done a lot of writing, but there was something at the middle missing.

Then somehow I came across the difference between the Hebrew idea of knowing and the Greek idea of knowing and in that moment everything fell into place. I realized that though intellectual knowledge has likenesses to all the senses, the Greeks were thinking of it more by analogy with seeing, whereas the Hebrews thought of knowing more as if it were hearing. We typically think of knowledge like the Greeks. The Greek word *idea* has the same root as *video* in Latin, meaning *I see*. We say "I see" to mean "I understand." We speak of ideas as images and *view*points. We describe them as clear, brilliant, and dazzling. Our language is shot through with figure, which "show" our visual bias. We're so immersed in it that we don't realize it's a bias—you know, like everything's wet if you grow up like a fish.

Once you have an alphabet that lets you represent sounds on a two-dimensional sheet of paper, and then develop writing by hand, and then, further, develop print, you almost can't help locking ideas into space. You tend to put an exaggerated value on surface as a means for storing and locating and conveying information. You start drawing outlines, diagrams, and systems. Eventually, after a few hundred years of this people naturally think that words were always on some kind of surface like paper, that they came from such surfaces and belong there.

I wasn't aware of how visualistic my own thinking was until I "saw" how the Hebrews regarded knowledge and I "discovered" they were doing something different. Since the Hebrews thought of knowing more by analogy with hearing, learning tended to mean listening to someone. They thought even of things as speaking, not only as showing themselves, but as declaring themselves.

Yadha' in Hebrew means *to know* in the sense of to know your way around. It means to have savvy. It is something that has to do with the human lifeworld and human behavior.

Knowing for the Greek means to be able to explain. It means to analyze, to take apart, to show the different pieces of. It's a very abstract knowledge. Our Greek visualist bias shows when we try to provide a rational explanation for everything. This can't always be had, and the attempt to set it up becomes more and more suspect the closer we get to the source of life. There is a kind of wisdom you cultivate in not being excessively rational.

RIEMER: "Explain" or "show" also means to communicate knowledge. Then the ability to communicate knowledge must be an essential part of knowledge.

ONG: Yes, that's right. The Hebrews just didn't think much about explaining. It's notorious that there was no science among the Hebrews. They were event-minded. History-minded. People-minded. The ancient Greeks were too, by contrast with modern technologists, but by contrast with the Hebrews they show up as abstractive. Most early cultures were like Hebrew culture. The Greeks break with the rest of mankind here.

Hebrews were event-minded and thus were tuned in on sound because sound is the only sensory field that always indicates something is going on. Sound is current, that is, running. Sound is contemporary. Sound is transient and exists while going out of existence. Even in saying "existence," by the time I get to *-tence*, the *exist-* is gone. You can't stop sound or freeze it in flight. If you do stop sound, you have silence. What this all means, then, is that if you hear a sound, you are hearing something that's acting. Sound is an event in motion.

The fact that the Greeks and Hebrews thought of knowing in such different ways made great differences in the way they learned and lived. Today, when we want to remember a number of things, we make a checklist. We have dictionaries and reference books where we can "look up" facts. Even when they had the alphabet, most early peoples didn't do much "looking up." They "recalled" for the ear, as their pre-literate ancestors had done. Verse meters or rhythms and rhymes were memory aids. In such a culture, you can easily see how age and wisdom go together. Old people got a lot of respect often because they were memory banks—human storehouses for information.

The great axis in my Ramus work is the shift from an orally oriented culture to a visualist culture. Ramus bridges antiquity and modern technology because he intensified and accentuated the visualist element in verbal cognition. What made this possible for him was the printing press.

A prominent feature of Ramus' work is the dichotomized outline. He'd take a subject like "dialectic" and divide it into "invention" and "judgment." Then he'd divide "invention" into two more parts and do the same for "judgment." Then he'd divide each of the resulting parts into two more parts and so on and on. Ramus didn't know it but he was working out a crude computer flow chart. He dropped memory as a part of rhetoric because his diagrams and outlines are an elaborate memory system. That's what a computer is. It "remembers" data.

RIEMER: It must have been awesome standing on the verges of such a vast sweep of human history. How did it make you feel?

ONG: I felt awfully excited. I started writing. I put out quite a few articles about this before my big books appeared. I just couldn't hold it in.

RIEMER: Some teachers say there's no longer any need to teach writing because film and sound will take the place of books.

ONG: Writing is here to stay. The media never destroy each other. They reinforce one another. But they also interact and remake each other. This fools people. Many think a new medium is simply added to the old without any change in the old. This is the kind of person Marshall McLuhan likes to get at and does get at. Many people think that when you write you simply can put down what you talk. But no. You don't think the same way when you write. That's why people who talk with ease can find it difficult to write. Once you do write, however, some of your writing habits or styles feed back into your speech. People who write begin to talk as though they were writing, just as I'm doing now to a degree.

RIEMER: I revise a lot when I write, trying to break clichés and searching for more exact language. These taped interviews are showing me how much my writing habits have influenced my speech. I sometimes sound like I'm stammering.

ONG: When talking and writing interact, neither is the same any more. It's quite likely that people who know how to write talk more than the ones who don't.

Now our talk today is the talk of inner-directed people. We are social-minded, as earlier oral man was, but he couldn't think of any other option. Men had to be social-minded before writing because people came together precisely to talk and to hear talk. Talk was where the action was, where thinking was. People in an oral society are interested in events because early people didn't have science. We're interested in events, not because we don't have science, but because we've got so much science.

TV news reporting gives you a sense of participation largely because of the voice and sound effects. The picture generally supports the voice, not vice versa. Any studio man will tell you you've got to have the sound. A live picture doesn't really live unless somebody is talking about it.

RIEMER: Remember when Apollo 11 failed to transmit pictures? People stayed at their sets anyway, listening to the astronauts talk.

ONG: That's right. They have to talk up there on the moon. You can't read a weather map on television like you can read it in the papers. You've got to have somebody reading it to you. It's talk that gives you this sense of participation.

The reason for this is that sound unifies its listeners. Readers are all split up, but an audience is one group. "Audience" is a collective noun. There is no singular collective noun for readers, and you can't form one because that's not the kind of thing readers are. "Readership" is not a true collective noun, but an abstraction.

RIEMER: Editors and publishers, I notice, get shrill and uptight about Marshall McLuhan. They think he's proclaiming the death of print.

ONG: They are mistaken. Television and radio will help print. When print was invented, did it destroy writing? Just the opposite, and print is here to stay. Like writing is. New media do not cancel out the old. They build on them, reinforcing them and—this is what most people miss—radically changing their mode of existence and operation. But in their changed form the old media are stronger than ever.

In classical antiquity, people wrote a lot, but they didn't read much. Once we got print, it became necessary to have universal literacy. Everybody had to know how to write. Print didn't destroy writing. It forced people to learn to write. It interacted with writing. Now people began to write for print. The classical example of someone writing for print is James Joyce's *Finnegans Wake*. This has to be for print because with all his tricks of orthography we could never possibly get two manuscript copies that were even reasonably like one another.

RIEMER: The film *Ulysses* had trouble with that.

ONG: Of course it did. That's right. When man started writing for print, his writing style changed. Even now when you write letters to friends that are not to be printed, there's an influence from print. Print didn't destroy the oral world, but it changed it. Our oral world is that of an inner-directed, chirographic people. Now that we have entered an electronic age, it is increasingly necessary for almost everybody to print. That's the typewriter. Television has to have writing and print in back of it. But neither writing nor print are what they used to be before the radio, the telephone, the phonograph and television. Look what we—you and I—are doing now in taping this interview.

What's going on here will produce a printed book. Electronic tape is supporting print. We're using talk and writing (for editing), and electronics and print. Yet the book produced will have been "written" by no one.

RIEMER: Not in the usual sense of "writing a book."

ONG: It will represent an interaction between talk and taping and writing and more talk and taping and writing and finally print. The only way I can characterize such a fascinating end product is to call it a "presentation." It's typical of our culture today.

RIEMER: The writing after taping will be a more accurate writing.

ONG: Yes. You can get a certain kind of accuracy with this. Right.

RIEMER: Another difference is that you and I have different, perhaps conflicting images of the ultimate reader of this book. I might be thinking of a reader who's unfamiliar with Jesuits but open and friendly. You might be worried about a hostile reader. Your image could affect what you tell me. You'd tend to be more guarded, more defensive, more suspicious. I hope to avoid a conflict of reader images by having you address me instead of the tape, because when you address the tape, you are addressing your image of the reader and not mine. Of course, in order to address me you have to trust me, and I have to give you confidence that I can be trusted.

ONG: Yes. The use of present-day media such as tape complicates our relationship to the ultimate reader. I am saying things to you to be taped in order to be typed out, edited, and printed. You are asking me questions in order to get me to speak in this complex. I know that what I say will have something to do with what ultimately appears on the printed page, but I am not quite sure in what way. So we cannot entirely avoid the conflict by our own personal friendship. No matter what, for our present purposes I am not talking really just to you. Still, friendship and our personal presence to one another can establish a tone.

RIEMER: The Jesuits were founded in 1534 during the lifetime of Ramus. Your particular studies should give a certain special understanding of the changes troubling the American people and the Society of Jesus today. Marshall McLuhan has said the Society was founded on literacy and is therefore in trouble. Is McLuhan right?

ONG: Let me break your question in two. As for the Society being founded on literacy, yes, in certain ways. We have written Constitutions and we make a lot of them—so does the United States of its *Constitution*. The British historian Denis Brogan likes to point out that in the United States we actually quote the *Declaration of Independence* and the *Constitution* in court, whereas if you quoted the Magna Carta in England, they would think you were crazy. The English have a stronger feeling for common law, for the way people talk and the way people do. But we, here, believe in writing. Americans have the most literate culture the world has seen. Comparably, in the Society of Jesus we specify that we cannot appeal to custom against our written law. This is rather contrary to what had been a normal thing in canon law and the religious tradition. It shows that we come from a very chirographic culture. People in such a writing culture know that they can put things down in writing and that operations can be conducted on that basis.

But early members of the Society of Jesus were also quite oral because the old oral traditions of classical antiquity continued in our schools right up to Romanticism. You never tested a person in those times by asking him to write something. Testing was always oral. It was the Renaissance that brought to the fore the old classical idea of the "rhetor"—orator, the public speaker. Consequently, you have the stress on eloquence that marks Renaissance and therefore Jesuit education. Jesuits are writing-oriented and speculation-oriented, but we're also activists.

Now the second part of your question, that the Society was founded on literacy and is therefore in trouble. I don't know. Being troubled is part of human existence.

Fortunately, our tradition has always been that of adjustment. We've been very free-falling. We've never had any particular way of dressing. We are largely in education today in the U.S., but this was not our initial purpose.

The Society was founded to do whatever the Church needed done. We are becoming much more conscious of that now than we were, say, in the past thirty or forty years. We used to say it just as we've always said we were free agents unfixed in any special work. But now we're thoroughly conscious of it. Right now we're hanging loose in our activities and watching for major adjustments, though we do of course have to be true to commitments we have made to others. There's a lot of new programming going on now in the Society.

RIEMER: The telephone company is severely based on written rules. Have you ever tried to get any information from an operator beyond what she was instructed to give you? Dealing with big companies today is more and more frustrating because the companies make sure there is no capricious deviation from their written rules by programming the rules into a computer.

ONG: You always have to complement written rules. In the Society of Jesus the complement or counterpoise is the constant personal relationship between the superior and everybody in the province or the house that he's in. This is an oral thing. You do have direct oral communication all through the Society. This has always been cultivated and always will be. The Society is fathered institutionally in a literacy structure, but there's a conscious effort to complement the written Constitutions with things they don't have. We have the Constitutions, but the superior can dispense from them. We are founded on literacy, but literacy is not the ultimate thing.

RIEMER: Has the Society's concept of obedience to superiors changed?

ONG: It isn't waved around as a flag, perhaps, the way it used to be. We are concerned that the flow of information from the members of the Society to superiors be kept open so that the commands of the superior are responsive to actualities of life. There is a great deal of talk about this, but it really isn't new, because the Constitutions provided for this quite specifically. One of the distinctive things in the Constitutions is that subjects are supposed to tell superiors if they have difficulties. There is more concern that this go on today, but that again is where the Society of Jesus is responding to the general structures of the society outside. Obedience is structured into that situation of lots of up-and-down communication.

RIEMER: Two black Jesuits interviewed elsewhere in this book [*The New Jesuits*] say that Jesuits in their spiritual training are sensitized to examine their consciences for subtle personal imperfections while remaining insensitive to gross social wrongs. Does a bias for self-awareness and introspection result from literacy?

ONG: Yes. Inner-directedness goes with a writing culture. Before people knew how to write, they didn't think things out for themselves. There was nothing that corresponded to study as we think of it today. If you were to be in contact with the articulated thought of another person, he had to be there, you had to be talking to him. Thinking was not the lonely occupation it became once we got writing.

People were examining their consciences long before Christianity—there were the Ten Commandments, for example. But you didn't have a stress on the examination of conscience as a reflectively controlled and directed activity, at least no stress that amounted to very much, before say around 1500. At about this time you do. Suddenly, you have all kinds of manuals for examining your conscience. There were lists of sins in the Middle Ages, but they were minor lists compared to the ones that came out at this time. The technique of introspection now became extremely developed.

The *Spiritual Exercises* show how deeply interiorized and inner-directed Jesuits are. The *Exercises* were to bring a man to make up his own mind all by himself in the presence of God. St. Ignatius cautions directors not to interfere with the one they are helping through the

Exercises. Let him make up his mind. You can give him suggestions to think about but he is going to have to do the deciding.

But inner-directedness doesn't only mark the Society of Jesus. It's characteristic of everything that came out during that period right after the development of printing. It's part of Protestantism and the Protestant ethic, too.

RIEMER: I have an optical illusion with the terms "inner-" and "other-directed." I keep wanting to think they mean introvertive and extrovertive or introspective and extrospective, as if "inner" were really "inward." I have to make a conscious effort to realize that inner-directed means self-directed or self-starting or self-motivated. Does the inner-directed person find it hard to socialize his thoughts? I mean, can he communicate?

ONG: Oh, yes. Inner-directedness is not antisocial. By inner-directedness I mean an attention to oneself in all one's dimensions. This includes, very deeply, the social dimensions. The drive comes from within but moves out.

RIEMER: Epictetus taught self-awareness.

ONG: Yes. Epictetus was a Stoic, and Stoicism connects at certain points with the Christian tradition quite well. Of course, there's a lot self-awareness in everybody all the time. No self-awareness, no human being. But the kind of stress that you get on it at this time is connected with writing and the intense literacy of the Middle Ages.

RIEMER: Did people who lived before print and writing have personal prayer?

ONG: Prayer was always to a degree personal, but in significant ways not so personal as it became later after writing and print really took hold. Earlier, prayer was much more communal. The thinking was much more communal. In human cultures before writing, you didn't have individual thinkers who figured things out alone. All men's thought had to advance more or less at once. And prayer was likely to be felt as something that was done within the community.

Much that was later interiorized remained somewhat external, in certain ways. In the early books of the Bible, you have a ritual of purification, for instance, for touching a dead body. No one was exactly guilty of wrongdoing here, yet this contact was an impurity something like that of sin. Quite external, and yet it had to be treated somewhat as sin was. Then much later you get to where Jesus tells people that the things that come out of the heart are the things that dirty man. You see? We're becoming more clearly interiorized by this time. Exterior behavior counts, but largely because it connects with interior consciousness.

Anthropologists talk about the difference between a shame culture and a guilt culture. In a shame culture the pressures are more external, in a guilt culture they're more from within. Today, we're other-directed something like earlier man. We tend to measure ourselves by what other people do. But it's not a question of unreflective conformity so much as it was earlier, because we still have our inner-directedness. We study other people consciously, whereas the tradition-directed man simply conformed without any particular study. David Riesman has spelled out much of this very well in *The Lonely Crowd*, where he explains the tradition-directed character, the inner-directed character, and the other-directed character. These occur that way in roughly temporal sequence.

RIEMER: Was there more of a chance for dialogue before writing and print were developed? I'm referring to the Buber kind of I-Thou dialogue, the attempt to reduce false images in communicating with others. I believe we get many of our false images of each other because of our visual, therefore surface, orientation.

ONG: The frames of reference are so different. Human relations are human relations, so undoubtedly individuals related to one another very warmly from earliest times. They certainly could not, however, be as articulate about their relationships as we can.

Dorothy Lee did a study some years ago on the concept of the *I* among the Wintu, an Indian tribe. Every human being says "I," but when the Wintu says, "I" he feels himself significantly in context with many other people. We don't so much. In early oral culture, a man couldn't ever get quite as far away from other people as we can. Privacy is a modern invention. Earlier cultures had very little privacy. In a tribal culture it might be a we-you relationship rather than an I-Thou. There is some of the I-Thou there, but it's very socialized.

A former student of mine who came back after a couple of years with the Peace Corps in Nigeria told me about the linguistic isolation of the people she lived with. They couldn't talk to anybody if they went thirty-five miles from their village. People beyond that distance all spoke a foreign language. What she missed most for herself was privacy. Everybody knew all the time what she was doing every moment of the day. The only way she could be private was to go to her little hut, and there wasn't anything in there, nothing to do.

There is no word in ancient Latin for what we today call a family, that is, a husband, wife, and children, who are felt as a unit, with everything else in the whole world outside this unit. The word *familia* in Latin means a household.

RIEMER: That concept of *familia* is still strong in Italy. It also includes animals. I have a paper written by a seven-year-old Italian child taking his toy dog to the doctor. He asks his aunt, "Who will pay?" His aunt says, "You will." "But l have no money," he says, and she answers: "But it's your dog." Then he answers, "The dog is not an outsider. The dog is one of us."

ONG: *Familia* included all the people that worked in and around the house, the hangers-on, everybody. There was just no way for a family in our sense—husband, wife, and children all alone—to have privacy. We don't have the old kinds of extended family structure much in America any more except among our poor.

RIEMER: In my first letter to you a long time ago, I asked whether dialogue might not take the place of eloquence as the objective of a Jesuit education. We need the dialogic person much more than the eloquent person today. Eloquence, today, seems almost a selfish luxury. You wrote that it would take too much in the space of a letter to answer. Can we talk about it now?

ONG: I don't remember your asking me that question, but I think that to a degree what you suggest is true. What we are developing now in the Society of Jesus is people who are good at dialogue. Today you have to use dialogue. This is the typical modern approach. On the other hand, I think that you can exaggerate the irenic possibilities of dialogue. There is a certain point where you have to put your cards on the table and say, "This is where I stand."

RIEMER: But that's the point when dialogue truly begins. So long as you hide your cards you're faking or masking or bluffing. All these tactics prevent dialogue from happening. I don't think of dialogue as having irenic possibilities because you can end up enemies. The dialogue in marriage may lead to divorce. The dialogue in the Society may result in an ex-Jesuit.

ONG: But dialogue is open. When you contrast dialogue with rhetoric, the rhetorical man doesn't have an open mind. A man who is defending a criminal in court doesn't have an open mind. He maintains his man is innocent, and the prosecutor maintains he's guilty. The rhetorical stance is not an open-minded stance. It is the stance of a person who has taken a position. Now the favored stance today is an open-minded one. However, we have to start from a position, and it is completely fraudulent to maintain that you have an absolutely open mind when you start. But you can have a relatively open mind. The dialogic approach means you don't know where you are coming out. You stand to be modified by the other man; he stands to be modified by you.

RIEMER: Community life is probably the deepest source of problems for the Society right now. Is this true, and is it related to what we are talking about?

ONG: Yes. Yes, it is. It comes about with the younger people. They are the ones who chiefly have the problem. The Society's structures were ordered largely to earlier writing-and-print culture, but our younger people have grown up in a culture that is much more oral. They look more for a kind of warm community. In the older structure there was a great warmth, but it was restrained. Everybody was doing his particular kind of work in a very firm structure of behavior, having meals and common reading at a certain regular time—for we had reading aloud during many of our meals—the litanies and common prayer together. You felt a great sense of community because you knew that there was a personal bond uniting the individual to the superior and in that way to the others through the superior. There were personal relationships among individuals too, but you didn't have the feeling that it was necessary to get the whole community together and talk things out all at once. Now that's the kind of thing that young people come with today. It's that way in the colleges, too.

RIEMER: But older men, too, complain about the absence of community feeling. By "older" I mean men about forty.

ONG: In my experience, it's uncommon for a man in a higher age bracket—say over sixty-five—to complain in quite that fashion unless he picks it up from the young and recognizes the need for it now.

Forty is about the breaking point, I guess. Those around forty have been caught more than others in change. The forties probably feel it more intensely than the very young do today.

RIEMER: Some of the forties I've talked with don't even live in the community as I knew it to be.

ONG: The Jesuit tradition in the United States has been far more communitarian than in most other places. Our communities here are generally larger than Jesuit communities in Europe, and our activities used to be much more community-oriented.

There's a curious dialectic in evidence today. Some people who talk about community also talk about "doing your thing," and really don't live in communities. It's very strange. I suspect there may be some compensatory mechanism at work there, as there has been in similar situations in the past.

RIEMER: Some Jesuits have some married couples as friends. Some find their friends in student groups and some find their friends among the lay professionals they work with. My point is that a community is where one's heart is and their hearts are with their friends.

ONG: I'm sure I exist in a great many communities. I feel close to all sorts of in-groups, besides those in my own classes and student groups. And I trust many feel close to me. But my real home community is the Society of Jesus and the Jesuit community at Saint Louis University. I draw on it for other communities.

RIEMER: Whether McLuhan is right or wrong about literacy, the Society of Jesus is indeed in some kind of trouble. There is a shifting of things. Changes are being made, and if those changes are troublesome—that's trouble.

ONG: That's right.

RIEMER: What do you think the trouble comes from?

ONG: I think many troubles in the Society of Jesus and the Church and in the civil order all come from the same thing. Human society is going through a reorientation process because of the technologizing of life. Technology affects not only the physical world but also our mental world. Because of technology, we're overwhelmed with awareness. In our day technologized man knows where all human groups are all over the world. He knows more history than ever before. He is torn by feelings both of unity and diversity in the human family. He has discovered that earlier living structures were rather provincial.

So far as you can say one thing about the changes disturbing the world, that's what you'd have to say. This is something Teilhard de Chardin used to point to. Earlier people didn't know where the rest of the human race was. We do. And once in a while some of them are on the moon.

RIEMER: When you say "provincial," are you referring to tribal differences?

ONG: No. I mean provincial in the sense of limited. People think of Emerson in Concord and how he was in touch with his past. But he was in contact with only a narrow band of the past. We're in contact with a past of all human beings all over the world, in a depth that was unimaginable before. The Vietnam situation is connected with this. A technologized society like ours can no longer believe that any group of people are complete villains. This was quite easy for Americans to believe in World War I. The Kaiser and the Huns were real villains. Or even World War II, the Japanese. But even in World War II men had difficulty in believing Hitler or Nazism was as bad as it was.

RIEMER: Or that there was any villainy in our own men.

ONG: That's right. Now this is the problem in Vietnam—one of the many, many problems. The Viet Cong can more easily believe that we are total villains. I suppose many of them really do. Just as we used to believe of those we fought. But they don't hate our technology. And this is the kind of tension we're getting. You see everybody in a technologized culture is trying simultaneously to relate to everybody at once.

There's a dialectic in this. Because we live in the large structures provided by technology, by television, for example, we deliberately make structures that are small to complement this. So you will see Jesuits working with little groups.

We're in trouble, but I don't see that the Society of Jesus is in any distinctive kind of trouble. It's the trouble that the human race is in. If Jesuits weren't in this kind of trouble too, then we wouldn't be with it.

I don't want to sound smug about this, but because of my work the things that are going on now somehow haven't surprised me too much. I've felt the need to make some adjustments, but a great deal of my adjusting has simply meant to push along on lines I'd already started on.

RIEMER: What things are "going on now"? Could you specify one or two things?

ONG: Oh, I suppose existentialist thought, personalistic philosophy and intergroup and interpersonal relations, minority revolutions, outsiders becoming insiders. Things like that.

RIEMER: Some well-known priests have been leaving the ministry. When this happens, does it affect you?

ONG: Yes, this affects me. It affects everybody. I cannot judge the individual's own motives, but one of the ways it affects me is by knowing the shock this sort of thing inevitably causes and the tremendous hardships it imposes on people in the Church. The more prominent a man is, the more that sort of thing ordinarily affects us.

You can't talk about these things much because you have to be charitable and you don't know what individual problems are. When you do know, your knowledge is confidential, not yours to disclose. Consequently, there is relatively little public talk in the Church about defections. There is some, but considering the number of them, it's always struck me that the amount of talk is quite limited and often guarded even when it pretends to be "frank." In general, I think this is a good thing. One respects an individual's privacy, and especially his privacy before God. But, nevertheless, this kind of thing concerns me because of the blow it is—you have to speak frankly—to the faith of a great many people.

RIEMER: Maybe they're requiring people to stand on their own faiths, and not on images of strong people.

ONG: Yes. People now do have to stand more on their own feet. They have to interiorize their faith, live in God's presence personally. We should have been doing this all along. So what happens is that people are being put to a test today that they were not put to before. But it's not good to put people to a test just to put them to a test.

RIEMER: It may not be a scandal. A good jolt may be just what some of them need to settle their convictions. I think they have a chance to become more authentic people.

ONG: Yes, but it still shakes them. Jesuits are very much inner-directed. We are supposed to stand on our own feet. Examine our own conscience.

This is in all Catholic spirituality, but it's been a special mark of Jesuit spirituality. Today we are in an other-directed society. I think Riesman, in *The Lonely Crowd*, had this right. We look to other people and are constantly trying to get support from them. This is one of the problems of all younger people today. But there may not be that much support for you in other people. You just have to face this fact. Just because you want to talk things out, doesn't necessarily mean that you get the kind of support you need.

Younger Jesuits speak much more readily about religion than we did earlier. Probably not more, though, than what was done in the earlier Society of Jesus. But their support has to come both from the inside and the outside.

Many of the younger people—not all, by any means—find it hard to be alone. But unless you can be alone, you don't have anything to say. This is one of the paradoxes of human existence. You don't know what it feels like to be me. I don't know what it feels like to be you. We are completely isolated from one another, in a sense, but this is the only situation in which communication is possible.

RIEMER: It is only when you understand what silence is that you know what sound is.

ONG: That's right. Sound emerges from silence. And not vice versa.

RIEMER: You've been able to get a lot of foundation money for your work. But you still live in the community and take your support from the Society, is that true?

ONG: Of course. And when I'm on a grant, I don't live in any high style. I use grants for what they are given for—specified work. Meanwhile, I practice poverty like anyone else. Occasionally, I have quite a large income other than grants, and this income I always simply turn in to the community. And that's that. My life isn't materially affected at all by the kind of income I get from, for instance, visiting professorships and lectureships. That's all community money, for our corporate apostolate, for work for others. Your apostolic value, though, is not a matter of how much money comes through your activities.

The only things for which I have to ask superiors for money are ordinary personal needs—clothes, occasionally books, sometimes a supply of offprints of my own articles, medical or dental attention, and so on.

Poverty has to maintain itself in fresh forms, but some religious today are naive in not recognizing that many practices long standard in their way of life bear quite clearly witness to poverty. I was mentioning to a layman recently our experiments with smaller communities. He asked, "Isn't this some kind of luxury? Living together in sizable groups is a way of living cheaper." The practice of living in large communities at the site of one's work is one quite evident way of practicing poverty or of trying to practice it, though not necessarily the only or the best way. Any businessman is perfectly aware of this. Small communities may be useful. But we should be more aware than perhaps we have been of what our various ways of living have already been saying.

RIEMER: Do you have a secretary?

ONG: I have a student who works for me part-time. Many religious in the past have had secretaries when their apostolate required it. St. Thomas Aquinas, I know, had one—one who couldn't type though. We use secretaries because we need more technological help. Certain kinds of work can be turned over to individuals who have particular skills. Other work can be done by machines. There will be more and more of this, but I don't see that this creates any really new difficulties in the practice of poverty.

RIEMER: What do you think of Jesuits working on secular campuses?

ONG: Except for serving as visiting professors, I feel that by and large teaching by a priest on a secular campus is not as effective as working in our own institutions. Your presence is minimized. Our institutions tend to maximize it. I've taught on a lot of secular campuses, you know. However, there are many exceptions to this general rule.

RIEMER: Dan Berrigan says Jesuits go into a school and accept it on its own terms and never think to challenge it. He feels there are times when they ought to challenge those structures.

ONG: He's right. We get lost. You don't amount to that much. One trouble is that a priest permanently on a secular campuses may get occluded as a priestly witness—though not if he is a Father Dan Berrigan doing his highly apostolic and highly visible work. It's one thing to be Berg Professor of English at New York University and have your name listed in the catalogue ahead of everybody in the department, to be lionized for one year. Everybody knows you're there as "our Berg Professor." You're the star. (There will be another star next year.) But it's another thing to go into a department, to live there ten or twenty years and maybe lose distinctive witness value as a priest and religious. In a Catholic institution the milieu helps sustain your identity. There can of course be other ways of managing elsewhere.

Faculties of high schools, colleges, and universities in the United states are populated by hundreds—perhaps thousands—of Protestant ministers who have left the ministry or are relatively inactive in it. No one even knows that they are or have been Protestant ministers. Ministerial dedication can grow invisible. This happens a little less easily to Catholic priests because of the structure of priestly dedication, especially celibacy in the Catholic Church, but it can and does happen.

RIEMER: When you lecture in secular institutions, do you ever wear a necktie?

ONG: No, unless clerical dress is prohibited by civil law. In circles where I move I am known this way. Other priests and religious may find their cases different.

Some say that a Roman collar distances you from people, but my experience has simply not borne this out. After all, it's not a spectacularly different form of men's dress. I've taught as visiting professor at secular and state universities all over the country and abroad, and it is certain that in many cases a Roman collar made it easier for people to relate to me. High definition often adds appeal, and especially today, when costume is often favored over dress.

So I would constantly have to explain why I'm wearing a necktie. And I don't have time to explain why I'm wearing a necktie.

RIEMER: When I was in the Society, there was a hero group, some very brilliant men were destined to become the Jesuit philosophers and theologians. They got the best teachers and got their prime time. Lesser students were given the clear and distinct impression that they were not qualified to philosophize because they were not professionals. One of these very elite students, now an ex-Jesuit priest, told me he had had straight A's from kindergarten to law school and all through the Society. But now at age fifty he feels he wasn't educated. He had learned all the required structures charted by all his schools. Now he's trying to find himself.

ONG: This is very real, I think. That attitude towards the heroes in philosophy was a real problem. It was not due to a defect in the philosophy itself, but to a lack of openness, a somewhat narrow idea of what philosophy was. I think we suffered from that a great deal. The philosophy taught at Saint Louis University when I was studying it there was very good. It could have tied in with even more things than it did tie into, but it didn't because many of the people teaching it had a very specialized idea of what philosophy was. Precisely one of the things that it could have tied in with is the thing in your interests that makes you like the work of a psychologist such as Piaget.

I don't think our problems were any greater than those in any other kind of educational system. In many ways less. I hit Saint Louis University when St. Louis Thomism rose to its first crest, quite vigorously historical and structurally sensitive in the hands of the good teachers. What I learned studying philosophy at Saint Louis University made my work on Ramism possible and has given me a permanent edge over many colleagues around the world. The advantage of the kind of philosophical training we were given was that if you got it, if you studied it, you knew the central intellectual tradition of all Western culture.

But you didn't really know that was what it was unless you knew a lot of things outside of philosophy too. So you had something that was a wonderful tremendous asset, provided you could open it up. That's just what many people then failed to do. Others succeeded. Today philosophy is beautifully open here, and I think strong at the same time. One of the most brilliant students I've ever had—she was offered around fifty thousand dollars in fellowships upon receiving her B.A.—told me that perhaps her biggest advantage in the Department of English at Harvard over other graduate students was the philosophy and theology she got at Saint Louis University. So many graduate students in other fields need to get into philosophy in their work and prove to be complete innocents. They have no firsthand knowledge of central features of their own intellectual traditions.

RIEMER: What difference do you see between learning and education?

ONG: We use both those words in various senses. When you say "education," you imply involvement with another person. You can say a man is "self-educated," but then you make him into two people—*he* educates *himself*. A self-educated person is his own leader. But when you say "learning," you don't think about another person being there. It's thought of as an activity that originates within the individual.

RIEMER: I wonder whether education might look into the person and his individual capacity for development, whereas learning has to do with a certain tradition or with systems and abstractions that have to be acquired?

ONG: We do have that distinction too. Education involves a personal relationship, whereas learning is a transaction between you and a body of knowledge, which is a *thing*.

RIEMER: Learning, therefore, would be more prominent in a print culture, because you do have structures of knowledge collected in books et cetera.

ONG: Right. It would. There is a distinction in French between *l'enseignement* and *l'éducation*. *L'enseignement* is just teaching, instruction. *L'éducation* is the total development of a person.

RIEMER: Are you satisfied with the Society's own training curriculum as it now is?

ONG: It's undergoing such tremendous change that nobody quite knows where it will come out. You can never be satisfied with any structure of education, because every structure has advantages and disadvantages. As society changes, the disadvantages begin to get greater or lesser, and you have to make adjustments. There is no perfect way of educating, that's the first thing.

There were many advantages in the way in which we were educated in the Society of Jesus. Everybody had a common store of knowledge, and therefore shared a common background. This was why you didn't need the amount of personal discussion that you have in the Society today. You already knew a lot of things that were in the other people's minds. You could go off with assurance, developing your own intellectual community. Also, remember that the Society saw to it that many of us received advanced degrees in secular schools, too.

The problem with the older system was that for many people it was too closed and too provincial. It wasn't necessarily so, because many people kept an open mind to things outside and were able to develop. The difficulty today is that with the wide variety of knowledge that Jesuits have to have, the common core is likely to suffer. I think we will have some kind of real problems here regarding the feeling of identity around a core of shared knowledge.

RIEMER: Jesuit community will suffer?

ONG: Yes. I think one of the real reasons for having meetings and discussion groups is the diversity of the knowledge content of our minds. We need this kind of personal unity more than in the past. It's a new way of acquiring a community sense.

RIEMER: So that the Jesuit image of "I" is changing?

ONG: Yes, it is somewhat.

RIEMER: If you feel you have a common store of knowledge with other people, isn't that "I" different from the "I" you have when you all have different kinds of knowledge?

ONG: That's right. There is a sense of "I" and a sense of community in both cases. But the way in which the two are structured into one another is quite different. Let's see if we can spell that out. Earlier, our sense of community was maintained by a certain number of rather formalized activities, which were, however, deeply interiorized by the individuals. That was important. They were interiorized because you did them out of obedience, an obedience that was not merely external but humanized and interiorized in faith. You made the formalized activities yours. I'm referring to things such as an exact daily order, the common refectory reading. These things may not always have been the most appealing in the world, but you were doing them out of obedience, and you knew that others were doing the same thing that way too.

RIEMER: And in silence there was a very taut closeness about it.

ONG: Yes, the silence is important. Although we communicate with words, real understanding lies in the silences in between. So silence, the right kind of silence, is a deeper kind of communication than speaking. Human speech is defective. "The word of the Lord remains forever." This is exactly what the human word does not do. The human word is, of its very nature, evanescent. Silence for us remains. It is something enduring, and consequently, it is in our silence too that our communication is like God's. It is like God's in another way when we speak.

RIEMER: Also you had one set of rules of behavior. In a context of silence you could see deviations and attitudes toward that rule. Through these you got to know a lot of people and their slightest differences.

ONG: That's right. Extremely well. You knew their personalities. We had stories that were always told about personalities in the earlier days of the community. Such stories are not told so much any more because there isn't a very clear-cut norm against which you can measure the deviations. Now this is not only in the Society of Jesus but in the world at large.

RIEMER: I saw an article lamenting the loss of the eccentric in England. Do you think the eccentric is on his way out?

ONG: To a degree, yes. Because the eccentric is *in*. Today, you see, you have to be an outsider to be in. So any kind of deviation is standard now.

Until recently our training had firmly external structures that were deeply interiorized in the mature religious. Those firm external structures included the heritage of scholastic philosophy and theology. Given this formalized intellectual heritage, you had a good base for developing later on, provided you could open it up. Of course, as we've said, not everyone succeeded in relating it to things outside itself. Some did. Some didn't.

Today the "I" and the "we" is somewhat different. We didn't use to talk about the "we" very much. Now we talk about it a lot. We talk about community. We try to hold people together less by a formalized structure and more by talking about being together. In primary oral cultures men did not self-consciously talk about being together. They were together because they didn't have any alternative. Today, we talk about being together. We program our social side. We plot our togetherness in our secondary oral culture, the oral culture coming after print.

I think we've really discovered something here in our conversation. The generation problem in the Society of Jesus is felt more intensely than in many other places in human society. The older Jesuits have great difficulty in adapting to this other-directedness. Not all of them, because some understand it and go along with it. But some find it hard.

We're going to have to adjust to other-directedness. Some Jesuits nostalgically try to detect little drifts back to older patterns, but there's no going back. On the other hand, it's a mistake to pretend that we're going to get along just by working things out in discussion groups. You can go so far with this, but then somebody has to make the decision.

Earlier Jesuits would not have consented to this kind of interview such as we're having now. We would not have opened up our somewhat private affairs for other people to read in a book. Not that there was anything to be ashamed of. You just felt that some things ought to be kept private.

RIEMER: Families had more secrets, too.

ONG: Yes. Now everybody discusses everything. So this is not peculiar to the Society of Jesus. The whole Church has opened up this way and so have other institutions in the larger human society. This is the trend toward other-directedness.

RIEMER: There seems to be little formal concern for *tactus*—regulations governing touch in the novitiate.

ONG: I think there was a great deal of sense in rules regarding *tactus* in the context of our training.

RIEMER: It just occurs to me that *tactus* and silence work together. Silence without *tactus* could have been wild!

ONG: That's right. *Tactus* and silence work together to isolate the individual. Yes of course. This is interiorization. It threw the individual in on himself. But in the context of a community, interacting.

RIEMER: This seems to have achieved what sensitivity sessions appear to be striving for. The leaderless sensitivity groups flounder. Have you been to any of these?

ONG: No, I haven't had much urge to, frankly. However, I'm pretty close to this sort of thing and have a pretty good idea of their purpose and how they work. It's super-other-directedness, of course, but, as you say, it doesn't work unless you have someone to program it. Which means that you may have someone operating on other people. Often such leaders are just getting people to verbalize the way they want them to. They almost have to be geniuses to do anything else. There aren't that many geniuses around.

RIEMER: John Glenn Gray in *The Warriors* discusses how soldiers threatened by death in battle are comrades rather than friends. You don't utterly reveal yourself to a comrade, and it's not expected that you do. But you may still die for a comrade. Gray believes it's the strong fear of death that makes the relationship. Remove two comrades from that context of war, and they wonder how or why they ever got along together.

ONG: There are some analogies in the Society, but there is a difference. One of the problems everywhere today is that with the extended irenic structures in our technological culture it's hard to keep close to the fact of death. Unless you're neurotic. It sounds strange to speak of irenic structures, with all the violence we indulge in and advertise. There's a paradox here. Most other cultures could not tolerate our shows of violence: not enough irenic counteragents.

RIEMER: When you say "irenic structures" do you mean forces working towards peace?

ONG: I guess irenic is a little less positive than peace. By irenic structures in society, I mean largely the forces suggesting that life can be lived without a great struggle. Except in sports, we deinstitutionalize antagonisms, officially that is. Even amidst violence, cooperation overwhelms us. The cooperation needed to build one air-conditioned skyscraper, put on one TV network show, run a modern city or university for one day, is virtually incalculable. Not to mention the moonshot.

RIEMER: Why are they "structures"? Are they attitudes?

ONG: I'll try to spell that out. For example, all academic education used to be polemic, roughly until the Romantic movement. A German Jesuit teaching in Xavier High School in New York recently told me joshingly—but he meant it too—"These boys here all want their teacher to be their friend. When I was in school everyone knew that the teacher was your enemy." But he was a purely ceremonial enemy. The same teacher who was your enemy in class could be the man you went to afterwards with your confidences and who was very sympathetic and understanding.

The old *Ratio Studiorum* for Jesuit schools used to encourage competitive learning. It calls this contest method *aemulatio*. The idea wasn't original. The *Ratio* just took what all education all along had been doing. The contest or competition has been identified as typically Jesuit, but it is no more typically Jesuit than using Latin in the schools used to be.

In the *Ratio Studiorum* of the Society, it says that the boys are not to be allowed to bring their daggers into the classroom. This shows that the ritualized violence of the classroom not only reflected, but also sublimated the real violence outside of school. Now, today, according to a more recent general trend in education, you shouldn't pit pupils against one another but simply pit them against a standard. We're supposed to take all the personal contest out of learning. Don't let students feel they're competing with each other. That's one aspect. Another is the pupil-teacher relationship I just mentioned. The relationship now is supposed to be one of understanding and there's no real struggle involved in it. Student union negotiations and student arbitration boards are also irenic structures.

These things are good, don't get me wrong. I'm not saying you shouldn't have irenic structures. You should have all that you can. I wouldn't favor going back to the old style of education. On the other hand, despite irenic tactics polemic is also here to stay in one way or another. Every Marxist knows, as every Christian should know, that life is a struggle. There's always a polemic going on at some level. Some people rise to the top in General Motors or in the SDS [Students for a Democratic Society], and others don't. Life is still competitive, but today we're encouraged not to see the polemic aspects of society.

RIEMER: And yet they are all around us.

ONG: They are. We don't ritualize polemic—again, except in sports. So it may hurt us more. Our education system today tends to mute polemic in its formal structures. We're Dewey-ites. So polemic asserts itself informally in demonstrations and confrontations—which themselves are now institutionalized, of course. But unadmittedly.

RIEMER: All right. I understand "irenic structures" now. Are Jesuit communities breaking up because the men don't feel drawn together by the threats of a hostile world?

ONG: I had begun before to say how the irenic structures in our technologized culture distracted us from feeling we were under the threat of death. Yet all Christians are called to martyrdom and *are* under this kind of threat, really. We should be. We should be ready to die for Christ. But since this seems rather remote today, the feeling of comradeship, not only in the Society of Jesus, but in the Church suffers from an illusion of security.

Comradeship, though, is not all we have in the Society of Jesus. There's also friendship. But the revealing of oneself has been structured strongly to superiors, though not exclusively so. Your superior is to be personally interested in you. Of course, so are other individuals, too, but there's a very specially open channel of communication between the individual and his superiors. Here in one's openness is where the love is expressed. This is one way you know there is love among the people who are your companions. They have the same relationship to the total community through the superior.

But there is a great deal of this basic relationship of comradeship. We're all in the same boat. Many difficulties of the Church come from our somewhat falsified irenic structures. Our technological culture is more irenic than any that went before it; just the same, human society isn't really as irenic as we make it out to be.

RIEMER: Your bibliography as of 1968 lists over half a dozen books and 276 articles. Of course it doesn't mention classes and lectures. How much time of your day goes to work?

ONG: This is almost as bad as a question in the worst questionnaire I have ever received. It asked, "How much time do you spend thinking?"

I don't know how many hours I spend working. A lot of my work is thinking. In actuality, work and play are not entirely separate. Certainly not for me. My work is varied: teaching, counseling, ministerial activity such as hearing confessions or preaching, celebrating Mass—the liturgy, *leit-ourgia*, the work of the people of God—serving as consultor for scholarly foundations and inner-city work. All this as well as writing. I need time for private prayer, so I get up early, and for just being with people. That's not work. My reading is largely work in that it's purposeful, though at times in a random, relaxed way.

RIEMER: What do you do for fun?

ONG: Besides work? Work can be fun even when it's hard. I practice random recreation, I suppose. An art gallery, theater, or symphony once in a while. Occasionally, I go out trout fishing. There's a place about an hour and fifteen minutes from our residence at Saint Louis University. I'll go there maybe five or six days a year. Slosh and climb around the stream all day. Flies only. I don't do other systematic exercise like playing tennis. I tend to run upstairs, and I guess I use up calories that way. I used to feel guilty about not doing systematic exercise. Being inner-directed, I thought somehow I was supposed to. But I got over that. I don't see why you have to. I'm rather against systems, you know.

RIEMER: Do you enjoy eating?

ONG: I'm always hungry. I suppose I'd get fat if I ate all sorts of stuff. I could eat a lot more than I do. I skimp on fattening foods.

RIEMER: Dan Berrigan was the first Jesuit I'd known who knew something about making food. He said he'd learned it living in France.

ONG: Marshall McLuhan tells this story on himself. He and his wife frequently had Wyndham Lewis as a dinner guest. One evening Lewis called about an hour before dinner and asked what was going to be served. Ham. And what sort of wine? Marshall mentioned some popular table wine, and Lewis said, "Well, I'll come another night."

I don't make an art of cooking, nor an issue of having food prepared this way or that way. Yet I suspect I know something about food from my father. He was from New Orleans. He wasn't a big eater, but he was extremely demanding regarding the quality of his food. And variety. Any and all domestic and exotic dishes, arcane even. Mother was less demanding, but perfectly happy to venture anything. My brother Dick and I are completely omnivorous. Dick is like my father. If he sees a menu and there's something there he's never eaten, he gets that. So do I. The only reason I've never eaten rattlesnake meat is that somehow I've never yet had the chance. Dick ate it first chance he got.

RIEMER: I once tested children with herbs. I found that where children were afraid to try spices that were strange to their culture it was because their fathers were very cautious—meat and potatoes people.

ONG: Overprotected. My father would have regarded that as very vulgar and childish. Meat and potatoes. Extremely timid and very fearful. I mean really. It isn't human. For man, eating demands maturity, the ability to assimilate and enjoy a variety of things. It's a way of learning to like all the different people who prepare and eat these things.

RIEMER: I believe that a person's attitudes about beginnings, his openness to adventure and novelty and innovation are formed in early childhood and largely through eating.

ONG: Oh, I agree. That was an important part of my training actually. I didn't know it at the time. But I believe it was.

All my life I've been interested in learning processes. This is tied in with an interest in art and doing things that would turn people on. I guess too, I'm a kind of spoiled biologist. I feel very rooted in nature and I am interested in growth processes. Wherever I am, I'm constantly noting the terrain, the kinds of trees, the birds. It was that sort of thing—a part of Romanticism—that used to be pretty completely absent from Catholic thought generally and from the central philosophical teaching at Saint Louis University, although it is included there now very much. My whole intellectual career, from one point of view, has been the establishment of this connection between the Romantic process-oriented, nature-loving side of knowledge and the structured side of knowledge. And neither of these seem to me sufficient unto itself. But I guess if I had to choose one, I'd choose nature.

RIEMER: Did you see English as a field where you could combine both the Romantic and structured aspects of knowledge?

ONG: I guess when you shake it all down, I felt it this way. I had majored in Latin as an undergraduate. At one point, although I loved the language and literature very much, as I still do, I simply despaired of ever knowing as much about an ancient poem as I could know about an English poem. You just don't have that amount of information coming to you from it. But for my intellectual life and purchase on present actuality and modern media, I couldn't do without Latin.

RIEMER: I should have said "language" instead of "English."

ONG: All right. I'd answer yes, here too. I'm interested in language because it's the meeting ground of these two: process and structure. I guess you could put it that way, though I've never put it that way before even to myself. People in English label me philosophical. The people in philosophy seem to feel I'm philosophical, but I think some of them tend to resent me because I don't do it the way some of them do. I'm constantly being misclassified. Or I'm asked to classify myself, and I don't know how. Some people think I'm an anthropologist or a sociologist or a philosopher or a theologian. Occasionally, a professor of French. In principle, I'm a professor of English, but in my own way. I don't particularly see why a person has to first classify himself and *then* do something. I've been told I teach and practice Onglish.

RIEMER: I have a feeling now at the end of these interviews that you're lonely.

ONG: That I'm lonely? I don't think I am.

RIEMER: There's a certain tone that runs through the tapes that sounds like loneliness. It might be fatigue. I understand you've just given fifty university talks as guest lecturer for Phi Beta Kappa. Or is it that inner-directedness is a lonelier condition than other-directedness.

ONG: Well if it is, I don't mind it. No, I really don't think I ordinarily give that impression. In fact, most feedback I get tells me the opposite. I have believed that others find me friendly and sociable, at least to a normal degree. I hope I've not been wrong. But I feel that I can support loneliness, with God's help, when it's called for. We all need a little loneliness to be human. And to be Christian. Spiritual life demands isolation as well as community. Our faith is communal, but we are also alone before God, each of us. I suppose I have a lot of inner-directedness, that could be what gives you that impression.

Now you don't want to trust me too much here because I'm talking about myself, and first of all, I've never said this to anybody until you brought it up. But when you think of it, my inner-directedness might look like loneliness. Writing is terribly lonely, as you know yourself. I'm trying to write a book to be read by thousands—so everybody get out of the room! But I don't feel oppressed with loneliness. If people do think I'm lonely, then I'm not: their concern has cured me.

RIEMER: Are there areas of your work, say in Ramus or communication, you'd like to see others carry out and extend? Areas you don't have time yourself to do?

ONG: Yes. The whole business of sensory perception is badly neglected in psychology, strangely enough. The implications of sensory perception and the phenomenology of sensory perception need a lot more investigation. Speculative theology, too, could be advanced by such investigation. Our understanding of the Word of God as Word is underdeveloped. And so are other central related doctrines, such as the Trinity and the Incarnation.

I have carried forward some of the leads from my Ramus books myself in *The Presence of the Word*, published in 1967 by Yale. Others, K. G. Hamilton, or Frances Yates in her fascinating book, *The Art of Memory*, have fed leads from the Ramism books into their own original research. Just recently, a French-Swiss institute for research and innovation in education, projected a study in learning aimed at trying to find out why we teach what we do and why we teach it the way we do. This calls for tough research into intellectual history and into shifts in priorities among the senses. All of this connects with my work on Ramism.

It was twelve years ago that my books on Ramus came out. When you publish a book, you think everyone reads it the next day. Mere vanity. Ideas take time to get around. But it's encouraging if at some point others find your ideas useful for their own thinking. Scholarly writers need encouragement. It can be a lonely business.

Work Cited

Gray, John G. *The Warriors*. Lincoln, NE: U of Nebraska P, 1959.

Hamilton, K. G. *The Two Harmonies: Poetry and Prose in the Seventeenth Century*. Oxford: Clarendon of Oxford UP, 1963.

Ong, Walter J. *The Presence of the Word*. New Haven and London: Yale UP, 1967.

—. *Ramus and Talon Inventory: A Short-title Inventory of the Published Works of Peter Ramus (1515-1572) and of Omer Talon (ca. 1510-1562) in Their Original and in Their Variously Altered Forms*. Cambridge, MA: Harvard UP, 1958.

—. *Ramus, Method, and the Decay of Dialogue*. Cambridge, MA: Harvard UP, 1958.

Riesman, David, with Reuel Denney and Nathan Glazer. *The Lonely Crowd: A Study of the Changing American Character*. New York: Doubleday, 1950.

Yates, Frances A. *The Art of Memory*. Chicago, U of Chicago P, 1966.

3

Hopkins' Sprung Rhythm and the Life of English Poetry (1941/1949)

> Soun is noght but air y-broken,
> And every speche that is spoken,
> Loud or privee, foul or fair,
> In his substaunce is but air.
> —The egle to Chaucer in *The Hous of Fame*

"In the winter of '75 . . . I had long had haunting my ear," so Gerard Manley Hopkins writes to Richard Watson Dixon, "the echo of a new rhythm which now I realized on paper. To speak shortly, it consists in scanning by accents or stresses alone" (*Correspondence* 14. Oct. 6, 1878).

This was Hopkins' celebrated "sprung rhythm," christened by its author with a name that is at once vigorous as the rhythm itself, colorful but disenchanting, and, for the better or worse fortune of the rhythm it designates, not a little hoydenish.

In the case of Hopkins, it may be possible to convict Chaucer's eagle of understatement. For sprung rhythm, which characterizes most of Hopkins' poems, is so integral to the whole poetic texture where we find bedded his deep-rooted raciness that we may expect an investigation of it to prove altogether more fruitful than an ordinary pursuit of metrics. Investigation here should be capable of something more than physical measurements, than counting the pieces of broken air. This is plain not only from the rhythm itself as heard, but from the remarks about it winding through Hopkins' correspondence in a trail that, for all its apparent errancy, hints at a secret consistency on a level that explanation so far has not reached.

Investigation is needed. We can gather, for instance, with W. H. Gardner in his article on *The Wreck of the Deutschland*, which touches on the movement of Hopkins' verse as closely as any study so far, that sprung rhythm "is virtually a stress-meter derived from two main sources—the 'irregular' choruses of Milton's *Samson Agonistes* and the free rhythms of popular jingles and nursery rhymes" (127). But why is it also, to cite Hopkins' own statement, "the rhythm of common speech and of written prose, when rhythm is perceived in them"? (*Poems* 5). Certainly this latter pedigree, which is often neglected, outranks the former, which is frequently enough cited; furthermore, if the two pedigrees are connected, because the rhythm of the Samson choruses, the rhythm of nursery rhymes, and the rhythm of prose are the same, such a connection is not by any means evident.

Hopkins' remarks on his new rhythm are often oblique, *obiter dicta*, and since the appearance of the four volumes of his papers, others' comment or study in the vicinity of his rhythm has simply taken similar oblique paths with regard to the rhythm itself. Moreover, an accumulation of prosodic detritus against which I. A. Richards protested some years ago (203), has further obscured the view; and statements such as Dr. Richards' that Hopkins "gave himself complete rhythmical freedom," while they brush aside the detritus ("the absurdities of prosodists"), do not leave fully lighted the vistas they have opened. What is Dr. Richards' "complete rhythmical freedom"? To say what the movement of Hopkins' poetry is not—it is not what prosodists ordinarily try to count, it is free from this thing they would make rhythm out to be, it has "complete rhythmical freedom"—this is to say something, and in the present case something worthwhile. But it is to open the proper question, not to close the discussion. Sure now of one thing it is not, we may still wish to know what the movement of Hopkins' verse is.

The present study attempts to account for Hopkins' sprung rhythm and at the same time to design a key to his vast number of scattered remarks about the rhythm by showing both his practice and his comment on his practice against a general pattern of development in English verse.

I. The Ways of Discovery

In opening a discussion of Hopkins' verse, first steps must be taken carefully so as to avoid false starts. Even yet there are plenty of such starts possible, and a preliminary excursion through Hopkins' papers will be necessary to recognize them for what they are and to find the proper point of departure.

The Question of Old English

At first sight, one of the most promising starts is the indisputable connection, often enough observed, between Hopkins' sprung rhythm and
Old English verse. As we shall see, this connection leads us, in a way,
toward explanation, but the way is so roundabout as to be misleading. It
is easy to mention the connection without adverting to the fact that,
instead of providing explanation, it really raises a sprawling genealogical
problem. In Hopkins' day, knowledge of Old English was not easy to
come by, and the nature of Old English poetry by no means entirely clear.
It was not until 1885, ten years after the writing of the *Deutschland*,
Hopkins' first sprung rhythm poem, that Eduard Sievers first published in
Paul und Braune's Beiträge his "Zur Rhythmik des germanischen
Alliterationsverses," the definitive work setting forth—and that in
German, in which Hopkins shows little interest—the structural principles
of Old English poetry.

Late in 1882 Hopkins admits that he does not know for certain
whether his sprung rhythm occurred in Anglo-Saxon verse: it does, he
says, "so far as I know—I am enquiring and presently I shall be able to
speak more decidedly" (*Letters* 156. Oct. 18, 1882). A month later
Hopkins writes that he is (only then) learning Anglo-Saxon (*Letters* 163.
Nov. 26-27, 1882).

Hopkins' acquaintance with the work of William Barnes, "good soul,
of Dorset-dialect poems," looks promising at first sight but goes little further in the way of explaining the connection of Hopkins' new rhythm with
Old English. Barnes had indeed published in 1849 an Anglo-Saxon collection, but Hopkins nowhere mentions it. His acquaintance with Barnes
seems to have been confined principally to the latter's own Dorsetshire
dialect poetry: but even if this poetry were capable of suggesting sprung
rhythm to Hopkins, his interest in it was too slight to matter. He writes in
1879, again after the completion of the *Deutschland* and other sprung
rhythm pieces, that he had never read any of Barnes' poems since his own
undergraduate days "except the one quoted in Gosse's paper" (*Letters* 87.
Aug. 14, 1879). Everything else in Hopkins' acquaintance with Barnes is
too late to help account for sprung rhythm. At the instigation of Patmore,
Hopkins later went over more of Barnes' Dorsetshire poems, but this was
in 1885, when sprung rhythm was ten years old (*Further* 218 to Patmore.
June 4, 1886; *Letters* 221. Sept. 1, 1885). His acquaintance with Barnes'
An Outline of English Speech-Craft (*Letters* 162-163. Nov. 26, 1882),
with its insistence on "pure" English and its abhorrence of Latinisms
might possibly have accounted for some of Hopkins' idiom that seems the
fiber of his verse movement, had Hopkins' acquaintance with the book

been possible earlier. But the work did not appear until 1878; Hopkins' idiom was well matured in 1875.

There remains *Piers Plowman* as apparently Hopkins' only means of establishing contact with Old English poetry before his sprung rhythm was already formed. This late fourteenth-century poem preserves enough of the early Old English rhythmic movement to make it a possible source, and Hopkins mentions it often. But even the part played by *Piers Plowman* in introducing the new rhythm to his ear, and still more in furnishing him a *detailed* theory, is highly questionable. It is true that in his lecture notes prepared in 1873-1874 he quotes a few lines from the poem. In 1880, however, he writes Bridges that he had not studied it enough to know whether or not it employed triple time in its verse (*Letters* 107. Sept. 5, 1880); and it is not until two years later that he reports, "I am reading that famous poem and am coming to the conclusion that it is not worth reading" (*Letters* 156. Oct. 18, 1882) .

With this last remark, we finally come upon Hopkins' first definitive statement, repeated when he wrote "in '83 or not much later" (Bridges 100) the Preface now published with his *Poems*, that "the old English verse seen in Pierce Ploughman" is in sprung rhythm. (*Poems* 6; *Letters* 156. Oct. 18, 1882). Clearly, this by no means explains the source of Hopkins' rhythm: it simply states a fact that Hopkins had discovered.

The Question of Later Authors

Similarly, with regard to specific authors after the Old and Middle English periods, Hopkins' treatment of their sporadic manifestations of sprung rhythm is on altogether too undecided a basis to indicate that they were really sources: often Hopkins cannot make up his mind whether they use sprung rhythm or not. He mentions Milton so often in his correspondence that it has been easy to suspect he derived his rhythm from Milton, especially from the *Samson Agonistes*, and the ease of making this conjecture has obscured the fact that Hopkins nowhere says that he learned sprung rhythm from Milton. Rather, he approaches Milton as one who judges, not as one who learns, and he can never quite make up his mind whether Milton's rhythms are sprung or not. The *Samson* choruses, which Hopkins first mentions in his now printed papers on April 3, 1877 (*Letters* 38), are, he writes to Bridges later the same year, "intermediate between counterpointed and sprung rhythm," but in the same breath he adds, "In reality they are sprung" (*Letters* 45. Aug. 21, 1877). Later, he calls Milton "the great standard in the use of counterpoint," but states definitively that Milton did not use sprung rhythm: "When . . . secondary or 'mounted rhythm,' which is necessarily a sprung rhythm, overpowers the original . . . you reach simple sprung rhythm. Milton must have known this but had reasons" for not going so far (*Correspondence* 15. Oct. 6, 1878).

It is well to remember that the interest Hopkins shows in Milton's rhythms is not all his own. A large part is the reflection of the interest of Bridges, his constant correspondent, who was on his way to writing *Milton's Prosody*.

Shakespeare is the one cited in Hopkins' letters at the first mention of anything promising to develop into sprung rhythm. This occurs in a post-script to Bridges just before Hopkins enters the novitiate:

> I hope you will master the peculiar beat I have introduced into St.
> Dorothea. The development is mine but the beat is Shakspere—e.g.
> Why should thís desert be?—and
> Thoú for whóm Jóve would swear—where the rest of the lines are
> eight-syllabled or seven-syllabled.
> (*Letters* 24-25. Aug. 7, 1868)

As indicated by Hopkins in at least one of the versions of his poem, the beat is:

> I bear a basket lined with grass.
> I´ am só light´ and fair´
> Men are amazed to watch me pass
> With´ the básket I beár. (*Poems* 141)

This looks promising, but with this particular beat other authors besides Shakespeare are associated in Hopkins' lecture notes for rhetoric made in 1873-1874 (*Notebooks* 221-48). In these notes, although he does not use the term "sprung," Hopkins describes a kind of verse that is unmistakably that destined to become in his hands the new rhythm. This is the "stress verse," verse that builds with stresses only, disregarding how many other syllables there may be. Hopkins contrasts it with quantitative verse, such as classical Greek and Latin, and with "counted" or "numbered" verse, which regards the total number of syllables, stressed and unstressed. He mentions that the rhythm of verse without count of sylla-ble, that is, the pure stress rhythm like that he was later to make his own, is to be found in the ancient Saturnian Latin verse and in *Piers Plowman*. In *Piers*, he notes, each half-line gets two beats commonly, but sometimes three or four. He goes on to say that such stress or beat rhythm can be found occasionally in Shakespeare, Campbell, and Hamilton, quoting from them four, one, and four lines respectively. There are other unusual-ly acute observations on this verse that regards only stress without taking into account the total number of syllables—we shall come to some of these remarks later—and finally Milton is mentioned as having "made experiments in accentual counterpoint," as (with Hopkins' own marks)—

Hóme tó his móther's hóuse prívate retúrned

This is the only line from Milton quoted in the lecture notes, although Hopkins tells Dixon that he had paid "a good deal of attention to Milton's versification" when the notes were being got up (*Correspondence* 13-14. Oct. 6, 1878).

Derivation and What It Means Here

When these lecture notes were being assembled in 1873-1874, sprung rhythm was undoubtedly in the offing, and, indeed, the lectures may well have been occasion for Hopkins' giving full attention to the rhythm—it was only a year later that the *Deutschland* appeared, after Hopkins had had the echo of the new rhythm "long . . . haunting" his ear. Yet it is impossible to state that Hopkins "derived" his rhythm from any of the authors mentioned in these lecture notes, for the passages he quotes here give every evidence of being *loci* that Hopkins could cite as instances of his rhythm rather than "sources" for it. "Single lines and single instances of it [sprung rhythm] are not uncommon in English and I have pointed them out in lecturing," he writes Bridges (*Letters* 45. Aug. 21, 1877), quoting from these same authors and others. The Shakespeare passages early connected with *St. Dorothea*, which are really the most promising as genuine sources, are too meager to account for sprung rhythm as such. Hopkins appreciates this and in his lecture notes simply lists them, without special mention, with the other lines that serve merely as instances.

It seems true, then, to say that Hopkins' statement giving the most definite information about the source of the new verse is the one quoted earlier: "I had long had haunting my ear the echo of a new rhythm" (*Correspondence* 14. Oct. 6, 1878). Conclusions that Hopkins' meters derived, or that he even thought they derived, from their being used in this or that particular author are wide of the mark. Hopkins testifies only to the fact that the new rhythm was "haunting" his ear. It might be said that he noticed *what* it was when it was already in his own possession, after he had already picked it up. Whether Hopkins himself could have named all the really proximate sources, we simply do not know. This much is certain: the real sources of a rhythm that makes such a radical claim on a language as that of being the rhythm of the language's prose can hardly be narrowed to one or two authors or to nursery rhymes, though these may provide quite valid instances of the rhythm's appearance. Sources for a rhythm with such roots must be more widespread than that. If Hopkins' claims for his rhythm are acceptable, he must have been, consciously or unconsciously, hearing it everywhere.

Whether Hopkins' first susceptibility to the movements of the new rhythm was occasioned by his speculating on its possibility or directly by his hearing it, is not at all evident from his printed papers and perhaps will always remain an unsolved question. At any rate, once his enthusiasm for sprung rhythm had begun, about the time he set down the *Deutschland*, he began to find it in more and more places. This is hardly strange, for had the rhythm that Hopkins found been other than something basically widespread, it would very likely not have been the sort of thing that could have worked. For, practically speaking, there can be no question of a poet's introducing into a language the bases of a rhythm—various stresses, lengths of syllables, other hinges on which a language turns. He can utilize what is there, perhaps change it subtly. But the rhythms of a language are already rooted when the poet arrives, and the real question to be answered concerning Hopkins' sprung rhythm is, What was this thing he was discovering all around him? or What is the life of this rhythm in the language, what are its claims on our speech?

This is the sort of question Hopkins himself was gradually solving. Where the new rhythm came from and what its implications were Hopkins was at first not sure. The *St. Dorothea* piece he associated with Shakespeare in 1869 is an important but only equivocal hint and an entirely inadequate explanation of what was to come. But by 1873-1874 Hopkins certainly had a skeleton theory erected for a verse that counted stresses only and disregarded the number of syllables in a line. A theory so stated was capable of differentiating the "new rhythm" from other rhythms that had been the ordinary concern of metrists. But that was all. What was the full economy of such a pure stress verse in English, Hopkins could not yet answer. His ear had caught a rhythm, and he could describe it. But it would take time to know how it would work, what organization it demanded, just as it would take time to know the principal places where it might be found.

From here on, Hopkins begins listening for the rhythm and listing instances of its occurrence, blocking in areas of theory as he proceeds. Leaving the theory for later discussion, we can remark not only that *loci* of the rhythm increase in number as Hopkins becomes more familiar with the rhythm by using it himself, but also that *loci*, such as that of ordinary rhythmical prose, of the most likely important sources (because they were most commonly in his ear or in anyone's ear) are mentioned latest in Hopkins' discussion of his discovery.

The crisis is reached in 1882-1883. By 1882 Hopkins had come to the point where he was ready to give his sprung rhythm a brief and tentative history in a letter to Bridges: he suspects that it

> existed in full force in Anglo saxon verse and in great beauty; in degraded and doggerel shape in *Piers Ploughman* . . . ; Greene was the last who employed it at all consciously and he never continuously; then it disappeared—for one cadence in it here and there is not sprung rhythm and one swallow does not make a spring. (I put aside Milton's case, for it is altogether singular.) (*Letters* 156. Oct. 18, 1882)

This is the skeleton of the view given in the Preface published with his *Poems*, but this Preface, written as we have seen within approximately the next year, lists as additional *loci* of the rhythm weather saws, nursery rhymes, and songs—and caps all with the astonishing and sweeping statement that sprung rhythm "is the rhythm of common speech and of written prose, when rhythm is perceived in them" (*Poems* 5).

Thus we come upon the inevitable question with which we began. If this sprung rhythm is, being the rhythm of prose, the commonest and most ordinary rhythm of the language, how did it happen that Hopkins did not from the first give it its fullest pedigree by stating such a fact? In 1877 he was still writing to Bridges that it is not the rhythm of prose but "the nearest to the rhythm of prose" (*Letters* 46. Aug. 21, 1877). The answer lies in Hopkins' only gradually opening awareness of the genealogy of his own new rhythm and of the rhythm's economy and connections.

Although in his 1883 Preface he says everything in summary when he says, "It is the rhythm of common speech and of written prose when rhythm is perceived in them"—although this indeed "caps, clears, and clinches all," this statement still needs its implications developed. With things at such a pitch, however, in the press of work that in his own case as in that of Brother Alphonsus,

> Could crown career with conquest while there went
> Those years and years by of world without event

Father Hopkins himself went quietly to God, "lover of souls, swaying considerate scales." This was in 1889. Had he lived longer, he might have explained more: "And there it is," he writes Bridges:

> I understand these things so much better than you: we should explain things, plainly state them, clear them up, explain them; explanation—

except personal—is always pure good; without explanation people go on misunderstanding; being once explained they thenceforward understand things; therefore always explain: but I have the passion for explanation and you have not. (*Letters* 275. May 25, 1888)

A frank avowal and the truth. For Hopkins was always trying desperately to explain his rhythmic practices. But the mass of brief comment dispersed through his letters and his all-too-brief Preface leaves much explaining still to be done.

Hopkins' misunderstandings of Greek and Latin rhythmic usages, which derived from the mistakes of scholars of his age, led his speculation on classical meter over unsafe ground, as Father John L. Bonn explains. Since Father Bonn's work discusses separately what here might have proved a troublesome enough distraction, the matter of Greek and Latin meters need not enter the present study. Fortunately, Hopkins was not constructing a rhythm on Greek theory, however much Greek theory may have provided him false analogies in Greek for his rhythm. The validity of his work is independent of speculation on Greek metric: Hopkins knew sprung rhythm because he *heard* it in English.

We must keep in mind the cardinal problem, which, despite the direction taken by much thought on the matter, is not why Hopkins is different, but why he is not different. Hopkins' poetry, which is not separable from the vehicle of his rhythm, has a hold on the English language as unshakable and as permanent as that of St. Thomas More, Shakespeare, Donne, Dryden, or, indeed, quite absolutely, anyone else at all, though his grasp may not be so ample as the grasp of some of these. Now Hopkins' differences from his contemporaries are obvious. But simply to be different is no virtue. The virtue of Hopkins' difference and the thing that wants explaining lies in the fact that in an age when most of the major poets— major at least with regard to their contemporaries—were out of contact with a living language, Hopkins was able to reestablish contact with one.

Scott, Southey, Landor, Arnold, Rossetti, Swinburne, much of Tennyson—and Newman, to take a poet whose importance is lesser but whose basically religious views of reality were the same as Hopkins'— these have little life to supply the serious poet of the present century. A minor poet of the seventeenth century, such as King, is likely to be far more alive today. But upon the appearance of his poems in 1918, Hopkins' work was found to have carried forward a fecund vitality into a new age that its author had not lived to see.

Hopkins, rhythm and all, had taken up his position at a place over which the living current of the language was moving, when men whom his age thought great were, as it latterly appears, stogged to the right and to the left in drying sloughs. This is what needs explaining. The question is not the one often heard: How did Hopkins break with tradition? Hopkins is in a tradition—or he could not have survived. Nor is it, What did Hopkins invent? For, though many men have found a tradition, no one yet has invented one. Hopkins' entire discussion of his rhythm, as we have seen, evinces that he found something, his ears were opened, and once they were, he began to hear about him more and more evidence of the same thing.

Our question, then, can be put this way: What did Hopkins come upon?

II. Another Economy in English Verse

From speech, from music, or from the mere miscellany of activity about him, man's ear is being fed constantly with a complex wave of sound. Though sound is "noght but air y-broken," the texture of this wave, when its source is speech, can be exceedingly rich and variable, and in its manifold many patterns of diverse kinds and diverse degrees of fixity can be discovered—patterns noticed or made by adverting to pitch or to phrasing or to syllabic length or to the number of syllables or to the strange phenomena grouped together under the title of stress or accent, which is something easily recognized but, with its variable mixtures of pitch and force, not easily defined or even described. Sound pattern, and hence verse, can exist in terms of any of these things or of combinations of them, or in terms of other things as well.

The Alternating Stress

One pattern in English speech, at least in Modern English speech, is quite easy to identify. For English, as we pronounce it, demands, with a few exceptions to be noted later, a stress of some sort on every two or three syllables: that is, however few the stresses demanded by sense may be, other stresses are scattered through English speech so that generally no more than two syllables pass without one. If at least every third syllable takes a sense stress, this will serve: thus we would say *And nów let us gó* or *And nów let ús go*, as the sense might demand. But if the sense demands no particular stress on any special word or words in a group of monosyllables such as this, we ordinarily must put stresses on some of the words anyhow, making our own one or another of the possible alternating stress patterns: we would hardly say, as a Frenchman speaking English might say, *And now let us go*, with all the syllables equi-accented and only a slight tonic elevation on the last. Or again, no matter what the sense of a phrase in which the word occurs, we pronounce polysyllables with alternating stresses, the longer the word, the greater the number of stresses. Thus we say *in"com-mu"ni-ca-bil'i-ty*, or perhaps *in"com-mu"ni-ca-bil'i-ty"*. This rule is general enough to set up throughout our speech the feeling for alternating or pulsing between syllables that are stressed and syllables that are not. We may call the stress this feeling demands, the alternating stress.

In non-versified speech the pattern of this alternating stress and its correlative slack is irregular. Thus we might scan (since the alternating stress asserts itself with some flexibility, other scansions would be equally admissible in places):

> Foūrscŏre ănd sēvĕn yēars ăgō ŏŭr fāthĕrs broŭght fŏrth ŏn thĭs cōntĭnēnt ă nēw nātĭon, cŏncēĭved ĭn lībĕrtȳ, ănd dēdĭcātĕd tō thĕ prōpōsĭtĭŏn thăt āll mĕn āre crĕātĕd ēquāl.

Now, one way of writing English verse is to create a regular rhythm by so arranging words that the alternating stress sets up a quite regular beat of stress-slack, or stress-slack-slack, and so on. Thus in Gray's *Elegy Written in a Country Church-Yard*:

> The Curfew tolls the knell of parting day;
>   The lowing herd winds slowly o'er the lea;
> The plowman homeward plods his weary way,
>   And leaves the world to darkness and to me. (90)

Or in Spenser's "Mutabilitie" cantos:

> When I bethinke me on that speech whyleare
> Of Mutabilitie, and well it way. (Bk. VII, Canto viii, p. 676)

Here the alternating stress sets up a simple one-two beat like that of very elementary, unsophisticated, measured music—how far actual time is an element of the beat need not concern us here; we need only note that the beat pattern is somehow an element—and once the beat is set up, it may be varied by reversing or making undecided occasional slack-stress "feet" so long as the variations are not great enough to destroy the measured rhythm. Thus Shakespeare in *Sonnet 33* (reversed foot):

> *Stealing* unseen to west with this disgrace; (p. 33; italics added)

or in *Sonnet 30* (undecided feet):

> And with *old woes new wail* my dear time's waste. (30; italics added)

Sometimes this beat of the alternating stress is so marked in its timing that it admits either one or two slacks indiscriminately, the two when they occur receiving each approximately half the time of one. For instance, Coleridge's *Christabel*:

> The lovely lady, Christabel,
> Whom her father loves so well,
>
> .   .   .   .
>
> She had dreams all yesternight
> Of her own betrothed knight;
> And she in the midnight wood will pray
> For the weal of her lover that's far away. (116)

With proper allowance for this latter kind of verse, it is plain that the verse made from the alternating stress—we call such verse, with Hopkins, "common" or "running" rhythm (*Poems* 1)—determines the number of syllables in a line in determining the number of alternating stresses.

The Breakdown of Alternating Stress

With regard to this kind of rhythm, Hopkins' "new rhythm" is evidently "sprung." This running rhythm limps badly in a passage like this from stanza 8 of the *Deutschland*:

> Is out with it! Oh,
> We lash with the best or worst
> Word last! How a lush-kept plush-capped sloe
> Will, mouthed to flesh-burst,
> Gush!—flush the man, the being with it, sour or sweet,
> Brim, in a flash, full!

Or again in stanza 13:

> And the sea flint-flake, black-backed in the regular blow.

The reason for the breakdown here of running rhythm, the rhythm of the alternating stress, derives from the fact that the general rule that English speech proceed by stresses alternating with one or two slacks between them cannot always be observed in English. The place where it most commonly cannot be observed is where the sense demands that two stresses be juxtaposed: *lush-kept*, or *plush-capped*, or *flint-flake*. From the particular effect that arises here in contrast to the demands of running rhythm, Hopkins designates this other rhythm as "sprung" (*Correspondence* 23. Feb. 27, 1879).

Often, indeed, even this juxtaposition of stresses yields to the general tendency of English to proceed by alternating stresses and slacks. In the first place, occasionally the juxtaposition of two stresses will be taken care of by a complete break in the rhythmic structure. When there is opportunity for such a break, as, for instance at the end of a phrase or clause or sentence in prose, the juxtaposition of two stresses means nothing: one rhythm is stopped and another started again. Moreover, when there is not an occasion for this kind of pause, we can adjust two juxtaposed stresses to the feeling for alternation of stress and slack in either of two ways: (1) we may add equivalently a slack, after the first syllable by pausing slightly between the two syllables or by drawing out the first; or (2) we may, in a certain context, make one accent actually predominate.

An example might be that used by lexicographers: *The room is airtight. Airtight* is one of the not uncommon English words that varies its accent precisely for purposes of rhythmic adjustment, "according to the rhythm of the syllables in the context" ("A Guide" ix). Careful advertence will show that the feeling for alternating stress easily intrudes in the example just cited, so that either (1) between the beginning of the syllable *air-* and the beginning of the syllable *-tight* there is a prolongation of time that produces at least a felt pause (so that saying *The room is airytight* would not change the timing), or else (2) the word tends to become *airtight'* or *air'tight.*

The meter generally heightens one or the other stress in this second way (*airtight'* or *air'tight*) when running rhythm uses equi-accented words; if such words must really remain equi-accented, running rhythm usually will not use them at all. Hopkins was aware of this and bridled at it, setting down as a virtue of his sprung rhythm its ability to assimilate juxtaposed stresses. In some running rhythm measures, indeed, the two stresses are given full value, as in the third line at the opening of Coleridge's *Christabel* (this third line, like all the other lines, has a total of four stresses):

> 'Tis the middle of night by the castle clock
> And the owls have awakened the crowing cock.
> Tu——whit!—— tu——whoo!
> And hark, again, the crowing cock,
> How drowsily it crew. (116).

(See Hopkins' comment in *Correspondence* 21. Feb 27, 1879.) But this is somewhat unusual. Running rhythm, for the most part, is averse to two or more consecutive stresses, and hence Hopkins seizes on the more general affinity of his sprung rhythm for such stresses as a characteristic feature roughly differentiating it from most alternating stress measures. Differences between it and the *Christabel* rhythm have to be worked out in more detailed formulae. But there are differences: Hopkins says only that the *Christabel* meter "might be developed into" sprung rhythm (*Correspondence* 21. Feb. 27, 1879) .

Hopkins' juxtaposed sprung rhythm stresses are to be found, for example, in the last two words in this line from stanza 20 of the *Deutschland:* "Christ's lily and beast of the waste wood," or in the last three in this line from stanza 11: "The sour scythe cringe, and the blear share come."

Almost all the instances of his new rhythm that Hopkins first rehearses are cases of these juxtaposed stresses marked by him as such (*Notebooks* 235-36; cf. *Letters* 24-25. Aug 7, 1868):

> Shakespeare—
>> Toád that únder cóld stóne
>>> and—
>> Sleép thou fírst i' th' chármed pót
>>> and—
>> Why should thís désert bé
>>> and—
>> Thoú for whóm Jóve would swéar–;
> Campbell—
>> As ye swéep thróugh the déep.

Without arguing over the validity of these instances, we can see plainly here what Hopkins was taking note of. His "new rhythm" he describes later as being based on the principle that only stresses, and not stresses and slacks, are counted. Hence these juxtaposed stresses are not its only manifestations: it may manifest itself as well by merely unequal numbers of slacks between stresses. But the juxtaposed stresses are symptomatic. Ordinarily they are not found in running rhythm as such. From their characteristic abrupt effect—by no means the only effect of sprung rhythm—Hopkins takes the name for his new verse (*Correspondence* 23. Feb. 27, 1879).

Sense Stress

The working of these consecutive sense stresses shows the effect of sense interpretation in overruling on occasion the tendency in English toward an alternating stress. The sense stress is important on an even larger scale in determining another group of sound units in English apart from those made by the alternating stress. Syllables that carry a sense emphasis, particularly if this is very marked, tend to pull surrounding syllables to themselves, forming units with the sense stress as a core; or a sense stress by itself may even constitute a unit of this sort. One resolution into such units—other resolutions are possible, for units will vary somewhat with varying interpretations—might be indicated thus, the virgules marking off the unit formed around each stress:

> Foúrscore and seven | yéars ago | our fáthers | brought fórth | on this cóntinent |a néw nation, | concéived in liberty, | and dédicated | to the propósition | that áll men | are creáted | équal.

Or, in a highly dramatic style (with rather marked pauses at the virgules):

> Fóurscore| and séven| yéars| agó| óur| fáthers| bróught| fórth| on thís| cóntinent| a néw| nátion,| concéived | in líberty,| and dédicated to the proposition| that áll| mén| are creáted | équal.

This patterning is not entirely independent of the pulsing or alternating stress, for many stresses here would be picked up by the alternating stress, which, as we have seen, utilizes sense stress without being restricted to it. Yet it is apparent that this kind of rhythm is not that of the alternating stress as such: this rhythm does not merely utilize sense stresses; it grows out of them, is constituted by them alone. It arises when the sense is being wrung out of the words. If this rhythm were somehow built up into verse, the basic rhythmic movement of such verse would not be constituted by (at least implied) stresses placed evenly along a line that thereby flows steadily in one direction and is thus styled iambic, or trochaic, and so on. Rather, it would be assembled from units that are heavy stresses alone or heavy stresses with slacks on either or both sides: reversed or "antispastic" effects are *of* this rhythm, not variations on it.

Now, from units of this sort Old English verse is made. And, although we have seen that the fact does not argue Old English as a source, from the same kind of units is built the sprung rhythm of Gerard Manley Hopkins. The following analysis is based on this hypothesis.

The Affinities of Old English and Hopkins

The comparative study of two independent bodies of verse separated by such wide intervals as Old English verse and Hopkins' can be productive of more valuable results than might otherwise be hoped for. It will be seen again and again in the following analysis how apparently accidental features arising spontaneously in both Old English verse and in Hopkins' sprung rhythm appear by this very fact for what they really are—not accidental at all, but integrated parts of an economy that must be seen as a whole before we can know what sort of thing Hopkins discovered.

Affinities Rooted in Interpretive Speech

The resemblance of the two bodies of verse is deepest in the relation of each to dramatic delivery, to the spoken language. The case for Old English has been made by Professor Kemp Malone:

> The rhythm of Old English verse grew naturally out of the prose rhythm, by a process of heightening and lowering. . . . The lifts [*hebungen*, stresses] in a line of verse regularly coincided with syllables which would (or might) take stress if the line were read as prose; in like manner, the drops [*senkungen*, slacks] coincided with syllables which would (or might) be without prose stress. (74)

Hopkins' final conclusion that his sprung rhythm was "the rhythm of common speech and of written prose, when rhythm is perceived in them" (*Poems* 5) comes to the same thing. He remarks earlier that his verse "is oratorical, that is the rhythm is so" (*Letters* 46. Aug. 21, 1877).

The great regularity of alternating stress that makes running rhythm is not a virtue in prose. The existence of a very marked pattern relatively independent of sense is out of keeping with prose psychology. But prose can operate effectively with pure sense-stress units. These are intimately connected with interpretation: increase in feeling tends to heighten and draw out the stress and countenances hurrying over unimportant syllables so that otherwise disparate units come to be equivalent to one another. In this fashion, if the equivalence of the units is made only a little more marked than it might be in prose, the passage from the *Gettysburg Address* already quoted could slip into a kind of Old English verse rhythm. Thus it might be arranged with four stresses to a line:

     fóurscore | and séven | yéars | agó |
     óur | fáthers | bróught | fórth |
     on thís | cóntinent | a néw | nátion |

As verse this is weak-kneed and perhaps somewhat footless, but it makes evident the tendency prose enjoys. The difference between rhythmically patterned prose and verse, as Hopkins observes (*Notebooks* 221), can be only one of degree. This is true to some extent even in the case of running rhythm, when freed from the label of rhyme: there are the passages in Shakespeare that may be intended either for verse or for prose. But in sense-stress patterning the difference between prose and verse is less marked because sense-stress rhythm differs from running rhythm in this important psychological feature: whereas emotion does not naturally re-assort words so that the alternating stress is placed evenly to produce running rhythm, emotion does naturally heighten the irregular sense stresses and in doing so can assert its tendency to rhythm by balancing the weight of the segments of speech of which these sense stresses form nuclei. This is what happens in the passage just cited when read as scanned. The connections here indicated bring out the all-important fact about this rhythm, the fact that fixes its psychological bearings and stabilizes it as emotional currency: heavy stressing, dramatic interpretation, high feeling are the life of the rhythm itself, so much so that the more dramatic the rendition of a passage becomes, the more marked the rhythmic movement is. The converse of this statement is equally true and perhaps more important: the more the heavy stress that constitutes this rhythm is brought out, the more the sense clears and the feeling rises.

Specious Differences and Real

This is a point of great difference between the rhythm of these sense-stress units and running rhythm. In the latter, sense stress often reverses and plays against the (running rhythm) pattern, and bringing out the sense makes this rhythm less marked, as in the line Hopkins quotes from Milton:

Hóme tō hǐs móthěr's hoūse prívāte rĕtúrned. (*Notebooks* 241)

I use the marks ‾ and ˘ to mark the stresses and slacks respectively of the fixed running rhythm pattern (to which the real stresses and slacks do not always correspond); the marks ´ and ˟ to mark stresses and slacks, respectively, considered as incorporated in sense stress rhythm, including Hopkins' sprung rhythm. Stress marks on Hopkins' verse are his own unless it is otherwise indicated.

Even where the sense does not thus reverse the rhythm, bringing out each metric stress heavily does not help the sense, but rather makes the rhythm monotonous and distasteful. The reason is plain. These stresses are not all really closely connected with sense or feeling. Thus in Gray's

Elegy, if the running-rhythm pattern is read like a sense-stress pattern so as to be very marked, it becomes intolerable and makes the sense difficult to follow:

> The Cúrfew tólls the knéll of párting dáy;
> The lówing hérd winds slówly ó'er the léa;

Since their units have one stress each but a varying number of syllables, the lines of Old English verse or of Hopkins' sprung-rhythm verse can be distinguished from those of running rhythm by the fact that they count only stresses, whereas running rhythm, the rhythm of the alternating stress, counts the total number of syllables per line. Hopkins, as has been seen, occasionally points out his sprung rhythm by means of this difference, and it is common to differentiate Old English verse from later English verse on the same basis. But this guide can prove to be vicious as well as serviceable, for it diverts attention from the deep-seated psychological disparities between the two rhythms. Difficulty arises if the supposition is encouraged that the stress that Old English or Hopkins' sprung rhythm counts and the stress that running rhythm counts are the same thing, for they are not. That they are in part alike adds confusion, for the psychological values of the two patterns are at opposite poles. Moreover, unless the divergent polarity of the two systems is pointed out, many phenomena of the Old English-Hopkins rhythm appear as mere adventitious accretions instead of what they are, parts of an ordered verse management.

The case for Old English is clear. The stress of its verse is always the sense, or interpretive, stress. Thus Jacob Schipper says in *A History of English Versification*:

> Each hemistich must have two syllables which predominate over the rest in virtue of their logical and syntactical importance and have on this account a stronger stress. (30)

And Dr. George T. Flom notes in his *Introductory Old English Grammar and Reader*:

> Here in every case [of the examples cited] the accent in the successive measures coincides absolutely with the natural accent. . . . Thus it is seen that the metrical stress always rested upon the important word and the naturally accented syllable. Weak words . . . could not have the rhythmic emphasis. (152-53)

Hopkins' *obiter dicta* regarding the stress in sprung rhythm show an early awareness that this stress was not that of running rhythm. Not only does he insist that in sprung rhythm stress alone, not stress as alternating, is essential to a foot (*Correspondence* 39. Jan. 14, 1881), but he also notes that the sprung rhythm is "more *of* a stress" than that of running rhythm, "in which less stress is laid" (*Correspondence* 39. Jan. 14, 1881; italics Hopkins' own). But to establish further the identity of Hopkins' sprung rhythm stress with the sense stress here described will require close collation of his many and scattered remarks, with one another and with the operation of stress in his verse and in other verse of a similar nature. To this collation we now turn.

Hopkins' persistent plea for oral, interpretive reading of his poems shows that this "more *of* a stress" was, just as the stress in Old English, the dramatic or interpretive stress. He tells Bridges:

> You must not slovenly read it [*The Loss of the Eurydice*] with the eyes but with your ears, as if the paper were declaiming it at you. For instance the line "she had come from a cruise training seamen" read without stress and declaim is mere Lloyd's Shipping Intelligence; properly read it is quite a different thing. Stress is the life of it. (*Letters* 51-52. May 21, 1878)

We know from a letter to Dixon that Hopkins wanted the line here mentioned to be read, "She had cóme from a crúise tráining séamen" (*Correspondence* 40. Jan. 14, 1881). This is plainly the way the sense of the verse would demand. The other rhythm that Hopkins evidently wanted to avoid is suggested not by the sense but by an alternating stress pattern induced by the first half of the line (˘˘ — ˘˘ —),which would make the whole line read, "shĕ hăd cōme frŏm ă crūise trăining sēamĕn." Only the sense stress pattern fits into Hopkins' stanza, which requires a four-stress line where this one occurs.

Hopkins, indeed, wanted more than "rhetorical" reading for the higher tension of poetical rendition. The sense emphasis is a more intense thing here than in oratory, for the pitch of feeling to which his poetry rises makes its performance demand "not reading with the eye but loud, leisurely, poetical (not rhetorical) recitation, with long rests, long dwells on the rhyme and other marked syllables, and so on. This sonnet [presumably *Spelt from Sibyl's Leaves*] shd. be almost sung: it is most carefully timed in *tempo rubato*" (*Letters* 246. Dec. 11, 1886).

An interesting gloss on these quotations that, by linking his verse with oral delivery, confirm the primacy in it of sense emphasis, is Hopkins' own half-shamefaced admission to Patmore that he made his verse orally and only wrote it down "with repugnance" (*Further* 231. May 12, 1887).

There is evident throughout Hopkins' writings a marked sensitivity to the difference between kinds of stress that indicates his ability to feel sense stress as different from other kinds and thus as a stress that can be used apart from others to construct a rhythmic pattern. The "lightsome French or Chaucerian rhythm," he writes, is used by Dixon; but, he adds thoughtfully, "Chaucer properly read is heavier stressed than we think" (*Correspondence* 78. Oct. 23, 1881). His description of *To what serves Mortal Beauty* as "common rhythm highly stressed" (*Poems* 113) points both to the same sensitivity to differences in kinds of stresses and to a realization that common rhythm ordinarily is not stressed highly. Moreover, keeping in mind his earlier remark that sprung rhythm uses "more *of* a stress," we read with interest his statements to Bridges that sprung rhythm "lends itself to expressing passion" (*Letters* 92. Oct. 8, 1879) and that in the *St. Winefred's Well* fragments, "as the feeling rises the rhythm becomes freer and more sprung" (*Letters* 212. April 1, 1885). Set against the earlier remark, this means that as the dramatic emphases assert themselves under the influence of feeling, the rhythm becomes more of a sprung rhythm. The dramatic stress makes the sprung rhythm pattern.

There is, moreover, no difficulty in seeing how a sensitivity to the value of the heavy or dramatic stress is at one with Hopkins' whole attitude toward poetry. For him a poem was not to be grafted on language, but grown from it. Rhythm, if it is a mode of conveying feeling, gains by being drawn out of the interpretive stress, for this stress naturally mounts with the feeling. This line of thought accords with Hopkins' remark to Bridges that

> the poetical language of an age shd. be the current language heightened, to any degree heightened and unlike itself, but not (I mean normally: passing freaks and graces are another thing) an obsolete one. This is Shakespeare's and Milton's practice and the want of it will be fatal to Tennyson's idylls and plays, and to Swinburne, and perhaps to Morris. (*Letters* 89. Aug. 14, 1879)

Hopkins tells Bridges in the same place that he avoids inversions

> because they weaken and because they destroy the earnestness or inearnestness of the utterance. Nevertheless in prose I use them more than other people, because there they have great advantages of another sort. Now these advantages they should have in verse too, but they must not seem to be due to the verse: that is what is so enfeebling (for instance the finest of your sonnets to my mind has a line enfeebled by inversion plainly due to the verse, as I said once before "'Tis joy, the falling of her fold to view"— . . .). . . . . So also I cut myself off from the use of *ere, o'er, wellnigh, what time, say not* (for

do not say), because, though dignified, they neither belong to nor ever cd. arise from, or be the elevation of, ordinary modern speech.

It might be noted that Hopkins' "what while we, while we slumbered" in *The Leaden Echo and the Golden Echo* arises not from any Spenserian archaizing but from dramatic disturbance.

With an extraordinary consistency, Hopkins' musical sensibilities reflect the same bent as his poetic. He is an admirer of the Church's plain chant, which is eminently the elevation of speech (*Letters* 214. Apr. 1, 1885). (It is, indeed, interesting to speculate what the effect would have been on him had the Solesmes Benedictines' work of restoring the original chant been completed before his death so that the real rhythm of the chant would have been available to him in its fullness.)

It does not come as a surprise that the mind in evidence here would hit upon a rhythm built from the interpretive, sense stresses that are a normal mode of conveying feeling in English and that tend themselves to become more prominent as the feeling rises. "Why do I employ sprung rhythm at all?" Hopkins asks, apparently echoing a query of Bridges':

> Because it is the nearest to the rhythm of prose, that is the native and natural rhythm of speech, the least forced, the most rhetorical and emphatic of all possible rhythms, combining, as it seems to me, opposite and, one wd. have thought, incompatible excellences, markedness of rhythm—that is rhythm's self—and naturalness of expression—for why, if it is forcible in prose to say "lashed:rod," am I obliged to weaken this in verse, which ought to be stronger, not weaker, into "lashed birch-rod" or something?
>
> My verse is less to be read than heard, as I have told you before; it is oratorical, that is the rhythm is so. I think if you will study what I have here said you will be much more pleased with it and may I say? converted to it. (*Letters* 46. Aug. 21, 1877)

Similarly, he writes to Dixon later that he believed his rhythm was based on "a better and more natural principle than the ordinary system, much more flexible, and capable of much greater effects" (*Correspondence* 14-15. Oct. 6, 1878). His claim that his poetry had a popular style, which claim amused Patmore (*Further* 207. Patmore to Hopkins, Apr. 5, 1884), derived largely from this same conviction that its rhythms grew naturally out of normal emotional language.

In the light of these texts, it is unmistakable that Hopkins consistently views his rhythm as a rhythm derived not from any stresses, but from high stresses important to sense, from the strong stresses that arise in the normal rhythms of emotional prose. This picture coincides with the picture we have of the rhythm of Old English poetry. Further examination of the practice of Hopkins and the Old English poets confirms this conclusion, showing, as we shall see, that the rhythms are identified with one another in a surprisingly intimate fashion.

Juncture of Sense-Stress Units

Whether we take a prose passage such as that from the *Gettysburg Address* already used, or a passage of Old English poetry, or one of Hopkins' sprung rhythm poems, it is noteworthy that there is a great variation in the ways in which the sense units of the sort indicated articulate with one another. Although sense-stress verse seems to demand that the time intervals between stresses, generally speaking, be felt as being somewhat equal, the spacing of the slacks within these time intervals between the stresses will follow various arrangements, depending on the varying amount of time required for the pronunciation of different syllables, natural pauses or rests in or between certain words or syllables, various ways of counterbalancing minor accents, and so on. Thus all sorts of rhythmic complications and syncopations can arise, like those of a very complicated and varied dance figure.

For instance, longer units are enunciated relatively faster, and monosyllabic units are drawn out and perhaps receive compensating emphases, as in the arrangement of the *Gettysburg Address* passage, which may stand as a prose counterpart of Hopkins' poetry—

$$\text{Fóurscore} \mid \text{and séven} \mid \qquad \text{yéars} \mid \text{agó} \mid$$
$$\text{óur} \mid \text{fáthers} \mid \qquad \text{bróught} \mid \text{fórth} \mid$$

—or as in Hopkins' *Spelt from Sibyl's Leaves* (with scansion developed from Hopkins' own incomplete marks):

$$\text{. . . . . Héart,} \mid \text{yŏu róund mĕ} \mid \text{ríght}$$
$$\text{Wĭth:} \mid \text{Óur} \mid \text{évĕnĭng} \mid \text{ĭs ŏvĕr ús;} \mid \text{óur nĭght} \mid \text{whélms,} \mid \text{whélms,} \mid \text{ánd} \mid \text{wĭll}$$
$$\text{énd ŭs.}$$

(I indicate here one possible resolution into sense-stress units, although, in view of the close interlocking of the units in actual rendition, the virgules dividing them off from one another are elsewhere in this paper usually omitted.) Moreover, the various internal movements of these sense units—rising, falling, rocking—are not leveled off into a simple one-two or one-two-three pattern, but all the natural variety of spoken utterance as such is incorporated into the verse movement.

The intricate ballet is perhaps the best analogy. We could take as representing the sense-stress units small groups of individual steps ranging, let us say, from one to four (or more) steps each. The individual steps (in verse the stress and slacks) in these groups would be some longer, some shorter, and would represent in timing quarter, eighth, and sixteenth notes, for example; these would be arranged in various groupings, perhaps with some pauses included, and with a kind of ictus or principal step (corresponding to the stress) placed within each group, but not necessarily always in the same position with regard to the other steps (slacks) in the group. These groups of steps, then, to form a complete ballet, would be woven together so as to engage with a rhythmic background. The principle would be, in general, to keep the ictuses (stresses) at rather equal distances, except when some special syncopation is desired, and to work the slacks in as they naturally fit best by making minute adjustments. Similarly, in verse the sense-stress units would be woven together across a rhythmic background, which would vary from poem to poem, being perhaps now a kind of 4/4 time, now 6/8, or again something like the free rhythm of plain chant (as, for instance, the opening line of *The Leaden Echo and the Golden Echo*).

Normal pronunciation, which does not permit the complete equalization suggested by regular stress and slack alternation, does allow minor adjustments in accentuation and timing depending on the rhythmic context of the sense-stress units. This is plain in prose, where at one time a phrase will be pronounced one way and at another time another, the timing within a phrase being always somewhat *ad libitum*. When sense-stress units are woven into a rhythmic setting, these minor adjustments will be made according to the rhythmic background, but because they are adjustments of the usual sort, they will not destroy naturalness of utterance.

Here, of course, a given number of slacks between two stresses will not necessarily demand always the same pattern. Everything will depend on the timing that pronunciation demands. There will be hovering on some syllables and complete rests here and there, such as normal enunciation sprinkles with great freedom all about our speech, as well as special adjustments in timing and accentuation that high feeling may demand. Some slacks will themselves receive various minor accents. (Professor Malone has commented on varying weights of stresses in Old English verse [74-80].)

Thus, for instance, in the *Spelt from Sibyl's Leaves* passage just scanned, the second syllable of *evening* would be a kind of grace note, as also might be the *is*, which yields to its common tendency to suppress its vowel. But the other slacks have more time and weight. Poems like *The*

Windhover and the *Deutschland* are full of examples of elaborate rhythmic variations of the sort described: the syllables might be represented
variously as something like quarter notes, eighth notes, sixteenths, grace
notes, and there will be a variety of rests to correspond.

All this makes the organization of a line in this kind of rhythm a matter for delicate workmanship, as Hopkins was well aware. There must be
accommodation to a marked rhythm without loss of the natural timing
and stressing that words can demand. Indeed, the natural movements
must be built up instead of de-emphasized. Speaking of the sprung
rhythm pattern superimposed on certain other verse patterns, Hopkins
observes that the beats of the sprung rhythm are "so subtly hung and distributed and balanced that scarcely any two are alike" (*Notebooks* 236).
This is indicative of his recognition of the rhythmic complication of
which we have been speaking, as is also his remark, already cited, that a
sonnet, *Spelt from Sibyl's Leaves* most probably, "is most carefully timed
in *tempo rubato*" (*Letters* 246. Dec. 11, 1886). "Robbed time," with its
reference to the lengthening of some notes at the expense of others, is an
excellent label for the variegated and often syncopated effects resulting
from the combination of protracted sounds with shorter ones in the unlike
groupings of sense-stress units.

Of course, this kind of rhythmic complication, which can arise by
virtue of the variable sense-stress units we have been considering, is foreign to the simple throbbing of pure running rhythm. It demands sensi-
tivities other than those demanded by running rhythm, a sense of complex
timing. This, too, Hopkins was aware of. Because of Bridges' lack of this
sense, Hopkins complains to him: "Since the syllables in sprung rhythm
are not counted, time or equality in strength is of more importance than
in common counted rhythm, and your times or strengths do not seem to
me equal enough" (*Letters* 81-82. May 26, 1879).

In a letter to Dixon, Hopkins shows his feeling for his sprung verse
as a product assembled out of units consisting of stresses with their adher-
ing slacks. In this letter, he speaks of "an easily felt principle of *equal
strengths*," that

> supposes not only that, speaking in the abstract, any accent is equal
> to any other (by accent I mean the accent of a word) but further that
> each accent may be considered to be accompanied by all equal quan-
> tity of slack or unaccented utterance, one, two, or more such unac-
> cented syllables; so that wherever there is an accent or stress, there
> is also so much unaccentuation, so to speak, or slack, and this will
> give a foot or rhythmic unit, viz. a stress with its belonging slack. But
> now if this is so, since there are plenty of accented monosyllables,

and those too immediately preceded and followed by the accents of other words, it will come about that a foot may consist of one syllable only and that one syllable has not only the stress of its accent but also the slack which another wd. throw on one or more additional syllables, though here that may perhaps be latent, as though the slack syllables had been absorbed. What I mean is clearest in an antithesis or parallelism, for there the contrast gives the counterparts equal stress; e.g. "sanguinary consequences, terrible butchery, frightful slaughter, fell swoop": if these are taken as alternative expressions, then the total strength of *sanguinary* is no more than that of *terrible* or of *frightful* or of *fell* and so on of the substantives too. (*Correspondence* 22. Feb. 27, 1879)

In stating here, "by accent I mean the accent of a word," Hopkins shows clearly that he is not concerned with the alternating stress, which may in some words occur three or four times.

His marking of strong stresses, pauses, quivers or circumflexions (one syllable read as two), syllables to be huddled together, and so on are all attempts on Hopkins' part to indicate by a notation not a strange manner of reading, but how the rhythmic adjustment actually works out in a heightened, feeling enunciation. See, for example, the facsimile of the *Harry Ploughman* autograph (in *Letters* opposite 262; cf. Bridges' remarks in *Poems* 95). The presence of such marks provides further evidence of the workings of the sense-stress economy we have been describing.

A similar organization seems to be quite evident throughout Old English measures, where the articulation of units in which the stress always followed the sense resulted in a verse that Professor Malone calls "an instrument subtle and sophisticated enough," by reason of the fact that "systematic alternation of lift and drop was avoided, presumably because of the mechanical, monotonous rhythm that such an alternation all too often produces" (80).

The question of the juncture of the sense-stress units with one another to form a complex whole goes to the very heart of sense-stress rhythm. We are here in the realm of rhythmic complication such as the simple throb of running rhythm does not know. But the detailed theorems according to which the articulation of the sense units with one another is carried out, although of capital importance for the complete understanding of sprung rhythm, would be too intricate to be worked out in the broad outline being sketched in this present study. It has seemed worthwhile to sketch the broad outline first, confining attention to the presence of the sense units themselves rather than looking to the more minute details of their organization. (But see the note at the end of Part 2.)

Hovering Accents

However, within the sense-stress units themselves, a special manifestation of rhythmic complication in Hopkins merits some special attention.
This is the effect achieved—again the closest analogy is perhaps dance
movement—when two successive stresses are used almost as one pro-
longed stress. Often managed with the aid of a simple device, repetition
of the vowel sound of the first stressed syllable in the second so as to minimize the syllabic break (*beak-leaved* or *tool-smooth* below), this quasi-
prolongation is rather distinctive of sprung rhythm, which here proceeds
with successive stresses, not after the manner of running rhythm by
reducing one equivalently to a slack, liquidating it within the fixed pattern, but by balancing the two against one another so as to make of them
a kind of one. The verse can often be read with two juxtaposed accents
almost equal so as to constitute a single hovering stress. Thus *beak-leaved*
or *tool-smooth* or *bleak light* in *Spelt from Sibyl's Leaves* (the stress marks
are mine):

> Ónly the béak-lèaved bóughs drágonish| dámask the
>   tóol-smòoth bléak lìght; bláck,
> Ever so black on it.

The reader of Hopkins will recognize this effect as very common. It is
also perhaps a feature of Old English, as in the examples scanned by
Schipper as *Béowùlf* or *hrĭng-nèt* (28). So in *The Seafarer*:

> síþas sécgan hú ic geswíncdàgum. (line 2; Krapp and Dobbie 143)

The use of such a hovering accent by Walt Whitman has been noted by
Dr. Sculley Bradley (437-39). It is significant that Hopkins considered
Whitman's verse "an irregular rhythmic prose" at times quite near highly
wrought sprung rhythm (*Letters* 155, 157. Oct. 18, 1882).

Reversal of Movement

It is in keeping with the principle of equal strengths that the units in a line
of sense-stress verse need not all proceed in the same direction. Some
may have the stress at their beginning, some at their end, some toward
their center—all this without constituting exceptions to the movement,
since this incorporates the units not as moving in any particular direction
with alternation of stress and slack, but simply as more or less equal
weights, each with a stress as the core. The operation of this law has been
seen in the scanned *Gettysburg Address* passage. The operation of the

same law in Old English leads Schipper to classify Old English half-lines into ascending, descending, and ascending-descending (35), and leads Professor Malone to note how the drops (*senkungen*, slacks) serve both to lead up to and to lead away from the lifts (*hebungen*, stresses) (80). The same law is seen in operation in the passage just scanned from *Spelt from Sibyl's Leaves*, and can be observed throughout Hopkins' sprung rhythm verse. And Hopkins' own explicit statement of the law's exerting its force in his sprung rhythm presents the clearest possible evidence that he conceived this rhythm in terms of what we have described as sense-stress verse. Hopkins' practice of scanning with the stress always first in the "foot" was a mere convenience, and Hopkins recognized it as such (*Poems* 1-2, 3-4), as he had also recognized his earlier practice of scanning with the stress last to be a mere convenience:

> though it is the virtue of sprung rhythm that it allows of "dochmiac" or "antispastic" effects or cadences, when the verse suddenly changes from a rising to a falling movement, and this too is strongly felt by the ear, yet no account of it is taken in scanning and no irregularity caused, but the scansion always treated, conventionally and for simplicity, as rising. . . . Bridges in the preface to his last issue says something to the effect that all sorts of feet may follow one another, an anapaest a dactyl for instance . . . : so they may, if we look at the real nature of the verse; but for simplicity it is much better to recognize, in scanning this new rhythm, only one movement, either the rising (which I choose as being commonest in English verse) or the falling (which is perhaps better in itself), and always keep to that. (*Correspondence* 40. Jan. 14, 1881)

Of course, the sense stress need not be always irregularly placed among the syllables. It may for special effects alternate with slacks quite regularly, as in the line from *Spring and Fall* which scans (my marks):

Bý ănd bý, nŏr spáre ă sígh.

Predilection for Antithesis

From the complexity of rhythmic structure within each unit, it might be expected that the organization of sense-stress verse on the stanzaic level would remain relatively simple. In Old English it does. The patterns used here were regularly confined to antithetical or antiphonal arrangements of half-lines with two stresses in each, occasionally shrunk to one or extended to more than two stresses (Professor Malone notes many lines with three, five, six, or even seven). And among the many points of agreement of Hopkins' verse with Old English, none is more remarkable than the uncanny tendency to fall into similar half-line patterns.

Developing an intricacy of organization set deep within the economy of the language—the kind of "intricacy" found in villanelles and rondels only disgusted him, and "I wish we were rid of them," he writes Bridges (*Letters* 277. May 25, 1888)—Hopkins' sprung rhythm veers decidedly toward the Old English antiphonal movement. His discussion of parallelisms already noted has an obvious relation to this movement. Moreover, he deliberately favors alexandrines in sonnets (*Letters* 157. Oct. 18, 1882; 203. Jan. 1, 1885; cf. 212. Apr. 1, 1885; 80. Apr. 22, 1879; 92. Oct. 8, 1879), and his treatment of them there is telling. *To what serves Mortal Beauty* has the halfline breaks *marked* with a virgule. This shows Hopkins' tendency to use alexandrines for the precise reason that they break in the middle, and not in such a way as to conceal their tendency to do so, a tendency that indeed has bothered most poets. Similarly, the *Moonrise* fragment (No. 65) has its lines divided, as does *That Nature Is a Heraclitean Fire*. *Spelt from Sibyl's Leaves*, too, is divided into four-stress half-lines, which Hopkins would consider as alexandrines, since he held that in these latter "each half line is by nature a dimeter; two bars or four feet, of which commonly one foot is silent or lost at the pause" (*Letters* 212. Apr. 1, 1885). Indeed, Hopkins' feeling for dimeters in alexandrines makes his alexandrine verse movement correspond more closely than ever to Old English, for it introduces an antiphonal movement into each half-line and eliminates from his alexandrines the three-beat unit that would be unusual in Old English as a fixed pattern.

In accord with the general principle that the complexity of rhythmic structure within each unit of sense-stress verse calls for simplicity of stanzaic structure, we should expect something to happen if a complicated stanza form were attempted. So it does. Hopkins' most ambitious stanza form is the sonnet, and here it is that the dissolution into simpler half-line antithesis takes place.

Hopkins himself supplies the obvious explanation of the impulse of sense-stress rhythm to develop antithetical movement when he explains to Dixon in the passage already cited above that the correspondence of units in this rhythm "is clearest in an antithesis or parallelism" (*Correspondence* 22. Feb. 27, 1879). (His remarks on the four-beat line in common use in English, despite the promise of the subject itself, yield little or nothing of value here—*Letters* 119-20. Jan. 26, 1881).

Operation of the grammatical parallelisms to which Hopkins here refers is evident throughout Old English poetry. It can be seen for instance, in the last verses of *The Wanderer*, in the *Riddles* (for example, "The Nightingale"), or at the opening of *The Seafarer*:

earfoðhwile	oft þrowade
bitre breostceare	gebiden hæbbe,
gecunnad in ceole	cearselda fela,

. . . .

dyde ic me to gomene,	ganetes hleoþor
ond huilpan sweg	fore hleator wera,
mæw singende	fore medodrince.

(lines 3-5, 20-22; Krapp and Dobbie 143-44)

Stretched Lines

Even the rhythmical variations that Hopkins calls "hangers" or "outrides" establish another *rapport* with Old English verse. Just as Old English admitted occasional "long lines"—lines with more than four stresses—so Hopkins occasionally stretches his lines with his "hangers" or "outrides," which he describes as "one, two, or three slack syllables added to a foot and not counting in the nominal scanning," so called "because they seem to hang below the line or ride forward or backward from it in another dimension than the line itself " (*Poems* 4-5; cf. 107). At first Hopkins thought these could be used only in counterpointed rhythm (a mixture of common rhythm and sprung—*Letters* 45. Aug. 21, 1877), but he soon describes them as "natural to Sprung Rhythm" (1883 Preface in *Poems* 4). The correspondence of hangers or outrides and the Old English long lines can, I think, be pushed closely only at the cost of great subtleties, but it is plain that both Hopkins and the Old English poets had here in common at least the practice of varying rhythm by lengthening verses.

Hopkins' lengthening also includes what he calls "burden lines." Thus in *Harry Ploughman*:

> .   .   .   . Back, elbow, and liquid waist
> In him, all quail to the wallowing o' the plough;
> 's cheek crimsons; curls
> Wag or crossbridle, in a wind lifted, windlaced—
>   See his wind— lilylocks —laced;

The last line here is a "burden line," and indeed it appears from his marks in the manuscript reproduced in facsimile in the volume of letters to Bridges (*Letters* opposite 262), that Hopkins perhaps even intended it as an outride, in which case outrides and burden lines would come to merge into one another, as they do at least in part in being both expansions or extensions for rhythmic effect.

The extreme of psychological effectiveness in the use of line lengthening is found in *The Leaden Echo and the Golden Echo*, where the nervous protraction of the opening line dramatizes the drive of high emotion that will not be brooked:

> How to kéep—is there ány any, is there none such, nowhere
> known some, bow or brooch or braid or brace, láce,
> latch or catch or key to keep
> Back beauty, keep it, beauty, beauty, beauty, . . . from vanishing
> away?

Hopkins nowhere does intelligible and intense feeling a greater service than when he defends here the choice and position of "Back" (*Poems* 113).

Thunder, Echoes, and Chimes

The economy of the rhythm we have been describing is hardly reducible to rules of thumb. However, since the reason for this is not that the rhythm is amorphous, but that it is alive and flexible with the life of high perception and feeling—"stress is the life of it," and this stress is the stress of dramatic interpretation—we can at least observe that the economy of the rhythm demands the heightening of stress. Regarded in perspective with this fact, the alliteration and assonance, the partial rhymes and other echoes, the consonantal clangor—all the heavy arms with which Old English verse equipped itself and which are likewise present up and down Hopkins—these become understandable. The recurrence of these devices with the revival of Old English rhythms by Hopkins hints that the devices are not adventitious ornament in sense-stress verse. As a matter of fact, they are invaluable helps to the poet in bringing out what dramatic interpretation he wants (for dramatic interpretation, on which stress depends, is always somewhat *ad libitum*), and in enabling him to build up the intensity of the stresses so that the pattern may be evident despite the variable and often large number of slacks between stresses.

The working of these sounding devices is observable in any Old English poetry. *The Seafarer* opens:

> Mæg ic be me sylfum   soðgied wrecan.
> siþas secgan,   hu ic geswincdagum
> earfoðhwile   oft þrowade
> bitre breostceare   gebiden hæbbe.

gecunnad in ceole   cearselda fela.
atol yþa gewealc.   . . . .
(lines 1-6; Krapp and Dobbie 143)

In the second half of the second line here, alliteration both cues in and builds up the stress on -*swinc*-. The heavy consonantal load -*ft þr*- in the short half-line "oft þrowade" works to the same end: the echoes of the sounds amplify one another in the hearer's ear. In brief, the more we allow the necessary mechanics of the language to operate here, the more the sense is clarified, the more the feeling mounts, the more marked the rhythmic movement becomes. Rhythm and interpretation interlock, and monotony is no danger because of the free-jointed movement of the verse loosed from syllabic count.

Similar analyses can be repeated throughout Hopkins. We find in *Harry Ploughman*:

Breathed round; the rack of ribs; the scooped flank; lank
Rope-over thigh   .   .   .   .   .   .

This can be compared with a line such as this from the Old English *Genesis*,

Abrægd ða mid ðry bille,   brynegield obhread,
(*Genesis* line 2932; Krapp 86)

and there is found similar alliteration, assonance, internal rhyme, all working to the same end of leading in with great force the sense-stressed syllables.

This force, in Hopkins as in Old English, is cumulative. By the use of alliteration, partial rhyme, assonance, and consonantal bunching not only on the syllables with the sense emphasis but throughout the verse as well, the emphases of the sense stresses require a proportionately greater heightening so that often very heavy verse emerges, as in *Harry Ploughman*:

In him, all quail to the wallowing o' the plough;
's cheek crimsons; curls
Wag or crossbridle   .   .   .   .   .

The heavy consonantal load '*s ch*—, made heavier than usual by the elision, in combination with the long *ee* of *cheek* forces a very heavy stress onto the first syllable of *crimsons* because the sense demands that this latter word receive more emphasis than *cheek* (*Letters* opposite 262). So, for example, in the Old English *Phoenix*:

Swa se gesælige (line 350a; Cook 62)

the *se* receives some additional prominence because of an alliteration with the preceding *swa*, but the second and third syllables of *gesælige* must override the effect of this alliteration and hence demand relatively stronger stresses.

Hopkins has drawn a red herring across his own trail—not without effect—in his remark to Dixon that the *Deutschland* uses "certain chimes suggested by the Welsh poetry" he had been reading (*Correspondence* 15. Oct. 6, 1878). If this is taken to mean that the rich texture of sound in Hopkins is a conscious importation that is not a growth integral to the management of the English verse he is writing, it is entirely misleading. For it is within his verse itself that the elaborate network of Hopkins' sound effects gathers its strength and has its meaning. Hopkins himself writes to Bridges that he got the chimes only "in part from the Welsh" (*Letters* 38. Apr. 3, 1877), and his mention of them to Dixon occurs while he is explaining how *natural* his new system is. The Welsh influence undoubtedly helps account for the relatively richer chiming of Hopkins' verse as against Old English, but beyond this it does not go.

The integrating value of assonance, alliteration, and the other sound equivalences comes home when one reads *London Snow* or the other poems done by Bridges in Hopkins' "new rhythm" as Bridges conceived it. Examination of these poems shows how much the neglect of Hopkins' rich overlaying of echo on echo results in the loss not of a grace but of the rhythm's self. See Hopkins' criticism of Bridges' sprung rhythm, *Letters* 71 (Feb. 22, 1879); 81-82 (May 26, 1879); 111 (Oct. 26, 1880); 122-123 (Feb. 5, 1881); *Further* 187, to Patmore (Nov. 14, 1883).

A more surprising, because an apparently less essential yet exact point of resemblance to Old English, is to be found in Hopkins' theory that all vowels alliterate with one another. The agreement with Old English here is underlined by Hopkins' firmness in holding to his theory—he argued it out with Patmore—and his explicit statement concerning its origin:

> I should like you to reconsider the matter of alliteration in vowels. To my ear no alliteration is more marked or more beautiful, and I used to take it for granted as an obvious fact that every initial vowel lettered to every other before ever I knew that anything of the sort was practiced in Anglo-Saxon verse. I cannot agree that this alliteration

is destroyed by using the same vowel. . . . How this alliteration arises is, I know, very hard to say, but to my ear there is no doubt about
the fact. (*Further* 183-84. Nov. 7, 1883)

Schipper follows Sievers in explaining the alliteration of unlike vowels in
Old English by supposing a glottal catch missing in Modern English, in
which language, we are told "the harmony or consonance of the unlike
vowels is hardly perceptible . . . and does not count as alliteration"
(Schipper 14). This theory rests on the supposition that perception of
"harmony or consonance of unlike vowels" is carried on independently of
any particular artistic economy. But we are used to alliteration in a standard type of context where it is a grace. Do we know how to look for alliteration that is more integral to verse? What would it sound like if we
heard it? In Hopkins' case an ear attuned to modern verse organized like
Old English is taken by the same resemblance in the current language that
caught the ear of the Old English poet.

Development, But No Shift in Direction

Correspondences between Hopkins' rhythms and Old English are remarkable enough so far, but they do not stop with the pointing of similarities,
however remarkable these may be, for even the characteristic features of
Hopkins' verse that are not found in Old English are, for the most part,
explainable on the same grounds as the similarities themselves and operate in accord with them. This is to say, the same principle that we have
been invoking to explain the characteristics of Old English and of
Hopkins' rhythms—the fact that both develop from interpretive or sense
stresses in the language—serves also to explain a great many of Hopkins'
individual "peculiarities."

Hopkins' Rhymes

With the odd petulancy that always pinches the genuine appreciation he
has for Hopkins, Bridges objects to the latter's rhymes. Now rhymes Old
English verse had not used to any extent. Rhyme came into English when
the Old English sense-stress verse was being displaced by running
rhythm. Hence Hopkins, in introducing rhyme into sense-stress verse,
was transplanting it from the special culture in which it had grown to a
new. The notion that this fact might to some extent change the appearance
and function of rhyme Bridges seems never to have entertained. He might
have been helped to the notion by Hopkins' desire that his sprung rhythm
poems be in most cases not broken at the end of lines, where the formal
rhyming occurs, to the extent usual with poems in running rhythm
(*Letters* 86. Aug. 14, 1879; cf. *Correspondence* 40. Jan. 14, 1881; *Poems*

4), as well as by the whole movement of Hopkins' sprung rhythm verse. But Bridges—though we must not forget to remember him gratefully for his gift of Hopkins' poems nor fail to appreciate his genuine affection for their author—seems indeed never to have known Hopkins' verse in full movement. His persistent stumbling over "exaggerated Marianism" or over "sonic perversion of human feeling, as, for instance the nostril's relish of incense 'along the sanctuary side'" (Bridges had his mind made up that emotion was forced if it ran in "theological or sectarian channels"), or his frequent detours around "unpoetic lines" and excursions after peccadillos for argument (see Bridges' notes in *Poems* 96-100)—all this must have so mingled with annoyance his progress through any one of Hopkins' poems that his powers of perception were seriously dissipated.

Had Bridges' perception been freer to operate, he might have observed that what happens in the rhyming of words at the end of lines in Hopkins' verse is, on the whole, not particularly remarkable within the great skeleton of internal rhyme, assonance, alliteration, and other sound echoings bracing the entire verse structure. Thus in a typical passage from *Spelt from Sibyl's Leaves*, the end rhymes are only fuller developments continuous with effects built everywhere into the verse:

> Only the beak-leaved boughs dragonish | damask the tool-smooth
>   bleak light; black,
> Ever so black on it.   Óur tale, O óur oracle! | Lét life, wáned,
>   ah lét life wind
> Off hér once skéined stained véined varíety | upon, áll on twó
>   spools; párt, pen, páck
> Now her áll in twó flocks, twó folds—black, white; | right, wrong:
>   reckon but, reck but, mind
> But thése two; wáre of a wórld where bút these | twó tell, each
>   off the óther; of a rack
> Where, selfwrung selfstrung, sheathe— and shelterless, | thóughts
>   agaínst thoughts ín groans grínd.

Moreover, sprung rhythm lines vary so much in syllabic length that it is most often impossible to anticipate the exact place of a rhyme's occurrence: the rhyme loses inevitability, as, for instance, in the first four lines of *The Windhover*:

> I caught this morning morning's minion, king-
>   dom of daylight's dauphin, dapple-dawn-drawn Fal-
>   con, in his riding

Of the rolling level underneath him steady air, and
    striding
High there, how he rung upon the rein of a wimpling wing.

This all means that the perfect chiming of endings is not so much demanded, for endings are not felt as belonging so closely to one another.

In the light of this principle the consistency becomes apparent in
Hopkins' frequent demand that sprung rhythm poems be read through
with less break at the line endings than is the case with running rhythm
poems: "the scanning runs on without break from the beginning, say, of a
stanza to the end and all the stanza is one long strain, though written in
lines asunder" (*Poems* 4). The same principle explains the fact that

> it is natural in Sprung Rhythm for the lines to be *rove over*, that is for
> the scanning of each line immediately to take up that of the one
> before, so that if the first has one or more syllables at its end the other
> must have so many the less at its beginning. (*Poems* 4)

This means that Hopkins' nominal scansion with stress first is preserved
by considering slacks at the beginning of a line as going with the last
stress of the preceding line and not being extra-metrical.

The special applications of this principle to certain relatively swift
four-beat measures (such as *Spring and Fall*) are too detailed for attention here (*Letters* 120. Jan 26, 1881; see note at the end of Part 2.)

The nature of the sprung rhythm stress, which is "more of a stress,"
and the whole economy of a verse that it dominates again provide the
explanation and justification for rhymes such as *eternal* and *burn all*, or
and some and *handsome* that nettle Bridges (*Poems* 99). The same is true
of rhymes that break words, such as *king-* (*king-dom*) and *wing* in the
opening lines just quoted from *The Windhover*, and *overbend us* and *an
end, as-* (*an end, as-tray*) in *Spelt from Sibyl's Leaves:*

Her fond yellow hornlight wound to the west,| her wild
    hollow hoarlight hung to the height
Waste; her earliest stars, earl-stars, | stárs principal over-
    bend us,
Fíre-féaturing heaven. For earth | her being has unbound,
    her dapple is at an end, as-
tray or aswarm, all throughther, in throngs; | self ín
    self steepèd and páshed—quíte
Disremembering, dísmémbering | áll now. . . .

Hopkins' practices here are understandable when viewed in their relationship to all the parts of the closely geared machinery: line endings are less marked, exact rhyming has therefore less purpose, and the force of the stresses in a context already ringing with verbal echoes brings out resemblances that would be lost elsewhere. It is worth noting in this connection that Dr. Henry Lanz's recent studies have shown how imperfect forms of rhyme work better where accent is heavy (94-100). Russian, for instance, which shows on Dr. Lanz's oscillograph records as a language of relatively intense explosive sounds, uses assonance where other languages use rhyme. Plainly, there is a parallel here with the English verse that takes a markedly heavy stress. In keeping with such a fact, we find Hopkins, who despised eye-rhymes but not imperfect rhyme and assonance (*Notebooks* 244-48), insisting on the interpretive reading of his verse as the test for his rhyming. The kind of reading that sprung rhythm demands makes his rhymes work. "My rhymes," he writes to Bridges, "are rigidly good—to the ear" (*Letters* 44. Aug. 21, 1877). And, discussing the matter later, he adds:

> Some others again there are which *malignity may munch at* but the Muses love. To this class belongs what you quote. You will grant that there are things in verse which may be read right or wrong, which depend for their effect upon pronunciation. (*Letters* 180. May 11, 1883)

How badly Bridges failed to follow Hopkins in the latter's discerning sensitivity to sound is apparent when one compares Bridges' remarks on Hopkins' rhymes (*Poems* 98-99) with the discussion of rhyme in Hopkins' lecture notes on rhetoric (*Notebooks* 244-248).

Omission of the Relative

The place accorded dramatic stress in sprung rhythm likewise helps explain even such "peculiarities" as the omission of the relative pronoun at which Bridges munches again, though this omission in Hopkins is rare enough to deserve little comment. Omission of the object relative pronoun is a common English practice: *the man I saw, the room he lived in.* But the omissions in question are of subject relatives: "O Hero [that] savest," or "Squander the hell-rook ranks [that] sally to molest him" (*Poems* 97-98). Now, the speaking of the phrase "O Hero that savest" with heavy stresses on the *He-* and *sa-* will show the tendency of the relative to disappear: it can, in feeling delivery, easily become "O Hero 't savest," and in the breaking of deep emotion drop altogether. Similarly with the other line Bridges quotes.

Bridges' explanation does Hopkins justice in stating that these omissions were not "carelessness in Gerard Hopkins," but that Hopkins

> banished these purely constructional syllables from his verse because they took up room which he thought he could not afford them: he needed in his scheme all his space for his poetical words, and he wished those to crowd out every merely grammatical colourless or toneless element. (*Poems* 97)

Bridges' use of the expression "poetical words" shows a mind veering far off the line of thought that holds that "the poetical language of an age shd. be the current language heightened." We wonder how Bridges' distinction between constructional and poetical would explain the stresses Hopkins often marks on prepositions. The distinction is, at best, pointless. Hopkins omitted relatives at times, not because they are not "poetical," but because in language highly stressed and emotional they may really tend to be crowded out. This is "the current language heightened." Hopkins' building with dramatic stress (both lines quoted by Bridges are from sprung rhythm poems) explains his practice: he was carrying forward—how advisedly need not be argued here—a tendency that that stress creates.

Unusual Sense Stresses

The same emphasis on dramatic interpretation explains a practice of Hopkins to which little attention has been paid but to which attention will at some time surely be diverted. This is his marking of stresses in places unusual for sense stresses. It is true that most of the instances of stress marks inserted by Hopkins in his poems are self-explanatory: the rhythm of sense-stress verse is not always unambiguous, and in places Hopkins wishes to indicate his preference for one interpretation over others that would be easily suggested and that would scan, too. Thus, in general, he marks the metrical stress, as he indicates at the foot of the *Harry Ploughman* manuscript, "in doubtful cases only" (*Letters* opposite 262). Often the mark indicates an interpretation dictated by unusual emotional pitch, as the stress on *and* in *Spelt from Sibyl's Leaves*:

> .   .   .   .   .   Heart, you round me right
> With: Óur évening is over us; óur night   whelms, whelms,
>   ánd will end us.

But an instance like this in the first line of *Spring and Fall* brings at first sight more difficulty:

> Márgarét, are you gríeving
> Over Goldengrove unleaving?

If this is sprung rhythm, how justify the stress on the last syllable of *Margaret*? Does not theory here dissolve into a fiction? Sprung rhythm uses sense stresses, and is not the sense stress here on the first syllable of the name? Is it not true that the ordinary way of emphasizing a polysyllable is to stress the member with the principal accent? The ordinary way, yes; but not the only way. The answer here lies, I think, in the thoughtful deliberation that marks the emotion of this poem and that brings to the interpretation an unusual second heavy accent as the speaker begins slowly and pensively. This second accent need not have the exact physical volume of the first, although it should be heightened psychologically at least. There is no need to explain this kind of enunciation in any other way than by noting its natural place in emotional speech. The touch here is exquisite. Other examples of a second metrical stress added by the feeling to a polysyllable may be found in Hopkins, for instance, in *Spelt from Sibyl's Leaves* on *dismembering* (and *disremembering* as well, though Hopkins has not made this explicit with stress marks, probably because the stresses are not juxtaposed):

> . . . . . For earth | her being has unbound, her
>   dapple is at an end, as-
> tray or aswarm, all throughther, in throngs; | self ín
>   self steepèd and páshed—quíte
> Disremembering, dísmémbering | áll now. Heart, you
>   round me right
> With: Óur évening is over us; óur night | whélms, whélms,
>   ánd will end us.

This is again "the current language heightened," and other cases of unusual accent in Hopkins are explainable as being the same sort of thing.

It is plain, then, that sense-stress rhythm, when it utilizes stresses that would ordinarily be only alternating stresses, does not do so without making them in context equivalently sense stresses. Thus in a line such as "Over Goldengrove unleaving," where the stress of the sprung rhythm coincides exactly with the regular alternating stress and hence with a running rhythm, the line is read not as such lines are read in running rhythm with the regular beat in the background, to be got away from as much as possible, but it is read with the stress heavy and prominent. The regularity of beat, which is not intrinsic to the rhythm, is simply explainable as arising from other sources, in the present case perhaps the suggestion of

the senseless back-and-forth motions of a numbing grief and the measured sobs of the little Margaret. This regularity, which would become
monotonous and shortly destroy altogether the feeling of a real sense
stress, is lifted in the next line of the poem.

Rhythm Which Is Feeling's Self

Finally, what has been said of the parts of Hopkins' rhythm may be said
of the whole, of the sweep and the ring that is its very self,

> .   .   .   .   the strong
> Spur, live and lancing like the blowpipe flame, (*Poems* 69)

that gives it life. For in the last analysis, the power driving this "line of
masculine expression" is nothing other than the interpretive stress of the
language assimilated in its full force, allowed its full play. The secret of
this verse is that its rhythm thus bears up under the most emotional declamation. Hopkins' intensity, his dramatic suppression of words, his tele-
scoping of grammatical structure, are possible and are demanded because
with them and in them the interpretive stress mounts in value, and thus
the rhythm grows. In brief, Hopkins' language and structure are what they
are because his rhythm can support the kind of feeling for which such language is a normal vehicle. He is "strange" only to those not used to this
pitch of emotion in verse. His language and structure are genuine, are
commonly found in extrapoetical emotional contexts, and are foreign
only to a "continuous literary decorum" (Bridges in *Poems* 96). They are
"the current language heightened." If they are more than some verse will
stand, because this idiom reaches heights in its stresses and lows in its
slacks that would entirely dismember the poetry of an Edmund Spenser,
they are the concomitants of feeling that provide the movement on which
Hopkins' rhythm thrives. Thus in the *Deutschland* (stanzas 7 and 8):

> The dense and the driven Passion, and frightful sweat;
> Thence the discharge of it, there its swelling to be,
> Though felt before, though in high flood yet—
> What none would have known of it, only the heart, being hard at bay,
>
> Is out with it! Oh,
> We lash with the best or worst
> Word last! How a lush-kept plush-capped sloe
> Will, mouthed to flesh-burst,
> Gush!—flush the man, the being with it, sour or sweet,
> Brim, in a flash, full!   .   .   .   .   .

If the poem calls for shouting, the shouting need not be kept imaginary for fear the beat of the rhythm will go. Shout, declaim, and you will only have thrust this rhythm home. So, too, if the shout should need to die to a whisper, as in Poem No. 71:

> Strike, churl; hurl, cheerless wind, then; heltering hail
> May's beauty massacre and wisped wild clouds grow
> Out on the giant air; tell Summer No,
> Bid joy back, have at the harvest, keep Hope pale.

Or there may be neither whisper nor declaim, but only a light passage in *The Woodlark*, with its bright rhythmic movements integral to entirely other feelings and tones:

> 'The blue wheat-acre is underneath
> And the braided ear breaks out of the sheath,
> The ear in milk, lush the sash,
> And crush-silk poppies aflash,
> The blood-gush blade-gash
> Flame-rash rudred
> Bud shelling or broad-shed
> Tatter-tassel-tangled and dingle-a-dangled
> Dandy-hung dainty head.
>
> .   .   .   .
>
> And down . . . the furrow dry
> Sunspurge and oxeye
> And lace-leaved lovely
> Foam-tuft fumitory
>
> .   .   .   .
>
> Through the velvety wind V-winged
> To the nest's nook I balance and buoy
> With a sweet joy of a sweet joy,
> Sweet, of a sweet, of a sweet joy
> Of a sweet—a sweet—sweet—joy.'

All this is the language of high feeling, and the rhythm. As Professor Malone has remarked of Old English, this is "an instrument subtle and sophisticated enough." And "stress is the life of it." Hopkins, who had a knack for happy expressions, never hit upon a happier. "In sprung rhythm the stress is more *of* a stress." The key to the understanding of the movement of Hopkins' sprung rhythm verse is the recognition that this stress, unlike that of "common rhythm," is not the stress that the mechanics of English make us want to put on every second or third syllable—though it may often coincide with this—but the stress of declaim, the stress of interpretation, the stress that grows from sense and feeling. On this stress the verse lives.

Note.—Since the present study was written, the *Kenyon Review* for the summer of 1944 has appeared with four Hopkins anniversary essays, one of them an interesting study entitled "Sprung Rhythm," by Harold Whitehall. Deriving from the theory that Professor William Ellery Leonard advanced some years ago for Old English and drawing on the work done in ballad measures by George R. Stewart, Jr. (I believe, although the reference, as it is given, is to a "G. B. Stewart"), the article advances the thesis that sprung rhythm is really a system of dipodics, feet conceived of as equivalents of musical 4/4 time.

In Parts 2 and 3 of the present study, I have attempted only to put sprung rhythm in a general rhythmic setting without going into details either in stress scansion or time equivalents. Dr. Whitehall is undoubtedly correct when he says that in treating stress independently of time, English metrics has abstracted too far. Whether Hopkins' time equivalences that I have considered from the point of view of dramatic emphases, can be reduced in whole or in part to "dipodies" is worth consideration. There is evidence for it in Hopkins' discussion of four-beat measures (*Letters* 119-20. Jan. 27, 1881) as well as in the apparent movement of many of his poems, and in his tendencies to binary development to which I have drawn attention.

But there is much evidence against it. It is hard to believe with Dr. Whitehall that sonnets like *Carrion Comfort* are really to be read in lines of four units and that the five-stress reading that Hopkins commonly intended for sonnets not in halved six-stress or eight-stress lines is therefore spurious. Other places, for example, in *St. Winefred's Well* and *The Leaden Echo and the Golden Echo* seem to resist fiercely any Procrustean tailoring. And how are we to get stanzas 29 and 31 and 35 of the *Deutschland* to lie down in the same dipodic bed?

Moreover, if Hopkins' sprung rhythm is always dipodic, the counterpoint in running rhythm must be dipodic, too, for by sprung rhythm Hopkins meant the kind of rhythm found in this counterpoint (*Correspondence* 15. Oct. 6, 1878; *Poems* 5). Can we hear dipodic rhythms over Milton's pentameters listed by Hopkins? Again, how is it that the rhythm of ordinary speech must be dipodic? For it, too, is a sprung rhythm (*Poems* 5). The very fact that Hopkins found sprung rhythm in Old English is at best an equivocal argument for the dipodic theory since it is exceedingly doubtful that Hopkins read Old English poetry in a rhythm not formally proposed for it until well within the twentieth century.

Hopkins' description of the way he wants his verse read (*Letters* 246. Dec. 11, 1886) confirms his awareness of the value of time in rhythm, but does not help in the reduction of all sprung rhythm time to dipodies.

The difficulty, which we must honestly face, is that in the manifold of sound that is speech, there are many patterns. Sometimes a simple one is obviously emphasized. But at other times more subtle patterns exist. Such patterns may tend to dissolve into simple patterns even when this dissolution is not desired or desirable. Piano players know how triplets intended to equal together the time of a quarter note will, if one is not careful, dissolve into an eighth and two sixteenth notes. The Kyrie of the ordinary Gregorian Requiem Mass all too easily slips into the 6/8 time to which a poor performance distorts it. If we hold a frame of fours in our mind, a set of "dipodies," we can find ourselves slipping all sorts of movements into it.

There remains, however, the possibility of some kind of correlation between a dipodic movement, a hypothetical basic time pattern against which normal irregular English speech rhythms have their being, the counterpoint on ordinary English running rhythm, and the peculiar effects of Hopkins' sprung rhythm, including the relation of his stresses to sense and his picturing of reversed feet as part of the real movement of verse (*Poems* 1) . Is what I have called sense-stressing a syncopation of, a kind of compromise with, a basic rhythm represented in another way by alternating stress? These questions, involving the greatest psychological subtleties, are not easy to answer. Further study is still needed.

III. Not Birth, But Resurrection

With the knowledge, then, that Hopkins' sprung rhythm is a rhythm built out of the dramatic or interpretive or sense stresses of the language, a rhythm the units of which are sense stresses each with its belonging slacks, and with the understanding that the "peculiarities" of Hopkins— his lines weighted with alliteration, assonance and other *retentissement*, his tendencies toward antithetical verse movement, his use of rhyme, the very sweep and lancing of his verse, "the roll, the rise, the carol, the creation," even to his variations of meter by "outrides" or "hangers" or by burden lines—with the understanding that all this is not mere ornament here but the stuff that "gathers to a greatness" to form the substance, the organism, the essential machinery and the accomplishment of a delicately adjusted rhythmic mechanism, just as phenomena of the same order had gathered to form the early sense-stress verse of Old English—with this understanding we return to the earlier question, What did Hopkins find? It is not enough to say that he found the kind of basis for rhythm that Old English had used, for this does not give all the credentials of his rhythm. To be understood, Hopkins' discovery must be seen in its relation to conditions in his own time, which themselves are only understandable as the live ends, the wave front, of a long past.

As a matter of fact, the rhythm that Hopkins found has a history in verse that is not restricted to Old English. (Since it is plainly always bound close to English prose, from its history in this medium we prescind.)

Two Rhythms at Once: Counterpoint

Since running rhythm and sprung rhythm are concerned with different elements in the language, there is the interesting chance that they may coexist in one piece of verse. Verse with both rhythms would be such that we could attend now to one rhythm, now to another. Early in his discussions of sprung rhythm Hopkins pointed out instances of the coexistence of the two movements, calling the verse that employs both at once by the fortunate name of "counterpoint" verse. Counterpoint, he says, arises in running rhythm with the reversal of "two feet running, especially so as to include the sensitive second foot" (*Poems* 3; *Correspondence* 15. Oct. 6, 1878). Thus it arises in a line such as

Hóme | tŏ hĭs móthĕr's | hóuse | prívăte | rĕtúrned,

cited by Hopkins from Milton (*Notebooks* 241; *Correspondence* 15. Oct. 6, 1878; *Paradise Regained* iv, 639) (The scansion marks here are mine, but are based on Hopkins'.) Here the variations that the running rhythm allows can be taken as setting up a pattern of their own. Moreover, they are rooted in the sense stress. If such patterns based on this irregularly placed stress existed by themselves, that is, if only the kind of rhythm that is here called the reversed rhythm were heard, we should have sprung rhythm.

In a passage redolent of Hopkins down to details of diction, Bridges notes in *Milton's Prosody* the confusion possible when the two kinds of verse concur. The system of counting only stresses to the neglect of syllabic enumeration

> is a perfectly different system from that which counts the syllables. It seems also the most natural to our language; and I think that the cause of this distinction not being recognized is the fact that stress cannot be excluded from consideration even in verse that depends primarily

on the number of syllables. The two systems are mixed in our tradition. . . . But if once the notion be got rid of that you must have so
many syllables in a line to make a verse, or must account for the
supernumerary ones in some such manner as the Greeks or Latins
would have done, then the stress will declare its supremacy; which, as
may be seen in Shakespeare and Milton, it is burning to do. (72-73)

Hopkins' diction is repeated by Bridges, perhaps unconsciously: Hopkins
had written to Bridges that if earlier poets had known of sprung rhythm,
"they would have used it. Many people, as we say, *have been 'burning,'*
but they all missed it" (*Letters* 156. Oct. 18, 1882, italics mine). Bridges
does not discuss his pure-stress verse here precisely in terms of sense
stress. If he had, it would be plain that the persistent absorption of sense
stress by the alternating stress of English explains the confusion that he
decries: sense-stress verse and alternating-stress verse are always alike
and never quite the same.

Hopkins calls attention to the fact that a second or counterpointed
rhythm can arise in running rhythm but not in sprung (*Letters* 45. Aug.
21, 1877; *Poems* 4). The reason is plain. The sprung-rhythm pattern is
based on the sense stress. But the real or basic running-rhythm pattern,
while not based on the sense stress, always includes it, never runs counter to it. Hence, reversals of stresses and slacks that make a counterpointed rhythm can arise only when a regularly alternating basic pattern is
imported to a given line from the other lines of the poem. The sprung-
rhythm pattern is never fixed enough for this, and such importation can
therefore only be accomplished in a poem the basic rhythm of which is
the running rhythm.

Now all this could be mere drumming at the higher poetical mathematics were not the roots of Hopkins' rhythm struck so deep into the language. As it is, the principle of counterpoint opens English poetry along
its center and from end to end.

Hopkins had no idea how far this was true. By academic profession a
Greek scholar who disclaimed wide reading in English literature
(*Correspondence* 87. Oct. 29, 1881), he knew English poetry only as confined pretty closely to the recognized authors, who, for reasons to be noted
later, were precisely the ones least likely to exhibit strong counterpoint.

Middle-English Survivals of Sense Stress

Sense-stress rhythm did not disappear from English with the advent of the
Normans. This is a well known fact. The first volume of Saintsbury's
History of English Prosody turns on a discussion of the persistence of the
Old English rhythm within the later running rhythm that spread through

English from Medieval Latin, French, and, later, Italian grafts. This persistence is not merely a matter of isolated poems such as *Sir Gawain and the Green Knight*, here and there reverting consciously to the old forms. It enters far deeper into rhythmic perception than that. Hopkins' guess that Chaucer "properly read is heavier stressed than we think" (*Correspondence* 78. Oct. 23-25, 1881) has been substantiated by the conclusions of the late John M. Manly and Edith Rickert, which help relate the movement of Chaucer's verse to the "rough," heavy sense-stress rhythms of Old English. "It is still uncertain," they conclude in the eight-volume collation of the *Canterbury Tales* manuscripts,

> whether Chaucer's versification should always have the regularity assumed for it by the scholars of the late nineteenth century. . . . Current theories of Chaucer's versification are based, not upon the text as found in the MSS or as established by critical processes, but upon an artificial text made regular by all the devices at the disposal of the scholar. (2:40-41)

The line from the Prologue, for instance, which is usually given as

Hath in the Ram his halve cours yronne

should be deprived of the smoothing final *e* so as to read,

Hath in the Ram his half cours yronne, (3:3)

in which one observes a movement remarkably like an Old English line:

Háth | ĭn thĕ̆ Rám | hĭs hálf còurs | y̆rónnĕ̆. |

The alliteration in evidence in this line is too common in Chaucer and, as we shall see, in later poets to be dismissed as coincidence.

Renaissance Survivals

To omit the century following Chaucer's death, when the force of Old English rhythms is heard on every side, in the early sixteenth century Bishop Gavin Douglas' translation of the *Aeneid* overlays the decasyllabic running rhythm, which it seems to follow, with an unmistakable heavy sense-stress pattern, complete with the alliteration, consonantal weighting, and complex echoings of sound that help constitute sense-stress rhythm. If one halves its lines, the verse becomes practically indistinguishable from Old English in rhythm:

Ǎnd áll | ǐn váne | thǔs quhíle Ěněǎs | cárpǐt, |
Ǎne blústěrǎnd | búb| ǒut frǎ thě nórtht | bráyǐng |
Gáne | ǒur thě foírschìp| ǐn thě bák sàil | dýng. |

. . . .

Héich ǎs ǎne híll   thě lǎw ǒf wáttěr brák,
Ánd ǐn ǎne héip   cǒme ón thǎme wǐth ǎne swák.
Sǒme hésǐt hóverǎnd   ǒn thě wállǐs hýcht,
Ǎnd súm thě sǒwnchǎnd sée   sǒ láw gǎrt lýcht,
Thǎme sémǐt thě ěrd óppǐnǐt   ǎmýd thě flúde;
Thě stówr w̌p búllěrǐt   sánd ǎs ǐt were wúid.
(Bk. 1, lines 6-18; Douglas 2:28)

In this same period, Skelton's typical short lines, his "ragged rhymes,"
are largely sense-stress, often again developing the usual alliteration:

Ǐt wǎs sǒ prétty̌ | ǎ fóle |
Ǐt wǒuld sýt | ǒn ǎ stóle |
Ǎnd lérned | ǎftěr my̌ schóle |
Fǒr tǒ képe | hǐs cút, |
Wǐth, Phýllǐp, | kěep yǒur cút. | (1:54, my italics)

It will be seen that these skeltonics, from *Phyllyp Sparrowe*, include a
rhythm like the Old English antithesis, each line here being equivalent to
an Old English half-line. Skelton's *Speke Parrot* is even more markedly
counterpointed with sense stress. The declaim is evident in this heated
diatribe against Wolsey, and the sense-stress pattern has the common tendency to move in fours. Breaking the lines like Old English, we get:

So myche raggyd ryghte   of a rammes horne;
  So rygorous revelyng   in a prelate specially
So bold and so braggyng,   and was so basely born;
  So lordlye of his lokes   and so dysdayneslye;
So fatte a magott,   bred of a flesshe flye;
Was nevyr suche a ffylty gorgon,   nor such an epycure,
Syns Dewcalyons flodde,   I make the faste and sure. (2:24)

The alliteration cannot be missed.

Analysis of the verse of the period of Wyatt and Surrey shows how
firmly the Old English half-line held the language even when a conscious
attempt was made to establish the syllabic count imported from Latin
sources. Thus in a sonnet attributed to Surrey or Vaux, a marked sense-

stress pattern, alliteration and all, overlays the running rhythm; and the lines can easily be broken to bare the sense-stress movement, as in "The Frailtie and Hurtfulness of Beauty":

Bríttlĕ̈ | bĕáutiĕ̈, | thăt nátŭre | măde so fráil,
Whĕreŏf thĕ gíft | ĭs smáll, | ănd short | thĕ sĕasŏn, |
Flowring today,   to morowe apt to faile,
Tickell treasure,   abhorred of reason,
Daungerous to dele with,   vaine, of none auail,
Costly in keping,   past not worthe two peason,
Slipper in sliding   as is an eles taile,
Harde to attaine,   once gotten not geason,
Iewel of ieopardy   that perill dothe assaile,
False and vntrue,   enticed oft to treason,
Enmy to youth: that most may I bewaile.
Ah bitter swete   infecting as the poyson,
Thou farest as fruit   that with the frost is taken:
To day redy ripe,   to morow all to shaken.
(Arber 10, italics mine)

It has been the fashion to dismiss such verse as this as being merely crude and stumbling, on the assumption that Wyatt, Surrey, and others must have been trying to write syllabic-count verse. Since the original draft of this present study, D. W. Harding has ably contested this assumption. He finds that often Wyatt "positively chose the pausing line composed of dissimilar rhythmical units," and Harding believes it an untenable theory that would hold that Wyatt's was only a stumbling performance (99).

There is not this much alliteration in most of Wyatt and Surrey, but there is enough, and enough out-and-out antithetical movement to point to part of the answer to the question that has persistently troubled metrists: What were Wyatt and Surrey trying to do?

Elizabethan Drama, the Great Reservoir

It is not strange that the movement of a rhythm based on the declamatory stress should be most effectively preserved on the Elizabethan stage. For, to say the truth, it is practically impossible for running rhythm to be recognized if blank verse is declaimed as the sense demands. Whatever Elizabethan and Jacobean convention may have been, when the sense is given full play in Shakespeare's blank verse, the rhythm becomes indistinguishable in kind from the rhythm of Shakespeare's high stage prose. The same is true of Fletcher, Webster, and the rest. Hopkins, indeed, mentions a playwright, Greene, as the last to use sprung rhythm consistently, but the other playwrights, with the exception of Shakespeare, he gives little evidence of having read: concerning Marlowe's works, he writes Bridges, "I could flog myself for being so ignorant" (*Letters* 227. Oct. 2, 1886).

To confine illustration, for brevity, to one dramatist, Shakespeare is full to bursting with sense-stress movements, often cued in with alliteration and other sound echoes, even in his early plays. *The Comedy of Errors* yields many passages such as this that can be arranged like Old English by halving the lines:

> And *p*iteous *p*lainings   of the *p*retty babes,
> That mourn'd for *f*ashion,   ignorant what to *f*ear,
> *For*ced me to seek delays   *for* them and me.
> And this it was,   *for* other means was none:
> The *s*ailors *s*ought   *for* safety by our boat.
> (I. i.73-77, italics mine)

But the later plays are even richer in examples, such as:

> Lów-cròokĕd | cúrt'sĭes | ănd báse | spániĕl-făwnĭng,
> (*Julius Caesar* III. i. 43)

or

> Thĕ wéariĕst | ănd mŏst lóathĕd | wórldlў | lĭfe |
> Thăt áge, | áche | pénŭrў, | ănd ĭmprĭsŏnmĕnt |
> Cănn láy | ŏn nátŭre | .   .   .   .
> (*Measure for Measure* III. i. 130-132, italics mine)

In many passages, the running decasyllabic rhythm is almost completely concealed under the sense-stress movement, which is loaded with echoes:

> .   .   .   . Gone already!
> Ínch-thĭck, knée-dèep   ŏ'er hĕad ănd éars ă fórk'd òne!
> Gŏ, pláy, bŏy, pláy: thў móthĕr plăys, ănd Í
> Pláy tóo;   bŭt sŏ dĭsgráced ă părt, whŏse íssŭe
> Wĭll híss mĕ tŏ mў gráve: cŏntémpt ănd clámŏur
> Wĭll bĕ mý knéll.   Gŏ, pláy, bŏy, pláy   .   .   .   .
> (*The Winter's Tale* I. ii. 185-90, italics mine)

Prosodists have frequently called attention to the tendency of modern English decasyllabics to use lines with three or four real stresses (Baum 155; Tillotson 125). Indeed, it seems altogether likely that its ability to take on the sense stress movements inherent in the language since Old English is one of the principal reasons for the success of heroic blank verse. Passages such as these last need not be here multiplied from Shakespeare or the other dramatists, for, especially in the most feeling passages, they are easy enough to find.

In the Dramatic Tradition: Wit Poetry

Now the strange fertility of Elizabethan drama seems largely attributable to the fact that keeping contact with it meant keeping contact with heavily counterpointed verse. The debt that the metaphysical poets, particularly, owe the drama is definitely connected with the survival of sense-stress rhythms. Terence Heywood has observed that

> masculinity and ruggedness were, as we know, a special cult of the metaphysicals. It is probable that Hopkins would not have considered Dryden "the most masculine of our poets" had he known Donne. . . . To me it seems certain, though I know that some still doubt it, that Donne and many of his followers were striving for a natural speech-rhythm in English poetry. (20; cf. Short)

It would perhaps be helpful to emphasize that Donne and his followers, as well as Jonson and his—and from these two fountainheads the stream of wit flows—*had not lost contact* with a natural speech rhythm, that their verse perpetuated the sense-stress design that, without perhaps being fully conscious of the fact, they had inherited from the first poets of the language.

It is certainly more than a coincidence that almost universally the lyrics of the metaphysicals, or, more inclusively, the wit poets, do not meditate but talk. They fall naturally into the tones familiar on the stage, where one character is addressing another. This inspiration is observable in the titles typical of Jonson's lyric pieces: *To Dr. Donne* or *To My Mere English Censurer* or *To My Booke-seller*, which last, for example, begins with the characteristic conversational tone:

> Thou that mak'st gaine thy end, and wisely well
> Call'st a booke good, or bad, as it doth sell,
> Use mine so, too: I give thee leave . . . . . (3)

Sometimes the dialogue is with the audience, as in *Her Triumph* from *A Celebration of Charis in Ten Lyric Pieces*, which opens, "See the chariot at hand here of Love" (91). Even Jonson's epitaphs, like his famous songs such as *To Celia*, preserve stage presence and address.

This same attitude carries over into the poetry of the Sons of Ben. Thus Herrick's *Corinna's Going a-Maying* is spoken directly to Corinna and echoes Jonson's brusque vigor:

> There's not a budding Boy, or Girle, this day,
> But is got up, and gone to bring in May.
> A deale of Youth, ere this, is come
> Báck, ǎnd wi̊th *Whíte-thòrn* ládĕn hóme. (69)

It is evident from the way he turns into his last stanza that Carew's elegy, *Maria Wentworth*, is conceived in his mind as a direct address; the last line slips pretty much from the running rhythm pattern and at the same time turns to echoing:

> Learn from hence, Reader, what small trust
> We owe this world, where virtue must,
> Fráil ǎs oŭr *fl*ésh, crúmblĕ tǒ dúst. (79, italics mine)

So, too, George Herbert writes with a sense of declaim and a quite loose alternating-stress movement even in such a poem as *The Collar*, where meditation sends him not into a reverie but into the heart of a dispute:

> I struck the board and cry'd, "No more!
> I will abroad."
> What, shall I ever sigh and pine?
> My lines and life are free; free as the road
> Loose as the winde, as large as store.
> Shall I be still in suit? (1:175)

And Donne, though neither a dramatist nor a Son of Ben, is almost invariably in his lyric pieces talking to someone, while counterpoint grows unmistakably. *The Computation* ends (I halve the lines):

> Yĕt cǎll nǒt thís lóng lìfe;   Bŭt thínke thǎt Í
> Ǎm, bў bĕing déad, Ĭmmórtǎll;   Cǎn ghósts díe? (1:69)

And in *Love's Alchemy*:

> Sǒme thǎt hǎve déepĕr dígg'd   lóves Mỳne thĕn Í
>
> . . . .
>
> Bút shoŭld Ĭ lŏve, gĕt, téll,   tíll Ĭ wĕre óld. (1:39)

The poetry of wit, with its tone of direct address, is the principal non-dramatic vehicle in which the sense-stress rhythms of the language are carried on. The habit of direct address moves forward to Pope, whom F.R. Leavis has discerningly identified as the last of the line maintaining connections with Jonson or Donne (Leavis 71, 91). Pope does not uniformly use the tone—for instance, in the romantic pieces such as *Eloisa to Abelard* it is missing—but in his better pieces he does: the *Epistle to Dr. Arbuthnot* opens with

> Shut, shut, the door, good John! fatigued I said:
> Tíe ŭp thĕ knóckĕr; săy Í'm síck, Í'm déad. (3:241)

Pope is still able to utilize the variegated speech rhythms of the language for poetical purposes, but in this he stands apart from nearly all his contemporaries.

Spenserian: The Other Tradition

For another line of poets had learned other manners. Within a rhythmic tradition such as that which was carried from Old English into Elizabethan times, it was natural for his contemporaries to single out Spenser as "the new poet." For into the tradition Edmund Spenser hardly fits. Something might be done to introduce him in part into the tradition on the score of "Februarie" and "Maye" in *The Shepheardes Calender*, although this is uncertain, but all the important rhythmic achievements of this poet tend to divert English verse into pure running-rhythm channels with no sense-stress tributaries.

We are so close to the Spenserian tradition even yet that it is difficult to realize the extent of the revolution Spenser effected. His full influence in establishing the eighteenth- and nineteenth-century feeling for a "continuous literary decorum," which so easily associated itself with the quiet throbbing of the smooth alternating-stress verse he perfected, is only beginning to be recognized as comparable to that of his greater disciple Milton, for whom he had everywhere paved the way. Saintsbury was not only making a supposition common in his day, but he was calling attention to a fact when he said that Spenser was the Joshua who brought English prosody into its promised measure and rhyme (1:351). Saintsbury's supposition would find little support now: that Spenser's achievement was inevitably progress is at best a gratuitous assumption. But the importance Saintsbury assigns to Spenser is not exaggerated. To appreciate the revolutionary effect of Spenser's verse, we need only look to the diffidence of Elizabethan prosodists toward the "feet" that become the stock in trade of prosody in the late Spenserian tradition we have known. And to see the extent of his influence long after his death, we can recall that all the poets disapproved of by the eighteenth century, and by the nineteenth following its lead, have uniformly been those who are outside the Spenserian tradition. Generally speaking, to the eighteenth and nineteenth centuries rhythmic crudity was equivalent to non-Spenserian verse movement. It is significant that eighteenth-century prosody outlaws alliteration (Saintsbury 3:541).

It is a simple fact that the smooth Spenserian rhythms cannot stand much sense interpretation or declaim. But no need for declaim was felt by the Augustans. The demand was for a standard currency, a guaranteed emotional tender insured against inflation. Since it provided this, the Spenserian tradition cannot be said to have achieved nothing: it does one of the things that poetry can do. And yet the reduction of all poetry to this sort of thing was bound to be disastrous. This reduction forms one facet of the "dissociation of sensibility" that T. S. Eliot has described (247) and that took place when Spenser's influence was in the ascendency. Here, indeed, the language was developed (along a simple enough line), but the feeling became more and more vulgarized as it became more and more standard, less responsive to its object, for no matter what their object, all vehicles had to follow the same road, not because it reached the destination, but because it was smooth. Of course, this road runs out in album verse and poetry as a "polite accomplishment." Moreover, this is the road that leads verse off the English stage: as verse in general loses ability to declaim, the age of prose drama is ushered in.

It is difficult not to believe that the taste for smoothness that remained an accepted touchstone of good English poetry from Dryden's day, when Mr. Waller had only lately improved our numbers, till some time around the turn of the present century, is intimately associated with the whole intellectual milieu of this period. In this bright and shining world of a successful Newtonian physics, a Cartesian mathematical solvent for all reality, and a naive materialism, there is something that inevitably gave body to a "continuous literary decorum." Like the decimal measurement systems, Spenserian smoothness represented great achievement to the enlightened mind.

The effects of Spenser's canonization persist on all sides in Hopkins' age. They appear in the fact, already mentioned above, that Hopkins, reading the English poetry ordinarily read in his day, never came across the greater bulk of the poetry that would have interested him most, as the natural antecedent of his own. They are manifest in Saintsbury, who, proclaiming in his *History of English Prosody*, "It is the 'Progress of Prosody' that the present writer, not being able to 'sing,' is ambitious to 'say'" (2:26), considers it a foregone conclusion that in the march of progress, Spenser is the Joshua. The same tradition accounts for the judgments of a Sir Sidney Lee in the *Dictionary of National Biography*. Without a glance aside at Gavin Douglas or Skelton, Sir Sidney hits with predictable accuracy on Sackville's *Induction* as the greatest poem between Chaucer and Spenser. It "has no rival" (18:586). The reason is not hard to find: it is almost the only thing like Spenser until Spenser himself.

Other evidence is available in the development of the lyric. In the Spenserian tradition, the lyric of Jonson and Donne, which had built on the strength of declamatory stress a strong idiom of counterpoint now regarded as making the verse too rough, had been discarded in favor of the staid and sober ruminations of Akenside and the Wartons. The tone of direct dialogue is replaced at best by bursts of apostrophe before an audience either unconscious or absent. It is here rather than in the twentieth century that poetry begins talking to itself. And this tradition was in possession when Hopkins put in his appearance. How thoroughly it had proscribed an oratorical delivery by its exclusive exploitation of running rhythm is evident in any representative poem, such as Shenstone's *The School-Mistress*:

> Ah me! full sorely is my heart forlorn,
> To think how modest worth neglected lies;
> While partial fame doth with her blasts adorn
> Such deeds alone, as pride and pomp disguise;
> Deeds of ill sort, and mischievous emprise!
> Lend me thy clarion, goddess! let me try
> To sound the praise of merit, ere it dies;
> Such as I oft have chaunced to espy,
> Lost in the dreary shade's of dull obscurity. (2:333)

Any tendency to develop a pattern built on sense-stress here is entirely masked by the steady drone of the Spenserian meditative machinery. Indeed, the only sense or feeling that can exist here is that capable of moving with the special motion of this verse. Earlier verse had not all known such a restriction: this movement was only a phase in the varied rhythms found in the dramatists, even in their lyrics. But in the eighteenth and nineteenth centuries it pretty well held the field all the way from light lyric pieces to Thomson's staid heroics. It is little wonder that the mind that restricted poetry to this sort of thing should be disgusted with Donne and embarrassed to discover in itself a liking for Shakespeare.

Hopkins' Discovery

In this picture of the poetic heritage of Hopkins' world lies the answer to the question, What did Hopkins find? Hopkins found a tradition in English poetry that was older and stronger than the one in possession in his day. He found a rhythmic tradition that could cut under and around the "running" or "common" rhythm of the nineteenth century, not because his new rhythm was the ancient rhythm of English—this would be a fact of no value in itself—but because it was a rhythm still inherent in the language and only suppressed by an artificially sustained tradition. It is indeed strange that between the period when we find Shakespeare's "cabined, cribb'd, confined" and

> If it were done, when 'tis done, then 'twere well
> It were done quickly, ...

and the later period that finally brought Hopkins' "hearts' charity's hearth's fire" or "And the sea flint-flake, black-backed in the regular blow," there is almost nothing to compare with these passages. The place in poetry where such things fit was kept tightly locked. Certainly such expressions were not entirely foreign to speech—though they may have been more foreign to it than we suspect—but the kind of poetic rhythm in favor left them no room. Hopkins opened a place for them.

In opening this place, Hopkins' achievement was not quite alone. After the dramatists and the wit poets, there had remained tendencies to maintain in English poetry the strength of the sense-stress rhythms. (We must remind ourselves continually that these are not *entirely* unlike those of the "smooth" or "reformed" numbers of running rhythm, and hence only rarely will verse be free of at least equivocal instances of them.) There was the case of Milton, who as a young man had, in *Comus*, trafficked in the livening rhythms of the stage, but who—as he himself later acknowledged, telling Dryden that Spenser was his "original"—had turned away to the rhythms of the non-dramatic tradition. With, however, a scholarly sophistication unknown to Spenser, he had overlaid the Spenserian numbers with a heavy counterpoint and had finally in his *Samson* choruses gone so far as to sacrifice almost completely the rhythm of the alternating stress. But life was gone: under the spell of the epic theory, Milton had fallen upon a coagulating poetic idiom that passed stiff and unyielding to the hands of his successors. Nevertheless, Milton being an approved author, his work came to Hopkins' attention.

The eighteenth century, after Pope, had been pretty destitute of sense-stress rhythms, but latterly there had come Burns, cultivating the habit of direct address, and the sense-stress counterpoint revives once more with the life of the declamatory verse. Burns' strength, which lies in his satirical pieces, is apparent in *To a Louse*:

> Ha! whare ye gaun, ye crowlin' ferlie!
>
> . . . .
>
> My sooth! right bauld ye set your nose out,
> As plump and gray as onie grozet;
> O for some rank, mercurial rozet,
> Or fell, red, smeddum. (74)

With its three successive stresses tempting the rhythm far from an alternating stress, the last line here is as much a surprise as the first.

Burns is followed by Blake, with his "rhymeless pindarics" and *The Fairy,* which is in genuine skeltonics:

> Sŏ ă Fáirў súng.
> Frŏm thĕ léaves Ĭ sprúng;
> Hĕ léap'd frŏm thĕ spráy
> Tŏ flée ăwáy;
> Bŭt ĭn mў hát cáught,
> Hĕ sóon shăll bĕ táught. (122)

And there was Southey's *Thalaba* and Shelley's *Queen Mab*, done in what was much later to be called free verse, as well as other pieces like those noted by Hopkins, or like Shelley's *A Dirge* ("Rough wind that moanest loud") interesting for a tendency toward juxtaposed stresses. There are stirrings, too, of a new life in Byron, a defender and imitator of Pope. And the Keats of the mature odes picks up a kind of counterpoint verse unknown since the Elizabethans. Lines in the *Ode on Melancholy* can be divided to expose the Old English antiphonal pattern:

> Nó, nŏ, gŏ nŏt tŏ Léthĕ,   néithĕr twíst
> Wólf's-bàne, tíght-ròoted,   fŏr ĭts póisŏnŏus wíne;

or

> Ănd féed dèep, déep   ŭpŏn hĕr péerlĕss éyes.
> (3:184, italics mine)

In the *Ode on a Grecian Urn* there is this heavy counterpoint:

"Béautў̆ is trúth, trŭ̈th béautў̆," thä̆t is áll
Ye know on earth, and all ye need to know. (3:157)

The whole nineteenth century witnessed a general movement toward this "rougher" verse, a movement that culminated perhaps in Browning, where a revival of counterpoint brings in again sound echoes. Certain lines in *The Ring and the Book*, for example—there are plenty of others— might be halved as four-stress lines:

> *Flúng* with ä̆ *flóurish!*　　　Bŭ̈t rĕ̈pén̆tăn̆ce, tóo.
> Bŭ̈t púre ä̆nd *símplĕ̈*　　　*sórrŏ̈w* fŏ̈r láw's brèach
> Rather than blunderer's-ineptitude?
> Cardinal, no!　　Abate, scarcely thus!
> 'Tï̆s thĕ̈ *fáult*, nót　　thä̆t Ĭ dáred trỳ ä̆ *fáll*
> With Law and straightway am found undermost.
> But that I failed to see, above man's law,
> God's precept you, the Christian, recognize?
>
> *Ćollў̆ mў̆ ców!*　　Dŏ̈n't fídgĕ̈t, Cárdin̆ä̆l!
> (XI, "Guido"; 577)

Apart from the lines divided here, the verse, as is usual with Browning, is not smooth. Had Browning's idiom been more genuine, less pretentiously offhand, its gawkiness less "flung with a flourish," his achievement might have partaken of Hopkins'. As it is, Hopkins says discerningly of Browning's verse, "I greatly admire the touches and the details, but the general effect, the whole, offends me, I think it repulsive" (*Letters* 137. Sept. 17, 1881), and he has little patience with "the scarecrow misbegotten Browning crew" (*Letters* 111. Oct. 26, 1880).

Songs, Saws, Nursery Rhymes, Other Special Survivals

While these developments were taking place, sense-stress rhythms had persisted here and there in out-of-the-way places where the tradition of smoothness in verse was not enforced: in songs, including the ballad, where because the verse was subordinated to music great regularity had never been demanded (musical measure has always been able to salve errancy in syllabic count); and in weather saws and nursery rhymes for which no one had bothered to construct metric containers. But there were other odd places, for wherever departure was made from the usual running rhythm, the sense-stress pattern had a chance to assert itself. The various attempts to reproduce Latin or Greek quantitative meter in

English seem to fall back in reality on a sense-stress rhythm. George Canning pays unconscious tribute to the methods of sense-stress verse when his lampooning attack on Southey's experiments in quantitative meter slips into alliteration and a movement not unlike Old English four-stress verse:

> *N*eedy *Kn*ife-grinder!   *wh*ither are you going?
> *R*ough is the *r*oad, your *wh*eel is *ou*t of *o*rder—
> *Bl*eak *bl*ows the *bl*ast; your *h*at has got a *h*ole in't,
>   So *h*ave your *br*eeches. (20, italics mine)

The same tendency to support with characteristic sense-stress devices the irregularity of pattern that these "classical meters" attempt is found in Tennyson's *Ode to Milton* done in "alcaics":

> O *m*ighty *m*outh'd inventor of harmonics,
> O *s*killed to *s*ing of *T*ime or E*t*ernity. (267, italics mine)

The same thing had been observable in the "classical meter" of the Renaissance, as in Richard Stanyhurst's *A Prayer to the Trinity*:

> *B*lessed I iudge *h*im that in *h*ert is *h*ealed,
> Cursed I know *h*im, that in *h*elth is *h*armed (133)

But here one notes a more marked tendency to reproduce the Old English four-stress line so noticeable elsewhere in the poetry of Stanyhurst's contemporaries.

In turning from the verse of the simple alternating stress, the nineteenth-century writers were all in one way or another falling back on the sense-stress patterning that is so much the bone and sinew of English rhythm. Evidence of the revival of the pattern is often in individual instances equivocal, but the evidence in the whole body of English verse toward the end of the nineteenth century as against the middle of the eighteenth is unmistakable. Moreover, there are such signs as the alliteration to be found here and there. This is probably for the most part entirely unconscious, it is not uniform throughout the poems, and yet it comes in quite too persistently to be accidental. It is the old functional alliteration asserting itself again, as it had asserted itself in Old English and was to assert itself in Hopkins' sprung rhythm. It is the alliteration that poets fall back on as a natural help to heighten stress for sustaining a rhythm not built on a regularly pulsing beat.

After Hopkins

But the current of the tradition in which the gaunt and lovable figure of Hopkins stands even managed to flow around him and move ahead before he was discovered in midstream. For with the "free verse" that appeared some decades following his death but before the publication of the *Poems*, sense-stress rhythm was pretty thoroughly revived. It is difficult indeed to see anything else in the movement of this verse, which it used to be the fashion to call "strophic." Certainly the rhythm is looser than is usual with Hopkins, and perhaps than is usual with Old English, but in the absence of a regular alternating-stress beat, the sense stress remains as the core to which the movements of the verse are attached. Bridges' remarks are again in place here:

> Immediately English verse is written free from a numeration of syllables, it falls back on the number of stresses as its determining law: that is its governing power, and constitutes its form. (*Milton's* 72-73)

Thus in the typical free verse of H. D.'s *Pear Tree*, the lines are loosely organized Old English half-lines:

> Sílvĕr dúst
> líftĕd frŏm thĕ́ éarth,
> híghĕr thăn mў̆ árms rèach,
> yóu hăve móunted.
> Ó sílvĕr,
> híghĕr thăn mў̆ árms rèach
> yŏu frónt ŭs wĭth gréat màss;
> nŏ flówĕr ĕvĕr ópĕned
> sŏ stáunch ă whíte lèaf,
> nŏ flówĕr ĕvĕr pă̆rtĕd sílvĕr
> frŏm sŭch ráre sílvĕr!
> Ŏ whíte péar,
> yŏur flówĕr-túfts,
> thíck ŏn thĕ́ bránch,
> brĭng súmmĕr ă̆nd rípe frùits
> ĭn thĕir púrplĕ héarts. (84-85)

The pattern here is somewhat flexible; the next-to-last line, for example, might perhaps be read with more stresses. But despite such possible variations, a two-stress pattern survives. Again, in Ezra Pound's *Dance Figure* we find the same movement:

Ĭ hăve nŏt fóund thĕe ĭn thĕ ténts,
Ĭn thĕ brókĕn dárknĕss.
Ĭ hăve nŏt fóund thĕe ăt thĕ wéll-hèad
Ămŏng thĕ wómĕn wĭth pítchĕrs. (73)

These are instances of free verse done in a plain two-stress design, which is extremely common and at the same time exhibits sense-stress patterning more clearly than the complex forms. The latter are too varied for separate treatment here.

T. S. Eliot's *Murder in the Cathedral* asserts once more the claims of structural alliteration (I break the lines to show the tendency to an Old English four-stress pattern):

THOMAS

Nó! Shăll Í   who *kéep* thĕ *kéys*
Ŏf *héaven* ănd *héll*,   sŭpréme ălŏne ĭn Éngland,
Whŏ bínd ănd lóose,   with *pówer* frŏm thĕ *Pópe*,
Dĕscénd tŏ *désíre*   ă *púniĕr pówĕr*?
Délĕgăte tŏ *déal*   thĕ *dóom* ŏf *dămnátiŏn*,
Tŏ cŏndémn kíngs,   nŏt *sérve* ămŏng théir *sérvănts*
Ĭs mў ópĕn óffĭce.   Nó!   Gó

TEMPTER

Thĕn Ĭ léave yóu   tŏ yŏur fáte.
Yŏur *sín* sóars *sún*wărd   cóvĕrĭng *kíngs*' fálcŏns.
(30, italics mine)

Before this, the direct influence of Old English could of course be felt in Ezra Pound's near-literal translation of *The Seafarer* and elsewhere.

IV. The Ambit of Hopkins' Achievement

Hopkins, then, had found the tradition of a sense-stress rhythm, which we may also call the declamatory rhythm or the interpretive rhythm of English—a rhythm inherited from Old English as one of the bases of verse until the "reform" and "smoothing" of English numbers, principally under the influence of Edmund Spenser and his followers. Basically, this sense-stress rhythm is a rhythm that grows not from the tendency of English to stress every second or third syllable (whether sense demands this stress or not), but from the tendency of each sense-stress especially in emotional utterance, to constitute itself a kind of rhythmic unit, either alone or together with a varying number of slack syllables that may pre-

alone or together with a varying number of slack syllables that may precede and/or follow it. These rhythmic units can be of more or less equal weight while retaining great variety of movement—falling, rocking, or rising—and various lengths.

Perpetuated largely in the playwrights and in the line of wit poets, who preserved the tone of direct address in their verse and with this the preeminence of sense stress associated with stage delivery, this sense-stress rhythmic tradition persisted quite noticeably as a secondary or "counterpointed" rhythm until Pope, and was, indeed, never quite eliminated even at the height of the Spenserian influence during the eighteenth and nineteenth centuries. During these lean years, sense-stress rhythm survived after a fashion in out-of-the-way places such as songs and popular saws and nursery rhymes (more genuinely, it seems, in the songs than in the saws or rhymes—but this would take long to show). Hopkins notes it in these places. It also persisted in a way in various metrical experiments. Always different from and always somewhat like the "running" or "common" rhythm of English, this sense-stress rhythm is ready at all times to assert itself in English verse, especially when syllabic count is neglected. In Hopkins' day it was reviving to some extent in places other than his own verse.

The rhythm had existed all the time in prose, in the rhythms of speech where the restraint of reformed numbers was not felt. Hopkins himself finally came to understand this. Even before he did, he realized the hold of the rhythm on the language ("I do not claim to have invented *sprung rhythms* but *sprung rhythm*," he tells Bridges, *Letters* 45. Aug. 21, 1877), but the reading menu that his age prescribed kept Hopkins from ever knowing how much the forces back of sprung rhythm had normally made themselves felt in English verse.

This limitation of his knowledge did not stop accomplishment, for Hopkins' rhythmic achievement was primarily the work not of theory but of an extremely keen ear aided by a singularly open and objective mind, and it was made possible by the unusually true and consistent sensibility reflected in Hopkins' understanding that "a perfect style must be of its age" (*Correspondence* 99. Dec. 1, 1881-Dec. 16, 1881).

Hopkins' achievement in reviving sense-stress rhythms is largely traceable to this understanding. On the strength of it, he turned in his poetry to language that is the normal tender for emotion, a currency heavy with the Anglo-Saxon small change of the English tongue. Hopkins' preference for the short word is apparent in every line of his verse.

General neglect of the longer Latin derivatives is indeed not essential to sense-stress rhythm. "Free verse" has never been remarkable for

Anglo-Saxon preferences, and its rhythm is no less sense-stress because the stresses consequently occur at a greater distance from one another than is usual in Hopkins, who is able to say of his own sprung rhythm verse that it uses more than three successive slacks only "for particular rhythmic effects" (*Correspondence* 40. Jan. 14, 1881). Moreover, an Anglo-Saxon vocabulary is, conversely, quite consonant with the smooth rhythms of Gray's *Elegy*, which in many stanzas can be convicted of no more Latinity than Hopkins' *That Nature Is a Heraclitean Fire*.

And yet, beyond the shadow of a doubt, Hopkins' diction does make the characteristic movements of his verse more unmistakable. By and large, the number of sense stresses in English decreases as words become longer, since each word, no matter how long, ordinarily is ready to receive no more than one sense stress. Filled with short words, and thus adaptable to a high proportion of sense stresses, Hopkins' verse moves so as to underline heavily the principles on which it is based. Stresses are packed close together to form a kind of condenser that gives each stress a higher charge than other diction might do. This is eminently stress verse. And it is stress verse all the more because of Hopkins' revivification of the alliteration and other sound echoes that make the verse of high stress live. Hopkins succeeded in reaching to the very "inscape" of his medium. His achievement is its "clearest-selved spark."

The focal point in Hopkins' own view of his work is his recognition of the occasional co-existence of two patterns in English verse, a phenomenon that he calls "counterpoint." For this is implicit recognition of the fact that since two distinct rhythms can be attended to, the one rhythm that, isolated, is sprung rhythm, is based on a different thing in the language than is running rhythm—not entirely different, but different enough.

Hopkins' rhythm will be understood only when this fact is appreciated. It will not be understood by being explained in terms explicitly or implicitly those of a rhythm that depends on components of language on which it itself does not depend. It will certainly not be understood by being explained merely in terms of the "feet" that, borrowed in an unfortunate hour from classical prosody, have generally trod under any adequate understanding even of English running rhythm.

Hopkins himself has been charged with such short-sighted comment. Dr. Richards speaks of his explanation of sprung rhythm as a "curious way . . . of eluding a mischievous tradition and a spurious question, to give them a mock observance and an equally unreal answer" (203). But it is a serious mistake to judge the terms in which Hopkins explains his sprung rhythm apart from his own discussion of them in his lecture notes, a discussion that inoculates his whole terminology with a distinction and subtlety sufficient to immunize it against the usual suppositions of the "tradition." The more valid criticism of Hopkins' explanation is not that it is unreal, but that it is undeveloped; the consistency of its manifold implications is not made clear.

It is this consistency that the present study has attempted to point out and explain in connection with Hopkins' verse itself.

Neither will Hopkins' sprung rhythm be understood by concentrating attention on his "atrocious rhymes," or his "over-reaving" or his other "peculiarities" without regarding his rhythm as a whole. This is Bridges' mistake, and it ends only in bickering. For the apparent incidentals of Hopkins' echoings, stretched lines (outrides and burden lines), neglect of perfect end-rhyme, and "over-rove" lines are all part of the rhythm Hopkins employs, and at least in germ are likely to be associated with this rhythm in other poets.

Rhythmic integrity makes for great complexity, and hence Hopkins' "sprung rhythm" will be understood first by being heard. Explanation had better wait on love. If it does, the reader will be more than receptive, for he will know that, however great Hopkins' rhythmic achievements, he has others to his credit, too.

Works Cited

"A Guide to Pronunciation." *Webster's Collegiate Dictionary*. 5th ed. Springfield, MA: G. and C. Merriam, 1938.

Baum, Paul F. "The Character of Anglo-Saxon Verse." *Modern Philology*, 28 (1930-31): 143-56.

Blake, William. *The Poetical Works of William Blake*. Ed. John Sampson. London: Oxford UP, 1914.

Bonn, John L. "Greco-Roman Verse Theory and Gerard Manley Hopkins." *Immortal Diamond: Studies in Gerard Manley Hopkins*. Ed. Norman Weyand. New York: Sheed and Ward, 1949. 73-92.

Bradley, Sculley. "The Fundamental Metrical Principle in Whitman's Poetry." *American Literature*, 10 (1938-1939): 437-59.

Bridges, Robert. *Milton's Prosody*. Oxford: Henry Frowde 1901. [In the same volume with *Classical Meters in English Verse* by William Johnson Stone].

—. "Notes to Poems." *Poems of Gerard Manley Hopkins*. Ed. with Notes Robert Bridges. 2nd ed. London: Oxford UP, 1930.

Browning, Robert. *The Complete Poetic and Dramatic Works of Robert Browning*. Boston: Houghton Mifflin, 1895.

Burns, Robert. *The Complete Works of Robert Burns*. Ed. Alexander Smith. New York: Thomas Y. Crowell. [no date].

Canning, George. "*Sapphics*: The Friend of Humanity and the Knife-Grinder." *Poetry of the Anti-Jacobin*. With notes by Charles Edmonds. London: G. Willis, 1854.

Carew, Thomas. *Poems of Thomas Carew*. Ed. Arthur Vincent. London: George Routledge and Sons [no date].

Coleridge, Samuel Taylor. *The Poetical Works of Samuel Taylor Coleridge*. Ed. James Dykes Campbell. London: Macmillan, 1914.

Cook, Albert Stanburrough, ed. *The Old English Elene, Phoenix, and Physiologus*. New Haven: Yale UP, 1919.

Donne, John. *The Poems of John Donne*. Ed. Herbert J. C. Grierson. Oxford: Clarendon P, 1912-1915.

Douglas, Gavin. *The First Buik Eneados*, 6-18, in *The Poetical Works of Gavin Douglas, Bishop of Dunkeld*. Ed. John Small. Edinburgh: William Paterson, 1874.

D[oolittle], H[ilda]. "Pear Tree." *A Book of Poems for Every Mood*. Ed. Harriet Monroe and Morton Dauwen Zabel. Racine, WI: Whitman Publishing, 1933.

Eliot, T. S. *Murder in the Cathedral*. New York: Harcourt, Brace, 1935.

—. "The Metaphysical Poets." *Selected Essays, 1917-1932*. New York: Harcourt, Brace, 1932.

Flom, George T. *Introductory Old English Grammar and Reader*. 2d ed. Boston: D. C. Heath, 1930.

Gardner, W. H. *"The Wreck of the Deutschland," Essays and Studies*. (English Association 21, collected by Herbert Read). Oxford: Clarendon P, 1936.

Gray, Thomas. *The Poetical Works of Gray and Collins*. Ed. Austin Lane Poole. London: Oxford UP, 1917.

Harding, D. W. "The Rhythmical Intention in Wyatt's Poetry." *Scrutiny*, 14 (1946): 90-102.

Herbert, George. *The Complete Works of George Herbert*. Ed. Alexander B. Grosart. London: private printing, 1874. ("The Fuller Worthies' Library").

Herrick, Robert. *The Poetical Works of Robert Herrick*. Ed. F. W. Moorman. Oxford: Clarendon P, 1915.

Heywood, Terence. "Gerard Manley Hopkins: His Literary Ancestry." *English* 3 (Spring, 1940): 16-24.

Hopkins, Gerard Manley. *The Correspondence of Gerard Manley Hopkins and Richard Watson Dixon*. Ed. Claude Colleer Abbott. London: Oxford UP, 1935.

—. *Further Letters of Gerard Manley Hopkins*. Ed. Claude Colleer Abbott. London: Oxford UP, 1938.

—. *The Letters of Gerard Manley Hopkins to Robert Bridges*. Ed. Claude Colleer Abbott. London: Oxford UP, 1935.

—. *Notebooks and Papers of Gerard Manley Hopkins*. Ed. Humphry House. London: Oxford UP, 1937.

—. *Poems of Gerard Manley Hopkins*. Ed. with Notes Robert Bridges. 2nd ed. London: Oxford UP, 1930.

Jonson, Ben. *The Poems of Ben Jonson.* Ed. Bernard H. Newdigate. Oxford: Shakespeare Head P, 1936.

Keats, John. *The Poetical Works and Other Writings of John Keats.* Ed. H. Buxton Forman and Maurice Buxton Forman. New York: Charles Scribner's Sons, 1938.

Krapp, George Philip and Elliot van Kirk Dobbie, eds. "Seafarer." *The Exeter Book.* New York: Columbia UP, 1936. ("Anglo-Saxon Poetic Records," 3).

Krapp, George Philip, ed. *Genesis,* in *The Junius Manuscript.* New York: Columbia UP, 1931. ("Anglo-Saxon Poetic Records," 1).

Lanz, Henry. *The Physical Basis of Rhyme.* Stanford CA: Stanford UP, 1931.

Leavis, F. R. *Revaluation.* London: Chatto and Windus, 1936.

Lee, Sidney. *Dictionary of National Biography.* Ed. Leslie Stephen and Sidney Lee. London: Oxford UP, 1921-1922.

Malone, Kemp. "Lift-Patterns in Old English Verse." *English Literary History* 8 (1941): 74-80.

Manly, John M. and Edith Rickert. *The Text of the Canterbury Tales.* Chicago: U of Chicago P, 1940.

Pope, Alexander. *The Works of Alexander Pope.* Ed. Whitwell Elwin and William John Courthope. London: John Murray, 1871-1889.

Pound, Ezra. *Selected Poems.* Ed. T. S. Eliot. London: Faber and Faber, 1934.

Richards, I. A. "Gerard Hopkins." *Dial* 81 (Sept., 1926): 195-203.

Saintsbury, George. *A History of English Prosody: From the Twelfth Century to the Present Day.* 2nd ed. London: Macmillan, 1923.

—. *A History of English Prosody.* 3 vols. London: Macmillan., 1906-1910.

Schipper, Jacob. *A History of English Versification.* Oxford: Clarendon P, 1910.

Shakespeare, William. *The Complete Works of William Shakespeare.* Ed. Sidney Lee et al. Cambridge, UK: Cambridge UP, 1907.

Shenstone, William. *The Works in Verse and Prose of William Shenstone, Esq.* London: R. and J. Dodsley, 1764.

Short, R. W. "The Metrical Theory and Practice of Thomas Campion." *PMLA* 59 (1944): 1003-1018.

Skelton, John. *The Poetical Works of John Skelton.* Ed. Alexander Dyce. London: Thomas Rodd, 1843.

Spenser, Edmund. "The Fairie Queene." *The Complete Poetical Works of Edmund Spenser.* Boston: Houghton Mifflin, 1908.

Stanyhurst, Richard. "A Prayer to the Trinity." *Translation of the First Four Books of the Aeneis of P. Virgilius Maro: With Other Poetical Devices Thereto Annexed* [1582]. Ed. Edward Arber. London: 1880. ("The English Scholar's Library of Old and Modern Works," No. 10).

Surrey [?]. "The Frailtie and Hurtfulnes of Beauty." *Songes and Sonnettes (Tottel's Miscellany).* Ed. Edward Arber. London: 1870.

Tennyson, Alfred, Lord. *The Poetic and Dramatic Works of Alfred, Lord Tennyson.* Boston: Houghton Mifflin, 1898.

Tillotson, Geoffrey. *On the Poetry of Pope.* Oxford: The Clarendon Press, 1938.

Whitehall, Harold. "Sprung Rhythm." *Kenyon Review* 6 (1944): 333-54.

4

The Province of Rhetoric and Poetic
(1942)

The literature of all ages is inextricably wound up with rhetorical and poetical theory. This is true even of a time like the present, when rhetorical theory often proceeds by a kind of negation of formal rhetoric. The conscious avoidance of certain devices not only is impossible without the substitution of others, but is itself based on a theory. We can avoid certain techniques, but not technique. Though we may have cultivated a horror of naming our tools, which earlier artists did not know, we still retain some knowledge of how to use them. Hence rhetoric and poetic remain with us.

But rhetorical and poetical theory has most often failed to find the location of the boundaries within which each of these two arts operate. Current studies in literary history have not placed the lines of demarcation any more accurately (Baldwin, *Ancient, Medieval, Renaissance*; Clark; Crane 253-76). Although the literary historian's distinctions between rhetoric and poetic have been more or less sufficient for his immediate purposes, there is still need to settle more definitely how a poetical work differs from a rhetorical one. The investigation of this question falls rather to the lot of the philosopher than to that of the literary historian, and hence the present discussion will be properly philosophical.

I

Those things in the world that are made by man, being artifacts and not as such possessed of any substantial forms of their own, are differentiated from one another in a variety of ways: in terms of a variety of accidents that they possess, as when I speak of square artifacts, or black artifacts; in terms of the material, that is to say, the second matter in which they have their being, as when I speak of works of stone or works of iron; and finally in terms of their final causality—and this is the way in which we most generally speak of them—as when I speak of a table or of a gun or of a fountain pen.

175

Differentiation of the works of man in terms of final causality will proceed according to the more or less perfect participation of these works in this principle. (Final causality, form, accident, etc., are of course to be taken analogously when we are referring to artifacts.) Thus we have the division into works of non-servile or fine arts and works of servile arts. The former are more perfect in the order of final causality in that they are ordered directly to the speculative intellect, to man's enjoyment as things of beauty, and are therefore destined only indirectly for other use, although their contemplation is of course governed by prudence.

Over against these works of fine arts, we have the works of those arts such as the machinist's or the paint manufacturer's art, which works are not directly for contemplation but means to further ends.

Rhetoric Ordered to Action

Within this division of works of art in terms of final causality the division between works of rhetoric and works of poetic falls. There is no need to quibble over words. Rhetoric has some unpleasant meanings that interfere, but the meaning that is here attached to rhetoric is a traditional and accepted one. All that is asked is that the reader look to what is meant here by rhetoric—call it what you will. For, if we take rhetoric to signify what Aristotle took it to signify—"the ability to find the available means of persuasion with reference to any subject whatsoever" (*Rhetoric* i. 2. 1. 1355b)—works of rhetoric must be ordered to the production of action in another individual and to action in the sense of something other than contemplation. Works of rhetoric have their finality, then, only in terms of that action to which they are ultimately directed. There is another art, that we call poetic, which produces works ordered to contemplation and to no other direct end, that is, works of beauty. Such works are produced simply to be enjoyed by the one contemplating them.

It is to be noted that this rhetoric and this poetic are logical arts directive of the acts of the intellect itself. It is true that there is what we may call a general poetic, an inclusive order of those arts directed to the production of works for contemplation, which has a kind of unity derived from the community of end realized in such works. This order of arts, or general poetic, breaks down into poetic in the ordinary sense, sculpture, music, painting, and so on.

To this general poetic there corresponds another order of arts that we may call a general rhetoric and that includes those arts that may produce action in others not only by intellectual persuasion but by means other than the significative use of words. The sales agent who installs fluorescent lighting to put his customers at ease and thus indirectly persuade them to buy an automobile is practicing this general rhetoric.

However, the rhetoric and poetic that govern the formal use of words (as significative sounds) are both individual arts. They are logical arts, for each is not only a *habitus* of the intellect (all arts are this), but a *habitus* directive of the operations of the intellect itself. And yet they are not of the same species of logic as that according to which science (*scientia*) proceeds; for the connections in the logic of rhetoric and of poetic are not the necessary connections that exist in the logic of demonstration.

It will help to schematize a text from St. Thomas Aquinas (*in I Anal. Post.*, Lect. 1; see Figure 1).

There are many points of difference among these arts that a scheme such as the one given here does not bring out. See, for example, Averroes (65a): "*Ars quidam Rhetoricae affinis est artis Topicae: quoniam ambae*

Ars logica directs the acts of the intellect itself (*actus rationis*).
Ars logica is diversified as are *actus rationis*:

	Treated by Aristotle in:
I. *Intelligentia indivisibilium*	*Praedicamenta (Catgoriae)*
II. *Compositio vel divisio*	*Perihermenias*
III. *Discursus*	Other logical treatises as follows:

Art, like nature, acts in three ways, and the third act of the intellect has therefore a three-fold diversity, with corresponding arts:

A. *De necessitate (cum certitudine)*	*ars logica judicativa*	*ex forma syllogismi:* *Analytica Priora* *cum forma ex materia syllogismi: Analytica Posteriora*
B. *Frequentius*	*ars logica inventiva*	
1. *In pluribus*		
a. *Cum probabilitate*	*dialectica*	*Topica (Dialectica)*
b. *Cum suspicione*	*rhetorica*	*Rhetorica*
c. *Cum existimatione*	*poetica*	*Poetica*
2. *In paucioribus*	*sophistica*	*De Sophisticis Elenchis*

Figure 1

unum finem intendunt, qui est eloqui cum alio, et quo neutra istarum artium homo secum ipse utitur, sicut est Dispositio artis Demonstrationis: sed utitur eis cum alio." [That particular art of Rhetoric is related to the arts of the Topics, since both seek the same goal, which is to speak eloquently with another; in so doing, a person uses neither of these arts for himself, as disposition is of the art of demonstration, but instead uses them with another.] In Figure 1 the connection between the members of the syllogism in *logica judicativa* (or *demonstrativa*) is a necessary one. As we proceed downwards in Figure 1, the connections are seen to become progressively looser. In dialectic (disputation) they require probability. The rhetorical syllogism, or "enthymeme," requires only suspicion—for this degree of certitude is sufficient to induce a man to act. In poetic, the logical connection is merely feigned, for the poet is making his connection. Certain and probable connections—more probably (*"cum probabilitate"*) or less probable (*"cum suspicione"*)—exist independently of the poet and hence are not his to make. The sophistical argument, of course, does not really conclude and resists conclusion, so that it is lower on the scale than even the merely assumed argument of poetic.

Rhetoric, then, and poetic both differ from the logic of the sciences in that neither requires certitude for its arguments. (Historical works occupy a special place by the side of science. History is not science, though it constantly approaches science, as a calculus to its term.) Rhetoric must more closely approximate certitude in its conclusions. Poetic contents itself with a logic that is very thin: its argumentation is treated as though it concluded, and this assumption suffices. Furthermore, although rhetoric and poetic are distinct arts directive of the third operation of the intellect, no given work is the product of such an art alone. The works of these arts, as they stand concreted in matter, are erected by other arts as well, arts that are directive of the physical structure out of which such things are made, as, for instance, an art that directs the rhythmical use of words, and so on. It is the aggregate of all these arts necessary for the production of a work of rhetoric or poetic that is often meant by "rhetoric" or "poetic," and it is such an aggregate that we have called a "general rhetoric" or a "general poetic." A book professing to teach rhetoric may, then, treat of many things other than the enthymeme and the example, and thus present a composite of several arts. Quintilian's *Institutio Oratoria*, for instance, is a composite of this nature. See, for instance, his treatment of gesture (xi. 3, 65 ff.). Quintilian, who was a rhetorician without being a philosopher, defines rhetoric as *"bene dicendi scientia"* (ii. 15. 34, cf. ii. 15. 38). Not only is Quintilian's rhetoric a composite of many arts, but his *"ars"* and *"scientia"* are other things than St. Thomas'.

II

An important phenomenon in literary history is the persistent confusion of poetic with rhetoric or with demonstrative logic (see, for example, Baldwin *Ancient* 100, 229; *Medieval* ix, 24, 39; Clark 35-37). Poetic and rhetoric are confused when, in an attempt to strengthen its logic, poetic is made to proceed by means of the rhetorical enthymeme and example. Such an attempt can only result in something neither fish nor flesh—a poetic whose works are ordered to the practical intellect. Nevertheless, this sort of monster can be fathered on every age since Plato's. It comes into being when poetry is taken to be a direct means of persuasion, either because the defense of an art that creates objects simply for contemplation is felt to be impossible, or because the common association of certain other arts with both poetic and rhetoric obscures the true position of these latter arts. Since the works of both poetic and rhetoric are concreted in matter that is words, these arts gather around themselves a system of satellitic arts that are often the same for both rhetoric and poetic, arts such as that which governs the production of oral sounds. The fact that these arts are found in connection with both rhetoric and poetic tends to obscure the fact that in each case they are serving a different purpose.

Judicative Logic and Poetic

The confusion that constantly tends to arise between poetic and the logic of demonstration that governs the sciences (including philosophy) is likewise of some importance. Clearly distinct from a work of rhetoric, a philosophical work, which proceeds according to *logica judicativa* and may be taken as typical of all scientific works, is not so easily distinguished from a poetical work. A philosophical treatise, like a poetical work, is directed to the speculative intellect. But in what way? The philosophical is concerned with the communication of something that has its existence independently of the words used to communicate it, and, while the poetic use of language communicates truth too, it is truth that does not exist in its totality as entirely independent of the language in which it is conveyed. The logical connections are made by the poet. They are fabricated ("*cum existimatione*"). Consequently, since they do not exist of themselves necessarily, assent to the argument of a poem must be induced by something other than the truths with which the poet deals, so that these truths are apprehended by the intellect with some special kind of cooperation on the part of the senses and emotions that is dependent on the very words in which the truths are presented. Insofar as a work acts independently of the words in which it is presented, it tends toward the scientific treatise.

Gerard Manley Hopkins, S.J., a poet highly conscious of technique, had an artist's characteristic awareness of this special mode of operation in poetry:

> Poetry is speech framed for contemplation of the mind by way of hearing or speech framed to be heard for its own sake and interest even over and above its interest of meaning. Some matter and meaning is essential to it but only as an element necessary to support and employ the shape which is contemplated for its own sake. (249)

It should be noted, however, that what the poet makes is not independent of the truths he makes it of. The truths he employs are not the poetry, and he can use great truths to make poor poetry indeed, but he cannot make great poetry without great truths. Neither stone nor straw is of my making; nevertheless, although I can badly botch a piece of stone construction I attempt, a better house can be made of stone than of straw. For all this, the poet can utilize any material for he is not making houses but simply things: his art is in a way coextensive with being.

Now, in the confusion of poetic with rhetoric and with demonstrative logic, it is always poetic that tends to disappear. And the reason for this is not far to seek. The principal domestic struggle of Western culture has been between a philosophically centered and a rhetorically centered regimen. The forces engaged have been the champions of the speculative intellect versus the champions of the practical intellect. On this basis was waged the struggle between Socrates and the Sophists, the struggle that led to John of Salisbury's *Metalogicus*, and the struggle that was echoed in Swift's *The Battle of the Books*. The victory has gone first to one side and then to another. Under the Roman Empire and until the eleventh century the rhetoricians were in the ascendency, but by the thirteenth century philosophy seemed destined to win out, only to receive a sharp set-back when rhetoric triumphed and made the Renaissance (Haskins 93-126).[1]

Meanwhile poetic has had to eke out an existence in occupied territory. Philosophy is eminently speculative. It will do no work. Rhetoric is eminently practical. It will do a work that is itself productive of some work on the part of others. Poetic is practical, but its work is not. It runs shortly to a dead end. Its work is for the speculative intellect here and now, ordered further only indirectly by reason of prudence. Hence, tucked away in its tight little corner, poetical composition has never been accorded the

[1] For a thorough and enlightening treatment of the conflict between philosophy and rhetoric that runs through the history of Western civilization, I am particularly indebted to some unpublished work of Professor Etienne Gilson made available in a course of lectures delivered recently by Dr. Bernard J. Muller-Thym at Saint Louis University.

prominence in any curriculum that either rhetoric or philosophy have, and even when rhetoric has fallen on evil days, as it had in the thirteenth century and as it more or less has now, it is still, in a position to bestow largess on poetic, which, as an art, is consistently neglected in schools.

Poetry's Results—Indirect

The defense of poetry depends not on what its works do directly, but on what they do indirectly. Because so many well-meaning but unobserving persons insist on defending it for the direct results it produces—a line of defense that is untenable—neglecting the entirely valid argument that the organization that a schooled appreciation of poetry imposes upon the human being is something that cannot be attained independently of words of poetic (or of music, painting, and so on), we are continually having the wrong thing defended or the right thing defended for the wrong reasons. This difficulty is, of course, chronic, and will remain so, for the indirect results that works of poetic bring about in the human being are known only to those who have had experience of them.

It will be seen, then, that the contrast between poetic and scientific writing is a more basic one than that between verse and prose. In the one case the difference arises from final causality, while in the other it is merely of accidental origin, dependent upon and ordered to the purpose that the work is to serve (Hopkins 249-51). This should be a commonplace. It has been said over and over again from Aristotle's time on (*Poetics* i. 7-12. 1447b), even by persons whose discussions are critical rather than philosophical, as, for instance, Coleridge (ch. xiv. 2. 5-13—esp. 10). But it represents a stand that is continually being challenged.

There is, of course, a connection between verse and poetry, as there is between prose and scientific writing. Scientific writing, as has already been said, is concerned with the communication of something that has its existence independently of the words used to communicate it. Hence any configuration of those words lies outside the realm of such writing. If a scientific work is written in verse, the configuration is truly an ornament added to the scientific content of the writing. In poetry, however, the verse functions as an intimate part of the work itself. Apart from what special significative force verse rhythms may themselves exert (as in rhythmic onomatopoeia), they constitute a part of the object to be contemplated. Their relation to the "logical" content is close in a work where the connections in such content are, like the verse itself, of the author's own making.

Poetry in Prose

But this is not to identify verse with poetry, for prose, too, may be written to produce a work for contemplation. Such a work would be poetry in the sense in which this word is used here. No more is it to identify verse with one particular kind of rhythmic patterning (as, for example, with the syllable-counting systems of Homer, Virgil, and most English poets after the Conquest, as against the antithetical patterning of Hebrew poetry or the stress patterning of Old English or modern "free" verse).

Rhetoric, falling between *logica judicativa* and poetic, favors a prose development, for the rhetorician, although he deals with that which is not necessary (or certain), is not the "maker" that the poet is. His logic is not as intimately connected as the poet's is with the words in which it is concreted.

It is seen, then, that poetic is distinguished from rhetoric by the relative tenuousness of its logical connections. The logic of poetic and of rhetoric follows the end to which each of these arts is directed—the former to the making of a thing for contemplation, the latter to the production of action in another. Both poetic and rhetoric are distinct from the logic of the sciences in that their arguments do not proceed with necessity, although rhetoric approximates the necessary in a way that poetic does not.

However, as a matter of fact, most writing is a composite, not only in the sense that arts other than those that govern the operations of the intellect are needed in order that a given concrete piece of writing take form, but also in the sense that a given piece of writing will often partake of the nature of many kinds of writing at once. In most of what may be designated as poetry there is a considerable mixture of special pleading that is nothing more or less than dialectic or rhetoric. Again, what we would ordinarily call a poem may de facto convey scientific as well as poetic truth, although it is not as a poem that it does so. And a politician who should be practicing rhetoric may introduce a fact for its own sake. Finally, writing ostensibly scientific can and often does become a plea to take this attitude toward the subject, or that. Works of rhetoric, poetic, and science do not exist in the concrete in separate works. We must generally rest satisfied with calling a thing a poem because it is mostly a poem, or a political speech a work of rhetoric because it is nearer to that than it is to anything else.

Works Cited

Aristotle. *Poetics.* Trans. and ed. S. H. Butcher. London: Macmillan, 1898.
—. *Rhetoric.* Trans. J.E.C. Welldon. London: Macmillan, 1886.

Averroes. *In Libros Rhetoricorum Aristotelis Paraphrasis*. Venetiis: apud Iuntas, 1574.

Baldwin, Charles Sears. *Ancient Rhetoric and Poetic*. New York: Macmillan, 1924.

—. *Medieval Rhetoric and Poetic*. New York: Macmillan, 1928.

—. *Renaissance Literary Theory and Practice*. New York: Columbia UP, 1939.

Clark, Donald Lemen. *Rhetoric and Poetry in the Renaissance*. New York: Columbia UP, 1922.

Coleridge, Samuel Taylor. *Biographia Literaria*. Ed. J. Shawcross. Oxford: Clarendon P, 1907.

Crane, William G. *Wit and Rhetoric in the Renaissance*. New York: Columbia UP, 1937.

Haskins, Charles Homer. *The Renaissance of the Twelfth Century*. Cambridge, MA: Harvard UP, 1927.

Hopkins, Gerard Manley. *The Note-Books and Papers of Gerard Manley Hopkins*. Ed. Humphrey House. London: Oxford UP, 1937.

John of Salisbury. *Metalogicon*. Trans. Daniel D. McGarry. Berkeley: U of California P, 1955.

Quintilian. *Institutio Oratoria*. Trans. H. E. Butler. New York: G. P. Putnam's Sons, 1921-1922.

Swift, Jonathan. *A Tale of a Tub: Written for the Universal Improvement of Mankind. To Which Is Added, an Account of a Battel Between the Antient and Modern Books in St. James's Library*. London: Printed for John Nutt, 1710.

Thomas Aquinas. *In I Analyticorum Posteriorum. In Aristotelis libros Peri hermeneias et posteriorum analyticorum: expositio, cum textu ex recensione leonina*. Ed. Raymundi M. Spiazzi. Taurini: Marietti Editori, 1955.

5

Historical Backgrounds of Elizabethan and Jacobean Punctuation Theory (1944)

The disputes centering about the oratorical value of sixteenth- and seventeenth-century punctuation in England have hinged mostly upon a study of printed texts current in Elizabethan times or shortly after. Professor Charles C. Fries, in a monograph surveying the whole of the discussion about Shakespeare's punctuation, notes that "some significance attaches to the fact" that all of the five Elizabethan and Jacobean grammarians whose theories he adduces to help settle the dispute "refer to the use of these terms, *comma, colon*, and *period*, in classical rhetorical theory" (80).[1] And yet, in considering the question of sixteenth- and seventeenth-century punctuation, no one has investigated the systems of pointing that were associated with classical rhetorical theory and that may have been carried with that theory through the Middle Ages into Elizabethan and Jacobean England. Until an investigation of this matter is made, we are likely to be guilty once more of the pernicious practice of reading history backwards, understanding phenomena in terms of what succeeded them instead of what preceded, and explaining in terms already at hand for us phenomena that are not reducible to these terms.

This study presents, first, a survey of the punctuation theories and rules that had long influenced the practice of authors and scribes before the sixteenth century, and, second, it attempts to show the direct bearing of these theories and rules on the systems of punctuation taught in late sixteenth- and early seventeenth-century England. The result is, I believe, a marked change in perspective in our view of Elizabethan and Jacobean practice.

---

[1] Fries reviews the bulk of the literature, which need not all be listed here. Among the more important writings on Elizabethan and Jacobean punctuation might be mentioned Simpson (*Shakespearean*, "Bibliographical"), Lee (64-67), and Alden.

I

The grammarians of the early Christian era, who during the Middle Ages and for some time thereafter more or less monopolized their field, almost always insert in their treatises some notes on marks of punctuation, which they call "*distinctiones*" or "*positurae*." The sections measured off the pauses that close the sections, and the marks that indicate the pauses are all designated by these same terms.

The marks of punctuation are invariably of three kinds: (1) the *distinctio* or *positura* proper, corresponding analogously to our present period; (2) the *media distinctio* (*media positura, mora, submedia distinctio*), sometimes analogous to our semicolon, sometimes to our colon, sometimes to our comma, and representing an intermediate pause between that of the *distinctio* proper and that of (3) the *subdistinctio*, which is for the most part analogous to our comma. These three marks are written respectively above the line (*ad summam litteram* or *ad caput litterae*), somewhat above the line (*ad mediam litteram*), and on the line (*ad imam litteram*). These marks, for which the grammarians occasionally give the Greek as well as the Latin names (στιγμη [stigmē], στιγμη μεση [stigmē mesē], 'υποστιγμη [hypostigmē]) derive from the Alexandrian schools of the third century B.C. (Thompson 60-61). Thompson notes how the scribes confused the marks with one another, and himself makes the 'υποστιγμη [hypostigmē] equivalent to the semicolon and the στιγμη μεση [stigmē mesē] to our comma (60), whereas most authorities have it the other way around. See, for instance, Liddell, Scott, Jones, and McKenzie (2:1645, 1896). Sometimes the early grammarians, too, are not very clear in this matter. The kind of equivalence to expect between these marks and those of present-day punctuation will come out in the course of the present study.

It is clear from the grammarians that these marks were designed primarily to meet the demands of oral reading or of declamation, and to meet them on a very practical level. They are breath marks, like the breath marks in musical scores. The fourth-century *Ars Grammatica* of Diomedes, from another part of which Percy Simpson has cited in the work mentioned above, tells us that punctuation marks are to indicate "opportunity for taking breath" (*copiam spiritum reficiendi*) (in Keil 1:437). In another *Ars Grammatica* of the same century, Dositheus says that the *distinctio* is "a mark indicating a rest, which gives an opportunity for recovering the breath in reading in order that it may not give out with prolongation [of the speech]" (*silentii nota, quae in legendo dat copiam spiritus recipiendi, ne continuatione deficiat*) (Keil 7:380).

Speaking of the *positura* or *distinctio* as that which the marks of punctuation indicate, Cassiodorus notes in his sixth-century *Institutio de Arte Grammatica* that this is a "suitable pause in a duly measured delivery" (*moderatae pronuntiationis apta repausatio*) (Keil 7:215).

The oratorical considerations uppermost in the minds of these early grammarians are undoubtedly tied up to a degree with grammar and syntax (Croll 454). But in the case of all three punctuation marks that the early grammarians mention, the clarification of the syntax is coincidental. The grammarians are interested primarily in the exigencies of breathing. It is convenient to place the breath pauses, and consequently the punctuation marks, where they will not interfere with the sense. But interest in both breathing and sense is quite independent of formal attention to grammatical structure. In an early treatise published as *Excerpta Donatiani: Fragmentum*, we find, for example, that the anonymous author recognizes the relation of the *distinctio* to sense, but places its temporal aspect first (*distinctio est temporis et sensus finitio*), noting also with regard to the *mora* that it first "refreshes the reader" (*reficit lectorem*) while at the same time it affords a means of insight into the sense (*simulque sensibus lumen accommodat*) (Keil 6:273). The author says nothing of grammatical structure. Practically, the policy of these grammarians means that the marks will in a rough way and sporadically follow the syntax. That is all. The marks do not exist primarily to bring out the syntax, and similar syntactical arrangements do not always call for similar punctuation. Indeed, with the exception indicated for the period in the next paragraph below, so far as I have been able to find, these grammarians never refer to the position of a punctuation mark in terms of grammatical structure. For the most part, they are content to indicate where a *distinctio* may (not where it must or must not) occur, and if one wishes to breathe oftener than would be usual, there is no objection, apparently, to inserting the marks "*ex abundanti*" (Diomedes, in Keil 1:437).

The syntactical element in the early punctuation theories intrudes in a special way in the case of one stop mark, it is true, but only by a kind of attraction that is due to the fact that it is convenient to make the principal breathing pause coincide with sentence endings. Thus of the three points of punctuation, the *distinctio* proper, or full pause, more than any other mark finds a counterpart in modern punctuation—the period. Since the less prominent pause marked by the *distinctio* (*positura*) *media* could occur in a greater variety of grammatical situations, the role of the *distinctio media* as a breathing mark remained unobscured. In his fourth-century *Ars Grammatica*, Donatus' general directions for using this mark are evidently dictated by very practical considerations concerning the breathing mechanism: he merely says that it should be used toward the middle of the sentence (*ubi fere tantum de sententia superest, quantum iam diximus*) (in Keil 4:372). In the next century, Sergius, one of Donatus' many followers, adds that the *media distinctio* exists for purposes of respiration *(propter respirationem)* (in Keil 4:484-85). The *Ars Grammatica* of Cledonius clearly states that the *positura media* is for "*dilatio respirandi*" (in Keil 5:34). In the *De Arte Grammatica* that Henry Keil ascribes to Maximus Victorinus, the mark is prescribed for use in order to give the reader time for breathing (*respirandi spatium*) (6:192). And our anonymous author adds that the *mora* (*distinctio media*) is a "*requies animi*" (6:273).

The *subdistinctio* admits the greatest variety of syntactical settings with the early grammarians. Rules for its insertion are extremely broad when translated into grammatical terms and leave no doubt that it is conceived of as an oratorical breath mark. Its position is governed not by the sense or structure, but by how much of the sentence remains to be spoken, for this shortest of pauses and the mark that indicates it are prescribed for use when there is not far to go to complete the sentence (*ubi non multum superest de sententia*) (Donatus, in Keil 4: 372).

The tradition represented by these early grammarians was continuous through the Middle Ages. Donatus was of course the favorite author. Not only do we find commentaries devoted to his work, such as the seventh- or eighth-century *Cunabula Grammaticae Artis Donati* (Migne, *Patrologia Latina* [hereafter, *P.L.*] 90:613 ff.) and the *Commentum Einsidlense in Donati Artem Minorem* (Hagen 230-31) preserved in a tenth-century manuscript, but his name came to be used as a common noun (in English under the form "donet" or "donat": Murray 3:599) to designate a grammar textbook or primer. And other early grammarians were not neglected. The twelfth-century *Anticlaudianus* of Alanus de Insulis refers to Donatus, Aristarchus, and Priscian (*P.L.* 210:508). Hugh of St. Victor's *Didascalicon* of the same period refers the student to Donatus, Servius, Priscian, and Isidore of Seville (Buttimer 46). Cassiodorus, Diomedes, and others were likewise well-known (Baldwin 87, 95, 130).

The continuity of the early grammatical tradition is attested to not only by the constant reference of medieval authors to writers of the early Christian era, but by the retention of the early orthographical theories and terminology in new treatises composed throughout the Middle Ages. These new treatises, however, did not pass on the older tradition entirely unchanged. In the same treatises that reflect the earlier views, the writers lean more and more toward a recognition of sense as a determinant of punctuation. Near the opening of the seventh century, Isidore of Seville in his *Etymologiae* had said that the *"positura"* was a device for marking off the sense into the colons, commas, and periods (*figura ad distinguendos sensus per cola et commata, et periodos*) (*P.L.* 82: 95) This is a mixture of the old and the new. Punctuation is becoming more closely associated with sense, while at the same time it is still thought of as marking off sections of speech into the traditional oratorical units, which Isidore associates with breathing. For he notes in the place already cited that the marks are called *"positurae"* possibly "because there the voice is 'set down' for the duration of a distinction" (*quid ibi vox pro intervallo distinctionis deponitur*), and that the comma is inserted where the sense is not complete and nevertheless one has to breathe (*et tamen respirare oportet*).

Alcuin, some two centuries later, in his *Grammatica* says simply that the *"positurae"* are points to make clear the sense (*puncti ad distinguendos sensus*) (*P.L.* 101:858). In the twelfth century, John of Salisbury notes in his *Metalogicus* that the sense is marked off by the *"positurae"* (5:51). But John has not divorced himself from the earlier grammarians. He, too, uses their terminology—not only *"positurae"* but *"distinctio,"* *"media distinctio,"* and *"subdistinctio"* as well, and he still conceives of the sense in oratorical, not syntactical segments—the "colon," the "comma," and the *"periodus."*

The tendency of the marks to shift more and more from a temporal breath-mark value to a sense value in later medieval theory is of some importance, but is itself carried over from the earlier grammarians. The dual purpose of the marks, as has already been explained, was really incipient in their very early use, especially in the case of the *distinctio* proper, but the original emphasis made the marks serve primarily the purpose that breath marks serve today in a musical score, the three marks allowing respectively three breath pauses of varying lengths. When sense punctuation first comes in, it arises in opposition to, as well as in conjunction with, this system of breath-marking. And thus we have in existence side-by-side, two systems, more or less blended with one another, neither of which, however, is conceived of as we within recent years have conceived of a syntactical system. As yet there is no mention of grammatically structural units. Neither has the punctuation concerned itself as yet with any niceties of dramatic interpretation, although the whole system, characteristically for a thing so well within the rhetorical tradition, is concerned primarily with spoken rather than written works, which must be considered as spoken before punctuation for them can be determined.

However, today *A New English Dictionary*, for example, says that "The function of the comma is to make clear the grammatical structure,

and hence the sense of the passage" ("Comma"), and that the colon is a
"punctuation-mark . . . usually indicating a *discontinuity of grammatical
construction* greater than that marked by the semicolon, but less than that
marked by the period" ("Colon"; italics added). Similarly, Genung (328-
29) notes that the comma "is the mark of the closer dependent clause,"
etc., and prescribes it "when a long or involved subject is finished, ready
for its verb; . . . when a constituent clause is of subordinate, not coordi-
nate significance" (cf. Genung's remarks on the office of punctuation,
325-26). These examples need not be multiplied.

II

The treatment of punctuation that we have just summarized sheds considerable light on the condition of orthographical marks in Elizabethan
and Jacobean times. The whole classical-medieval tradition is easily recognizable in the late sixteenth- and early seventeenth-century English
printed texts that treat of punctuation, and the case can hardly be decided
for or against elocutionary punctuation in Shakespeare or elsewhere
before the evidence concerning this early tradition is in. Indeed, until this
evidence is in, the issue to be decided is not itself clear. In his monograph
Mr. Fries says:

> The question at issue in this discussion of punctuation is whether the
> pauses indicated by the punctuation have been placed as dictated by
> the syntax and structure of the sentences or whether they are dra-
> matic pauses indicating elocutionary emphasis and placed with no
> relation to structural divisions. (76)

This statement of the question is based on a review of the pertinent literature and is representative of the tenor of the discussions so far. But, if the
earlier system survives in Elizabethan and Jacobean England, it is quite
possible to have a punctuation that is based neither upon "syntax and
structure" nor upon simple elocutionary emphasis. As we have seen, in
the earlier tradition punctuation indicates neither the syntax nor the
niceties of delivery, but is rather a device *serving primarily the exigencies
of breathing* in discourse, considered basically as oral, with due respect
only secondarily for the demands of sense. To show the effects of this
view on Elizabethan and Jacobean notions of punctuation, I will examine
the viability of the early tradition and then indicate how the survival of
the tradition bears on our understanding of the textbook discussions of the
time. The practical use of punctuation is not reexamined here, but, as Mr.
Fries observes (81), it must have some connections with the theory
expounded by textbooks.

From the evidence in texts that between 1582 and 1640 treat of punctuation, there is little doubt that there survived not only—in varying degrees—the terminology of the earlier system that we have been treating, but also a recognition of the primacy of breathing as a determinant of punctuation. Richard Mulcaster in his *Elementarie*, published in 1582, notes that the comma, colon, and period, together with the parenthesis and the "interrogation"—all these taken as punctuation marks and not as units of discourse—

> ar *helps to our breathing*, & the distinct *vtterance* of our speche . . .
> & therefor com here in note, bycause theie ar creaturs to the pen, &
> *distinctions to pronoūe by*, & therefor, as theie ar to be set down with
> iudgement in writing, so theie ar to be vsed with diligence in the right
> framing of the tēder childes mouth. (167; italics added)

Like the earlier writers, Mulcaster here conceives of the comma, colon, and period as marking off segments of discourse rather than as primarily making clear the sense, and these segments are those demanded by breathing and distinct utterance. Breathing comes first. Discussing the separate marks, comma, colon, and period, he says:

> *Cōma*, is a small crooked point, which in writing followeth som
> small branch of the sentence, & in reading warneth vs to rest there,
> and to help our breth a little . . . *Colon* is noted by two round points
> one aboue the other, which in writing followeth som full branch, or
> half the sentence . . . *Period* is a small round point, which in writing
> followeth a perfit sentence, and in reading warneth vs to rest there
> and to help our breth at full. (167)

Except for the "perfit sentence" in the case of the period, there is no direct reference to either syntax or sense here, but reference to breathing persists.

George Puttenham in *The Arte of English Poesie* (1589) gives more place to sense as a determinant of punctuation, but does not neglect to mention breathing as well. He notes that it is

> requisit that leasure be taken in pronuntiation, such as may make our
> wordes plaine & most audible and agreable to the eare: also the
> breath asketh to be now and then releeued with some pause or stay
> more or less: besides that the very nature of speach (because it goeth
> by clauses of seuerall construction & sence) requireth some space
> betwixt thē with intermissiō of sound, to th'end they may not huddle
> vpon one another so rudly & so fast that th'eare may not perceiue
> their difference. (73-74)

How loosely "your three pauses, *comma, colon, & periode*" are connected with either syntax or sense is shown when Puttenham says that
they appertain more to oratory than to verse, where there are plenty of
pauses without them since "euery verse is as it were a clause of it selfe"
(i.e., demands a pause at its close) (76, 75).

Thomas Heywood, in *An Apology for Actors* (1612), gives some
additional evidence when he says that university dramatic performances
teach the participant "to speake well, and with judgement to observe his
commas, colons, and full poynts; his parentheses, his breathing spaces,
and distinctions" (29). The "commas, colons, and full poynts" here may
be oratorical sections instead of marks; if they are, the term "full poynts"
shows that there is a connection between these sections and punctuation
marks in Heywood's mind. And "breathing spaces," it will be noted, are
thrown in here with the rest of Heywood's miscellany.

The most detailed and conclusive evidence for the preservation of the
earlier attitudes toward punctuation is in *The English Grammar* of Ben
Jonson. The last chapter of the *Grammar* is headed "Of the Distinction of
Sentences" and treats of "one general affection of the whole [discourse],
dispersed thorough every member thereof, as the blood is thorough the
body," which affection "consisteth in the breathing, when we pronounce
any *sentence*" (9:316).[2] To breathing and to sense as related to breathing
and the exigencies of the speaking voice, Jonson, like the early grammarians, confidently ascribes the origin of punctuation:

> For, whereas our breath is by nature so short, that we cannot contin-
> ue without a stay to speak long together; it was thought necessary as
> well for the speaker's ease, as for the plainer deliverance of the
> things spoken, to invent this means, whereby men pausing a pretty
> while, the whole speech might never the worse be understood. (9:
> 316)

The roots of Jonson's theory of punctuation lie quite bared in his definitions of the various "distinctions":

---

[2] C. H. Herford and Percy Simpson (2:424-28) discuss the variations of the
Cunningham-Gifford text (which was based on the 1692 edition of the *Grammar*) from
the original printing of the *Grammar* in the 1640 folio, which they note itself reproduced
the *Grammar* "very incorrectly" (417). The *Grammar* has not yet appeared in the Herford
and Simpson edition, but the Cunningham-Gifford edition, which I have used as the basis
of the present discussion, serves the purpose here even better than a new collation since it
represents a revision that brought the text up to date in 1692 (Herford and Simpson 2:424)
and thus shows the tradition we are interested in persisting to a much later date than that
of Jonson's death in 1637.

A *comma* is a mean breathing, when the word serveth indifferently, both to the parts of the sentence going before, and following after,
and is marked thus (,)

A *semicolon* is a distinction of an imperfect sentence, wherein
with somewhat a longer breath, the sentence following is included;
and is noted thus (;).

And the "distinction of a perfect sentence," which may be either a
"pause" (our present colon) or a period, "hath a more full stay, and doth
rest the spirit" (9:317). We recall that the fourth-century *Ars Grammatica*
of Diomedes had said that punctuation marks gave "*copiam spiritum reficiendi*" (9: 350). The phrase is still sacrosanct.

Jonson also discusses the interrogation "note" and the mark of "admiration," our present exclamation point (9:318), and although these points
are not of equal antiquity with the others, we are left in no doubt about
the general affinities of Jonson's system: "These distinctions," he says,
"as they best agree with nature, so come they nearest to the ancient stays
of sentences among the Romans and Grecians" (9:318).

Finally, in Simon Daines' *Orthoepia Anglicana* (1640), we find the
older tradition continued when the author explains the relative time of the
stops by an analogy between the marks of punctuation and rests in music.
Speaking of the relative values of the individual points, he says:

> I remember my singing-Master taught me to keep time, by telling
> from 1, to 4, according to the nature of the time which I was to keep,
> and I found the practice thereof much ease and certainty to me, till I
> was perfect in it. The same course I have used to my pupils in their
> reading, to inure them to the distinction of their pauses, and found it
> no lesse successefull. (71)

This time-value of the marks is connected in the early grammarians,
as we have seen, with the breath-mark system, and Daines otherwise
unmistakably connects the stops with the exigencies of breathing,
although he also occasionally hints at their use for elocution or dramatic
interpretation, as in these remarks on the comma:

> The *Comma* hath its place at the foot of the line, and is marked with
> a semi circular forme like an halfe Moone decrescent, thus (,) The
> use onely in long sentences, in the most convenient place to make a
> small pause for the necessity of breathing; or in Rhetoricall speech-
> es (where many other words are used to one effect) to make a kinde
> of Emphasis and deliberation for the greater majesty or state of the
> Elocution. (70)

There is other evidence of Daines' being still under the influence of the early system: for instance, the new "Comma-colon" (semicolon) is of use in "long winded sentences," and Daines scruples about treating the apostrophe among the "points" because "for pause of time, it hath none belonging to it" (70, 72-73).

This is not to say that Daines' punctuation system is the same as earlier systems. When we read in the passage given above of the use of the comma for "Emphasis and deliberation," as when Daines says that the parenthesis demands a pause "as little as may be; exacting rather a distinction of *tone*, than distance of *time*" (72), we see a punctuation that might subserve the nice nuances of delivery. The function of punctuation, never quite simple, is becoming more manifold in Daines as well as in some of his contemporaries. The same interest in tone found in Daines is exhibited by Charles Butler in *The English Grammar* (1634), where punctuation is also given a markedly syntactical function. In Butler the "Primari Points"—the period, colon, semicolon, comma, and four others—show the tone, sound, and pauses of words (58-59, cited in Fries 77). In a somewhat similar fashion, Alexander Gill, treating of accent in his *Logonomia Anglica* (1621), notes that punctuation serves to indicate (rhetorical) accent because it brings out the sense (*"Accentui inseruiunt interpunctiones: quia illae vt sens aperiunt, ita, quantu possunt accentui viam sternunt"*: 135), although this remark, thrown in at the end of the chapter on accent, should perhaps be taken as simply an indication of the relation of punctuation to accent without the implication that this relationship defines the principal function of punctuation. Of these last three authors, the first, Daines, as we have seen, shows unmistakable connections with the earlier tradition. Gill in his brief passage at least notes that the points in English are the same as among Latin writers (*"Eaed sunt nobis quae Latinis, & usus idem"*: 135). And even with Butler, who was a bold innovator in other ways (for example, in spelling and typography), the length of the pause for each mark remains a major factor, although the older system is wearing pretty thin.

From this examination of textbooks, the late classical-medieval theory emerges as the unnoticed factor that has scuttled the attempts to explain Elizabethan and Jacobean punctuation. The principal dispute about this punctuation springs from two hitherto irreconcilable facts. (1) The punctuation of late sixteenth- and early seventeenth-century England in practice, and in theory, too, is evidently not syntactical or "logical." (2) And yet, as Professor Raymond Macdonald Alden has shown in the case of the Shakespeare Folios and Quartos, the elocutionary theory is not satisfactorily substantiated by the actual practice; moreover, if we favor the view of those who assert that the punctuation is elocutionary or interpretative, one "who attempts to trace the development of our system of punctuation as that system is expressed in the grammars of the last three hundred years receives an impression quite different from that of these assertions" (Fries 83-84). The present study shows that this *impasse* is to be explained by the fact that behind the punctuation theory of the time, which was based on a mixed set of principles, there was a factor that is not included under either a syntactical or an elocutionary system as these systems have been understood. This factor was the original theory of the late classical and the medieval grammarians, for whom punctuation was first of all a system demanded by the exigencies of breathing in oral delivery and only secondly (at first rather negatively) a means of interpreting the sense. Lying at the background of Elizabethan and Jacobean theory, this view of punctuation accounts for a practice that is loose by either syntactical or elocutionary standards.

Keeping its roots in spoken instead of in written discourse and rather forced onto the latter, the older system of the early grammarians in its Renaissance developments that we have examined here, has more affinity with elocutionary punctuation than it does with syntactical. Of all the Renaissance English authors cited by Mr. Fries (75), who makes out a case for structural punctuation while admitting the possibility of an elocutionary system, only one, Charles Butler, has an unmistakably syntactical punctuation theory. With the other authors, the more or less loose system of the early grammarians, since it regards the actual pauses of delivery rather than the more simply conventional pauses of syntax, could incidentally fall in here and there with dramatic elocutionary emphasis, although it would not of set purpose concern itself with any of the niceties of interpretation.

Despite the growing deference to sense and an occasional reference to syntax, the most telling characteristic, then, of Elizabethan and Jacobean punctuation theory remains the fact that it never cut itself loose from the traditional view of punctuation as basically a physiological rather than either an elocutionary or a syntactical (logical) device. The fact that man has to breathe had been a primary consideration at a time when all discourse, in keeping with the rhetorical tradition, was conceived of as a thing spoken rather than written. With regard to actual practice in the age of Shakespeare and Jonson, we can reasonably assume that it conformed in some way to the prevailing theories, once allowance is made for the compositors' and "correctors'" errors; and, indeed, this allowance, in view of the elasticity of the theory itself, need not, perhaps, be so great as we once supposed.

Works Cited

Alanus de Insulis. *Anticlaudianus. Patrologiae cursus completus. Series Latina.* Ed. J.-P. Migne. 217 vols. Paris: [s.n.], 1855.

Alcuin. *Grammatica. Patrologiae cursus completus. Series Latina.* Ed. J.-P. Migne. 217 vols. Paris: [s.n.], 1855.

Alden, Raymond Macdonald. "The Punctuation of Shakespeare's Printers." *PMLA*, 39 (1924): 557-80.

Baldwin, Charles Sears. *Medieval Rhetoric and Poetic.* New York: Macmillan, 1928.

Buttimer, Charles Henry. *Hugh of St. Victor's Didascalicon.* Diss., Catholic U, 1939. Washington, DC: Catholic UP, 1939.

"Colon." *A New English Dictionary.* Oxford: Clarendon P, 1897.

"Comma." *A New English Dictionary.* Oxford: Clarendon P, 1897.

Commentum Einsidlense in Donati Artem Minorem. Supplementum. Ed. Herman Hagen. Leipzig: Teubner, 1870.

Croll, Morris W. "The Baroque Style in Prose." *Style, Rhetoric and Rhythm: Essays by Morris W. Croll.* Ed. J. Max Patrick and Robert O. Evans with John M. Wallace and R. J. Schoeck. Princeton: Princeton UP, 1966. 207-33.

Cunabula Grammaticae Artis Donati. Printed with the *Opera Didascalica* of Bede, Sectio ii a, "Dubia et Spuria." *Patrologia Latina*, Ed. J.-P. Migne. Paris: J.-P. Migne, 1844-1864. Vol. 90: 613 ff.

Daines, Simon. *Simon Daines' Orthoepia Anglicana.* Ed. M. Rösler and R. Brotanek. Halle a. S.: Max Niemeyer, 1908. ("Neudrucke Frühneuenglischer Grammatiken," 3).

Diomedes. *Ars Grammatica. Grammatici Latini.* Ed. Henry Keil. Leipzig: Teubner, 1857-1780.

Donatus, *Ars Grammatica. Grammatici Latini.* Ed. Henry Keil. Leipzig: Teubner, 1857-1880.

"Donet." *A New English Dictionary.* Ed. Sir James Murray et al. Oxford: Clarendon P, 1897.

Excerpta Donatiani Fragmentum. Grammatici Latini. Ed. Henry Keil. Leipzig: Teubner, 1857-1880.

Fries, Charles C. "Shakespearian Punctuation." *University of Michigan Publications: Language and Literature*, Vol. I, *Studies in Shakespeare, Milton and Donne.* New York: Macmillan, 1925.

Genung, John Franklin. *The Working Principles of Rhetoric.* Boston: Ginn, 1900.

Gill, Alexander. *Alexander Gill's Logonomia Anglica.* Ed. Otto L. Jiriczek. Strassburg: Karl J. Trübner, 1903. ("Quellen und Forschungen zur Sprach- und Cultur-geschichte der Germanischen Völker," 90).

Hagen, Herman, ed. *Supplementum.* Leipzig: Teubner, 1870.

Herford, C. H. and Percy Simpson. *Ben Jonson.* 2 vols. Oxford: Clarendon P, 1925.

Heywood, Thomas. *An Apology for Actors.* London: The Shakespeare Society, 1841. (From the edition of 1612 compared with that of W. Cartwright).

Isidore of Seville. *Etymologiae. Patrologiae cursus completus. Series Latina.* Ed. J.-P. Migne. 217 vols. Paris: [s.n.], 1855.

John of Salisbury. *Metalogicus. Joannis Saresberiensis Opera Omnia.* Ed. J. A. Giles. Oxford: J. H. Parker, 1848.

Jonson, Ben. *The Works of Ben Jonson.* Ed. F. Cunningham after W. Gifford. London: Bickers and Son, 1875.

Keil, Henry, ed. *Grammatici Latini.* 8 vols. Leipzig: Teubner, 1857-1880.

Lee, Sir Sidney, ed. *The Year's Work in English Studies, 1919-1920.* London: Oxford UP, 1921.

Liddell, Henry George, Robert Scott, Henry Stuart Jones, and Roderick McKenzie, eds. *A Greek-English Lexicon.* Rev. ed. Oxford: Clarendon P, 1940.

Migne, J.-P., ed. *Patrologiae cursus completus. Series Latina.* 217 vols. Paris: [s.n.], 1855.

Mulcaster, Richard. *Mulcaster's* Elementarie. Ed. E. T. Campagnac. Oxford: Clarendon P, 1925.

Murray, James, ed. *A New English Dictionary.* Oxford: Clarendon P, 1897.

Puttenham, George. *The Arte of English Poesie.* Ed. Gladys Doidge Willcock and Alice Walker. Cambridge, UK: Cambridge UP, 1936.

Sergius. *De Littera, De Syllaba, De Pedibus, De Accentibus, De Distinctione Commentarius [in Donatum]. Grammatici Latini.* Ed. Henry Keil. Leipzig: Teubner, 1857-1880.

Simpson, Percy. "The Bibliographical Study of Shakespeare." *Oxford Bibliographical Society: Proceedings and Papers,* I (1922-1926): 33-41.

—. *Shakespearian Punctuation.* Oxford: The Clarendon Press, 1911.

Thompson, Sir Edward Maunde. *An Introduction to Greek and Latin Paleography.* Oxford: Clarendon P, 1912.

6

The Jinnee in the Well-Wrought Urn (1954)

I

This is the age that has repudiated books about the girlhood of Shakespeare's heroines. Criticism in the English-speaking world within the past few decades has made it its business to guarantee the autonomy of the work of art as constituted within its own limits. Every effort has been made to clear the art object of accretions, to focus attention on it as freed of irrelevancies concerning the author's life, his friends and his problems, or of errant speculation about the previous or subsequent history of characters, if any—from all that might be styled the personalist irrelevancies adventitious to the work of art in its own totality. The effort has been reasonably successful. The once undisputed popularity of biographical excursion has been severely curtailed. It maintains itself with effort even in concert program notes.

The compulsions responsible for the present emphasis are many and complex, and they operate in quite diverse quarters simultaneously. The conviction that it is neither the potter who made it nor the people, real or fictional, to whose lives it is tangent, but the well-wrought urn itself that counts, has been fed indifferently out of studies of Donne or Pope or Coleridge, out of trenchant criticism working through contemporary literature, out of theory spun from clues picked up in St. Thomas Aquinas, and from innumerable other sources. Indeed, the ability it manifests to pick up nourishment almost anywhere at all is convincing testimony to the essential truth of the conviction in question: it is in accord with facts as they are.

In a sense, the current emphasis on the work of art as such simply exploits by reaction a special weakness of nineteenth-century criticism such as Hazlitt's or Lamb's. Associated with commitments of rhetorical theory through long centuries, this weakness was not even new. But the present age found it singularly ripe for attack, and the past few decades

199

have, by a kind of inner compulsion, set themselves to forging weapons for the antipersonalist armory. This compulsion is discernible in T. S. Eliot's submersion of the individual's subjective talent in an objective tradition (of which, to be sure, the subjective talent is simultaneously the expression), and in the attack launched by F. R. Leavis and others against a criticism based on measuring fictional characters by "real life"—by their seeming adaptability to ultrafictional projection. The same compulsion is seen everywhere in the persistent emphasis of American criticism as represented by such work as that of Cleanth Brooks or Kenneth Burke.

But a change of heart, however carefully defined, is setting in, as a close reading of recent critical credos, such as those of Leslie Fiedler or of Richard Chase, shows. The compulsion to beat the personalist horse loses force as the impression gains ground that he has shown no unambiguous signs of life for a long while. Beating him becomes a bore, and we want something newer and more interesting to do.

However, it is not quite clear to me, nor perhaps to many others, that the horse is really dead. A phenomenon so universal and persistent as the personalist deviation in criticism, it would seem, still deserves rather more explicit consideration than it has received. It has been written off in places at which it might well have been looked into. Personalist deviationism is, after all, not merely the last infirmity of feeble sensibilities. Dr. Johnson, who is honestly admired by most objectivist critics and is cited by Mr. Fiedler as a practitioner commonly acknowledged as extraordinarily good, not only stands for an approach to literature that is frankly moral, in a distressingly simplified fashion, but could state bluntly to Boswell that "the biographical part of literature is what I love most." (The personalist horse does seem dead and shrunk to a heap of bones when we try to imagine a present-day critical collection with *that* for a title-page motto.)

This is not to say that the personalist approach to a work of art is to be advocated. If I may be permitted a personal deviation of my own, I myself subscribe wholeheartedly to the practice and theory of focusing primarily on the work of art itself and feel no desire to defend the personalist approach as a substitute technique. It is not defense of the personalist drift, but explanation, that is needed. The personalist deviation is here to stay, not only in program notes but in serious discussions of literature that, apparently unaffected by recent critical trends, continue to pour from the presses. For some it may be a racking experience to own that the personalist approach is still established as the dominant approach in most classrooms. But there it is, all the same.

However objectionable, the personalist approach manifests a persistency that itself clamors for explanation. If the urn really is the issue, why is it always in peril of being overlooked or tossed aside? If you so much as whisper that there is a jinnee in the urn, most onlookers will be only too willing to drop the urn without further ado. Broken, it will let the jinnee out, and they can ask him a few questions. While decrying the tendency to behave this way, we may be excused for asking what accounts for the presence of the tendency in the first place.

II

There are countless ways in which works of art fray out into personalities and thus give the personalist distraction a foothold within the art object itself. The most obvious, that of character in literature or even in the plastic arts, is both so straightforward and so complicated—with the curious susceptibility characters exhibit even for getting themselves psychoanalyzed—that it hardly need be mentioned. But there are other footholds, some closely approximating to this. There is the autobiographical strain that persistently fertilizes fiction. Or there is the obverse autobiography of a Scott Fitzgerald, where not only are the novels cut to the measure of the author's life, but this life itself is lived to the measure of the novels—type and antitype are generated not only simultaneously but reciprocally as well.

Or there is the fact that groupings of works by author have a tough and ready viability not found in groupings by classes. The body of works by Shakespeare—plays, sonnets, and other poems all together—forms a whole in a way more integrated than that formed by the body of Elizabethan sonnets or by Elizabethan drama. *Sweeney Agonistes* belongs with "Tradition and the Individual Talent" in a way it does not with Pound's *Cantos* or with a poem by Auden.

Or again, there is the fact that the final stage of interest in a poet's work creates inevitably the poet's shrine, which is consecrated to the poet's person and thus may as well be his birthplace as something more readily connected with his works. The Shakespeare Memorial Theatre is at Stratford, not on the south bank of the Thames. Or, once more, the personalist distraction intrudes itself by reason of the sense of communion that rides through the contemplation of a work of art. At the threshold of consciousness, there hovers the awareness that others, or at least another, knows this work in the intimate way that I do. What would be an intrusion on our attention, if only an object were concerned, is thus transmuted into a sharing in terms of this injection of personality, however vague it may be. One wonders if there could be any artistic experience at all if the contemplator were a human being entirely alone in the universe.

This is not all. The very genesis of works of art is often—perhaps always and necessarily—derivative from personal relations and tensions.

That the muses are conceived of as persons and not as clouds or waves bears testimony to a state of mind elusive but real. Certainly the artistic impulse is at a kind of peak when the person-to-person relationship takes possession of the whole field of life in a crisis terminating ordinarily in marriage. For the great majority of persons, this is the only time anything like artistic creativity even remotely threatens in their lives. Even those whose creative activity persists testify to the earlier period of intensification of impulse and the readjustment demanded for continuation. There is Villon's verse testament executed "en l'an de mon trentiesme âge," or Mr. Eliot's pertinent remarks about those who want to continue to write poetry after their early youth. The crisis adverted to here is one that hardly exerts itself so immediately in the case of scientists.

Even where there is readjustment and the period of artistic impulse associated in one way or another with entrance upon the plenary personal relationship of marriage is past, the personal drive continues in the production of works of art. Frank accounts of artistic development, such as Stephen Spender's recent account, throughout are replete with personal relations and tensions, which, again, would have an entirely different status in the life of a mathematician or physicist or perhaps even a metaphysician.

It would be hard to disprove the statement that the impulse to produce a work of fine art simply cannot arise except within a framework of personal give-and-take, a *you-me* situation, set up within the artist's mind. The lack of artistic impulse among animals is a simple corollary of the dead quiet that Rilke found so terrifying in the animal eye. J. S. Mill's attempt to define poetry as something not heard but *over*heard is largely traceable to the impulse of the abstractionist, scientific mind to extricate poetry from the network of personality in which it is involved. But the attempt is successful, or at least titillating, precisely in so far as it removes the sensorily ascertainable audience and replaces it with a mysterious audience suggesting the bottomless depths of a pure personality, disengaged from the crudities of sense perception and existing only in the vibrant tension that makes a *me* separate from a *you*.

Creative activity is often—again, perhaps always—powered by the drive to accomplish, in terms of the production of an object of art, an adjustment or readjustment in certain obscure relationships with other persons. The state of protest in which artistic activity is so often framed is evidence of how matters stand here. Only persons are liable to protest. You cannot protest to a fact or to an object. Although you speak of protesting against it, you can only protest about it to some one. In a discussion of Lionel Trilling's recent book, R. P. Blackmur very properly suggests the artistic sterility of a feeling for systems—impersonal things—and the fact that existing politics is good not *for* literature, but "to *aggravate* literature" (41). These sensitively conceived remarks underscore the value of high-potential person-to-person situations in generating the artist's product.

Even critical activity is dependent on this person-to-person situation for its coming into being. Another way of putting this is to say, as it is commonly said, that criticism is a social activity in a way in which scientific activity is not. Although in science there is question of background, there seems to be no question of a personal *mise en scène* as a condition of scientific activity in the way in which there is in critical activity. Even when questions as to who says what about whom are not obvious at the surface, issues involving such questions are likely to be found in the depths, where the wells of criticism, like those of the poem, are driven deep in the personal situation in which the critic finds himself. The goddess of criticism is a kind of in-law of the muses, and there is some question of an underground passage between the watering places to which she brings her devotees and the springs of Helicon.

III

The artistic situation differs from the scientific, against which it is helpful to set it here, precisely in centering about an externalized, manmade object. The persuasion that the object itself must be primary is thus both sound and promising. But the object is not free of involvement in tragedy simply because of its primacy as object. Although it stands solidly—or pretty solidly—on its own feet, it is nonetheless a harbinger of disappointment and of death. For once we have granted to the work of art the kind of autonomy that the artistic situation demands, once we have decided to allow it to slough its irrelevancies, which would dissipate its own objective being in the confusion of personal issues out of which it perhaps arose, a further question presents itself: Is it not in the last analysis cruel to face a human being with merely an object as such, a being that is less than a person? As soon as contemplation enters beyond a certain stage of awareness, is not the human being going to be unsatisfied if be cannot find another, a person, a *you*, in whatever it is he is concerned with?

It seems that he is going to be unsatisfied, precisely in so far as he drives this contemplation of the object to its ultimate—in so far as he takes it in its maximum of seriousness. We consider here the case not of passing attention to a work of art but the case of plenary attention, serious and protracted and repeated. Contemplation of this sort involves love, and the question is whether it can be carried on, or how far it can be carried on, without some suggestion of reciprocity. Projected into an unpeopled void, love becomes only the ultimate refinement of self-torture. And while it is true that contemplation of a minor object of art may not involve the full psychological mechanism of love in all its complications, still, in proportion as the object of art pretends to be serious, it at least sets in motion this tremendous mechanism, which demands for full satisfaction the reciprocity of another person.

Man's deepest orientation is personal. He cannot give himself fully in an outpouring of love unless someone else is *there*, with at least the capability of giving a self in return. Otherwise, psychological disaster threatens—the disaster that takes such heavy toll of serious writers or artists.

The morass of personality that surrounds the work of art in ways only briefly hinted at here establishes the personalist aberration as a permanent threat. As contemplation enters upon a more serious stage, the human being is driven by the whole economy of what it is to be man to find opposite himself, in that which he contemplates, a person capable of reacting in turn. This drive is primordial and will not be denied. It can be deflected from the object, as it ordinarily is, by a refusal to take the object in total seriousness, by a smile, a shrug of the shoulders, by an acknowledgment, if only subconscious, that somewhere or other the poem will break down, will ultimately reach a point at which it is incapable of eliciting further love—unlike a person, who can go on eliciting love without limit.

When the personalist aberration sets in, or in so far as it sets in, the resolution of the state of tension is otherwise effected. The movement of love goes on, but persons—the characters of the novel, the artist himself responsible for the object, the peopled parlor where the Ming vase was displayed, or the woman who ran her fingers over the cool jade—will begin to haunt the attention, not as within the work of art itself but as constituted more and more in their own right. This personalization is, of course, unsatisfactory, even to the compulsion from which it derives. It is only an evanescent appeasement, for these persons do not exist in the present situation controlled by the object, and it is an existent and responsive person that human nature demands. But the personalist drive, if still frustrated, has had a kind of say.

The nature of the frustration here can be misunderstood. It turns not on the fact that the work of art is man-made but on the fact that it is an object. Drilled at least from the time of Walter Pater to focus all aesthetic questions on the man-made art object, we are likely to overlook the fact that the fundamental impasse here presents itself at a more basic level than that of art itself, and that the impulse to focus the difficulty at the level of art is only another manifestation of the tendency to keep the potential of personality around an object at a maximum. The art object, with its immediate social context, is an easier point than the natural object at which both to study and to project the personalist aberration. That for both operations we today automatically avail ourselves of the object of art rather than of the natural object testifies perhaps to the waning power of the imagination in our present culture.

In more primitive cultures, it has been otherwise. It has been otherwise in the earlier history of the culture of the West. The nature cults react to the impasse created by the person-object situation not only on the artistic, but upon the natural level as well. Hebrew and early Christian critiques of the nature cults of antiquity attack the cults precisely on such ground. In the analysis offered by the writer of the Book of Wisdom, it is man's orientation toward personality that has betrayed him in his contemplation of natural objects, so that be pretends that the objects themselves are persons, imagining "either the fire, or the wind, or the swift air, or the circle of the stars, or the great water, or the sun and the moon, to be gods that rule the world." The pre-Hellenic nature cults are accused of pretending to close a circuit where it cannot be closed, of failing to own that the person-to-person drive must push on past the person-object situation to find a response that plays back. While the objects of nature are indeed redolent of Person, the Person must be not in, but beyond them. The error lies in the self-deception that tries to turn the object into a person instead of squarely facing the impasse.

Centuries later, this same critique is extended to the Greco-Roman world and given additional dimensions by Paul in the opening of his Letter to the Romans. Men have allowed themselves to be misled in imputing what is proper to the invisible and incorruptible God (personality as such is not visible, the human person, in so far as merely visible, being rather like an object) not only to human beings but to birds and four-footed animals and creeping things. Here the aberration of idolatry, of misplaced personalism, is presented as intimately connected with other deep psychological displacements. The deterioration of the sexual aspect of marriage in an idolatrous society is not a mere accident, for treating objects like persons and persons like objects suggests a basic imbalance sure to make itself felt in this deepest of human personal relationships.

IV

It would be difficult to assign the precise differences between the place of the artist and the art object in contemporary society and their place in the Judaeo-Hellenistic world. It is, however, certain that the shifts that have produced the modern world have radically altered the focus of the personalist crisis. Men are less and less inclined to impregnate inanimate nature with personality, at least in any crass fashion, although it is well to recall that in Mr. Eliot's later poems, as H. Marshall McLuhan has recently pointed out, the quite convincing speakers seem to be sections of the landscape. Even apart from reflections suggested by this and the many related phenomena that everyone can think of, it would be too simple to maintain that the old apotheosis of natural objects has simply been removed and the apotheosis of the objects of human art put into its place. But it is certain that a great shift has taken place from the former to the latter kind of apotheosis.

Between Greco-Roman times and the present, the crudity—indeed, the childishness—of almost all medieval and Renaissance purely rhetorical theory, which stands in such strange contrast to the sophistication of theological, philosophical, and even, within its limits, what we might today call the paraphysical or paramedical theory of the same periods, and which lags far behind rhetorical practice, betrays the fact that through the Middle Ages and the Renaissance the object of art had not aggregated to itself any large concentration of serious intellectual issues. No especially crucial questions attached to objects of art, not because earlier ages had an adequate apparatus of theory for explaining away the questions, but rather because the object of art failed, it would seem even in the case of serious artists, to become in any urgent way the psychological crux for things. It was idolatry of nature, implemented indeed by art, but only implemented, which long remained the real threat. The idolatry of art seems only during the Renaissance to have begun to appear as something more than a mist on the horizon.

Whatever the complete details of its history, the shift in emphasis from nature to art has matured today in connection with several related phenomena. There is the elaboration of rhetorical and esthetic theory that has marked the past few centuries, there is the cult, half-explicit but quite real, of the artist who is martyr to his craft and burnt up wholly in its service, and, finally, there is the present insistence on focusing the object of art itself to the careful exclusion of its personalized periphery.

The first of these phenomena, the elaboration of theory, is simply testimony to the fact that the work of art itself is now somehow capable of focusing the central issues of human existence. The second points immediately to the personalized aspect of these issues, for in figures such as those of Kafka or Proust or Joyce—at least as they exist as symbols in men's minds, for, as to their persons, we cannot presume to frame a definitive answer—we find the human being who has given himself to the work of art so completely as to blur the distinction between himself and it, presenting himself to it, as though it were a person, in an act of total abandonment, and thus endowing it, by what must be the ultimate fiction, with the marrow of his own abrogated personality. For the devotee of the martyr-artist, the blurring here is accomplished not at the periphery of the work of art by shading this periphery out into personalities, but rather at the very center of the work, where the personality of the artist has so annihilated itself as to be defined by nothing more than the work. The autobiographical bias in the work here does not stand in relationship to a life retained in its own right as real. The autobiography has consumed the life in its telling. The real life has been terminated in a foundation sacrifice: a human being has been put to death in order to serve as the ultimate substructure of the artistic edifice. To serve even the cause of the natural fertility that underlies the fertility of art, neither Moloch nor any other Baal could ask for more.

It is in association with such phenomena as these that the present insistence on the autonomy of the art object acquires its high seriousness. The concentration on the object is hardly a passing infatuation of a school of critics. It is a specialized focus of a persistent problem at the center of human life. If the object of art has become less religious today in being less often explicitly directed toward an extratemporal goal, it has also become more religious in bearing more directly the weight of religious issues. The object-person question pressing on the art object today is not a mere prop tangential to human living. It is the axis, the quiet pole that bears the weight and movement of all.

The assertion that in works of art it is the object itself that counts thus treads such crucial ground that it must be made with great honesty, which means with circumspection and humility. Not only the truth of the situation, but its awkwardness as well, must be faced. This awkwardness derives from the fact that, farfetched as it may seem when applied to less important works of art, the principle apparently holds that, in a valid but not exclusive sense, each work of art is not only an object but a kind of surrogate for a person. Anything that bids for attention in an act of contemplation is a surrogate for a person. In proportion as the work of art is capable of being taken in full seriousness, it moves further and further along an asymptote to the curve of personality.

The very insistence on the object-existence of the work of art, the insistence that it be set off from another reality, clean and self-possessed. involves an anomaly. For it is not an object, but a person who is self-possessed. It is only persons who, in their deep interiors where no other creature can enter, are cut off clean from the rest of the world, poised alone. The object situation itself is really the crux, the ultimate impossibility—a situation that by its very structure points away from itself to another world of persons, which carries in itself its own dissolution. The very way in which we envision the object-situation as clean, cut off, is derived not so much from the object as from our own personalist bias. We have forgotten the lesson of Gestalt psychology. This is humiliating for those who must deal with objects, as we all must. But it will do no good to blink the facts and pretend that they are otherwise. And it will perhaps do no harm to understand and sympathize with the recurrent impulse—shall we say, of the undergraduate?—to get away from it all and back into the vibrant world of personalities again.

The fact is that, in the last analysis, as a matter of full, serious, protracted contemplation and love, it is unbearable for a man or woman to be faced with anything less than a person—and thus, tragically, even partway unbearable to be faced only with other human persons, where the personal relationship is inevitably enmeshed in material situations involving objects, and where even the human being, measurable, definable, partakes of the nature of object at the same time that he is person. In all our moves, our motivation, perhaps in secret and by indirection, bears toward the countermove, hopes to find itself really a countermove. Our great fear is that we are not being loved. Our gaze on the object, we peep anxiously from the corners of our eyes, alert for someone's response somewhere.

This situation keeps the jinnee in the urn and promises to keep him there for good. Try as you may, he will not be exorcized. What is worse, he will always threaten to prove more interesting than the urn itself. For he is a person, or—since it is hard to be certain about jinn, themselves folklore creatures grown out of the person-object crisis and representing an ambiguous and unsatisfactory compromise, for some Moslem writers make them angelic or demonic persons, but others mere diaphanous animals—at any rate, if he is not a person, he behaves enough like one to betray the bias of the human heart.

Works Cited

Blackmur, R. P. "The Politics of Human Power." *The Lion and the Honeycomb: Essays in Solicitude and Critique.* New York: Harcourt, Brace, 1955. 32-42.

Spender, Stephen. *The Creative Element: A Study of Vision, Despair, and Orthodoxy Among Some Modern Writers.* London: Hamilton, 1953.

—. *The Destructive Element: A Sudy of Modern Writers and Beliefs.* Philadelphia: A. Saifer, 1953.

Trilling, Lionel. *The Liberal Imagaination: Essays on Literature and Society.* Garden City, NY: Doubleday, 1953. (Original 1950).

7

Ramus: Rhetoric and the Pre-Newtonian Mind (1954)

Peter Ramus is known to the world today chiefly as a reformer, in logic an anti-Aristotelian, in rhetoric not only anti-Aristotle but anti-Quintilian and anti-Cicero too. However, Ramus thought of himself not only as a revolutionary, but also as a champion of the past. Revolution was for him confusedly synonymous with return to the past, for the issue of reform with him, as with many of his contemporaries, was tied up emotionally with the notion of recuperating what had supposedly been lost since the times of antiquity. He taunts the medieval and Renaissance Aristotelians with the earlier achievements of Quintilian and Cicero, both these with the still earlier "laws of method" proposed by Aristotle, to which they do not conform, only to taunt Aristotle himself with the achievements of his master Plato (see Ramus *Aristotelicae animadversiones* fol. 2^V ff.; "Scholae rhetoricae" in *Scholae* fol. [k_6], preceding col. 233, 344 ff.).

Part of the confusion in Ramus' mind was due to the economy of the revolutionary mentality itself. The professed revolutionary carries about in himself the germ of retrogression. Everyone's future grows out of his past, but for the revolutionary the past too often tyrannizes over the future. Specializing in the overthrow of the past, the revolutionary sees everything in terms of this overthrow, which is to say, everything in terms of the past itself. For this reason, the study of a revolutionary often demands to be understood in terms of his past even more than the study of other types of persons.

Study of Ramus has been neglected because we have for centuries been deliberately inattentive to the immediate past out of which he grew. His opponent, Antonio de Gouveia, taunts Ramus, saying that everybody in Paris knows whose works he has raided for the material in his *Dialectica* (Gouveia 787-88; see Schegkius 61). But apart from Aristotle and Melanchthon, the names that Gouveia mentions—Johannes Caesarius, Hegendorphinus, Titelmannus—mean nothing to us. The chief source of Ramus' *Dialectica* and indirectly of the Talon Ramist *Rhetorica*, and thus of the hundreds upon hundreds of editions of Ramus' own works and the hundreds of other editions of his followers, is Rudolph Agricola. But since his death, in the fifteenth century, Rudolph Agricola has never been accorded more than a monograph, and his principal claim to attention is his tendency to get himself confused with his more famous namesake George.

The scholastic logicians, in whose tradition Ramus had been trained and against whom he says his reform—and, incidentally, the whole humanist movement at Paris—was directed, are to us, with few exceptions, not even names. We have heard vaguely of Buridan, but the Belgian Dulardus, the Frenchman Pierre Tartaret (or Tataret), the tremendously influential Scot John Major, his more mysterious compatriot John Caubraith, the Spaniard Juan de Calaya, and most of their equally important confrères are sunk in oblivion. Yet theirs is the central linguistic tradition of the Western world. Out of this tradition there stares the dim figure of Ralph Strode—Chaucer's "philosophical Strode"—and of the most important personage of all, Peter of Spain. This is the unknown milieu into which Ramus' revolution was faced and in which it has its meaning.

Our knowledge of the early logical and rhetorical tradition is seriously handicapped by the specialization of our interests in the past. This specialization has taken several characteristic turns, the first of which can be indicated by taking a sharp look at so familiar an object as the *Short-Title Catalogue*. If the *Short-Title Catalogue* had attempted to list all the books by British authors published during the period it covers up to 1640, it would have had to be at least twice its present size. It has been kept to its present dimensions by limiting its inclusion of Latin works. However, most of the writing in the period up to 1640 was in Latin. Moreover, what was not written originally in Latin was often translated into Latin and went through more editions in Latin than in the vernacular in which it was first written. In the schools most of the teaching was not only *of* Latin and Latin literature, but also actually *in* Latin—at least in principle—from the very lowest grades. Except for his "lesse Greeke," Shakespeare studied practically nothing but Latin in school. When he did study something else, he studied it, as he studied Latin, in Latin—unless his masters were remiss, as some masters no doubt were. But remissness in this respect called for initiative, for the textbooks, even for such things as arithmetic, were in Latin, too.

The *Short-Title Catalogue* limits its inclusion of Latin works by omitting all such works published by British authors outside England, Scotland, and Ireland. This gives its listings an artificially provincial tone, for one of the advantages of writing in Latin was that it gave work first published in England a larger circulation and greater influence. Thus, it happens that in terms of the general intellectual climate the works excluded by the *Short-Title Catalogue* are often more important than the ones included. Because he wrote in Latin, Ralph Strode, Chaucer's friend from Oxford, was already appearing in Venetian editions of the incunabula period and exerting an influence on Italian thought impossible for his fellow-countryman Chaucer.

It made little difference where you published Latin works. In the early 1600's the Ramist Anglican bishop of Derry, George Downham, found Frankfort-on-the-Main a more convenient publishing center for his works than London or anywhere else in Great Britain. These Frankfort editions are quite as common today in old British libraries as are editions of the same or similar works printed less frequently in London. Whether or not we connect it with nineteenth-century jingoism, the specialization of the *Short-Title Catalogue* has given prominence in our minds to the works that were often regarded by their authors as the least important of their creations.

Specialization has taken another form in the case of our study of scholasticism. Despite the prevailing impression, scholasticism as a whole has not been studied exhaustively over the past few decades. What has been studied is a certain kind of scholasticism, the scholasticism of theologians, and of a select group of theologians at that. Very few "scholastics," if by that we mean teachers of philosophy in the period called scholastic, were theologians. Still fewer of the students of this period ever studied any theology at all. They studied mostly the scholasticism of the arts course. The scholasticism that most students knew has never appeared in modern editions.

Who, we might ask, were these students who studied arts-course scholasticism? They were not only those preparing for theology, but also those preparing for law and medicine—medicine was the higher course most intimately connected with arts course scholastic philosophy. Most especially, however, those studying arts-course scholasticism were those arts-course students preparing themselves for everything or for nothing at all—just attending the university. All in all, perhaps three fourths of the scholasticism of the Middle Ages and the Renaissance was studied in the arts faculty.

This arts scholasticism was almost entirely logic and physics. Of metaphysics there was almost none—at least as prescribed in the arts curricula and studied directly. There was much implied metaphysics, particularly in "physics," as, for instance, in the tracts *De anima,* but, as a separate discipline the arts professors seem not to have liked to handle metaphysics. Alone, it veered too close to theology, which was not their field at all. Hence they kept it rather as tangent to physics, as a genuine meta-physics—with the result that this metaphysics has a quite different tonal-ity from even scholastic metaphysics today.

Their chariness of problems touching theology reminds us that these arts professors as a group were not by any means all priests, as we may be sometimes inclined to suppose they were. Indeed, priests were the only class of men some of whose members were positively excluded from being professors of arts, for Paris University statutes excluded from the arts faculty all members of religious orders, so that the only priests who could act as masters of arts were secular priests. The arts faculty as such had no theological interests. Its teachers were masters of arts—or, for cer-tain courses, bachelors of arts, apprentice teachers in their mid-teens—often studying for a medical degree at the same time, or perhaps for a the-ology degree, rather less likely for a law degree (to undertake the study of law one did not need an M.A.). The arts-course professor could also be a master of arts who with only that degree made teaching his life work—such was Peter Ramus. These teachers of arts were people with the priv-ileged, rather indefinable social status of Chaucer's Clerk of Oxenford.

The condition of our knowledge concerning arts-course scholasticism as this touches Ramus and the linguistic attitudes he exploits can nowhere be more strikingly seen than by looking to the case of Peter of Spain, a contemporary of St. Thomas Aquinas, but a physician rather than a the-ologian, whose work, the *Summulae logicales*, became probably the most influential of all medieval scholastic textbooks. At Paris, where Ramus ("Pro philosophica" in *Scholae* col. 1049) tells us nearly one third of the philosophy course was spent studying Peter of Spain, so that the word for the first-year philosophy students was *summulistae*, this logician-physi-cian ranks in university documents alongside Aristotle (Denifle and Chatelain 4:728-29). The term *summulistae* had been in official use for at least some hundred years by Ramus' day. It occurs (*"artistas, maxime Summulistas, et Logicos"*) in the decree of Louis XI in 1464 for the gov-ernment of the College of Navarre, which was to be Ramus' college (de Launoy, 1:170 Pars I, Lib. II, cap. ix). In unofficial use, the term may well go back to the early fourteenth century or even the late thirteenth. Peter of Spain's influence was comparable in other universities. Scores of edi-tions of his work appeared everywhere after the invention of printing—a count that does not pretend in any way to be complete has numbered some 160 by 1530 (Mullally 132-58). But after 1530, near silence ensued, and by the end of the century it had become total. This situation prevailed till our own day. This is the man at the very center of the tradition against which Renaissance humanism took form. With the rest of the tradition, he dropped out of sight and memory during Ramus' lifetime with a dismaying finality. We think of the Renaissance as a revolution, but our first-hand knowledge of what the revolution took place against is close to zero and has been since the Renaissance itself.

At the risk of being a little too sweeping, we can here attempt a description of the arts-course intellectual milieu in which the Ramist dialectic and rhetoric take shape, making our description as relevant as possible to the Ramist tradition itself. (See Rashdall for the best approach to the pre-Ramist educational tradition.) We must imagine a milieu in which, of course, logic played a dominant role. This is the logic that we have been taught to call decadent, without knowing very well in what the decadence consists—understandably, since we have had no editions in which to examine the logic for some four hundred years. The decadence is often imagined to consist in a preoccupation with distinctions, but first-hand acquaintance with the logic does not give us precisely that impression. There are treatises studied, such as Boethius's *De divisione*, which treat distinctions at some length, and there is some treatment of distinction in Aristotle's *Organon* itself. But any real obsession with distinction is not easy to detect. If this logic is decadent, it is decadent in the sense in which non-Euclidean geometry or any pure mathematics is decadent or in the sense in which modern logistic is decadent. It simply goes its own way in speculation without regard for the practical use to which the speculation can perhaps be put. It evolves all sorts of complicated descriptions of complicated logical situations. In Peter of Spain's famous "Treatise on Supposition" we encounter this sort of "rule":

> It is impossible for a general term, functioning as a predicate, to have simple suppositional value and to be movably or immovably indeterminate when there is a universal sign in the subject of an affirmative proposition, as in the statement: "Every man is an animal." The reason for this is, as Porphyry indicates, that everything which is predicated of something is either greater than or equal to that of which it is predicated—and he had essential predication in mind. (Mullally 13)

This kind of detailed fence-running represents much the same kind of logic, recent studies have remarked (Boehner xii-xvi; Mullally v), as is found in the modern logistic of Carnap and others. The easiest way, perhaps, to form a notion of the high and late medieval arts course and of the intellectual climate in which it existed is to imagine a university course made up principally of a logic such as Professor Carnap taught in itself and as applied to physics. Like many modern logicians, Peter of Spain, in a fashion that cannot be detailed here, but is connected with the way he manipulates the predicaments, or categories, develops in his logic a strong mathematical torque. The way for Newton's mathematical physics was here being prepared, not by training in mathematics—that was to come later—but by a kind of pretraining in forming concepts in terms of quantitative and spatial analogies. The subject and predicate, as in the passage from Peter of Spain just quoted, were sized up as being "greater" or "lesser" than one another.

In this logical tradition interest in making distinctions shows up, indeed, in a special way in the technique of disputation that before the Renaissance took the place of written exercises almost completely. In the disputation process, indeed, distinctions were exploited—but again it is hard to discover any infatuation with them. When Ramus, in one of his rare amusing passages, makes fun of disputation procedures, he makes fun of the formal way of putting objections and responses rather than of the practice of making distinctions ("Prooëmium" in *Scholae* cols. 1087-96). Ramus himself was infatuated, as perhaps no one else—except one or another of his followers—has ever been, with making distinctions, and if making distinctions is a mark of scholastic decadence, then Ramus, the anti-scholastic, can lay claim to being the most decadent scholastic of all times. But "decadence" is a chameleon term and often confuses issues under the guise of emotionally simplifying them. Moreover, in Ramus' case there is something far more interesting than decadence or the lack thereof—the matter of *what* Ramus is interested in distinguishing, for at this point his interests represent the very culmination of the scholastic tradition that ejects him on the world.

What, then, is Ramus interested in distinguishing? Not angels dancing on the points of needles—the average arts professor kept angels at a good arm's length. Not "entities," or *entitatulae*, in any way that would give much meaning to the often quoted, but hard to explain, razor associated with William of Ockham, *entia non sunt multiplicanda sine necessitate*. Ramus, true heir of arts-course scholasticism, is interested chiefly and primarily in distinguishing the arts and/or sciences one from another and in distinguishing within these arts and/or sciences their separate parts.

This is one of the culminating points, if not, indeed, the chief culminating point, of the medieval arts course and the point at which this arts course helps generate the modern interest in scientific method. The study of logic in the scholastic tradition had been built around Aristotle's *Organon*, and this collection of most of Aristotle's logical treatises had kept in more or less continuous agitation questions concerning the different kinds of logic—the logic of dialectic, rhetoric, sophistic, poetic, and science—as well as questions concerning the interior structure of the various disciplines to which one or another of these logics applied. Throughout the centuries these questions were agitated, but they were not solved; that is, no generally accepted solution was arrived at that would be served up uniformly to all arts-course students by all arts-course professors. In Ramus' day, the various answers that had been generated were still proliferating. Ramus has one notion, Jacques Charpentier another, Adrien Turnèbe a third, and Melanchthon still one more.

The reasons for the lack of a universally accepted solution are manifold and rather respectable, on the whole. First, Aristotle's discussion had itself been conducted with a full awareness of the complexity of the linguistic situation, and not only his answers but also his very formulations of the questions are most often tentative, frequently downright puzzling, and almost always entirely too cagey to be open to the kind of whipping-boy interpretation that Ramus (or, in our own day, Korzybski) put on them—with documentation which at best is kept slender. Second, the philosophy program of three and one-half years, only one of which, Ramus tells us ("Pro philosophica" in *Scholae* col. 1049), was in his day devoted to the *Organon*, at Paris, scarcely gave time for a really adequate treatment of this not very systematic bundle of treatises discussing complicated questions concerning the various kinds of knowledge treasured by the human mind. University professors were aware of the difficulty here and came more and more to acknowledge it openly. In the early sixteenth century Juan de Celaya (fols. ii ff.) begins his lectures on Porphyry's *Isagoge* or introduction to Aristotle's *Organon* by explaining that he will follow the "modern" fashion of not treating at the beginning the question whether *logica* is a science or not, since such a thorny question is more fit to conclude than to begin a course in logic.

Third, apparently genuinely profound treatment of philosophical problems in the arts course was precluded by the youth of the students, if not of the professors, throughout the whole medieval and Renaissance history of universities (or of scholasticism—for there is no practical distinction whatsoever between the two histories, the university and the scholastic tradition being exactly the same thing). Students became masters of arts, which meant that they completed everything the university had to offer by way of courses in grammar, rhetoric, logic, and all philosophy, by the time they were approximately twenty. The University of Paris had actually been forced to leave statutes on its books to forbid anyone from actually teaching, M.A. or no M.A., before he was twenty years old (Denifle and Chatelain 1:78). And Ramus himself brags that he could turn out M.A.'s at the age of fifteen at his Collège de Presles better than the average university product ("Pro philosophica" in *Scholae* col. 1022).

If we marvel at the youth of the universities, we may marvel still more at the curious development of human intellection it manifests: the whole intellectual community that has produced the modern scientific world was fascinated with the problem of the structure and interrelation of the sciences before it had given many of these sciences a satisfactory content. But a historical fact is a historical fact, and this phenomenon is such a fact. It brings home to us the curious economy of human intellection, which first approaches its problems over the most abstract route—which, if often the most fruitless, is also the most direct route—doubling back only when it finds it must. At any rate, this abstract approach to the sciences, the attempt to determine their interrelation and structure before most of them were given satisfactory content, is the prelude to all our modern scientific and linguistic attitudes. It is the overture of modern scientific method. Nowhere else in the history of mankind and only after such a prelude does the symphony or the cacophony of the modern world appear.

Ramus has been arraigned for confusing logic and dialectic and for erecting the wrong kind of distinctions between both these things and rhetoric (Nelson). But seen in this real historical setting, Ramus shows no particular genius for confusing these things. He turns up in a confused situation, and his professed attempts to better the situation only perpetuate the confusion. He can be blamed, perhaps, for giving chaos a new lease on life. The huge problem of the regimentation of the sciences that swirls out of the Middle Ages and around him was too much for any professor caught in the arts-course tradition. Or at least, for any we know of so far. It is true that St. Thomas Aquinas had notions on the structure and interrelation of the sciences painstakingly thought out and matured—notions far from complete, but astute, carefully elaborated, cautious, and open to tremendous further development. However, like most of those reared in the scholastic tradition, Ramus did not make a point of studying St. Thomas, who was a theologian and, one knows, matured his notions in the long course—often twelve or even fifteen years—of theology, working out from theological problems a metaphysics and a kind of epistemology that is scarcely a part of the arts course scholastic tradition at all.

Ramus' preoccupations and confusions derive, often with astonishing directness, from the arts-course scholasticism in which he was trained. With reference to arts-course authors, not for nothing did his contemporaries call him the *usuarius*, the usufructuary, the man living off the income of property belonging to someone else. When he drives trenches right and left between the sciences, taking as his motto, in a revealing analogy, "Solon's Law" that regulated building developments in ancient Athens—a foot's margin for a wall, two feet for a house, and so forth

("Scholae rhetorica" in *Scholae* cols. 255-56)—Ramus is only continuing the preoccupation with assorting the sciences that began with the medieval study of the *Organon*.

When he says that dialectic and logic are the same thing, he does so, not because he feels called to overthrow an old order in favor of a new chaos, but because for more than two centuries university students in every part of Europe, particularly at Paris, Peter of Spain's alma mater as she was Ramus', had found in their introduction to logic, that is, in Peter of Spain's *Summulae logicales*, no distinction between logic and dialectic at all (Mullally xxi). (The *Summulae logicales* have been edited by I. M. Bochenski, O.P.; Mullally gives the most significant part of the work, *Tractatus Septimus*, also known as the *Parva logicalia*, in the complete Latin text with a parallel English translation.)

Similarly, when Ramus makes no clear-cut distinction between *ars* and *scientia*, this is not only because no clear-cut distinction is maintained in Cicero and Quintilian, but more precisely because this same *Summulae logicales* seems specifically to identify the two in its opening words, which, after a few biblical phrases and a bit of St. Augustine, form probably one of the most recurrent expressions throughout the Middle Ages and the Renaissance: "Dialectic is the art of arts, the science of sciences." ("*Dialectica est ars artium, scientia scientiarum, ad omnium methodorum principia viam habens*"—Peter of Spain, fol. 2^v.) Mullally (xxi and lxxiv) points out that this definition is reminiscent of Cicero's *Brutus*, (cap. xli-xlii). The definition is also echoed by Ockham and many others. Peter of Spain had not made clear whether he meant the "science of sciences" to be a synonym for or a supplement to the "art of arts." Very likely he was uncertain himself and wanted to blur the question. Certainly arts-course scholasticism as a whole had maintained the suspended state of mind, and it is a serious mistake to import a nicer terminology out of St. Thomas Aquinas or St. Albert the Great or any other author and call it "scholastic" without further ado.

It is impossible to consider Ramus' rhetoric apart from the background of scholastic dialectic and logic out of which it grew. This follows, indeed, from Ramus' own reiterated principles, which set up dialectic and rhetoric: as correlatives of one another, limiting one another's possessions, since between them were distributed the "laws" or "matter" hitherto held conjointly by a jumble of ill-assorted arts. But it follows even more imperiously from the psychological bent of Ramus' own mind, which, while not that of all scholastics, is certainly that of his own scholastic predecessors of the arts course at Paris and many other universities. Melanchthon, Ramus' great competitor and posthumously his enforced partner, once remarked that there was no medieval corruption of rhetoric as there had been of dialectic: the medieval authors had been relatively inactive on the rhetorical front, and "no authors are extant except the best"—that is, Quintilian and Cicero, chiefly (*"Nulli enim extant autores nisi optimi"* [s.l]. The complete passage from Melanchthon is given in translation in T. W. Baldwin, 2:9). This is true, but it meant for Melanchthon, as for Ramus, that his own handling of rhetoric, deriving necessarily from a mentality inherited from his immediate predecessors, whom he affected to despise, but whose influence he could not abdicate, was colored by the dialectical or logical tradition that was in all but complete possession of the field in the youth of Melanchthon, Ramus, and their contemporaries.

Indeed, humanism with its program calling for a controlled vocabulary and a carefully policed classical style, is a product of scholastic scientism almost as much as a reaction against it. No one can mistake the different accent when the same ground is covered by these professed devotees of the classical rhetoricians, who forswear scholasticism with bell, book, and candle, and by the classical rhetoricians themselves. The Renaissance rhetoricians, almost to a man, have a pronounced dialectical twang that contrasts with the smoother, more random, and often inconsistent observations of Cicero.

It is true that Ramus can be quite as inconsistent as Cicero ever was. But he cries loudly and incessantly in favor of consistency, which for him is an obsession in a way it could not be for either Cicero or Quintilian. Ramus' *Brutus' Problems* (*Brutinae quaestiones*) and *Evaluations of Quintilian's Rhetoric* (*Rhetoricae distinctiones in Quintilianum*) are both nothing but long and circumstantial diatribes against the alleged inconsistencies and lack of "method" in Cicero and Quintilian, respectively.

The dominance of dialectic in setting the rhetorical climate was also guaranteed by a fact about which we sometimes do not like to think. Through the Middle Ages and the Renaissance, rhetoric was a subject for little boys. Practically speaking, it had no existence for students after they were ten or twelve (later, perhaps, fourteen) years old. It was taught as a chore often by young masters of arts who were studying other subjects themselves, or even, perhaps, by still younger bachelors, also studying. Neither the Middle Ages nor the Renaissance rhetoric courses were sophistic or Attic schools for orators, late finishing schools polishing off their prospective graduates for immediate entry into active political life. Despite the campaigning of Erasmus and others, the rhetoric course mostly remained a propaedeutic to logic, philosophy, and thereafter professional studies. After the arrival of the universities, a training capped by rhetoric was never more to be known. Even Johann Sturm's Strasbourg Gymnasium soon became a university in name, as it had been already in inclination, and the Jesuit colleges evolved very early a university structure, with philosophy, not rhetoric, at the top. Harvard, which started as a Renaissance college, followed exactly the same pattern.

This does not mean that rhetoric was not an important subject or that it did not involve very important attitudes toward language and life in general that stayed with students forever. But it does mean that Ramist and other Renaissance rhetoric must be viewed in the whole complex educational picture of which it is a part and which we find so much difficulty in piecing together.

Renaissance rhetoric is, first of all, a means of teaching boys style, that is, Latin style. It is conceived practically, even when it fails to be practical. Melanchthon's justification for his statement that "dialectic presents things unclothed, rhetoric adds elocution as clothing" is typical: "Although many object to it, I am not against this distinction," he says, "for the reason that it can be grasped by youngsters," and, he adds, because it is etymologically consistent, if not with regard to the word "rhetoric," at least with regard to the word *elocutio.* (*"Dialectica res nudas proponit: Rhetorica vero addit elocutionem quasi vestitum. Hoc discrimen etsi nonnulli reprehendunt, ego tamen non repudio, quia et ad captum adolescentium facit, et ostendit, quid Rhetorica maxime proprium habeat, videlicet elocutionem, a qua ipsum Rhetorices nomen factum est."*) (13). Intellectually, this position may make us wince, but Melanchthon's reason—"because it, can be grasped by youngsters"—lies at the base of whole philosophies, from Ramus to John Dewey.

In the writings of St. Thomas there is a carefully thought out theoretical position for rhetoric as one of the probable logics directed toward a practical rather than a speculative end. That is not the kind of thing we have here. As it existed in the ancient world and as it emerged in the Middle Ages, rhetoric has no commonly accepted theoretical position. The implications of the position it actually did have, as the science that added "ornamentation" or clothing to naked thought, were not thought out by most of those who taught or studied rhetoric. Rhetoric existed as a curriculum subject, not because anyone had a clear-cut theoretical grasp of how to define it, but simply because somehow or other as a practical discipline it fitted into the reality of the curriculum. Moreover, rhetoric fitted into the curriculum at a level that did not encourage speculation about it. Youngsters who studied it were in no condition to profit from a philosophical discussion of what rhetoric was, and most of the writing about rhetoric comes to rest, directly or indirectly, at the level of these same youngsters. There is no explicitly grasped theoretical position at all, although there is an implied one, one with tremendous consequences.

To catch sight of this position, one will often find it less profitable to spin out the philosophical implications of one or another remark made by a rhetorician than to cut under such remarks to find the general frames of thought, the modes of conceptualization, the ways of conceiving reality that determine the direction taken by the rhetorician's thought when he feels he is going about his business of being a practical teacher. When we try to do this in the case of Ramus and the Ramists, we are driven back immediately to arts-course scholasticism and its own distinctive frames of thought as the machinery out of which the Ramist development, dialectical and rhetorical, is almost automatically to flow.

Arts-course scholasticism is, as has been earlier remarked here, a scholasticism of logic and physics—of a physics often erroneous and laced with too much logic, but nevertheless definitely a physics, and of a logic decidedly more oriented psychologically toward physics than toward metaphysics. This orientation of logic can be considered in Peter of Spain's *Summulae logicales*, doubtless the most important preparation for the Ramist dialectic and rhetoric. "This is the book of the *Summulae*," the influential John Major (or Mair) was telling his Paris auditors soon after the opening of the sixteenth century, when young Pierre de la Ramée came up to Paris, "[this is] the door to all logic, the usefulness of which is plain from its very definition. . . . Dialectic, which is also called logic, is ordinarily defined thus: It is the art of arts, the science of sciences" ("*Iste est Summularum liber, totius logices ianua: cuius utilitas ex eius definitione et proxime dicendis nota evadet. Dialectica, quae et logica dicitur, sic definiri solet: est ars artium, scientia scientiarum*") (fol. IIII, Libellus I, tractatus ii).

One historian of philosophy described the *Summulae logicales* as "a dialectical fencing manual" (de Wulf 2:85), but one need only read a little of it to perceive that it is scarcely this at all. This work is not concerned primarily with telling you what move to make when your opponent threatens to pink your predicate or to run through your entire major proposition from *S* to *P*. Rather than a book on practice, it is a kind of summary adaptation of Aristotle's quite theoretical *Organon*, with a new medieval development on what is known as "supposition" (*suppositio*) and associated subjects tacked on at the end. At the risk of some misunderstanding, we can describe Peter of Spain's special fashion of presentation as a kind of dephilosophizing, or demetaphysicizing of logical questions in favor of a treatment of those aspects of logic that can be summed up diagrammatically or by means of some sort of quantitative analogy.

For example, Peter of Spain not only passes over the difference between a dialectic concerned with what is merely probable and a logic of strict scientific demonstration, but he similarly disregards the crucial issue that forces itself on him concerning the difference between terms that are univocal and admit of classification by genus and species in categories and terms that are analogous—such as "being" or "one"—which cannot be fitted into one category rather than another. This issue is central and must be faced at least once in any theoretically grounded logic, but for Peter of Spain it does not even exist as a problem. He throws everything together higgledy-piggledy, without a pause for explanation, making "being" a genus just like "animal" (Mullally xxx). Similarly, the problem concerning the universal concept, which Porphyry had at least raised, is for Peter of Spain equally nonexistent. As inevitably happens when this problem is not squarely faced, the author of the *Summulae logicales* ends by saying all sorts of things, but to all intents and purposes treating the universal as a thing outside the mind just like an individual horse or dog (Mullally xxxi-xxxii). The epistemological problems raised by the *Posterior Analytics* of Aristotle are likewise brushed quickly aside.

By contrast with this lack of interest in the basic and recurrent problems of philosophy, Peter of Spain becomes tremendously preoccupied with all possible intricacies of problems of another sort. This can be seen in his "Treatise on Supposition," which forms the new part of the *Summulae logicales* representing a medieval development and which Ramus says formed almost the entire content of the first-year philosophy course at Paris. Here the problems in which Peter of Spain specializes reveal an intense interest in the quantitative or quantified aspects of propositions. The signification (*significatio*) of a term is the concept in the mind for which the term is a sign; but the *suppositio* is the actual individuals for which the term "stands" or "supposes." In the proposition "Man is a rational animal," the "man" supposes for all the individual men in the world. This kind of consideration opens questions such as what happens to such a proposition when another individual is born or dies and, by tying up logic with such head-counting, stresses the points at which logical operations resemble the jockeying of counters on a checker board or abacus.

This tendency to specialize in spatial, quantified conceptualization that bulks so large in the *Summulae logicales* gives a clue, if we did not have one already, as to what is forcing the particular kind of development that we find in this work, so important in the history of Western thought and the development of the modern mind. Here is being evolved a logic and by implication a whole attitude toward language that will govern rhetoric, too, that can be taught to bright little boys—for exactly the same reason that surprisingly complicated kinds of mathematical reason can be taught to bright little boys. In this kind of logical world the metaphysical depths are carefully filled in. After this the problems—or rather what is left of them—are handled legitimately, for the most part. If we disregard the falsification occasioned, if not actually caused, by omissions, there is really very little wrong with the positive development here, nothing decadent—as far as it goes. Very little more decadent, certainly, than in mathematical logic today. But there is a narrowly specialized way of considering the logical processes. The quantitative imaginative constructs that implement this specialized viewpoint are not too much for a bright fifteen-year-old, or possibly even a twelve-year-old—for the same youngster, that is, who would be completely at a loss in sighting even the problem at issue in a genuinely philosophical discussion about language.

The force at work here in shaping this logic is so elemental that we can miss it completely: the demand for a logic that can be absorbed by a youngster in his teens. Once we are aware of the imperiousness of this demand, some of the most characteristic and puzzling developments in the medieval logic that prepares the way for Ramist logic and rhetoric begin to open to us: the specialization in categorization, for example, or the tremendous interest in sophistic. These are things assimilable by boys. We recall that John of Salisbury remarked about sophistic that there was nothing easier to explain to youth (quoted in Mullally xcvii).

It was easy to explain to youth, so you had it in the arts of discourse. The same reason, as we have seen, accounts for Melanchthon's distinction between dialectic and rhetoric, which was practically Ramus' distinction, too, and which was not far from being the distinction of most of the educated world for centuries. The accent on youth explains even more than we might at first blush think, when we advert to the fact that before the rise of the universities in the Middle Ages the sciences had never catered to youth in the way in which they were made to do from then on.

What we have called the quantification of logic went hand in hand with the emphasis on physics rather than metaphysics in the scholasticism of the arts course and with the orientation of this course as a whole toward medicine. Law students did not need to complete the master of arts degree, and theologians were constantly campaigning for an abbreviated arts course so as to get more quickly to their specialized studies. The doctors of medicine took the arts course more seriously, and it is no accident that Ramus' philosophical opponents—Jacques Charpentier, Jean Riolan the elder, and Jean Quentin—were M.D.'s, as many of Ramus's followers and his own star pupil Nicolas de Nancel were to be. Peter of Spain had been a physician himself. Peter of Spain's posthumous reputation for black magic, which grew out of his great reputation as a physician, was not dimmed by the fact that he had been Pope (John XXI) for six months before he was killed by a falling roof. He had been connected with the papal court as physician to his predecessor, and while Pope he found time not only to concern himself with Nominalism at Paris but to issue documents on alchemists as well.

The implications of the scholastic physics, which the medical interests did so much to sustain, have been sounded a little in studies that have pointed up the connections of one or another old theory—the theory of impetus, for example—with more modern developments. But the larger psychological implications of medieval and Renaissance physics remain to be explored. These implications connect intimately with the quantified logic we have just mentioned. We know that the difference between the old arts-course scholastic physics and the far superior Newtonian physics lay largely in the explicit reliance on mathematics in the latter. The difference was not simply that the early physics was metaphysical, the later mechanical. The early physics was, if anything, too mechanical—as in the case of the impetus theory of the Parisian School of Buridan, Albert of Saxony, and Nicholas of Oresme, who seem to have conceived of the impetus as a kind of thing that lay inside the body that had acquired it. Such an objectified "impetus" was better fitted mechanically to push things along. Aristotle's theory of propulsion, which this had replaced, was in a way even more mechanistic. He seems to have conceived of the air as continually closing in behind and pushing an arrow when it had left the bow (Butterfield 11 ff.). From this kind of conceptualization Newtonian theory was a movement toward at least a more refined sort of mechanics.

This all may seem a far cry from rhetorical theory, but in reality it is only a fraction of an inch distant. Whether at Paris or at Oxford or at Salamanca, rhetoric was uniformly taught by masters of arts who had been put through this arts course. Peter of Spain and the arts course in which he plays such a representative role form the common background of Ramist and anti-Ramist, of semi-Ramists, of Philippo-Ramists, and of the collusionists of every stripe who plied back and forth between any and all of these camps.

The rigidity in Ramist rhetorical theory, the counterpart of the rigidity in Ramist dialectic, and the quality that helps produce the Puritan plain style have their roots here. The sources and the implication of Ramist rhetoric in the development of the Western sensibility have long been a major puzzle, and many have found it hard to believe that a theory of "ornamentation" of language could be proposed with the downrightness or crudity that seems to be found in the Ramist tradition. The puzzle has been increased by the fact that Ramism does not seem to add anything to the ingredients in the huge rhetorical and dialectical broth that the centuries had brewed, but rather to be merely some sort of rearrangement of the ingredients in the old recipes (Tuve 331).

This is, in a sense, even more true than has been generally realized, although it is likewise more true than has generally been realized that the century-old ingredients are undergoing in Ramism a real, if subtle, change corresponding to the changes in other areas of awareness in the Western world. The epistemological naivete in the Ramist attitudes toward language, the tendency to envision concepts as clipped off neatly from all association with imagery and to relegate them as total abstractions to the field of Ramist "dialectic," where they were thereupon treated as things, to be "opened," Ramus says, like closed baskets (*Dialecticae* fol. 18^V), the corresponding impoverishment of rhetorical theory that, on the one hand, maintained that to these abstract "arguments" rhetoric added ornament, or what Ramus's literary lieutenant Omer Talon liked to call *lumen*, but that, on the other hand, is quite unable to explain what this "ornament" can be that is added to naked truth—these things have sometimes been discussed as though the impasse arrived at here were particularly Ramist. It is not at all; it is the heritage of the scientism of the medieval arts course and of the structure of the university educational system.

Back of the Ramist rhetoric and the Puritan notion of a plain style is the arts course in which logical development takes its curiously quantified form as a preparation, not for metaphysics, but for Newtonian physics. The Puritan doctrine of plain style is puzzling, not because it rests on some well-thought-out theory plunged deep in a metaphysics that escapes our blunt twentieth-century minds, but because it rests on attitudes and habits of conceptualization that its proponents did not understand very well and are not necessarily consistent, as a well-thought-out theory should be, but that are nonetheless subtly connected with the whole complex intellectual ferment producing the modern mind.

In the university educational system as a whole, logic and linguistics in general were occasionally given a well-thought-out treatment, but this was for the most part a peripheral treatment occasioned by work in theology or medicine. It is in the interest in symbolism in these traditions that the seeds of a mature theory of language are contained. The theologians were interested in "typology," by which the meaning of Old Testament history is seen as matured in the actual historical events of the life of Christ. The physicians were interested in the human body and in all physical reality from a physical and symbolic view simultaneously. A voluminous tradition specializes in analogies between the human body, or microcosm, and the macrocosm, or universe, as well as in the general symbolic valences of the physical world. Thomas Brown's treatise on the mysteries of the quincunx is exceptional, not because of its subject, but rather because through some happy accident, unlike the hundreds of similar treatises, it is not written in Latin. This whole medical tradition has, of course, obvious connections—psychological, philosophical, and, I am inclined to think, also historical—with the present work of Jung and others on symbolic archetypes.

Within these two traditions, logical and rhetorical theory could retain or regain the suppleness that the mechano-scientistic bent of arts-course scholasticism was constantly tending to deny it. Here we find persistent, if not ubiquitous, exploitations of Aristotle's notion of the various kinds of logic—scientific, rhetorical, dialectic, and sophistic—that, as Peter of Spain's *Summulae* show us, the arts course tended to nullify and that Ramus makes the central objective to be destroyed by his curricular reform. But even when rhetorical theory was allowed a promising suppleness, it seldom overcame the handicap of being a subject for little boys, and however supple, it tended to remain rudimentary.

This is the intellectual setting in which Ramism arose—I speak of the setting in terms of theory and the determinants of theory. The teaching and the practice of rhetoric, at least by the Renaissance, was another thing. But Ramism was, before everything else, a theoretical reform, and its practical effects were shaped, rather more than is usual with such things, by its theory.

All this we should have been prepared more readily to see had we not entertained so many undemonstrable presuppositions concerning the past out of which grew Ramism and much in the Renaissance, that is, concerning the nature of arts scholasticism—that, considered in terms of the large number of those who studied it, was most scholasticism. Once we become aware of this background in many of its implications, we can see why Ramism—with its ideas opened like baskets, its arguments "glued" together in judgments, its methodized syllogisms, and its tropes and figures strung deftly through the whole—can often wear an expression so strangely familiar to us. The Ramist view of language exhibits the hallmarks of mechanistic views always, such as we find two centuries later in the associationist philosophers and can find all about us today: an engaging downrightness, based more or less obviously on rather crude spatial analogies that reveal themselves by a passion for charts or sometimes for more subtle schematizations, which turn out nevertheless to be little more than caricatures. In Ramus' case the characteristic symptom, although not by any means the most profound manifestation, of the real state of affairs is the dichotomized table—there are enough of these in print in Ramist works to extend, if laid end-to-end, for miles. These are the things that have their serviceableness in presenting material to youth, but that, philosophically, are so lethal, rendering unwelcome anything that cannot be so represented. For reasons that are assignable, but cannot be gone into here, undue attachment to these spatial images seems to be psychologically inevitable in any mentality that makes too much of distinctions or of "clear" ideas; in this way Ramus is the forerunner, if not exactly the cause, of Descartes.

But for all its naiveté, the quantitative manner of conceptualization is not to be neglected. It deserves serious study. Ramism alerts us to the fact that the psychological preparations for the modern specialization in quantity, in mathematical physics and all that goes with it, good and bad, has roots which are far deeper and rather more definitely assignable than we have thought. Ramist rhetoric is an event in an historical and psychological framework that we can grasp only by bettering our notions of what its antecedents really were.

Works Cited

Baldwin, T. W. *William Shakspere's Small Latine and Lesse Greeke.* 2 vols. Urbana, IL: U of Illinois P, 1944.

Bochenski, I. M., ed. *The Summulae logicales.* Turin: Marietti, 1947.

Boehner, Philotheus. *Medieval Logic.* Manchester, UK: Manchester UP, 1952.

Butterfield, Herbert. *The Origins of Modern Science.* London: G. Bell, 1950.

de Celaya, Juan. *Expositio . . . in librum Predicabilium Porphyrii.* Paris, 1516.

de Gouveia, Antonio. *Opera iuridica, philologica, philosophica.* Ed. Iacobus van Vaassen. Rotterdam, 1766.

de Launoy, Jean. *Regii Navarrae gymnasii Parisiensis historia.* Paris, 1677.

de Wulf, Maurice. *Histoire de la philosophie médiévale.* 6th ed. Louvain: Institut Supérieur de Philosophie, 1936.

Denifle, Henri and Emile Chatelain, eds. "Reformatio universitatis Parisiensis facta per Cardinalem legatum Guillelmum de Estoutevilla" (1452). *Chartularium universitatis Parisiensis*, IV. Paris, 1897.

Major, John. *Introductorium in Aristotelicam dialecticen, totamque logicen . . . nuper . . . repositum.* Paris, 1521.

Melanchthon, Philip. *Elementorum rhetorices libri duo, recens recogniti ab autore.* 1572. (Copy in my possession).

Mullally, Joseph P. *The Summulae logicales of Peter of Spain.* Notre Dame, IN: U of Notre Dame, 1945.

Nelson, Norman E. *Peter Ramus and the Confusion of Logic, Rhetoric, and Poetry.* Ann Arbor, MI: U of Michigan, 1947. (University of Michigan Contributions in Modern Philology, No. 2.)

Peter of Spain. *Summulae logicales cum Versorii Parisiensis clarissima expositione; parvorum item logicalium eidem Petro Hispani adscriptum opus.* Venetiis: P. Sansovinus, 1572

—. *Summulae logicales.* Ed. I. M. Bochenski, O. P. Turin: Marietti, 1947.

—. "Tractatus de Suppositione." *The Summulae logicales of Peter of Spain.* Ed. Joseph P. Mullally. Notre Dame, IN: U of Notre Dame, 1945. 2-19.

—. *Tractatus Septimus (Parva logicalia). The Summulae logicales of Peter of Spain.* Ed. Joseph P. Mullally. Notre Dame, IN: U of Notre Dame, 1945.

Pollard, Alfred W. and G. R. Redgrave. *A Short-title Catalogue of Books Printed in England, Scotland, & Ireland and of English Books Printed Abroad 1475-1640.* London: The Bibliographical Society, 1946.

Ramus, Peter. *Aristotelicae animadversiones.* Paris, 1543.

—. *Dialecticae institutiones.* Paris, 1543.

—. *Scholae in liberales artes.* Basle, 1569.

Rashdall, Hastings. *The Universities of Europe in the Middle Ages.* New ed. Ed. F. M. Powicke and A. B. Emden. 3 vols. Oxford: Clarendon P, 1936.

Schegkius, Iacobus (Iakob Schegk or Iakob Degen). *Hyperaspistes responsi ad quatuor epistolae Petri Rami contra se editas.* Tubingen, 1570.

Tuve, Rosemond. *Elizabethan and Metaphysical Imagery.* Chicago: U of Chicago P, 1947.

8

Ramus and the Transit to the Modern Mind (1955)

Pierre de la Ramée, or, as he is better known, Petrus Ramus (1515-1572), presents to the present English-speaking world an interest that is only with difficulty understandable in France or in most other Continental countries. The reasons for the interest are complex, but all more or less intimately connected with the tendency of the Anglo-Saxon mind, ever since the time of the medieval logicians, to generate philosophical thought out of linguistic analysis. Hybridized with the aestheticism that the late nineteenth-century English-speaking world learned largely from France, this tendency has produced today in England, and even more in America, a literary criticism of a sort relatively unknown in France itself. On the Continent generally, the best literary criticism is part of an overtly personalist dialogue that begins in the salon and may end anywhere in the cosmos. In America, and to almost the same extent in England, the best literary criticism—or at least a great part of it—often professes to begin with a rigorous consideration of a particular work of art in terms of its own integrity as an object of attention, to the exclusion (at least in principle) of all personality, and ends by generating—if not explicitly, at least by implication—direct examination of the conditions of knowledge itself and ultimately a kind of metaphysics.

This kind of criticism has grown particularly strong within the past decades and, with it, the feeling that the Renaissance, and the sixteenth century especially, was somehow or other a critical period with regard to linguistic attitudes, that during this period something happened in the way man talks about things, that somewhere after the sixteenth century a "dissociation of sensibility," to use Mr. T. S. Eliot's now well-worn phrase, had become discernible in the way man confronts the world around him.

Ramus is a man of the sixteenth century, and he is eminently a man concerned with language, with the traditional arts of expression—grammar, rhetoric, and logic. As the first and only professor of eloquence and philosophy at what was soon to be called the Collège de France, he stood on the middle ground between linguistics and metaphysics, a kind of humanist-scholastic. If he is himself no real thinker, all the more reason why the flurry his works created deserves looking into. This flurry is not to be underrated, for an international inventory of his works (Ong *Inventory*), which has long been wanting, reveals the astonishing total of nearly 800 separately published editions (including some adaptations) of single or collected works by him or his collaborator, Omer Talon (Audomarus Talaeus, ca. 1510-1562)—close to 300 editions of the important *Dialectic* alone. Counting separately each of the works in these 800-odd volumes (some of which include more than one item), one gets a total of some 1100 separate printings of individual works. All but a few of these fall in the century roughly between 1550 and 1650.

In the nineteenth century, two sizable studies of Ramus had appeared, one by Charles Waddington, and the other by Paul Lobstein. Lobstein's sober and discerning work is restricted to Ramus' posthumous *Commentariorum de Religione Christiana Libri Quatuor* and concludes that theologically Ramus stood for a mild Zwinglianism that is in the long run quite uneventful. Lobstein is quite right. Ramus' significance certainly does not lie in theology. This one and only theological work out of his sixty-odd separate productions was never printed by any other than the Wechel firm at Frankfort-on-the-Main. Its chief significance appears in Theophilus Banosius's preface, which dedicates the work to Sir Philip Sidney; and the significance consists in a curious deformation of theology. For, as Banosius proudly remarks, Ramus here attempts to reduce religion itself to an "art" like the arts of expression—grammar, rhetoric, and logic—an event truly momentous if we only examine the long-neglected history of arts scholasticism and its connection with the sixteenth-century passion for "method," or with Calvin's *Institution de la religion chrétienne* and its patently schoolroom-type title.

Waddington's work is more ambitious than Lobstein's, and the valuable mass of facts he assembles merits more competent exegesis than that which he provides. His resolution of the issues is almost exclusively personal and moral, often to a passionate and even neurotic degree. There are good people and bad people, and Ramus was one of the good ones. The real issues are hardly exposed, for Waddington gives no evidence of reading either the people Ramus reacted against, headed by Peter of Spain, Pierre Tartaret (Tartaretus or Tateretus), and the like, or Ramus's chief source after Cicero, Rudolph Agricola. Characteristically, Waddington can completely miss the significance of a sixteenth-century term such as *hypothesis*, while making a passionate issue of it (355). The medieval and Renaissance meanings of *thesis* and *hypothesis* were largely controlled by the use of these terms in rhetoric. A non-hypothetical science was not an observational science, as Waddington suggests, but precisely a deductive science. (See Ramus's adversary Iacobus Schegkius 124.) It should be said in Waddington's favor, however, that Ramus is not in any sense simple to explain. As a paper on Ramism in the Netherlands read at the recent International Congress of Philosophy at Brussels makes clear (Dibon), Ramism is radically eclectic and often hard to distinguish from other movements, even those it professes to be against.

The most pretentious study of Ramism since Waddington and Lobstein is Frank Pierrepont Graves' *Peter Ramus and the Educational Reformation of the Sixteenth Century*. This work is the best all-round brief of the positive content of Ramus' various works, and it will remain permanently useful. Unfortunately, the background in which it sets the works is, at best, sophomorically conceived, without any sense of the real movement of intellectual history and with a repetition, sometimes word-for-word, of Waddington's moral indignation as a substitute for historical perspective. Waddington had seen Ramus as a sixteenth-century Victor Cousin; Graves makes him a sixteenth-century John Dewey, forcing on the technical legal term *usuarius* the unheard-of meaning of "utilitarian" and even "pragmatist" (57). The 1922 thesis of M. Robert Barroux at the École Nationale des Chartes, "Pierre de la Ramée et son influence philosophique," is far more intelligently provocative in handling the context of Ramism, for it suggests the huge perspectives in which Ramus' "method" is set, perspectives that open into the very center of the intellectual heritage of Western man.

However, with the occasional articles, mostly German, that have appeared in the past century, all these studies by Waddington, Lobstein, Graves, and Barroux remain rather isolated from one another. Present-day interest in Ramism in the English-speaking world is a different kind of thing. It is rather communal; and it tends to regard Ramism not as a mere *cause célèbre* admitting of revival from time to time, but rather as a phenomenon or symptom that, studied dispassionately, may yield helpful and perhaps even startling information concerning intellectual history and the formation of the modern mind. This present-day interest received its greatest stimulus when Professor Samuel Eliot Morison produced his *Harvard College in the Seventeenth Century* as a part of the Harvard tercentennial celebration in 1936, publishing at the end of the second volume lists of the theses defended at Harvard from 1643 to 1708. These theses are thoroughly scholastic in any acceptable twentieth-century meaning of this term; but they are also, particularly in the earlier period, most decidedly Ramist. *"Sola Dialectica Concrescit cum Seipsa et cum Omnibus Aliis Artibus"*

[Dialectic alone increases with itself and with all the other arts], *"Grammatica Est Perfecta sine Rhetorica Non Contra"* [Grammar is perfect, even without rhetoric], *"Linguae Sunt Artium Gratiâ"* [Languages exist by the grace of the arts], *"Bene Metiri Est Cujusque Magnitudinis Proportionem et Affectionem Perspicere"* [To be measured well is to perceive the proportion and emotion of its magnitude]—these titles we read among the theses for August 9, 1653. Earlier, in 1647, there was *"Res Est in Loco, Tempus in Re"* [A thing is in space, time in the thing]—a thesis that reveals the box-inside-of-box formulation typical of Ramist "analysis."

The weird sound of some of these assertions—*"Rhetorica Est Affectuum Hortus"* [Rhetoric is the garden of feelings], a 1653 thesis emended in 1691 to *"Rhetorica Est Affectuum Syren"* [Rhetoric is the quicksand of feelings] or *"Dialectica Est Sol Microcosmi, Argumenta Sunt Logici Radii"* [Dialectic is the sun of the microcosm, syllogisms the rays of logic] or again *"Methodus Intelligentiae Parens Est, Magistra Memoriae"* [Method is the parent of intellect, the teacher of memory] (1653)—fell tantalizingly on ears in the English-speaking world trained by twentieth-century interest in metaphysical poetry to expect the unexpected in sixteenth- and seventeenth-century linguistic attitudes. They suggested that the interior of the early New England mind certainly did not correspond to the accepted description of this mind drafted by a chauvinistic nineteenth-century liberalism using the past as a mirror for itself. In 1939 Professor Perry Miller of Harvard produced a new description in his revolutionary work, *The New England Mind*, where, among other things, the Ramist tradition was given its full due and placed in the largest context it had ever been placed in: New England Augustinian piety, the Scholastic heritage, the New Englander's persuasions about the nature of man and his relation to God, the question of rhetoric and the plain style, and of God's covenant with New England. Three years before, the same year as Morison's work, Professor Hardin Craig of Stanford University had published *The Enchanted Glass: The Elizabethan Mind in Literature*, which provided a further discussion of Ramism in the cis-Atlantic English-speaking world, describing Ramus as "the greatest master of the short-cut the world has ever known." This work has been followed by others, which also depend on Miller's fuller treatment, such as Rosemond Tuve's *Elizabethan and Metaphysical Imagery*, Sister Miriam Joseph's *Shakespeare's Use of the Arts of Language*, and T. W. Baldwin's two-volume *William Shakspere's Small Latine and Lesse Greeke*, and several other works with large sections on Ramism and its effect on the literary sensibility of the sixteenth and seventeenth centuries.

As a result of these and recent shorter studies, interest in Ramus and Ramism is now at its maximum in the English-speaking world (Nelson;

Duhamel, "Logic," "Milton's"; French; Howell; Ong, "Hobbes," "Methodism," "Johannes Piscator," "Fouquelin's"). This concentration of interest is perhaps as it should be, for, although as a movement Ramism had its greatest vogue in Germany (largely because its specious encyclopedism made it attractive to the often newly organized and somewhat starry-eyed German universities), it had its second greatest vogue in the English-speaking world, in the British Isles, the American colonies, and among the exiles in the Low Countries, where it had also an indigenous history, fed from both the German and the British sides (Ong *Inventory*). After his death in 1572 in the massacre on St. Bartholomew's Day, Ramus ceased to have much direct importance in his own country. This fact was connected with religious differences; but it cannot at all be explained by them alone, for, although Ramus had become a Protestant toward the end of his life, Ramism, as has been indicated above, does not directly engage theology (its strong but subtle theological implications were never really adverted to by contemporaries and represent tendencies widespread among Catholics, too). The weakness of Ramism in France is connected with the fact, which the tabulation of the editions of the *Dialectic* and the *Rhetoric* will make clear, that when it later reached its full strength, Ramism did so as a dialectic more than as a rhetoric, whereas at the earlier period, when Ramus was accepted in France, he was accepted rather as a rhetorician—the greatest Latin orator since Cicero, thought his colleagues, who were possibly right. The reason for this state of affairs is fascinating but too complicated to be gone into here.

As scholars in the English-speaking world have suspected, the significance that Ramism has for our age can be largely described in terms of developments with the more or less complementary fields of dialectic and rhetoric. Medieval arts scholasticism—that is, scholastic *philosophy*—in the large regarded dialectic, to which it commonly assimilated logic (McKeon), not as the art of thinking but, following the Ciceronian tradition, as the art of discourse (*ars disserendi*), with all the equivocation that this ample view implied. One could never be sure whether dialectic and/or logic governed only certain, formal, scientific reasoning, or whether it governed also, and in the same fashion, all the intellectual elements in all speech. In the *Summulae logicales* of the thirteenth-century Peter of Spain—which, in its historical consequences, is probably the most important scholastic work of all times, since, directly or indirectly, it controlled arts scholasticism at Paris and through Northern Europe until Rudolph Agricola projected his topical logic toward the end of the sixteenth century—dialectic is *described* as an art having to do with probabilities; but it is *treated* as an art dealing with certainties like those in mathematics—

except for the astounding fact that the topics (which had classically to do with probabilities) are thrown in without explanation for good measure. This picture is complicated by the connection of dialectic in practice with scholastic dispute and, even more importantly, with the pedagogical tradition of the northern universities, where dialectic or logic is likely to be viewed as the art of teaching rather than as the art of thinking.

As the art of discourse or speaking, or of teaching, dialectic or logic had a definite connection with the audile and with words as sounds, with the definite personalist and existentialist implications that attach to a world of voices. Ramus arrives on the scene at the time this dialectic is being "simplified" in an operation that is among the most complicated and critical and central in the whole history of the human mind and out of which grows preoccupation with method and the whole modern mechanistic-minded world, for it must not be forgotten that, in theory and to a great extent in fact, dialectic or logic controlled all the other arts or sciences or curriculum subjects. This simplification of logic is connected with the humanists' determination to provide something adapted to the capacities of children, for humanism is pupil-centered, whereas the northern universities, essentially teachers' unions, were teacher-centered, tending to see their pupils not in terms of the pupils' capacities here and now, but as aspirant pedagogues. But the simplification is even more deeply related to a widespread and mysterious shift from the audile to the visile in the whole way of thinking about cognition and the nature of man. At the end of this shift, by the eighteenth century, God will become in the minds of many curiously mute, and by that fact depersonalized, a mere mechanic, a celestial architect, a mason, whose laws concern not the human consciousness but the ranging of objects in space. Man's notion of what he himself is will undergo a corresponding shift in emphasis.

The details of this shift from the audile to the visile cannot be described apart from a much fuller treatment of Ramism than is possible here, for they are extremely complicated and profound. But they are unmistakable. It is within this shift that Ramus turns up—an eloquent man, voluble and learned besides, but so innocent of genuine philosophical insight as to be an unwitting catch-all for the tendencies of the age that more discerning men often tried to resist or at least to understand and control. As one observes Ramism in its historical unfolding, beginning with Rudolph Agricola and his replacement of the old scholastic logic or logistic with a logic of "places" (commonplaces or *loci*) even more mechanistic in implication, and developing through Ramus himself and into German philosophical "systems" conceived by analogy with Copernican space and into English "Methodism" (Ong, "Methodism"), it becomes possible to assign what, I believe, is the central significance of Ramus and Ramism, at least for our own age.

Ramism is above all, although not exclusively, a manifestation of the subtle and apparently irresistible shift sacrificing auditorily oriented concepts for visually oriented ones that sets in with medieval scholasticism and on which most of the characteristic manifestations of the modern as against the ancient world depend. This shift is intimately connected with the scholastic emphasis on a logic that, as against more purely Aristotelian logic, was a kind of logistic (Boehner), and on physics—a bad physics, but physics nevertheless, taught to millions of schoolboys from the thirteenth to the sixteenth century and later on a scale the ancient world had never even approximated. The shift is equally connected with the scholastic build-up of the teaching profession. It is connected with the invention of printing, with the emergence of book titles in their postincunabular form, with the development of a sense of format for communication encouraged by printing, with the humanists' attitude toward language—a thing controlled by the *written* word, the word committed to space, not by *living* speech—as well as with the belief that all revelation was contained in a book.

The shift manifests itself in Ramism particularly in Ramus' complete divorce between dialectic and rhetoric. For Ramus appears on the scene just when dialectic (or logic) was shifting from an art of discourse, as Cicero had had it and as Ramus' Latin definitions nominally have it, to an art of thinking or reasoning. As an art of discourse, dialectic had suggested an interplay of personalities, a give and take in an existentialist situation. As an art of thinking, it was carried on in the privacy of one's own head and in a fashion more and more diagrammatic, with greater and greater reliance on spatial analogies and a more or less overt desire to dispense with words as words, since these annoyingly hint that in some mysterious way thinking itself is always carried on in the presence—at least implicit—of another. The meaning of the well-known Ramist tables of dichotomies is to be sought here in the drift toward spatial analogies of any and all sorts. With dialectic separated from rhetoric as a kind of intellectual diagrammatics, rhetoric is left in absolute control of the world of sound as sound. But even here, the spatial imagination gains control, and rhetoric comes to be described as a kind of ornament conceivable in mechanico-spatial terms.

Such are the issues which Ramism involves and such the issues within which the sixteenth-century and seventeenth-century madness about method swirls. The study of Ramism shows the utter fatuousness of considering Bacon or Descartes as the fountainheads of interest in method.

They are not the start but the culmination. Ramus was older than Francis Bacon by two generations, and it is quite evident that in Ramus' day the question of method had been long at the boiling point. The method crisis had set in in the scholastic period. We sometimes forget that the only place in the entire history of human thought where our "modern methodology" (which culminates in the H-bomb) emerges is after the scholastic age, as we sometimes forget, too, that most scholasticism was not theology at all and most scholastics were not priests.

The study of Ramism makes it evident that to understand the history of method we have to abandon our own favorite lines of explanation and get back to the issues as they really existed. The basic issue was not the struggle between inductive and deductive method, for there never was any serious or concerted opposition to inductive method but, if anything, too much respect for it—philosophers commonly took it for granted that induction was essential groundwork and therefore that it was easy to do and needed no special attention. The basic issue was the struggle between sound and sight, between habits of thinking based on listening to voices and habits of thinking based on looking at surfaces, between living in a world inhabited by persons who talked back and living in a world occupied by passive objects scattered in "systems" through the new Copernican space. The real obstacle in the way of fuller inductive development was not deduction but the voice and person of the teacher, who kept talking all through the scholastic centuries. The way in which teaching actually blocked observation in dissection as practiced in medical lectures has been shown by Herbert Butterfield (32-33). This situation is symptomatic of the whole state of mind at the time. But this same teacher proved all-important, nevertheless, in paving the way for a more inductive approach, since his incessant talking helped reduce the dialogue of dialectic to a monologue and thus was a preparation for the more complete elimination of personal components in the scientific situation in favor of an "objective," apersonal approach.

The great crisis of the sixteenth century is set in these strange perspectives, and Ramus' famous anti-Aristotelian reform of logic lodges here, too. Ramus' attack on logic was an attack not on deduction—nobody ever deduced with the fanaticism of a Ramist—but on that bedrock of intellectual life, the curriculum. This is why the teachers' unions that we call universities reacted, for logic was not only the art of discourse but a fortiori the art of teaching, by which curriculum subjects were, at least nominally, organized. In the opening words of Peter of Spain's *Summulae logicales*, dialectic was defined as "*ars artium et scientia scientiarum*"—where *ars*, and even *scientia*, is in effect a curriculum subject. Renaissance educators seldom reversed this ruling. Ramus' wild desire to attack the curriculum was accompanied by no remarkably discerning solutions of the difficulties, which were real, although his practical reforms in teaching methods, like those of many others in his age—Vives, Sturm, the Jesuits—were common-sense and in some measure effective. Ramus's overpowering drive, which he shared with many contemporaries, was a deep-seated, unconscious yearning for simplification, which expressed itself finally and characteristically within the Ramist economy in diagrams—there are whole folio volumes by Ramists in which every word and phrase is spitted on a dichotomized table, deployed in a spatial relation to the other words and phrases.

This drive toward the spatial, this reinforcement of the visile component of cognition, is a drive toward the construction of the observational, depersonalized collection of objects in terms of which we picture the world today, because it is a drive to think of things as surfaces, objects, rather than as symbols or as persons with voices. But the drive in Ramus' case is completely blind: he has no noteworthy expressed partiality for an observational approach at all. What he wants is "arts," something to know that is clear, distinct, set down once for all in a book, and, in the last analysis, picturable—the visile Ramus is the forerunner of the visile Descartes here. At this point, the way is prepared for "objectivity" by the death of the element of dialogue in dialectic. The two-part Socratic personal interchange is gone, and even the monologue of the teacher is gone—in other words, persons and voice are gone. An art is now a "thing," not a possession of the mind but something with surface, like the rest of the coming Newtonian world.

Works Cited

Baldwin, T. W. *William Shakspere's Small Latine and Lesse Greeke*. 2 vols. Urbana: U. of Illinois P, 1944.

Barroux, M. Robert. "Pierre de la Ramée et son influence philosophique." *Positions des thèses*, École Nationale des Chartes. Paris: Librairie Alphonse Picard, 1922. 13-20.

Boehner, Philotheus. *Medieval Logic*. Manchester, UK: Manchester UP; Chicago: U. of Chicago P, 1952.

Butterfield, Herbert. *The Origins of Modern Science*. London: G. Bell and Sons, 1950.

Craig, Hardin. *The Enchanted Glass: The Elizabethan Mind in Literature*. Oxford: Blackwell, 1966. (Originally 1935)

Dassonville, M.-M. "La genèse et les principes de la dialectique de Pierre de la Ramée." *Revue de l'Université d'Ottawa* 23 (1953): 322-59.

Dibon, P. "L'influence de Ramus aux universités neerlandaises du 17e siècle." *Actes du XIème Congrès Internationale de Philosophie* 14 (Bruxelles, 1953): 307-11. ("Complèment au Vol. 12").

Duhamel, Pierre Albert. "The Logic and Rhetoric of Peter Ramus." *Modern Philology* 46 (1949): 163-71.

—. "Milton's Alleged Ramism." *Publications of the Modern Language Association of America* 67 (1952): 1035-1053.

French, J. Milton. "Milton, Ramus, and Edward Phillips." *Modern Philology* 47 (1949): 82-87.

Graves, Frank Pierrepont. *Peter Ramus and the Educational Reformation of the Sixteenth Century.* New York: Macmillan, 1912.

Howell, Wilbur Samuel. "Ramus and English Rhetoric: 1574-1681." *Quarterly Journal of Speech* 37 (1951): 299-310.

Joseph, Sister Miriam. *Shakespeare's Use of the Arts of Language.* New York: Columbia UP, 1949.

Lobstein, Paul. *Petrus Ramus als Theologe.* Strasbourg, 1878.

McKeon, Richard. "Rhetoric in the Middle Ages." *Speculum* 17 (1942): 1-32.

Miller, Perry. *The New England Mind: The Seventeenth Century.* New York: Macmillan, 1939.

Morison, Samuel Eliot. *Harvard College in the Seventeenth Century.* Cambridge, MA: Harvard UP, 1936.

Nelson, Norman E. *Peter Ramus and the Confusion of Logic, Rhetoric, and Poetry.* "The University of Michigan Contributions in Modem Philology," No. 2. Ann Arbor: U. of Michigan P, 1947.

Ong, Walter J. "Fouquelin's French Rhetoric and the Ramist Vernacular Tradition." *Studies in Philology* 51 (1954): 127-42.

—. "Hobbes and Talon's Ramist Rhetoric in English." *Transactions of the Cambridge [England] Bibliographical Society* 3 (1951): 260-69.

—. "Johannes Piscator: One Man or a Ramist Dichotomy?" *Harvard Library Bulletin* 8 (1954): 151-62.

—. "Peter Ramus and the Naming of Methodism: Medieval Science through Ramist Homiletic." *Journal of the History of Ideas* 14 (1953): 235-48.

—. *Ramus and Talon Inventory: A Short-title Inventory of the Published Works of Peter Ramus (1515-1572) and of Omer Talon (ca. 1510-1562) in Their Original and in Their Variously Altered Forms.* Cambridge, MA: Harvard UP, 1958.

Peter of Spain. *Tractatus Septimus (Parva logicalia). The Summulae logicales of Peter of Spain.* Ed. Joseph P. Mullally. Notre Dame, IN: U of Notre Dame, 1945.

Schegkius, Iacobus. *De Demonstratione Libri Quindecim.* Basileae, 1564.

Tuve, Rosemond. *Elizabethan and Metaphysical Imagery.* Chicago: U of Chicago P, 1947.

Waddington, Charles. *Ramus: sa vie, ses écrits, et ses opinions.* Paris: C. Meyrueis et ce, 1855.

9

Metaphor and the Twinned Vision:
The Phoenix and the Turtle (1955)

Metaphor, our generation likes to tell itself, is an omnipresent principle of language. What is the reason for the kind of primacy that metaphor enjoys in linguistic operations and that underlies its peculiar semantic effectiveness? No single answer can exhaust this fecund question, but I should like here to suggest a sort of answer that has hitherto not received the formulation it deserves and then consider *The Phoenix and the Turtle.*

I

Metaphor has many aspects, but for the present we may consider it, in a least-common-denominator definition, as the use of a term in a sense or signification improper to the term. Thus we include what all definitions or descriptions of metaphor somehow or other take into account: a kind of doubling, a bifocal quality. This twinning aspect of metaphor is implied as soon as we speak of an "improper" signification, which suggests a "proper" one. The term "improper" is not to indicate that the second signification is wrong, awkward, or only grudgingly allowed, although theories of metaphor have always suffered from a tendency to read this implication into the metaphorical situation. In metaphor, there is merely a signification that has a kind of priority, a prescriptive or presumptive right to the term for the simple reason that, in the hurly-burly of semantic activity, it somehow got prior hold of the term. In this sense, the second meaning has some of the disadvantages of an intruder.

While this is not to say that metaphors are embarrassing in the linguistic situation, it is perhaps to say that the linguistic situation itself is embarrassing, that the human way of knowing, which gives rise inevitably to linguistic symbolization, is involved in an impasse in which it can find and maintain its sense of direction only by somehow escaping from itself.

It is a commonplace that in metaphor a term does not abandon one signification for another, but rather stands related to two significations at once. When we speak of a certain man as a cur, the metaphor is effective in so far as we can keep the term "cur" attached primarily not to a man but to a dog. If the primacy of this original attachment is compromised, if the word becomes attached to the second meaning more or less directly so that the primary meaning is eliminated or at least is no longer effective—as when we speak of the foot of a mountain or the head of a table—the metaphor becomes spent, or even ceases to be a metaphor at all.

The doubling or twinning of two concepts that metaphor thus demands is a clue to the psychological and linguistic importance of metaphor. At the heart of the linguistic situation, there is another kind of twinning that human intellection must constantly seek to circumvent but that it can never succeed in escaping. This twinning is at the heart of all human operations of understanding. It is the judgment or enunciation or statement, the operation by which a subject is joined to a predicate to make a unit of discourse that has, as we say, *complete* sense.

Faced with an object, the human intellect is simply not equipped to assimilate it *en bloc*—not the object nor even any tiniest aspect of it. Man knows *componendo et dividendo*—by putting together and setting apart. Even after it has built up a reserve of symbols or concepts, if the mind is to get at the truth of a thing, it must always make two passes at it. One never suffices. The mind needs two items to set against one another. Looking at the object in the aquarium before us, "This," we say, laying hold of the thing intellectually in a sweeping, indiscriminate, unabstract way ("this" is a kind of pointing)—"This," we say, "swims," and with "swims" we have made another pass at the same object, caught it up again, only this time in a more precise kind of grip, one that clamps tighter the first, more haphazard, intellectual hold we had. We consider here only the simplest possible instance, but what obtains here always obtains: predicates specify, delimit, render more definite their subject, give it "form." By manipulating two items so that one thus for a brief instant controls the other we "know" in the full sense, we possess—for a brief moment—truth.

The object with which the intellect is concerned may be a huge disorganized landscape or a small, highly unified existent—our living, swimming organism. It makes no difference. The intellect must secure two separate footholds, one in the condition of subject, the other in the condition of predicate. In terms of a simple apprehension, a simple grasp, a simple concept, we cannot even pose the question of truth or falsehood. If a person says merely "star" or "arthritis" with no complementary subject or predicate even implied, it is impossible to broach the question as to whether what he is saying or thinking is true or not.

The fact that our decisive engagement with reality, the achievement of truth, is effected in some sort of twinning process throws light on the nature of concepts themselves—or, as they are also called, ideas or simple apprehensions. These things are destined to be coupled. They cannot stand on their own feet alone. They generate truth only by pairing with one another, as in the material world the most advanced form of generation is accomplished by the bi-polarized sexes, for human concepts are drawn from this world and behave accordingly. Our concept of "tree" or of "color" or of anything else, including complex concepts, which may also serve as subjects or predicates, such as "a nation of free men," "freedom from all contagious diseases"—each of these concepts is so formed as to be joined with other concepts in our intellectual operations. For everything we represent to ourselves as a concept can only turn up as a potential member of a pair of concepts, a potential part of an enunciation or judgment.

Now, as an intellectual device, the enunciation or judgment presents real problems. Its binarism—the binarism endemic in human intellection—is awkward, and such is the curiously introspective power of intellect that it can sense its own limitations here. Intellection is polarized to simplicity. It yearns to reduce everything to one principle, one starting point, not two. This polarization is so strong that the intellect wants to cut back of the enunciation itself, a poor, two-membered thing, Over the ages we can actually observe the human intellect as, by a chronic compulsion, it beats about for a simple apprehension, a single concept, an idea out of which it can draw everything. It wants a plenary or elemental experience of truth that is absolutely simple, a one. Out of this compulsion, all the philosophies of idealism are born, from Plato through medieval idealistic philosophies, through Cartesianism, down to Hegel and our modern world.

The attempts to base truth not on a compound—which is the result of perception—but on a supposedly simple thing come into the mind from no one knows where, will doubtless continue to the end of time. And critics will not be wanting as they have not been wanting in the past, to point out that the attempts are, however fruitful in many ways, ultimately involved in a fog of self-deception. Descartes' essay was indeed a dream, as it has been called, just as much, if not so overtly, as was Plato's theory of reminiscence. Any idealism is an escape from the real problem. Descartes pretends to develop an idea, but he does so, significantly, not by firing ideas one by one at his auditors but by firing enunciations or statements. His ideas, like everyone else's, come two by two. If the idea

itself is primary, it is indeed strange that it needs explaining, needs clarification, in what is supposed to be. a series of secondary or derivative
operations known as enunciations in which ideas turn up as dependent on
one another, not as absolutes but as parts, as pieces, in a construct.

The critic will indict Descartes of "angelism," reminding him that he
is trying to project into the human cognitive situation conditions that
philosophical speculation has better associated with cognition by "separated intelligences" or angels. In a world of "pure intelligence," where
intellect was not embedded in material existence, there would, indeed, be
no necessity for the composite thing called enunciation or judgment:
understanding would be effected immediately by a simple concept, an
intellectual monad, not a dyad. But of a concept such as this, one that
expresses truth in one sole grasp, we can have no direct experience. We
can talk of it, for we can envision it as the limit that our intellection moves
toward but that it is incapable of achieving. We can dream about the
whole science of field physics, let us say, as summed up in one word. But
to us, the word is quite ineffable. We cannot conceive it, let alone express
it. Were we instructed by some strange illumination how to form such
monad concepts, we should perhaps be destroyed by the travail that their
conception would entail. For us, relativity physics, however awe-inspir-
ing its conclusions, will remain like everything else we understand: a
series of principles and conclusions expressed in the composite structures
called enunciation or statements. If and when the more simple and gener-
alizing mathematical formulae now being sought are found, they will be,
like their predecessors, mathematical formulations figuring in enunciations, too.

About the further criticism of idealism, we need not be concerned, but
only with the persistent attraction of idealism for the human mind. A finite
being with an intellect is always too smart for himself. Inevitably, the
human intellect becomes acquainted with its limitations and hankers to circumvent them. Intellect has at least this much edge on non-intellectual
knowledge, that it can know that it has troubles when it has them. It thus
develops a curious nostalgia for something it has not really known, for the
greater unification of which its own activity bears a negative imprint.

II

At this point metaphor offers its tantalizing consolations. Metaphor, as has
been seen, is a doubling or twinning of intellectual vision, and as such
decidedly reminiscent of the double grasp at the heart of every enunciation.

Here we are taking metaphor in its simple form, as when I say of a
man, *That cur should not be allowed to continue in office*. It must be

understood that we are not considering the instances when metaphor is applied to a subject by means of a verb, as in the sentence *That man is a cur,* where there are questions extraneous to that of the metaphor itself. It is in the metaphor itself, independently of expressed predication, that the doubling here spoken of occurs. By the very fact that it occurs independently of a predicate, by a simple operation involving only one term, the metaphorical kind of twinning has from the point of view of simplicity and unification an advantage over the kind found in the full statement or enunciation. It suggests this latter twinning without being so overtly complex. It seems to do the work of an enunciation, but it also seems to be simpler in structure.

Actually, the metaphor does imply a kind of predication. We imply a proper term and implicitly predicate the improper term of it. It is as though I said, *That man, who is a cur, should not be allowed to continue in office.* But, since "cur" is predicated of man only by implication—for in the simple metaphor the "man" does not openly appear—the mind feels the impact of the two terms as practically one. This creates the impression of extraordinary unity or condensation, and it accounts for the brilliance, the glow of resplendent intelligibility that we sense in metaphor and that Quintilian long ago referred to as "light." Since the metaphor must be based on some similarity, however elusive, the impression of unity rests on more than a pure illusion. Often on not much more, for the similarity desirable here is of a curious kind, since the same term that unites the two concepts must also keep them distinct. Thus it is that the most farfetched or unexpected metaphors can be the most effective, provided that somehow the distance between the widely divergent meanings can be effectively bridged. Their divergence can then suggest the separation of subject and predicate terms without the actual complications that an expressed subject and predicate would necessitate.

The metaphor is thus an intellectual monad and dyad all at once. In it the mind senses the twinning suggestive of the enunciation, by which it is best equipped to lay hold of truth intellectually, but it senses this twinning in one single term, so as to suggest that the mind is, for once, functioning with single, not with double vision. The mind is pretty well eating its cake and having it, too. Which is only as it should be, for in non-metaphorical apprehension of truth, it never manages to eat to its complete satisfaction.

III

The explanation advanced here, which sees metaphor as a kind of economical or condensed judgment, suggests intimate connections between metaphor and poetry. For in some profound sense, poetic apprehension involves a condensed and simplified awareness, too. The vistas opened at this point are too extensive to be gone into fully here, but a brief example may be to the point.

The Phoenix and the Turtle has long seemed to me a poem in which metaphor rules with particular insistence. The economy of the poem comes so far under the control of metaphor that, in a twinkling, by a simple flick of attention, the theme of the poem converts into a metaphor of metaphor itself. The cardinal metaphors at work can be discerned at once. The phoenix, as suggesting change that is both death and birth, and the turtle, as symbol of devotedness moved by love, can be considered each as a metaphor with a particularly wide range of applicability—as potentially multiple metaphors. Like the archetypal symbols of Jung, these are capable of engaging reality at all sorts of levels simultaneously and indeterminately. They weave through the analogies of being, where "the dance along the artery/The circulation of the lymph/Are figured in the drift of stars." The exact reference of the phoenix and the turtle will depend on where you choose to pull them up for the moment by arresting your attention momentarily. They can be metaphorical terms for persons, for philosophical abstractions such as love and death, for mind and body, for Christ and the Church.

We cannot go into the means by which these and all the other possibilities are kept in agitation within this poem in a way such possibilities seldom enough are. We must note only the fact that the possibilities *are* kept alive, are not killed off by the disasters that can overtake a poem less well managed than this. Here the reader is not distracted by irrelevancies, but encouraged to let the metaphor grow and extend its range of applicability without particular limit.

It is while letting the metaphor grow that we may suddenly become aware that the phoenix and the turtle can fly off as symbols into a still further dimension and become a metaphor of metaphor itself, for the union of these two divergent terms—the "mutual flame" in which they are united—lends itself with surprising readiness to being taken as a symbol of the union of two terms that is the precise thing that metaphor realizes.

> So they loved, as love in twain
> Had the essence but in one;
> Two distincts, division none;
> Number there in love was slain.
>
> Hearts remote, yet not asunder;
> Distance, and no space was seen.

The way the symbolism accommodates itself here to metaphor should be no surprise, for, if what we have said of metaphor is true, the union of the two meanings in one term, the unity of the twinned vision, is as intimately and deeply involved in the meshes of being as are the kind of symbols here operating.

Metaphor, in its strange double focus, brings us quickly to the quest for unity that preoccupies the phoenix and the turtle and that conditions their appearance in this poem—the quest for unity set in motion by the mysterious structure of a composite being, man, nostalgic for a simplicity that he cannot find within his own consciousness, resentful of everything short of this simplicity, ultimately discontent with his grasp of truth in statements, which are poor, divided things like man himself, bearing the mark of their own destruction within themselves. Even when they contain no margin of error, when everything they assert absolutely true, our statements have a way of leaving us unsatisfied by not meaning so much as we had thought ourselves on the point of uttering. "One has only learnt to get the better of words/For the thing one no longer has to say."

The difficulty goes deep, for it lodges in the structure of human cognition itself. Hence it is not surprising that among the elemental, archetypal symbols he is operating with, Shakespeare encounters human reason itself, nonplused by the divided unities and the united divisions with. which it must deal:

> Reason, in itself, confounded,
> Saw division grow together,
> To themselves yet either neither,
> Simple were so well compounded
>
> That it cried, How true a twain
> Seemeth this concordant one!

Although more explicitly focused on something else, this last phrase hits off the metaphorical situation to perfection, because it touches the depths of the human situation out of which the need for metaphor grows.

10

Grammar in the Twentieth Century (1956)

I

If we believe the reporters on our educational system, there is no doubt that we live in a time when grammar has fallen on evil days. Certainly, in terms of earlier emphases, the neglect of grammar in our present educational tradition represents a major cultural attitude. Furthermore, the neglect cannot be accounted for as simply the unfortunate byproduct of blowsy educational theory, for educational theory, blowsy or not, has a history with extremely complicated and profound roots, some of the most profound and perplexing in human existence. The conspiracy theory, which traces all our ills back to a clique of subversives, will work even less well in intellectual history than in social and economic and political history. Grammar, as a matter of fact, has not been put aside by hostile forces. It has suffered a falling off among its own followers. Of recent years persons who in another age might have become grammarians have manifested very little inclination to do so. Grammar itself has lost its appeal and its nerve.

This failure of appeal and nerve had its beginnings much earlier than our generation. Already in the latter half of the nineteenth century Robert Browning had published his poem, "A Grammarian's Funeral," a typical Browning tour de force, for a grammarian was already by common consent the most impossible of all subjects for poetry. He was a dull subject at best, and the fact that in this poem he was dead did not make him any more interesting. Grammarians were almost always moribund. Browning's grammarian, who

> . . . settled Hoti's business—let it be!—
> Properly based *Oun*—
> Gave us the doctrine of the enclitic *De*,

247

was at the peak of his career

> Dead from the waist down.
> . . . The multitude below
> Live, for they can, there:
> This man decided not to Live but Know.

Moreover, it would be a mistake to think that the conditions reflected in Browning's poem apply only to the late nineteenth century. Its subtitle, "Shortly after the Revival of Learning in Europe," shows that the poem actually refers to conditions in the Renaissance, and these conditions were by definition a reproduction of still earlier conditions in classical antiquity, so that, if we can conclude from Browning and the humanists, the failure of nerve on the part of grammar traces to troubles that were present to grammar more or less from the beginning.

II

To understand in some measure what the loss of nerve on the part of grammar comes to, we can establish as historical points of reference two grammarians. The more distinguished, whom we shall come to only at the end of this essay, is the late Otto Jespersen, dean of recent English grammarians and creator of modern English grammar. The other, from whom we shall take our departure, while not so distinguished as Jespersen, is a typical representative of the general grammatical tradition as it existed before the past few generations. He is James Harris, a family connection of the Earls of Shaftesbury and a less distinguished spokesman for the Enlightenment, who at the very middle of the eighteenth century was writing on what he and his contemporaries called universal grammar.

Operating in the wake of scholasticism, Harris treats grammar as do most Western Europeans before Romanticism had achieved its full force. He is fascinated by the possibility of having "principles" with which everything in a particular area of knowledge can be connected—fascinated, that is, with the notion of structure, a notion, we might remark, closely associated with thinking in terms of spatial models. Harris' universal grammar was to be a structure containing the principles of all existent and possible grammars, and in the course of getting up what he conceived that this structure might be, we find him writing in 1751 as follows:

> Even in Matters of Art and *human* Creation, if we except a few
> Artists and critical Observers, the rest look no higher than to the
> *Practice* and mere *Work*, knowing nothing of those Principles, on
> which the whole depends.

Thus in *Speech* for example—All men, even the lowest, can speak their Mother-Tongue. Yet how many of this multitude can neither write, nor even read? How many of those, who are thus far literate, know nothing of that Grammar which respects the Genius of their own Language? How few then must be those who know GRAM-MAR UNIVERSAL; *that Grammar*, which without regarding the several idioms of particular languages, *only respects those Principles that are essential to them all?* (10-11)

Harris is informative for us not because he is profound—for he is not profound at all—but because he is a spokesman for a learned tradition. Dr. Johnson, who Boswell says considered Harris "a prig, and a bad prig," nevertheless respected him as a representative of such a tradition. So did others, for after both his and Johnson's death, the book from which our excerpt here is made, *Hermes, or a Philosophical Inquiry Concerning Universal Grammar*, was translated into French and published in 1796 by order of the French Directory as a kind of official expression of what the enlightened mind was supposed to think about language and grammar.

The passage quoted here follows Harris' explanation of how, in any and all philosophizing or scientizing, man must move up from "effects" that he encounters most immediately to "causes" that he finds are the last things he comes upon, although they must necessarily in themselves precede their effects. In this present passage, Harris is indicating precisely this movement from "effects" up to "causes" or "principles." He is saying here, in effect, that oral speech is the effect of reading, reading the effect of writing, and writing the effect of grammar. Or in reverse, the principles of grammar "cause" writing, writing "causes" reading, and reading "causes" oral speech. This altogether shipshape account blinks entirely the simple fact that so far are reading and writing from "causing" speech that most men who have lived in the world have done all their speaking and the evolution of language has pursued nearly its entire course without reading or writing at all. Harris would certainly have owned this had he thought of it here. The interesting fact is that he did not even think of it. It seemed to him natural that grammar should be derivative more immediately from written than from spoken language.

Harris' presuppositions and outlook can be paralleled in a thousand places in the world around him, and not only in the eighteenth century world, but all the way back through antiquity as far as we can go. The mentality to which they bear witness is memorialized in the very term "grammar" itself, which comes from the same stem as the Greek word *graphein*, to write, and thus insinuates always, despite the most industrious semantic policing, that to study grammar is to study written rather than spoken language. This mentality is part of a much more widespread supposition, seldom articulated but generally operative, which only recently has become unpopular: namely, that any scientizing of speech involves first silencing it and thus removing it from the world of sound and fixing it in the world of space.

Studying written speech is, of course, far simpler than studying spoken speech, and it is not strange that the early attempts to scientize speech, almost without exception until just a few years ago, veer toward the consideration of written or literary language exclusively, disregarding or slurring over the fact that this is language at second remove. Thus, for example, although Diogenes Laertius and Priscian make some distinction between the *figura* or shape of a letter and its *potestas* or pronunciation value, this distinction is exceptional, is not really held to even by those who make it (Robins 13-14), and means very little indeed in the learned tradition as a whole. Indeed, Priscian's very proffering of this distinction shows that his approach to sound is through letters themselves: sound is taken not as existing in its own right but as a derivative of letters. It exists at second remove.

This degradation of sound is a regular by-product of an unreflective graphic culture, and has many parallels in such a culture. Thus from Cicero to Ramus and beyond into our own day, it has been common to think of "parts'" of words as letters—marks laid out in space—rather than as what we today call phones or phonemes. The terms and the concepts of "phone" and "phoneme" are very recent formations, new in linguistic equipment. "Letter" or *littera* is a very old piece of equipment, and a concept much easier to form. Similarly, "linguistics," formed by reference to the Latin *lingua*, tongue, with the explicit suggestion of sound, attests a new way of scientific thinking. "Grammar," built on the notion of writing, attests the old. To be sure, there was from ancient times a linguistic study called *rhetoric* or *rhetorica* (root in *er* or *ere*, "I speak"), but wherever this achieved a status of its own independent of grammar, it had to do with a study comparable not to grammar in any sense or to modern linguistics, of which grammar is a part, but to public speaking and/or the modern study of literature.

III

Given the nature of oral speech and of writing, it is possible to discern convincing reasons why early grammar should have veered consistently toward the written rather than the spoken word. Nothing is more evanescent than sound, which has its being only while it is in process of perishing. *Verba volant, scripta manent* [Words fly, writing remains]. If sound is metamorphosed or reduced to spatial equivalents by writing, the resulting product has, if not eternal duration, at least a repose that suggests imperishableness. Science favors fixity or repose. It has a nostalgia for the unchanging. Hence scientific-type knowledge involves concepts formed by reference to space rather than to time: it is interested in "structure" or "patterns" or "principles" ("first takings"—*primus-capio*) to which other items are "reduced" (brought back) or "referred" or "related" (carried back).

When sound itself is explained scientifically, it is processed in terms of this sort, after having been metamorphosed into spatial equivalents such as wave lengths, intensity indications, and the like. Science must consider fluidity by freezing it, in one way or another. It is thus understandable that the first scientific attack on language should have been made where language was already rigidified, that is on written speech. By the same token, we are not surprised that early grammar tends to be rather exclusively normative, interested not merely in observing and reporting, but specifically in prescribing what people ought to do when they use language. They ought to use it according to the norm of those who *write* it—and to avoid the usage of those who merely talk it, for, in contrast to modern descriptive grammar, more humble in its approach to linguistic fact, early grammar shows practically no interest in living colloquial speech (Robins 4, 38).

In view of the close connection between the scientific and the scriptural outlook, it is not at all surprising that, so far as we know, the first scientific treatment of language, far from antedating the invention of writing, does not come until a long time after writing is established. There is also a curious feedback here, for if it is processing in spatial terms that makes language at first amenable or inviting to scientific analysis, scientific analysis itself, whether it is concerned with language or anything else, can hardly come into being before a graphic culture, for writing gives the needed fixity to the constructs required by scientific analysis. It is impossible to keep a definition entirely unaltered in a completely oral culture. It is impossible even in a manuscript or a typographical culture, but here at least something more like permanence can be maintained.

However, if at first it is written language that inspires linguistic and grammatical science, this science can ultimately be brought to bear on the spoken language itself in the way in which modern descriptive grammar and other branches of linguistics seek to do. But study of the spoken language is much more difficult than study of the written record. It involves taking not what is already fixed in space and working it up into other structural patterns, but taking what is fleeting in time and working it up into structural patterns. As has been seen, to do this inevitably involves fixing sound in some way or other—for example, with the oscillograph, which can reduce the flow of sound to patterns of waves in space that can be "frozen" into charts. This is, in many ways, a more serviceable metamorphosis than the metamorphosis effected by the alphabet or by character writing, for it obviates the innumerable misleading impressions regarding the nature of speech that writing of any sort, and particularly alphabetic writing, creates and perpetuates. With more ingeniously contrived and flexible spatial models, such as those that wave analysis or phonemic analysis provides, linguistic treatment of spoken languages can become more and more precise, more subtle, and more adequate.

Nevertheless, however refined, any reduction of sound to the fixity of space is still a degradation of sound. It seems that the need of science to make such reductions to fixed patterns means that it will never be able quite to catch up with the oral and aural linguistic reality. For there is a kind of incompatibility not only between sound and space, but more profoundly, between the process of communication itself and reduction to a static form. Communication is something that goes on, not something that simply perdures. Because of this it has a natural affinity for the fluid world of sound, where, if the flow does not continue, everything perishes. In such a world, communication, which takes place always between persons or depths, not objects or surfaces, has its normal material mode of existence. The space world may supply more fact of the object sort, more surface to observe, but it is poor in personalist resonance.

Space is simply not so communicative as sound. The closest spatial equivalent of voice is not posture, but gesture, and by comparison with voice even gesture is half dead: it can be stopped, as voice cannot, and leave a kind of permanent remainder in the medium in which it exists. Gesture can be resolved into a succession of spastic poses that do not go on but merely perdure. In so far as grammatical analysis, even of living, spoken language, must reduce language in terms such as "structure," it must reduce language in some sort, directly or indirectly, to such spastic poses. There must be "conjunctions" like couplings on railroad cars, "prepositions" or words "put before" other words, "interjections" or words "thrown between" other words, "adjectives" or words "thrown against" nouns, and so on. Even the verb, which is the word par excellence, the predicate or category—or, to take the root meaning of these two words, Latin-based and Greek-based respectively, "that-which-is-cried-out"—even this verb must be analyzed as "complementing" or "filling out" the subject. In this context "nouns" are degraded from the status of "names" or cries, to "things."

It is true that these old parts of speech are far from exhaustive or complete as tools of grammatical analysis. Evolved gradually by the early grammarians to deal with Greek speech and later adapted with moderate success to Latin, they do not, as we know, serve adequately even for Modern English or for Standard Average European generally. But the schemes which supplement or supplant these parts of speech, while often much more adequate and true to the genius of language, all seem inevitably to labor under the same difficulty of seeking to *envision* or to reduce in terms of spatial models what is essentially not visual at all, but auditory. If you are going to scientize language, this you must do.

Improved linguistic terminology is, if anything, even more diagrammatic than that of unreconstructed grammars. The term "context," so assertive today, meaning something like what-is-woven-together, just as much as the term "syntax" (a "setup" or "array"), is dependent for its formation on a patently spatial model. It is a picture term. Other neologisms are no better. Seeking to approach linguistic facts in as unprejudiced a manner as possible, J. R. Firth, followed by R. H. Robins and others, in analyzing a given language, does not look for "parts" of speech either in general or in particular, but for what he calls "formal scatters" of any sort (Firth 62; Robins 91-99). These are to be described, and the terms of the linguistic analysis are to be derived directly from these descriptions. "Formal scatters" is a fascinating term, for it shows, first of all, an awareness of the disability from which all analysis and particularly linguistic analysis, suffers: the disabilities attendant on freezing things in terms such as "part" or "form" (etymologically associated with the notion of "outline"). Particularly in the initial stages terminology must not be too formal, too rigid, too inadaptable. We shall then not look for speech "forms," which we presumably should have set up in our minds in advance. Rather, we must look for "scatters," which are things that we encounter without preparation. But they must be *formal* scatters! The form has indeed been de-emphasized, at least temporarily, but it has to be there after all. We may have determined not to analyze the language in question into "forms" or any other terms given beforehand, but we have determined to find its "structure," and therefore have assumed that it has *some* kind of structure—in other words, we have come to it convinced that even the sound pattern must be reduced or tamed or metamorphosed by being reinterpreted by analogy with things in space—where we have simply replaced form or "outline" with structure or "setup."

I do not wish to appear to be making fun of the notion of "formal scatters." It seems to me that this approach to language is a good one, better than those of which I know that it supplants. I only wish to point out the limitations of any analysis of language. There is something in the realm of sound that eludes the very idea of analysis itself. Ultimately—we cannot go into this here—it is the element that belongs to the world of persons, who obviously cannot be "broken down" by analysis. When we approach even spoken language scientifically, we reduce it in one way or another in terms of "structure," which means in terms of space. We take communication out of the world where it has its real existence and treat it in terms of analogies and models. In reducing sound to structure, we can handle it very accurately and discriminatingly. In terms of "structure" we can account for everything there is here—except for the mystery of sound itself. A whole volume of diagrams of sound waves makes no noise. There is indeed nothing that we can do about this situation except recognize it, and with it the poverty—which is not at all the same as inaccuracy—of any scientific treatment, not only of sound, but of anything.

IV

The modern approach to grammar, with its awareness of the fact that linguistic performance is primarily oral performance and only derivatively graphic—"grammatical" in the basic etymological sense—carries with it an awareness, or the possibility of an awareness, of the limitations in the scientific approach to reality. This awareness of the limitations of science is very much a part of modern life, where it paradoxically accompanies a confidence in the possibilities of scientific achievement within limited fields. We live in an age that, if not entirely free of brashness in its scientific enthusiasms, has grown increasingly aware of the limitations of what had once been thought to be all-conquering scientific fact and theory. Classical or Newtonian physics has been discovered to be a certain kind of physics, supplemented or transcended by relativity and quantum physics. Euclidean geometry is accurate, but it is now known to be a special geometry for special situations that does not exhaust geometrical possibilities at all. Aristotelian logic is a marvelously accurate logic, but as Lukasiewicz has painstakingly worked out, one designed for certain special situations and far from adequate for the analysis of all thought structure. What was once taken to be "universal grammar" has been discovered to be not universal at all, but a special grammar fairly adequate for the Greek language and quite incapable of accounting satisfactorily for performances in languages unrelated to Greek.

A sense of the limitations of grammar has thus developed in conjunction with a sense of the limitations of all science. But in the case of grammar this discovery of limitations has been associated with a new awareness of the primacy of the spoken over the written word. As is perhaps apparent from what has already been said, recognition of the fact that grammar has ultimately to deal with speech and with sound has not only been associated with a sense of the limitations of science, but has strongly reinforced this sense. Sound is more important in language than anywhere else, and sound as sound exhibits curious resistance to scientific treatment. Attention to the vocal as vocal normally brings some kind of awareness of the limitations endemic to notions of "structure," that is, to nonvocal frames of reference.

Now any mature consideration of communication must include an awareness of the psychological meaning of sound as sound, and thus, to cut short what is already a long story, we must frankly admit that a mature consideration of communication must by the same token gnaw away at the foundation of grammar itself in so far as grammar is interested in what can be interpreted as structure and diagram. Indeed, in developing the general awareness of the particularity and limitations of science, the mature study of language plays a leading role, perhaps the leading role. Grammar has in a sense succumbed to the maturing of language study. While we recognize the need for studying languages in terms of fixed forms, and the necessity of teaching normative grammar at the primary- and secondary-school levels—and even at higher levels, unfortunately, as a therapeutic measure—we can no longer attach to these forms so much importance as earlier ages did. It is no longer possible in our day and age to have the unshakable confidence in the adequacy of schematic models of language—which are ultimately space-models of language—that earlier ages had. Scientific awareness must be complemented here by other awarenesses, by poetic or existentialist or phenomenological awarenesses that give insights into linguistic phenomena while they preserve at the same time the sense of profound mystery with which such phenomena are involved.

V

All this suggests that the misfortunes of grammar in our schools cannot be dealt with intelligently if we think of them as the result of wrongheadedness or stupidity or even perhaps moral fault on the part of those who supposedly "control" our education. The failure of nerve on the part of grammar, the hesitancy to enforce rules, may be and is a bad thing when one is supposed to be teaching normative grammar. But it is to a great extent understandable. It arises out of a tremendous complex of causes, which none of us completely fathom but which we can do something to understand. Like other large-scale cultural developments, the swing away from grammar—a swing that can certainly be overestimated, and often is, but that seems in many ways quite real—is part of a pattern too extensive and ramified for any one person or group of persons to "control." We are in some ways apparently at the end of the Gutenberg era, the age that climaxed the structural approach to language and perfected the printing press, reducing once resonant words to items on a mass production assembly line and bringing us to think of a book no longer as a record of utterances or cries emanating from a living person, but as a structured object or thing.

We should be naive, however, if we expected the structural approach to language to go. Far from it. The human mind does not forget or put aside its former achievements, but builds on them. Indeed, we might conjecture that there will be more and more attempts at describing and otherwise investigating language in terms of structure, more and more schemata of language, more and more elaboration of classifications—allomorphs, morphemes, articulatory phonetics, phonemics, "bundles and fascicles of isoglosses," "assortments of isoglosses" (Gleason 293), and so on. But here the very multiplication and proliferation of the structures that are used to interpret language will bear witness to the elusiveness of the linguistic situation as a whole when approached through scientific analysis.

Moreover, as the number of languages subjected to analysis increases, the structures serving for interpretation will have to be more and more enlarged. At this point, another cause of the present grammatical malaise can be indicated. It is nothing other than the growing global consciousness of mankind, the human race's growing self-consciousness and self-possession. It was easy to be devoted to Greek grammar when that part of the human race that was in Southern Europe was not aware where the rest of mankind was, or even that there was a rest of mankind. Now that we know, or can learn, a little of the linguistic of Hopi or Shona or Bassa, the enthusiasm for the older closed grammar systems must yield to more open or elastic schemata.

The present situation has not merely multiplied the items with which grammar and other divisions of linguistics must deal. The developing global consciousness of the human race has also placed a new accent on communication, which is to say on language as functioning, on language as living rather than as frozen in grammatical analyses, and thus ultimately again on that mysterious thing, sound. The old concept of universal grammar, involved with Harris' and others' naive approach to language through writing, has consequently badly suffered. We had promised earlier to compare the eighteenth-century universal grammarian, James Harris, with a modern grammarian, the late Otto Jespersen, and can turn to this comparison now. In Jespersen's famous work, *The*

Philosophy of Grammar, first published in 1924, we find the notion of a universal grammar yielding to that of "living grammar"—a term that forms the title of Jespersen's first chapter. The essence of language, Jespersen begins by observing,

> is human activity—activity on the part of one individual to make himself understood by another, and activity on the part of that other to understand what was in the mind of the first. These two individuals . . . should never be lost sight of if we want to understand the nature of language and of that part of language which is dealt with in grammar. But in former times this was often overlooked, and words and forms were often treated as if they were things or natural objects with an existence of their own—a conception which may have been to a great extent fostered through a too exclusive preoccupation with written or printed words, but which is fundamentally false. . . . The spoken and the heard word is the primary form of language. (2)

At this point Browning's dead grammarian comes to life. Jespersen here is making a declaration in favor of freedom and in favor of communication itself. By the same token, it is a declaration in favor of the internationalism toward which all men and all communication must move. It promises not an easy universalism of communication, but one which is more universal than that of a statically conceived, so-called universal grammar. Is it entirely an accident that the most eminent modern English grammarian and the champion of vocal sound over mechanized silence should be not an Englishman or even an American but a Dane? Jespersen's devotion to a language outside and beyond his own registers the drive toward internationalism which linguistic studies today frequently foster.

Jespersen's view here is, moreover, representative of most modern grammarians', who, however they may differ in various theoretical details, commonly agree that grammar must study primarily voice, not writing. Jespersen's philosophy of grammar may not be perfect, and it is certainly not complete, but in so far as he and others today acknowledge the primacy in communication of the living world of sound, they are keeping language in a condition where it can continue to be serviceable to twentieth-century man, and to man of the twenty-first and of the thirtieth centuries. Moving ahead out of the Gutenberg era, even as we perfect our primitive translating machines, we have also to face the fact that communication is ultimately rooted not in things, but in persons. Like persons, it is alive with a mysterious interior life, so that what is most meaningful in it radically resists being "structured" at all.

Works Cited

Firth, J. R. "The Technique of Semantics." *Transactions of the Philological Society of Great Britain* (1935). 36-72.

Gleason, Jr., Henry A. *An Introduction to Descriptive Linguistics.* New York: Henry Holt, 1955.

Harris, James. *Hermes, or A Philosophical Inquiry Concerning Universal Grammar*, 2nd ed. rev. (London, 1765). [The first edition was dated 1751.]

Jespersen, Otto. *The Philosophy of Grammar.* London: George Allen and Unwin, 1924.

Robins, Robert H. *Ancient and Mediaeval Grammatical Theory in Europe.* London: British Book Centre, 1951.

11

Voice as Summons for Belief: Literature, Faith, and the Divided Self (1958)

> Memory believes before knowing remembers. Believes longer than recollects, longer than knowing even wonders.
> —WILLIAM FAULKNER, *Light in August.*

> Everything that we believe, we believe either through sight or through hearing. Sight is often deceived, hearing serves as guaranty.
> —ST. AMBROSE, *Commentary on St. Luke*, Book 4, Chaper 5.

> A Presence is never mute.
> —PIERRE TEILHARD DE CHARDIN, S.J., private notes.

I

Any discussion of literature and belief must at some point enter into the mystery of voice and words. In a sense every one of man's works is a word. For everything that man makes manifests his thought. A dwelling or a spear tip communicates even when communication is not particularly intended. A building or a tool, we say, "shows" thought. In this, it is a kind of word, a saying of what is in one's mind.

In the fine arts, communication is even more intense, for the *raison d'être* of works of the fine arts is some sort of communication. As a "word," a painting may be polysemous and mysterious. Yet it remains something that some person has projected outside himself and made accessible to others. It externalizes something conceived within the artist—although not fully conceived, indeed, until it was in some way externalized—in order that this something may be assimilated into another or others, or at least may be available for such assimilation.

In this a painting is both like and unlike a word. For, if a word is an externalization, it is not so external as this. A word can live only while actually issuing from the interior, physical and psychic, of the living individual. As soon as it has passed to the exterior, it perishes. Returning toward its speaker, a word is not a word, but only an echo. "Words, after speech, reach/Into the silence." No spoken word can exist in its entirety all at once, but only bit by bit.

On the other hand, in so far as words are formed within us, they are destined for externalization. One might conjecture about intelligences with ineffable private words that remain forever media of interior contemplation and cannot be projected to the exterior. But the fact is that our natural interior words or concepts are not of this sort. If we can conceive a thought within ourselves, it is the sort of thing our fellows—the more perceptive ones, anyhow—can enter into. If we can think it, others can, too. Depth analysis has made it more evident than ever that there is no private language, even of inarticulate symbols. In so far as we speak to ourselves in any way, others are capable of sharing our thoughts. To conceive something interiorly is to process it for externalization.

If a painting is in some sense a human word, an exterior saying of something conceived interiorly, much more is a work of literature a word. For it is not only, as a totality, a word, but the stuff of which it is compounded is words. The canvas and oils and ground clays and salts with which a painter works are not of themselves means of expression, although they can be made so. But the words with which a speaker or writer works are themselves means of expression, and, no matter what we do with them, this they must remain.

This fact, banal enough in itself, is occluded by our present tendency to think of literary works as objects. Under one of their aspects, they are objects, of course. As a painting or sculpture or even a dwelling, while essentially an object, is also in a more subtle sense a word, so a literary work, while consisting of words and being in its own totality a word, is also in a more subtle sense an object. But it is well to remind ourselves how subtle this sense really is. Would an illiterate society, where verbal expression could be given no vicarious existence in space through writing or printing, be able to think easily of songs or orations as objects?

In a society where the only known word is the pure, evanescent spoken word it is easier to think of objects as words than it is to think of words as objects. This is the mentality revealed in the Old Testament and even in the New. It is the mentality of the primitive peoples studied by Benjamin

Lee Whorf and others. Even in John Donne's day, when typography was established but had not laid so tight a hold on society as it has in the days of neoscholasticism and the New Criticism, a poem, circulated in manuscript, was associated with rhetoric rather than with an artifact. Literature was expression. "The play's the thing," says Hamlet. But it is not a "thing" in the sense of an object. It is a "thing" to move the "conscience of the king." Moving or persuading was one of the offices of rhetoric.

II

When we say a literary work is a "word," we mean that it is some thing that is said or spoken. In our typographical culture, of course, this saying or speaking must be understood in a special sense. For in such a culture the greater bulk of literary production never finds its way out of the silence of the manuscript or the printed page. Probably the only persons who actually pronounce aloud the words of novels or of most poems written today are proofreaders, whose experience while reading proof, whatever else it may be, is hardly literary; and, alas, most of what is written never gets so far as the proofreading stage. Nevertheless, in an acceptable sense silent writing is a form of speaking, as silent reading is a form of hearing.

Speaking and hearing are not simple operations. Each exhibits a dialectical structure that mirrors the mysterious depths of man's psyche. As he composes his thoughts in words, a speaker or writer hears these words echoing within himself and thereby follows his own thought, as though he were another person. Conversely, a hearer or reader repeats within himself the words he hears and thereby understands them, as though he were himself two individuals. This double and interlocking dialectic, so beautifully described by Louis Lavelle in *La parole et l'écriture,* provides the matrix for human communication. The speaker listens while the hearer speaks.

The fact that the speaker listens to himself and the hearer speaks to himself shows that communication is not effected between individuals related to each other as we might imagine a broadcasting station and a receiving set to be. In wireless transmission there is a center of emission and a center of reception, one active, the other passive, and there is movement of impulses from one to the other. Because it has this simple structure, broadcasting is not at all communication in the human sense. It is an aid, a tool of communication. In the human situation, matters are quite different. The center of emission is a kind of receiving center, too, and cannot emit its words properly unless it is at the same time receiving them. Similarly, the receiving center has to be a kind of center of emission, for it receives its words by imagining them as emitted. One consequence of this is that it is fallacious to imagine that words are capable of being reduced to impulses.

Every human word implies not only the existence—at least in the imagination—of another to whom the word is uttered, but it also implies that the speaker has a kind of otherness within himself. He participates in the other to whom he speaks, and it is this underlying participation that makes communication possible. The human speaker can speak to the other precisely because he himself is not purely self, but is somehow also other. His own "I" is haunted by the shadow of a "thou" that it itself casts and that it can never exorcise. In "The Secret Sharer," that strangely existentialist story from a preexistentialist age, Conrad's hero is painfully aware that the refugee from justice whom he has secreted on board his ship is his double, a symbol of his own interior division and of his alienation from himself. The stranger-double is somehow there in the captain's own cabin because the captain himself feels himself a stranger on his own ship, and this because he is a stranger to himself in his own soul. The same double is party to the captain's conversations with other men. When a visitor from another ship, come aboard to look for the refugee, speaks too low, the captain explains, *"As . . . I wanted my double* [concealed in the cabin] *to hear every word,* I hit upon the notion of informing him [the visitor] that I regretted to say that *I was hard of hearing"* (italics added). It was essential that the double participate secretly in the conversation. But to effect this participation, the captain had to attest a deficiency in his own powers of communication.

Conrad's profoundly symbolic tale is a kind of allegory of human existence. It reveals a rift, a limitation inside our own beings, but a rift that opens its own way to salvation—for it is a rift which comes from our bearing vicariously within ourselves the other with whom we must commune, and who must commune with us, too, and thereby compensate for the rift, the limitation, in our persons. The other within must hear all, for he already knows all, and only if this other, this *thou,* hears, will *I* become comprehensible to myself.

A literary work can never get itself entirely dissociated from this I-thou situation and the personal involvement which it implies. For a literary work to exist in the truest sense, it does not suffice that there be code marks, which we know as letters, printed on paper. A drawing can exist on paper, in space, in a way in which a literary work cannot. A drawing can be assimilated in an instant, at a glance. For a literary work to be what it really is, words must move in sequence, one after another, in someone's consciousness. The work must be read or heard, re-created in terms of communication touching an existent person or persons over a stretch of time.

The manner of this literary communication is, of course, complicated in the extreme. As compared with real dialogue between two persons, a literary performance—a story or a poem or a play—has a special objective quality, signalized by the fact that the author himself stands outside the work, as Shakespeare's own person stands outside his plays. In this way the literary work is like a drawing. It is in a sense something that the author has extruded and thereupon left. This same impression is not given by the words spoken in a personal conversation in which persons find themselves actually involved through the process of daily living. The words in such conversation are less exteriorized.

The symbol of the exteriority of a literary creation is the mask, for in such a creation the author does not communicate directly but through a kind of covering or disguise, fictitious persons or characters, who are more or less in evidence and who speak his works. As T. S. Eliot remarks, poetry "is not the expression of personality, but an escape from personality" (43). A literary work is a sign of special alienation, for wherever we have literary creation some sort of mask inevitably appears. In *The Sound and the Fury* Faulkner nowhere emerges as Faulkner in the way he does in his Nobel Prize speech. The bard who sings the ballad is not the same person who sits down to eat afterwards. The courier who brings news by word of mouth is. The orator, being partly creative, both is and is not the same.

In the case of the drama, the communication is still more complicated by another echelon of persons coming between the writer and his audience, the actors themselves. Actors are real persons, but they perform not as the persons they are, but as persons they are not. They have at times worn masks, to show that they are not themselves, but something other. Yet, is it not highly indicative that the word for mask, *persona* (that-through-which-the-sound-comes), has given both to the ancients and to us the word for person? It is as though this ability to take on the role of another shows the actor's own humanity, shows that the other is already within him, and is, indeed, the shadow of his most real self. Ortega y Gasset points out that the brute animal is pure *alteración,* pure "otheration," in the sense that he cannot enter into himself. Man is not pure "otheration," because he can enter into himself—and yet, by the same token, he can find in himself and recognize by contrast the echoes of the personal other, the "thou," the alienation or *alteración* that is there. Thus acting a role, realizing in a specially intense way one's identity (in a sense) with a someone who (in another sense) one is not, remains one of the most human things a man can do. No brute animal can act a role.

Unable to recognize himself, he finds it impossible to recognize what by contrast with self is other. By the same token, he has nothing against which to set a role so that it is a role.

III

Voice is the foundation for role-playing among men in the sense that the use of voice and its understanding, as we have seen, forces man to enter into others. From this point of view, it is not strange that as literature develops in the course of history, roles become more manifold and more complex. Homer's Odysseus plays a great many roles, but how many more are played, and played designedly, by the modern Ulysses, Leopold Bloom? And how many more, still, are played by the voice whom the reader hears—it does not matter here whether or not he knows that the work is by James Joyce—narrating the story *Ulysses?* Over and beyond all the other roles in which it is involved (those of Bloom and of all the other characters) is the voice playing the role of mocker, making fun of itself?

Whatever the answer, a role cannot exist outside a context of belief, and it is my purpose here to discuss how it is that since voice demands role-playing, taking the part of the other within who is not ourselves, it demands belief as well, and how it is that belief is thus not something superadded to communication and thought, but something endemic to all human thinking, so that the question of belief and literature is really a specific variant of the general question concerning belief and communication in general, and ultimately concerning belief and human thought itself. All human intellectual activity implies belief because it implies faith in the possibility of communication and faith in someone with whom we can communicate.

Here one must make the well known distinction between belief as opinion and belief as faith. Essentially, as Gabriel Marcel points out, belief as opinion is belief *that* and faces toward what it is concerned with as toward an object or "thing" or "fact" (a truth considered as a thing), as when I say, "I believe that tomorrow will be rainy," or "I believe that this book would sell well." Belief as faith, on the other hand, is belief *in* and faces toward a person or persons, as when I say, "I believe in Matthew," or "I believe in God." Belief as opinion is impersonal and should be impersonal, for its whole rationale is its "objectivity." Even if it is concerned with a person, it treats the person "objectively," not as someone to commune with but as an object to be measured. Thus, "I believe that Matthew is a competent reporter." Belief as faith, on the contrary, is personal in cast, and must be.

However, despite these contrasts between opinion and faith, it is no accident that the term "belief" is used for both, since opinion and faith are indissolubly related by the commerce they carry on with each other. Thus, although belief as faith basically is belief *in* a person, it is also possible to believe *in* a thing or an object by giving it a personalist cast. Thus, "I believe *in* this book" erects the book into more than object. It makes of it a cause, with all the personal issues that this involves. It throws down the gauntlet on behalf of the author, whereas "I believe that this book would sell well" does not necessarily do so. Conversely, to believe *in* a person (belief as faith) involves a certain belief *that* what he says (in so far as he understands and controls it) is true.

Moreover, it appears that any belief *in* (belief as faith) not only is directed toward a person but also involves in one way or another his truthfulness, his "word." This is shown in part by the fact that one cannot believe in a liar as a pure liar (if such a man can exist). But something more profound than this negative example is involved. For belief in a person is ultimately an invitation to the person to respond. As Gabriel Marcel has pointed out in *The Mystery of Being* (2:68-84), belief in a person may include all sorts of beliefs *that*, varying from mere conjectural opinion (thus I believe that my friend will act considerately) to the acceptance of the truth of something of which I do not have direct knowledge (thus belief in God includes the acceptance of the existence of God as a truth, belief *that* God exists). But belief in a person includes also much more than this. To believe *in* God is to look for a response from Him. The construction of our expression and thinking with the term "in"—a construction found in many languages other than English—is significant here. It suggests that somehow in believing *in* someone, we enter into him. He is not merely an "object" of belief with whom our belief terminates. He is an interiority into whom our belief penetrates and with whom it enables us to commune. The expression suggests the same interpretation of I and thou that, we have seen, underlies all human communication.

This brings home to us the fact that all communication—and, indeed, all our thinking, which is learned and developed only through communication with others—goes on in a context of belief. For when we speak, we invite response. If I expect no response, no Yes, no No, no riposte of any sort, at least internal, I do not normally speak at all—unless I am losing hold on myself, am distraught, or am not in my right mind. Now, any expectation of response is in some way a declaration of belief in the person or persons to whom I address myself. It is recognition of a presence to whose word I can, in turn, attend, and in whom I can thus believe through the acceptance of what he has to say.

Since belief, either as opinion or as faith, includes some sort of acceptance or commitment without full "objective" evidence, belief as faith, or belief *in*, surpasses belief as opinion, or belief *that*. Belief as opinion moves toward knowledge of objects, but, since it has not sufficient contact with objects to amount to full knowledge, it is essentially deficient and vulnerable. Belief as faith moves toward knowledge and love of persons, and since persons cannot be known as objects at all, no matter how intimately they are seized, the lack of "objective" evidence here is not the liability that it is in the case of belief as opinion.

This situation can be restated in terms of the way in which belief as opinion and belief as faith differ with regard to their relationship to words. Belief as opinion tends to do away with words in so far as it is ordered to "objective" knowledge, which has to do with things that do not speak. Belief as faith, on the other hand, since it has to do with persons, tends not to eliminate words, but rather dwells in words and feeds on them, since they are manifestations of persons. Furthermore, in so far as communication with persons is better, more human, and, we might add, holier than contact with objects, belief as faith outclasses belief as opinion. Opinion is styled belief because it can be thought of as analogous to belief as faith. But belief as faith is simply belief in its purest form. For, short of direct observation, the best contact we can have with objects and "facts" is not opinions about them gleaned from imperfect evidence, but faith regarding them—that is, knowledge derived from our acceptance of the word of other persons who have this knowledge by direct observation.

Of the knowledge that individual men have today, almost all of it is grounded in faith. The knowledge of scientists themselves is almost all grounded in faith, well founded and rational faith in the reports of their fellow scientists, but faith nevertheless. Of the scientific knowledge that any man has, only a tiny fraction has been achieved by his own direct observation. For the rest, he has good reason to believe *that* it is true because, within the limits of their competence, he believes *in* his fellow scientists reporting on their work or reporting reports of the work of others. Thus, even in the most "objective" of fields, in actuality the word of persons is more pervasive than factual observation. Science itself cannot live save in a network of belief. Even in science, where fact is more determinative, presence is nevertheless more pervasive than fact.

IV

Against this background, the question of belief in literature can be raised. A survey of current writing in English on this question shows that it is pretty well all concerned with literature as involving belief *that*. The grounds of the question are staked out in terms of Coleridge's "willing suspension of disbelief," so that the problem becomes, as in Richards' *Practical Criticism,* How can one who does not share Donne's Christian faith enter into his sonnet "At the Round Earth's Imagined Corners Blow"? Or to adapt Richards' terminology, How can one share Donne's beliefs emotionally while not sharing them intellectually?

This focus of the question of belief in literature is legitimate. However, we must remember that it considers belief as concerned with a kind of object or "thing," excised from any personal context. The notion of response to a presence, manifested by voice, drops out entirely, although such response seems intimately a part of literature. Objects cannot elicit response to a voice in the way in which persons can, and when we treat belief in terms of the object of belief exclusively, response becomes attenuated to behavior, and its correlative is not voice, but stimulus in the Pavlovian pattern of stimulus-response. It is significant that Professor Richards not only concerns himself with "willing suspension of disbelief," but also, perhaps not entirely out of line with Coleridge's thinking even here, regularly discusses literature in terms of the way words "behave," as though words were not cries, but "things," visible objects. We have a right, of course, to speak of words in terms of this analogy, but let us not forget that it is an analogy.

Without attempting to deal with the question of belief on these grounds, I should like to set it up on other grounds and to examine it there, not with a view to providing utterly conclusive answers, but to improve our perspectives and to reveal how limited some of our common views of this problem really are. Let us recall that in the last analysis, any utterance, even a scientific utterance, is the manifestation of a presence that cannot be "grasped" as an "objective" of knowledge can be, but only invoked or evoked. The most abstruse mathematical theorem remains always and inextricably within this framework of utterance, for it originated as something communicable and remains always something that someone *says* to others or, in special cases, to himself. But since in the case of scientific utterance the vocal element is minimized, we can treat such utterance readily as an object and speak with ease of "grasping" or "not grasping" it, as we might an object. Thus, we grasp or we do not grasp the meaning of the formula $E = mc^2$. But we know how difficult and unconvincing it is to apply the notion of "grasp" to a poetic work. The notion can, of course, be applied to some extent. We can speak of "grasping" *Hamlet* or *The Marriage of Heaven and Hell* or *Absalom, Absalom!* But so to speak is not very satisfactory, not convincing. It seems much more real to speak of the response that these works evoke from us. The "evocative" quality—which is to say, the "calling" quality—is paramount in a work of real literature. Literature exists in a context of one presence calling to another.

This is a context of faith, no matter how much there may be in an individual work that outside the work we can know by direct evidence. Indeed, here faith achieves a special intensity (and simultaneously a special attenuation) in so far as the voice that invokes us as present and evokes our response is in a way more a pure or self-subsistent voice because of the "objective" quality of the literary work as such, its detachment from the poet, who as an individual is disassociated from the work by his literary mask. There is a special kind of dialectic at work here. In so far as the work is objectified, set apart from the existent writer who gives it being as a kind of well-wrought urn is detached from its creator, its evocative effect becomes more poignant. Thus Yeats went to the Japanese Nō plays for "more formal faces," explaining that "a mask [even taken metaphorically] . . . no matter how close you go is still a work of art." Joyce's progress from *Stephen Hero* through *A Portrait of the Artist* to *Ulysses* and *Finnegans Wake* is progress from personal involvement to artistic detachment, and as the masklike detachment grows, the evocative quality of the work, its pull on the sensibilities of the reader, grows. Because Poe can never achieve so great a detachment, because his personal problems and neuroses show through—to those, at any rate, for whom Poe's English is their native language, as it was not for Baudelaire and Mallarmé—the evocative quality of his work remains less poignant than that of Joyce or, to take another American, that of Faulkner.

We might ask why this is. If voice is an invitation to response, in what sense can the invitation become more insistent when the speaker wears a mask? To see what is involved in this question, one must consider the peculiar conditions of person-to-person communication, which is implemented by the use of voice. Human persons are of themselves distant from one another in the sense that they cannot enter entirely into one another's consciousness. The sense of distance attending on personal or I-thou relationships has been elaborated by recent writers such as Lavelle, Heidegger, and Buber, but once it is stated it needs no great explanation, for we live with this sense all the time. In dealing with another person, I am always dealing with one whom I cannot entirely fathom and with whom I cannot enter into direct communication quite like the communication I enter into with myself. His sense of self remains outside my direct awareness, and yet I can feel its aura and know that there is some interiority with whom I am dealing.

My contact with this interiority is mediated by exterior phenomena that implement commerce between interiors. This commerce is most readily maintained by voice. Voice is the least exterior of sensible phenomena because it emanates not only from the physical, but also from the divided psychological interior of man and penetrates to another physical and psychological interior where, as we have seen, it must be re-created in the imagination in order to live. Unlike a picture, it lives by its contact with these interiors—when they are gone, it is gone.

Still, for all this interior orientation, even a voice is an exterior something. It achieves its effect through an exterior medium. Our way of hearkening to one another, and thus our sense of presence, necessitates a kind of breakthrough. We penetrate into a "thou" through a something which is neither "I" nor "thou," through a medium over which the action emanating from one person exercises an effect on another. Even direct physical contact involves an externalizing medium, for our body is, in a sense, not so much our self as is our consciousness. Even in its interior, our body is somehow the "outside" of us.

The exteriority attendant on communication is what gives point to the mask in dramatic performance and, analogically, in all literature. Although it modifies the presence that manifests itself most poignantly in voice, of itself the mask is not vocal, but a medium manifest in space. It does not modify the voice of the character (presence, person) as the mute modifies the sound on a violin. Even though masks may occasionally affect voice projection, to do so is not the mask's primary function, for it is patently objectified as a visual phenomenon and produces its characteristic effects by being seen. It stands for that in the person-to-person situation that is nonvocal, noncommunicative, nonpersonal, remote, alienated.

In the preliterate world, where the eye is especially subservient to the ear, masks themselves are felt as belonging rather more to the world of voice than they are today, or perhaps are caught up more thoroughly into the world of voice, and aesthetic distance tends to disappear. For the Wintu, Dorothy Lee has noted, Coyote, Buzzard, and Grizzly Bear are bewilderingly man-and-animal. Although the wearer of a wolf mask among preliterates is not a wolf, he somehow really participates in wolfness. In this situation, where the object-world is not clearly differentiated from the world of voice and person, belief has not the depth of meaning it enjoys in a literate society, for the same reason that science itself has not: the two are confounded with each other, for the dialectic that sets them apart with some precision has not yet sufficiently progressed.

This seems to have been the state of affairs with the very early Greeks in their ritualistic use of masks. Later, with the great tragedians, real characters appear, and the masks worn become devices establishing aesthetic distance, *alteración,* limited more definitely to the universe of space. For space separates, whereas voice unites. As this evolution takes place, the number and complexities of roles, and of literary forms, proliferate. The means of controlling and differentiating characters and forms have been developed as the tension between the vocal and the visual grows. For this tension the mask is the symbol, or in a later day costume and make-up, a mitigated form of mask.

As the tension between visual and vocal grows, and with it the use of the truly dramatic character and the formalized separation of drama from life, there grows also, paradoxically, an awareness of the foundation in real human existence for dramatic character. A character in a drama is a person set off, advertised as other. Yet this state of being-set-off, this remoteness in the midst of intimacy, is found in real life, too, and experience of drama teaches us to recognize the fact. Each man is always in some degree a mask to other men, more consciously so today because of the progressive reflectiveness that mankind develops in its passage through history.

The sense of being-set-off is not annihilated by intimacy. Indeed, it is heightened and realized in its fullness through intimacy because of the very interiority that makes possible intimacy between persons. As a unique and induplicable individual abiding in the depths of your own interior consciousness, you are in a way more other to me than even inanimate objects are; and this despite the fact that I can carry on a dialogue with you and cannot carry on a dialogue with inanimate objects. For in assuring me of my closeness to your consciousness, this dialogue assures me also of the uniqueness of your consciousness and of its ultimate inviolability—of the fact that, naturally speaking, I can never know what it is to be you, can never share this ultimate experience of yourself with you. Of course, I cannot know what it is to be an object either—a rosebush or a canary—but neither can the object know what it is to be itself, so that this lack of knowledge on my part does not prevent a quite full knowledge of the object. Object-being includes no experience of self to be shared. What uniqueness the object has is reflected from the outside. In the case of a person, however, his experience of his unique self is constitutive of his most intimate self. Yet it is this very experience that intimacy cannot fully share.

V

These considerations throw some light on what happens to the personal charge carried by a voice in the case of a work of literature—of poetry, let us say, to take a relatively pure instance of literature. In a poem, the voice is there, but "objectified" in such a way as to mask the real person who uttered it in the first place and any other real person who utters it after him. A poem thus advertises the distance and remoteness that, paradoxically, are part of every human attempt to communicate, and it does this in so far as it is under one aspect "objective," an "objective correlative," objectlike, which is to say, nonvocal. But under a certain aspect only, for under another it is not objectlike since it is attempting to communicate very hard indeed.

Given the effective drive toward communication, the more the remoteness between the voice that working within this drive really creates the poem (that is, the voice of the writer) and those who hear or read it, the more evocative the work becomes. The drama is the most evocative and personal of all literary forms. In it living persons on a real stage really speak to one another; and yet, here the remoteness between point of origin and point of assimilation has actually been increased because the number of masks has been increased: in a performance of *Othello,* besides the mask or masks that Shakespeare as author wears, there is the mask of a character that each performer wears and that makes him precisely a *dramatis persona,* a person or mask in the drama. The reason for the corresponding heightening of effect seems to be the fact that all communication takes place across barriers, or is an attempt to crash through barriers, namely, the barriers that bar the ultimate compenetration of the "I" and the "thou." Provided that communication is going on, the interposition of further barriers has a tantalizing effect. It teases us to more vigorous attempts, sharper alertness, greater efforts at compassion or sympathy. One thinks of the poignancy achieved by the device of the wall in the story of Pyramus and Thisbe.

But certain other parallels might be adduced to show the intensification of the personal charge by the interposition of a mask or other barrier. A major one is in the religious history of Judaism and Christianity, where, moreover, the connection becomes evident between person and mask, on the one hand, and faith, on the other. Compared with Aristotle, who thought it impossible that God should concern Himself at all with human affairs, Hebrews and Christians know God in a highly personal fashion. Yet they know Him by faith, which is in a kind of mask, "through a glass darkly." Moreover, in the Christian dispensation God reveals Himself more personally to man when the Second Person of the Trinity, Whose personal name is the Word as well as the Son, takes to Himself a human nature that masks His divinity. His passion, where even His human nature is seen through the mask of death, is memorialized in the Eucharist, where the human and divine natures of the Word are both masked under the appearances of bread and wine, which also by symbol-ic separation of His Body and Blood masks His human death itself. But this "masking" only heightens the personal relationship between God and man, for through the Eucharist the personal union of Christians in the Person of Christ and thence in the other two Persons of the Godhead is realized and perpetuated. Although not applied to what we are discussing here, this sense of the Eucharist is highly operative in Christian tradition. It accounts for a favorite name of the Eucharist, Holy Communion, that is, Holy Togetherness. Its implications are elaborated by St. Thomas Aquinas and other theologians, who point out, moreover, that the conse-cration of the elements in this sacrament of sacraments is effected not by any sign in space, but by *words* given us by the Word of God. The whole setting for this series of masks is one of communication of the most per-sonal sort, in a universe of words and of faith, where sight is always at one or more removes from full reality.

VI

The masks in literature are generally assumed by one party to communi-cation rather than by both. The playwright and the actors, who are the communicators, assume the masks—the playwright a metaphorical one and the actors real ones or their equivalent in costume and make-up. By contrast, the hearer is present in his own person. Were he to put on a mask, he would become a part of the play, a *dramatis persona.* As it is, although the actors and the play may enrapture him, carry him somewhat out of himself, they do not make him into a quasi-other person. The act on his part that corresponds to the masking on the part of the communi-cators is simply his act of belief, in the sense of faith; and belief here is not at all tantamount to opinion. One has no "opinion" that Sir Laurence Olivier is Hamlet, and no "opinion" that Ophelia's death is real. Belief *that* is relatively meaningless here. This belief is more radically belief *in,* and such belief is not pretended.

But belief in whom? In whoever are the persons behind the masks. In the actors and the playwright all together. The act of faith, or belief *in,* is an invitation to them to respond as persons, to give themselves in and through truth. While there is also a certain faith in the audience that play-wright and actors both have, a belief *in* the audience, an invitation to the audience to respond—for this faith, as we have seen, accompanies all human communication—nevertheless this faith of the playwright and the actors is less obviously faith than that of the audience. The reason is the curious one-way nature of artistic communication, the fact that no real dialogue takes place, that the audience itself has no occasion or opportunity to speak. The audience's response is hidden, as the act of faith on the part of the playwright and actors is correspondingly hidden. The response of the playwright and actors, on the other hand, to the audience's faith is the play itself, which is far from hidden since the audience's act of faith is quite obvious.

In response to the audience's act of faith the playwright and the actors give themselves in and through truth. How the truth is contained in the words of the play—or, *mutatis mutandis,* in the poem or other piece of literature—and, indeed, what the truth in question really is, may be a very mysterious matter. This is to be expected. The truths arrived at by faith, natural as well as supernatural, are not noted for readily admitting of clear-cut statement or of clear-cut assimilation nor for being entirely evident to everyone, even to those of good will. They often submit reluctantly or not at all to full articulation, for they have to do most intimately with persons to whom we address ourselves. If they are neatly articulated, they are taken not on their own evidence but on the evidence of a person to whom we address our act of faith; and it is hard to articulate a person. For a person whom we are addressing nature provides us no distinctive word while we are addressing him save the strange noun-substitute or name-substitute or pro-noun "thou," which is not a name at all but changes its entire meaning with each different person we apply it to.

Our belief in a play or a poem is thus an invitation to the persons involved in composing it and presenting it to us either to say something worth our while or to betray our trust in them as persons. It involves a kind of openness to them and to their meaning at all levels, to what Professor Philip Wheelwright in *The Burning Fountain* styles "depth experience." If certain details of a poem seem unacceptable to us in terms of belief *that,* the voice of the poem, coming through the mask of its speaker (as well as through the masks of any characters he may have introduced) teases us on, so that beneath any disagreement with detail there persists the conviction that something worthy of assent is being said, into which the otherwise unacceptable detail may somehow be fitted. If we cannot believe in Prospero as a real magician, we can believe that the playwright is using him to convey some further word or truth to us.

In *La parole et l'écriture* Louis Lavelle makes much of the "world" as language. For communication to be possible there must be a world shared by our individual consciences so that by naming the objects in this world we can break through our solitude and communicate with one another. When a child believes that he knows something as soon as he can name it, he is not entirely wrong. For when he can name it, he can use it for what it is worth, as a means of communicating with others. That which is neither you nor I, once it is known, becomes a link uniting you and me. This is true not only of the natural world that we apprehend through our senses, but also of poetry and of literature in general. Poetry is often involved and mysterious, but by its very existence within our ken it is destined to communicate. Indeed, its communication is in one sense communication par excellence, the most intimate communication. John Stuart Mill's notion, Romantically rooted, that poetry is something that is overheard is a not too happy attempt to deal with the intimacy that poetry can effect: so intimate is the union of hearer and poet that it is as though the hearer as other were not there. The opinion sometimes expressed that poetry or art in general is basically not communicative at all is connected with the dialectical situation in which estrangement (the mask of the poet) and intimacy (achieved when the mask is somehow penetrated) are so strangely compounded.

If a poem is likened to an object in the world, it must be likened to an object already named, processed for purposes of communication, if named with a quite mysterious name. "Poetic truth," which seems so difficult to bring to earth, to isolate, to state clearly, and which is also so strangely intimate, has its roots in a sense of communion with other persons, persons perceived through masks, yet somehow decidedly there, who have believed in us enough to invite us to this uncommonly intimate response and in whom we, in turn, are called on to believe.

We come to the conclusion that any belief *that* involved in literature is subservient to belief *in*, that the most basic meaning of belief in literature has to do not with belief in the sense of opinion, which regards objects and facts (truths treated as objects), but with belief in the sense of faith, which regards person-to-person relationships, invitations and response, and truth with reference to these relationships. This conclusion is, I believe, nowhere more strikingly evident than in the situation that has obtained for some years in twentieth-century poetry. The withdrawal of the serious poet (or of the serious artist generally) has been commented on *ad nauseam*. Withdrawal from what or into what? Into himself, we are told. Yet we are faced with the striking fact that serious readers of poetry today favor no other type of poetry so much as this poetry of withdrawal. The conclusion would seem to be that readers like nothing better than to follow the poet into his retreat. Everybody wants to be alone together; and this is not strange. There is no doubt that in our age, which has evolved, among other things, a mass culture and mass media of communication, intimacy is also in many ways better served than it has ever been before. Certainly the human race is more conscious of itself as a whole and has developed its dialogue about intimacy and communication more than at earlier periods in human history. We have a more highly perfected vocabulary and more advanced means of articulation about this subject than ever before. However aware earlier man may have been of persons and of the "I-thou" situation, the philosophy known as personalism is a twentieth-century creation, just as thoroughly a product of our age as technology or television commercials. In this climate belief *in* becomes very meaningful. In terms of belief as we have viewed it here, the serious modern reader wants to believe in his poets more than ever before. This would seem to indicate that in the age of television voice is in some ways regaining a prestige over sight, that we are at the end of the Gutenberg era.

Works Cited

Ambrose, St. *Sancti Ambrosii Mediolanensis Opera: Pars IV Expositio Evangelii Secundum Lucam, Fragmenta in Esaiam.* Turnholti: Typ. Brepols, 1957.

Conrad, Joseph. *The Secret Sharer.* Ed. Daniel R. Schwarz. Boston: Bedford Books, 1997.

Eliot. T. S. "Tradition and the Individual Talent." *Selected Prose of T. S. Eliot.* Ed. F. Kermode. New York: Harcourt Brace Jovanovich, 1975. 37-44.

Faulkner, William. *Light in August.* New York: Modern Library, 1950.

Lavelle, Louis. *La parole et l'écriture.* Paris: L'Artisan du Livre, 1947.

Lee, Dorothy. *Freedom and Culture.* Englewood Cliffs, NJ: Prentice-Hall, 1959.

Marcel, Gabriel. *The Mystery of Being.* 2 vols. Trans. G. S. Fraser (vol. 1) and René Hague (vol. 2). Chicago: H. Regnery, 1960.

Richards, I.A. *Practical Criticism: A Study of Literary Judgment.* New York: Harcourt, Brace, 1950.

Wheelwright, Philip. *The Burning Fountain: A Study in the Language of Symbolism.* Bloomington: Indiana UP, 1954.

Whorf, Benjamin Lee. *Language, Thought, and Reality: Selected Writings.* Ed. John B. Carroll. Cambridge, MA: Massachusetts Institute of Technology P, 1956.

12

The Barbarian Within:
Outsiders Inside Society Today (1962)

I

The outsider theme is both an old theme and a preoccupation and symbol of our time. Earlier ages are aware of individual characters as outsiders—Lear or Ulysses or Job. But our interest in the outsider penetrates through individual characters to the pure abstraction itself. Besides a movie, two earlier recent books, one by Richard Wright and one by Colin Wilson, have taken as their title the unqualified term *The Outsider*, which has also become the name of a quarterly announcing itself as "vigorous" and "new." How new it can be is questionable, in view of the many other exercises in the dialectic of the "in" and the "out" that of late have been flooding the market. From the lowbrow, middlebrow, and highbrow tastemakers of Russell Lynes (an aggressive early in-and-out sponsor) one moves through David Riesman's inner-directed and other-directed (or outer-directed) characters and Vance Packard's status seekers (outsiders pushing in), on through the "U" and "Non-U" people of Nancy Mitford's set into the utter explicitness of the Benton and Schmidt *In and Out Book*, which tells what is IN and what is OUT in capital letters.

Externalism has become established orthodoxy. At an increasing number of levels, being "way out" has replaced being "in" as the most trenchant expression of "belonging," of social acceptance. All support for such expression is not merely journalistic or faddist—the latest manifestation of popular un-think. Outsidedness has been the concern of some of our most serious and humanly meaningful contemporary thinking. In the modern world, farthest out of all (and hence really in) are the heady but truly intellectual heights of the existentialist dialectic of self-versus-other (inside-looking-out versus outside-looking-in) that dominates so much of the profoundest thinking of our time. On the other hand, this same externalism works itself out in ways that are patently democratic in the grossest sense, and even commercial: Grove Press has certainly found the existentialist in-and-out game one of the most lucrative developments in twentieth-century philosophy.

One of the remarkable features of the outsider theme as it charms us today is its appeal to the few and the many conjointly. Outsiders make headlines not only in the *Evergreen Review* and the *Chicago Review*. They make them in the daily press as well, and with a frequency attesting the alacrity with which the average "decent" American secretly identifies with those who are "out." Teen-age outcasts especially, such as American neighborhood toughs, British teddy boys, and their equivalents the world over, are more than ever before staples of the city desk. Youth itself, of course, is an element never entirely "in," and by contrast with these unhappy youngsters, outsiders because of inexperience as well as misbehavior, the middle-aged gangster has lost news appeal, having become in some quarters almost a symbol of security.

The accent on youth in the American heritage (no one is allowed to dress like a real grandmother any more) and the prolongation of adolescence made necessary by a technological civilization's demand for a protracted period of formal education doubtless helps further interest in the outsider question. But so do other things in the United States, such as the American's haunting remembrance of the abandoned fatherland of his ancestors, the still vicariously felt experience of the lonely frontier, and the present American (and global) preoccupation with "integration," racial and other, that represents a concerted effort, if as yet not always a successful one, to bring the outsider in.

Interest in social outcasts is of course not new and not restricted to the United States. It reaches back through Richard Hovey's and Bliss Carman's shabby-genteel *Vagabondia* literature of the 1890's on past Daniel Defoe's *Moll Flanders* and *Robinson Crusoe* (social ostracism Romantically transmuted into geographical isolation), through Renaissance rogue literature, the medieval Francois Villon and his goliard brethren, on through Apuleius and even Homer, for whose Odysseus the prototype seems to have been a more ancient character of the clever-rogue-and-outcast type. And the story of paradise lost itself ends in exile, long a preoccupation of Hebrew and Christian thought, literature, and prayer. *To thee do we cry, poor banished children of Eve.*

Nevertheless, today's interest in the outsider is somehow special, intensified by the structure of society in a newly populous planet whose inhabitants, by contrast with their ancestors of a few millennia, or even of a few centuries, ago, are now for the first time living with an awareness of the global dimensions of human relationships. The mass media of communication, and more particularly the electronic media of instantaneous telecommunication that bring the news on the quarter hour, have made it normal for individuals to participate daily and even continuously in significant activities of the entire human race over the face of the globe. In technologically advanced societies—and all societies will soon be such—it is necessary and inevitable for individuals so to open their interior consciousnesses to outside goings-on. The interior of the individual is called on today, as it never was until recently, to live through at each moment the ongoing exterior activities of the entire human race.

Technology—by no means so simply and purely exterior as is sometimes supposed—has established this new interior-exterior frontier. In the images that technological society projects for itself through its public communications media such as the press, radio, and television, mankind somehow finds itself divided quite naturally into the "beat" and the "square" on the basis of insideness and outsideness, participation and nonparticipation, belonging and rejection.

The beatnik is such a society's deliberate outsider, the voluntary reject, the calculatingly uninvolved. I take "beatnik" here as referring to the figure, partly real and partly a symbolic transformation, embodying the patterns of behavior, real and imaginary, that have given this concept its currency in our day. The beatnik's quick reduction of everything to classes (not only beat and square, but the whole assembly-line vocabulary of chick, cat, and the rest) even in direct address (where the other has no proper name but becomes simply "Man") and his avoidance of direct or complete statement (Man, like you can't help it) are calculated to advertise that he is keeping out—and "way out"—that he is not committed to any person, for all real commitment is personal at root. But action is impossible outside some context of commitment, and the beat's maneuvers to establish himself as solidly "out" with regard to society as a whole unavoidably establish him as solidly "in" with other "beats."

The beatnik, however, is never so "way out" with regard to "square" society as he might like to think, for he is inextricably involved in this society's highly developed communications media, and indeed could not find or sustain his own peculiar ambitions without such media. He needs phonograph records and tape, radio and television awarenesses, and the ability to roam in high-speed cars (modern transportation is largely a communication device) over great highways that could not be constructed without today's close-knit communications and could not be made to function without the electronic instruments needed to patrol them. The beatnik's intense kind of outsideness is unthinkable before human society has developed the special complementary insideness that comes from its present tight intercommunication system. A paleolithic beatnik was impossible.

Involvement with mass communications has resulted finally in the assembly-line beatnik. Despite their in some ways unquestionable externality, mass communications nevertheless give the human race today its minute-to-minute awareness of itself as a whole. Aware through its press, radio, and television that it is spawning beatniks unwittingly, society becomes reflective about the process. The beatnik is seized on as a symbol to be consciously exploited, with beatnik night clubs and beatnik parties for the kiddies (costumes are encouragingly inexpensive). At this point, inevitably, the cult of the outsider moves back inside, and big business undertakes the mass production of beatniks. A St. Louis firm advertises nationally its zip-collar sweatshirt with "beautiful official Beat Generation emblem" that gives you "your chance to join the exclusive Beat Generation" for $4.95 plus $1.95. Exclusiveness sells widely.

Life magazine a few years ago blessed the mass production of beatniks by running a special feature on the beats for its consumer-culture clientele, picturing as in a department-store advertisement the equipment necessary for a beat "pad," with all items numbered and labeled—primly and condescendingly, so that *Life* readers can be reassured that this is not themselves, but also with consumer's guide accuracy giving the same readers to know what is the real thing and what isn't, so that if they *should* just want to set up a beat "pad" of their own on a do-it-yourself basis, they could be sure to do it right and not lose status.

By eliciting this kind of hypocrisy from his would-be censors, including *Life* magazine, the beat can nurse a wry, but decisive, victory. For, wrong as he may be, the beat is invulnerable to any attack that implies that he is wrong because his critic is right. There is always in human society and in my own life something that warrants criticism and withdrawal. The outsider can only laugh when he hears others say that he is wrong in his withdrawal because the insiders are so good. He has been inside, or at least has looked in, and he knows they are not. A self-righteous insider cannot win. Only if, like Dostoevsky's Underground Man, he faces up to the full truth about himself can the insider hope to meet the threat the beatnik poses. To meet this threat the insider must abandon all complacency. The insider must acknowledge complicity with the beat. He is not so different as he likes to pretend to be. After all, the beat items so carefully inventoried by *Life* are many of them part of ordinary family living: hi-fi loudspeaker, Italian wine bottle, empty beer cans, ill-tended house plant. This is not only San Francisco's North Beach; it is America. The insider may as well avow his likeness to the beatnik—his fascination has already given him away. He must avow that he himself has faults, grave ones, and that society has, too, and he can only protest that even so, society has claims.

Of course, such a realistically harsh appraisal of society makes the insider in some sort an outsider, too. To this extent, the beatnik can claim achievement, for to this extent his achievement is positive: he has brought the squares to acknowledge their own involvement in the forces that have produced him, and to acknowledge that the established order is not entirely good and in this life never will be.

II

The outsider-insider dialectic is by no means entirely new. It is endemic to the West's understanding of its own culture and appears in many guises, most notably in the dialectic of Greek and non-Greek, or Greek and barbarian.

Barbarian and outsider, however, if closely related, are not entirely the same. Of the two, outsider is the more thinned-down, the more geometrized—and by the same token the more easily manageable. The concept of the "outsider" is both striking and poignant because of its gruesome starkness: it represents what is essentially the plight of human existence in terms of unadorned geometrical position. We are fascinated by the idea of being "in" or being "out" because we find it incongruous and mildly intolerable that one person be estranged from another simply because the two are on different sides of something represented as a mere physical border—a door, a fence, a wall, perhaps a "line" (party or color), or whatever it is that maintains an inside and an outside. Position with regard to a mere object should not define human relations. We are fascinated by the gruesome concepts that imply that it does.

Barbarian is a more complex concept to analyze, and certainly more rewarding. It developed not merely in terms of a spatial analogy, but seemingly out of what is more subtle and human, a cultural relationship focused in linguistic behavior. The original barbarian was the man who could not speak Greek. *Barbaros* is seemingly an echoic word, imitating the supposed sound of strange tongues—the Latin *balbutiare*, to stammer, appears to have similar roots. Defined in terms of speech, the barbarian is defined not in extrahuman, geometrical terms, but in terms derived from human life itself, from the eminently human activity of verbal communication.

The communication system to which the barbarian finds himself referred and by which he is defined is not the one he knows. Those inside this communication system, the Greeks, who are the ones bestowing on him the name barbarian, take toward him a depreciatory attitude. They imply that he is badly off because he does not know Greek, that he is aware of this fact, and thus that he would like to know Greek and be integrated into Greek civilization if possible. From the Greek point of view the barbarian is thus in one way a projection of Greek self-confidence. But also, in another way unavoidably implied by this first, he gives evidence of the Greek lack of self-confidence manifested by the need for admiration. The Greek draws assurance from the admiring glance of the barbarian whom he professes to despise.

This Greek-barbarian situation dramatizes in its own way the human condition of interdependency. It is a special case involving the quest of security and integrity within a dialectic of inferiority and superiority. The barbarian, as the Greeks considered him, is a peripheral man, insufficient to himself, camped outside a civilization that he feels—however dimly and resentfully—promises him greater integrity than the civilization that was his own by birth. He may be more or less articulate about his position. The barbarian on the Greek perimeter may have expressed—and we can conjecture probably did express—positive scorn for the Greeks. But in so far as he was on his own barbarian terms caught up into Greek civilization, he registered his sense of dependence (subconscious though it may have been) upon the Greeks. As a raider, the barbarian is dependent upon the civilization upon which he makes inroads. To this extent, the Greeks were justified in their assumption of superiority, even when they may have been going down in defeat: their riches were being preyed on— and this was proof that they were indeed riches.

What were the riches of the Greeks? When we think of the Greeks as contrasted with barbarians, we think not merely of their material wealth, but much more of their cultural self-possession, a kind of cultural self-containedness. And there is warrant for this, at least if we regard those within ancient Greek civilization who profited from it most, the ten per cent or so who, like Sophocles, Socrates, Plato, and Aristotle, were on the top, not slaves. These achieved what they achieved from the growth within their culture—and thus within themselves—of a kind of integrity or wholeness of view. But one might add that the Sophists were barbarians in so far as they viewed law as extrinsic force and thus that historic ancient Greek civilization in its entirety was far from "Greek" in the technical antibarbarian sense—but nevertheless in a way that is historically meaningful, for the Greeks civilization did consist in a kind of wholeness of view or integrity, such as Werner Jaeger has explored in his *Paideia*. Greek integrity was limited, of course, much more filled with holes, of which the Greeks themselves were often aware, than poorly informed rhapsodizers about Greek "rationality" allow, as Eric Robertson Dodds has shown in *The Greeks and the Irrational*. The Greeks knew that they had no really coherent answers worked out for many basic and essential questions. "I was evil from birth," says Oedipus—thereby showing that Sophocles' tragedy cannot really be fully accounted for by Aristotle's *hubris* or any known rational explanation. In his massive work, *The Odyssey: A Modern Sequel*, Kazantzakis provides a good sample of something very like the ancient Greek mind protracted into our own day—independent, zestful, vigorous, sometimes to the point of boring us with its effusions, thoroughly incomplete, but unflagging in its determination to be self-reliant, even when it does not fully know what self-reliance can mean.

How far one can push this integrity in historical detail has been and perhaps still is matter for painstaking investigation. Here the point is that, as contrasted with the barbarian, the Greek felt within his culture a germ of integrity. A germ is not adequate, of course, and the Greek, like all men, was basically insecure. Nevertheless, in so far as he was Greek and not barbarian, he was one who was willing to live with his insecurity. One can ask for no more as a starting point.

Although any culture (and every society has a culture) possesses some integrity that it seeks to maintain, when we speak of a culture as barbarian by comparison with Greek, we refer to it as turned somehow outside itself for a larger integrity that it is seeking. Integrity has to be built from within, but the process of building it is a social transaction, and a reciprocating one: the child develops his integrity as a response to that which he senses in his elders, particularly his parents, and these, in turn, develop their integrity further by living with the efforts of their children. At the very moment when the son is living up to the expectations of the father, the father is in another way most intensely living up to the expectations of his son. In either case the process is dark and obscure, for integrity is of the deep interior, but the process is also in a way exteriorizing, for the model that urges us on to establish our own integrity is "other," is in some sense "out there."

This exterior element in the process of establishing integrity is heightened by the fact that in human affairs the response of interior to interior has to be effected through external means. One of the most evident of such means is sheer imitation or annexation of something belonging to another. Such annexation is a well known phenomenon in the case of individuals: the child who apes his father or older brother, the Oxford students who, consciously or unconsciously, used to imitate Newman's mannerisms. Certainly such annexation is one of the phenomena manifest in those we think of as barbarian. As contrasted with the Greeks, the Romans were barbarians in this sense—as indeed were all the cultures outside the Greek that later took on a Hellenic cast. The cultured Roman, from Cicero on, remade his language out of Greek sources, described it with the help of a grammar derived from Greek (the Romans had no way of theorizing about their language as it really was, but only through analogy with the Greek), and indeed often used the Greek language itself when moving in sophisticated society. This is not to say that all elements in Roman life were in the present sense barbarian: there were Roman Stoics who could be regarded as in some way Greeks, if (as has been successfully maintained) rather small-souled ones, because of their insistence on inwardness and self-reliance. Yet even here two things must be noted: first, a Roman Stoic was necessarily a barbarian in the sense that the Stoa itself was originally a Greek school, not a Roman; second, the Stoic aim is in a sense security rather than integrity, since it seeks to avoid or assuage all personal tensions and to minimize risk—the Stoic advocated never making a wager except on a sure thing.

Medieval Western Europeans have long been called barbarians with reference to the ancient Romans (and indirectly to the ancient Greeks). Everywhere in Europe they uniformly carried on their most consciously cultural pursuits not in their own tongues, but in the language of the ancient Romans, and, to give their cultures some kind of continuity with Greco-Roman culture, they "fixed" their histories (as in the legend deriving the British race from a Brutus supposed to be Aeneas' great-grandson) and even their political institutions (as in the case of the quasi-fictitious concept of the Holy Roman Empire).

As a Christian, medieval man felt a conscious superiority to the ancients, but this conscious superiority sat uneasily upon a strong subconscious inferiority. Men of the Middle Ages went to the Latin translations of the ancient Greeks to explain to themselves elements in Christian doctrine for which their own intellectual resources were all too inadequate. The ancient Roman culture had not had the integrity that the medieval Western European liked to impute to it. It was highly derivative from Greek and its lack of self-containedness evident from this fact was only made more telling by the admixtures of Arabic culture that accrued to it before it came into medieval hands. But the barbarian's type of insecurity, bred of a need for integrity and a kind of despair of finding it within himself rather than within the more sophisticated culture with which he had established contact, led him to project an integrity into something outside himself on which he fastened.

In accord with this barbarian frame of mind, medieval man habitually viewed the pursuit of knowledge as some kind of recovery effort, an exploitation of what others somehow already knew. Not only did the philosophers (a rubric that included physicists and mathematicians—in fact, all learned men except students of language, medicine, law, and theology) together with the physicians, the lawyers, and the theologians teach by commenting on texts, but even the poets looked to *auctoritas* or "authority" for source material and details as well as for the whole warrant and structure for their productions. A creative writer today may turn to Sophocles or to John Donne as a source of plot or character or tone, but he does not ordinarily in the course of his work refer the reader, as Chaucer and his contemporaries do, to what is said by "the book" or "my author," citing sources as part of his very process of telling his story.

The "others" to whom medieval man imputed the command of knowledge on which he drew were commonly his more or less distant predecessors. Their knowledge was uniformly in a peculiar condition, being accessible only in manuscript form, where it was permanently removed and insulated from dialogue and incapable in itself of the kind of development that dialogic exchange offers. Moreover, with his underdeveloped historical sense, man in the Middle Ages was unable to make the kind of correction in earlier thinking that is possible when thinking is assessed in terms of its historical context. Under these conditions the use of *auctoritas* by scholastic philosophers and theologians took a turn that involves what we today should consider calculated dishonesty. To the author one was following, one imputed a kind of inerrancy, sometimes to the extent that when the author's works said something with which one could not agree, one pretended that they said—or at least meant—quite the contrary. By the thirteenth century this practice had become a kind of convention, and seems to have disturbed no one. What was really at stake was not at all the exact sense of Aristotle's or another's words, such as the present-day scholar would want to ascertain, but the ability to maintain the conviction that one's "authority," Aristotle or another, had in his possession some sort of genuinely *integral* vision.

Under these circumstances it is not surprising that Western European man in the Middle Ages appears often unaware of the fact that he had himself made real, and often tremendous progress over his predecessors. The striking advances in logic that were effected by Peter of Spain and those medieval logicians who followed him and that carried this science far beyond where it had been left by Aristotle seem not to have struck the medieval mind generally as advances at all, and it is only today with the work of Duhem, A. C. Crombie, Anneliese Maier, and others that we are becoming aware of medieval progress in optics, physics, and related fields. By and large, the medieval mind took for granted that earlier man knew all sorts of things even when there was no record of his having expressed them.

Perhaps the most spectacular evidence of the barbarian imputation of omniscience to a preceding culture is seen in medieval interpretations of the first chapter of Genesis. Here the Hebrew concept of the world, vague and thoroughly unscientific, and left that way in the presentation of a divine revelation concerned principally with supramundane matters, pictures the earth as more or less flat, with waters somehow heaped around its sides up and over the "firmament," or solid element in the heavens, which keeps the water from coming down when it is not raining and lets it through when it does rain. Medieval theologians pretty much *en bloc* managed somehow to read into this text the cosmos as Aristotle and Ptolemy imagined it: our earth as a globe made up of the four "elements" earth (soil), water, air, and fire, and surrounded by a series of concentric, transparent spheres that consisted of a fifth, inalterable element and bore successively the moon, Mercury, Venus, the Sun, Mars, Jupiter, Saturn, and the fixed stars. This construct was entirely foreign to and in fact quite irreconcilable with the Hebrew view of the cosmos. The medieval mind reconciled the two anyhow.

As a Christian, medieval man had to acknowledge that the ancient pagan vision of creation had been incomplete. But the barbarian Christian was terribly distressed if he had to own that the vision was utterly mistaken. He needed to believe in its integrity. Somewhere, somehow, in the past there had been someone who had everything straight in every direction and dimension in which it was given him to see, at least in principle. There are of course a great many such barbarian Christian minds among us still today—perhaps nowhere more than among American Catholics.

The barbarian type of insecurity that assuages its pangs by finding outside itself an order or integrity by which it can live appears intimately connected with the development of modern science, which has its confused but unmistakable beginning in medieval European culture. Science offers us a purchase, elaborately structured, on the actuality outside us, enabling us to make external order permanently our own. One of the striking phenomena of medieval and Renaissance thought, which I have attempted to document in my *Ramus, Method, and the Decay of Dialogue*, is the preoccupation with establishing schematic relationships among the various "arts" and other areas of knowledge, even though the knowledge being ordered was in many cases so sketchy as to be virtually nonexistent. There is not and, I suspect, never will be a complete science even of physics, much less of mathematics, totally developed, with all its parts and possibilities exhausted. Yet already in the twelfth and thirteenth centuries men were treating of the structure and interrelation of the sciences as wholes, undismayed by the fact that they had not one single integral science worked out with what we today could consider even an approximation of reasonable completeness. Fascinated with the idea of an integrating structure, of which they had found circumstantial suggestions in the world around them, they could not forego the pleasure of elaborating comparable structures—however prematurely—in what was closer to them, their knowledge itself.

The scientist truly humble about his science, as most scientists are, is a Greek, willing to live with acknowledged insecurity, not a barbarian. But the populace remains, probably always, barbarian in the image of science that it projects. For the popular press, the mythical thing called science has all the answers, or soon will have. It is a kind of totality, an integral something. Such a popular image of science, generated perpetually in the minds of the less informed even as the more informed are discarding it, will persist because there is some foundation for it. Science is born of a vision of completeness. As Alfred North Whitehead has suggested, the Judaeo-Christian milieu provided the foundation for science by teaching that God made absolutely all reality outside Himself and that He was infinitely wise, so that ultimately there was available somewhere a complete explanation of everything down to the least detail, however long it might take man to find it. The integrity of all science, its completeness, is thus ultimately in the intellect of God. But in a further and very special sense science provides in a kind of exterior form minor visions of completeness in the hypotheses which the scientist "projects" outside himself and outside the ambit of his knowledge, afterwards testing to find whether the facts match the projection. The scientist here is radically barbarian in this sense: he looks for integral explanation in a truth that he does not in fact formally possess, but that he proposes as a mere "let us suppose."

The medieval complex of barbarianism comes to a marvelous maturity in St. Thomas Aquinas' view of theology. Unlike most medieval theologians, St. Thomas thought of theology itself as somehow an integral science. His science of theology not only offers in some measure a framework of integrity somehow outside one's own self and yet susceptible to personal appropriation by study, as other sciences do, but unlike other sciences, draws its own first principles or origin from a kind of ultimate "outside" in the sense that these principles come from outside the entire created world, directly from divine revelation, from the Word of God, although from the Word as Incarnate in the created world. At this point, that from which theology borrows its integrity of course ceases to be exterior, for faith comes through the Word, Jesus Christ, to the interior of the individual soul. Yet the integrity of theology, if real, is indeed borrowed, and theology itself remains, as compared with the teaching activity of the Church, a barbarian production. Erasmus was right on this score, although wrong in using barbarian as a narrowly depreciatory term.

The barbarian question becomes a live and vivid one in the Renaissance. By contrast with the medieval man who preceded him, the Renaissance humanist was something of an antiscientist and definitely considered himself an antibarbarian. It is true that he achieved a sense of community with the ancients that medieval man had not had. Rudolph Agricola, Hegius, Erasmus, and their congeners and epigoni felt and somehow conveyed to others a sense of ancient Greek and Roman authors as still living influences, so that communing with them became for a time something very like dialogue, despite the disabling effects of preoccupation with written records of thought and expression.

This success of the humanists is often described in terms of a reaction to medieval man's failure to establish contact with the ancients. The humanists stumbled upon a mine of manuscripts that medieval man had not known. To a certain extent this is true. And yet medieval man had maintained a great deal of contact with ancient authors, as modern scholarship more and more makes evident. The relative success of the humanists was rather in great part due to the nature of the medieval contact—to the fact that it was barbarian in the sense that medieval man often imputed to the ancients the awed deference of an inferior to a superior. John of Salisbury and others can be cited as instances of medieval men who were not barbarian in this sense. And they are cited rightly, for they protest quite vocally against too great subservience to ancient writers. But the urgency of their protest attests the tendency on all sides to be too subservient.

John of Salisbury and others like him are medieval representatives of the tendency that became more marked in the Renaissance, when the ancients were viewed with less deference and more real man-to-man respect. Of course, the Renaissance, too, provides instances of too great subservience to antiquity, but its more typical spokesmen are men such as Ben Jonson, whose advice that one value the knowledge of the ancient Greeks and Romans but at the same time raid them as though one were their master sounds extraordinarily high-handed by comparison with the unquestioning deference of the typical medieval formulary rhetorics such as those of Matthew of Vendome and Geoffrey of Vinsauf.

It is ironic but inevitable that the humanists, genuinely antibarbarian as they proposed to be, could not manage in the last analysis to be truly Greek, but assimilated themselves in the large to the Romans (barbarians from the Greek point of view). The fact is highly significant that despite the early sixteenth-century advocacy of Greek as at least the equal of Latin, it was always Latin that dominated in the Western humanist milieu. C. S. Lewis is quite right in *English Literature in the Sixteenth Century, Excluding Drama*, which is volume three of *The Oxford History of English Literature,* when he says of the humanists that "the desire was for order and discipline, weight, and decorum; and men rightly felt that these qualities were to be learned from the Romans rather than the Greeks" (24). Order and discipline, weight, and decorum are matters on which the barbarian, making his way up in the world, is likely to put a high premium. They are the virtues of the bourgeoisie, often taken as typifying the intelligent barbarians within an intellectual culture. Indeed, "discipline" itself refers to what is proper to the disciple or learner.

This alignment of the humanists with Romans rather than Greeks is, moreover, a product of their own history. As descendants of barbarians, they had not been able to negate their own ancestry, however much they may have thought they were doing so. They did not abandon but merely revised their fathers' ambitions. They still felt themselves outsiders in that they looked to a culture other than their own for their integrity, for although they were able for a time to identify themselves with this culture, that of ancient Greece and Rome, with an intensity that minimized their outsideness, they were in reality more widely separated from it by time and social institutions than their more patently barbarian fathers had been. Indeed, the increased distance between them and ancient Rome accounts in a large measure for their overarticulateness about ancient Roman culture. The orientation toward the ancient world that had, after all, been a dominant feature of medieval culture, was becoming less automatic. One had to shout louder to reach the ancients as they receded into the distance.

Under these circumstances it was inevitable that the old formalism would again set in. By the seventeenth and eighteenth centuries, the works of the ancients with which the humanists had managed to carry on a simulated dialogue came to be regarded quite commonly as a body of writings guaranteeing almost magically to those "formed" through the educational process that integrity that even the earlier barbarian devotion to science could no longer promise so convincingly, since under the impact of the new cosmology the older scientific world found itself, as John Donne saw it, "all in pieces, all coherence gone."

Much could be said about the Catholic-Protestant situation of the sixteenth century in terms of the Greek-barbarian theme—indeed, altogether too much to admit of inclusion here. In so far as it parallels to some extent the opposition of humanist to scholastic, the opposition of Protestant to

Catholic corresponds to that of Greek to barbarian—and partakes of the same ambivalence. Early Protestants aligned themselves with antiquity and against medieval barbarianism by ambitioning a return to a presumedly pure primitive Christianity, and in this sense were Greek.

But this same recourse to a culture other than that in which they were nurtured reveals not the Greek, but the typical barbarian cast of mind—a "pure" primitive Christianity being an utterly typical barbarian projection. Hand in hand with the barbarian rejection of the indigenous culture goes the Protestant rejection of nature as totally corrupt. At this point the Protestant stand is barbarian, whereas the Catholic acceptance of nature and the Catholic insistence that God acts through Christ with a grace that transforms the human soul intrinsically (not merely extrinsically, or through imputation, as in classic Protestant doctrine), appears as Greek. The situation is further complicated by the fact, a commonplace today, that whatever their disavowals, sixteenth- and seventeenth-century Protestants as well as Catholics were deeply imbued with "barbarian" scholastic philosophy even when they were denouncing it. Altogether, perhaps nothing would reveal the tangle of complications that make up the Reformation and later the Catholic Counter-Reformation more intriguingly than the application to the situation of the Greek-barbarian theorems. But the application would be an almost endless undertaking.

In the generations since the humanistic-scholastic tiff, no larger cultural issues have raised so explicitly the barbarian question. Nevertheless, in treatments of subsequent history the theme is constantly returned to, for whatever insights it may afford. A great many disturbing movements, not a few of them successful, have been labeled as "barbarian": free enterprise, progressive education, civilization in the United States generally, and more recently Nazism, Fascism, and Communism. The entire revolutionary momentum itself, which gathered its forces several centuries ago in the depths of the Hebrew-Christian psyche and has since spread to all mankind, has been seen by some as purely barbarian in its roots and manifestations. So has almost anything that has impinged from the outside on Western culture, for better or for worse.

III

In the title of his book, *The Holy Barbarians*, Lawrence Lipton can shock the uninformed by calling barbarians "holy" because in its popular application and even in serious cultural analyses until rather recently the term barbarian has been taken as automatically depreciatory. But recent analysts have grown increasingly aware that it can be neuter in implication. Barbarians turn out rather regularly to be the custodians—often the only custodians—of the culture on which they prey. And if they transform such cultures, transformation is inevitable and can well be good, since no non-barbarian or "Greek" culture is anything more than a quite limited human achievement, destined by its very limitations to be transmuted into something else. Of course, transformation of a culture can also be bad, but this is not necessarily due to the fact that its transformers are barbarians. It can be due to certain positive defects that the culture may have. We must continually remind ourselves that every culture is probably in some way barbarian with regard to every other, although in varying ways and degrees, and that every culture that cannot survive contacts with other cultures is by that very fact certainly limited, for mankind is obviously destined to possess itself as a whole. Two adjoining cultures cannot be kept out of contact with each other, and if one or the other feels the need to keep out of contact this fact itself manifests a defect, a lack of self-possession.

To say that a culture is barbarian, therefore, as this term is taken here, is to say neither that it is good nor that it is bad. It is to say that it feels that the integrity it seeks is in some way possessed by, or enshrined in, or symbolized by a culture outside itself to which it must adapt.

To the Greek, barbarian is a derogatory term because the barbarian is an outsider. But the term is far more derogatory by implication in the mouth of what we may call a "practicing barbarian," one who regards Greek culture as a paramount good, something to be emulated at all costs. Since for such a man all that he is not is good, by inference he himself is bad. The inference, of course, is not true. For no culture is worth uncritical and unselective emulation.

For the advance of civilization barbarians may be necessary. They supply vigor, for a properly administered inferiority complex can compel high achievement. And they force discrimination. No culture is worth preserving just exactly as it is. All cultures need improvement, and need it rather badly, and the operations of barbarians on a culture, whatever the immediate effects, can result in a sorting out of what is valuable from what is not.

The very concepts of Greek and barbarian are aids to discrimination. For the Greek-barbarian disjunction cannot be applied to any cultures simply or en bloc. There are no complete Greeks or complete barbarians, only partial ones. There are no total outsiders of any kind. These dialectically related concepts, Greek and barbarian, like other similarly related concepts such as classic and Romantic, are useful precisely because they do not fit the whole of a given situation but fit the situation only in part—that is, they are useful largely because of the ways they do not fit. In saying that a culture is Greek, one is forced to say how it is so by contrast with some certain barbarianism, and vice versa, since every culture (like every person) is both Greek and barbarian, so that one is saying nothing until one has worked out a specific ground for a statement involving these terms. If every culture is both Greek and barbarian, nevertheless no two cultures are Greek or barbarian in exactly the same way.

This is rather strikingly evident in the case of contrasting cultural groups today, and notably in the case of the United States and the Union of Soviet Socialist Republics. Khrushchev's pronouncements that have taken the United States as the measure of technological achievements— "*We* are going to outdistance *you*"—are typical examples of the barbarian outsider's defense mechanism in the face of a culture that he envies. On the other hand, the American reaction to the Russian educational perform- ance also shows signs of the barbarian's defense mechanisms. This com- posite of reactions suggests that with regard to technologically contrived well-being Americans are not barbarians at all, but the ultimate Greeks. Such well-being is felt as interior to American culture, so that in realizing a reign of material sufficiency, Americans feel that they are drawing on nothing at all beyond their own interior resources. To be surpassed in the production of material well-being really distresses Americans seriously, not so much because it gives them to feel that they are being deprived of material comforts as because of something deeper: they are losing some- thing of their own interior orientation. But the material well-being native to the American psyche is an import in Russia, the object of calculated striving supported by a self-consciously materialistic system of thought that the Russians have annexed and that strikes an American, rightly or wrongly, as a bit naive, however effective it may prove.

At the same time, however, with regard to intellectual achievement, Americans tend to be barbarians, viewing—not ungrudgingly—such achievements as existing at their optimum in cultures other than their own: in Europe or in the past or in the future, or even—the abiding "other" in American life—in nature. It does Americans no harm at all to be told or to tell themselves that other cultures have better ways of train- ing the mind than they do. They want to believe this. The smart of such a conviction distresses Americans not at all, but simply drives them, as nothing else could, to better their own educational procedures.

In activity connected with education, American life presents several facets of a curiously obvious barbarian cut. Most spectacular perhaps is the rash of Greek-letter associations distinctive of American universities and colleges. Membership in these associations certainly ensures no very effective contact with ancient Greek civilization—most members can rec- ognize few letters of the Greek alphabet beyond those naming their own organization, and the latter only if they are capital letters. But membership does confer the "Greek" status of being "in." The associations are commonly styled fraternities (brotherhoods) or sororities (sisterhoods) to make this fact plain. The Hellenic facade is deliberately maintained. Interfraternity or intersorority or inter-fraternity-sorority groups are commonly referred to as "Panhellenic" groups of one sort or another, and students who do not belong to the fraternities or sororities are referred to as barbarians or "barbs." Greeks are in and barbs are out. Membership in the Greek-letter associations is achieved by passage through initiation rites closely (if unconsciously) paralleling the *rites de passage* of primitive societies that anthropologists have described as marking entrance into a new state of being.

It is, of course, tempting to write off all this self-conscious Hellenism as a mere "accident." College age is sure to be an age of initiations. It is so everywhere. Someone started Phi Beta Kappa in America, and the Greek letter ideas "somehow" caught on. But there are no such "accidents." The "somehow" cries for explanation of one sort or another. There must be a reason why this idea, and not others, swept all before it. And one does not have to cast out all other explanations to observe that one reason could well be the deep drive within the American to move from the barbarian status in which he feels he is born (for no one is born into a fraternity or sorority, but always adopted) into that of a true Greek, however confused or even unconvincing this imputed Hellenism might be. In college or university the drive manifests itself with full academic explicitness. Early American education was like other Western education in being centered around the study of Latin and Greek, skill in the latter being rarer and an indication of greater prestige—or of being further "in." But only in America did the implications of the early classical educational system (a barbarian system, of course, in America as elsewhere) hit home with this peculiarly obvious force.

Another phenomenon in the American academic world of interest on a similar score is the high concentration of scholastic philosophy in the United States, where a scholasticism or neoscholasticism more or less connected with its medieval counterpart is far more widespread than in any other country of the world. In so far as scholasticism, as explained above, called forth from the humanists the charge of barbarianism, the vigor of its modern counterpart in the United States is worth noting. The vigor is due to no one cause but rather to a combination of various circumstances—but that does not mean that it is fortuitous. The culture of the United States favors this particular "barbarian" mode of thinking in ways often intriguing even though indirect or coincidental.

One of the chief circumstances favoring such thinking has turned out to be the American devotion to a liberal education in the sense of a protracted general education, a devotion that itself evinces a desire to strengthen assurance that an individual really "belongs." For the most part, in other countries, the teaching of philosophy as a part of a liberal or general education is restricted to the secondary schools, where alone general education is purveyed, it being assumed that the student can be inducted into the full range of essential knowledge early, so that the university remains exclusively a specializing organ. But in the educational system of the United States, where general education persists even at the university level, scholastic philosophy is made part of the Catholic program of *higher* education and in Catholic institutions is taught to all students who aspire to undergraduate degrees.

The effect of neoscholasticism in the United States, moreover, is not restricted to Catholic circles. The University of Chicago, for example has known strong, if somewhat ambiguous, neoscholastic influences under Robert M. Hutchins, Mortimer Adler, Richard McKeon, and others, and has developed a school of literary criticism manifesting strong neoscholastic traits. The typically American "Great Books" programs often show high interest in scholastic and neoscholastic works. Professors Jacques Maritain and Etienne Gilson, distinguished deans of European scholastic philosophers, have been annexed by North America, the former being long established at Princeton and the latter teaching regularly at Toronto, where American students flock to his classes. The recent intensive study of the influence of scholastic logic and formal rhetoric on English literature has been done largely in American universities such as Harvard, Yale, Columbia, North Carolina, Saint Louis University, the Catholic University of America, the University of Chicago, the University of Illinois, and the University of Wisconsin. More than other groups, Americans like to write and to read books such as *The Thirteenth, Greatest of Centuries* (Walsh). But the historical roots of scholasticism in the United States do not lie only in Catholic ground. American Puritanism itself was in great part scholasticism, as Perry Miller and others have shown. And the American mind, although a many-faceted thing, reflects in not a few of its facets a formal, apersonal, and schematic pattern that attests connections with much in the scholastic heritage.

Looking also beyond educational circles, one might say that although certain aspects of life in the United States are of course not barbarian, doubtless American life is best described as barbarian rather than Greek in its overall cast. The special position in history of the American north of the Rio Grande makes him an established outsider: he is the one who more than any other set himself up outside Old World society. He has long looked to this society—perhaps too long-as his measure of achievement. It is interesting in this connection that visitors in Europe from the United States are so often drawn to Germany as to the culture closest to that of the United States. Germany is a focus of barbarian culture in Europe. Tangent to the classical world from antiquity and always drawn to Mediterranean culture by a powerful inferiority complex (*los von Rom!* has stirred the German spirit in its intimate depths), the German-speaking world remains psychologically outside—further outside than the British Isles, which had been an integral part of the ancient Roman culture. The tension between modern Germany and ancient Greece is documented in books such as E. M. Butler's *The Tyranny of Greece over Germany.* And yet the same German-speaking world has performed the typical barbarian role of preserving the exterior civilization it seizes on: German scholarship, rather more than Italian scholarship and far more than Mussolini's grandiose imperial scheming, has kept alive ancient Rome and Greece.

The Latin American, less likely to be impressed by Germany when he visits Europe, is in certain discernible ways less barbarian than his neighbors north of the Rio Grande. For in Latin America European culture encountered a country far more populous than that which constituted the present United States and Canada. The relationship of the emigrants to the Europe that they had left was complicated in the extreme by a new relationship with masses of people around them who were not European at all. The immigrants were outsiders to two cultures, that which they had left and that to which they had come, but because they were more inclined to view the indigenous American culture as barbarian, they felt themselves less barbarian with regard to Europe, where, moreover, as South Europeans they preserved close historical continuity with classical Mediterranean culture. The South Europeans in Latin America were emissaries of the Greeks at the outposts of civilization. The Latin-American psyche, at one level, has thus retained a continuity with the European experience that Americans north of the Rio Grande do not know.

The strong commitment to the future that has always been part of the United States psyche identifies it in a still further way as barbarian. For the barbarian can be seen quite readily as the man of the future. He is the man who is viewed as not having anything to offer out of his own past or present, and whose achievement thus lies necessarily in the future if it lies anywhere at all. To the barbarian, all the glories of the *past* and *present* empire *will* fall.

This raises the question as to the relationship of barbarianism and what might be called Nietzschean man in the sense of the man who insists on living at the edge of things somewhat disdainful of past and present, peering prophetically into the future. Is such a man a barbarian? Is he one who must prey on something not himself? Such a Nietzschean is a barbarian certainly in so far as his effectiveness depends on his ability not simply to find truth but also to astound the bourgeois—but a kind of inverse barbarian, since he desires not to learn from the "others" (the bourgeois), but to make them unlearn what they think they know. But the bourgeois himself is even more consummately barbarian if he believes that by maintaining his "way of life" he is preserving a well established and permanent security or "well established order" (and much more if he believes that he is *re*-establishing it) rather than that he is working toward such security. For the conviction that order is here—which contrasts markedly with the Greek willingness to live with a certain order in a context of disorder—shows only that one has smugly identified oneself with a merely hypothetical or projected order of an imagined Greek instead of living the more strenuous and upsetting life that consists in working toward an order never to be obtained in this life. For total security is never the possession of any living man, who must work out his salvation in fear and trembling to the very end of his life—and much less is it the possession of any human culture organized by these perilously organized individuals. Anyone who thinks of integrity as being in reality an actually achieved possession must be thinking of it by implication as someone else's, for he should know that it is patently not his or his culture's. Thus in this sense his is the barbarian's view, measuring things by an integrity that someone else is supposed to have.

In so far as Nietzschean man is willing to live with the fact that the reality of human life, the node that we actually hold in our possession, is never fully ordered, that the possibility of chaos is built in, he is willing to live with a limited integrity—and to that extent is Greek. But in so far as he situates a hoped-for integrity in the dream of a future *Uebermensch*, a Superman, he is a barbarian of the most hopeless sort. And in so far as he denies God, he is not being barbarian where he should be. Because if we must have integrity from another—as we must—the other is not the mere future, but God, Who is here now.

IV

As the newer nations and hitherto "backward" groups of men take their place more and more in the sun, the barbarian issue comes more alive than ever. Are the Indians of South America barbarians? In a basic sense, it appears not. In Latin America they preserve their own pre-Columbian civilization, at least to a great extent. American Indians in the United

States and Canada, on the other hand, perhaps because of their small numbers from the beginning, have been more barbarian, but not so much as another group, American Negroes, who, in so far as they are one of the subcultures making up the United States, have been true, vigorous, aggressive, progressive barbarians, making the culture that was once largely that of white Europeans alone more and more their own (while contributing to it massively themselves) until, as has been said more than once, they become the most American of all Americans.

In other countries, however, as less advanced peoples come into contact with modern technological civilization, they are less barbarian today than they would have been in an earlier age. For the age of barbarianism in the strict sense has passed, in that mankind has matured to the point where each culture and subculture is highly reflective about itself and about all cultures and their relationships to one another. The barbarian's adulation of another culture is now tempered with global consciousness. The "other" culture is no longer so much "other" as it used to be, and hence is approached more critically.

Moreover, to the Greek, the barbarian as such is no longer so entirely "other." The outsider can now claim the interest of the insider precisely because of his otherness. Society reaches out to the outcast not too generously yet, but more generously than ever before, at least in those countries where social betterment has become a major concern. Race-relations work is a special instance of what happens when man becomes sufficiently reflective about the question of otherness. The development of a personalist philosophy in our day provides the most clear-cut instance of improved interest in the other, for at this point the quest for the universal (that which is not other, but the same) in being yields to attempts to deal with what is utterly "other" and induplicable, the person, the person's commitments, and the particularities of history.

At this point the fate of the beatnik becomes most tortuously ironic. A professional outsider, he becomes of paramount interest to philosophers themselves precisely because of his declared intransigence. He is a kind of barbarian in reverse, for he insists that he, the outsider as outsider, is the real Greek who has the integrity that the insiders or squares have sacrificed to a cheap security. The beatnik's reversal of role here is not due merely to perversity or intransigence. It is in a way inevitable, for it corresponds to a profound reversal within thought itself. In classic philosophic thought grown out of the Greek world into the present, the focus of interest has been the universal, the nonunique, the duplicable, which has by and large been taken to be the sole subject of true science and philosophy. But this approach to reality has been under siege as recent philosophical developments of a phenomenological and personalist or "existentialist" cast have pressed the cause of the individual and unique with a vigor never evident before. Hitherto, the unique was the outsider, philosophically inconsequential. Today the philosophical spotlight covers him inexorably as he struts and frets his hour upon the stage. Indeed, the philosopher's interest would be even greater if the beatnik were only as unique, as far out, as he would like to be.

What is more, the beatnik knows all this. He knows that the squares have an interest in him, which is even an academic interest. *A Casebook on the Beat* (Parkinson) has recently been published by Thomas Crowell Press to implement study of the outsider in society today. The beatnik cannot avoid knowing that his outsideness guarantees that he is really in. But this makes him less an outsider, and hence less interesting. At this point his real motives become garbled to the point of total unmanageability. Does he really want to be out only in order to be in? Or does the fact that being out, he is really in only annoy him and make him push harder than ever to be out? No one knows. The difficulty in assessing his motives is, in fact, built into the motives themselves, because his very revolt is an assertion of the state he revolts against. The beatnik is caught in *the toils that ensnare every man who sets up a program that at its heart is negative.* Such a man is derivative in his very assertion of independence, and his program is an elaborate self-delusion at heart.

And yet the beatnik is highly significant for our age. His revolt in its very futility and his consequent plight illustrates what is evident on many other scores: the barbarian's case is weakening, for man's global consciousness is growing so that other civilizations themselves are all in a sense our own, no matter what or where they are. For the same reason, of course, the Greek's case is weakening, too, since all civilizations must look outside themselves more than ever now to other cultures. The historical awareness that marks all the serious thinking of modern man is an awareness of otherness, and this means that it includes an awareness of the limitations of our own achievements. The beatnik's trouble is that it is no longer possible to be a barbarian without being a reflective one.

Furthermore, as man's relationship to time has changed with the accumulation of knowledge that enables him to write history, he has increased his sense of the richness of his immediate milieu and in doing so has found much of his otherness at his finger tips. In earlier ages, university lecturers were expected to spend their time commenting on the work of others who had to be far removed from themselves in time. Medieval and Renaissance professors of medicine commented on Galen, who flourished in the second century of the Christian era. St. Thomas

Aquinas commented on Peter Lombard, who had died about 1160, and, although St. Thomas Aquinas himself died in 1274, his works did not displace Peter Lombard's in many places until several hundred years later. This academic system of speaking into the more or less distant past continued well into the age of Kant. And when the English language was introduced as a subject for university study during the nineteenth century, Old English came in first. But today, while we do not neglect the past (much more available to us than it ever was to earlier man), we focus more and more on the present that because we know so much more fully than earlier man its connections with the past, presents itself to us as a rich and varied manifold. We find otherness around us, and are Greeks and barbarians with regard to our own times.

And thus if in some ways the barbarian-Greek tensions are lessening in society, in another way they remain. There is barbarian and Greek permanently in us all. Each of us is divided between his drive inward and his drive outward, between self and other. The ultimate other is God—and yet this is no relief, for *this* Other is to be found chiefly within. When we achieve our integrity in Him, it is interior, but still does not come from ourselves. He is ours when we are His.

Here there is special hope for the Christian. If his relationship to God is in a sense that of barbarian to Greek, this relationship has been tempered by Christ, for it has been brought to fruition in His Person. It is no accident that the Christian climate was the one which initially made assimilation of barbarian by Greek and of Greek by barbarian feasible on a large enough scale to fix the term "barbarian age" classically in the early Christian era for good. The Christian climate is a climate in which tensions do not die but come to fruition, a climate not of indifference but of active conciliation. The Christian is in the world but not of it. He is an outsider living from within.

Works Cited

Benton, Robert and Harvey Schmidt. *The In and Out Book.* New York: Viking Press, 1959.

Butler, Eliza M. *The Tyranny of Greece over Germany: A Study of the Influence Exercised by Greek Art and Poetry over the Great German Writers of the Eighteenth, Nineteenth, and Twentieth Centuries.* Boston: Beacon Press, 1958. (Originally published 1935)

Carman, Bliss and Richard Hovey. *Songs from Vagabondia.* Boston: Copeland and Day, 1894.

Crombie, Alistair C. *Augustine to Galileo: The History of Science, A. D. 400-1650.* Cambridge, MA: Harvard UP, 1953.

Dodds, Eric R. *The Greeks and the Irrational.* Berkeley: U of California P, 1951.

Duhem, Pierre M. *Le système du monde: Histoire des doctrines cosmologiques de Platon à Copernic.* 10 vols. Paris: A. Hermann, 1913-59.

Jaeger, Werner. *Paideia: The Ideals of Greek Culture.* 3 vols. Trans. Gilbert Highet. New York: Oxford UP, 1939.

Kazantzakis, Nikos. *The Odyssey: A Modern Sequel.* Trans. Kimon Friar. New York: Simon and Schuster, 1958.

Lewis, C. S. *English Literature in the Sixteenth Century, Excluding Drama.* Oxford: Clarendon Press, 1954.

Lipton, Lawrence. *The Holy Barbarians.* New York: Messner, 1959.

Lynes, Russell. *The Tastemakers.* New York: Harper, 1954.

Maier, Anneliese. *On the Threshold of Exact Science: Selected Writings of Anneliese Maier on Late Medieval Natural Philosophy.* Ed. and trans. Steven D. Sargent. Philadelphia: U of Pennsylvania P, 1982.

Mitford, Nancy. *Noblesse Oblige: An Enquiry into the Identifiable Characteristics of the English Aristocracy.* New York: Harper, 1956.

Ong, Walter J. *Ramus, Method, and the Decay of Dialogue: From the Art of Discourse to the Art of Reason.* Cambridge, MA: Harvard UP, 1958.

Packard, Vance. *The Status Seekers: An Exploration of Class Behavior in America and the Hidden Barriers That Affect You, Your Community, Your Future.* New York: D. McKay, 1959.

Parkinson, Thomas Francis, ed. *A Casebook on the Beat.* New York: Thomas Crowell, 1961.

Riesman, David, with Reuel Denney and Nathan Glazer. *The Lonely Crowd: A Study of the Changing American Character.* New York: Doubleday, 1950.

Walsh, James J. *The Thirteenth: Greatest of Centuries.* New York: Catholic Summer School Press, [1907].

Wilson, Colin. *The Outsider.* Boston: Houghton Mifflin, 1956.

Wright, Richard. *The Outsider.* New York: Harper & Row, 1965. (Originally published 1953)

13

Review of *The Singer of Tales*
(1961-1962)

Lord, Albert B. *The Singer of Tales*. Cambridge, MA: Harvard UP, 1960. Pp. xvi + 309.

This is a most informed and informative work. Basically, it is a book on the epic tradition. "This book is about Homer. He is our Singer of Tales. Yet, in a larger sense, he represents all singers of tales from time immemorial and unrecorded to the present. Our book is about these other singers as well. . . . Our immediate purpose is to comprehend this manner in which they compose, learn, and transmit their epics" (vii).

But this is far from just another book on Homer, and for two reasons. First, the materials out of which it works derive from sources still living, the nonliterate bards still active in South Slavic regions, particularly among speakers of Serbocroation and Bulgarian in modern Yugoslavia. And the materials are quantitatively and qualitatively altogether exceptional, being the distillation of a staggering number of epic texts, translations, and commentaries, as well as interviews with individual singers, all now being published under the joint auspices of Harvard University Press and the Serbian Academy of Sciences. Much of this epic material derives from collections of recordings completed by Professor Lord after they had been begun by the late Milman Parry, whose "oral theory" concerning the Homeric poems is well known to classicists and who launched into the making of recordings by the thousands when he was teaching classics at Harvard University in the 1930s. It is the unprecedented spread of its documentation that makes this work so valuable.

Second, the importance of this book comes from the fact that its report on the oral-aural cast of mind relates not merely to Parry's "theory" but also to a great many other recent areas of study: modern linguistics (with its primary focus on the spoken word rather than on written texts), folklore and cultural anthropology, phenomenological philosophy, and contemporary scriptural study and biblical exegesis. Many of the distorting frames of reference that ages of manuscript-oriented and typography-oriented culture and scholarship have elaborated are here definitively dismembered and seen for what they often are—irrelevancies and unwitting falsifications not merely of answers but also of problems. These out of the way, the fuller significance of oral composition as such is here entered into with gusto and discernment. If Professor Lord's book is itself of necessity a production of a chirographic and typographic culture, it shows such a culture finally aware of its own built-in squints—and to this extent freed of them by that informed reflectiveness that is the only natural therapy available to finite intellects to remedy their finiteness and that is truly liberal and liberating in the very best sense of these words.

Typographically preconditioned minds, many of them, are likely to show themselves unsure and querulous in the presence of this and similar studies in which the landmarks they had been taught to take for granted are done away with as useless. The fact is that only with extreme difficulty can the oral performance that this book investigates be talked of at all meaningfully in our civilization, for the very concepts in which purely oral performance must be thought of are often missing from our minds and are contrary to our analytic habits. Most of our conceptual apparatus for handling verbal performance, such as "literature" or "creativity," is here both disabling and falsifying. Literature, which means either something written or at the very least something conceived of by analogy with what is written, does not exist at all in a preliterate culture. The basis for such a conception—writing—is simply unknown. And thus to think of a sung story from the oral-aural tradition as "literature" is to be insensitive to what the story really is. It is true that the modern singers of tales with whom Professor Lord is concerned know of the existence of writing even when they are illiterate, and are influenced by it in varying degrees, as Lord's evidence concerning the effect of song books on some singers spells out in painstaking detail. However, the work of even these latter-day singers grows demonstrably out of a tradition that is historically and fundamentally oral-aural, radically preliterate; it is not merely developed retrospectively by literates practicing antiquarianism.

Thinking of a story or tale from an oral-aural culture as composed *for* performance can engender errors as serious as those engendered by thinking of it as "literature." In the oral tradition, a tale or story is not composed *for* performance but *during* performance, while it is being sung. Recording shows that no one performance or singing is quite like another. Here there is no possibility of having an "author" distinct from the performance: the two are necessarily always one. This suggests a certain spontaneity or originality, but one must be very careful here, for this singing is not artistic "creation" either. Quite the obverse: even an original song sung for the first time—and of course there have been such songs—is, in this epic tradition, essentially a re-application of pre-existing formulae and themes by a particular singer (each singer has his own ways of utilizing the formulae, his own oral-aural "signatures") to one more particular "matter" or situation. One can well think of a story in this oral tradition as a child does when he teases an adult to "tell" a story, not expecting that the adult will "create" the tale but simply that he will bring into the here and now, will make accessible, *the* story that inevitably "is" already in existence somewhere, but without being thought of as in writing or in print. Like the chirographic presuppositions supporting the concept of "literature," the Romantic presuppositions back of the concept of artistic "creation" are simply missing in the original epic world as reported by Lord. Classical concepts of "invention" as drawing "matter" out of a "store" of commonplaces (*topoi, loci communes*) are considerably closer to the preliterate mind. (The Renaissance revival of the topical logics, the logics built around the "places" drawn on by invention, which I have attempted to deal with in my *Ramus, Method, and the Decay of Dialogue*, was thus in a sense the final shower of sparks released by an old oral-aural world as it was plunging from the epic firmament into the sea of a typographical civilization.) A civilization dominated by print, the great conservator, puts a premium on originality, but an oral-aural civilization values the innovator less than the conservator, who serves as a counterpoise to its impermanencies.

Although the first part of this book devotes itself to "theory," its unprecedented spread of documentation makes the "theory" in fact largely exposition of phenomena at hand as Professor Lord works through the performance and training of singers, the formula, the theme, originality and tradition, and finally the divergence of written from oral tradition. Matters heretofore conjectural are approached in terms of direct and for the most part seemingly indisputable evidence. What is meant by verbal accuracy can here be tested by recordings of the same illiterate singer singing what he considers to be the same tale at intervals of some seventeen years, or, in another way, by singers performing a song new to them after they have heard it only once! In these repetitions the accuracy of substance is astounding, if less than perfect, and is quite understandable when it becomes apparent how any performance must be a concatenation of formulae and themes of which all singers have an abundant store. Because these formulae and themes are common property—although always with individualist variations of "style" for each singer—the very substance of any story is in a way common property even before it is told.

Chirographically trained persons, and even more those typographically trained, are likely to interpret the singers' remarkable ability to repeat as an optimum development of rote memory. But quite wrongly. Rote memory, in the ordinary sense of word-for-word matching of long passages like that of two printed pages from the same type form, has nothing to do with this reproduction, for it is hardly envisaged by the singers as a desideratum. Indeed, it is not envisaged by them at all, since the very idea of such rote memory is based on experience with writing.

One of the major incidental values of this book is the evidence it adduces to show that not only is literacy no help to the singer of tales, but that it is a positive disability, since the whole "feel" for epic song is destroyed as soon as one thinks of one's performance as matching a written and fixed text—which has *nothing* to do with the *original* oral tradition, being a later development, adventitious and distracting.

Lord's exposition inevitably impinges on a certain type of critical speculation, that concerned with the mode of existence of a literary work—*Where* is *it?* This speculation is here revealed for what it is, the product of a manuscript and typographical outlook. For the compulsion to think of verbal performances as necessarily represented by a single verbal something or other that is in some sort of place proper to itself is apparently inoperative in the more oral-aural cultures from which epic tradition derives. This is not, of course, to say that such speculation is meaningless or misleading. It is needful and helpful. But it is also a specialized, culturally conditioned kind of speculation.

The second half of this work treats successively Homer, the *Odyssey*, the *Iliad*, and, more cursorily, various problems in the study of medieval epics, notably *Beowulf*, *La Chanson de Roland*, and the Greek epic *Digenis Akritas*. The treatment of these epics is often suggestive rather than exhaustive. In the light of detailed exposition of oral performance, new lines of thought are developed concerning organization and interrelationships. But standard major questions are also broached.

Having painstakingly set forth what an oral poet does, Lord concludes that "there is now no doubt that the composer of the Homeric poems was an oral poet," for "the proof is to be found in the poems themselves" (141)—that is, in the presence of the oral forms and procedures that familiarity with oral performance renders evident. These oral forms and procedures are obvious enough in *Beowulf* and other epic or epic-like medieval work, Lord points out in detail, drawing in the case of *Beowulf* on the recent work of Francis P. Magoun, Jr, and Robert P. Creed.

Readers who have not followed Lord's detailed analyses of oral forms and procedure will nevertheless be struck by material in the book's several appendices, notably by "The Song of Milman Parry," composed (that is, sung or performed) by Milovan Vojii Nevesinje on the twentieth day of September, 1933. Here the skilled use of the epic formulae to celebrate Parry's visit to Yugoslavia as well as his own person as he prepared to embark for America again on the "Saturnia" (the song names the modern ship without embarrassment) creates an atmosphere unmistakably heroic and even Homeric, despite the seemingly less than Homeric dimensions of its subject. Nowhere is the genesis of the epic effect in the epic form and procedure more evident than in this performance, which converts a present-day classical scholar's return to his homeland into an epic song, a minor—if slightly shabby—*Odyssey*.

Lord's placing of the Homeric question in a circumstantially described oral-aural setting does not, of course, solve all the Homeric problems, although it helps us to formulate many of them more adequately. In this setting, the question of multiple authorship for the *Iliad* and the *Odyssey* as conceived by Separatist theory based on the suppositions of a chirographic culture is meaningless. Every performance of every epic in an oral tradition is both different from every other and of a piece with others. Prescriptive rights to fixed versions or parts are out of the question, for unless we remove the epic from oral tradition by writing it down, no fixed versions or parts even exist. Given this state of affairs, however, the basic epic problem becomes a particularly sweeping one: Why should epos or oral performance of epic have been set down in writing at all? Why should epos ever be transmuted into literature? It is indeed hard to say. Alphabetic writing appears to have been initially useful for such things as account keeping, not for recording what individuals sang aloud. Lord suggests that a wave of intense scribal activity was sweeping across the Mediterranean and that the Greeks, like the Hebrews and others, were caught up in it, fascinated by the fixity that writing conferred on utterance. Doubtless the human drive for permanence in utterance, as Lord proposes, *any* permanence, even the partially misleading one of writing, was operative here.

As to why the epics known as Homer's should have become the most famous ones, Lord proffers the interesting suggestion that one reason may well have been their length. The length of a singer's tale varies from performance to performance, according to the occasion. Wide experience with singers of tales suggests, surprisingly enough, that singers who can sing the longest songs are likely to be the best singers. They have greater "invention"—which means that they have a more fecund store of formulae and themes, the pieces constituting an epic: their structures simply have more to them than do the sparser structures of less voluble bards.

Epic Cycle songs in Homer's day, as it appears, commonly ran to some 7000 lines—as against Homer's own 27,000! The extreme length of the *Iliad* and *Odyssey* suggests a very special occasion, and Lord proposes (153-54) that the occasion could very well have been dictation to a scribe. Dictation, allowing a song to be strung out over several days, was a challenge to do a full-dress oral performance such as had perhaps never been done before—and Homer met the challenge best of all singers. This hypothesis situates the two great Greek epics grown out of an oral-aural world at the borderline between the doomed oral-aural culture and nascent manuscript culture.

A wealth of more specialized questions is also treated in this work—questions, for example, concerned with the length and structure of epic lines, the "thrift" in use of formulae achieved by singers today and by Homer, and even the question of Homer's blindness. Lord indicates that there can exist some connection between being blind and being a singer of tales. He and Parry found blind persons who had turned to folk singing as something for which their disability is no evident handicap. On the other hand, their best singers were definitely not the few blind ones whom they encountered. But the possible connection between blindness and a bardic vocation is real enough to keep the question of a blind Homer quite alive.

This book also makes it clearer than ever how epic survivals are being pushed today further and further back into the hinterland, where they will eventually vanish. Literature has won. Singers of songs are relicts of another age. Yet they have helped make us what we are today, and their very difference from ourselves helps us to understand by contrast what we ourselves are. This study is particularly fascinating and informative as we stand at the dawn of another age when literature itself is entering a new phase of existence in a new communications complex dominated in the strategic areas by electronic media.

Works Cited

Creed, Robert P. *Reconstructing the Rhythm of Beowulf.* Columbia: U of Missouri P, 1990.

Magoun, Francis P., Jr., ed. *Béowulf and Judith: Done in a Normalized Orthography.* Cambridge, MA: Harvard UP, 1959.

Ong, Walter J. *Ramus, Method, and the Decay of Dialogue: From the Art of Discourse to the Art of Reason.* Cambridge, MA: Harvard UP, 1958.

14

Review of *The Gutenberg Galaxy* (1962)

McLuhan, Marshall. *The Gutenberg Galaxy: The Making of Typographic Man.* Toronto: U of Toronto P, 1962. Pp. vi + 294.

Interest in the work of Marshall McLuhan has been more intense than uniformly diffused. Those who have had the good fortune to get hold of a copy of an earlier book of his, *The Mechanical Bride*, or who know his work with the periodical *Explorations*, form a group of enthusiasts strung all through the English-speaking world. This writer has met them from New York to California—and in London, Cambridge (England), Oxford and Paris. The present book should make his thought much better known.

McLuhan's voice is always the voice of the present calling into the past, a past that he teases into reacting ebulliently and tellingly with present actuality in his readers' minds. *The Gutenberg Galaxy* is concerned with changes in communications media, moving out of the past through our age into the future. Its axis is a huge assemblage of cultural phenomena—social, intellectual, political, and other—coincident with the appearance of typography.

Typography, as McLuhan abundantly shows, was in one way the cause and in another way the result of a profound interior revolution of the human spirit, establishing sets of mind that were unknown in earlier, more oral cultures, and that we are only now on the verge of understanding. Typography, in his view, is still commonly regarded as merely effecting a multiplication of manuscript materials. This is to think of a new invention in terms of what it supplanted, not in terms of what it is—as people used to do when they thought of the automobile as a "horseless carriage."

But at the same time, we are standing on the verge of a new post-typographic age dominated by electronic means of communication, which we are having still greater difficulty conceiving of on its own terms. "Every technology contrived and *outered* (uttered) by man has the power to numb human awareness during the period of its first interiorization" (153).

307

The present work, like much of McLuhan's utterance, is prophetic in the classical sense of this term. It is the result of a live realization of a truth that at least partially transcends immediate powers of utterance and that, as uttered, will affect hearers diversely. Those whose antennae are as sensitive as McLuhan's will be overjoyed at this high degree of articulateness about a vast range of mysteriously linked cultural phenomena. Others, completely dominated by the habits of thought incident to the typographical society that McLuhan is standing off from and evaluating, will either be unable to make head or tail of what he is saying or will reject it with some show of hostility.

If the human community is to retain meaningful possession of the knowledge it is accumulating, breakthroughs to syntheses of a new order are absolutely essential. McLuhan aids one such breakthrough into a new interiority, which will have to include studies of communication not merely as an adjunct or sequel to human knowledge, but as this knowledge's form and condition.

> The new electric galaxy of events has already moved deeply into the Gutenberg galaxy. Even without collision, such coexistence of technologies and awareness brings trauma and tension to every living person. Our most ordinary and conventional attitudes seem suddenly twisted into gargoyles and grotesques. Familiar institutions and associations seem at times menacing and malignant. These multiple transformations . . . are the normal consequence of introducing new media into any society whatever. (278-79)

What further syntheses lie ahead remains to be seen. But we shall have to work, as has the author of *The Gutenberg Galaxy*, to open all the sweeping vistas we can.

Work Cited

McLuhan, Marshall. *The Mechanical Bride: Folklore of Industrial Man*. New York: Vanguard P, 1951.

15

Review of *Preface to Plato* (1964)

Havelock, Eric A. *Preface to Plato*. Cambridge, MA: Belknap P of Harvard UP, 1963. Pp. xiv + 328.

The frontiers of several fields of research meet in this rich and germinal study. Professor Havelock is concerned with Greek epic poetry and Plato's attack on it, with the whole of the Greek *paideia* as it existed before and after Plato, with the technological problems of communication, and, finally, with the emergence of Plato's doctrine of "forms" in its total cultural setting.

In brief, Havelock's point is that Plato's attack on poetry is integral to his philosophy as such if we see poetry as what it really was in his day. Plato's doctrine of forms emerges as a vindication of a new way of thinking, namely abstract philosophy, because Greek society was shifting in Plato's day from a stage of craft literacy, in which some persons knew how to write as others knew how to make vases or to make ships, to a stage of general literacy, in which the ability to write radically affected the storage of knowledge and thus altered man's entire view of his lifeworld.

Havelock reviews the evidence (49-52) showing that the Greek alphabet was introduced only around 720-700 B.C. and that thereafter (relatively) full literacy took over three centuries to achieve (294, etc.). Homeric epic belongs to the age when Greek culture was functionally oral, when knowledge was generally not stored in written records. The earlier Mycenaean script, if it survived at all on the margins of Homer's culture (as it probably did not), was of negligible currency and serviceability. Availing himself abundantly of the insights into epic composition and into the psychology of oral tradition made available by the Parry's and Lord's exhaustive studies of modern illiterate Yugoslavian epic singers and by the now many related studies, Havelock points out that, nevertheless, commitment to the spoken word was far more drastic in Homer's day than in modern Yugoslavia, which is at least governed by literates, as Homer's Greece was not. In Homer's society poetry func-

tioned not simply as literature does now, but as a political and social
necessity (125), a practical aid serving the business of government itself
(94, 134, 139).

A society in which oral performance was the sole mechanism of
recall naturally generated at many points typical elements picked up by
epic technique—set themes and formulaic modes of expression adaptable
to metric patterns. Epic poets were thus the greatest adepts at what was a
widespread general skill: thematic and formulaic oral performance. The
poet's basic social function was not simply to entertain or recall, but
rather to repeat incessantly the accumulated wisdom of the culture, for
without constant repetition, the wisdom would vanish. Under these conditions, the content of tradition becomes completely typical in order to
implement memory. The genius of the epic poet lies not in "creativity"
but rather in the extreme skill with which he plies a common craft.
Traditionalism, not originality, makes him a center of cultural power.
Homer's value as a poet coincided with his value as an oral encyclopedia,
the great storer of knowledge performing at a time when knowledge could
not be encoded in any more abstract form because it remained unwritten.

In this setting, the hero is not merely a literary creation but a social
and cultural necessity, since the tribal encyclopedia of an oral culture cannot handle abstractions but must deal with persons and events.

> The psychology of oral memorization and oral record required the
> content of what is memorized to be a set of doings. This in turn pre-
> supposes actors or agents. Again, since the content to be preserved
> must place great emphasis on public and private law, the agents must
> be conspicuous and political people. Hence they become heroes. All
> non-human phenomena must by metaphor be translated into sets of
> doings, and the commonest device for achieving this is to represent
> them as acts and decisions of especially conspicuous agents, namely
> gods. (171)

Thus oral culture positively favors polytheism. And it of course dis-
courages formal philosophy, or renders it impossible. Havelock further
notes (188) that it also encourages visualization, for acts and their agents
can be "pictured" as principles and categories cannot. As compared, however, with literate culture, which subjects the word itself to visual apprehension in space, oral culture minimizes the visual in verbalization proper and maximizes sound.

This is the world against which Plato set himself (with of course a
comprehension less explicit than Havelock's today) in ousting the poets
from his ideal state and in launching his campaign for thinking based on
pure "forms" or "ideas." The poet had been a real *paideia* or encyclope-

dia for orally oriented Greeks—and Homer, even when used as the basic *paideia* of an increasingly literature culture was studied by being memorized, that is, was made to function as an oral encyclopedia still. Thought and society could rest on such bases no longer, so Plato felt.

Plato's permanent relevance to human thought and culture, his perennial appeal, appears in Havelock's perspectives as due in great part to the fact that he stood at the point in history when the function of poetry as tribal education was being transferred to prose. The mind itself was moving from a world of set themes, drastically economized formulaic expressions, rhythmic rocking, and paratactic organization to a prose state of causal connectedness. At another level or pitch, the state of relative innocence found in traditional oral culture (in which there were minimal body-spirit tensions and minimal personal guilt feelings, for too much reflection blocked the flow of verbalization in which memory had to reside) was being succeeded by a state of personal reflectivity, of increased drive toward the interior and exploitation of personal responsibility and guilt. Motivation was being interiorized. In the process, pleasure was more and more disqualified as a principle of cultural continuity. Previously, learning had been achieved by listening to the poet sing. Learning henceforward was to involve more interiorized personal effort, that is, was to become more like "work." (In primitive cultures "work" is relatively unknown as a category of activity distinct from other types of activity.) Poetry henceforward was not to be so diffused through the entire social complex: it could be regarded as "different," nonconceptual, nonrational, nonreflective, ecstatic, and Plato did so regard it. As a controlling *paideia*, it belonged to an age when distinction between an individual thinker and an objective world was less operative.

Plato's "forms" or "ideas" derive from the effort to establish this world of "objects" apart from man and his ethos, to found the world that would lead eventually to that of science. The "ideas" represent the maximum distancing of objects from man. They appeal to the new need, induced by general literacy, which dispensed with the necessity for constant oral recitation—the need to establish relations in terms of causal connections rather than narrative vividness.

Professor Havelock is able to show how the work of Hesiod is in very precise ways intermediate between that of Homer and Plato. Descriptive cosmology (and geography) lies between the person-and-event world of oral epic, on the one hand, and true philosophizing, on the other. Such cosmology and geography of course had initially to be in verse because Hesiod's society, post-Homeric but pre-Platonic, was a dominantly oral one still, and his work could be preserved only if it was cast in mnemonic verse form.

Havelock's thesis is a sweeping one and, on the whole, utterly convincing, tying in with the findings of an increasing number of recent psychological, historical, philosophical, and cultural studies. Literacy induces interiorization of the self, detribalization. In bringing out the self-discipline imposed by advance in civilization, the thesis of course parallels that of Freud in his *Civilization and Its Discontents (Unbehagen—Its Discomforts* would be a better translation), although it is infinitely better documented historically than Freud. Havelock says little or nothing about the shift in the ratio of the senses involved when the spoken word is transmuted to a spatial, alphabetic construct, and vision thereby heightened at the expense of hearing, nor does he advert to the limitations of the alphabet in processing sound, so patent to modern linguists. But his work is so seminal that he could not possibly touch on all the chains of thought it initiates. It was a good thing that Milton did not know all that Havelock and others working in allied fields know today, or he would never have written *Paradise Lost*. He would have understood how, for all its magnificent splendors, its relative failures were built in by the state of the media of communication and corresponding social and psychological structures endemic to the seventeenth-century and later sensibilities. Epic is most at home in an oral world.

The Hermes on the dust jacket of this book, incidentally, appears to be swinging not a cup and goblet, as a dust jacket identification states, but a cup and wine pitcher *(oinochoë)*.

Work Cited

Freud, Sigmund. *Civilization and Its Discontents*. Trans. and ed. James Strachey. New York: W. W. Norton, 1962.

16

Oral Residue in Tudor Prose Style
(1965)

I

We have recently been growing more aware of the differences between oral cultures and literate cultures. The massive work of H. Munro Chadwick and Nora Kershaw Chadwick traces the emergence of literature out of preliterate oral performance. In *The Singer of Tales*, Albert B. Lord follows up the work of Milman Parry on Yugoslavian singers of epic tales and brings the results to bear on Homer, *Beowulf*, and other epics, showing conclusively that not only is the oral epic independent of literacy but that it is also dependent on illiteracy—if an individual knows how to read, at least in twentieth-century fashion, he cannot render the truly oral form. And in his brilliant *Preface to Plato,* Eric A. Havelock traces the emergence of the Greek philosophical mind to the shift from an oral (Homeric) culture to alphabetization. The effects on modes of thought inherent in the successive media of expression—oral speech, analphabetic writing, alphabetic writing, letterpress printing, the electronic media, wired and wireless—have been studied in some detail, and we know something of the effect of (alphabetic) writing on the ability to perform abstract analysis and to exercise individually controlled thinking as against communally controlled think thinking (Carothers, Opler, Durand).

The full effects of our new sensitivity to the shift in media, however, have hardly begun to be felt in literary history and criticism. For example, in his magnificent and germinal work *European Literature and the Latin Middle Ages*, Ernst Robert Curtius pays almost no attention to the media as roots of culture and/or style. Yet without being aware of it, Curtius is deeply involved in shifts in the media. If by nothing else, this is shown by his casual statement that "every true humanism delights simultaneously in the world and in the book" (315). Such a statement links the very existence of humanism to the medium of writing and simultaneously disallows any claim that most of mankind in the past might have to be humanistic. Thus the biases generated in chirographic and typographic culture will assert themselves until they are quelled by reflection. Today, devotion to books, if it is unreflective, does not liberate but enslaves our minds. A liberal education today must include reflection on the significance of writing and print, situating these media and all their works in their historically patterned sequences.

When we speak of a sequence of media, we do not mean that new media of communications annihilate their antecedents. When men learned to write, they continued to talk. When they learned letterpress printing, they continued both to talk and write. Since they have invented radio and television, they have continued to talk and write and print. But the advent of newer media alters the meaning and relevance of the older. Media overlap, or as Marshall McLuhan has put it, move through one another as do galaxies of stars, each maintaining its own basic integrity, but also bearing the marks of the encounter ever after.

Manuscript and even typographic cultures thus sustain traces of oral culture, but they do so to varying degrees. Generally speaking, literature becomes itself slowly, and the closer in time a literature is to an antecedent oral culture, the less literary, or "lettered" and the more oral-aural it will be. Thus, it is to be expected that the oral residue in Tudor literature is, by contrast with most writing in comparable genres today, heavy in the extreme. Indeed, the interaction between oral tradition, writing, and the relatively new mode of alphabetic typography can be used to define some of the most salient characteristics of Tudor style, both as this was consciously cultivated in the highly rhetorical Tudor milieu and as it was actually achieved.

This chapter is concerned with oral phenomena in Tudor literature, but its main interest is in oral residue rather than in consciously cultivated oral effects. Oral effects, such as conversational elements in literary style, approximations of informal speech patterns, the use of dialogue, can be imported into written composition at will. They occur in Tudor writing, too, although, with the exception of dialogue, rather less frequently than in comparable writing today. Oral residue is another thing. By oral residue I mean habits of thought and expression tracing back to preliterate situations or practice, or deriving from the dominance of the oral as a medium in a given culture, or indicating a reluctance or inability to dissociate the written medium from the spoken. Such residue is not especially contrived and seldom conscious at all. Habits of thought and expression inseparable from the older, more familiar medium are simply assumed to belong equally to the new until this is sufficiently "interiorized" (McLuhan 24, 54, 58) for its own techniques to emerge from the chrysalis and for those more distinctive of the older medium to atrophy. Thus, for example, early type designers laboriously cut punches for the myriad ligatures that had been a godsend to scribes but were only encumbrances in typography.

In assessing the forces at work to preserve oral states of mind and the techniques that went with them, we must not forget the extreme novelty of alphabetic writing in the total duration of human cultures. Oral composition, more or less formalized, apparently belongs to the entire time span of the human race, going back perhaps well over 500,000 years. By contrast, in Tudor times, alphabetic writing was around three thousand, or perhaps three thousand five hundred, years old. The "interiorization" of alphabetic writing under such conditions could quite understandably be far from complete, and could remain far from complete even with the extraordinary intensification of chirographic effects being brought about by printing. Print was closer to chirography than to speech and reinforced some of the psychological effects of chirography at the very time it was succeeding only poorly in interiorizing itself as a genuinely new medium (poets felt it a profanation of their written lines to have them printed, just as Plato had once felt it a profanation of the spoken word to have it written).

The study of oral residue in Tudor prose could be carried much further than it will be here. Here we shall concentrate on the Latin problem faced by the humanists in its relation to the oral set of mind and on certain features of Tudor style, some macroscopic and some microscopic, connected with the cult of *copia* and of the commonplaces, a cult itself involving highly oral elements connected with the humanist Latin tradition. This approach to style differs from that taken by Croll, Williamson, and others concerned with the Ciceronian, Senecan, baroque, and other parallel classifications. It does not dispense with Croll's type of analysis, but simply looks at the situation in other perspectives.

II

The rhetorical tradition that in the academic world had so largely controlled the concept and practice of expression from antiquity strongly supported the oral set of mind in Renaissance culture. Rhetoric, which is at root simply the Greek word for oratory, governed far more than oratory as such. Poetry, highly "rhetoricized" in the Middle Ages, was commonly thought of as more or less ruled by the orator's art (McKeon 28-29; Howell 4-6, 40, 274-76), and letter-writing manuals, which proliferated in the sixteenth century under the influence of Erasmus, Vives, Melanchthon, Junius, Lipsius, Macropedius, and Hegendorff, commonly prescribed, in accord with medieval *artes dictaminis*, that letters themselves be organized in the same fashion as orations, proceeding from exordium, through statement of proposition to be proved, proof, and refutation of adversaries, to a peroration or conclusion (see Humiliata, esp. 261-62). Scholarly treatises of all sorts had an oratorical coloring. For example, Rudolph Agricola's work on the art of dialectic or logic, *De inventione dialectica libri tres*, like other comparable humanist treatises, in the 1571 Strasbourg edition and others as well, dutifully featured a *peroratio*, labeled as such, at its conclusion.

In accord with the rhetorical outlook, students were almost never taught objective description or reportorial narration: the object of education was to get them to take a stand, as an orator might, and defend it, or to attack the stand of another. Everyone is now aware that partisanship was encouraged by dialectic, the art of formal debate, but even scholars often fail to observe that it was encouraged even more by addiction, real or fictional, to oratory. In either case, the partisanship was thought of as functioning in an oral setting: debate or persuasion was felt as an oral-aural undertaking. Over all the teaching of expression, even though writing was much employed, there hung a feeling that what was being taught was an oral rather than a written mode.

Rhetoric, despite its deep involvement in the written medium, retained its earlier, expressly oral contours intact: normally it included as one of its five parts *pronuntiatio* or delivery—which meant oral delivery—as well as memory. The Ramists managed finally to discard this latter (memory), but not the former (oral delivery), although, like the others, they actually devoted little enough space to delivery in their rhetoric textbooks. This avowed commitment to the oral flew in the face of the fact that Latin, the language of the schools (and *a fortiori* its satellite Greek and far dimmer satellite Hebrew), had been completely controlled by chirography for almost a thousand years—Latin here meaning that part of the ancient linguistic tradition that had been artificially preserved from the normal oral processes of development resulting in the romance vernaculars.

Apart from the association of Latin with rhetoric as an art, this last mentioned fact, that Latin was totally controlled by writing no matter how much it was used for speech, produced other special kinds of drives toward the oral within the academic world. This can be seen in the attention given to promoting *copia*. *Copia* does not translate readily into English. It means abundance, rich flow, as well as ability, power, resources, or means of doing things. The quest for *copia* could express the whole humanist dream of "an eloquence that would cover the whole range of the human mind" (Bolgar 273). But there is something curiously relevant to the oral-aural outlook suggested by the humanists' affection for *copia* as expressive of their educational and intellectual ideals. Fear of failure in *copia* is close to the oral performer's fear of hesitancy—for abundant flow is more critical to the orator, who cannot call time out, than it is to the writer, who can and does. Renaissance works proposing expressly to develop *copia* are often curiously elementary. The *copia* that they assure is often that which would come in great part from normal nonacademic oral activity in the case of the vernaculars.

This is evident in the works of Erasmus, the largest and most important collection of material undertaking to supply *copia*. Significantly, Erasmus' more than four thousand *Adages* and his eight books of *Apophthegms* are collections not of writings, but specifically and professedly of sayings (which have been written down, to be sure, but are thought of still as things spoken). The adages are proverbs or anonymous popular sayings; the apothegms are sayings attributed to individual persons, more carefully tooled, frequently—but by no means always—gnomic, sententious, and witty. Often, however, the so-called adages prove not to be proverbial at all: Erasmus puts into this collection merely ways of saying things, *modus loquendi*, the Latin equivalents, for example, of "whiter than snow," "blacker than pitch," "sweeter than honey," "softer than the ear lobe." He is providing the small change picked up in the vernaculars largely through oral chit-chat, but hard to come by when one learns a language so chirographically and typographically committed as Latin was.

Erasmus' most basic workbook for Latin learners, his *De duplici copia verborum et rerum commentarii duo* (in some editions, . . . *libri duo*) is less ostensibly but quite as really meant to serve in place of the informal oral patter from which basic fluency in a language normally derives. It is a collection of phrases and of recipes for accumulating and exploiting expressions, examples, and indeed any sort of material that might later be worked into what one might want to say. Made up chiefly of informal jottings, it hurls at the teacher or pupil in cloying abundance thousands of ways of varying Latin words or phrases and of varying thought. For example, over one hundred and fifty different ways of varying in Latin the term *delectarunt* ("has delighted") in the statement, "Your letter has delighted me very much" are shot at the reader in one uninterrupted blast, followed by some two hundred ways of saying in Latin, "I shall remember you as long as I live" (1: columns 23-30).

Erasmus' *Colloquies* or sample dialogues have a similar oral orientation. The humanists were desperate to get youngsters to speak Latin, as is evident from school statutes (Baldwin 1:75) and from individual boyhood careers, such as that of the young Thomas More, whom William Roper writes of not as being "taught Latin" but as "brought upp in the Latyne tongue" at St. Anthony's in London (Roper 5). The *Colloquies* provide models of what little boys might talk about—or so it was hoped—once they were sent away from their families to be free of the company of women, who normally knew no Latin.

Erasmus' other works extend and buttress this make-up program for fluency. Significantly, most of the classical works he edited were collections of one sort or another: Aesop's *Fables*, Epiphanius' *Lives of the Prophets*, Sophronius' *Lives of the Evangelists*, St. Jerome's *Lives of the Evangelists*, Lucian of Samosata's *Dialogues* and other works, Pliny's *Natural History*, Plutarch's *Works*, and Suetonius' *Lives of the Twelve Caesars*. These—among other purposes they obviously serve—help supply, the anecdotal substructure always deficient in a language only deriv-atively oral.

Erasmus undertook to make antiquity current by moving it as close to the oral world as he could. Although he himself was a textual critic, he was irresistibly driven to establish a community of conversation and of personal interchange—in Latin, of course, for this was his medium of communication not only in letters and learned treatises but in face-to-face contact with his friends in the More circle and elsewhere. Despite his residence in England, we must remember that Erasmus never troubled to learn English.

Erasmus' educational purposes were of course complex, and it was certainly his intention that the springs of invention, which he had pooled for his age largely single-handed, should give life not merely to speech but to writing and print as well. Indeed, the humanists' programs stress written rather than oral performance. Our point here is not that the humanists were as intent on oratory as the classical rhetoricians and writers had been, but rather that the humanist program gives evidence of concern—very often unacknowledged—with building up the oral presence of Latin, partly because the humanists were influenced by the oratorical orientation of the ancients whom they read, partly because the literary tradition was in their day still continuous to some extent with the ancient oratorical tradition, and partly because one of the problems with Latin was the atrophy of its oral roots over a millennium. Erasmus' quest of *copia* was tied in with all these considerations—most often not at all expressly.

Erasmus' quest of *copia* was that of the age. From his collections, the waters of invention flowed off in all directions and seemingly without stop. On the basis of the admittedly tentative listings in the *Bibliotheca*

Erasmiana, presented by its editors in 1893 (Haeghen) with its thousands upon thousands of entries as a "simple questionnaire," one can estimate that well over six thousand editions of one or another of Erasmus' works have been put into print. Erasmus was not merely an individual writer: he was an institution, and as such a relict of an oral culture that despite the humanists, and partly because of them, was no longer viable.

III

In his extraordinarily well documented work on epic song, Albert Lord has contrasted the oral with the literary in terms of text, grammatical structure, and ideas or themes. He notes that in the oral "text" expression is chiefly by means of formulas, with the bulk of the remainder formula-like or "formulaic" and very little nonformulaic expression. In a literary text, on the contrary, we find few formulas and only a bit of the formulaic, leaving us with nonformulaic composition. Oral composition or grammatical structure is typically nonperiodic, proceeding in the "adding" style; literary composition tends more to the periodic. Oral composition uses ideas and themes that are well established and can be rapidly maneuvered in standard patterns by the bard; literary composition uses typically newer themes or combines older themes in ways more novel than are usually found in oral composition (Lord 130-31). The differences between oral and literary are, of course, not absolute, in that any single feature of either kind of composition can be matched from time to time in the other, but the differences are clear in the sense that in sufficiently extended passages the incidence of distinctive features is notably different in the two kinds of composition.

Although Lord is writing primarily about the epic, what he has to say here is based on the known mechanics and psychology of oral and literary composition taken more or less generally. In the light of his observations and of what has just been noted about the state of Latin as a medium and focus of training in expression, it becomes possible to reinterpret much in Tudor English prose style as residual oralism, in part endemic to the native tongue because of the still largely nonliterary, oral grounding of this tongue, and in part due to positive encouragement from the oral residue and emphases in Latin.

Here we can resuscitate a concept long moribund and unexploited by Lord, but highly serviceable to sum up and focus Lord's points for our present purpose. Oral composition is essentially "rhapsody" (Greek *rhapsoidia*), that is, a stitching together, in the original meaning of this term as applied by the Greeks to their epic song—and by Englishmen well through the seventeenth century to loose collections of material of all sorts.[1] The epic singer is not a memorizer in our post-Gutenberg sense of the word, but a skilled collector. He works unavoidably with a deep sense of tradition, which preserves the essential meaning of stories. But he has no fixed text to reproduce, such as we take for granted in a typographic culture. Instead, he possesses an armory consisting of formulas or metrically malleable phrases (together with near-formulas or "formulaic" expressions), and of themes or situations—the banquet, the messenger, the demand for surrender, the challenge, the invitation, the boast, the departure, the arrival, the recognition, and so on (most of these still occur today in the Western, clearly a regressive art form). Formula and theme are the stuff that the epic singer rhapsodizes or "stitches" into his oral epic fabric, never worded exactly the same on any two occasions.

But rhapsody was not restricted to poetry. The classic orator proceeded in much the same rhapsodic way as the ancient bard, and so, in theory, did his Renaissance followers. Doctrines of invention, rhetorical and dialectical or logical, had encouraged the view that composition was largely, if not essentially, an assembling of previously readied material. The humanists had reinforced this view with their doctrine of imitation and their insistence—not new in actuality but only in conscious emphasis—that antiquity was the storehouse of knowledge and eloquence. Bolgar has shown how humanist educational procedures enforced the assumption that the classics were writings that could be dismembered into bite-size pieces for reassemblage into new configurations. Indeed, he has made the point that the humanist achievement consisted largely in transferring into the modern consciousness the best of classical antiquity largely by just such a process of decomposition and recomposition (Bolgar 271-75, 295-301).

Operationally, this rhapsodic view of literary composition found its center in the doctrine of the commonplaces to which one can relate so many of the tactics advocated and practiced by Tudor prose writers. The doctrine of the places was applied to poetry, too (generally taken as a form of rhetoric), but was developed mostly for prose use. It was a complicated and at certain points inconsistent set of assumptions, views, and prescriptions (Lechner 65-131), but the part of it relevant here is its advocacy of the advance preparation of material that could be inserted as occasion offered into whatever one was composing.

---

[1] "For Metaphysicks, I say that Aristotles Metaphysicks is the most impertinent Booke (*sit venia*) in all his works; indeed, a rapsodie of Logicall scraps."—[Thomas Barlow? 4]. This assertion clearly echoes Ramus' accusation that Aristotle's metaphysics was only theology sieved through dialectic (or logic—the two terms were synonymous for Ramus). See Ong (190).

The Greeks, and following them, Cicero and Quintilian, advocated that the orator get up in advance a repertory of *loci communes* or commonplaces—little purple patches on loyalty or treachery, or friendship or decadence ("*O tempora! O mores!*") or other themes "common" to any number of cases or occasions for insertion into an oration as opportunity offered. As has been seen, the classical oration was the product of a situation, typically an oral performance even in the case of so literate an orator as Cicero, who wrote out his orations only after he had delivered them—sometimes, it appears, years afterwards (Petersson 92-94). For such a performance a stock of commonplaces was the equivalent of the epic singer's stock of formulas and themes, although a literate orator such as Cicero might make incidental use of writing in ways in which illiterate bards and orators did not. Quintilian reports on the writing out of commonplaces in order to decry it, but Cicero appears to have known this practice and also to have taken notes during trials at which he was to speak (although of course he did not use them in the course of the speech itself) (Quintilian 1:239-41; Petersson 92-93). Commonplaces, however, even when written, belonged to the oral tradition in that they stocked the imagination with material accessible on the spur of the moment. Moreover, in their use, as in all oral performance, the question of originality as a virtue does not even arise. The oral traffics in the already known. Only in the early nineteenth century, when the residue of oralism had greatly diminished as its major depository, Latin, lost effectiveness, does "commonplace" become a generally derogatory term. Commonplaces could of course be composed by the orator himself or garnered from other writers—the germ of the commonplace book, so much in use in Tudor times, lies here.

Following Aristotle and other Greeks, Cicero and Quintilian also wrote of *loci communes* or commonplaces, in another, deviously related, sense, as headings, sources, or "seats" *(sedes argumenti)* "common" to all sorts of subjects, to which one could betake oneself to discover arguments to prove one's point: headings such as genus, species, cause, effect, related things, opposed things, and so on. Special or "private" places or headings had been devised to supply arguments specifically for law, physics, medicine, and other subjects. In practice, common and special places or topics were often intertwined in the many competing lists of places that filled the dialectic or logic and rhetorical textbooks. The use of the places was far more attended to than the often flimsy theory got up to support their existence (Ong 116).

In either this latter meaning (headings) or that earlier mentioned (prefabricated purple passages), the commonplaces were an answer to the

need for fluency that the orator, like the epic singer, felt much more acute-
ly than the writer, since as has been seen, oral performance, once begun,
cannot be interrupted with impunity as written composition can. Thus the
Tudor retention and intensification of interest in the commonplaces suggests a need, felt if not articulated, to attend to expression in an oral rather
than chirographic frame of reference.

IV

It is well known that one of the major features of Tudor prose—and poetry, although this is not our direct concern here—was a tendency to a
loosely strung-out, episodic style. Episodic, loosely serial organization is
observable in a great spectrum of forms from controversial literature
(Fish, More, Tyndall) through the chroniclers who for the time serve as
historians, in prose fiction (Nashe's narrative in *The Unfortunate
Traveller*, the romances of John Lyly, Robert Greene, and Thomas
Lodge), and on through "characters" and that most distinctively Tudor
product, the essay. This tendency to feature strung-outness, the collection
as such, under various guises, is not taken into account in the ordinary
analysis of Tudor prose in terms of Ciceronian, Attic, Senecan,
Euphuistic, or baroque style. The tendency suggests the somewhat dis-
jointed, nonperiodic Senecan style, but chiefly in the latter's meandering
phrases rather than in its moments of gnomic intensity.

The perspectives earlier sketched here invite us to see the looseness
of Tudor style as residual oralism, even when it may also be in part an
imitation of written models. The Tudor writer was by literary and cultural heredity in great part rhapsodic. For him written expression had never
been so fully detached from the oral as it was to be shortly when the new
invention of letterpress typography had its fuller effect. His was thus a
marginal position, and it deserves more study as such. Here we shall
undertake only a survey of some typical manifestations of loose,
"adding," organization.

One of the most prominently oral phenomena of this prose is its
reliance on the "formulary" structures discussed by Howell (138-46). It
should be noted that we are referring here not to a formula in the sense of
Lord and Parry, as "a group of words that is regularly employed under the
same metrical conditions to express a given essential idea" (Lord 30), but
rather to formulas for a sequence of elements in a passage of some
length—to organizational formulas. Such organizational formulas provided, among other things, for an ordered progression through a list of
topics in praising or blaming a character: for example, Richard Rainolde's
The Foundacion of Rhetorike (1563), an adaptation of the *Progymnas-*

mata of the fourth-century Greek rhetorician Aphthonius, a favorite textbook in Tudor schools, specifies that for the praise of an individual person one should eulogize in succession his country, ancestors, education,
"actes" (*res gestae* or achievements, that is, his use of gifts of the soul, of
the body, of fortune), concluding with some comparison that would show
to the advantage of the subject of eulogy (folios xl^r-xliii^v). The relationship between this approach to composition and the oral procedures discussed by Lord as mentioned above is evident enough. Aphthonius has
codified in writing an oral institution.

The *de casibus virorum illustrium* (the fall of great men) pattern that
persists in works such as St. Thomas More's *Richard III* can be regarded
as a special type of formulary writing: a foreordained sequence of rise,
triumph, and fall. The persistence of *de casibus* formulas in the Middle
Ages (alongside other equally schematized patterns for lives of the saints)
(Stauffer 3-32) and its gradual demise through the Renaissance can be
regarded from one point of view as marking the transit to a less orally
controlled culture.

The formula, in a larger sense, goes even further than this, controlling
the pattern of the oration proper, the master prose genre. For the oration,
approved rhetorics prescribed from two parts (Aristotle's minimum in the
Rhetoric) to seven parts (Thomas Wilson's prescription in *The Arte of
Rhetorique*), the minimal two being always statement of the case plus
proof. To these two can be added an introduction, a summary of the case,
division of the proof, refutation of adversaries, and conclusion. Within
this set formulary order other subformulas tend to grow. These consist of
special groups of commonplaces (in the sense of headings or classes of
arguments). For although the places as sources of "arguments" properly
belong only to the proof, such is the force of the commonplace frame of
mind that the commonplaces serve to structure other parts of the oration
as well. Thus Curtius (85-91) discusses the special topics or places used
for the introduction or exordium (the first part of the oration when four or
more parts are taken as normative) and the peroration or conclusion (the
last part). Curtius is concerned directly with the Middle Ages, but there is
no significant difference here between medieval and Tudor practice.

The parts of the oration imposed formulary structure on much other
prose writing besides the oration itself, including not only letters (as
already mentioned), but also learned treatises and narrative. Sidney's
Apology for Poetry, for which Sidney also used the title *The Defense of
Poesie*, and which consists largely of literary theory, is organized as an
oration. This organization is neither a happenstance nor a tour de force.
Sidney really thought the work out in oratorical form, as its title, *Apology*

or *Defense*, a technical term, makes clear. Here Tudor criticism of literature, despite the fact that it is itself literature, written composition, and
concerned essentially with literature as such (for Sidney views poetry as
basically, although not exclusively, literature, something normally composed in writing) is nevertheless cast in a preliterate, oral form. For examples of oratorical organization in narrative, there are Nashe, Lyly, and
many others.

Allied to the use of formulas for overall structural organization is the
use of epithets and of material from commonplace collections. This use
suggests medieval techniques of amplification and in varying degrees
marks virtually all styles of the Tudor period, poetry as well as prose.
From More through Hooker, the reader is showered with adages,
apothegms, standard incidents of all sorts to illustrate a moral or prove by
example—the fall of Icarus as an example of the overreacher, Pyramus
and Thisbe, Brutus the betrayer, and so on, ad infinitum. Every possibility in life was covered by hosts of standard sayings or incidents, which
obtrude more in some styles than in others and are satirized in some, as
in Nashe's, but are almost always before the reader's eyes. The shower of
epithets and examples is pleasant and even beautiful, rainbow-hued at
times, but it is curiously unlike what is advocated in post-Romantic writing. Our knowledge of the sources of examples and sententious sayings
is improving with works such as that of Professors DeWitt T. Starnes and
Ernest William Talbert on Renaissance dictionaries. But we have hardly
scratched the surface of the vast collections of quotations available in the
sixteenth century—the greatest number of them, I should estimate, deriving in one way or another through publishers at Basel, the long-standing
headquarters for Erasmian forces. We are becoming more aware of the
reliance of many Tudor writers on handbooks for their classical echoes
and allusions. It would appear that the glut of collections from classical
authors that flooded the Renaissance—and gave it further continuity with
the Middle Ages and their passion for florilegia—fed an appetite that was
still largely created by a residual oralism in expression. The oral performer favors use of a well-known phraseology. The humanists' insistence on imitation and the typographers' ability to multiply lists of
cullings effectively and cheaply combined for the moment to give the
orally oriented mind a new lease on life, although ultimately typography
was to spell its doom.

Another type of oralism marks the highly figured styles of the Tudor
period, from More and Lyly through Nashe. These are clearly devised for
their effect on the ear and thus are oral in a real sense, but one not exactly
our direct concern in treating of rhapsodic oralism. Titillation of the ear is

not necessarily residual oralism: it can be a new and conscious sophistication. More akin to rhapsodic tradition are certain special features of the figured styles, most notably their use of epithets, found so abundantly in Lyly, as in many of his contemporaries: "this new kind of kindness, such *sweet* meat, such *sour* sauce, such *fair* words, such *faint* promises, such *hot* love, such *cold* desire, such *certain* hope, such *sudden* change," or "the *soft* drops of rain pierce the *hard* marble" (65-66). Such usage is very close to the oral formulas of which Lord has made such careful analyses.

In part, of course, Lyly's style connects directly with oral performance, deriving not only from figured oratorical style generally but in particular, very probably, from the style in the orally presented lectures of John Rainolds at Oxford (Ringler). But Lyly's use of epithets has also direct sanction in the Tudor collections of epithets got up to assure *copia*. In one of the most influential collections, the *Epitheta* of the Parisian rhetorician Ioannes Ravisius Textor (1480?-1524), Elizabethan schoolboys, for whom Textor's *Epitheta* and his related collection *Officina* were prescribed, could find epithets by the thousands for all things under heaven and many above: Apollo is accorded 113 epithets, love 163, death 95, and so on through entries which include Africa, the river Alpheus, the arts themselves, to touch only on a few of the hundreds under the letter "A" (Textor). Baldwin (349, 394-95, 519) cites school statutes and British editions of Textor's *Officina* and *Epitheta*. Of course, the far more numerous Continental editions were also known to schoolmasters in the British Isles, as can be seen from inscriptions in surviving copies today. This approach (designed directly for Latin, but strongly influencing English) strikes us as weird. But it is, among other things, designed to sate the oral appetite for adequate and proper formulas.

Many other instances of oral residue could be discussed here. One could note the formulary aspects of decorum, or the very insistence on decorum itself as evidence of a formulary frame of mind. Deloney uses Lyly's euphuistic formulas to cue in the speech of his rare characters from the nobility, such as the Earl of Shrewsbury's daughter, Margaret, in *Thomas of Reading*. Or one could also note the large-scale use of parallelisms that are formulaic in a highly oral way, often incremental, certainly "adding" in form. Such are many of Sir Thomas Elyot's expressions in *The Boke Named the Governour*: God shows "wisedome, bounte, and magnificence," man's estate is "distributed into sondry uses, facilities, and offices," man is exposed to "the fraude and deceitfull imaginations of sondry and subtile and crafty wittes," one is urged "to enserche and perceive the maners and conditions" (1:4, 6 [Book 1, chapter 1], 60 [Book 1, chapter 10]). This multiplication of synonyms is of course due to nervousness about the adequacy of English words—it is a mannerism in translators—but it appears to be also in part residual oralism. One could note also the use of dialogue, which is not inserted into the narrative to give color and "interest," as it might be today, but which serves to cast up sociological or economic or psychological issues—for example, in More's *Richard III* or, in Deloney, the speeches of characters summing up the plight of the country or their own problems, social, economic, or psychological. In the absence of appropriate sciences such issues could hardly be caught in any other way than in direct, oratorical address stating more than merely personal issues in the guise of personal concerns. But multiplication of instances carries us too far afield for a brief survey. The examples we have adduced, however, may provide sufficient background for some possible conclusion about oral residue in Tudor style.

V

This summary discussion of what we have styled oral residue in Tudor prose has not been concerned with what might ordinarily be thought of as typically oral elements in prose today. Oral elements today are typically those introduced more or less openly into a medium of expression felt primarily as written. They are, in a way, extraneous, although they are by the same token more obviously oral than was the case with the oral residue we have here touched on. Today's prose is often shot through with idioms calculatingly echoing oral performance at any and all levels—for example, in Joyce or Hemingway or Faulkner. It has a special kind of oral richness that decorum inhibited in the most permissive Tudor prose, where slang and colloquialisms are mostly avoided in so far as they can be identified in a language still little subject to written control. (One must make some exception for Thomas Nashe and for the playwrights.) At the same time, however, these same twentieth-century writers are definitely using a written or typographical medium rather than the oral medium as their overall matrix: although *Finnegans Wake* can be read aloud and listened to with great enjoyment, and *The Sound and the Fury* echoes voice within voice like an aeolian Chinese puzzle, neither could have been conceived or executed as oral performances. By contrast, the *Iliad* and the *Odyssey* not only were so conceived, but had to be in order to be what they are.

The oral elements we have been considering in Tudor prose are akin to those in the *Iliad* and the *Odyssey*. They are not among the oral elements that Tudor writers may have consciously introduced into their prose as oral. Rather, they are elements that Tudor writers automatically favored largely because these writers were close to a far more primitive—and by this I do not mean unskilled—preliterate mode of expression. These oral elements survived centuries of manuscript culture because in the teaching and practice of expression this manuscript culture retained very live connections with the old preliterate oral-aural world. In particular, the persistence of oral residue was favored by the study of Latin that governed so largely the writing of English prose. Latin sustained the rhetorical—which is basically oratorical and thus oral—cast of mind. The stress on *copia* that marked Latin teaching and that was closely associated with rhetorical invention and the oral performer's need for an uninterrupted supply of material favored exploitation of commonplaces. The use of these in turn made for the "adding" or "rhapsodic" style that survives in so much Tudor writing as it had in medieval "amplification," and that is not adequately accounted for by the ordinary discussion of Tudor stylistics.

It should be subjoined that certain institutions surviving from oral-aural culture other than those concerned with formal language study also favored the oral cast of mind and the survival of oral elements. The most important of such institutions was the orientation of all academic instruction toward oral performance: written exercises were in use (and that a restricted use) only for the learning of Latin (and Greek and Hebrew), after which the student, whether in arts (philosophy), medicine, law, or theology, was tested only by his oral performance in disputation or oral examination. Outside the academic world, the oral cast of mind was also sustained by special vernacular practices, such as the singing of ballads.

Much of what we have called oral residue in Tudor prose does not, as we have treated it, differentiate Tudor prose from that of earlier ages, although closer study could very likely show that there were indeed many points of difference. But what we have treated as oral residue here does differentiate Tudor prose from what was soon to follow it. The features here noted become more and more attenuated through the seventeenth and eighteenth centuries until their virtual disappearance with Romanticism. The loose episodic structure, in particular, which is one of the central characteristics of oral style, was on its way out as narrative worked its way toward the modern novel and short story, and as devices such as Ramist "method" charmed the mind with prospects of organization that were basically visual, chirographic and, even more, typographic.

Despite the fact that it can be discerned readily in preceding ages, oral residue is of special importance on the Tudor scene, for, in one genre at least, the world of the Tudor writer shows a more massive concentration of oral residue than that of earlier ages. This is in its commonplace collections. The sequel of medieval collections of exempla and other such material, these collections reach their apogee in the two centuries following the invention of printing. The new typographic medium offered previously unheard of opportunities to the impulse of the orally oriented performer to have as much as possible on hand so that he would be prepared to extemporize in absolutely any eventuality. Sixteenth-century and seventeenth-century printed collections of commonplace material are so utterly countless that no one has ever attempted even a preliminary survey. They were the last flash of activity from the orally oriented mind, which had proved viable in manuscript culture, but was soon to be reduced to insignificance when the visualization induced by writing was both supplemented and eventually transformed by print.

Works Cited

Baldwin, T. W. *William Shakspere's Small Latine and Lesse Greeke.* 2 vols. Urbana: U of Illinois P, 1944.

[Barlow, Thomas?]. *'A Library for Younger Schollers' Compiled by an English Scholar-Priest about 1655.* Ed. Alma DeJordy and Harris Francis Fletcher. Urbana: U of Illinois P, 1961. (Illinois Studies in Language and Literature, Vol. 48).

Bolgar, Robert R. *The Classical Heritage and Its Beneficiaries.* Cambridge, UK: Cambridge UP, 1958.

Carothers, J. C. "Culture, Psychiatry, and the Written Word." *Psychiatry* 22 (1959): 307-20.

Chadwick, H. Munro and Nora Kershaw Chadwick. *The Growth of Literature.* 3 vols. Cambridge, UK: Cambridge UP, 1932-1940.

Croll, Morris W. *Style, Rhetoric, and Rhythm.* Ed. J. Max Patrick and Robert O. Evans, with John M. Wallace and R. J. Schoeck. Princeton, NJ: Princeton UP, 1966.

Curtius, Ernst Robert. *European Literature and the Latin Middle Ages.* Trans. Willard Trask. New York: Pantheon Books, 1953. Bollingen Series 36.

Durand, Gilbert. *Les Structures anthropologiques de l'imaginaire.* Paris: Presses Universitaires de France, 1960.

Elyot, Sir Thomas. *The Boke Named the Governour.* Ed. Henry Herbert Stephen Croft. London: Kegan, Paul, Trench, 1883.

Erasmus. *De copia verborum ac rerum commentarius primus . . . secundus* [table of contents, *De copia verborum ac rerum libri duo*]. *Opera omnia.* Leyden, 1703-1706.

Haeghen, Ferdinand van der. ed. *Bibliotheca Erasmiana: Répertoire des oeuvres d'Érasme.* Nieuwkoop, B. de Graaf, 1972. (Original 1893)

Havelock, Eric A. *Preface to Plato.* Cambridge, MA: Belknap P of Harvard UP, 1963.

Howell, Wilbur Samuel. *Logic and Rhetoric in England, 1500-1700.* Princeton, NJ: Princeton UP, 1956.

Humiliata, Sister Mary. "Standards of Taste Advocated for Feminine Letter Writing, 1640-1797." *Huntington Library Quarterly* 13 (1950): 261-77.

Lechner, Sister Joan Marie. *Renaissance Concepts of the Commonplaces*. New York: Pageant P, 1962.

Lord, Albert B. *The Singer of Tales*. Cambridge, MA: Harvard UP, 1960. Harvard Studies in Comparative Literature, Vol. 24.

Lyly, John. *Euphues: The Anatomy of Wit: Euphues and His England*. Ed. Morris William Croll and Henry Clemons. London: George Routledge and Sons, 1916.

McKeon, Richard. "Rhetoric in the Middle Ages." *Speculum* 17 (1942): 1-32.

McLuhan, Marshall. *The Gutenberg Galax: The Making of Typographic Man*. Toronto: U of Toronto P, 1962.

Ong, Walter J. *Ramus, Method, and the Decay of Dialogue*. Cambridge, MA: Harvard UP, 1958.

Opler, Marvin K. *Culture, Psychiatry, and Human Values*. Springfield, IL: Charles C. Thomas, 1956.

Petersson, Torsten. *Cicero: A Biography*. Berkeley: U of California P, 1920.

Quintilian. *The Institutio Oratoria . . . With an English Translation*. Trans. H. E. Butler. London: William Heinemann, 1920. (Loeb Classical Library).

Rainolde, Richard. *The Foundacion of Rhetorike*. (1563). Introduction Francis R. Johnson. New York: Scholars' Facsimiles and Reprints, 1945.

Ringler, Jr., William A. "The Immediate Source of Euphuism." *PMLA* 53 (1938): 678-86.

Roper, William. *The Lyfe of Sir Thomas More, Knighte*. Ed. Elsie Vaughan Hitchcock. London: Humphrey Milford, Oxford UP, 1935. (Early English Text Society, Original Series, No. 197).

Starnes, DeWitt T. and Ernest William Talbert. *Classical Myth and Legend in Renaissance Dictionaries: A Study of Renaissance Dictionaries in Their Relation to the Classical Learning of Contemporary English Writers*. Chapel Hill: U of North Carolina P, 1955.

Stauffer, Donald A. *English Biography before 1700*. Cambridge, MA: Harvard UP, 1930.

Textor, Ioannes Ravisius. *Specimen epithetorum*. Paris: Henricus Stephanus. 1518. [The second edition (Paris: Reginaldus Chauldiere, 1524), published posthumously under the editorship of Ioannes' brother Iacobus, and the many subsequent editions were entitled *Epitheta*.]

Williamson, George. *The Senecan Amble: A Study in Prose Form from Bacon to Collier*. Chicago: U of Chicago P, 1951.

17

Written Transmission of Literature (1967)

Literature involves skilled, imaginative verbal performance, on the one hand, and writing, on the other. Originally these two were separate developments. Primitive verbal performance reached a high degree of skill and artistic virtuosity in tales, oratory, and song thousands—perhaps hundreds of thousands—of years before writing was even thought of. Writing first came into existence not to record or foster verbal virtuosity, but to meet practical needs such as account keeping. Only long after the invention of writing did it occur to man to record in writing a performance of storyteller, speechmaker, or singer, and finally to make up songs and tales and other such literary works with writing instruments in hand.

Oral Roots of Literature

Written composition thus began as an adaptation to a new medium of skills perfected in another, quite different medium. Until very recently, this fact and its implications have not been fully appreciated even by scholars. The scholarly study of skilled verbal activity focused initially on written verbalization, that is, on texts, and necessarily so, for only with the advent of recording machines in the past few decades has scholarly study of oral expression become generally practicable. As a result of preoccupation with written texts, all artistic verbalization has long been thought of as "literature" (from *litterae*, letters of the alphabet), that is, basically as something written. Some oral performance can legitimately be so considered: oral delivery of plays, for example, is vocalization that matches a written document. But the concept of "literature" has been extended beyond such warrant. Oral performance in cultures with no knowledge of writing at all has been thought of as a form of "literature," and even great scholars have commonly used such chimeric concepts as "oral literature" (that is, "oral writing"). The result has been not merely a confused nomenclature but also a radical misconception of what oral performance is; for thinking of it as somehow "literature" entails thinking of it as, at least in some obscure way, a variety of writing—writing that somehow failed to

331

get committed to paper. Primitive oral performance is no such thing. Oral performance, arising before the idea of writing even existed, enforced and thrived on techniques, effects, and attitudes—highly specialized themes, repetitiveness, indifference to "originality"—that writing was to render increasingly nonfunctional, distasteful, and to some extent obsolete.

As direct study of purely oral performance has developed in recent years, ways have been devised for conceiving of such performance as it actually was or is in itself rather than by analogy with writing. As a result, the vast differences between skilled verbal performance of genuine, purely oral preliterates and skilled verbal works produced pen-in-hand—i.e., literature proper—have begun to be more fully understood. Proportionately with our understanding of the oral prehistory of literature, our understanding of literature itself and of written transmission has improved. The written transmission of literature can be seen to involve several distinct but interrelated questions. First, what brought about the writing down of elaborate verbal expression, which for thousands of years had been an exclusively oral affair? Second, what happened to the "matter" when expression shifted from oral to written? That is, was the same "thing" (incident, plot, characterization, attitude toward life, worldview) that had been communicated in oral performance also communicated when writing took over? Third, what happened to the forms of expression, in the sense of genres, as the use of writing developed? Finally, how have the oral and the written influenced one another? These questions are interconnected and will be discussed conjointly.

Beginnings of Writing

Understood as skilled imaginative verbalization involving writing, literature is dependent upon the development of true script, that is, of a relatively elaborate and supple system of signs usable for communication.

Systems before Script. Pictures such as the paleolithic paintings in Altamira, Spain, and Lascaux, France, however astonishingly imaginative, can hardly be considered in any sense literature, although they may be taken to have something vaguely to do with the misty origins of pictographic script. Similarly, other records of the *aide-mémoire* type, such as Inca *quipus*, Australian notched sticks, or North American Indian wampum belts, while they may in a sense tell a story, are hardly literature. Neither are the picture stories of the Ewe of West Africa or the "winter count" calendars in which Dakota Indians kept records of successive winters by inscribing on a buffalo hide a symbol for a major event in each winter (30-Dakotas-killed-by-Crows winter, smallpox winter, sun-eclipse winter, etc.).

Earliest Scripts. To the best of our present knowledge, scripts, or true writing systems, first appeared among urban neolithic populations: cuneiform scripts among the Sumerians *c.* 3500 B.C., Egyptian hieroglyphics *c.* 3000 B.C., Minoan pictographic *c.* 2000 B.C., Minoan (Mycenaean) "Linear B" script *c.* 1200 B.C., Indus Valley script *c.* 3000 to 2500 B.C., and Chinese script *c.* 1500 B.C. The alphabet, the most important script of all, since it undertakes to reduce sound itself most directly to spatial equivalents, was developed *c.* 1500 B.C. in the Eastern Mediterranean region. From there it spread around the Middle East, Europe, and Asia; all alphabets in the world derive from the original Mediterranean invention. In the New World, Mayan script seemingly appeared only *c.* A.D. 50, and Aztec script, about A.D. 1400.

The principal incentive to the development of scripts was generally the need for groups of persons living in concentrated, urbanized centers to keep records of property, personal and public, or of various functions. The record keepers were commonly public officials, often religious functionaries, such as priests or temple attendants. Of the probably more than 250,000 Mesopotamian cuneiform inscriptions now known, more than 95 per cent deal with economic transactions. In many cultures, laws were the first written works to which some literary value can be assigned, although the relationship of these written "laws" to actual practice is not always clear. Many early scripts, Linear B for example, never reached the point where it was possible to use them for anything except the crudest lists. They were pictographic, or largely so, and they could deal only with what was rather directly picturable.

From Script to Literature. However, in scripts such as Egyptian hieroglyphics, cuneiform writing, or the Chinese character system, pictography had developed into a syllabary or partial syllabary. These scripts could be used for imaginatively nuanced expression such as skilled oral performance had long employed, and thus for literature in the strict sense of the term. Above all, the simple serviceability of the alphabet made the development of literature possible, although at the sacrifice of some of the visually based richness that Chinese characters and comparable pictographic systems can achieve by the fact that their characters always retain at least some remote picture value even when denoting relatively abstract concepts. The Chinese character for "good," for example, is a combination of the characters for "woman" and "child," although the spoken word for good, *how* [*ha*U], has nothing to do with the word for woman, *nü* [*ny*], or the word for child, *dzuh* [*dz*], and hence does not of itself evoke the concepts occasioned by the written word.

Within some 1,500 years or so of the appearance cuneiform writing, the earliest known script, the Sumerians, who developed this writing and bequeathed it to the Assyrians and Babylonians, had a sizable corpus of works that can be considered truly literary in the sense of being imaginatively evocative. Their monumental inscriptions constitute a kind of history; about 3,000 known clay tablets, chiefly from *c.* 2000 B.C., contain literary matter, consisting of myths, hymns, prayers, epic tales, proverbs and aphorisms, lamentations, and love songs. A single clay tablet of *c.* 2000 B.C. lists 62 different titles, and another Sumerian catalogue brings to nearly 90 the total of known titles of different Sumerian epics.

The Beginning of Literary Genres

It is a mistake, however, to suppose that early literary productions were written works in the sense in which a novel today is a written work. Writing, once it was invented, took possession of language only slowly. Given the psychic and cultural structures of early man, reading itself was difficult, particularly when carried out in complicated non-alphabetic scripts. Even when, as among the ancient Babylonians, it was prescribed by law that all except the lowest class of people learn to read and write, it appears that the prescription was often not observed. After the Greek alphabet came into use probably *c.* 700 B.C., Greek society took some 300 years to pass from a state of craft literacy, when writing was a skill practiced by a certain group, as shipbuilding or stonemasonry might be, to a state of general literacy, when the ability to read became an asset to the ordinary citizen. Reading habits long remained largely painstaking and "myopic," proceeding word by word and often entailing much vocalization, so that, through much of the Middle Ages, the reader's voice was commonly audible even when he was reading to himself. Early manuscript illustrations often helped alleviate the strain readers felt: they distracted from the text more than they explained it.

Under such conditions writing was not at first really written composition, but rather oral performance in transcriptions that exhibit sometimes more and sometimes less influence of the new medium of writing. The impulse to write down oral performance was doubtless a product of the impulse to keep records; the invention of writing encouraged this. Transcription of oral performance was at first very difficult; the performer was necessarily trained to pace his production much faster than an attendant scribe or he himself could write (if he was literate, as he might exceptionally be), and his ability to recall and perform was closely tied to this pacing. One possible way in which this problem was solved was to sing a brief passage and then pause so that the scribe could write it out, then another brief passage with a pause, and so on—a procedure that would almost certainly produce a text not quite the same as that of a full-blown normal oral performance.

Division of Genres. Understandably, most if not all early literature thus falls into the preliterary genres, which H. Munro Chadwick and Nora Kershaw Chadwick, ranging through a vast amount of world literature in *The Growth of Literature,* have classified in two basic groups: (1) works relating to individuals specified or unspecified, heroic and nonheroic, including (a) narrative poetry or saga intended for entertainment, (b) poetry (rarely prose) in the form of speeches in character, (c) didactic poetry or prose, (d) poetry (seldom prose) of celebration or appeal (panegyrics, elegies, hymns, prayers, exhortations), and (e) personal poetry (rarely prose) relating to the author himself and his surroundings; (2) works impersonal or general in character, including (a) antiquarian, (b) gnomic, (c) descriptive, and (d) mantic compositions. Reproducing such genres, the earliest works in writing retain the typical features of expression demanded for elaborate oral performance but destined to become less operative as writing gained strength; these features include a fixed and highly selective economy of themes, formulas, and formulaic elements out of which oral performers "rhapsodize" or stitch together their recitations (see Lord "Literature"), loose narrative structures, standardized archaisms—which Aristotle took for granted as belonging normally to poetry, since he found them in the epics he knew—and many parallelisms.

The high incidence of poetry found in earlier literature by comparison with that of more recent times is also a carryover from oral cultures. In these, verbalization was often highly rhythmic for quite practical purposes; in the absence of all records, oral speech itself functioned as a major mechanism of retention and recall, and thus was quite commonly given highly rhythmic and other "poetic" turns that facilitated such function. The balanced structure of the Beatitudes in the Sermon on the Mount (Mt 5:3, 4), for example ("Blessed are the poor in spirit / For theirs is the kingdom of Heaven. / Blessed are the meek / For they shall possess the earth"), represents a mode of expression and thought developed to facilitate oral retention and recall.

Concreteness of Oral Economy. The same dominantly oral economy kept early literature concretely imaginative rather than abstract. Abstract reasoning and thinking in terms of complex objective causality are minimized in oral cultures, for the amount and kind of information needed for scientific analysis cannot be accumulated in oral media. The result is that actuality is seized in terms not of categories so much as of events, particularly actions of human or anthropomorphized beings, which lend themselves to oral epic and other oral composition.

Results of the Use of Writing

Writing created new kinds of variability and new kinds of stability in the transmission of verbal performance. In oral tradition, special linguistic mixtures, more or less stylized, come into being. Thus the language of the *Iliad* and *Odyssey* is a special epic dialect originally brought into being by epic singers to serve their own necessities and ends. *Beowulf* gives evidence of a similar epic language preserving special archaic elements, but it also exhibits other kinds of dialectal variations clearly traceable to successive scribes. The single extant manuscript that preserves the poem was written *c*. A.D. 1000 in a language dominantly late West Saxon, but the text shows irregular admixtures of early West Saxon, Northumbrian, Mercian, Kentish, and Anglian. Significantly, one and the same word often occurs in different dialectal forms, thus indicating that the manuscript was recopied several times by various scribes who spoke different dialects and who sometimes changed the text before them to their own dialect and sometimes left it unaltered.

Textual Variations and Control. Textual variations are, of course, not restricted to dialectal irregularities. Additions and omissions occur in written copies of works, and attempts at control of manuscripts occur very early. In antiquity it was common to specify on copies of a work how many lines the original or standard edition contained (stichometry) or how many words or even how many letters. Josephus specified at the end of his *Jewish Antiquities* (A.D. 93) that its length is 60,000 lines (*stichoi*). Transmission of religious writings was often subject to extreme care: to avoid errors, sometimes each word was assigned a special position on each page in all copies, so that something like the effect of a printed text was achieved for a time at incredible cost of labor.

Textual control, however, was always exceedingly difficult in a manuscript culture, and not until the development of typography, and particularly of printing from movable alphabetic type, perfected in the mid-fifteenth century, did accurate reproduction of texts become feasible on a large scale. Modern textual study dates from the invention of print (see Ong "Humanism").

Printed texts reproduced from the author's own manuscript and, even more, under the author's supervision, can be extremely accurate. When the author's own manuscript no longer exists and editors must rely on copies, problems multiply, particularly if a large series of copies intervenes between the original and the extant manuscripts. Somewhat paradoxically, ancient texts that today show numerous divergent readings are often much firmer from a scholarly point of view than ancient texts that show no variations. When an old text has no variations, this almost always means that only one copy of the work is known, so that there is nothing to check it against. Chaucer's *Canterbury Tales*, with its many variants, is textually far more satisfactory than *Beowulf*, which has none because only one manuscript of it is known. With its many variants, the text of the Bible, extant in thousands upon thousands of manuscripts of varying degrees of completeness, some dating from even before the time of Christ (such as the Dead Sea scrolls), is a far better text than those of many secular works of Greek and Latin antiquity, for which our present text is based at times on only one manuscript, often copied out 900 years after the original, and occasionally lost since. For example, all known texts of the Roman poet Catullus (84?-54 B.C.) derive directly or indirectly from a single manuscript rediscovered at Verona shortly before 1323 and lost again by 1433. Except for the part known as *Scipio's Dream*, what is extant of Cicero's *De republica* derives from a single manuscript of the 4th century of the Christian era.

Bards, Authors, Patrons, Publishers. With the use of writing, the routes of transmission for the verbalized cultural heritage of a people change. The role of the bard becomes less significant, and he is gradually relegated to the more static and "retarded" sectors of society, a relic of the past. First scribes become important, then "authors" (authorship is made relatively little of in purely oral cultures, or at best is uncertain or confused), then patrons who support writers (at first individuals or religious institutions or governments, in our day also private foundations), and finally printers and publishers. Patrons, printers, and publishers often determine to a greater or lesser degree what is written; and how far or in what way what is written becomes known to readers. With writing, institutionalized religion becomes more important than ever as a transmitter of culture. Through the Middle Ages particularly, the preservation and copying of manuscripts was a major work of monastic orders.

Changes in Matter. As the use of writing grows, the matter inherited from oral tradition undergoes change. The hero, exalted by oral tradition as a figure in whose doings cultural values could be articulated and recalled, gradually becomes less obviously an embodiment of current cultural structures and more an abstract ideal. Eventually central characters are no longer exclusively public figures but also include more ordinary individuals, as in Balzac, Dickens, or Faulkner. The types in which an oral culture is forced to cast its memory very largely yield to greater particularizations. The literary imagination becomes more introspective, interiorized, and personal, less tribal, focusing on the tensions of individual conscience rather than on deviations from more exterior patterns of behavior as sources of human uneasiness. Such increasing interiorization of attention can be traced from Homer through Virgil and on through the Middle Ages and Renaissance into the present. At the same time, the findings of natural science are more attended to in the interpretation of human behavior. Within the past few generations the findings of sociology, biology, and psychology have been particularly exploited. Complexes of causalities— psychological, political, social, and other—are developed more deliberately and explicitly: organization becomes more strongly "linear." Scientific or "naturalistic" interests are aided by the development of techniques of exposition and of detailed description in which early literature was relatively weak. As knowledge of the natural world grows, the early literary preoccupation with religious questions becomes less exclusive and explicit, although the religious problem of man's existence remains, it would appear, at the center of literature, overtly or covertly.

Changes in Genre. With changes in matter come changes in genre. Literary forms that are more dependent on the written medium as such develop. The original categories, as mentioned above in the Chadwick classification, mostly persist in one form or another, although certain ones decline in relative importance, notably the purely didactic and gnomic (directive of human action), and poetry of public celebration or appeal. There is a notable increase of prose, as reliance on highly rhythmic forms of verbalization for conserving knowledge in oral culture decreases. The prose paraphrases of the earlier Norse heroic poems are developed, for example, in writing. Verse itself is given more elaborate designs. The verse of *Sir Gawain and the Green Knight* or Gerard Manley Hopkins' *The Wreck of the Deutschland*, for all the splendid sound effects of the latter poem in particular, obviously depends on writing. Plotting of stories is tightened and becomes more complicated, ultimately producing at one of its peaks the short story and the murder mystery and at another the extremes of complexity found in Faulkner's *Absalom, Absalom!* Drama, at least from ancient Greece on, generally depends on writing for its composition; although, like other forms, it long preserves close association with formally oral genres: Shakespeare's *Henry V* is one of countless plays of its time and earlier structured around extensive series of speeches just as old oral epics had been (one third of *Beowulf* is made up of speeches).

With writing, finally, distinctively chirographic designs are developed. Acrostic poems and alphabetic poems, each line beginning with a successive letter of the alphabet as in some of the Psalms or the Lamentations of Jeremiah, obviously depend on the existence of writing, although such poems are in greatest favor in cultures retaining a strong oral-aural cast of mind and a certain self-consciousness about literacy: in such cultures the alphabet as such has a strong appeal as another formula serving organization and recall. The letter (epistle) as a literary form is obviously the product of writing and is normally prose, thus contrasting with the formalized messages of preliterate cultures, which often had to be cast in some rhythmic or thematic-formulaic design, if they were moderately complicated, so that they could be recalled with acceptable accuracy.

Oral Effects in Written Works. The use of oral effects in written composition is frequent, but often different from that in purely oral performance. Dialogue composed in writing becomes over the centuries increasingly and calculatedly casual and colloquial, whereas in oral performance it is of necessity highly stylized, thematic, and formulaic. Sound effects are often more consciously elaborated than in oral production. Occasionally the picture presented by the text of a poem is integrated into the poem's meaning, as, for example, in George Herbert's "The Altar" and "Easter Wings," where the printed lines form the shapes of an altar and wings respectively. Much more sophisticated relationships between words as sound and their textual presentation have been achieved recently. A maximum interaction between oral-aural, visual, and kinesthetic elements is realized in a piece such as e. e. cummings' untitled poem on a grasshopper, where the reader, puzzling his way through the lines, finds himself involved in the same kind of situation as when on a walk through a field he sees an actual grasshopper idiotically dance into his disintegrating leap through the air and then abruptly compose himself again in full view:

```
                    r-p-o-p-h-e-s-s-a-g-r
                who

    a)s w(e loo)k
    upnowgath
                PPEGORHRASS
                            eringint(o-
    aThe) :l
            eA
                !p:
    S                                    a
                    (r
        rIvInG          .gRrEaPsPhOs)
                            to
    rea(be)rran(com)gi(e)ngly
    ,grasshopper;
```

In this performance words and letters are arranged and deranged so as to play a kind of visual and kinesthetic obbligato against the movement of sound. The poem cannot be read aloud, yet the sound, like the visible arrangement of the type, is functional.

Originality and Writing as Property. Another result of the use of writing is growth in the importance attached to originality and corresponding growth in the sense of writing as property. Originality, the ability to create something truly distinctive, meant little in oral cultures, where, indeed, it constituted a threat. Without records, oral cultures bend every effort to repeat over and over again what they know in order to keep possession of it, so that fidelity and invariability (never quite achieved) are among their major ideals in verbalizing. When writing transfers the burden of retention from oral repetition to the inscribed surface of a document, where a work can be "looked up" and gone over at leisure as often as the individual reader may want, the poet or other writer is freer to embark on original undertakings. When he does this, the sense that what he writes is his own begins to grow and is reinforced by the activity of booksellers, who were already operative in ancient literate cultures. With the invention of typography, the sense of literary works as property increases slowly—it was still not very widespread in Shakespeare's day, when what today would be considered plagiarism was taken to be only a demonstration of wide reading. The eighteenth century saw the beginning of modern copyright laws.

Learned Languages

Somewhat early in the history of literacy, as writing penetrated society more deeply, certain languages, such as Hebrew, Sanskrit, Greek, Latin, or Chinese, developed a "learned" form cut off from the mainstream of oral developments in which these languages themselves had first appeared. The learned form of the languages rigidified around bodies of written texts. Spoken forms of the languages, relatively free from written control, continued to develop into new vernaculars in ways previously normal for spoken languages generally, and more or less oral forms, such as ballads and folk tales, proliferate in these vernaculars. Gradually some of the vernaculars—those that have become today's "literary" or written languages—came more and more under scribal control. The learned languages were totally under scribal control from the time they ceased to be vernaculars, all their subsequent development being governed by written models, rather than by oral practice, for which writing had originally furnished merely a means of record, not a rule. Paradoxically, however, these learned languages sometimes perpetuated strongly oral-aural sets of mind, for the reason that they had become fixed in writing in an age when the total culture was highly oral-aural in cast. Thus the written Latin works studied in school vaunted both rhetoric, in its original sense of the art of public speaking, and the equally oral art of dialectic or formal academic debate because skill in public oral performance had been the aim of ancient Latin education, as of Greek. So long as Latin study dominated the curriculum in the West, it gave a more than normal oral tinge to the literary world. Renaissance manuals, for example, often specify anachronistically that letters (epistles) be organized as orations, and as late as the nineteenth century much literature has a decidedly elocutionary cast, not always to good purpose.

Writing and History

One of the most radical effects of writing is a change in the relationship between verbal performance and tradition. Memory is restructured. The thematic-formulaic memory of purely oral performers (whose trained memories were prodigious, but not verbatim) is replaced for a while by word-for-word mnemonic techniques, based on repetition of a written text. Memorization of writing, initiated toward the start of the chirographic stage of culture, reaches a peak in the typographic stage, which is early marked by development of the catechism, for religious and other subjects. Finally, in the present day, mechanical means of storage and recall are making vast ranges of knowledge extraordinarily easy of mechanical access and are further restructuring the memory and its functions. In imaginative writing, correlative developments can be detected: there is a tendency today even in fiction to minimize narrative continuity and to proceed by means of complex and involuted itemizations.

Writing makes history possible. With the understanding of the history of literature and its antecedents and of cultures other than the writer's own, now available on an unprecedented scale, writers turn, with a self-consciousness before unknown, to the past and to the diversity of cultures around them for both form and matter. The design of the Japanese *haiku* was taken over, not always very knowledgeably, by American and British imagist poets in the early twentieth century. Ezra Pound incorporates Chinese ideograms into his English-language *Cantos*. Joyce's *Finnegans Wake*, basically in English, achieves a new linguistic virtuosity and range by weaving countless other languages, past and present, into the text. With writers ranging through space and time for diversity, literatures of all nations and languages tend in many ways to grow together; international styles and fads have developed in the twentieth century as never before.

When viewed in its deepest perspectives, the use of writing has also brought about a radical restructuring of thought and thought categories and of the psyche itself. With writing, and even more with print, man is detribalized to a greater and greater degree and the isolated individual—the reader alone with his book or the writer at his desk—becomes a normal cultural type and, ultimately, a typical concern of literature in the present technological age. Verbalization is associated more and more closely with space and visualization—first on the written, then on the less variable printed page—rather than with its original habitat, sound. With the new electronic media of communication that are paraliterary or transliterary, such as the telephone, radio, and television, and with the increased use of person-to-person contact made possible by rapid transit, communication is reentering the world of sound in a new way. The effects on literature are seen already in a loosening of the linear structures (plot, for example) and in increased appeal of improvisation, or of seeming improvisation, similar to that once inseparable from early oral cultures.

Religion and Written Transmission of Verbal Performance

Like the Hebrew religion, Christianity came into being in an alphabetic culture with a strong residue of oral-aural institutions. The Bible includes a great many different types of works—history, allegory, poetry of celebration or appeal, hymns, prayers, gnomic and mantic writings, and other types—but all of these works exhibit, in varying degrees, a residue of oral-aural cultural attitudes and ways of thought and expression far more massive than anything ordinarily familiar in the literature of technological man. A long oral tradition formed and retained much of what is in the Old Testament and in the Gospels for varying periods before the material was written down, and even the most directly literary compositions in the Bible, such as the letters of St. Paul, are written in styles influenced or dominated by a highly oral cast of mind. It is noteworthy that Jesus, the Word of God, was Himself literate (Lk. 4:16-22; Jn. 8:6-8), but conveyed His teaching personally only by word of mouth. The New Testament is part of the Church's kerygma. It is not Jesus' own writing, of which we have none.

The written text of the Bible, however, has a certain maximum religious value. According to Catholic teaching, it is inspired, having God as its author, in the words of the Council of Trent and the First Vatican Council. How far this claim can be extended to the oral substratum of the Bible or to the antecedent literary documents on which the present books of the Bible at times depend is still a matter of active discussion. As knowledge of literary history has developed, the literary forms of the

Bible have been the subject of large-scale and highly informative study, especially since the mid-nineteenth century. Papal encyclicals such as *Providentissimus Deus* have encouraged continuation of such studies as basic to the understanding of the fuller meaning of the Scriptures in present-day perspectives.

Like other widely diffused religions (notably Judaism, Mohammedanism, Confucianism, and Buddhism), Christianity has encouraged use and study of the written word. More than this, however, Hebrew and Christian teaching regarding the positive religious significance of historical time enhances the value often placed by religions generally on written records; and the Christian doctrine of the Incarnation of the Word of God, Himself a Person and God, has given the *word* as such a unique value to the Christian mind. The alphabet, and with it the possibility of literature, secular as well as religious, was introduced by Christian missionaries to most of the non-Mediterranean European peoples as well as to the peoples of the New World. The Bible has influenced the literary development, religious and secular, of many languages more profoundly than any other single book. In English literature it has provided not only modes of expression (at first chiefly through the Latin Vulgate and then through vernacular translations, particularly the King James or "Authorized" version of 1611) , but also themes for almost every conceivable form of literature, notably lyric poetry, epic, and drama—from the Old English *The Dream of the Rood* (*c*. 900) through Abraham Cowley's epic *Davideis* (1656) to Archibald MacLeish's play *J.B.* (1958).

Bibliographic Note

There is no single book-length treatment of the matter covered in this article, but the following are some variously relevant works. Chadwick and Chadwick provide a nearly exhaustive worldwide survey of preliterate oral performance and early literature (but omit American Indians); it no longer has an entirely up-to-date conception of oral culture. Other sources include Diringer, Febvre and Martin, Havelock, and Thompson. McLuhan gives a racy survey, indifferent to some scholarly detail, but uniquely valuable in suggesting the sweep and depth of the cultural and psychological changes entailed in the passage from illiteracy to print and beyond.

Works Cited

Chadwick, H. Munro and Nora Kershaw Chadwick. *The Growth of Literature*. 3 vols. Cambridge, UK: Cambridge UP, 1932-1940.

Diringer, David. *The Hand-produced Book.* New York: Philosophical Library, 1953.

—. *Writing.* New York, Praeger, 1962.

Febvre, Lucien and Henri-Jean Martin. *L'Apparition du livre.* Paris, 1958.

Havelock, Eric. A. *Preface to Plato.* Cambridge, MA: Belknap P of Harvard UP, 1963.

Lord, Albert B. "Literature, Oral Transmission of." *The New Catholic Encyclopedia.* Ed. William J. McDonald. 15 vols. New York: McGraw-Hill, 1967.

McLuhan, Marshall. *The Gutenberg Galaxy: The Making of Typographic Man.* Toronto: U of Toronto P, 1962.

Ong, Walter J. "Humanism." *The New Catholic Encyclopedia.* Ed. William J. McDonald. 15 vols. New York: McGraw-Hill, 1967.

Thompson, J. W. *Ancient Libraries.* Berkeley: U of California P, 1940.

18

Preface to *Man at Play* (1967)

Rahner, Hugo. *Man at Play*. Trans. Brian Battershaw and Edward Quinn.
New York: Herder & Herder, 1967. Pp. xvi + 105.

Play should interest our contemporary world more than perhaps it does.
Not only in the United States, but all over the world man today is much
concerned with freedom, and the world of play is the world of freedom
itself—of activity for its own sake, of spontaneity, of pure realization.
Today, however, we seldom associate freedom with play. Freedom is
grim—something to be fought for, something that we feel may confront
us with antagonisms and even hatred instead of generating effusiveness
and spontaneity and joy.

This pugnacious understanding of freedom has been with us ever
since freedom became a "cause" at the opening of the modern age, and it
of course can be explained. But with or without explanation, it tends to
outlaw play, for if play has nothing to do with freedom, where can it lay
hold on life? When set against freedom instead of being associated with
it, play strikes us as inconsequential, beneath the adult's dignity, something one descends to or "indulges" in, something childish.

And yet play is at least the half of life. Play and work derive from the
same source in man's life world. When the infant first begins to use the
powers which are latent within him and by using them to develop them,
is he working or playing? When he flexes his muscles, crows and coos to
himself and others all day long, takes his first steps—is this *Spass* or
Ernst, "fun" or "for real"? There is of course no way of saying, for it is
both. And this is the situation, where play and work coincide, in which
learning (and life itself) is maximal. Educators have known this and have
tried to keep alive this initial situation or to recover it in the classroom,
making learning "fun." The Latin term *ludus* encapsulates the initial
infantile work-play situation: it means both play and school. Out of this
initial undifferentiated activity the two activities of work and play are
polarized—differentiated, but always in dependence on each other.

Work and play define one another by dialectical contrast. Certainly work is what is not play and play is what is not work. Yet only in a sense is this true. This is the way it is until you arrive at a peak situation, when suddenly everything is reversed: the best players in any game turn out to be the professionals, those for whom the game is in fact work, a means of livelihood, and the best workers in any field are those for whom their work is a kind of play—the mechanic whose job serves his desire to "tinker" with machines, the basic research engineer who is "playing around" with various possibilities for a huge industrial complex, the financier who "plays the market," the philosopher who likes to "play" with ideas.

It cannot be otherwise. For if work is truly human work, it is something for which man is fitted, something that he can do and do well, though it may exhaust him, cost him, take something out of him. Thus work is, like play, free in the sense that it truly comes from within, comes as a realization of human potential, as an effusion of activity spilling out from its immanent source. Work is an expression of freedom and joy. But this is what play itself is.

What then is the difference between work and play? Does work take more effort? Not necessarily at all, although it is more demanding in the sense that the worker is less free to determine when and where he will begin and end. But even here, only in a sense is this true. Certainly the player of a game is not free to start before the referee's signal, whereas the worker often is free to start his day ahead of time. The worker is generally far more free to continue past five o'clock than the player is to continue playing after the last whistle blows.

The difference is, of course, that in play the players set up or freely accept their own rules. In work, the rules are set by actuality itself, by "life," by the way things are. And yet even here the dialectical relationship of work and play asserts itself, for the rules in a game are made rigid in order precisely to make the play world an artificial imitation of the rigidity of actuality. The game must be serious, in its own way "for real," like life. The result is again paradoxical, for in a sense the rules of a game become more rigid than many of those in real life: no court administers the law so inflexibly as a referee administers the rules in an athletic event. The law itself gives a judge discretion far surpassing that of a sports official.

Play is imitation. It is "art." Yet for man art is essential for grasp of actuality. One learns what reality is through imitation. A little girl learns how to be a mother by "playing house." A teacher begins to teach when he first stands in front of a class and plays the teacher's role—"makes like" a teacher. There is no other way to learn how to work than to play at working. For man, imitation is the door leading into the real.

Thus when we look at the total field of human activity, the amount of play in it should hardly surprise us, although it does. Games are play (except in so far as they are a means of livelihood, too). Plays are play—but not really for the playwright or for the actor, both of whom work to produce a creation that is pure play only for the audience (although the audience often pays to see plays and thus puts into them a certain amount of work). All literature and art is of course play. Music is play. Ballet is play. Painting and sculpture are play. Much of architecture is play, though the play must be kept somewhat relevant or "functional." With the growing leisure afforded by technological society, we are going to have to make do with more play. This means we are going to have to take play more seriously.

When we turn to work activities to see which of them are mixed with play, we find they all are. We have always known this, in fact: life, we say, is a game. Moreover, the play element (to use Huizinga's term) in serious activity seems sure in one way or another to increase as the activity becomes more serious. The race of two great world powers into space, in its most serious aspects, is quite obviously play, stylized competition, *agonia*—this is why it is thought of all over the world as a "race," a sporting event. It is no accident that the most strenuous corporate technological effort that man has ever made coincides *in fact* with the activity that earlier man often *jokingly* imagined to be the most playful, the most pointless (play is aimed at nothing outside itself) of all activities, spontaneous to the point of being totally ridiculous: shooting for the moon.

Much of this we have learned from the insightful work of Johan Huizinga (a philologist who tried playing at being a social historian and philosopher, and of course succeeded), from F. J. Buytendijk, G. von Kujawa, and others. It should be obvious how apposite this literature of play could prove for Christian theology, which is concerned with a God who is good and thus "diffusive of himself," spontaneously and freely giving first existence and then redemption to his creatures, who are thus the result of his play—only not in any sinister sense, but in a positive and constructive sense. *Miris modis di ludos faciunt homines*, reads Plautus' *Rudens*, "In strange ways the gods make sport of men"—a passage that Gloucester virtually quotes in *King Lear*, "They kill us for their sport." These were the pagan gods. The one true God is no such God. His play is the giving of life, first by creation and then by redemption. "Though I walk in the midst of the shadow of death, I will fear no evil," sings the Psalmist, knowing that despite evil and suffering, God will somehow prevail. "I am come that they may have life and have it more abundantly."

In the present work Father Hugo Rahner has seized on the concept of play as a means whereby a historian of religion can explicate in a fresh way the freedom of the children of God, which is a participation in the freedom of God himself. God's activity toward and in all his creation is like that germinal, undifferentiated activity of the child, which is both work and play, both serious application and spontaneous activity for its own sake. Thus only those who "become as little children" can enter the kingdom of heaven. In the natural life of the child, however, the juncture of work and play is fragile and doomed: soon life will cleave in two, and work and play will drift apart, even though they never entirely lose contact with one another. With God such separation never comes. God's work is always play in the sense that it is always joyous, spontaneous, and completely free.

Here and there through earlier ages, in the Scriptures and elsewhere, this sense of play has entered into ascetic and devotional awareness. It has remained, however, for Father Rahner to pull together and interpret, with true historical imagination, what hitherto have been scattered, if often profound, observations. The thoughtful and, historically speaking, newly reflective love of play that Father Rahner's *Man at Play* evinces speaks well and hopefully for our own age.

Works Cited

Buytendijk, Frederik J. *Wesen und Sinn des Spiels: Das Spielen des Menschen und der Tiere als Erscheinungsform des Lebenstriebe*. Berlin: Wolff, 1934.

Huizinga, Johan. *Homo Ludens: A Study of the Play Element in Culture*. Boston: Beacon Press, 1955.

Kujawa, Gerhard von. *Ursprung und Sinn des Spiels eine kleine Flugschrift versehen mit Randbemerkungen eines Schilkbürgers*. Köln: E.A. Seemann, 1940.

19

Review of *Classical Rhetoric in English Poetry* (1971-1972)

Vickers, Brian. *Classical Rhetoric in English Poetry*. New York: St. Martin's P and London: Macmillan, 1970. P. 180.

This book undertakes a survey of the whole of rhetoric as the art emerges from classical antiquity and exerts its effect upon English literature from medieval times until it succumbs in the age of Romanticism. The author provides a concise history of rhetoric as well as an account of rhetorical processes, including the stages of composition, the parts of the oration, the three types of orations, and styles and genres. The functions of rhetorical figures are treated and some figures of rhetoric are exemplified in brief excerpts out of classical literature, the Bible, and English poetry from Chaucer through Pope. The book is both businesslike and sensitively humane, never slipping into the vapid antiquarianism that the more exotic features of rhetoric could encourage today. The final chapter shows how rhetorical analysis can be made to serve what are clearly twentieth-century projects, such as the assessment of the overall literary worth of a poem—a project too programmatically aesthetic and too holistic for pre-Romantic rhetoricians.

As an inclusive summary interpretation of a major influence on literature, Mr. Vickers' work makes up for deficiencies in many literary histories and perhaps most notably for that in C. S. Lewis' *English Literature in the Sixteenth Century*, from which Mr. Vickers selects his introductory quotation. For the late Professor Lewis, after devoting less than two eloquent pages at the start of his book to the transcendent importance of rhetoric in the production not only of sixteenth-century English literature but of all European literature before it, cavalierly dropped the subject immediately and for good, without mention of either the sixteenth-century writers on the subject or of the scores of twentieth-century scholars who have treated sixteenth-century and other early rhetoric. Mr. Vickers treats both

349

groups of authors and provides a useful bibliography, restricted understandably to books, for the articles on the subject are now legion. Most
scholars in this field have been Americans, and Mr. Vickers' British voice
is welcome among them.

With sensitive allowance for the needs of the present-day literary sensibility, the author approaches rhetoric as most writers on the subject do,
in terms of questions generated out of recent literary criticism and history of ideas: What did Aristotle or Cicero mean by rhetoric? How was it
studied in Quintilian's day? How did its study affect Shakespeare's dram-
aturgy? What were the figures of speech? How did they enter into
Sidney's or Spenser's poetry? And so on. But beneath such questions
there lie the deeper questions that scholars seldom broach: Why was rhetoric so massive a phenomenon? How could most writers of the past
devote themselves so utterly and unquestioningly to an "art" that to twentieth-century man appears meaningless and even somehow fraudulent?
What sort of world sense is implied in Dante's incredible esteem for rhetoric as "the sweetest of all the other sciences" (in the quotation from
Lewis used by Vickers as mentioned above)? Why for two millennia was
the oration generally taken to be pretty much the paradigm of all verbal
expression, so that even letters were designed as written orations? And
how could the age of Romanticism so abruptly and successfully scotch
this previously invincible and mysterious monster?

I have recently suggested in *Rhetoric, Romance, and Technology* that
Western culture can be conveniently divided into two periods, the
Romantic age (in which we still live and are destined to live for the entire
foreseeable future) and the rhetorical age, which reaches back in full view
for two thousand years and beyond that has excavatable roots extending
indefinitely into the primitive oral culture of all mankind. If rhetoric has
the potential thus to divide all human history, how can it possibly be
understood as simply a curriculum subject in our present sense of this
term? Can it truly be domesticated as one of the seven subjects in the trivium and quadrivium that are popularly supposed to have governed
medieval teaching? (I say popularly supposed because I have never been
able to identify a single real curriculum in medieval Europe that in fact
was organized to teach all of these seven "liberal arts" as they are enu-
merated in the educational mythology inherited from Martianus Capella.)
Rhetoric does indeed occur in the curricula in association with grammar
and, more loosely, with logic, but what appears in the curricula as rhetoric is obviously only the tip of an iceberg, the other eight-ninths of which
floats well beneath the surface of Western culture.

These deeper questions underlie all present discussions of rhetoric and must be dealt with. When they are not, rhetoric remains a historical surd, with no significant relationship to any human drives that one can empathize with or imagine as real. Unable to find a way to engage such questions or even to articulate them satisfactorily, scholars are likely to account for what strikes them as bizarre in rhetoric by projecting onto whole cultures one or another vice or sickness from which supposedly aberrant rhetorical developments spring. Rhetoric shows an "almost morbid tendency towards systems and rules," it is in one way or another often "repellent or frivolous," or "dreary and trivial," and so on. Vickers quotes, with admirable disapproval, these and other similar verdicts (61-89, etc.). He himself definitely rises above them, chiefly by showing how earlier rhetorical concerns, or at least some of them, are continuous with present-day literary concerns.

This is good, but it does not suffice for the submerged questions suggested above, or for others related to them. What is needed is, quite frankly, an anthropological, psychological, and cultural understanding of rhetoric as the massive and pervasive historical phenomenon it was. Rhetoric is basically an oral art with all this implies—*rhētorikē* in Greek means the art of oratory, public speaking. Rhetoric came to encompass writing only gradually and by quite unconscious and often awkward adaptation to changes in the complex of verbal media. And when it did assimilate writing to some degree (from Aristotle on), it helped keep writing closely bound to oral performance in a relationship quite strange to us today. As I attempted to point out a few years ago, the easily identifiable oral residue in Tudor prose style—preoccupation with *copia*, the use of epithets and other formulas, episodic or strung-together prose narration ("rhapsody" is the once well-known rhetorical term), and the like—is tied to the ascendency of rhetoric. In their handling of rhetoric, Renaissance educators are more than somewhat confused: they are training largely vernacular writers, but pretend they are training Latin orators, commonly retaining (oral) delivery as an integral part of rhetoric—though they then have precious little to say about it, if indeed anything at all.

Rhetoric has vast psychocultural roots that can no longer be neglected in assessing its relevance to literature. As Gilbert Durand has beautifully shown in *Les Structures anthropologiques de l'imaginaire,* rhetoric is intermediate between the imagination and the reason, moving consciousness from the semantic of minimally verbal symbols and of narrative-dramatic thought forms that one finds in all primitive cultures toward the essentially antithetic structures of formal logic, which of course itself cannot come into being without writing. (Durand's work here abuts on that of Eric A.

Havelock in the latter's *Preface to Plato*.) The features that are commonly taken to be particular weaknesses of rhetoric—euphemism, hyperbole, striking antitheses (these last not so sharp as the yes-no antitheses in formal logic)—are not aberrations, but as their persistence might suggest, belong rather to the texture and essence of rhetoric as such. So too, the upsurge of rhetoric in groups who feel themselves rising from oppression (for example, today among those of us Americans who are black) is not at all freakish, but is recurrent and normal in cultural history: rhetoric is of its very nature an instrument of hope as the human consciousness "rises." To oppressed peoples on the way up, rhetoric is essential.

Rhetoric is also essentially polemic (as poetry tinged with rhetoric is often found to be). This is because rhetoric is essentially oral at root, typically oratorical, and oratory is basically polemic. When you rise to make a speech, you are not undertaking an impartial investigation: you have your mind made up about a position. "Here I take my stand."

Rhetoric is also ceremonial. It developed in the past as a major expression on the rational level of the ceremonial combat that is found among males and typically only among males at the physical level throughout the entire animal kingdom, not simply among human beings. The ancient art of rhetoric did not and could not survive coeducation, which demands that the psyche reorganize itself in ways unknown and unknowable to oral cultures.

Rhetoric became particularly attached to Learned Latin, which the male psyche appropriated to itself as an extrafamilial language when Latin ceased to be a "mother" tongue (that is, was no longer spoken in the home by one's mother). Latin, spoken and written for 1500 years with totally negligible exceptions only by males, became a ceremonial language institutionalizing with particular force the ceremonial polemic that set the style for all education until Romanticism. For until the Romantic age, academic education was all but exclusively focused on defending a position (thesis) or attacking the position of another person—even medicine was taught this way. Pre-Romantic education was rhetorical and dialectical, dialectic and logic having developed out of rhetoric. (The British public schools, which trained for the verbal jousting of diplomacy, have long been typical Latin-bound schools.) As a result of these mysterious tie-ins around rhetoric, in curricula in the West these changes always occur in rapid succession, though not always conspicuously in the same order: Latin is dropped, rhetoric is downgraded (trial by disputation or debate is replaced by written tests), education substitutes self-fulfillment aims and procedures for agonistic aims and procedures, physical punishment (not accidentally but programmatically associated with the teaching of Latin for centuries) is outlawed, and coeducation is begun.

If this is interpreted to mean that rhetoric was the product of male chauvinism, then male chauvinism was essential for the maturing of intellect and culture. Whatever your interpretation, these are the forces you are dealing with when you undertake the history of rhetoric, deep movements within the human psyche in its relationship to cultural evolution. Although he does not broach the deeper questions suggested here, Vickers does treat rhetoric in a way open to the deeper questions, with some real relationship to our present lifeworld.

A few errors are to be regretted in the present book. Perhaps the most notable is the statement that in assimilating rhetorical invention and disposition to dialectic or logic alone, Ramus left "rhetoric with the remaining three parts: Elocution, Delivery and Memory" (40). It should certainly by now be pretty much a commonplace that Ramist rhetoric dropped memory as such and had only two parts, elocution and delivery, and that this binary structure is of the very essence of the art as Ramists conceived it. All the Ramists the author cites are quite specific that there are only two parts to rhetoric. And indeed there is now a quite considerable literature about the reasons for Ramus' dropping of memory as a "part" and the implications of this maneuver. The matter is discussed at length in Frances A. Yates' book, *The Art of Memory*. One can only regret the patronizing treatment of this and a few other major works by Mr. Vickers, who waves Miss Yates' magnificent and seminal study aside as "a rather wild analysis" (62). This is all the more unfortunate because Miss Yates treats rhetoric and allied phenomena with rare learning and with the profound discernment that is so imperative if we are to understand the *artes sermocinales* and their cultural and psychological and literary adjuncts in the depths out of which they cry to us today.

Vickers is quite right, incidentally, in his statement that much critical writing has been tendentious and ill-informed in identifying "Ramism" in sixteenth- and seventeenth-century authors, particularly poets, and in his insistence that Ramism is not all that distinctive. What makes Ramism interesting is not that it implements an always clear-cut revolution in stylistics with novel or advanced ideas, but rather the fact that it realigns the deeper psychological forces which had shaped rhetorical culture. (Ramus, incidentally, was himself no mean practicing rhetorician, being regarded by some of his contemporaries as the greatest orator since Cicero.) Ramist "method," proceeding from the general to the particular, was certainly not entirely new, for it is descended from the Porphyrean tree, but it marked the first viable alternative to the oration as a paradigm for organizing discourse. In a nondistinctive and even nondescript but real way, Ramist "method" lies at the root of modern encyclopedia articles and of most scientific or explanatory books today, including Mr. Vickers' and—Lord help us!—probably my own.

Works Cited

Durand, Gilbert. *Les Structures anthropologiques de l'imaginaire: Introduction à L'archétypologie Générale.* Paris: Bordas, 1960.
Havelock, Eric A. *Preface to Plato.* Cambridge, MA: Belknap P of Harvard UP, 1963.
Lewis, C.S. *English Literature in the Sixteenth Century, Excluding Drama.* Oxford: Clarendon P of Oxford UP, 1954.
Ong, Walter J. *Rhetoric, Romance, and Technology: Studies in the Interaction of Expression and Culture.* Ithaca: Cornell UP, 1971.
Yates, Frances A. *The Art of Memory.* Chicago: U of Chicago P, 1966.

20

Review of *Eighteenth-Century British Logic and Rhetoric* (1972)

Howell, Wilbur Samuel. *Eighteenth-Century British Logic and Rhetoric.*
Princeton: Princeton UP, 1971. Pp. xii + 742.

As the author puts it quite accurately, "The present history stands alone in its field" (9). It is the long-expected sequel to Mr. Howell's equally invaluable earlier work, *Logic and Rhetoric in England, 1500-1700.*

The "logic" and "rhetoric" of which this work treats are more elusive than those unfamiliar with the development of the subjects might think. Logic is more self-contained than most disciplines, but it has its own history, which has favored growth in certain directions and inhibited growth in others. Rhetoric, the matrix out of which logic first emerges, is less self-contained and registers even more directly and richly the evolution of social and psychological structures.

The present history focuses less on the internal development of logic than upon its development in relation to rhetoric and to the evolution of ideas. And with good reason. During the entire period that Howell's two books cover, discoveries in formal logic were apparently minimal to the point almost of nonexistence, not only in the British Isles but everywhere. In *A History of Formal Logic*, I. M. Bochenski can find almost nothing apart from Leibnitz's highly original work to report for this period except its lack of originality and its loss of contact with the mainstream of formal logical development, and even William Kneale and Martha Kneale, who take a more relaxed approach in *The Development of Logic,* and Wilhelm Risse, who in *Die Logik der Neuzeit,* I Band treats the sixteenth century in great detail, find little more. For all their continued preoccupation with logic, the years from 1500 to 1800 produced little, Leibnitz apart, to compare with the brilliant logical discoveries of the fourth century B.C. or the brilliant advances of the Middle Ages and later of George Boole (1815-1864) or Gottlob Frege (1848-1925).

Taking logic not as constituted by strictly formal structure but as what those who taught and used "logic" meant or tried to mean by the discipline, the present volume picks up at the point where the ancient understanding of logic as an art tied to communication and allied to rhetoric was replaced by an understanding of logic as an art of private inquiry, to which communication was more or less an additive. Dissociated from interchange of thought, logic was commonly taken to be a totally closed field with no history: it had been invented and completed by Aristotle. This conviction was shared not only by many textbook writers cited by Howell but apparently even by Immanuel Kant. The highly developed medieval semiotic had largely been forgotten, and John Wilkins, in *An Essay Towards a Real Character and a Philosophical Language* (London, 1668), could undertake to design scribal characters that would signify things and "notions" directly, independently of any language.

In this climate, one form of eighteenth-century British logic, represented by Henry Aldrich, Gerschom Carmichael, John Newbury, and others, held, though not slavishly, to what it considered an Aristotelian line, which Howell identifies largely with focus on deduction and which concerned itself with learned examination and presentation of known truths. This line of development was more or less entangled with Ramism, which was generally rejected or at least remodeled when it was recognized. The other form of logic, which Howell styles the "new logic," he identifies with interest in induction and scientific investigation by means of observation and experiment. Among the practitioners of the new logic were Thomas Reid, George Campbell, and Dugald Stewart. This logic reflected the emergence of the new science, of which Francis Bacon had been the herald, if hardly the master practitioner, and John Locke one of the chief allies. Locke's account of human understanding does much to feed the common eighteenth-century notion of thought as basically nonverbal and noncommunicative.

The history of rhetoric correlates with that of logic, but is intrinsically more complex because it links more directly with so much of man's lifeworld. The full-length, five-part rhetoric (invention, disposition or arrangement or judgment, *elocutio* or style, memory, and delivery) coming from ancient Greece and Rome survives in the eighteenth-century doctrines of John Ward, John Holmes, and others. It was often variously modified or adapted, and a stylistic rhetoric, a familiar concentrate of the third part of the fuller form, is found, too, for example, in Anthony Blackwall and John Stirling. But two new movements also get under way, which Howell labels respectively elocutionism and the new rhetoric. These are fascinating in their origins and implications.

The elocutionary movement began on the Continent in the early seventeenth century and was imported toward the end of the same century to the British Isles, largely through borrowing from the *Vacationes autumnales* (Paris, 1620) of the French Jesuit Louis de Cressolles, and the *Traitté de d'action de l'orateur* (Paris, 1657) of the French Protestant clergyman Michel Le Faucheur. (This elocutionary movement, incidentally, survived, at least residually, well through the twentieth century in the "elocution" contests still widespread after World War I and perhaps not unknown in some locales today.) Elocutionism in the British Isles received its major initial impulse from the orator, preacher, and "elocutionist" John Henley, abetted by the textbook writer John Mason and the actor Thomas Sheridan.

By "elocution" these and other "elocutionists" did not mean *elocutio* in its earlier sense of style, the third part of Ciceronian rhetoric. Rather, following the usage in Wilkins' *Ecclesiastes* (London, 1651), they used the term "elocution" to designate the fifth part of Ciceronian rhetoric, which before had uniformly been called *pronuntiatio* or *actio*, that is, oral delivery, including the use of both voice and gesture. The shift in the meaning of "elocution" came about, as Howell nicely shows, when the term "pronunciation" drifted from its original sense of delivery of an entire oration (a sense still retained when we speak of "pronouncing" a discourse) to its common present sense, the act or manner of articulating a word or words.

Many of the elocutionists made no mistake in their understanding of semantic history here: they knew that the sense they gave elocution differed from that of earlier *elocutio*. However, the same elocutionists, by no means the scholars that the Aristotelians and Ciceronians were, commonly made another mistake of major significance—they quite inconsistently believed, or at least implied, as Howell pointedly shows (202, 208, 233, etc.), that the entire program of ancient rhetoric, which in fact had been a program of pretty complete liberal education, coincided with their own understanding of elocution. That is to say, they supposed—what is unbelievable to even a casual scholar—that the rhetoric of Cicero and Quintilian and their congeners was designed chiefly to improve oral delivery and gesture.

The rise of elocutionism has long been a puzzling phenomenon, and Howell's account goes farther than any other to explain it. But in the details he so generously provides, one can discern certain additional patterns of development that he does not discuss and that carry the explanation even deeper, I believe. These patterns show how elocutionism arose, paradoxically, out of the new subjugation of oral delivery to the inscribed word, a subjugation begun with writing but maximized with print. Elocutionism was a symptom of a major readjustment in the entire noetic economy.

Howell makes clear (152 ff.) that "elocution" (in the sense of the fifth part of Ciceronian rhetoric, previously called *pronuntiatio* or *actio*) was stressed largely out of a need to improve reading aloud from texts, especially pulpit reading. But this indicated, first, that oral delivery was working in an economy quite different from that of earlier ages, when normally delivery was not from text at all, even a memorized text, but was instead the actual oral creation of an oration, with the help of the topics or "places" and of thematic and formulaic memory and perhaps a few notes, in the existential situation in which the orator found himself when he rose to his feet. Ancient orators, if they wrote out their orations at all, normally wrote them out after they had given them, sometimes years afterwards.

Second, the association of elocution with reading can throw new light on the shift in the meaning of memory between 1500 and the eighteenth century. Memory as a part of ancient rhetoric had not meant verbatim memorization of a text, but rather the recalling of the thread of argumentation planned for an individual oration and simultaneously the largely impromptu, more or less thematic and formulaic recall of commonplace material for "rhapsodizing" or stringing along this thread. In the mid-1500s Ramus had completely dropped memory as such in his reorganization of logic and rhetoric. He maintained that the "natural order" of things that his logic provided guaranteed automatic structuring of all discourse so that the old rhetorical planning and recall was unnecessary. But his real, unacknowledged, and indeed probably unconscious reasons for dropping memory, as I undertook to explain in *Ramus, Method, and the Decay of Dialogue* and as Frances A. Yates has further detailed in *The Art of Memory*, were somewhat different: first, Ramus' logic or dialectic was in fact itself a huge memory system connecting with a longstanding tradition of memory arts, and second, expression had become in his day more and more oriented to writing and print, where memory simply did not have the urgency it had in oratory.

The elocutionists indeed revived memory, as Howell points out, for they obviously did not think always of delivery as simple oral rendition from a text in front of the speaker. But their memory was in fact quite text-oriented. For Thomas Sheridan, both as an actor and as an elocutionist, memory tended to be primarily, if not exclusively, mere memorization—verbatim repetition of a text—quite a different thing from what the old rhetorical memory had been. The elocutionists thus did not actually revive the old rhetorical memory, but substituted for it something adapted to the extramental knowledge storage and retrieval systems begun with writing and maximized by print.

Third, the association of elocution with reading has fascinating implications if we think of it in terms of what Howell reports as a "cultural problem" (156), namely, the relationship between English and its Scottish speakers. The Scot Alexander Wederburn "could write English, as well as Latin, with tolerable purity" (157-59), but he had difficulty making his spoken English understood south of the border. He turned in desperation to the elocutionist Sheridan, among others, for help in tailoring his oral performance to his written. (Sheridan was not only an elocutionist but an Irishman transplanted to London and thus, incidentally, well experienced in adapting other pronunciations of English to that preferred in England.) The tables, as we can see, are turned here: in the old rhetorical pattern, linguistic performance had been focused on and maximized in the oral world, of which writing had been merely an offshoot; here linguistic performance was first brought to a degree of perfection by work with the printed page, from which the word was recycled into the oral world. Rhetoric had been the product of relatively unadulterated orality; elocutionism arose when there was question of returning the nonoral to the oral.

The elocutionist movement, in short, shows in striking ways how the oral management of knowledge, threatened ever since the invention of writing, was by now thoroughly debilitated. (Romanticism would mark its virtual demise.) By the close of the eighteenth century orality as a way of life was in effect ended, and with it the old-time world of oratory, or, to give oratory its Greek name, rhetoric. The demise of rhetoric marked probably the greatest break with the past that Western culture had ever experienced, and it ushered in, as I have tried to show in *Rhetoric, Romance, and Technology*, both modern technology and the Romantic movement.

Howell notes a further puzzling fact regarding elocution or delivery that could also be explained in terms of shifts in media: in the seventeenth century all the other four parts of the old rhetoric were under attack, only delivery was immune (152). On reflection, this suggests that all the other four parts were being adjusted to a typographic noetic economy. Even memory, which the Ramists had simply discarded, as we have seen, could be adjusted to print, though print made memory less needful: instead of the old thematic-formulaic recall in living, growing, existential situations, memory now came typically to mean verbatim oral repetition of a text on a page. (The increasing uselessness of such activity would not strike home for a couple of centuries.) Of the five parts of rhetoric, only delivery (*pronuntiatio* or *actio* in the centuries-old earlier terminology, "elocution" in the eighteenth century) remained typographically irreformable.

Oral delivery was oral delivery: there was no way to convert platform performance as such into the alphabet. So the rhetoricians of the sixteenth and seventeenth centuries either gave delivery short shrift in textbooks subconsciously adjusted to a post-oral noetic economy, or else treated it at length for just what is now uniquely was, something oral, voiced. Among other things, this meant that all the old oral drives in human expression (and there were many still) had now only one effective outlet left, "elocution." No wonder elocution grew so large.

And no wonder elocution and elocution contests quickly went under with the advent of electronic broadcast media—public address systems, radio, television—that impinged directly on the sound world. Delivery not only could be adjusted to such new media, but it had to be adjusted to them. Whereas writing and print were visual, the new electronic broadcast media were oral. They remodeled delivery. By World War II the old declamatory oratory was outmoded. A new coefficient in oratory, woman's speaking voice, was given the same volume and range as man's. The sweeping gesture, the grand style, calculated to project a message without mechanical assistance to an audience of thousands, passed away over the next few decades. On television now, public address is tête-à-tête even to an audience of millions on seven continents. And with public address systems, it is not much different even with thousands present before a speaker in an auditorium. He can whisper to them and be heard. He is simply a speaker. Orators are no more.

The second eighteenth-century movement in rhetoric, which Howell calls quite appositely simply the "new rhetoric," proves equally fascinating. The new rhetoric was continuous with the old in its concern with popular communication (logic had been for the intellectual elite) and with the traditional three kinds of oratory. But as logic withdrew from the ancient, medieval, and Renaissance world of thinking-via-discourse into the Cartesian solitudes advertised by writers such as Wilkins and indeed, in effect, by John Locke himself, rhetoric moved into the vacuum to deal with learned expression and all other kinds as well. Through Adam Smith, who migrated into economics from his professorships of logic and moral philosophy, and through George Campbell, Hugh Blair, and others, rhetoric at last became a general theory of literature (conceived of now typically as writing and print, not as oral discourse). By the late nineteenth century, this new rhetoric would ultimately give birth to today's departments of English and other languages and literatures. The second rhetorical movement thus also opens into a vast new world.

The history that Mr. Howell here so learnedly and circumstantially unfolds will provide material for years of reflection on the part of historians of ideas and culture, as well as of the noetic and verbal arts themselves. It is invaluable for what lies at the very center of all history: the story of the origins and growth of consciousness, of the "rise" of consciousness, which is to say the story of the evolution of the human psyche as man related to himself and to what is beyond himself through the course of time.

Works Cited

Bochenski, I. M. *A History of Formal Logic*. Trans. and ed. Ivo Thomas. Notre Dame, IN: U of Notre Dame P, 1961. (Original German edition, 1956).

Howell, Wilbur Samuel. *Logic and Rhetoric in England, 1500-1700*. Princeton: Princeton UP, 1956.

Kneale, William and Martha Kneale. *The Development of Logic*. Oxford: Clarendon P of Oxford UP, 1962.

Ong, Walter J. *Ramus, Method, and the Decay of Dialogue*. Cambridge, MA: Harvard UP, 1958.

—. *Rhetoric, Romance, and Technology*. Ithaca, Cornell UP, 1971.

Risse, Wilhelm. *Die Logik der Neuzeit*. 2 Bande. Stuttgart-Bad Cannstatt: Fromann, 1964.

Yates, Frances A. *The Art of Memory*. Chicago, U of Chicago P, 1966.

21

Why Talk? A Conversation about Language with Walter J. Ong Conducted by Wayne Altree (1973)

ALTREE: "Language" is a vast territory, intellectually and geographically. There are all kinds of "languages," not just English, Italian, Swahili, and so on, but computer languages like Fortran. We hear more and more about the languages of bees and porpoises and other animals. Still, man has been called "the language animal." Is language truly what distinguishes him from other animate beings?

ONG: Well, certainly language, if you understand what it really is, does distinguish man from other living beings. Human language is a very mysterious thing. It's creative, and it's creative in a distinctively human way. It directs man beyond himself. It enables him to direct the things around him beyond themselves.

What do I mean when I say language is creative? Well, we can see if we reflect that there is no single way to report anything that goes on. There are, potentially, an infinite number of ways. In a very interesting essay, "Grammar and Meaning," at the beginning of the *American Heritage Dictionary of the English Language*, Professor Richard Ohmann gives an instance, which I believe he worked up himself, to show how language is creative. I'm not going to use his exact words, but I'm going to use his ideas and his example.

Suppose you give to twenty-five people a simple little picture and ask each one to report what he sees. One person will say—and I am referring to the picture that Professor Ohmann worked with, although these descriptions aren't the exact ones that he recorded—one person will say there is a bear in a telephone booth and a man waiting outside. Another person will say a motorist has parked his car along the highway and is waiting impatiently while a bear is making a telephone call. Another will say a grizzly bear is in a telephone booth with the phone to his mouth and ear and an irate motorist is stomping around outside. When you have your twenty-five different samples from twenty-five different people, you can be virtually certain that no two would be worded exactly alike.

ALTREE: How many different wordings could you have?

ONG: We can speak to that question because Professor Ohmann, who likes to play with computers, has done a little computing with his story. Suppose you take twenty-five actual statements about this little picture that describe it adequately, accurately, truthfully, grammatically, running not more than twenty-five to thirty-five words. Now restricting yourself to the lexical resources of these twenty-five statements—that is to say, just the words that you find there, not all the English words that could be used, because these twenty-five statements would not by any means have used all the words you could use for the picture—ask yourself how many statements you could make in English that would adequately, truthfully, and grammatically describe this picture.

ALTREE: You want me to guess? I have no way of estimating.

ONG: Well, I have already asked this of a good many people. They often will guess 1,000 or 2,000, maybe a brave soul will say 25,000. This is the kind of problem you can put on a computer, and Professor Ohmann did, working with twenty-five typical sentences. It comes out 19.8 billion different statements, all describing this one limited state of affairs. I talked to Professor Ohmann about this a year or so ago, and he said, "Well, that's a conservative figure. As you know there is a certain leeway even on computers, and this is on the low side of the leeway." And of course if you used all the words available in English for a description of the picture instead of restricting yourself to the words in the twenty-five sentences, you would have far more than 19.8 billion different statements.

One can often dispute complex computer programming. But nothing here depends on an exact figure. Let's think of other comparable situations. Suppose you go to a library like the main library here at Saint Louis University. I believe there are some 800,000 volumes in the Pius XII Memorial Library. Suppose you copy out from all those books every sentence that is not a quotation from one of the other books and that consists of thirty words or more. Do you think it's at all likely that you'll have two sentences that are the same? Most persons can sense how extremely unlikely, or virtually impossible, it would be. You see, language is creative. There isn't just a thing out there that comes out in words. You have to relate it to other things if you are going to say something about it.

ALTREE: I hope you aren't saying that everything we say is relative, or how can we know what we're hearing?

ONG: No, we are not talking about false statements at all here. We are talking of statements about the bear-and-motorist picture that any informed person looking at the picture can test for truth: 19.8 billion true statements. The number of false statements would have no limit. You see, when you make a statement about something you observe, you have to select certain items in your perception and relate them to other things you know. A machine can't really do this the way a man can. A man has experience, a man has memory. A machine's so-called memory is only a retrieval mechanism. Man's memory is alive. It churns back through time, dreaming up unprecedented categories, hunting for relations between his thoughts, feelings, perceptions—real relations, or only imaginary ones, or both.

But this is a very complex thing we are dealing with. Many people have the idea that language works this way: Out in front of us there are a lot of little marbles, every one distinct from everything else, and this is what "reality" is. And concepts are little marbles, only they are in our minds. There is a little marble in our mind for every marble outside. For each concept there is an external word I shoot toward you. It carries the concept into your mind. That isn't what language is at all. Concepts and words aren't that easy to distinguish. And both are entirely different from things. Words are symbols.

ALTREE: What terminates the possibilities of creativity, if anything?

ONG: You mean why is it just 19.8 billion and not more? Well, it would be more of course if you used all the words in English. You can say "grizzly bear," or you might say "Kodiak bear," if it is a Kodiak grizzly and you know enough about bears to be this specific. What actually bounds the number of true statements you can make is the existential situation in which we actually are here and now, which is bounded by history. The situation has certain specific limitations. I know only so many words, you know only so many words, in English. Even this number can grow: My vocabulary can grow. Yours can grow. The total English vocabulary can grow. English is a growing thing, developing all the time, but at any given time always limited. You can express truths in English today that Shakespeare's age could not express.

ALTREE: It's staggering to think that there are so many billion more ways to describe that bear than there are people to talk about him. But doesn't that fact, in itself, lead us to important questions about those human beings?

ONG: Indeed it does. One of them involves another point I want to make about reporting. When someone says, "The reason I said that is because that's the way it really is," this can be true. But it doesn't say very much, because I want to know why he picked this one out of the 19.8 billion or more possibilities. If he simply says that the reason was that's the way it really is, that reason applies to all the rest of the 19.8 billion as well. The reasons for this particular choice among possible true statements, you see, are going to be largely subjective, which doesn't mean untrue. It means that your choice is made in terms of your own history, and the history of the people you are talking to.

Any kind of reporting has to be extremely subjective, not in the sense that it's necessarily untrue, but in the sense that the man who is doing it has to pick out what he reports in terms of his own knowledge and his relation to his listeners, real or imagined. If he's never heard of a grizzly bear, he won't call the animal a grizzly bear, but maybe just an animal. If he's an expert on grizzlies, but knows his audience has never heard of them, he may call it just a bear. Unless he wants to impress them. This means of course that the théâtre-vérité, the theater-of-truth kind of reporting, documentary reporting, is in a way the most subjective reporting we can get. With more than 19.8 billion ways to report each situation truly, the documentary reporter chooses one for reasons outside the situation, reasons in himself and his presumed audience, for documentaries are made for specific audiences.

The less subjective narrative is the kind that has a plot as well as the situation outside the reporter, a plot in the standard sense—anything from *Oedipus Rex* to a murder mystery, a narrative structure organized by forces within itself. Plot removes the story from the tyranny of subjectivism. "Little Red Riding Hood" has a structure independent of those who tell it. Its plot goes the way it does because its symbolism fits widespread psychological structures. As long as the person is trying to structure a story as a story and not to string items together "the way they really are," he can keep himself out of it to a large extent, whereas if he is trying just to report random facts, he has to select, and what he selects is what *he* selects.

Of course, news stories are consciously structured: newspaper stylesheets prescribe what kind of things to write about and how. *Time* magazine prescribes the how even more: their stories are somewhat modeled on Hemingway plots as well as on Hemingway style, as Professor Walker Gibson has shown in his *Tough, Sweet, and Stuffy*. The truth they report is of a special, limited kind.

ALTREE: Then choosing and language go together?

ONG: Yes. The question of choosing among alternatives is of course an essential part of language.

ALTREE: Why don't you talk about that in a little more detail?

ONG: When you are reporting, you are necessarily transfixed with the necessity of making choices. When you make a choice, meaning immediately intrudes. Language, you see, is a search for meaning, and meaning is a particularly human kind of search. Language shows the transcendental nature of actuality. Man is not satisfied with just things. He wants to project things beyond themselves. He wants to find the way they connect with something else, with the other things he knows and with the things that he doesn't know, because man himself is directed beyond himself. No man is satisfied with this world we live in. This is a curious thing about human nature: we just aren't satisfied with our world in itself, and we can't even imagine a world that we would be completely satisfied with. Our wildest imaginings are still unsatisfactory. Philosophers have talked of the "best possible world." "Best" indicates that even such a world is not self-contained: it is referred to other, presumably less good worlds so that it will show up by comparison as best. St. Augustine gets at this point talking about God, "Our hearts are restless till they rest in Thee."

There is nothing around us that works fully, perfectly, closed off in itself. So we always want to relate every little thing we find to something else, beyond it. First of all, we try to relate it to the other things around us that we know. And then we try to relate it to more philosophical and more religious meanings. Language, with the thinking that accompanies language, is a sign of human dissatisfaction. The utilitarian view of language is extremely artificial, contrived, and doesn't stand up even under laboratory conditions.

ALTREE: What were you referring to when you talked about psychological structures?

ONG: When I talked about psychological structures, what did I say . . .
oh, that a plot follows human psychological structures? What I had in
mind there was this, to take an example that everybody knows. If you
look into Sophocles' play *Oedipus Rex*, you can find there the kind of
psychological structures that a psychoanalyst reports when he talks about
the Oedipus complex. The reason people tell stories is related to the way
in which during their lifetime they develop psychologically from infants
to adults. We all follow the same general pattern of development, and
story plots ring true with us in part because they relate to the symbolic
organization we find to correspond to actuality as we work our way
through existence.

But although you can find a kind of common denominator in the sort
of things that depth psychology talks about, even these vary from age to
age. The way in which an Oedipus complex works in the twentieth century (particularly with a phenomenon like women's lib) is not exactly the
way it operated within ancient Greece, although the ways are related.

This point comes out very clearly in a seminar in which I am
involved. I am still Professor of English, but I have a secondary appoint-
ment as Professor of Humanities in Psychiatry in the Saint Louis
University School of Medicine. For over four years now, Dr. Charles K.
Hofling, Professor of Psychiatry, and I have been giving a seminar on
psychiatry and literature for the M.D.'s who are doing their residency in
psychiatry and for a selected group of our graduate students who are
doing doctorates in English. We study the psychological structures in literary works. You can see similarities between the structures in the literature of the ancient world and that of today, and you can also see the way
in which history has changed the structures. The basic relationships—for
example, that of man and woman, or father and child, or individual and
society—are still there, but they show up in quite different guises.

ALTREE: Does this continuity of psychological structure have a parallel
in the internal structure of language? Or, more directly, is there a universal grammar?

ONG: Well, man's thinking about this has gone through several stages.
Through the Middle Ages, the Renaissance, and the Enlightenment,
scholars felt strongly that there was a universal grammar. Then there was
a feeling that there wasn't any universal grammar. And now many of the
best linguistics specialists are pretty well convinced that there is a very
simple basic universal grammar. All languages have a subject and predicate, for example, though these manifest themselves in different ways.

ALTREE: I think that's important because otherwise it would seem that the relationship of any language to actuality is random.

ONG: Well, the relationship is not random. A few generations ago some scholars suggested that every language ran off in a different direction and, if you learned to think in Chinese, you could never relate your Chinese-language thinking to English. Well, with the experience you have with Chinese, Wayne, you know that isn't true.

ALTREE: No, many people can relate English and Chinese thinking even though the two languages are different. But not enough people have had to think in both to bring the two languages together.

ONG: Right. Although English and Chinese haven't yet influenced each other very much, languages do tend to grow together. Take English and French. English grew itself into many French thought-forms at the time of the Norman Conquest.

Let's take an even better example—English and Latin. In Shakespeare's day you couldn't learn medicine unless you knew Latin, because there wasn't a stock of English words to express medical concepts. It would have been like trying to learn atomic physics today in Potawotomi. There is no way to express atomic physics in Potawotomi, but you could develop Potawotomi to handle atomic physics. You could develop any language to handle it. So English-speaking people could develop English to teach medicine, and they did. We borrowed all kinds of words from Latin and Greek: "anatomy," "physiology," "cardiac," "medicine" itself. Any language, if you give it a chance, will annex any other language it needs. Theoretically, I suppose, one language could incorporate the resources of all the others, given time and effort.

You can explain in English certain verb tenses that do not exist in English, but in doing so you are likely to form concepts based on the way the other language works and to this extent expand English to accommodate the other language.

A given language is never a closure of existence, but an opening into existence. Any one language is one of many possible windows into reality. It gives you certain options that you can use, and they aren't always the same options, even in languages as closely related as English and French. You can say certain things in French that you can't say in English. You can say some things in English that you can't say in French.

For example, there is no word in French that covers what "smooth" refers to in English. In English I can say "My face is smooth. This asphalt tile flooring is smooth. The lawn is smooth, and the pane of glass is smooth." There is no one word in French that will work the way this English word does for all those. You'd say something like "*La vitre est lisse*," "the glass is a slick-smooth." You'd probably say that my face, if I've shaved recently, is "soft smooth"; perhaps you'd say, "*La figure est molle.*" To the lawn, too, you'd probably apply the same word: "*La pelouse est molle.*" If you saw an asphalt tile floor, you'd say, "*Le plancher est uni,*" meaning that it is put together out of little pieces that are so well joined that if you run your fingers over them you don't feel the joints very much—"*uni.*" Now since we can't say that about asphalt tile very economically in English, we don't pay very much attention to that sort of thing. But what if we wanted to say it a lot? Well, we'd do what we've done in other cases. We'd borrow from the French.

Take a word like "milieu," which means both the middle and what you are in the middle of—what surrounds you with you in the middle. It's an idea that you could not quite get across in any other single English word. "Surroundings," by comparison, tends to suggest something at a slight distance. So we just appropriate the French word "*milieu*," build it into English. Languages are pirates: they constantly raid one another.

ALTREE: In these terms, is one language bound to be better than another?

ONG: Well, English is a very advantageous language because it has such a highly developed vocabulary, the largest vocabulary in the world, it appears. Consequently you've got more options. Since new words come into being daily and are hard to track down, no one knows exactly how many English words there are—the 1969 *World Almanac* asserts that there are "some 800,000" and that well-educated users often manage with a speaking vocabulary of 5,000 or so of these. *Webster's Third New International Dictionary* treats some 450,000 words but notes it could have included "many times" that number. Whatever the ultimate statistics, English has achieved this advantage of a vast vocabulary by borrowing from scores of other languages. Its mongrel vocabulary is one of its greatest assets. In this connection, purity of language is utter nonsense.

ALTREE: Anthropologists are pious about this and say that there are no superior languages.

ONG: There aren't any, in a very real sense. All languages we know are indescribably complicated. A hundred years ago even scholars used to think naively that primitive peoples had simple languages. They don't. As a matter of fact, the longer a language is used and the larger the number of its users, the simpler in some ways it may become.

Mass languages, such as English, used by over 300,000,000 people, are new phenomena, of course. Even today, many if not most languages are used by no more than a few thousand people. But with the build-up of population in the past few thousand years, mass languages have come into being: English, Chinese (although Chinese is really a group of related languages and not one language—still, one of these Chinese languages, Mandarin, has more native speakers than English), Spanish, Portuguese, Hausa (spoken by over 14,000,000 West Africans), and so on. In these languages a kind of simplification can set in, but they are still complicated.

All languages have strict grammatical rules. We know now, for example, that the dialect of English that is used in the black ghetto in the United States—though you might say dialects, because there are small variations from place to place—has an elaborate grammar with fixed rules of the same sort as those in Standard American grammar. It's just a different grammar. For instance, in black-ghetto dialect you say, "He busy." For certain reasons and with certain definite rules, you don't use the verb form "is" here and in many other places where Standard American would use it. "He busy" means he is busy now and it won't last very long. You can also say, "He be busy," which means he is really occupied, he is all tied up. We are beginning to work out these grammars now, and they are all complicated. If you grow up learning black-ghetto English, you learn a grammar with its own invariable and very strict rules, some of which are the same as and some of which are different from the Standard American dialect spoken by the larger number of us.

ALTREE: You said something earlier about all languages being complicated when they came into being. Could you be specific about some of the complications?

ONG: I shouldn't say that all languages were complicated when they came into being because we don't know how languages came into being. But it is true that of all the languages we know, the most primitive languages are complicated, just as complicated by and large as any other language. Their grammatical rules are extremely elaborate, and the nuances they can express are extremely delicate.

In some languages you can tell in the verb what we can't tell in English by a verb form—whether this action is difficult or just beginning or about to begin or likely to end pretty quickly or whether it is tied up with something else or is a free action, and so on. There are many other possibilities. Very primitive as well as advanced languages do things of this sort.

ALTREE: All these options, all these possibilities, make language not just complicated but far more rich than we usually think of its being. In fact, we don't think much about language per se.

ONG: Yes, it's tremendously rich. I said earlier that words aren't signs, but that they are symbols. There is a difference here that is very important if we are going to understand what a rich thing language is. When we think that words are signs, we think of them as just standing for something: I want milk, and I put a word out there, just "milk." You take the word "milk" away and somebody puts a cup of milk there and that's the way language works. That's what might be called the utilitarian view of language. But language isn't utilitarian in just that way.

There is a very interesting story, a true story, about a so-called wild boy who was found some generations ago in France. The story is reported by Susanne Langer in her book *Philosophy in a New Key* (119-21). Victor, the so-called Savage of Aveyron, was found by a French doctor, E. M. Itard, and was supposed to have grown up in the woods among animals. As happens in most such cases when they are investigated, this was found not to be true, but at any rate he was a retarded youngster of some sort. He didn't know how to talk, and Itard undertook to teach him.

Well, Itard had a very bad case of utilitarianism. He taught Victor to say the word *"lait,"* French for milk. What he wanted the boy to do was to say *"lait"* when he wanted milk so that the milk would be given to him. Itard discovered that this wasn't what happened. He said, "It was not till the moment, when, despairing of a happy result, I actually poured the milk into the cup that he presented to me, the word *lait* escaped him again, with evident demonstrations of joy. . . . It is evident from hence, that the result of the experiment was far from accomplishing my intentions; the word pronounced, instead of being the sign of a want, it appeared, from the time in which it was articulated, to be merely an exclamation of joy." Well, how unresponsive can you be? It was an exclamation of joy because it was an exclamation of knowing, of meaning opened by language.

Helen Keller, the late well-known deaf and blind author and lecturer, wrote about this kind of knowing. It suddenly dawned on her as a little girl, she said, when her teacher, Miss Sullivan, was working with her in the presence of water running over Helen's hand, that there was a *word* "water," that *this was* water, that somebody else *knew* what water was, and that now she herself knew. The concept and the word and its application to a subject and the communication all came at once. Looking back to Dr. Itard's youngster Victor, we can recognize that what Victor was saying was in effect, "This is milk, this is milk, this is milk." He knew what the word meant, knew what it meant to know, and wanted to feel his knowledge as shared. The doctor, that unfortunate utilitarian with his distorted view of language, completely missed what was going on. He really had a vending-machine concept of language you put a word in and something comes out.

Now this ties in with something we said earlier. Words are symbols. The word "lait" or "milk" is not milk. It isn't the same thing. It is a representation, a re-presentation. The milk is presented to you, but then you have to re-present it in your mind. The word, a sound, signals and supports what is going on in the consciousness, the thought.

Now, words and thoughts are not the same things, but they are related to one another. We have to have both an interior concept, something in our consciousness, and an exterior word, a sound, precisely because we can't deal with this brute thing outside us on its own terms. But the concept is not exactly like what it re-presents. It is not tied down in time and space the way the objects of our senses are. I can look at some milk over here and say, "This is milk," and I can look at some milk over on the other side of the table and say, "That is milk." The two quantities come together in that term "milk." But they are completely different bodies of liquid in two different places. You are in another world when you are dealing with concepts, and it is concepts that the words enable us to express

ALTREE: Do words or thoughts come first?

ONG: To answer that, we can reflect on our own experience. What happens when a youngster, a little child, learns to talk? Almost everyone has observed the process. Children enter into a lalling stage when they make noises—"goo, goo" and such—for hours on end. The human being is the only animal we know that does this. No other animal plays with random sounds with such intensity. An infant creates around himself a universe of noises he can control. And the tendency to make sounds in this constructive, creative, playful sort of way is, I think beyond a doubt, related to what is distinctive of man, his consciousness, his self-consciousness, his intelligence, the thing that enables him to say "I" and to think thoughts, to relate things to other things beyond them.

So a child enters this lalling stage. One day he makes a noise that sounds something like "mama," perhaps free-wheeling or perhaps in mimicry. If he is lucky at the time he happens to say "mama," there is outside him but near him a nice, big, warm thing that picks him up from time to time. With the sound "mama," he gets picked up and chucked under the chin and kissed. It's all a rather pleasant experience. Later on he happens again to say "mama" and this pleasant experience happens again. And it happens again and again. But the nice things don't happen unless there is this big, warm thing outside. If he says "mama" when this big, warm something is not around, nothing happens.

Remember, as William James said, for a child the world at first is a big, blooming, buzzing confusion. He doesn't have the things that are outside him distinguished in the nice way in which we distinguish things. He doesn't see trees and flowers and automobiles; although his visual images may be clear, he can't sense what goes with what. And so with other senses besides vision. But gradually, you see, as he says this word and this big, nice, warm thing picks him up, he begins to recognize this big, nice, warm thing as something different from all other things. And he begins to relate it to this word "mama" and the word begins to become a word because he begins to form a concept in his mind of "mama," which isn't really mama because it can be there when she isn't. It re-presents her, even when she isn't present. And it can be related, as we'll see, to other things. So words and concepts come into being simultaneously. All our speech and thinking go back to this kind of situation.

Some psychologists would explain all this as "reinforcement." The child is being rewarded for saying "mama," and thus his tendency to say it is being reinforced. True enough, but reinforcement is not the point here. What is significant is not that he says "mama" more often, but that he is changing inside, being brought more to life. At the end of the process, saying "mama" is quite different from what it was at the start. The word is a real word now, not just a sound, for a thought is now connected with it.

ALTREE: Can we think without words?

ONG: For a human being, thought is impossible without some kind of verbal context. Now I'm not saying that all our thoughts come in words. Certainly they don't. I don't know what I do when I am thinking. A few years ago one of the stupidest questionnaires I ever received included the question "How much time do you spend each day thinking? Hours? Minutes?" I raised such a noise about this question that the people who got up the questionnaire sent a special emissary around to find out what the trouble was and mollify me. I told him what the trouble was: I don't know exactly what I'm doing when I'm thinking. I can't tell when I start and when I stop. But I do know this: the context of thinking is words. If I hadn't learned words like "mama," I could never have got started thinking. And my thoughts are not in good condition, they are not at the optimum, until I have them in words. Then I know what I am thinking, what I mean. How can I tell what I mean until I hear what I say? It's by formulating my thoughts in words that I bring the thoughts to maturity.

Note, this means that we don't have any completely private thoughts, doesn't it? The words that I use to formulate my thoughts are not my own. All language is public. All our thinking is public in the sense that it shapes up in a public medium—language. What is truly our own is not thought, but will. When I determine a course of action, when I make up my mind to do or not to do, to accept or reject—that determination is mine far more than my thoughts are. "A penny for your thoughts." I can in a way "give" you my thoughts, share them. If I "give" you my decision, I simply tell you what it is. I don't share it. It's mine for keeps. Gerard Manley Hopkins speaks of the will as "the selfless self of self, most strange, most still." And, anticipating Sartre by two or three generations, he notes how much one's decisions enter into the self: "What I do is me." Our decisions are what we are held responsible for. Not our thoughts, except in so far as we build them into decisions. Thoughts themselves are not really that much our own.

ALTREE: Language isn't a system of items that are symbols in the sense that nonlinguistic symbols are: for example, international traffic signs. It is a system that provides an opportunity to construct that indefinite number of sentences that you were speaking about, isn't it? Now, what about that? It seems to me you are explaining language here in a historical, cultural sense, in a diachronic way. But there is a horizontal dimension to this, too.

ONG: There is. You remember Itard's case of the little boy who would say "*lait*" when a cup of milk was in his hands. You have seen children in this situation: they point to something, and they say "tree," and what they are saying in effect is, "This is a tree." Now psychological studies, for example Paula Menyuk's *Sentences Children Use*, show that children commonly learn predicates first. This means, you see, that you don't learn a word all by itself; you learn it in at least implicit relationship to a subject. And the subject and predicate relate to each other as no other paired items do. No other thing in human experience is quite like this relationship.

In a significant way, a predicate is more intensely a word than a subject of a sentence is. In Latin, "*verbum*" means word, but it also means verb, the predicate part of a sentence. Our term "verb" comes from the

Latin *"verbum,"* which itself comes from the same early Indo-European root that gives us our English term "word." Suppose you make a sentence of a gesture and a word. You point to someone and say, "Lawyer." Normally the hearer will understand "lawyer" in the verb part of the sentence, as a predicate: the gesture means "this" or "this man" and the word means "is a lawyer."

The subject you can indicate much more readily just by pointing, because it is less verbalized than the predicate. Although the subject is rich in implications, these are concealed: in itself the subject is less processed intellectually and verbally than the predicate is. One of the ways to put this is in terms of Aristotelian philosophy: the predicate relates to the subject as the form to matter. The subject is indeterminate, relatively blah. And the predicate determines it. The predicate is more specific, precise, in a special sense more alive.

So there is a kind of living relationship of words to one another. They don't come into existence all by themselves, but with other words. One fatal thing in thinking about language is to think that words are like little things, little marbles or tickets, receipts exchangeable for things. The real reason why that is fatal is that words are basically sounds, and here we have to go into something that is really mysterious.

All human beings have languages, and the languages are all in sound. You don't make statements by drawing pictures, or by giving off odors, or flavors, or heat and cold, not even by making gestures, although gestures get closer to the sounds. You can express yourself in all the senses, all the sensory fields, but there is a special relationship between sound and thought. And that is why words are sounds.

ALTREE: Yes, I can see that. It's why our discussion is about "talk," not just words, but the sounds of human talk. But why are words sounds? Are there physiological or psychological reasons?

ONG: Nobody knows the complete story here. I've tried to write a little about it in *The Presence of the Word*, but I really know of almost no one else who does. It's perhaps too close to us.

Let's take a look at a few things here. First of all, it is obvious enough that words are basically sound. When you write words, you are making marks that enable you to make sounds aloud or in your imagination. Even deaf and dumb people get themselves integrated into the world of verbal sounds indirectly. They learn to read lip motions connected with the production of sound and to read words initially organized in the sound field and permanently related to sound.

The importance of sound and thought is dramatically illustrated by the case of those born deaf. Before we had the very sophisticated methods for training deaf people that are used, for example, at Saint Joseph Institute for the Deaf here in St. Louis, a pioneer in these methods, deaf persons were always subnormal intellectually simply because their ways of getting into the sound world were so indirect that they could never get their thinking up to par. This was so even when there was nothing wrong with them except that they were deaf.

ALTREE: You are suggesting that hearing, sound, is in some way a special sense, at least in human beings. Would you explain?

ONG: Sound is different from any of the other sensory fields in that it indicates the present use of power. Sound shows that something is going on, something is happening, power is being used. A primitive hunter can see a buffalo, touch a buffalo, smell a buffalo, and taste a buffalo when the buffalo is completely inert, and in fact dead. But if he hears a buffalo, he had better watch out, something is going on. Sound means power.

This truth is caught in folklore as well as in the philosophy and theology of the past and the present. Homer speaks of "winged words." This means words fly away, they are evanescent. But it also means that they are powerful: you have to be strong to fly. In the Bible we find this sense of the word developed with extreme sophistication. "*Dabar*" in Hebrew means a word and it means an event—both. So God's word is God's action, his breaking into history, an event, a happening.

A word is an event, it is a happening.

Only literate people who can be desensitized by their literacy (literacy sensitizes in some ways, but desensitizes in others) can think of a word as other than a happening. If a person knows nothing about writing, a word to him means a sound. Sounds are events. A sound exists only when it is going out of existence. When I say the word "existence," by the time I get to the "*-tence*" the "*exis-*" is gone. It has to be gone or you couldn't understand me. This used to bother St. Augustine a lot, and it bothers us, but that's the way it is.

Writing is a kind of faking. I can write the letters of the word "existence," and the letters are all there at once, but the word really cannot be. Words are inescapably tied into time. This is why they are alive, why they are strong, why they are powerful: they are actions.

And our thinking is the same way—time-bound. When I say, "I know geometry," that means I can run it through my mind. It doesn't mean that I am thinking of everything in geometry simultaneously, but that I can fish the theorems of geometry one by one out of memory and can run them through my consciousness. So our thinking is tied in with memory, with recall, with voluntary recall (which a computer doesn't have), with movement through time. Our thoughts run in parallel with sound: like sound, they are events.

Let's go back to the power of words. The hunter, remember, can see, touch, smell, and taste a buffalo when the buffalo is inert, even dead. If he hears a buffalo, it's a different matter: the buffalo is doing something. Sound signals the present use of power. Scholars sometimes say that primitive peoples naively associate words with power. It is such scholars who are naive: if you think of real words, of sounds, not of letters on a surface, words are always an indication of power-in-use. When Genesis says, "God said let there be light and there was light," it is registering a feeling for the word as signaling power.

It is often also said that primitive people think that words give you power over things. Adam named the animals and thereby felt he acquired power over them. Well, I hope that advanced technological people also think words give power over things, because they do. No words, no advanced technology. Can you imagine mastering chemistry without knowing any chemical terms? Words do give you power over things. Without them we are unable to cope with existence. You can't understand or manage anything effectively until you've got a minimum of words to enable you to cope with it. To manage human life, you have to have symbols.

Words have power in human relations, too. I can say to you, "You are my agent," and that makes you my agent, and what you do may get me into real trouble or keep me out of it. That is tremendous power. Words get things done.

Now thought has a relationship to this kind of world. This is where our thought lives—in this world of power, of ongoing activity. Thought cannot be represented as just a movement of counters in some kind of spatial field. Unless we think of words in terms of sound and unless we think of thoughts, of thinking, in alliance with sound, as events, we are not thinking about thought the way it is.

It's disquieting, isn't it, to think of words as always vanishing, going out of existence? But is that the whole story? To answer this and other deeper questions about words and what they are, it helps to think of words religiously, because words have to do with man's deepest instincts. We manage some of our finest insights into the nature of words by comparing man's word to God's word. The power of man's word gives it some resemblance to God's word, which, in the Bible, both in Jewish and in Christian teaching, is presented as of limitless power. But the Bible also says the word of the Lord remains forever, and this is exactly what man's word does not do; it does not remain, but vanishes.

ALTREE: But is there anything about our speech that remains?

ONG: Yes, there is. Silence. Silence is part of our speech. Our speech has to include silences. All human speech is articulated, which means it is not constant emission of sound, but is always interrupted sound. Words are interrupted by being divided into syllables. And sentences are divided into words, and we pause more or less between many words.

ALTREE: We are likely to pause at the ends of certain phrases and at the ends of sentences.

ONG: Yes, that's where we got punctuation originally. As late as Ben Jonson's grammar, first published in 1640, three years after his death, punctuation marks were still said to indicate pauses for breathing. This is the way the ancient grammarians had thought of punctuation. Today we think of punctuation in terms of sentence "structure"—as though an utterance were something architectural, put together in space: we sometimes diagram sentences. Such diagramming can be advantageous. But it is at least one remove from actuality. Jonson still regarded sentences not as architectural constructs but as sayings, sounds. Punctuation marked silences.

Modern linguistics studies the meanings of certain kinds of silences. Often a silence after an utterance is where we achieve understanding of the words that went before. Like now. . . . Our memory, in its depths, works in silence.

So speech is a transaction between sound and silence. Silence endures. You can "hold" it, "keep" silence, as you cannot keep a sound. But man's words interrupt the duration of silence, and his words, as we have seen, unlike the word of the Lord as explained to us in the Bible, do not remain forever. Writing addresses itself to this disability of our words: it undertakes to make the word of man endure, last. Writing commits the living, powerful word-in-sound, the word that is living and powerful but also evanescent, fleeting, flying away, to the quasi-permanence of space. We say "quasi-permanence" because materials cannot be absolutely permanent: even stone, like books, rots away. Books disappear in curious fashion sometimes. In the Middle Ages, one abbot writes another and asks, "Would you please send me your copy of Peter Lombard's *Sentences* because a bear just ate up ours." Books were written on parchment and parchment could get damp and rather ripe, and smell good to a hungry bear. There is a good bit of protein in parchment.

Books are destroyed also in countless less spectacular ways. There is a kind of permanence though, in writing: a text can be copied, multiplied. If you transcribe or print enough copies you hope that one or another will survive for an indefinite period of time.

So writing commits these words to space. But to do so, it makes words less real, pretends they are something they are not: quiescent marks.

ALTREE: I recognize that our topic is "Why Talk?" and not "Why Write?" But without going too deeply into writing, is it possible to discuss the relation between talking and writing? Certainly talking came first, but did writing, when it came along—fairly recently, incidentally—change talking? I know it did, but I'd like to hear how you relate the two.

ONG: Almost all our ancestors were illiterate, of course, because if man has been on earth somewhat more than 300,000 years (which is a pretty conservative figure), writing came in only yesterday. The first writing system, the cuneiform system of Mesopotamia, came into existence only about 3500 B.C.—less than 6,000 years ago.

True writing, script, is different from picture drawings. Nobody is ever going to know who drew the first picture or carved the first representation of something. This kind of thing is lost in remote prehistory. Pictures represent things, which can have any number of words attached to them. If I draw a picture of a bird, a French-speaking person will call it "*oiseau*," a German-speaking person will say "*Vogel*," an Italian-speaking person will say "*uccello*," a Spanish-speaking person will say "*pajaro*." Only an English-speaking person will call it what it really is.

Writing is different from pictures, that is, writing in the sense of a script. A script tells you what somebody says. It enables you to join a predicate to a subject as you can't do just by drawing pictures.

When writing converts the world of sound to a world of semipermanence in space, it changes a lot of things. By changing the way in which knowledge can be stored in words, it changes the way man can think. Until you had writing, you couldn't have a really scientific treatment of anything, say a treatise on medicine. The only way to have produced this kind of thing before writing would have been to have somebody recite a book on medicine, making it up as he went along—which can't be done. Once you have writing, you can write an organized treatise because you can put something down, go away from it, think it over, come back, and look at it, put the next thing down, and then review what you've done and put the next thing down, and so on. You get a highly developed linear, sequential thinking that goes on only in a very limited way in oral culture, not in this protracted way. Oral cultures typically organize thought in "sayings": formulas, proverbs, aphorisms, and the like. Once you get writing, this earlier organization is slowly phased out or minimized.

ALTREE: We hear a lot about new media today making the old media obsolete, eliminating the old. Is this what happens here?

ONG: No, it is not. A new verbal medium never cancels out the old. Many people think that a new medium simply eliminates what went before. You hear the assertion today that books are finished, that radio and television have replaced books. Well, anybody who thinks that is pretty well out of contact with actuality. Just drop into the ordinary bookstore, the drugstore, look in at the airport, in at the bus depot—in the old days I would have said look in a railroad station, but there's nobody there anymore—there are more books than ever. Quite clearly. More new ones, more reprints of old ones.

No, the new medium reinforces the old, but it changes it. We have to avoid two extremes. The new medium doesn't wipe out the old. On the other hand, the old isn't what it used to be anymore. Once you had writing, you could become familiar with the kind of sequential thinking that you do in writing. Then your talk could reflect the kind of thinking that writing enabled you to do. And indeed it had to, as my talk and yours is doing now. Ours is very literate talk. All educated persons' talk today is more or less literate, in the sense that it sounds more or less like writing. After writing took hold, purely oral talk was finished. Too bad, in many ways. For the purely oral has great beauties of its own. But you can't have your cake and eat it.

Similarly when print came along, print reinforced the earlier medium. Universal literacy, the ability of all to read and write, wasn't made necessary or even advisable by the invention of writing. It was made necessary by the medium that came after writing, that is, by print. But print changed the kind of things people wrote. It oriented the mind to "facts" rather than to sayings.

Today, in the new age of electronic media, the previous medium, print, is reinforced: it is necessary that virtually every educated person today know how to print, that is, use a typewriter, which is a way of printing, producing writing from pre-existing little types.

But print is also transformed by the new media. There are going to be more books than ever, but a lot of them are going to be talked books, like this book we are writing now—we tape an interview, edit it, cut things out, paste things in, probably do some retaping afterward to feed other things back into it, and then produce a volume like the one our readers will see before them, which, to be quite frank, presents the readers with something that nobody ever said and nobody ever wrote. We don't even have the words we need to talk about this kind of production. Who is the "author" of a book like this? There is no author in the ordinary sense of the term. You can't say, Wayne, that you are the editor or the author; I'm not the editor or the author. I suppose that in some way you are the master of ceremonies or the producer and I'm the cast.

ALTREE Some might say that a talked book is simply a way of getting a book out of someone who otherwise might not write the book. It takes some of the burden off.

ONG: Yes. But note that this is another reinforcement of the old medium by the new. The talked book makes possible more printed books than you would otherwise have. Which is to say, the oral electronic work (taping in this case) is producing more print than you would have without electronics.

Whatever we are or this book is, authors who write books in the older scriptorial fashion, who don't do a talked book, are going to want to make their written books have something of the kind of directness and informality that we achieve by such devious means this way.

It's paradoxical, isn't it, the way we plan informality? We work over the structure of the book to make it sound unstructured, to make it sound as though it's not a book, but relaxed talk. Essentially a book is not talk, and if you want to make it sound like talk, you really have to work hard at it. If you put offhand talk into print, it mostly doesn't sound like real talk, coming off the page. Or if it does, it's boring.

ALTREE: Do you think that's related to radio and television, where we have so much more talk? Most people hear the news; they don't read it, these days.

ONG: I suspect they both hear and read. But one of the commonest kinds of television show is called a talk show. Television is far more oral than its name leads us to think. A thing is what its history has made it. Movies, sound movies, are pictures with sound added. That's the way they came into existence. Television is radio with pictures added. You always have to have sound on television. Ask any television engineer. You can read a weather map on television, but do they ever let you? Never. You always have to have the pretty young girl or the sage old meteorologist to say it to you—the same thing you'd read out of the paper without any sound at all.

Television is definitely a talk medium. Print can give us news only after it's happened. Electronic media bring happenings to us when they are happening. This is why sound is important, even when you are using live visual shots. Because sight can give you a sense of quiescence, repose. Our sight is at maximum when its object is immobilized, whereas talk—sound—as we have seen, is always a happening, an event, something ongoing.

ALTREE: I know some people who insist on turning off the sound during a televised football game and turning on the radio, because the radio broadcaster will be much more specific and descriptive of details that may not show up in the picture. The television broadcaster feels that he can let you rely on the picture, which doesn't always work because if the camera isn't in exactly the right place, you miss the action. But the radio tells you.

ONG: Interesting. What you say suggests that a lot of the sounds we get on television, including the verbal commentary, are probably less effective for conveying information than we think and are there just because they are sounds, to give you the sense of present action. For example, imagine seeing a riot broadcast live on television without any sound. It would be very hard to feel that the broadcast was really live. If you had sound, even if only a musical background, it would be much easier to believe that what you see on the screen is really going on. Of course, it would be even more convincing if you got the sounds from the riot itself. But almost any kind of sound helps to give the sense of immediacy, of present action.

ALTREE: I certainly know what you mean about our being a sound people. Let's go back to the child learning to talk. How does he learn to say the things he does say without ever having heard these utterances? You know what I am getting at. Is there a language faculty? The child doesn't splatter all over the place. He knows almost intuitively and very early what's right in the use of language, what's wrong, what he can do, what he cannot do. He hasn't heard all the things said that he manages to say. But he has a sense of propriety. Now, he makes mistakes; but that's just because he's incompetent or forgets. How does he learn to say all these things he has never heard before?

ONG: There are several questions here. First of all, when a child learns a language, of course he makes mistakes, some of them very cute. My nephew's youngest daughter, Cindy, for a while was saying, "She's lost she's gloves." This is a very logical mistake to make, which you can surely account for very readily. And about the ways children learn. One of the ways is repeating the last words in utterances they hear adults make. They pick up from the tail end of things. But they do have a natural way of adapting and eliminating the mistakes, so eventually they end up without them. You simply have to say that a human being can do this. It is something distinctively human.

ALTREE: A second question is what have they got when they've got it?

ONG: This is what Noam Chomsky's work and that of other transformational grammarians or other generative grammarians attempts to answer. To put it roughly, transformational and other generative grammarians are trying to state in an abstract, formalized way the totality of the rules that a child or an adult carries unwittingly in his mind to enable him to do everything with a language that he does—formulate the rules so that you could put them all on paper, covering every possible combination of words. Well, it has been a noble effort, and they have gone pretty far, but they have just about given up completing the job because the refinements get too distressing after a while.

The fact is, though, that we do have an extremely complicated abstract apparatus that we carry around in our minds in a nonabstract way. I'm not a generative grammarian myself, so I'll just have to let it go at that.

ALTREE: I know you're not a structuralist, either, but would you please put them in our picture?

ONG: You're right, I'm not, but there is an analogy in structuralism, as Claude Lévi-Strauss and others propound it. For example, in a primitive tribe, where the anthropologist diagrams a tremendously involved family relationship, what the person in the tribe carries around in his mind is not exactly the anthropologist's description of it, but something more fundamental, not formalized, not articulated. We, too, know what uncle, aunt, daughter-in-law, and so on, mean generally without ever having diagrammed the relationships. Structuralism can refer to a variety of theories and procedures, but many of them turn on a persuasion that we operate in terms of very formal structures we are only vaguely aware of at best. These structures control social and linguistic behavior both. In this sense structuralism is really a kind of Romanticism, because it attends to areas in human awareness beyond or beneath fully articulated consciousness. But most thought and lifestyles are colored by Romanticism now, I suppose.

Structuralism, of course, moves out or attempts to move out from descriptions of social and language relationships to other human relationships and eventually to just about everything in human life.

When you raise the question of structuralism and some of the other suggestions that you have been raising here, Wayne, you suggest another point that is important. Words have a kind of dominance in human life. We talk about words having meanings. And in a sense human beings want to convert everything they do into words—in the very basic sense that we want all our actions to have significance, which means to be signs of something beyond themselves.

ALTREE: Physical actions, too, as well as mental operations?

ONG: Yes, when I make a gesture, for example, I want it to have meaning. This means to refer to something beyond itself, to be symbolic. Words have significance or meaning because they have more than just their physical being as sound: they bring in something else. The meaning of the word "liberty" is not just the word "liberty": the sound of a word brings in something more than what it itself is, physically. It is *meaningful*: full of something more than itself.

This is the way we want all our actions to be. We want our entire life to be meaningful. We want it to be referred to something beyond itself, to be related to other things, and, we generally imply, to something greater than itself. So our life and all of our actions are in this sense words in so far as they are significant, are meaningful; like words they move beyond themselves to point to something else, something beyond. Words, you see, have this curious outreaching character. They are constantly pointing to a beyond, something more, more, more.

Words are interiorizing. They relate things to my consciousness, but they also enable me to relate my consciousness to itself. And this is what is most deeply distinctive of man. Man can say "I." He can come back and take possession of himself, get hold of his own consciousness. The German poet Rainer Maria Rilke has something to say about the curious emptiness that stares out from an animal's eye. There is no kickback, nothing that fights back the way your eye, Wayne, fights back at mine. Beyond your eye—yes, deep inside anything locatable in your entire body—I feel a consciousness, I sense you, with the result that our relationship is a kind of struggle. I have to see, for example, whether you are buying what I say, and you are looking at me to see whether what I say makes any sense.

Each of us of course has a name that other people have given us. But each of us really knows that that name isn't "I." I am really not "Walter." That is really something that is given to me, not generated from inside me. You are really not "Wayne." You are really what you call "I" and what I call "you." And I am "I," what you call "you."

But—strange thing—I am "you" only when you are talking to me. When you are not talking to me, I am "Walter" or "he," not "you"; the person you are talking to about me is "you."

"I" and "you" are curious words. We call them pronouns, from Latin "*nomen*," which means a name, and "*pro*," which means in place of, instead of. A "*pro-nomen*" (pro-name, pro-noun) is something that is used in place of a name. Each of us is too close to himself to have a name for himself, because a name has a way of distancing things. We use "I" instead. And we come to this notion of "I" by talking—through words and the thought that goes with them.

I was with some very small children just a few days ago, and they presented a nice contrast. The older one was about four, and he could say "I," but the younger one was just two and couldn't say "I" yet. He could refer to himself by his first name, he could tell you who he was, give the name that others had given him, but he hadn't been thinking enough and talking enough to come to the point where he could enter into himself far enough to take hold of himself from inside. He had not yet found this "I" and hence could not say "I."

Animals below man do not have this problem. José Ortega y Gasset speaks of animals as suffering from what he calls "*alteración*" or "other-ation." Animals use signs as signals. Signals are not symbols as words are. A signal suggests one particular thing. A dog who responds to a signal doesn't think about the signal when the thing it signals isn't there, and he can't convert the signal into a word. So he can't mull over it, try it out in combination with other signals. Moreover, a dog can't enter into himself to get hold of himself in terms of "I." There is no "I" there. He is face-outward, to other things. His lack of inwardness is what brings Ortega y Gasset to say that an animal suffers from "otheration." So does a computer, even more so. Computer languages are quite different from the human languages that enable us to design computers. You can't put "I" on a computer. Or "you." A computer can't talk to a person.

ALTREE: I am troubled by one thing. Maybe it is a failure in understanding. It seems to me you have had a tendency to talk about language culturally or historically—language as habit-forming. Now all the young people, and it is part of our times, don't talk this way at all. I don't want to be tedious about this business of structuralism, but they will not find an explanation in the lapse of time and experience and so forth. This is a fact, not just a high-toned explanation of the current thinking of the younger generation that comes from Kenneth Kenniston or whoever.

I actually see this in the schools. It's a simple fact, but it is really consequential. There is a whole generation of English teachers who almost automatically think that words do not have meaning except in a frame. I think that is a very important point, especially when it comes to a consideration of the humanities. It disturbs me very much, and maybe I am obsolescent, but I automatically think about things historically. I automatically think about words and language as a singularity, explainable by history and such, and these teachers and students do not. They think of them as a part, not diachronically, but synchronically, horizontally.

ONG: If you are suggesting that many today think of language as structure, disregarding its historicity, of course I would have to admit that language is always structured. We can't deny that. And it has structures that are analyzable and that can be, in a way, pictured. On the other hand, it also has a kind of ultimate openness that shows that its structures are within something that is bigger than themselves.

All languages have histories. The only way to find out what a word means is to study its history. There is no other way. How have people been using it? What earlier meanings shaped its present meanings? And we can see, too, that there is no way of moving from an external event to a linguistic expression by pure structural maneuvers. Remember the scene with the bear in the telephone booth. You have to have a human interpreter who is creative. A computer simply cannot describe a happening. There is no way to program it to do it. You could program it so that it would do with one happening what a human being has done with one happening, but there is no way to get it itself to translate external goings-on into words, because it cannot be symbolically creative.

ALTREE: But all sorts of people today talk about the retreat from the word, George Steiner for one. Is there some reality to this? Have math, symbolic logic, science itself displaced the word as a mode of communication?

ONG: Well, it's no secret that George Steiner's thought and mine are fairly well attuned to one another, although we don't always talk about exactly the same things.

Yes, we tend to deal in mathematics and symbolic logic. Both math and symbolic logic are meaningless unless they are converted into ordinary words. There is a point at which the languages of mathematics and symbolic logic have to cross over into everyday language. They grow out of everyday language to start with. A computer cannot tell you, ultimately, what the results of its operation mean. They are only the results of a series of incredibly rapid local movements. Ultimately, a human being has to say what the computer work means.

On computers and in science generally, we conduct a great many quasi-intellectual operations at a distance from the spoken language, out of which the operations originate and to which they must return. To this extent we devocalize the word.

There are other ways, too, in which we devocalize the word. We reduce the word to space and maneuver its spatial parts silently. This reduction, however, had already begun with writing. It was intensified by print. With print, you can move around the types out of which you produce the reading material. Now we go further: we put bits of the reading material into motion. We have words on television screens that break up into little pieces, the letters moving around, turning upside down, crawling around like animals. These represent sounds, but sounds can't do this. So in that sense, the word is being—if we say lost sight of, we betray our visual bias—the word is losing its resonance in very real ways. But by reflecting on the situation, we can understand it and know that the spoken word is not truly lost but has entered into new interactions. You can't ever regain the past, but you can keep its values alive in your own way.

In another way we are gaining new resonances. In *The Presence of the Word* I have discussed the new world of electronic sound. With the electronic media voice has achieved a range never known before. One man can really talk to the entire globe all at once.

ALTREE: Your friend Steiner has said, "What save half-truths, gross simplifications or trivia can in fact be communicated to that semiliterate mass audience that popular democracy has summoned into the market place?" If that is a true description, what about the implications of this talking to mass audiences? Is that good sociology?

ONG: Mass audiences of the size we know—hundreds of millions—are relatively new in human experience. So are the mass languages they depend on. English is a mass language. It is spoken by hundreds of millions of people. When a language moves into this stage, it is a different kind of instrument from a language that is used by a little enclave of a few thousand persons, as many languages still are. A mass language can tend at certain points to operate in terms of or around slogans and images. Father William Lynch calls attention to this in his book *The Image Industries*, about such institutions as the press, movies, radio, and television, which project certain large, rather uncontrolled, magnificent figures around which we can group our knowledge and aspirations and often our unreal or false dreams. Products of the image industries can and do foster disastrous illusion.

Still, earlier use of language was not necessarily healthier. Primitive peoples can use their languages to work themselves into irrational and schizoid rage. Our difficulties are not worse than before, only of a different kind. We have greater possibilities for exploiting rather gross symbols, but also for understanding our problems. There is no convincing evidence that those subject to mass media are under more illusions than others, though they may be under different illusions. Studies show that children become critical of television advertisements at a very early age.

We do need to train as many people as possible to understand the projects of the image industries, to know how they function. For example, we need to interpret advertising. This doesn't mean necessarily to be hostile to it. It means to see what forces are really at work. They are not all sinister, though some may be. If you've been in the Soviet Union or other technologized countries with no commercial advertising, you are struck by the indirect service our advertising renders in giving a playful, invitational surface to public life. As a side-effect of its efforts to catch attention, advertising often cultivates a spirit of play. It is, paradoxically, often a relief from institutional suffocation. In the Soviet Union the public surface of life is all businesslike, ultraprogrammed. To Western visitors generally the U.S.S.R. seems like a barracks. This does not mean that advertising cannot have bad effects and bad side-effects, too, for it can. But its cultural effects are more complex than we commonly think, a mixture of the useful and the deleterious, of the viciously exploitative and the benign.

ALTREE: All languages are constantly modified, aren't they, in a lot of ways? There is an evolutionary trend in their adaptation to local conditions, to their environment. Besides, there are such great numbers of languages. Why this tremendous diversity in languages? We must have had more languages in the past than we have now because they disappear, but why this tremendous diversity in the whole spectrum?

ONG: Many have disappeared, and more are disappearing. They also
merge. When languages merge, though, the grammars don't merge much.
The vocabularies merge. By far most of our words in English are borrowed from other languages or manufactured from borrowed words, but
the grammatical history of English is basically Anglo-Saxon. A competing foreign language can bring simplification in grammar: the presence of
Norman French after A.D. 1066 in England helped simplify our declen-
sions. But we did not borrow Norman-French grammar as we borrowed
Norman-French words. The influence of foreign grammars can be real,
but it is often subtle and difficult to trace.

We are learning how to describe the development of languages in
greater and greater detail and even to describe laws at work. (Grimm's
Law about sound shifts is well known; it was one of the first laws found
to be at work in the evolution of the Indo-European languages.) But many
unanswered questions remain. We don't know how many languages there
were at the beginning. And we don't know really how human beings first
started talking.

We do know that languages respond to the environment, and in countless ways. Colors are a good example because in different languages they
vary. In French there is no adjective for the color orange. When a
Frenchman is faced with a color that an English-speaker would call
orange, he commonly tries to decide whether it is red or yellow. He can
say "the color of an orange," as we could say "the color of a banana." Or
he can say "oranged" ("*orange*") as we might say "bananaed." But
"orange" is not a color. On the other hand, the Frenchman has a color he
calls "flea"—"*puce*" is the French word. It means flea and also the color
of a flea. "This jacket is navy blue and that jacket is flea." We use "puce"
in English sometimes in women's fashions, borrowing from the French,
but we don't think of "flea" as a color.

The colors that a language uses are not derived from an abstract
analysis of the spectrum, but from objects that the environment makes
available. Purple for us means a kind of deep violet, but the Latin word
"*purpura*," from which our word purple comes, actually meant the kind
of deep crimson dye that the ancient Romans could get from a certain
shellfish, called "*purpura*," from the Semitic, via Greek. You remember
Lydia in the Acts of the Apostles was a dealer in this dye. "*Purpura*"
means the shellfish and the color produced from it. We're unfamiliar with
the shellfish and its product, and the color to which we attach "*purpura*"
or "purple" has shifted. I believe ours is more bluish than the Latin "*purpura*." So you can analyze to some extent, I suppose, the environment of
a people in terms of their way of sorting out colors in their vocabulary.

Naturally, there will be a fairly economical way in virtually all languages of saying "green," because you find at least some green plants everywhere you find man, except of course on the moon. But in various locales, many of the other colors may be more or less infrequent.

Influence of environment shows up in all kinds of ways in vocabulary. You often hear that the Eskimos have—generally some astronomical figure is cited—a thousand words, let's say, for different kinds of snow, but no generic word for snow. And the Arabs, you may hear, have a thousand words for camel, but no generic word. I am not sure what the facts are here, but minimizing generic terms and multiplying specific terms for major items in environment or culture are not peculiar to Eskimos or Arabs. Novices at football talk of "players," while the fan talks of linesmen, guards, centers, quarterbacks, broken-field runners—new specific terms are being generated all the time. For most people every horse is a horse, but for horsey people a "horse" tends to mean an adult male horse. Other representatives of the species are foals or fillies or brood mares, or whatever. Absence or infrequency of a generic word often means that you are in a very specialized culture or subculture, where people tend to know exactly what they are talking about.

ALTREE: Language, then, is a kind of window into reality, isn't it? It can show us characteristics culturally important to people. How much does language show about culture?

ONG: What language shows about culture is almost limitless. One new word, such as "astronaut," can reflect not only our interest in space exploration but also the historical relationship of English to Ancient Greek, from which the word is formed, as well as to Latin and French, through which the "*astro*" and the "*naut*" came from Greek into English. Otherwise we'd say "star-sailors," which is what "astronaut" etymologically signifies. You could also conclude something about the culture of the ancient Greeks—their familiarity with ships and so on.

ALTREE: This seems to suggest that to know a culture thoroughly you have to know the language of the culture. Should we teach more Chinese, for example, in the schools? Both to study culture and language itself?

ONG: Yes. Our ignorance of foreign languages is going to be an increasing disability of Americans in the next few years. By comparison with Europeans, and for understandable reasons, we were very badly off linguistically as of, say, thirty years ago. We are such a large country. Except for the edges of the United States—the northeast edge and the southwest edge—you have to go a long, long way to find a concentration of native speakers of any language other than English. A Frenchman or a German can move himself into another language group in just a few hours, maybe on a bicycle or even on foot.

We did quite well after World War II in improving our knowledge of foreign languages, having learned our lesson a bit. Right now, however, we are turning away from foreign languages. One reason, I think unfortunately, is a kind of narcissism from which American culture suffers at present, an unwillingness to study anyone but ourselves. But there is another problem here, too. Americans use a language spoken by several hundred million people, and with this size market, things that are done in other languages are likely to get translated into English quite quickly. Besides a high percentage of the original work in the humanities, in science, and in social sciences done across the world is done in English, simply because there are so many people who know it.

It is efficient and relatively inexpensive to translate into a large language. It takes as many persons to translate into Finnish, with its four and a half million speakers, as into English, with its more than 300,000,000 native speakers plus its millions of other non-native users. In fact, it takes more because you need to translate more things into Finnish, since a vast amount of the original work comes out in English and very little in Finnish. Finns are active intellectually, but their numbers are disablingly small. All this means that those who speak English are in a very favored position with regard to getting hold of new information, new theories, and so forth.

But no matter how many persons speak your language, it is still only one language and limited. A translation of a literary work never gives you all that is in the original, and it gives you some things that aren't. Knowing a foreign language provides you with a new window into reality and enables you to evaluate your own English-language views. I really don't see how anyone can teach English language or literature in depth without some knowledge of a foreign language, something to compare English to so you have some sense of what there is in English that's shared by other languages and what's specific to it, or so that you have some sense for the sorts of things that can be had in another language but not in English. These comparative views are extremely important. Without them, you are hemmed in. Foreign languages liberate—they have long been essential to a liberal education.

ALTREE: How many languages are there—or how many dialects?

ONG: There are a lot of languages in the world, certainly several thousand. It's difficult to count languages, for this reason: Suppose you have five villages next to one another, all speaking languages that in some sense are Italian. The people in villages #1 and #2, which are next to one another, can understand one another. The man in the third village, the one in the middle, can understand both of them, too, although he has a little more difficulty with #1 than he has with #2. He can also understand the two villages on the other side of him, villages #4 and #5, and they can understand one another. But village #2 can't understand #4 or #5, and village #1 can't understand #4 or #5 either. From the point of view of the man in the middle, there is only one language, with five dialects including his own, because he understands everybody around him, whereas from the point of view of the extremes, #1 and #4 or #5, #2 and #4 or #5, there are at least two languages.

Now for reasons of this sort, it is difficult to distinguish languages from dialects. Nevertheless, we can make some sort of arrangements for distinguishing languages in practice on the basis of intelligibility: two persons who cannot understand one another's speech at all can be said to speak two different languages. It is quite safe to say that there are several thousand languages in the world.

Americans seldom recognize the magnitude of the world's problems. Nigeria is a classic example. You could certainly gather in a room some thirty Nigerians of whom not one could understand what any of the others were saying unless he knew a language other than his mother tongue. A former student of mine spent two years with the Peace Corps in Nigeria, and her chief concern for the little tribe she worked with was that if her people went more than thirty-five miles from their village, there was nobody in the entire world they could talk to, unless they had learned a foreign language. We have to remember in speaking about languages that presumably this is the way all languages were in the beginning. Most languages still are the languages of small numbers of people and, as we've said already, have never become written languages at all.

Many Europeans, including highly educated Europeans, do not speak at home the way they speak in the schoolroom or on television. The dialect they speak at home is not a written language—there is no fixed way even to spell it. Such dialects are like ghetto languages in the United States, which aren't normally written, although there is some attempt to write them now. There are signs that dialects in Europe and elsewhere are disappearing, largely under the influence of the mass media. This is too bad, but there is not much you can do about it, because people tend to standardize. What will happen of course is that many of the features of these smaller languages, especially vocabulary, will be incorporated into the larger languages. And you can make taped recordings of disappearing dialects for later study.

But to get back to our subject, the failure to learn foreign languages is going to have a very damaging effect on the American character. It will tend to make us more egotistic than anybody ought to be—and we have problems with egotism already—and will damage our sense of reality, our ability to relate to other people, and our knowledge in general.

Another reason why language study is being given up is that it is hard. At least, this is a reason given by educators when it is dropped. You shouldn't study a subject just because it is hard, but on the other hand you shouldn't not study something just because it is hard. At the very time when it is most desirable that we relate to other people in the world, as the world is becoming more and more one culture, we are putting ourselves in a position where we can relate to other people only on our own terms. This has long been a major fault of Americans: we get along with everybody by adjusting them to ourselves.

A further reason given for dropping foreign languages is that their study is unreal—they have no immediate use. How much of what anyone studies has immediate use? Even in so practical, down-to-earth a field as engineering, how much has? Ask a fifty-year-old engineer. "Practical" courses are often the soonest out of date. We study largely to open ourselves up, to free ourselves from our limited horizons—to liberate ourselves. This is the point of a liberal education, education for freedom. And a new language—not only its literature, but even its grammar— opens new windows into existence.

You see, our national experience is unfavorable to us here. We feel that we are close to all the people in the world because we have absorbed peoples from every continent. But we forget that the ones who have come here are the ones who decided to become Americans. When we are abroad with other people who don't speak our language, we are all too likely to assume, and I have seen this over and over again, that all the people around us would be Americans if they only had a chance. As a matter of fact, they may not have the slightest desire to be Americans, and may even be repelled by the idea. If there is one way to make yourself unpopular, it's to assume that everybody else wants to be as much like you as possible.

The assumption that we are so privileged that everyone wants to be like us is a peculiarly American problem. We can get over it a little bit if we undergo the humiliation of trying to learn another language. If we are full human beings, we are called on to let ourselves be absorbed into other people's points of view as well as to welcome others into our country. It's a two-way street. There is a kind of American arrogance that we need to get over—all the more because it doesn't seem to us to be arrogance, but friendliness.

ALTREE: I think it's because the eclectic character of our culture makes many Americans feel a little insecure. Security comes with homogenization, so the second-generation immigrant doesn't want to talk his parents' language.

ONG: Yes, we have stressed standardization to achieve psychological security. There has been a real reason for this. No use blaming anybody because there is nobody to blame, but there is some point in seeing the disability you labor under so that you can do something about it.

ALTREE: You said it was hard to study foreign languages and so they are neglected for that reason sometimes. Isn't it also hard to study your own language? Isn't that one reason the study of our own language has been neglected, almost paralleling the neglect of the study of foreign languages?

ONG: Yes, this is true. It is hard to study your own language. Sometimes we don't think so. No less a person than Sir Philip Sidney in *The Defense of Poesy* wrote of English that "grammar it might have, but it needs it not, being so easy in itself." Sidney lived in Shakespeare's day. When he and Shakespeare were born there was no English grammar; nobody had ever written one. Englishmen, like all Europeans, thought of grammar in terms of Latin and Greek, which, from the point of view of a person who has grown up speaking English, of course are hard. But we have found out since that there is a very complicated English grammar, and that English seems "easy in itself" only to those who have grown up speaking it.

But even native English-speakers speak English with varying degrees of effectiveness, and one way to better yourself in speaking it is to study it. To better your language of course also means to better your thinking and to better your whole education. There is really no way to educate a person that does not take into consideration the improvement of his language.

ALTREE: And not just in the English class. This applies in history classes and elsewhere.

ONG: It applies in all of them. One of the problems faced by English departments in colleges and universities around the country is what happens after you do your best to get the students trained in English. At Saint Louis University, when our students finish freshman English, they have to take an exit examination, and if they don't pass it they have to take another course until they can pass this examination. We know that at the time we have certified them as passing the exit examination they are capable of quite good writing performances. But if faculty in the other departments don't demand good writing, all the effort that was originally put into the teaching of writing goes down the drain. Like others, I have found in my own experience that students write as well as you demand. Unfortunately, even in the best colleges and universities, good writing is not demanded by everyone on the faculty.

ALTREE: Then you assume the general idiom of communication must be kept in good order, precise, rich in vocabulary, figures of speech, and so on. It seems to me there has been a diminishment, a degeneration, in our cultural sensibilities. Not only do we abandon the study of language because it is a hard task, but increasingly there seems to be a tendency to emphasize that which is immediate, instantly popular, and so forth. Time has been preempted for other subjects.

ONG: We live in the first age that has ever engaged in an academic study of itself. The reason for this is that we live in an age that knows more than earlier ages have known about the past. At least it has access to such knowledge in books. Until you know a lot about the past, there isn't much to say about the present. It is like asking a fish to write a treatise on humidity. Everything is humid, everything is just as humid as everything else, so what are you going to say? All you can say is that everything is humid. In the water, even the sounds are humid.

But throw a fish out on dry land, and humidity becomes something to talk about—if he could only talk. Learn about a world different from the present, and the present becomes something to talk about. Once you know something about the past, you can see there are points at which the present is like it and points at which the present is different. You can trace classical influence, you can see the Hebrew influence, the Christian influence, the Romantic influence, and the influence of political and scientific developments, the influence of religious developments, and so on, and you can see how these things make us like the past in some ways and how they have changed us in other ways. As a result of our accumulation of knowledge about what is not our present, we can study our present. This kind of study is a new thing. Immanuel Kant, for example, either lectured on ancient philosophers, past philosophers, or he lectured on general principles. He didn't give courses in contemporary philosophy, much less on what philosophy will be ten years from now—as "futurologists" in our midst undertake to do.

Since we have this access to the present, we do study contemporary language and literature in school, which Shakespeare never did. Now I believe in studying the present world. For one thing, you have to get students in through their own door, and it is much easier for a student to relate to things that are in his idiom and in his own world than to something that's remote. However, if you are going to provide a liberal education, you also have to liberate the person from his own world so that he achieves some distance from it, knows other options. This makes it possible for him to understand his own position. To understand anything, we need both closeness to it and distance from it.

You have to help the student discover what some other kinds of things were like. Moreover, you have to show him how his own world—and language—got this way and how it might not have been this way if things had been a little different in the past and people had chosen different options, if things had developed in different fashion.

What I am saying boils down to this: you simply cannot hope to understand the present without understanding the past. But you can't hope to understand the past without understanding the present. Antiquarianism is out. The cry for relevance is important. This doesn't mean that you study the past to find out that Socrates is just like that fellow next door—which means you've probably learned nothing about either of them. But it does mean that you study the past in order to see how it relates to the present and how the present relates to it.

One of the difficulties, I think, in our culture right now is that since we are pretty good at analyzing ourselves and since we are so largely deficient in hard-nosed humanistic skills such as foreign languages, more and more students are opting for courses in things like American culture. I am all for courses in American culture. I study it and write about it quite a great deal myself. On the other hand, no one who knows only American culture knows very much about American culture.

ALTREE: I'm beginning to feel more and more somber: We don't know foreign languages nor the people they belong to. We opt for easy subjects at great expense to the humanities and so weaken the human nature that makes us ourselves. And earlier, you were talking about the specialization of language and the subjectivity of reporting. How do we understand each other? How does the "I" ever talk with the "you"?

ONG: When we are faced with the kind of paradox that you pose, the way the "I" relates to the "you," we must respond with another paradox. We speak to one another because each of us is alone. We form a unity with one another only out of isolation. Every human being lives in loneliness. You don't know what it feels like to be me, and I don't know what it feels like to be you. You do not know what "I" feels like to me.

The same is true of all human beings. Even a husband and wife never find out what it feels like to be the other. They try, they get awfully close. But no matter what, each of us remains isolated in his or her own consciousness, each one in his own little prison. And yet such isolated beings are the only ones on earth who can communicate. This is what a mere animal can't do. He can't say "I," can't enter into himself in isolation. So he has nothing to say. We can communicate, paradoxically, because we are completely different from one another.

We know one another by a kind of empathy, it is true. We know and we don't know what it means to be the other person. I know that being you means to be somehow like me without at all being me. But since every bit of me is me, what could be like me without being me? Knowledge gives out at this point, and we must, I think, speak quite simply of what we have to do about it. When knowledge gives out as a bridge, we make up for it with love. That is what you have to call it— love. Not only between husband and wife, or friends, but even in the more casual or routine kinds of social situations, love must still be present.

If I am going to communicate with anybody at all, in language or otherwise, there has to be a certain love between us or communication won't work, because the bridge won't be made. It's seldom that the love is pure, unmixed with other attitudes or reactions. But some love must be there. You have to give yourself to the other, assuming that the other person understands you and that you understand him. You in a way experience the other person.

It has become a kind of fad today to talk about having experiences. We are told to undergo or cultivate a great variety of experiences. But you don't have time for much experience. For any normal human being, 99.99 per cent of his experiences are vicarious. And the way you experience a real experience depends on your previous vicarious or imagined experiences. Any person who relies principally on his own direct experiences is impoverished. This is one reason why we read literature. This is why we use language. So that we can know experiences that we haven't directly had. This is what it is to be a human being, to be able to enter imaginatively and empathetically into countless experiences of others. A psychiatrist would go out of his mind if he had to have gone through all the experiences that he has to deal with. So would a priest hearing confessions. But you know what the others are talking about.

ALTREE: So when we talk here about language, we're not talking about a remote academic subject. There's a cultural crisis in the land, and language—talk—seems. to me increasingly pathological and unable to cope.

ONG: One part of the crisis is our relationship to ourselves—what we touched on earlier when we spoke of our desire to study ourselves and of the present trend to narcissism. Human consciousness is relentlessly reflective. We keep turning back more and more on ourselves. If you don't keep a complementary sense of distance—I prefer that term to objectivity—you are in trouble, and one of the major problems of contemporary man is achieving distance. We know the kind of person who tries to solve everything by having a sensitivity session and another sensitivity session—this may be all right, but at best close relationships—even if they are really achieved—are only half of life. We also need to be able to back off from ourselves, to assess ourselves and the actuality around us. Language enables us to do this, too.

ALTREE: Given this cultural crisis that we have been talking about, do you have any words of wisdom for the schools? Assuming the importance of language, assuming the schools' willingness to do something about it, what ought they to do in the present situation?

ONG: Of course there is one thing all schools ought to do, always—get better teachers. But that is hard, there aren't that many around. And improve the performance of those they have. Thank God we do have many excellent and dedicated teachers, but we just don't have enough of them. What should schools do? The trouble is when you are talking about language teaching, you are talking, really, about the core of the humanities, and one of the things you need here is the kind of confidence that can come only from learning. You have to *know*. So I think teachers should try to know more about language—which inevitably means about actuality itself. That's probably the basic need. When I say know more I don't mean in any rote way, but in ways that really face the difficulties. Too many teachers of language support themselves on intellectual crutches. We are particularly prone to this in America because we are so literate. I think beyond a doubt we are the most literate culture the world has ever produced. The Middle Ages were the most literate culture until their day. We have far outdistanced them.

We mythologize our culture as growing out of written documents—the *Declaration of Independence* and the *Constitution*—as no other nation on earth ever has. Many Americans, to judge by many student and teachers I have encountered, don't believe a word is a real word unless it is in a dictionary. Until then, even though people use it and know what it means, it's not a real word. It becomes real only when you write it down, or better when you print it in a dictionary. This makes the dictionary not an adaptable tool that you use for your own purposes, but a crutch on which you lean.

We have to be willing to face the fact that language is a growing thing. I am not at all urging that we don't study grammar—we have to study grammar. And we have to study the Standard English we need for getting along socially or in business and for most writing purposes. But let's give people the real reasons for the rules we may state. Don't say that two negatives make a positive in English, because most of the time they don't. "I ain't never going there." There is no native English-speaking person who thinks that means "I am going there." English grammar is not mathematics: in English negatives most often reinforce one another. Many languages work this way. There are of course certain conditions in which you can make one negative in English negate another—you might say, "The matter is not unimportant," meaning "The matter is important"—but often it doesn't work that way at all.

What we should tell boys and girls is that if you habitually say, "I ain't never going there," you can't get a job as a receptionist, and you can't get into medical school or succeed in politics. You can't get along because you show that you are unfamiliar with the mainstream of the language that you are operating in, that you are out of contact with the main line of effective thinking and feeling around you. Don't say that if it is "ungrammatical," people can't understand you, because most of them can understand what is "ungrammatical" very well. By "ungrammatical" we normally mean not conforming to the prestige grammar of the language. There are other grammars—even "I ain't never going there" is governed by a grammar, but it is a grammar out of touch with the main line of achievement in the English-speaking world. So I think one of the things to do is to approach the language realistically, but also in a firm way. For the demands of prestige grammar are often inexorable, Not mastering them may make you a social and intellectual cripple.

ALTREE: You are saying not all expressions are equal?

ONG: I am saying that it is false to say that many so-called nongrammatical expressions, nonprestige expressions, are unintelligible and therefore incorrect. And I am saying that they may have social and intellectual disadvantages. Teachers need to explain this as they teach prestige grammar, explain what is really meant by "correct" and "incorrect."

ALTREE: In the absence of anything really vital to say, they will say . . .

ONG: They will make a factitious rule that isn't really there.

ALTREE: And not in the ultimate attractive to students.

ONG: Yes, because students see through it. Like two negatives always make a positive. Such "rules" are ways of dodging the real problems. Grammar is more than a list of little "do's" and "don't's." It involves cultural attitudes, the whole person of the teacher. This can frighten teachers and does.

And if grammar can frighten teachers, literature can even more. If a work of literature is any good, it really does threaten your world somehow, it makes you look at the ultimate in life—the precariousness of human relations, the fragility and simultaneous inexorability of existence, the imminence of death. Then the work of literature resolves the threat. It resolves it of course at a literary level, not at an existential level. Literature does not of itself cure real psychological problems of readers, though it may be used in therapy, as a horseback ride or handicraft may be. But literature can threaten us psychologically. To teach it, you have to be able to face the threat it offers. And many teachers, as well as many students, are afraid to do this.

The relationship between language and actuality is delicate and complex and inescapable. It is difficult to talk about the sorts of things that we have been talking about here—about the way, for example, in which even a factual report of an event has to be creative. This upsets some people because they think that the objective world is thereby destroyed, that all reports are equally true. This is not so. If two reports of the same event flatly contradict one another, at least one of them is untrue. On the other hand, any report even of a fact is creative because there is never just one thing to say about anything. No matter how accurate your report is, there are other true things that could be said about the same event of fact—not contradictory but supplementary. There is no one-to-one relation between words and things. Remember the bear in the highway telephone booth with which we began.

Language is an organization of chaos. A person has to be able to face the chaos, in order to teach language. This is what is difficult to do. I don't believe people have this kind of insecurity when they are teaching certain other subjects—let us say geography or meteorology or mathematics. But when you get into something that is as close to man as language is, as deep within man's interior, where the great philosophical and religious questions resonate, you are dealing with vital matters. In the last analysis, the question of what language is, is a kind of total question. It seems to touch everything else in you. Man's idea of his own human existence, of what the sacred is, of what love and hate and human values are, of what God is, these are all tied up with language. God's word is of high significance in most religions. In the Hebrew tradition, God's word is divine power. Christians believe that God's word is actually a person, the Second Person of the Trinity, one God with the Father and the Holy Spirit. The Word became flesh in Jesus Christ. "In the beginning was the word." Dealing with words, man everywhere has found himself deeply involved in questions of time and eternity and of his own identity. A little language is a dangerous thing.

Bibliographical Note

Edwin Sapir's *Language* is still one of the best introductions to the study of speech. Some of Sapir's most important essays are available in his *Culture, Language and Personality.* In three thoughtful and full, but short lectures published as *Language and Mind,* Noam Chomsky discusses the richness and depth of linguistic performance and the way in which human speech transcends all "scientific" theories attempting to encompass it. *Introductory Readings on Language* (Anderson and Stageberg) provides a wide selection of readings from a variety of authors and generous bibliographies of further materials. For a well-written and simple textbook treatment, see Arlotto.

How language is learned is discussed by David McNeill. The relationship of dialects to social conditions is treated in a collection of studies, *Language and Poverty* (Williams), and more briefly in *The Social Meaning of Language* (Pride). The late Maurice Merleau-Ponty, in his *Phenomenology of Perception*, includes a chapter on "The Body as Expression and Speech," which is both profound and close to human experience.

Of Father Ong's books, the one most closely related to this conversation on language is *The Presence of the Word.* Other books of his including related material are *The Barbarian Within, In the Human Grain,* and

Rhetoric, Romance and Technology. More specialized in its research is his *Ramus, Method, and the Decay of Dialogue.*

Works Cited

Anderson, Wallace L. and Norman C. Stageberg, eds. *Introductory Readings on Language.* Rev. ed. New York: Holt, Rinehart, and Winston, 1966.

Arlotto, Anthony. *Introduction to Historical Linguistics.* Boston: Houghton Mifflin, 1972.

Chomsky, Noam. *Language and Mind.* New York: Harcourt, Brace, and World, 1968.

Gibson, Walker. *Tough, Sweet and Stuffy: An Essay on Modern American Prose Styles.* Bloomington: Indiana UP, 1966.

Langer, Susanne K. *Philosophy in a New Key: A Study in the Symbolism of Reason, Rite, and Art.* 3rd ed. Cambridge, MA: Harvard UP, 1969 (Original 1951)

Lynch, William F. *The Image Industries.* New York: Sheed and Ward, 1959.

McNeill, David. *The Acquisition of Language: The Study of Developmental Psycholinguistics.* New York: Harper and Row, 1970.

Menyuk, Paula. *Sentences Children Use.* Cambridge, MA: M.I.T. Press, 1969.

Merleau-Ponty, Maurice. *Phenomenology of Perception.* Trans. Colin Smith. New York: Humanities Press, 1962.

Ohman, Richard. "Grammar and Meaning." *American Heritage Dictionary of the English Language.* Ed. William Morris. New York: American Heritage, 1973. xxxi-xxxiv.

Ong, Walter J. *The Barbarian Within.* New York: Macmillan, 1962.

—. *In the Human Grain.* New York: Macmillan, 1967.

—. *The Presence of the Word.* New Haven and London: Yale UP, 1967.

—. *Ramus, Method, and the Decay of Dialogue.* Cambridge, MA: Harvard UP, 1958.

—. *Rhetoric, Romance, and Technology.* Ithaca and London: Cornell UP, 1971.

Pride, J. B. *The Social Meaning of Language.* London: Oxford UP, 1971.

Sapir, Edwin. *Culture, Language and Personality.* Ed. David G. Mandelbaum. Berkeley: U of California P, 1960.

—. *Language.* New York: Harcourt, Brace, 1949. (Original 1921).

Williams, Frederick, ed. *Language and Poverty.* Chicago: Markham Publishing, 1970.

22

The Writer's Audience Is Always a Fiction (1975)

> *Epistola . . . non erubescit.* [A letter does not blush.]
> —CICERO, *Epistolae ad familiares* 5. 12. 1.

> *Ubi nihil erit quae scribas, id ipsum scribes.* [Where there's nothing to write, write that.]
> —CICERO, *Epistolae ad Atticum* 4. 8. 4.

I

Although there is a large and growing literature on the differences between oral and written verbalization, many aspects of the differences have not been looked into at all, and many others, although well known, have not been examined in their full implications. Among these latter is the relationship, of the so-called "audience" to writing as such, to the situation that inscribed communication establishes and to the roles that readers as readers are consequently called on to play. Some studies in literary history and criticism at times touch near this subject, but none, it appears, take it up in any detail.

The standard locus in Western intellectual tradition for study of audience responses has been rhetoric. But rhetoric originally concerned oral communication, as is indicated by its name, which comes from the Greek word for public speaking. Over two millennia, rhetoric has been gradually extended to include writing more and more, until today, in highly technological cultures, this is its principal concern. But the extension has come gradually and has advanced *pari passu* with the slow and largely unnoticed emergence of markedly chirographic and typographic styles out of those originating in oral performance, with the result that the differentiation between speech and writing has never become a matter of urgent concern for the rhetoric of any given age: when orality was in the ascendancy, rhetoric was oral-focused; as orality yielded to writing, the focus of rhetoric was slowly shifted, unreflectively for the most part, and without notice.

Histories of the relationship between literature and culture have something to say about the status and behavior of readers, before and after reading given materials, as do mass media studies, readership surveys, liberation programs for minorities or various other classes of persons, books on reading skills, works of literary criticism, and works on linguistics, especially those addressing differences between hearing and reading. But most of these studies, except perhaps literary criticism and linguistic studies, treat only perfunctorily, if at all, the roles imposed on the reader by a written or printed text not imposed by spoken utterance. Formalist or structuralist critics, including French theorists such as Paul Ricoeur as well as Roland Barthes, Jacques Derrida, Michel Foucault, Philippe Sollers, and Tsvetan Todorov, variously advert to the immediacy of the oral as against writing and print and occasionally study differences between speech and writing, as Louis Lavelle did much earlier in *La Parole et l'écriture* (1942). In treating of masks and "shadows" in his *Sociologie du théâtre* (1965), Jean Duvignaud brilliantly discusses the projections of a kind of collective consciousness on the part of theater audiences. But none of these appear to broach directly the question of readers' roles called for by a written text, either synchronically as such roles stand at present or diachronically as they have developed through history. Linguistic theorists such as John R. Searle and John L. Austin treat "illocutionary acts" (denoted by "warn," "command," "state," etc.), but these regard the speaker's or writer's need in certain instances to secure a special hold on those he addresses, not any special role imposed by writing (Searle 24-28, where Austin is cited; see bibliography 146-48).

Wayne Booth in *The Rhetoric of Fiction* and Walker Gibson, whom Booth quotes, come quite close to the concerns of the present study in their treatment of the "mock reader," as does Henry James, whom Booth also cites, in his discussion of the way an author makes "his reader very much as he makes his character" (49-52, 138, 363-64). But this hint of James is not developed—there is no reason why it should be—and neither Booth nor Gibson discusses in any detail the history of the ways in which readers have been called on to relate to texts before them. Neither do Robert Scholes and Robert Kellogg in their invaluable work, *The Nature of Narrative*: they skirt the subject in their chapter on "The Oral Heritage of Written Narrative" (17-56) but remain chiefly concerned with the oral performer, the writer, and techniques, rather than with the recipient of the message. Yet a great many of the studies noted here as well as many others, among which might be mentioned Norman N. Holland's *The Dynamics of Literary Response* (1968), suggest the time is ripe for a study of the history of readers and their enforced roles, for they show that we have ample phenomenological and literary sophistication to manage many of the complications involved.

Among recent short studies exhibiting concerns tangent to but not the same as those of the present article might be mentioned three from *New Literary History*: Georges Poulet, Geoffrey H. Hartman, and J. Hillis Miller, as well as Gerald Prince, whose essay is concerned with the "narrataire" only in novels ("narratee" in a related English-language study by the same author as noted by him here) and with literary taxonomy more than history. Paul Ricoeur also addresses this topic.

So long as verbal communication is reduced to a simplistic mechanistic model that supposedly moves corpuscular units of something labeled "information" back and forth along tracks between two termini, there is of course no special problem with those who assimilate the written or printed word. For the speaker, the audience is in front of him. For the writer, the audience is simply further away, in time or space or both. A surface inscribed with information can neutralize time by preserving the information and conquer space by moving the information to its recipient over distances that sound cannot traverse. If, however, we put aside this alluring but deceptively neat and mechanistic mock-up and look at verbal communication in its human actuality, noting that words consist not of corpuscular units but of evanescent sound and that as Maurice Merleau-Ponty has pointed out (181-84), words are never fully determined in their abstract signification but have meaning only with relation to man's body and to its interaction with its surroundings, problems with the writer's audience begin to show themselves. Writing calls for difficult, and often quite mysterious, skills. Except for a small corps of highly trained writers, most persons could get into written form few if any of the complicated and nuanced meanings they regularly convey orally. One reason is evident: the spoken word is part of present actuality and has its meaning established by the total situation in which it comes into being. Context for the spoken word is simply present, centered in the person speaking and the one or ones to whom he addresses himself and to whom he is related existentially in terms of the circumambient actuality (Ong 116-17). But the meaning caught in writing comes provided with no such present circumambient actuality, at least normally. (One might except special cases of written exchanges between persons present to one another physically but with oral channels blocked: two deaf persons, for example, or two persons who use different variants of Chinese and are orally incomprehensible to one another but can communicate through the same written characters, which carry virtually the same meanings though they are sounded differently in the different varieties of Chinese.)

Such special cases apart, the person to whom the writer addresses himself normally is not present at all. Moreover, with certain special exceptions such as those just suggested, he must not be present. I am writing a book that will be read by thousands, or, I modestly hope, by tens of thousands. So, please, get out of the room. I want to be alone. Writing normally calls for some kind of withdrawal.

How does the writer give body to the audience for whom he writes? It would be fatuous to think that the writer addressing a so-called general audience tries to imagine his readers individually. A well-known novelist friend of mine only laughed when I asked him if, as he was writing a novel, he imagined his real readers—the woman on the subway deep in his book, the student in his room, the businessman on a vacation, the scholar in his study. There is no need for a novelist to feel his "audience" this way at all. It may be, of course, that at one time or another he imagines himself addressing one or another real person. But not all his readers in their particularities. Practically speaking, of course, and under the insistent urging of editors and publishers, he does have to take into consideration the real social, economic, and psychological state of possible readers. He has to write a book that real persons will buy and read. But I am speaking—or writing—here of the "audience" that fires the writer's imagination. If it consists of the real persons who he hopes will buy his book, they are not these persons in an untransmuted state.

T. S. Eliot suggests some of the complexities of the writer-and-audience problem in his essay on "The Three Voices of Poetry," by which he means (1) "the voice of the poet talking to himself—or to nobody," (2) "the voice of the poet addressing an audience," and (3) "the voice of the poet when he attempts to create a dramatic character speaking" (96). Eliot, in the same work, states that these voices often mingle and indeed, for him, "are most often found together" (108). The approach I am here taking cuts across Eliot's way of enunciating the problem and, I believe, brings out some of the built-in relationships among the three voices which help account for their intermingling. The "audience" addressed by Eliot's second voice not only is elusively constituted but also, even in its elusiveness, can determine the voice of the poet talking to himself or to nobody (Eliot's first sense of "voice"), because in talking to oneself one has to objectify oneself, and one does so in ways learned from addressing others. A practiced writer talking "to himself" in a poem has a quite different feeling for "himself" than does a complete illiterate.

Although I have thus far followed the common practice in using the term "audience," it is really quite misleading to think of a writer as dealing with an "audience," even though certain considerations may at times oblige us to think this way. More properly, a writer addresses readers—only, he does not quite "address" them either: he writes to or for them. The orator has before him an audience that is a true audience, a collectivity. "Audience" is a collective noun. There is no such collective noun for readers, nor, so far as I am able to puzzle out, can there be. "Readers" is a plural. Readers do not form a collectivity, acting here and now on one another and on the speaker as members of an audience do. We can devise a singularized concept for them, it is true, such as "readership." We can say that the *Reader's Digest* has a readership of I don't know how many millions—more than it is comfortable to think about, at any rate. But "readership" is not a collective noun. It is an abstraction in a way that "audience" is not.

The contrast between hearing and reading (running the eye over signals that encode sound) can be caught if we imagine a speaker addressing an audience equipped with texts. At one point, the speaker asks the members of the audience all to read silently a paragraph out of the text. The audience immediately fragments. It is no longer a unit. Each individual retires into his own microcosm. When the readers look up again, the speaker has to gather them into a collectivity once more. This is true even if he is the author of the text they are reading.

To sense more fully the writer's problem with his so-called audience, let us envision a class of students asked to write on the subject to which schoolteachers, jaded by summer, return compulsively every autumn: "How I Spent My Summer Vacation." The teacher makes the easy assumption, inviting and plausible but false, that the chief problem of a boy and a girl in writing is finding a subject actually part of his or her real life. In-close subject matter is supposed to solve the problem of invention. Of course it does not. The problem is not simply what to say but also whom to say it to. Say? The student is not talking. He is writing. No one is listening. There is no feedback. Where does he find his "audience"? He has to make his readers up, fictionalize them.

If the student knew what he was up against better than the teacher giving the assignment seemingly does, he might ask, "Who wants to know?" The answer is not easy. Grandmother? He never tells grandmother. His father or mother? There's a lot he would not want to tell them, that's sure. His classmates? Imagine the reception if he suggested they sit down and listen quietly while he told them how he spent his summer vacation. The teacher? There is no conceivable setting in which he could imagine telling his teacher how he spent his summer vacation other than in writing this paper, so that writing for the teacher does not solve his problems but only restates them. In fact, most young people do not tell anybody how they spent their summer vacation, much less write down how they spent it. The subject may be in-close; the use it is to be put to remains unfamiliar, strained, bizarre.

How does the student solve the problem? In many cases, in a way somewhat like the following. He has read, let us say, *The Adventures of Tom Sawyer*. He knows what this book felt like, how the voice in it addressed its readers, how the narrator hinted to his readers that they were related to him and he to them, whoever they may actually have been or may be. Why not pick up that voice and, with it, its audience? Why not make like Samuel Clemens and write for whomever Samuel Clemens was writing for? This even makes it possible to write for his teacher—itself likely to be a productive ploy—whom he certainly has never been quite able to figure out. But he knows his teacher has read *Tom Sawyer*, has heard the voice in the book, and could therefore obviously make like a *Tom Sawyer* reader. His problem is solved, and he goes ahead. The subject matter now makes little difference, provided that it is something like Mark Twain's and that it interests him on some grounds or other. Material in-close to his real life is not essential, though, of course, it might be welcome now that he has a way to process it.

If the writer succeeds in writing, it is generally because he can fictionalize in his imagination an audience he has learned to know not from daily life but from earlier writers who were fictionalizing in their imagination audiences they had learned to know in still earlier writers, and so on back to the dawn of written narrative. If and when he becomes truly adept, an "original writer," he can do more than project the earlier audience, he can alter it. Thus it was that Samuel Clemens in *Life on the Mississippi* could not merely project the audience that the many journalistic writers about the Midwestern rivers had brought into being, but could also shape it to his own demands. If you had read Isaiah Sellers, you could read Mark Twain, but with a difference. You had to assume a part in a less owlish, more boisterous setting, in which Clemens' caustic humor masks the uncertainty of his seriousness. Mark Twain's reader is asked to take a special kind of hold on himself and on life.

II

These reflections suggest, or are meant to suggest, that there exists a tradition in fictionalizing audiences that is a component part of literary tradition in the sense in which literary tradition is discussed in T. S. Eliot's "Tradition and the Individual Talent." A history of the ways audiences have been called on to fictionalize themselves would be a correlative of the history of literary genres and literary works, and indeed of culture itself.

What do we mean by saying the audience is a fiction? Two things at least. First, that the writer must construct in his imagination, clearly or vaguely, an audience cast in some sort of role—entertainment seekers, reflective sharers of experience (as those who listen to Conrad's Marlow), inhabitants of a lost and remembered world of prepubertal latency (readers of Tolkien's hobbit stories), and so on. Second, we mean that the audience must correspondingly fictionalize itself. A reader has to play the role in which the author has cast him, which seldom coincides with his role in the rest of actual life. An office worker on a bus reading a novel of Thomas Hardy is listening to a voice that is not that of any real person in the real setting around him. He is playing the role demanded of him by this person speaking in a quite special way from the book, which is not the subway and is not quite "Wessex" either, though it speaks of Wessex. Readers over the ages have had to learn this game of literacy, how to conform themselves to the projections of the writers they read, or at least how to operate in terms of these projections. They have to know how to play the game of being a member of an audience that "really" does not exist. And they have to adjust when the rules change, even though no rules thus far have ever been published and even though the changes in the unpublished rules are themselves for the most part only implied.

A history of literature could be written in terms of the ways in which audiences have successively been fictionalized from the time when writing broke away from oral performance, for just as each genre grows out of what went before it, so each new role that readers are made to assume is related to previous roles. Putting aside for the moment the question of what fictionalizing may be called for in the case of the audience for oral performance, we can note that when script first came on the scene, the fictionalizing of readers was relatively simple. Written narrative at first was merely a transcription of oral narrative, or what was imagined as oral narrative, and it assumed some kind of oral singer's audience, even when being read. The transcribers of the *Iliad* and the *Odyssey* presumably imagined an audience of real listeners in attendance on an oral singer, and readers of those works to this day do well if they can imagine themselves hearing a singer of tales (Lord 124-38). How these texts and other oral performances were in fact originally set down in writing remains puzzling, but the transcribers certainly were not composing in writing, but rather recording with minimal alteration what a singer was singing or was imagined to be singing.

Even so, a scribe had to fictionalize in a way a singer did not, for a real audience was not really present before the scribe, so it would seem, although it is just possible that at times one may have been (Lord 125-28). But as transcription of oral performance or imagined oral performance gave way gradually to composition in writing, the situation changed. No reader today imagines *Second Skin* as a work that John Hawkes is reciting extempore to a group of auditors, even though passages from it may be impressive when read aloud.

III

We have noted that the roles readers are called on to play evolve without any explicit rules or directives. How readers pick up the implicit signals and how writers change the rules can be illustrated by examining a passage from a specialist in unpublished directives for readers, Ernest Hemingway. The passage is the opening of *A Farewell to Arms*. At the start of my comment on the passage, it will be clear that I am borrowing a good deal from Walker Gibson's highly discerning book on modern American prose styles, *Tough, Sweet, and Stuffy* (28-54). The Hemingway passage follows:

> In the late summer of that year we lived in a house in a village that looked across the river and the plain to the mountains. In the bed of the river there were pebbles and boulders, dry and white in the sun, and the water was clear and swiftly moving and blue in the channels.

Hemingway's style is often characterized as straightforward, unadorned, terse, lacking in qualifiers, close-lipped; and it is all these things. But none of them were peculiar to Hemingway when his writing began to command attention. A feature more distinctive of Hemingway here and elsewhere is the way he fictionalizes the reader, and this fictionalizing is often signaled largely by his use of the definite article as a special kind of qualifier or of the demonstrative pronoun "that," of which the definite article is simply an attenuation.

"The late summer of that year," the reader begins. What year? The reader gathers that there is no need to say. "Across the river." What river? The reader apparently is supposed to know. "And the plain." What plain? "*The* plain"—remember? "To the mountains." What mountains? Do I have to tell you? Of course not. *The* mountains—*those* mountains we know. We have somehow been there together. Who? You, my reader, and I. The reader—every reader—is being cast in the role of a close companion of the writer. This is the game he must play here with Hemingway, not always exclusively or totally, but generally, to a greater or lesser extent. It is one reason why the writer is tight-lipped. Description as such would bore a boon companion. What description there is comes in the guise of pointing, in verbal gestures, recalling humdrum, familiar details. "In the bed of the river there were pebbles and boulders, dry and white in the sun." The known world, accepted and accepting. Not presentation, but recall. The writer needs only to point, for what he wants to tell you about is not the scene at all but his feelings. These, too, he treats as something you really had somehow shared, though you might not have been quite aware of it at the time. He can tell you what was going on inside him and count on sympathy, for you were there. You *know*. The reader here has a well-marked role assigned him. He is a companion-in-arms, somewhat later become a confidant. It is a flattering role. Hemingway readers are encouraged to cultivate high self-esteem.

The effect of the definite article in Hemingway here is quite standard and readily explicable. Normally, in English, we are likely to make an initial reference to an individual object by means of the indefinite article and to bring in the definite only subsequently. "Yesterday on the street *a* man came up to me, and when I stopped in my stride *the* man said . . ." "A" is a modified form of the term "one," a kind of singular of "some." "A man" means "one man" (of many real or possible men). The indefinite article tacitly acknowledges the existence or possibility of a number of individuals beyond the immediate range of reference and indicates that from among them one is selected. Once we have indicated that we are concerned not with all but with one-out-of-many, we train the definite article or pointer article on the object of our attention.[1] The definite article thus commonly signals some previous, less definite acquaintanceship. Hemingway's exclusion of indefinite in favor of definite articles signals

[1] The present inclination to begin a story without the initial indefinite article, which tacitly acknowledges a range of existence beyond that of the immediate reference, and to substitute for the indefinite article a demonstrative pronoun of proximity, "this," is one of many indications of the tendency of present-day man to feel his lifeworld—which is now more than ever the whole world—as in-close to him, and to mute any references to distance. It is not uncommon to hear a conversation begin, "Yesterday on the street this man came up to me, and . . . ." A few decades ago, the equivalent would very likely have been, "Yesterday on the street a man came up to me, and . . . ." This widespread preference, which Hemingway probably influenced little if at all, does show that Hemingway's imposition of fellowship on the reader was an indication, perhaps moderately precocious, of a sweeping trend.

the reader that he is from the first on familiar ground. He shares the author's familiarity with the subject matter. The reader must pretend he has known much of it before.

Hemingway's concomitant use of the demonstrative distancing pronoun "that" parallels his use of "the." For "the" is only an attenuated "that." It is a modified form of the demonstrative pronoun that replaced the original Old English definite article "seo." Both hold their referents at a distance, "that" typically at a somewhat greater distance than "the." *That* mountain you see ten miles away is indicated there on *the* map on *the* wall. If we wish to think of the map as close, we would say, "*This* map on this wall." In distancing their objects, both "that" and "the" can tend to bring together the speaker and the one spoken to. "That" commonly means that-over-there at a distance from you-and-me here, and "the" commonly means much the same. These terms thus can easily implement the Hemingway relationship: you-and-me.

This you-and-me effect of the distancing demonstrative pronoun and the definite article can be seen perhaps more spectacularly in romance etymology. The words for "the" in the romance languages come from the Latin word *ille, illa, illud*, which yields in various romance tongues *il, le, la, el, lo*, and their cognates. *Ille* is a distancing demonstrative in Latin: it means "that-over-there-away-from-you-and-me" and stands in contrastive opposition to another Latin demonstrative that has no counterpart in English, *iste, ista, istud*, which means "that-over-there-by-you" (and thus can readily become pejorative—"that-little-no-account-thing-of-yours"). *Ille* brings together the speaker and the one spoken to by contrast with the distanced object; *iste* distances from the speaker the one spoken to as well as the object. *Ille* yields the romance definite articles, which correspond quite closely in function to the English "the," and thus advertises the close tie between "the" and "that."

Could readers of an earlier age have managed the Hemingway relationship, the you-and-me relationship, marked by tight-lipped empathy based on shared experience? Certainly from antiquity the reader or hearer of an epic was plunged *in medias res*. But this does not mean he was cast as the author's boon companion. It means rather that he was plunged into the middle of a narrative sequence and told about antecedent events only later. A feeling of camaraderie between companions-in-arms is conveyed in epics, but the companions-in-arms are fictional characters; they are not the reader or hearer and the narrator. "*Forsan et haec olim meminisse iuvabit*"—these words in the *Aeneid*, "perhaps some day it will help to recall these very things," are spoken by Aeneas to his companions when they are undergoing a period of hardships. They are one character's words to other characters, not Virgil's words to his hearer or reader. One might urge further that, like Hemingway's reader, the reader or hearer of an epic—most typically, of an oral folk epic—was hearing stories with which he was already acquainted, that he was thus on familiar ground. He was, but not in the sense that he was forced to pretend he had somehow lived as an alter ego of the narrator. His familiarity with the material was not a pretense at all, not a role, but a simple fact. Typically, the epic audience had heard the story, or something very much like it, before.

The role in which Hemingway casts the reader is somewhat different not only from anything these situations in early literature demand, but also from anything in the time immediately before Hemingway. This is what makes Hemingway's writing interesting to literary historians. But Hemingway's demands on the reader are by no means entirely without antecedents. The existence of antecedents is indicated by the fact that Hemingway was assimilated by relatively unskilled readers with very little fuss. He does not recast the reader in a disturbingly novel role. By contrast, the role in which Faulkner casts the reader is a far greater departure from preceding roles than is Hemingway's. Faulkner demands more skilled and daring readers, and consequently had far fewer at first, and has relatively fewer even today when the Faulkner role for readers is actually taught in school. (Perhaps we should say the Faulkner roles.)

No one, so far as I know, has worked up a history of the readers' roles that prepared for that prescribed by Hemingway. But one can discern significantly similar demands on readers beginning as early as Addison and Steele, who assume a new fashionable intimacy among readers themselves and between all readers and the writer, achieved largely by casting readers as well as writer in the role of coffeehouse habitués. Defoe develops in his own way comparable author-reader intimacy. The roots of these eighteenth-century intimacies are journalistic, and from earlier journalism they push out later in Hemingway's own day into the world of sportswriters and war correspondents, of whom Hemingway himself was one. With the help of print and the near instantaneousness implemented by electronic media (the telegraph first, later radio-teletype, and electronic transmission of photography), the newspaper writer could bring his reader into his own on-the-spot experience, availing himself in both sports and war of the male's strong sense of camaraderie based on shared hardships. Virgil's *forsan et haec olim meminisse iuvabit* once more. But Virgil was telling a story of the days of old and, as has been seen, the camaraderie was among characters in the story, Aeneas and his men. Sports and war journalism are about the here and now, and if the story can be got to the reader quickly, the camaraderie can be easily projected

between the narrator and the reader. The reader is close enough temporally and photographically to the event for him to feel like a vicarious participant. In journalism Hemingway had an established foundation on
which to build, if not one highly esteemed in snobbish literary circles.
And he in turn has been built upon by those who have come later. Gibson
has shown how much the style of *Time* magazine is an adaptation of
Hemingway (48-54). To Hemingway's writer-reader camaraderie *Time*
adds omniscience, solemnly "reporting," for example, in eyewitness
style, the behavior and feelings of a chief of state in his own bedroom as
he answers an emergency night telephone call and afterward returns to
sleep. Hemingway encouraged his readers in high self-esteem. *Time* provides its readers, on a regular weekly basis, companionship with the all-
knowing gods.

When we look the other way down the corridors of time to the period before the coffeehouses and the beginnings of intimate journalism, we
find that readers have had to be trained gradually to play the game
Hemingway engages them in. What if, *per impossibile*, a Hemingway
story projecting the reader's role we have attended to here had turned up
in Elizabethan England? It would probably have been laughed out of
court by readers totally unable to adapt to its demands upon them. It
would certainly have collided with representative literary theory, as pro-
pounded for example by Sir Philip Sidney in *The Defense of Poesie*. For
Sidney and most of his age, poetry—that is to say, literature generally—
had as its aim to please, but even more basically to teach, at least in the
sense that it gave the reader to know what he did not know before. The
Hemingway convention that the reader had somehow been through it all
before with the writer would have been to Sidney's age at best confusing
and at worst wrongheaded. One could argue that the Hemingway narrator
would be telling the reader at least something he did not know before—
that is, largely, the feelings of the narrator. But even this revelation, as we
have seen, implies in Hemingway a covert awareness on the part of the
reader, a deep sympathy or empathy of a basically Romantic, nonpublic
sort, grounded in intimacy. Sidney would have sent Hemingway back to
his writing table to find something newer to write about, or to find a way
of casting his material in a fresher-sounding form.

Another, and related, feature of the Hemingway style would have
repelled sixteenth-century readers: the addiction to the "the" and "that" to
the calculated exclusion of most descriptive qualifiers. There is a deep
irony here. For in the rhetorical world that persisted from prehistoric
times to the age of Romanticism, descriptive qualifiers were commonly
epithetic, expected qualifiers. The first chapter of Sidney's *Arcadia*

(1590) presents the reader with "the hopeless shepheard," the "friendly rival," "the necessary food," "natural rest," "flowery fields," "the extreme heat of summer," and countless other souvenirs of a country every rhetorician had trod many times before. Is this not making the reader a recaller of shared experience much as Hemingway's use of "the" and "that" does? Not at all in the same way. The sixteenth-century reader recalls the familiar accouterments of literature, which are the familiar accouterments or commonplaces also of sculpture, painting, and all art. These are matters of shared public acquaintanceship, not of private experience. The sixteenth-century reader is walking through land all educated men know. He is not made to pretend he knows these familiar objects because he once shared their presence with this particular author, as a Hemingway reader is made to pretend. In Sidney, there is none of the you-and-I-know-even-if-others-don't ploy.

IV

To say that earlier readers would have been nonplused at Hemingway's demands on them is not to say that earlier readers did not have special roles to play or that authors did not have their own problems in devising and signaling what the roles were. A few cases might be instanced here.

First of all, it is only honest to admit that even an oral narrator calls on his audience to fictionalize itself to some extent. The invocation to the Muse is a signal to the audience to put on the epic-listener's cap. No Greek, after all, ever talked the kind of language that Homer sang, although Homer's contemporaries could understand it well enough. Even today we do not talk in other contexts quite the kind of language in which we tell fairy stories to children. "Once upon a time," we begin. The phrase lifts you out of the real world. Homer's language is "once upon a time" language. It establishes a fictional world. But the fictionalizing in oral epic is directly limited by live interaction, as real conversation is. A real audience controls the narrator's behavior immediately. Students of mine from Ghana and from western Ireland have reported to me what I have read and heard from many other sources: a given story may take a skilled or "professional" storyteller anywhere from ten minutes to an hour and a half, depending on how he finds the audience relates to him on a given occasion. "You always knew ahead of time what he was going to say, but you never knew how long it would take him to say it," my Irish informant reported. The teller reacts directly to audience response. Oral storytelling is a two-way street.

Written or printed narrative is not two-way, at least in the short run. Readers' reactions are remote and initially conjectural, however great their ultimate effects on sales. We should think more about the problems that the need to fictionalize audiences creates for writers. Chaucer, for example, had a problem with the conjectural readers of the *Canterbury Tales*. There was no established tradition in English for many of the stories, and certainly none at all for a collection of such stories. What does Chaucer do? He sets the stories in what, from a literary-structural point of view, is styled a frame. A group of pilgrims going to Canterbury tell stories to one another: the pilgrimage frames the individual narratives. In terms of signals to his readers, we could put it another way: Chaucer simply tells his readers how they are to fictionalize themselves. He starts by telling them that there is a group of pilgrims doing what real people do, going to a real place, Canterbury. The reader is to imagine himself in their company and join the fun. Of course this means fictionalizing himself as a member of a nonexistent group. But the fictionalizing is facilitated by Chaucer's clear frame-story directives. And to minimize the fiction by maximizing real life, Chaucer installs himself, the narrator, as one of the pilgrims. His reader-role problem is effectively solved. Of course, he got the idea pretty much from antecedent writers faced with similar problems, notably Boccaccio. But he naturalizes the frame in the geography of southeast England.

The frame story was in fact quite common around Europe at this period. Audience readjustment was a major feature of mature medieval culture, a culture more focused on reading than any earlier culture had been. Would it not be helpful to discuss the frame device as a contrivance all but demanded by the literary economy of the time, rather than to expatiate on it as a singular stroke of genius? For this it certainly was not, unless we define genius as the ability to make the most of an awkward situation. The frame is really a rather clumsy gambit, although a good narrator can bring it off pretty well when he has to. It hardly has widespread immediate appeal for ordinary readers today.

In the next period of major audience readjustment, John Lyly's *Euphues* and even more Thomas Nashe's *The Unfortunate Traveler* can be viewed as attempts to work out a credible role in which Elizabethan readers could cast themselves for the new medium of print. Script culture had preserved a heavy oral residue signaled by its continued fascination with rhetoric, which had always been orally grounded, a fascination that script culture passed on to early print culture. But the new medium was changing the noetic economy, and, while rhetoric remained strong in the curriculum, strain was developing. Lyly reacts by hyper-rhetoricizing his text, tongue-in-cheek, drowning the audience and himself in the highly controlled gush being purveyed by the schools. The signals to the reader are unmistakable, if unconsciously conveyed: play the role of the rhetori-cian's listener for all you are worth (*Euphues* is mostly speeches), remem-bering that the response the rhetorician commands is a serious and diffi-cult one—it takes hard work to assimilate the baroque complexity of Lyly's text—but also that there is something awry in all the isocola, apophonemata, and antisagogai, now that the reader is so very much more a reader than a listener. Such aural iconographic equipment had been functional in oral management of knowledge, implementing storage and recall, but with print it was becoming incidental—which is, paradoxical-ly, why it could be so fantastically elaborated.

Nashe shows the same uneasiness, and more, regarding the reader's role. For in the phantasmagoria of styles in *The Unfortunate Traveler* he tries out his reader in every role he can think of: whoever takes on Nashe's story must become a listener bending his ear to political orations, a participant in scholastic disputations, a hanger-on at goliardic Woodstocks, a camp follower fascinated by merry tales, a simpering read-er of Italian revenge stories and sixteenth-century true confessions, a fel-low conspirator in a world of picaresque cheats, and much more.

Nashe gives a foretaste of other trial-and-error procedures by which recipes were to be developed for the reader of the narrative prose works we now call novels. Such recipes were being worked out in other lan-guages, too: in French notably by Rabelais, whose calls for strenuous shifts in the reader's stance Nashe emulated, and in Spanish by Cervantes, who explores all sorts or ironic possibilities in the reader's relationship to the text, incorporating into the second part of *Don Quixote* the purported reactions of readers and of the tale's characters to the first part of the work. Picaresque travels, well known at least since Apuleius' *Golden Ass*, multiplied, with major audience adjustments, in English down through *Tom Jones*: the unsettled role of the reader was mirrored and made acceptable by keeping the hero himself on the move. Samuel Richardson has his readers pretend they have access to other persons' letters, out of which a story emerges. Journals and diaries also multiplied as narrative devices: the reader becoming a snooper or a collector of seeming trivia that turn out not to be trivia at all. Ultimately, Laurence Sterne is able to involve his reader not only in the procreation of his hero Tristram Shandy, but also in the hero's writing of his autobiography, in which pages are left blank for the reader to put his "own fancy in." The audience-speaker interaction of oral narrative here shows the reader in a new ironic guise—somewhat destructive of the printed book, toward which, as an object obtruding in the person-to-person world of human communication, the eighteenth century was feeling some ambiguous hostilities, as Swift's work also shows.

The problem of reader adjustment in prose narrative was in great part due to the difficulty that narrators long had in feeling themselves as other than oral performers. It is significant that, although the drama had been tightly plotted from classical antiquity (the drama is the first genre controlled by writing, and by the same token, paradoxically, the first to make deliberate use of colloquial speech), until the late eighteenth century there is in the whole Western world (and I suspect in the East as well) no sizable prose narrative, so far as I know, with a tidy structure comparable to that known for two millennia in the drama, moving through closely controlled tensions to a climax, with reversal and denouement. This is not to say that until the modern novel emerged narrative was not organized, or that earlier narrators were trying to write modern novels but regularly fell short of their aims. (Scholes and Kellogg have warned in *The Nature of Narrative* against this retroactive analysis of literary history.) But it is to say that narrative had not fully accommodated itself to print or, for that matter, to writing, which drama had long before learned to exploit. *Tom Jones* is highly programed, but in plot it is still episodic, as all prose narrative had been all the way back through the Hellenic romances. With Jane Austen we are over the hurdle: but Jane Austen was a woman, and women were not normally trained in the Latin-based, academic, rhetorical, oral tradition. They were not trained speechmakers who had turned belatedly to chirography and print.

Even by Jane Austen's time, however, the problem of the reader's role in prose narrative was by no means entirely solved. Nervousness regarding the role of the reader registers everywhere in the "dear reader" regularly invoked in fiction well through the nineteenth century. The reader had to be reminded (and the narrator, too) that the recipient of the story was indeed a reader—not a listener, not one of the crowd, but an individual isolated with a text. The relationship of audience-fictionalizing to modern narrative prose is very mysterious, and I do not pretend to explain it all here, but only to point to some of the strange problems often so largely overlooked in the relationship. Tightly plotted prose narrative is the correlative of the audiences fictionalized for the first time with the aid of print, and the demands of such narrative on readers were new.

V

The present reflections have focused on written fictional narrative as a kind of paradigm for the fictionalizing of writers' "audiences" or readers. But what has been said about fictional narrative applies *ceteris paribus* to all writing. With the possible[2] exception noted above of persons in the presence of one another communicating by writing because of inability to communicate orally, the writer's audience is always a fiction. The historian, the scholar or scientist, and the simple letter writer all fictionalize their audiences, casting them in a made-up role and calling on them to play the role assigned.

Because history is always a selection and interpretation of those incidents the individual historian believes will account better than other incidents for some explanation of a totality, history partakes quite evidently of the nature of poetry. It is a making. The historian does not make the elements out of which he constructs history, in the sense that he must build with events that have come about independently of him, but his selection of events and his way of verbalizing them so that they can be dealt with as "facts," and consequently the overall pattern he reports, are all his own creation, a making. No two historians say exactly the same thing about the same given events, even though they are both telling the truth. There is no one thing to say about anything; there are many things that can be said.

The oral "historian" captures events in terms of themes (the challenge, the duel, the arming of the hero, the battle, and so on), and formulas (the brave soldier, the faithful wife, the courageous people, the suffering people), which are provided to him by tradition and are the only ways he knows to talk about what is going on among men. Processed through these conventions, events become assimilable by his auditors and "interesting" to them. The writer of history is less reliant on formulas (or it may be he has such a variety of them that it is hard to tell that is what they are). But he comes to his material laden with themes in much vaster quantity than can be available to any oral culture. Without themes, there would be no way to deal with events. It is impossible to tell everything that went on in the Pentagon even in one day: how many stenographers dropped how many sheets of paper into how many wastebaskets when and where, what they all said to each other, and so on *ad infinitum*. These are not the themes historians normally use to write what really "happened." They write about material by exploiting it in terms of themes that are "significant" or "interesting." But what is "significant" depends on what kind of history you are writing—national political history, military history, social history, eco-

---

[2] "Possible," because there is probably a trace of fictionalizing even when notes are being exchanged by persons in one another's presence. It appears unlikely that what is written in such script "conversations" is exactly the same as what it would be were voices used. The interlocutors are, after all, to some extent pretending to be talking, when in fact they are not talking but writing.

nomic history, personal biography, global history. What is significant and, perhaps even more, what is "interesting" also depends on the readers and their interaction with the historian. This interaction in turn depends on the role in which the historian casts his readers. Although so far as I know we have no history of readers of history, we do know enough about historiography to be aware that one could well be worked out. The open-faced way the reader figures in Samuel Eliot Morison's writings is different from the more conspiratorial way he figures in Perry Miller's and both are quite different from the way the reader figures in Herodotus.

Scholarly works show comparable evolution in the roles they enforce on their readers. Aristotle's works, as has often been pointed out, are an agglomerate of texts whose relationship to his own holographs, to his students' notes, and to the work of later editors will remain always more or less a puzzle. Much of Aristotle consists of school logia or sayings, comparable to the logia or sayings of Jesus to his followers of which the Gospels chiefly consist. Aristotle's logia were addressed to specific individuals whom he knew, rather than simply to the wide world. Even his more patently written compositions retain a personal orientation: his work on ethics is the *Nicomachean Ethics*, named for his son. This means that the reader of Aristotle, if he wants to understand his text, will do well to cast himself in the role of one of Aristotle's actual listeners.

The practice of orienting a work, and thereby its readers, by writing it at least purportedly for a specific person or persons continues well through the Renaissance. The first edition of Peter Ramus' *Dialectic* was the French *Dialectique de Pierre de la Ramée à Charles de Lorraine Cardinal, son Mécène* (Paris, 1555), and the first edition of the far more widely used Latin version preserved the same personal address: *Dialectici Libri Duo . . . ad Carolum Lotharingum Cardinalem* (Paris, 1556). Sidney's famous romance or epic is *The Countess of Pembroke's Arcadia*. Often in Renaissance printed editions, a galaxy of prefaces and dedicatory epistles and poems establishes a whole cosmos of discourse that among other things, signals the reader what roles he is to assume. Sidney's, Spenser's, and Milton's works, for example, are heavily laden with introductory material—whole books have been devoted to the study of Sidney's introductory matter alone.

Until recent times the rhetorical tradition, which, with the allied dialectical or logical tradition, dominated most written as well as oral expression, helped in the fictionalizing of the audience of learned works in a generic but quite real way. Rhetoric fixed knowledge in agonistic structures.

For this reason, the roles of the reader of learned works until fairly recent times were regularly more polemic than those demanded of the reader today. Until the age of Romanticism reconstituted psychological structures, academic teaching of all subjects had been more or less polemic, dominated by the ubiquitous rhetorical culture, and proceeding typically by proposing and attacking theses in highly partisan fashion. (The academic world today preserves much of the nomenclature, such as "thesis" and "defense" of theses, but less of the programed fighting spirit, which its members let loose on the social order more than on their subject matter or colleagues.) From Augustine through St. Thomas Aquinas and Christian Wolff, writers of treatises generally proceeded in adversary fashion, their readers being cast as participants in rhetorical contests or in dialectical scholastic disputations.

Today the academic reader's role is harder to describe. Some of its complexities can be hinted at by attending to certain fictions that writers of learned articles and books generally observe and that have to do with reader status. There are some things the writer must assume that every reader knows because virtually every reader does. It would be intolerable to write, "Shakespeare, a well-known Elizabethan playwright," not only in a study on Renaissance drama, but even in one on marine ecology. Otherwise the reader's role would be confused. There are other things that established fiction holds all readers must know, even though everyone is sure all readers do not know them: these are handled by writing, "as everyone knows," and then inserting what it is that not quite everyone really does know. Other things the reader can safely be assumed not to know without threatening the role he is playing. These gradations of admissible ignorance vary from one level of scholarly writing to another, and since individual readers vary in knowledge and competence, the degree to which they must fictionalize themselves to match the level of this or that reading will vary. Knowledge of the degrees of admissible ignorance for readers is absolutely essential if one is to publish successfully. This knowledge is one of the things that separates the beginning graduate student or even the brilliant undergraduate from the mature scholar. It takes time to get a feel for the roles that readers can be expected comfortably to play in the modern academic world.

Other kinds of writing without end could be examined in our reflections here on the fictionalizing of readers' roles. For want of time and, frankly, for want of wider reflection, I shall mention only two others. These are genres that do not seem to fall under the rule that the writer's audience is always a fiction since the "audience" appears to be simply one clearly determined person, who hardly need fictionalize himself. The first of the genres is the familiar letter and the second the diary.

The case of the letter reader is really simple enough. Although by writing a letter you are somehow pretending the reader is present, while you are writing, you cannot address him as you do in oral speech. You must fictionalize him, make him into a special construct. Whoever saluted a friend on the street with "Dear John"? And if you try the informal horrors, "Hi!" or "Greetings!" or whatever else, the effect is not less but more artificial. You are reminding him that you wish you were not writing him a letter, but, then, why are you? There is no way out. The writer has to set up another relationship to the reader and has to set the reader in a relationship to the writer different from that of non-chirographical personal contact.

The dimensions of fiction in a letter are many. First, you have no way of adjusting to the friend's real mood as you would be able to adjust in oral conversation. You have to conjecture or confect a mood that he is likely to be in or can assume when the letter comes. And when it does come, he has to put on the mood that you have fictionalized for him. Some of this sort of adjustment goes on in oral communication, too, but it develops in a series of exchanges: a tentative guess at another's mood, a reaction from him, another from yourself, another from him, and you know about where you are. Letters do not have this normal give-and-take: they are one-way movements. Moreover, the precise relationships of writer to reader in letters vary tremendously from age to age even in intensively role-playing correspondence. No one today can capture exactly the fiction in Swift's *Journal to Stella*, though it is informative to try to reconstruct it as fully as possible, for the relationships of children to oldsters and even of man to woman have subtly altered, as have also a vast mesh of other social relationships that the *Journal to Stella* involves.

The epistolary situation is made tolerable by conventions, and learning to write letters is largely a matter of learning what the writer-reader conventions are. The paradoxes they involve were well caught some years ago in a Marx Brothers movie—if I recall correctly where the incident occurred. Letters start with "Dear Sir." An owlish, bemused businessman calls his secretary in. "Take this letter to Joseph Smithers," he directs. "You know his address. 'Dear Sir: You dirty rat . . . .' " The fiction of the exordium designed to create the *lector benevolens* is first honored and then immediately wiped out.

The audience of the diarist is even more encased in fictions. What is easier, one might argue, than addressing oneself? As those who first begin a diary often find out, a great many things are easier. The reasons why are not hard to unearth. First of all, we do not normally talk to ourselves—certainly not in long, involved sentences and paragraphs. Second, the diarist pretending to be talking to himself has also, since he is writing, to pretend he is somehow not there. And to what self is he talking? To the self he imagines he is? Or would like to be? Or really thinks he is? Or thinks other people think he is? To himself as he is now? Or as he will probably or ideally be twenty years hence? If he addresses not himself but "Dear Diary," who in the world is "Dear Diary"? What role does this imply? And why do more women than men keep diaries? Or if they don't (they really do—or did), why do people think they do? When did the diary start? The history of diaries, I believe, has yet to be written. Possibly more than the history of any other genre, it will have to be a history of the fictionalizing of readers.

The case of the diary, which at first blush would seem to fictionalize the reader least but in many ways probably fictionalizes him or her most, brings into full view the fundamental deep paradox of the activity we call writing, at least when writing moves from its initial account-keeping purposes to other more elaborate concerns more directly and complexly involving human persons in their manifold dealings with one another. We are familiar enough today with talk about masks—in literary criticism, psychology, phenomenology, and elsewhere. Personae, earlier generally thought of as applying to characters in a play or other fiction (*dramatis personae*), are imputed with full justification to narrators and since all discourse has roots in narrative, to everyone who uses language. Often in the complexities of present-day fiction, with its "unreliable narrator" encased in layer after layer of persiflage and irony, the masks within masks defy complete identification. This is a game fiction writers play, harder now than ever.

But the masks of the narrator are matched, not one-for-one, in equally complex fashion in the masks that readers must learn to wear. To whom is *Finnegans Wake* addressed? Who is the reader supposed to be? We hesitate to say—certainly I hesitate to say—because we have thought so little about the reader's role as such, about his masks, which are as manifold in their own way as those of the writer.

Masks are inevitable in all human communication, even oral. Role playing is both different from actuality and an entry into actuality: play and actuality (the world of "work") are dialectically related to one another. From the very beginning an infant becomes an actual speaker by playing at being a speaker, much as a person who cannot swim, after developing some ancillary skills, one day plays at swimming and finds that he is swimming in truth. But oral communication, which is built into existential actuality more directly than written, has within it a momentum that works for the removal of masks. Lovers try to strip off all masks. And in all communication, in so far as it is related to actual experience, there must be a movement of love. Those who have loved over many years may reach a point where almost all masks are gone. But never all. The lover's plight is tied to the fact that every one of us puts on a mask to address himself, too. Such masks to relate ourselves to ourselves we also try to put aside and with wisdom and grace we to some extent succeed in casting them off. When the last mask comes off, sainthood is achieved, and the vision of God. But this can only be with death.

No matter what pitch of frankness, directness or authenticity he may strive for, the writer's mask and the reader's are less removable than those of the oral communicator and his hearer. For writing is itself an indirection. Direct communication by script is impossible. This makes writing not less but more interesting, although perhaps less noble than speech. For man lives largely by indirection, and only beneath the indirections that sustain him is his true nature to be found. Writing, alone, however, will never bring us truly beneath to the actuality. Present-day confessional writing—and it is characteristic of our present age that virtually all serious writing tends to the confessional, even drama—likes to make an issue of stripping off all masks. Observant literary critics and psychiatrists, however, do not need to be told that confessional literature is likely to wear the most masks of all. It is hard to bare your soul in any literary genre. And it is hard to write outside a genre. T. S. Eliot has made the point that so far as he knows, great love poetry is never written solely for the ear of the beloved (97), although what a lover speaks with his lips is often indeed for the ear of the beloved and of no other. The point is well made, even though it was made in writing.[3]

Works Cited

Booth, Wayne. *The Rhetoric of Fiction.* Chicago: Chicago UP, 1961.

Duvignaud, Jean. *Sociologie du théâtre: Essai sur les ombres collectives.* Paris, Presses universitaires de France, 1965.

Eliot, T. S. *On Poetry and Poets.* New York: Noonday P, 1961.

Gibson, Walker. *Tough, Sweet, and Stuffy: An Essay on Modern American Prose Styles.* Bloomington: Indiana UP, 1966.

[3] In a briefer adaptation, this paper was read at Cambridge University, August 24, 1972, at the Twelfth International Congress of the International Federation for Modern Languages and Literatures. At the Center for Advanced Study in the Behavioral Sciences at Stanford, California, I have profited from conversations with Albert Cook of the State University of New York, Buffalo, and Robert Darnton of Princeton University, concerning matters in this final version.

Hartman, Geoffrey H. "History-Writing as Answerable Style." *New Literary History* 2 (1970-1971): 73-84.

Hawkes, John. *Second Skin.* New York: New Directions, 1964.

Holland, Norman H. *The Dynamics of Literary Response.* New York: Oxford UP, 1968.

Lavelle, Louis. *La Parole et l'écriture.* Paris: L'Artisan du livre, 1942.

Lord, Albert B. *The Singer of Tales.* Cambridge, MA: Harvard UP, 1960. Harvard Studies in Comparative Literature, Vol. 24.

Merleau-Ponty, Maurice. *Phenomenology of Perception.* Trans. Colin Smith. London: Routledge, 1962.

Miller, J. Hillis. "The Still Heart: Poetic Form in Wordsworth." *New Literary History* 2 (1970-1971): 297-310

Ong, Walter J. *The Presence of the Word.* New Haven and London: Yale UP, 1967.

Poulet, George. "Phenomenology of Reading." *New Literary History* 1 (1969-1970): 53-68.

Prince, Gerald. "Introduction à l'étude du narrataire." *Poétique* 14 (1973): 178-96.

Ricoeur, Paul. "What Is a Text? Explanation and Interpretation." *Mythic-Symbolic Language and Philosophical Anthropology: A Constructive Interpretation of the Thought of Paul Ricoeur.* Ed. David Rasmussen. The Hague: Martinus Nijhoff, 1971. 135-50.

Scholes, Robert and Kellogg, Robert. *The Nature of Narrative.* New York: Oxford UP, 1966.

Searle, John R. *The Philosophy of Language.* London: Oxford UP, 1971.

23

Typographic Rhapsody: Ravisius Textor, Zwinger, and Shakespeare (1976)

Commonplaces and Their Significance

Writing in *Chapters in Western Civilization*, Professor Paul Oskar Kristeller notes that "the frequency of quotations and of commonplaces repeated in the moral literature in the Renaissance gives to all but its very best products an air of triviality that is often very boring to the modern critical reader" (1:305). The Renaissance exploitation of commonplace material is of course not restricted to moral treatises. Such material shows everywhere through the Renaissance, from speculative theology and medical treatises, to lyric and dramatic poetry, where, however, its use is often less cumbersome than among the moralists. And at its best, in the "pointed" style that derives in part from Seneca, such material becomes brilliant, "illustrating" the subject with flashes of insight and wit.

A great many studies treat in one way or another what we may here style the commonplace tradition. Looking for the roots of the literary heritage of the West, in his *European Literature and the Latin Middle Ages* Ernst Robert Curtius devotes a great deal of attention to the various "topics" (*topoi* or *loci*, places, commonplaces) that have provided both themes and ways of managing themes to writers from classical antiquity on. Thus he treats the "topics of consolatory oratory," "historical topics," "topics of the exordium," and other "topics" explicitly labeled as such (79-105). Many of his chapter headings indicate that individual chapters are devoted to the discussion of further individual topics. Thus, "The Goddess Natura," "Heroes and Rulers," "The Ideal Landscape," "Poetry and Philosophy," "The Book as Symbol," and so on. A brief but tightly packed study by August Beck, "Die 'Studio Humanitatis' and ihre Methode," explains a great deal directly on the use of commonplaces, especially as prescribed in works on education, from Rudolph Agricola and Erasmus on to the time of Montaigne. Studies of sixteenth- and seventeenth-century writers, particularly by American scholars, who consti-

tute the largest group by far of experts on the rhetorical tradition, often
treat the commonplaces in various ways. One of the most thorough-going
of such treatments is T. W. Baldwin's monumental landmark, *William
Shakspere's Small Latine and Lesse Greeke*, which works patiently
through large numbers of commonplace collections in use in
Shakespeare's milieu by schoolboys as well as by adults. Sister Joan
Marie Lechner has provided an invaluable survey of Renaissance views
and practice in her *Renaissance Concepts of the Commonplaces*.

Out of these studies there emerges a major question: Why was the
commonplace tradition once so important, since it now seems so affected
and boring and aesthetically counterproductive? None of the studies just
mentioned, nor others like them, really broach this question. The question
can be answered only by situating the commonplace tradition in the
broader perspectives of noetic history, examining how the tradition
relates to the evolution of means of accumulation, storage, and retrieval
of knowledge, and thus eventually how it relates to the history of the
human psyche and of culture. This is what the present study undertakes
to do, working with a certain few significant Renaissance writers. Until
the commonplaces are related to the evolving noetic economy, they
remain antiquarian curiosities, quaint phenomena, whose obtrusiveness in
the past is no more explicable than their eclipse in the present.

"Commonplace" of course has several, more or less related, senses,
some of them quite technical (Ong, *Presence* 56-66, 79-87; Lechner;
Curtius). But in all its senses the term has to do in one way or another with
the exploitation of what is already known, and indeed often of what is
exceedingly well known. The "places" provided access to a culture's noetic store. In classical rhetorical doctrine, places (*topoi* in Greek, in Latin
loci) refer to the "seats" or, as we today would commonly conceptualize
them, to the "headings" to which one betook oneself to draw out of the
stock of knowledge the things one could say concerning a given subject.
These headings implemented analysis of one's subject: for a person, one
might, by a kind of analytic process, consider his family, descent, sex, age,
education, and the like; or, more generally, for all sorts of things, one could
look to definition, opposites, causes, effects, related matters, and so on.
This meaning of *topos* or *locus* or "place" is approximated still in our present term "topic" (from *topikos*, the Greek adjectival form corresponding to
the noun *topos*). In his *Rhetoric* (I. ii. 21-1358a) Aristotle notes two classes of "places": (a) "common" places, headings providing materials for any
and all subjects, and (b) "special" places, headings offering matter for certain individual subjects, such as law or physics. But this distinction was
too fastidious to survive the hurly-burly of rhetorical doctrine and practice,

where "places" (*loci*) and "commonplaces" (*loci communes*) were often used interchangeably (Ong, *Presence* 82).

A "commonplace" might also have another meaning, somewhat deviously related to this first: a "commonplace" could be a standard brief disquisition or purple patch on any of hundreds or thousands of given subjects—loyalty, treachery, brotherhood, theft, decadence (Cicero's *O tempora! O mores!* passage is a commonplace on this subject), and so on; these prefabricated disquisitions were excerpted from one's reading or listening or worked up by oneself (generally out of material taken or adapted from others). Quintilian explains this meaning of *locus communis* in his *Institutiones oratoriae* 5. 5. 12—cf. 1. 11. 12—after treating other usages of *locus* earlier in the same work (5. 10. 20).

Even in antiquity, as Quintilian testifies, commonplaces in the sense of standard brief disquisitions or purple patches were often committed to writing, and by the Middle Ages and the Renaissance came to be regularly stored in commonplace books or "copie" books or copybooks (books assuring *copia*, or the free flow of discourse essential for oratory). The medieval *florilegia* or collections of *exempla* and other useful bits for use in subsequent discourse belong to this tradition. To it can also be assimilated collections such as Erasmus' *De duplici copia verborum ac rerum,* where the entries are often less than disquisitions, being in many instances quite short expressions, mere phrases or turns of diction, such as the Latin equivalents of "white as snow," "soft as the ear lobe," for these phrases, too, are presented as stock ways of treating a particular subject, however briefly, got together for subsequent use. Many of Erasmus' works are collections of what in one way or another is basically commonplace material: thus his *Adagio,* his *Apopthegmata,* his *Colloquia,* the *De duplici copia verborum ac rerum,* the *Epigrammata* and the *Parabola sive Similia.* Moreover, his editions of collections of brief lives by Epiphanius, Sophronius, St. Jerome, and Plutarch are primary sources of commonplace exempla, as are also his editions of Lucian of Samosata's *Dialogi* and other works. As was the case with most humanists, Erasmus regarded reading generally as furnishing commonplace grist for the reader's own rhetorical mill. A great deal of his influence as an educator was due to the fact that he was the most influential collector of commonplace material the Western world has ever seen.

It is helpful sometimes to refer to commonplaces in this latter sense of garnered standard disquisitions or purple patches on a set subject as "cumulative" commonplaces, and to places or commonplaces in the earlier sense of headings as "analytic" places or commonplaces. By the term "commonplace tradition" I shall refer here to the practice, more or less reflective, of exploiting both analytic and cumulative places or common-places. "Commonplace collections" here refers to assemblages in writing or print of cumulative commonplaces, these latter being understood to include both lengthy passages and briefer expressions, down to mere *modus dicendi*; as in Erasmus' *De copia*, stocked in formulaic fashion out of the extant store of knowledge for further exploitation as occasion might demand.

As Eric A. Havelock has shown, the noetic economy of an oral cul-ture demands that knowledge be processed in more or less formulary style and that it be constantly recycled orally—otherwise it simply van-ishes for good unless it be discovered anew (36-60). The whole com-monplace tradition, an organized trafficking in what in one way or anoth-er is already known, is obviously part and parcel of the ancient oral world, the primitive human noetic universe, to which the Renaissance rhetorical doctrine of imitation also obviously relates. Elsewhere I have undertaken to show that the persistence of such material in more or less conspicuous form provides one rule-of-thumb indication of how oral or residually oral a given culture may be—which is also to say how oral or residually oral the culture's typical personality structures and its state of consciousness itself may be (Ong, *Rhetoric* 23-47).

Ioannes Ravisius Textor: Exemplary Collector

As an instance of some of the workings of the commonplace tradition in the Renaissance and a point of departure for reflection on the tradition, I should like to adduce here two collections of commonplace materials got up by a much neglected sixteenth-century French Neo-Latin writer, Jean Tixier, Seigneur de Ravisi, who latinized his name as Ioannes Ravisius Textor. Although Ravisius Textor was familiar to sixteenth- and early sev-enteenth-century schoolboys across western Europe—including, it would appear certain, William Shakespeare (Baldwin 2:391, 414-16, and index)—he remains a neglected figure today and indeed promises to be neglected even more effectively in the future, for he published in Latin and the knowledge of Latin is becoming less and less common even among scholars—a fact that we should by now frankly admit is severely warping many studies of the Renaissance.

Ioannes Ravisius Textor was born very likely around 1470, but per-haps as late as 1480, probably at Saint-Saulge in the Nivernais. He stud-ied at the University of Paris under his compatriot Jean Beluacus in the Collège de Navarre, with which Textor's entire life was thereafter identi-fied. There it was that he became professor of rhetoric, helping to make this college the best of all the Paris colleges for the study of humanities.

In 1520 he was elected Rector of the University, and in 1524 he died in Paris. Although a Nivernais by birth and a Parisian by adoption, Ravisius Textor, like many humanists, was international in his reputation and influence: editions of his works appear not only in Paris, Rouen, and Lyons, but also in Basel, Venice, Antwerp, Douai, and London.[1]

Few studies of Ioannes Ravisius Textor have ever appeared, and there is no definitive study at all, so far as I can ascertain. Another study of Ravisius Textor, and a valuable one, by McFarlane has appeared in the same volume in which the present study was originally published (Bolgar). There is a brief treatment of Ravisius Textor in Maurice Mignon. An earlier work by J. Vodoz treats Textor's *Dialogi*, which were written to be staged as *moralités, soties, et farces*, but, as would be normal or even inevitable at the time this work was done, of course says nothing about the influence of epithet-collecting or commonplaces on Textor's work. Vodoz (137) cites the *Roman de la rose* as a frequent source for Textor's ideas, but the complexity of Textor's sources is so little adverted to that one is unsure as to how directly operative this medieval romance as such actually was. A still earlier doctoral dissertation by L. Massebieau goes into the staging of Textor's comedies (that is, his *Dialogi*). Massebieau notes (47-48) some antecedents of Hamlet's gravedigger scene in Villon, Carolus Aurelianensis, Ravisius, and Reuchlin, but without reference to Ravisius's *Officina* or *Epithets*. He is aware of Textor's reliance on the commonplace tradition, as his remarks about what Textor takes "*ex communi fonte*" here shows (56): "*Quaecumque autem Ravisius aut excogitavit aut ex communi fonte hauserit aut quidem imitatus sit, at omnia libero impetu, vividisque verbis expressit, raro paganis nominibus respersa nec umquam circuitionum elegantiis oppressa*" [Well, Ravisius either thought something up or drew it from a common source or imitated it, but freely in his own way, and he expressed it in vivid words, rarely sprinkled with common terms or limited by any lack of tasteful terms]. The late Professor Don Cameron Allen (32-37) notes that in the 'Poetrie' section of his English-language work *Palladis Tamia*, Francis Meres borrows much of his material directly from Ravisius Textor. In reviewing ways by which Meres might have known Textor—and these are vast, for many editions were in circulation—Allen makes no mention of Thomas Johnson's work *Cornucopiae, or Divers*

---

[1] Including one London edition not listed in the Pollard and Redgrave Short-Title Catalogue, namely *Epistolae Ioannis Ravisii Textoris non vulgaris eruditionis: nunc recess in gratiam studiosae iuventutis multo quam antehac unquam emondatiores in lucem editae* (London: ex Typographic Societatis Stationariorum, 1628). I have not seen a copy of this edition, but a copy was listed for sale in Magga Brothers (London), Catalogue No. 901 (January 1966).

Secrets: wherein is contained the rare secrets in man, beasts . . . plantes,
stones, and such like . . . and not before committed to be printed in
English, newlie drawen out of divers Latins authors . . . Both the title and
the content of this work—it lists places that abound in various things and
places that lack various things, just as Textor's *Cornucopia* does (as
explained here below)—suggest direct derivation from Textor. But the
interweaving of commonplace collections makes such derivation a little
less than certain unless someone checks out the matter, as I have not
myself done. Hyder Rollins notes that Thomas Deloney's erudite anecdotes come from, among other sources, Johnson's *Cornucopiae*. And so
the *loci* yield their hold to generation after generation.

Textor's published works—all Latin, as we have just noted—include
mostly productions of a routine humanist sort: dialogues (written to be
staged, as they indeed often were), epigrams, letters, and editions of
Ulrich von Hutten's *Aula* and *Dialogus* and of other authors' works,
including a collection of short pieces on distinguished women by various
writers. The two works of Textor's to be glanced at here are his *Officina*
(a title that can be rendered into English as *Workshop*) and his *Epitheta*
(*Epithets*). These continue the copybook (*copia*-book) tradition of
Erasmus, whom Textor much admired, as his prefatory letter to his 1519
edition of Ulrich de Hutten's *Aula* makes clear (fol. *2), and as his brother Iacobus (Jacques Tixier de Ravisi) also indicates in his own prefatory
letter to his 1524 edition of Ioannes' *Epitheta* (fol. 2). The *Officina* and
the *Epithets*, like several of Erasmus' works, arrange in collections for
subsequent use bits and pieces out of Latin texts.

Collections of commonplace materials were used not only by orators,
poets, "philosophers" (including natural scientists), physicians, divines,
and others getting up "original" works under their own names, but even
more assiduously by other collectors in their own commonplace collections, published as well as unpublished. As the late Professor Don
Cameron Allen points out, a commonplace collection of similes in English
which gives us so much of our biographical material on some of the colorful literary hacks of sixteenth-century London, all of Meres' historical
examples (for his similes) come from Ravisius Textor's *Officina*, as most
of his similes themselves come from Erasmus' *Parabola sine Similia*.

Essentially the *Officina* is simply a dictionary of classified excerpts
or mini-excerpts from extant writing "examples" such as Erasmus' copybook program calls for. The excerpts present students with things to say
and Latin words to say them with. No Greek as such appears anywhere in
the work. Everything originally in Greek is put into Latin. The sources are
mostly the ancients, such as Virgil or Ovid, but also extend to Textor's

own contemporaries or near-contemporaries, such as Pontanus or Erasmus, with medieval writers of course scrupulously excluded. The content of the examples in at least ninety percent of the cases is concerned with antiquity even when the citation is from one of Textor's contemporaries, but on rare occasions citations from the later writers will have to do with a contemporary or near-contemporary matter, such as an event in the life of King Ferdinand of Spain.

The *Officina* first appeared in Paris in 1520 and apparently was not reprinted until 1532.[2] But after this date editions of the work in its entirety and in epitomes multiplied. More will be said of the editions later. One particular section of the *Officina* appeared frequently as a separate work under its own section title, *Cornucopia*. I have record of some thirty editions of the *Officina* in whole or in part, the last in 1626, with most editions appearing before 1600. Some editions, revised by Conrad Lycosthenes (Wolffhardt), appear under the title *Theatrum poeticum atque historicum: sine Officina.*

Certainly the *Officina* of Ravisius Textor is in many ways one of the most intriguing collections of commonplace material that was ever assembled. If the work were in French or English or German or any other modern vernacular rather than in Latin, it would certainly be a constant point of reference for literary commentators or curio seekers, or for connoisseurs of the unconsciously comic. In its studied pursuit of conspicuously useless detail it rivals even Burton's *Anatomy of Melancholy* or Sterne's *Tristram Shandy*, and in its nose for the bizarre it can compete with Rabelais. Textor is somewhat apologetic about the zany confusion of his work and in a set of elegiacs to the reader at the beginning sets out to disarm criticism by protesting that the *Officina* is not for "learned poets" but "for uneducated boys" (*rudibus pueris*) who are for the first time "sweating in the dust and still imbibing words in the course of elementary instruction" (1532 fol. Ai[v]). It is hard, however, to imagine the collection as being put directly into the hands of little boys, for, other reasons aside, the earlier editions of the *Officina* are large folios which would be very expensive even for masters. Probably masters used the work for self-improvement and as a teacher's manual.

As a dictionary of quotations the *Officina* differs from today's dictionaries most spectacularly in the nature of its headings. There are some

---

[2] *Io. Ravisii Textoris Officina partim historicis partim poeticis refertis disciplina* . . . ([Paris:] Reginaldus Chauldière, 1520)—copies in British Museum and Cambridge University Library. *Ioan Ravisii Textoris Officina* . . . *auctior additis ab ipso authore ante quam a vita excederit rebus prope innumeris* . . . *cui etiam accessit index copiosissimus...* ([Paris:] Reginaldus Chauldière, 1532)—copies in the British Museum and the Bibliothèque Nationale, Paris.

350 subject headings in the first edition of the book, with often large numbers of entries under each heading. The reader opening the first edition is plunged into a blood-bath perhaps suggesting that Textor was projecting into his subject matter some of the aggressions against oneself that the grueling work of a lexicographer can well generate (witness the case of Samuel Johnson, who in his *Dictionary* wryly defines a lexicographer— that is, himself and those like him—as a "harmless drudge"). Here are the first two dozen or so entries under which Textor ranges his selections of materials from writers in classical antiquity, translated from Textor's Latin and presented in exactly the sequence in which he gives them, beginning right after his preface. The reader (in Textor's plan, a little boy! *puer*) encounters first a list of suicides (all the cases from classical antiquity that Textor can find), then parricides, drowned persons, those who have given their names to bodies of water by being drowned in them, persons killed or dismembered by horses, persons killed by the fall of horses, those killed by serpents, those killed by boars, those killed by lions, those killed by dogs, killed by other beasts, individuals struck by lightning, dead from hanging and crucifixion, dead from thirst and hunger, consumed by fire, persons cast off precipices, dead from falling staircases, people swallowed up by the earth, individuals done away with by poison, victims of sudden death (such a heading shows that Textor's standards for close timing were pretty high), dead from joy and laughter, dead from too much food and drink.

Under each of these headings Textor gives a list of the individual cases he has read of. His research was not casual. He exhibits one hundred eighty-five suicides, eleven killed by dogs, and so on. Each instance is accompanied by an explanation that provides a varying amount of circumstantial detail for the case in question, together with references and quotations in many cases, though not in all.

In the particular sequence of headings just given, like items tend to cluster together, but elsewhere sampling of the classics is more random. One finds, for instance, a fairly sustained section on learned persons, and in rather intelligible succession such items as stonecutters (*sculptores*), engravers, statuary sculptors, marble cutters, painters, and pigments. But on the other hand one also encounters sequences such as the following (and I am giving these in the order in which they occur): trainers of monsters and wild beasts, the four elements, sycophants, buffoons, parasites, fat and thin men, famous and memorable gardens, public criers, sleepy people (*somnolentes*), fullers, the columns of Hercules. Every so often Textor avails himself of catch-all headings, such as "those famous for various things." He has further sections on geometricians, astrologers, various types of measures, lousy distemper (*morbus pedicularis*), men who smelt bad (a *topos* that I have found recurrent in collections of this sort), dwarfs, pygmies, the four harpies, various types of haircuts, brute animals to which statues were erected, arguments drawn from the impossible, various kinds of excrement, descriptions of a long time, descriptions of night, and a long strung-out list of various kinds of worms.

The part of the *Officina* labeled *Cornucopia* (1532 fols. LIX^V-XCIIII^r) is a little curio in its own right, constituting a major section of the book that outranks in size the sections under other headings. The title *Cornucopia*, or horn of plenty, is employed because this section is devoted exclusively to a catalogue of things that can be found in great abundance in specified places. Thus the reader here learns what countries abound in bees or cheese or cinnamon or whales, ants, iron, marble, and so on. The *Cornucopia* concludes with its own contrary, listing various things not found in various places. There is no gold in the Nile, alone of all rivers (a sweeping bit of information, but backed by classical references), there are no deer in Africa, no bears either, no swine in Arabia, "especially in the country of the Scaenites." (This transcendentalizing of an absolute denial seemingly defies logical clarification; there are none at all, especially in this place!) There are no eagles in Rhodes, no woodpeckers in the fields around Tarentum, there is no thyme in Arcadia, there are no mice in the island of Paris, no mountains in Portugal, no moles in Coronea, and finally, in England there is no oil or wine, only beer.

Ioannes Ravisius Textor's *Epithets* is a somewhat different but equally fascinating work. It is a collection of standard qualifiers and substitutes for nouns that a writer of Latin poetry imitating the classics might use— and of course that writers of French and Italian and English and German and other poetry also might use and did use, following the Latin. Like the *Officina*, the *Epithets* draws basically on ancient sources. The two medieval writers whom Professor McFarlane (84) notes that it includes, Martianus Capella (fl. 410-439) and Boethius (480?-?524) would seem to be medieval only by ascription, since the former was a younger contemporary (and fellow countryman) of St. Augustine of Hippo and the latter born only some fifty years after Augustine's death.

The first edition of the *Epithets*, called *Specimen epithetorum* (*An Exhibit of Epithets*) was put out in 1518 during the lifetime of its author. The second edition, although its title notes that it represents a revision done by its original author, came out posthumously in 1524, as mentioned earlier, under the supervision of the author's brother, Iacobus Ravisius Textor, who with quaint heartlessness observes in his introduction, "My brother was brought to an end before his revision was" (fol. *2^V).

In accord with Erasmus' example, as Iacobus Ravisius Textor tells us in his somewhat defensive introduction to the posthumous second edition, Ioannes collected his *Epithets* for boys an academic cut higher than those for whom he says the *Officina* was designed, that is, for those in the highest class in rhetoric engaged in doing exercises in themes for declamations or for dialogues, or other prose or verse ("*supremae classis rhetorices, quos convenit assiduis declamationum dialogorumque thematibus omnique tum solutae tum numerosae orationis genere exerceri*"—Preface, fol. *2ᵛ). The thinking behind the collection is obviously of a piece with the classical idea of rhetorical ornamentation. The *Officina* proffers more or less bare, hard ideas, "naked" thoughts, whereas the *Epithets* provides an assortment of options for giving the presumably bare or "naked" thought of the rhetorically untrained weaver of words a richer, more attractive—which is to say more commonplace!—texture.

The collection of epithets that Ioannes Ravisius Textor assembled is sizable. It runs to 311 leaves (that is, 622 pages) of folio size in the 1518 edition. Textor's industry appears to have flagged as he worked through the alphabet. *A* to *L* (10 letters, no *J* or *K*) take up fols. 1-206, *M-Z* (11 letters, but only two entries under *X*) take up only fols. 207-303, despite all the *S*s. (In comparison, large Latin dictionaries commonly divide almost evenly between *A-L* and *M-Z*.)

Running through these individual entries is far from a boring occupation today. The coins that Textor proffers have been worn smooth by use, but they still ring true in countless associations. In the *A*s the searcher for epithets can find 113 of them referable to Apollo, and 163 for *amor* (love). The complementary *bellum* or war merits a 36-page entry, and death (*mors*) has 95 epithets. Achilles warrants 48 epithets, such as—translated into English—tireless, untamed, trusted, furious. Africa is glowing, fertile, full of fords, bristling, teeming with wild beasts. The associations that countless poems and prose writings had established with Arabia are well recorded here. The inhabitants of the land, the Arabs, are rich in odors, palm-bearing, incense-collecting, tender, Oriental, wealthy, ardent, opulent, and so on. One thinks of Othello's dying declamation full of Arabia, wealth, odors, gums, and tender feelings. Coleridge's River Alph is here too, *Alphēus* in Latin. It is not sacred but it is definitely alien, clear, and swift. One could find here the accouterments and often the substance of thousands of poems of Western Europe through the Renaissance and indefinitely later.

Renaissance Interactions with the Commonplace Tradition

The management of commonplace material has a long and complex history, which can be sketched here and then brought into focus around

Textor's and related works. The source of the tradition, as we have noted above, is ultimately the primitive oral culture of all mankind. Memorable sayings from this culture—and in an oral culture, expression, and thought as well, not mnemonically patterned for recall to all intents and purposes does not exist—from simple turns of expression, epithets, and anecdotes to highly sophisticated aphorisms, gnomes, apophthegms, moralistic fables, and brilliant paradoxes, are woven from the ancient oral store into early writing, which in its most artistic forms continues the oral practice of reiterating and embellishing the already known. In this morass of commonly shared mnemonically structured knowledge there is no footing for anyone seeking an answer to the question, "Who first said . . . ?" Everybody is quoting everybody else, and has been for tens of thousands of years before the written records began, on purpose and with a feeling of achievement.

In classical antiquity, which remained always close to the primitive oral world, the use of commonplace material was always conspicuous and eventually, with the help of writing, had become the object of elaborate reflection, some of it more speculative, as in Aristotle's *Topika*, and some of it more practical, as in Cicero or Quintilian or Dionysius of Halicarnassus or Hermogenes. Despite the currency of writing, however, compilation of material, though not unknown in antiquity—conspicuous examples of compilation would be the Sapiential books in the Old Testament—was not highly developed before the Middle Ages. Ancient Greek and Roman authors wrote collections of biographies, such as those by Plutarch, and vaguely "encyclopedic" works treating individual words and subject matters (as in Pliny's *Natural History*). They did relatively little in the way of collecting excerpts. A good summary treatment, with references, can be found in the article, "Encyclopaedia." By contrast, the *Speculum* of Vincent of Beauvais (ca. 1190-1264), a famous medieval "encyclopedia," consists chiefly of excerpts from other writers. Following beginnings in the patristic period, the Middle Ages specialized in *florilegia*, collections of gnomic quotations, *exempla* (illustrative stories, historical or fictional), sermon excerpts, and other kinds of bits and pieces, culled from sources as distant as the Far East (the *Panchatantra*, a collection of beast fables ultimately from India, was taken over deviously by the Middle Ages in Europe as the *Directorium vitae humanae)*. The number of *florilegia* is so vast that no even moderately complete study of the genre, of even monograph size, has ever been published, nor has even an inventory of known or extant *florilegia* (see "Florilegia"). Titles would certainly run into the hundreds. Despite their scribal provenance, however, the contents of the inscribed medieval *florilegia* were often presented as "sayings" or orally conveyed narrative and were intended to be recycled through the oral world, just as the education in the universities, despite the fact that in many ways it was far more text-centered than education in classical antiquity (Ong, *Presence* 58-61), was calculated nevertheless to provide basically an oral formation for the student (Hajnal 64).

During the Renaissance, the commonplace heritage of antiquity and the Middle Ages became in many ways more important than ever before. First, by comparison with classical antiquity, the Renaissance needed to become even more self-conscious about commonplace material because Latin, normally the only language one studied and used in school (except for a generally quite small amount of Greek), was a foreign language to all its users and had been so for roughly a millennium. Bolgar (359) reports that, although in later editions of the Jesuit *Ratio Studiorum* Greek was to be begun simultaneously with Latin, in fact it was given only about one-sixth of the time given to Latin at the Jesuit college at Messing. Such proportioning of time appears typical of the better Renaissance schools; in the less good schools Greek got even shorter shrift (332-33). Unlike schoolboys in ancient Greece or Rome studying their vernacular Greek or Latin, and unlike schoolchildren today who address themselves to their own vernaculars in the classroom, Renaissance schoolboys normally came to the Latin that was the *pièce de résistance* of their academic menu with no store at all of common expressions or sayings from ordinary Latin conversation. These had to be artificially cultivated in academic circles.

Second, although the Middle Ages, for much the same reasons as the Renaissance, had had to exploit artificially a store of common Latin expressions or sayings, the Renaissance felt the need somewhat more keenly because of its keener and more self-conscious ambition to echo the Latin of classical antiquity. One had to be relatively sure that one's idiom, which included various *modus dicendi*, turns of expressions, Latin proverbs and comparisons and sayings, was more or less of a piece with that of classical antiquity. We need not exaggerate the Renaissance drive to Ciceronianism, which was usually relatively restrained in various ways, but we must acknowledge the existence and the real force of a desire to imitate ancient Latin quite closely. Good Latin writers, such as Erasmus, wrote not purely Ciceronian language, but they did not write in medieval style either, though they were influenced by the latter. They wrote their own classically toned Latin.

Third, in settling on the corpus of classical work as its more or less strict norm, the Renaissance fixed its attention on material visually stored and retrievable. Its lexical and linguistic base was not an orally possessed language as such, but a body of texts—a controlled and closed field, at least in principle more or less explicitly bounded. The adoption of this base was crucial in the history of commonplace materials, for it was to mark the beginning of the end of the commonplace tradition. Commonplaces had their deepest roots in the poetic needs of an oral world. The Renaissance preoccupation with texts, inherited from the Middle Ages but intensified by print, tended to shift the focus of verbalization from the world of sound to the surface of the page, from the aural to the visual. This is not to say there were not competing tendencies in the Renaissance, such as the accentuation of the oral fostered by the cult of the classical orator, but the effect of print was ultimately to prove overwhelming.

Various arrangements for visual retrieval of material in texts had been physically possible since writing was invented. Indeed, this was what writing was all about: words, though irreducibly sounds, could now be recovered by the eye (for reconstitution as sounds). But writing is far less effective than print in fixing verbalized material in space for widespread storage and ready visual access.

Once a fixed order is established in print, it can be multiplied with little effort almost without limit. This makes it more worthwhile to do the arduous work of elaborating serviceable arrangements and—what is all important—of devising complex, visually serviceable indexes. A hundred dictated handwritten copies of a work would normally require a hundred indexes, for the material would appear on different pages in different copies, whereas five thousand or more printed copies of an edition of a given work would all be served by one and the same index. Within a few generations after the invention of print, the index became a conspicuous feature of printed commonplace collections, much advertised on title pages (Ong, *Presence* 85-86).

Besides facilitating retrieval through indexing, the printed page also facilitated retrieval simply because it normally proved easier to read than most manuscripts. This was, of course, less true at the beginning of print. Earlier printed books kept close to the format and style of the manuscript with which they were competing: the pages were indubitably handsome, but not necessarily adapted to speed reading. However, as it gradually dawned on consciousness that printing was not just imitation handwriting, solid pages of close-set type gave way to pages with well-spaced words, the paragraph in the modern sense of this term—a unit of thought visually advertised by an indentation—was invented and became functional, and in countless other ways the feeling gradually developed that words could be arranged on a surface in ways facilitating visual retrieval

(albeit for processing in one way or another through the auditory world—
for words remain at root always sounds).

Development of the feeling for visual retrieval can be seen everywhere, but most spectacularly in the title pages of Renaissance books.
Everyone familiar with Renaissance editions will recall how an early title
page will often split even its principal words with hyphens, printing successive parts of the same word on successive lines in different sizes or
different fonts of type. An example—one of hundreds—would be the title
page of the first edition of Peter Ramus' final revision of his *Dialectica*
(Ong, *Inventory* opposite 192). The full title of this edition is: *P. Rami
Regii Professoris Dialecticae libri duo (The Two Books of the Dialectic
of Peter Ramus, Regius Professor)*. On the 1572 title page, the words are
dismembered. The first line presents, in upper-case type about 24-point in
size, the fragmented "P. RAMI RE-"; the next line drops to smaller upper-
case type, about 18-point in size, in which it presents the last two syllables of one word and the first three of another: "GII PROFESSO-"; the third
line, in 14-point upper-case type, provides the fourth syllable of one word
and the whole of another, "RIS DIALECTICAE," and the following line, in
10-point upper-case type, concludes the title with the two words "LIBRI
DUO." This last line is the first of the four to present the reader with words
not chopped into pieces.

The overall visual appearance of this title page is far from unpleasant. Quite the contrary, as an inverted pyramid arrangement of black
marks on a white surface, the page, which includes the printer's mark and
imprint, is aesthetically very pleasing and decorative. It would be attractive framed. It is, however, by present-day standards, not easy to read. As
soon as it is read aloud, it is understandable, but it does not come into the
visual field in such a way as to facilitate apprehension in lexical units
with the ease that later typography would demand. There is no sense of
what printers and advertisers today would call "display." The reason is
that the words are not thought of primarily as being picked off the page
as units by the eye, but rather as being made into units within the auditory imagination—or more likely, within the voice box, since many of
Ramus' contemporaries were, it seems, still reading aloud or in a mum-
ble when they read to themselves—with only casual relation to the visual. Presentation was improving somewhat. Words came soon to be set
with very evident spaces between them, as they were often not in early
print, but the verbal visual unit as such was still relatively weak.

In the gradual movement from the state of affairs typified by this
1572 title page toward a more functionally visual economy of verbalized
knowledge, collections of "places" prove to be a recognizable focus of

development. Vision is a fractioning sense, as Merleau-Ponty and others have remarked. So in its own way was the commonplace tradition, which, even in its original oral roots, had tended to fragment discourse into the bits assembled by oral narrators and orators—"rhapsodizers" or "stitchers," in the original Greek meaning of this term, who sewed together the commonplace bits out of which thought and discourse were made. It was not on the face of it unlikely that the fragmenting possibilities of the visual field would be exploited somehow when commonplaces were subject to the visual regimen of print. Some of the more complex ways in which this exploitation was carried out will be discussed here shortly, but it will be well to note initially the central interaction of the old oral commonplace tradition and the newly improved visual medium. This took place in the development in the index, just mentioned. Our present term "index" itself is an abridged form of the earlier *index locorum* (index of places) or *index locorum communium* (index of commonplaces) that one meets with in early printed books (Ong, *Ramus* 313-14). The elements into which an index breaks down a book are, basically, "places" in the text and simultaneously topics or "places" (*topoi, loci*) in the mind—in the physical world and in the conscious world both—thought of as pieces out of which a whole is constituted. The rhetorical and dialectical term "place" (*topos, locus*), conceptualized as some kind of vague region in consciousness or in a "field" of knowledge, here acquires a truly local habitation, becoming a gross physical reality, truly a place on a surface. *Topos* and *locus* could in antiquity also mean a place in a written text, though this meaning was less obtrusive than the rhetorical and dialectical meaning connected with invention (*inventio*) or "finding" arguments, as earlier noted here. With typography far more operative in noetic management, the locale was identical now upon thousands of surfaces, where a "unit" of verbalization and thought could be pinned down. The concept "place" had become thoroughly functional.

At this point an older primary oral world is dying out in a certain sense within consciousness and a new visual-verbal world is gaining credibility. The effects on the accumulation, storage, and retrieval of knowledge will be vast, as will the effects on the kind of knowledge to which the mind shapes itself. In the noetic economy, purportedly inert "facts" rather than intrinsically evanescent sayings will have the ascendancy as never before.

Evolution of Visual Retrieval:
Textor, Theodor Zwinger and Others

If we look at Textor's *Officina* and *Epitheta* in terms of knowledge storage and retrieval—there are of course other ways of looking at them—

their editorial history shows them to be in a way between the two worlds we have just mentioned, that of the old oral economy of early human cultures (to which composition by formula was indigenous) and the new visual world of the inscribed word, which had come into germinal being with the invention of writing and which in Textor's day was finally maturing through the newly developing alphabetic print of the West.

Modern cultures in certain parts of the world today are emerging from orality into print and into electronic culture at a rate hundreds of times faster than early modern Europe's and with full consciousness that was impossible in early Europe, of the evolution being undergone. These cultures manifest the same passion as that of the European Renaissance for collecting in print the proverbs and other formulaic sayings on which the earlier oral cultures always relied. Thus, for example, at Onitsha, Nigerian printers have been flooding the popular market with printed collections of proverbial materials (see, for example, Obiechena, Lindfors). Like their Renaissance counterparts, producers and users of these popular collections in Nigeria appear unaware that print makes cultivation of proverbs outmoded or even counterproductive, though Nigerian scholars are often exquisitely aware of this fact, as their Renaissance counterparts were not. The novels of Chinua Achebe, and of other African writers, counterpoint proverbial materials against growing technological developments, with great literary success.

In the ancient world of letters, which had remained more dominantly oral than its medieval or Renaissance counterparts, the commonplace tradition had kept the noetic store alive and accessible largely through actual oral performance. One mastered commonplaces largely by hearing them. Although it is true, as has been noted earlier, that Quintilian and others report and advocate some use of writing to implement oratory, antiquity did not compile written lists of things that had been said with the fervor later obsessing medieval Europeans, who, as we have just noted, set out to establish massive textual—which is to say visual—bases, such as *florilegia*, within their own attenuated latter-day orality. The Renaissance, for all its programmatic rejection of the Middle Ages, was actually generated and kept alive largely by the medieval addiction to texts as such. What we have seen in Textor is a sweeping design for textual (visual) management of the noetic store: precipitate out of all classical texts all the suicides, haircuts, sleepy people, astrologers, worms, or whatever, so that all of each class can be grouped together in space. The growing appetite for beginning the study of any field of knowledge with "history" in the sense of patiently recorded "examples" from the given field providing grounds for "induction," such as was advocated, for instance, by Francis Bacon, is certainly here receiving some encouragement that has seldom if ever been attended to. "Induction" is being encouraged here, subtly but really, by typographically supported developments within the commonplace tradition. The units are not individual observations or experiments, but bits of texts.

These developments show that the age's concern with particularities is not due simply to interest in physical science, that is, to interest in "induction" from individual experienced instances such as will lead to a universal scientific principle or "rule." Speculation about scientific induction there was in plenty in the Renaissance, as for that matter, there had been in earlier ages. But concern for particulars in the extramental world of the Renaissance patently intermingles here with a concern for textual particulars, which though outside the mind, on paper or parchment, in fact had to do with the mental world, since texts represented thought and its formulation and expression. In the case of Theodor Zwinger, to be discussed below, we see the two concerns merged or confused.

The new world of humanism and print in which Textor operated did not, however, immediately maximize all the fuller possibilities that print offered for particularized knowledge storage and retrieval. The new medium was too new, and many of the new procedures that it would ultimately make operative were slow to be realized. Successive editions of Textor's *Officina* and *Epithets* only gradually implement the possibilities of rapid visual retrieval inherent in print from the beginning. But this makes them all the more interesting, for despite the inertia in all cultural institutions, they do move eventually and inexorably toward more effective implementation.

We have already noted the often chaotic sequence of materials in the original text itself of the *Officina*. Comparable chaos rules the finding apparatus provided in the volume for pulling items out of the text. In the first edition of the *Officina* (1520), the headings are arranged at the beginning of the book in an index or table of chapters, not alphabetically but simply in their order of occurrence in the work. Visual retrieval is a matter of concern here, but not of urgent concern: the effort to expedite such retrieval is, by later standards, half-hearted. The 1532 Paris edition and subsequent editions, however, take visual access more seriously: they provide an introductory alphabetical index. The later editions of the *Officina* prepared by Lycosthenes further implement visual access by organizing the body of the collection itself into clearly defined sections. Don Cameron Allen's claim (23) that Textor's *Officina* is divided into seven major sections shows that he was using one of Lycosthenes' editions: the sections do not exist in Textor's original work.

Similarly, in the original edition of the *Epitheta*, entries themselves are presented in alphabetical order, but in a way that again shows that visual retrieval of material was still not attended to with full seriousness by later standards. Alphabetization is by first letter only: all the "a"s are together, but "al-" might occur before "ag-" or "ab-." This could indicate, and perhaps does to some degree indicate, haste in getting the material together. But that is not all. It is quite clear that alphabetic ordering as such is quite low in Textor's priorities, for he himself deliberately puts the entry on "Apollo" first of all and explains that he does so because, although alphabetically "Apollo" strictly belongs a little further down among the "a"s, it is most fitting that a collection of epithets for writing poetry should start with epithets that apply to the patron of poetry, Apollo (fol. 1). Hierarchy and the realities of the human lifeworld take ready precedence over mechanical alphabetic arrangement, which is to say over arrangement for fully implemented visual access.

Instances of casual visual organization of materials in this period can be multiplied indefinitely, as can instances of progressively better organization for visual retrieval. We shall content ourselves with some few more samples here. A work of the scholar and translator Raffaele Maffei (Raphael Maffeius Vollaterranus, 1455-1522), who is credited by Zwinger (*Theatrum* fol. [):( ):(4]) with being one of Ravisius Textor's chief sources, presents us with a clear case of alphabetization by sound rather than by letter: Maffeius' *Commentariorum urbanorum libri octo et triginta*, the British Museum copy (shelf mark 1437. w.3) that I have used here has no title page, but it does have a colophon. In Maffeius' book, a great mass of commonplace material, encyclopedic in scope and again, judged by later editorial standards, only partly digested, is introduced by various indices in which the letter *H*, not pronounced in Italian and no doubt considered by many Italians to be pronounceable only by barbarians, is printed but disregarded. Thus, for example, on fol. *3[r] we find this alphabetization: "Alyza, Halyzones, Haliartus, Alifa . . . ." The procedure makes sense, of course, but it also shows disposition to store the words on the page in terms of what they sound like rather than what they look like. Later Italian reference works, though they traffic minimally in the letter *H*, nevertheless commonly acknowledge its existence if not as a sound at least as a visually apprehensible item on the same footing with other letters, and alphabetize it accordingly. It will be noted also in this series of words, that the letters *I* and *Y*, being pronounced alike, are also treated as the same letter: "Halicarnassus, Halyz, Alyza, Halyzones, Haliartus, Alifa."

The casual alphabetization of Textor and the phonetic alphabetization of Maffeius would not be without precedent in manuscript tradition, and thus it is not surprising to find either kind in print. The point about their appearance in print is their brief tenure: this sort of thing is doomed by the new medium, which enforces strictly visual regularity as handwriting had not done. Today no editor would tolerate the casual approach to alphabetization taken in Textor's and other early printed works.

We can turn to a final sample that shows both the intense drive to assemble vast masses of commonplace excerpts and an attempt to organize them in another way for visual retrieval. The Basel physician and polymath Theodor Zwinger the Elder (1533-1588) undertook what was in many ways certainly the most comprehensively ambitious compilation of commonplace excerpts up to his time. His *Theatrum humanae vitae* is perhaps the world's largest single collection of commonplace excerpts. It went through five progressively enlarged editions between 1565 and 1604 (1565, 1571, 1576, 1586-1587, 1604), running to over 5,000 double-column folio pages of small type by the posthumous 1604 edition.

In this collection Zwinger marshals tens of thousands of single excerpts from extant writings to try to produce what today would be called groundwork for "scientific" history—he (11) calls it the work of "historian-rhapsodists" (*rhapsodi historici*), who ferret out and "stitch together" (*rhapsoidein* in Greek) the units of history, as the epic poets or other narrators "rhapsodized" or "stitched together" the themes and formulas out of the commonplace tradition in their oral performances. Zwinger may have picked up the term from Sabellicus, one of his many sources. Sabellicus uses the term *rhapsodic historiarum*, "a rhapsody of histories," in headings (e.g. fol. aaii) as well as in his *Prefatio* and his concluding "M. Antonius Sabellicus Democrito." There is no evidence, though, of any theory of his about *rhapsodia*. Sabellicus refers to various sources and has a general feeling that history is "woven" out of *exempla*—"*fartum et tectum inde opus*," "*a Venetiae civitatis conspectu totam . . . texui historiam*" (fol. [GGviii^V]). In Zwinger a new feel for the management of the textual store of knowledge in terms of constituent particulars is simultaneously in contact with the commonplace tradition (itemize and classify for re-use in discourse) and with some kind of more or less Baconian notion of scientific induction (itemize and classify to discover "rules" or "laws").

Zwinger's ponderous work is a product of the Basel milieu, not only financially, but also psychologically and genealogically. Zwinger's mother was the sister of the Basel printer Iohannes Oporinus and Zwinger had close personal connections with other printers: he lodged in Lyons for

three years with the printer Bering, was financed on a trip to Italy by the
Basel printer Peter Perna, and married Boniface Amerbach's sister-in-law
(see Karcher). The *Theatrum humanae vitae* (or, in the first two editions,
1565 and 1571, *Theatrum vitae humanae*) builds largely on the compil-
ing work undertaken earlier by Zwinger's father-in-law, Conrad
Lycosthenes (Wolffhardt), a continuator of Erasmus' compilations who
has been noted here earlier as editor of some late printings of Ravisius
Textor's *Officina*.

   In the last edition (1586-1587) of the *Theatrum humanae vitae* to
appear before his own death, Zwinger lists 510 authors as sources. His
son Jakob slightly enlarged the posthumous 1604 edition, which is dedicated to the Triune God—who else? Probably no mere creaturely dedica-
tee could have survived the now over 5,000 dense pages. Jakob added
new *exempla*, especially recent ones, and—an important point noted earlier and to be returned to later—improved the indices. These list 601
authors. The 1604 edition, with some slight variations, is largely a page-
for-page resetting of the 1586-1587 edition. The *Theatrum*, in all editions,
undertakes to treat universal history in terms of the good and evil of
mankind (1571, 10) and consists entirely of short excerpts from published
sources. By history in terms of the good and evil of mankind, Zwinger
appears in fact to mean a large proportion of everything that has ever happened, since there is little in the world which cannot be related directly or
deviously to man, for his good or evil. Zwinger's range is quite as indiscriminate as Textor's. The various sections of the work treat good and bad
things of the soul, of the body, good and bad chance occurrences, instruments of philosophy (grammar, rhetoric, poetic, logic), practical philosophical habits (including legislation, history, and worth or dignity), tem-
perance and intemperance, money, refinement (as opposed to flattery and
fastidiousness), religious and secular justice, mechanical skills (in artists,
workmen, craftsmen), the solitary, academic, religious, political, and economic life of man, not to mention other headings.

   In all subjects Zwinger casts his net wide. For example, in his chapter *"De prudentia inventrice bellica sive de strategematis"* (1586-1587, 7:
lib. iii), a title which we can render "On Inventive Prudence in Warfare,
or Stratagems," he includes material under the following classifications:
conscription of strong men; elimination of the cowardly; conscription
willy-nilly; conscription by wager; segregation of the suspect and perfid-
ious and rebellious; military haircuts and beards; deception of the enemy
by simulated victory, retreat, peace, friendliness, or by use of smoke,
snow, or statues, of fire, gestures, clubs, and noises of all sorts, or by use
of the human voice, either through shouting or through the utterance of

enigmas; the amassing and conservation of resources; treachery and desertion; the use and misuse of fortifications; the crossings of seas, lakes, rivers; avoidance of wild animals and snakes; kindness toward one's own forces; avarice and desire for booty; the hope of happiness, glory, victory, freedom; etc. His *exempla* include items such as an account of a betting system to recruit oarsmen for galleys (1586-1587, 7: lib. iii; 1768) and an anecdote (7: lib. iii) from Frontinus telling how Hannibal induced his reluctant elephants to cross the Rhone by having one of his men slash an elephant under the ear and then run to the river and swim across with the enraged elephant and all his elephant friends in pursuit (1811). A little later (7: lib. v), Zwinger is off in another direction with a series of anecdotes on the fervor of the Anabaptists (1946). He apologizes in his introduction for not doing a more comprehensive job, noting that collectors of "special places" (in Aristotle's sense, as contrasted with "common" places), such as those having to do with oratory or grammar or poetry or sepulchers or marriages or banquets, can do more thorough work than those who, like himself, are "rhapsodists" of universal history and thus attempt to excerpt and string together everything that was ever said on anything (1604, fol. [):( ):(5^V]).

In breaking down into excerpts and reorganizing the extant noetic store, Zwinger's aims and his epistemology are beyond a doubt not only typographically but also topographically conditioned. His title *Theatrum* . . . , matched in scores of other late sixteenth- and seventeenth-century "theater" titles (for example, theaters of botany, of chemistry, of celestial wisdom, of universal nature, of peace, of consumption [diseases], of God's judgments, of hydrotechnic machines, of politics, of poetry, etc.), advertises his visualist noetics. He explains that the twenty volumes of the *Theatrum* are in fact twenty scenes (1571, 32). Zwinger thinks of the printed page as a map on which knowledge itself is laid out. Over and over again he compares his work to that of geographers and cartographers. Like geographers, he describes only the larger places (*loci*) into which he wants to "distribute" his materials, relegating the "little places" (*locula*) to special supplements—"In suos locos distribuenda" (1604, fol. [):( ):(5^V]). The spatial implications in the classical notion of the *loci* as mental "places" where arguments can be located are realized with a vengeance here, as is true throughout the Ramist tradition (Ong, *Ramus* 310-13) in which, to a significant degree, Zwinger operates. The original "places" in the mind, a highly metaphorical conception, have here been transmuted into physical places on the printed page. Zwinger's ranging of *exempla* under titles (*tituli*) likened to the plotting of travels such as those of Alexander the Great and of Ulysses, and to the geometrical work of

Archimedes (1604, fol. [):():5^V]). In a like vein Peter Ramus had under-taken to organize knowledge in accordance with "Solon's Law," a build-ing code for ancient Athens specifying how far apart houses and walls and other structures had to be—the different bodies of knowledge were to be kept separate from one another in a similar way (Ong, *Ramus* 280-81).

Zwinger's concern for a topography of the mind goes hand in hand with an interest in physical topography. His works include a *Methodus apodemica*, in which he undertakes an outline of how to travel and to describe what one encounters. The work is remarkable for, among other things, a Ramist approach to art and art history: in a typically Ramist dichotomized diagram Zwinger analyzes Verocchio's equestrian statue of Bartolomeo Colleoni in Venice, plotting the statue in terms of its four causes (material, formal, efficient, and final) so thoroughly as to include a full historical treatment even of the vandalism to which the statue had been subjected (398).

The Basel physician was an omnibus dissectionist in the tradition which gives rise to, among other things, Burton's *Anatomy of Melancholy* and the scores of other "anatomy" titles of the age. The number of "anato-my" titles from the mid-1500s through the 1600s has never been calcu-lated, so far as I know. I have accumulated some thirty or so, quite inci-dentally, mostly of English works—anatomies of the mind, of valor, of abuses, of a lover's flatteries, of fortune, of sin, of the world, etc. There are many more anatomy titles of course in Latin and the other vernacu-lars. Passing references to the anatomy literature are to be found in Beaurline and in Höltgen, who treats Zwinger at some length and explic-itly connects the "anatomy" with Ramist dichotomized tables.

Zwinger is an outspoken admirer and follower of Ramus, whom he had known when the latter was visiting in Basel in 1569 and who praises Zwinger's *Theatrum* in his *Basilea* (18-19)—Zwinger is one of the rare Ramist doctors of medicine, for physicians were commonly the most adamant of Ramus' numerous opponents. Zwinger undertakes the organ-ization of his (ultimately) more than five thousand pages of material through Ramist dichotomized outline charts, which introduce each sec-tion of the *Theatrum humanae vitae* to show how the heads within the section and the quotations under each head all articulate. Charts on suc-cessive pages are linked to one another by asterisks or daggers or other typographical symbols, one of which will be affixed to one of the final brackets of a given page and then will recur at the head of the bracket dis-play on a subsequent page to indicate where the subsequent outline is to be hooked onto the preceding to continue the dichotomized divisions.

Visually neat, the result is so complicated as to be psychologically quite unmanageable. The reader is paralyzed by over-organized structural detail. And, in fact, although his *Theatrum humanae vitae* consists entirely of a fabric of citations in the full-blown commonplace tradition, Zwinger has lost all sense of the oral roots of the tradition. His excerpts are hardly conceived of as serving "invention," as providing matter to be fed back into the stream of discourse, the way Textor's had been. Rather, Zwinger's aim is to tidy up knowledge by collecting in snippets everything everyone has said with a view to arranging all the snippets in proper, visually retrievable, order, so that, in a historical "rhapsody," as explained here above, one can at long last find out why things are the way they are. Good Ramist that he was, Zwinger felt that somehow the thousands of quotations ranged "logically" in his text represented in some vague way the "structure" of the human lifeworld, the microcosm, and thus in some fashion, no doubt, the macrocosm as well.

The idea of diagrammatic organization has overwhelmed Zwinger without his quite knowing what has happened to him. The same idea would overwhelm many of his Swiss compatriots, for the typographic collecting drive and also the Ramist dichotomized outline appear to have enjoyed a vogue in Basel and elsewhere in Switzerland that they never quite achieved in other parts of the West. Zwinger's mentality may appear today curiously bemused in its addiction to noetic cartography, but the same drive toward consummate tidiness that produced this cartography would continue to manifest itself through the next two centuries in the Cartesian addiction to clarity and distinctness, and, even more conspicuously in the folding chart of knowledge, the *système figuré*, which at the opening of Diderot's and d'Alembert's *Encyclopedie* (1751-1772) epitomizes Enlightenment noetics.

In fact, the use of Ramist dichotomized outline diagrams, by Zwinger and so many others, for all its somewhat zany ineffectuality, was not entirely wrongheaded even though it had more limitations than Ramists might allow. For the Ramist outline would eventually have its day. In its binary organization, as anyone who knows computer programming sees immediately, the Ramist dichotomized outline is in fact nothing other than a computer flow chart. One can, however, hardly have a successful computer operation until one has a computer. This neither Ramus nor Zwinger had, but there can be little doubt that both would have welcomed one.

Ravisius Textor and his congeners, such as Zwinger, I hope it is clear, had no way of viewing what they were doing in the perspectives suggested here—which, it might be noted again, are by no means the only perspectives for viewing the commonplace enterprise of the Renaissance.

These perspectives appear useful largely because they help show how, with the emergence of typography, the human imagination, conditioned for thousands of years in the orally grounded commonplace methods of processing the noetic stores of a culture, was evolving new ways of organizing this store outside consciousness, in the silent tidiness of exactly duplicable, printed texts. Yet even after print, storage processes proper to the original oral culture or manuscript culture, with the latter's very heavy oral residue, persisted through many generations: that is to say, the drive to consider what had been said as demanding perpetual reiteration continued strong. Academia still felt the last thrust of the drive in *gradus ad Parnassum* or metrical Latin phrase books that persisted through the nineteenth century, providing schoolboys with set excerpts and expressions for the construction of Latin verse. Today in technological cultures, however, commonplace collections, or their equivalents, are quite peripheral to serious discourse, being restricted largely to dictionaries of jokes and of quotations compiled basically for desperate after-dinner speakers rather than for the serious playwrights, teachers, scholars, and scientists for whom Renaissance collections (and earlier collections) were typically prepared. In the Renaissance, the commonplace material to which Kristeller rightly draws attention was still part of the grist demanded for even the first-rate intellect.

An oral culture can make no lists of commonplaces, for lists demand writing, but, as has been suggested in the first section of this study, following Havelock, such a culture has as its commonplace collections the formal oral performances such as orations or narrative poetry or prose or other poetry, for these performances are most beautifully woven ("rhapsodized") textures of formulaic materials. The *Iliad*, it will be remembered, not only weaves together fixedly thematic and formulaic materials ("the rosy-fingered dawn," "the wine-dark sea," and so on), but actually includes a nearly four-hundred-line roster of the Greek leaders and their followers. This roster is presented in formulaic fashion itself, but it is a kind of oral equivalent of a list, an oral version of Ravisius Textor's and Zwinger's printed compilations. An oral culture's poems are the equivalent of commonplace collections (though they are other things besides).

It is of considerable interest that the Renaissance itself still preserved a strong sense that this is what poems and/or other "inventions" were, *inter alia*—assemblages of commonplace materials to which other poets could resort for the matter of their own poems. The Elizabethan anthology is typically presented to its reader not simply as an anthology would be presented today, that is, as a collection of works to enjoy. It is also presented as a collection of materials to be used. *Anthologia* is the Greek word for which the Latin *florilegium* is a calque: both mean etymologically "flower collection," for which the English equivalent is "posies," a term that figures in not a few Elizabethan collections of poems. The conceptual apparatus of "flowers" and "collecting" is tied in with the massive tradition of rhetorical invention (which includes poetic invention) running back into classical antiquity and thence to the oral sources of literature. "Flowers" imply the busy rhetorical "bee" who goes through the garden (or, at times, the forest) of invention to visit the "places" (*loci, topoi*) from which "arguments" are to be extracted. From the garden he gathers nectar to make honey (orations or poems). These themselves can be constituted as bouquets of flowers, in which "arguments" are artfully arranged now rather than naturally grown, and which are still interesting to industrious bees. One goes to an anthology thus conceived not merely to enjoy oneself but also to make out of what one can extract from the "inventions" there other "inventions" or poems of one's own. This is the ideology in play in the titles of anthologies such as John Bodenham's *Belvedere, or the Garden of the Muses* (1600) or John Proctor's *A Gorgeous Gallery of Gallant Inventions* (1578) or Clement Robinson's *A Handfull of Pleasant Delights* (1584).

In this tradition, with a certain effort, not entirely unwarranted, the commonplace book itself can be viewed as a kind of literary genre. If narratives taking shape within oral cultures, such as the *Iliad* or the *Odyssey* or *Beowulf* (or, in the present, the countless similarly formulaic tales and other verbal performances being transcribed in oral cultures everywhere today, particularly in the Third World), are collections of commonplaces in the sense of formulaic materials stitched together in a narrative frame, or if the classical oration is largely a collection of commonplaces framed for persuasion, the commonplace book is a collection of similar materials ranged in a more abstract frame. To this extent, Textor's two collections examined here and Zwinger's more ponderous assemblage and the hundreds of other collections like these three, are in a way more of a piece with the original oral epic than later epics are, such as Milton's *Paradise Lost* or even Virgil's *Aeneid*. (For the way in which Virgil studiously adapted orally based Homeric similes to the demands of written composition, see Carlson.) The collections of stock materials and the old epics belong to the same noetic world—the world of commonplace thinking. Milton has his share of stock epithets, but he was literate enough to want to minimize them if not to avoid them totally; for fully literate cultures, by contrast with oral cultures, teach their members that verbalization should avoid clichés. (In *The Faerie Queene*, however, it might be noted, for reasons that heretofore have never been fully explained, Spenser uses epithets with many of the techniques and with almost all the abandon of an oral poet, though this is a conspicuously literate poem.)

In these perspectives Textor and even Zwinger appear, if not as poets, which they certainly are not, at least in some sense as typographical equivalents of Homer—weavers, if not of tales, then at least of the elements of tales. For Homer, and oral poets generally, are more than poets are in technological cultures: they are also encyclopedists, the repositories for the culture's noetic store that they retrieve and organize by "weaving." It is interesting that Textor in Latin actually means "weaver," a meaning that its French form Tixier (Tissier—cf. *tisser*, to weave; *tisserand*, weaver) at least suggests. An individual's identity is deeply wrapped up in his name, and who knows the deeper forces of consciousness or of culture that may have helped steer this sixteenth-century humanist into his sometimes bizarre achievements? (One thinks immediately also of Ramus, whose name in both this Latin form and in its original French form, La Ramée, means "branch" and who specialized in branched dichotomized outlines or "ramifications" of knowledge, as has been noted here above.)

Effects on Renaissance Literature:
A Sonnet of Shakespeare's

Robert R. Bolgar has made the point that much Renaissance teaching of rhetoric, and particularly the doctrine of imitation, implies that a literary work consists of an assemblage of individually conceived parts (271-73). Although too much can be made of implications, this same piecemeal view of literary composition is obviously also implied by the doctrine of the commonplaces here discussed, and in a special way by the studied exploitation of epithets. For epithets—standard or expected qualifiers or substitutes for given nouns, encoding a certain amount of lore (the *sturdy* oak, the *clinging* vine, the *vain* braggart, etc.)—by and large, are the simplest or at least the smallest bits, the least divisible particles in a rhapsodizer's repertoire. A commonplace disquisition on, say, loyalty might run to a thousand words. An epithet is generally one word, a least common denominator, an atom, in commonplace composition. This is doubtless why Ravisius Textor's collection and others like it were useful for relative neophytes in the art of rhetoric. These collections provided the elemental particles of discourse.

If only because of this paradigmatic status of the epithet in the commonplace tradition, the effects of epithet collections on literature is a subject that warrants far more attention than it has received. Renaissance literature often intoxicates itself on epithets. In Book III, Chapter 38, of *Gargantua and Pantagruel*, Pantagruel and Panurge become dithyrambic over Triboulet's unparalleled qualifications as a fool, heaping up some 207 different epithets (some of them quite bizarre, rather than standard, qualifiers, but forced ironically to serve as epithets anyhow) to specify exactly what kind of a fool Triboulet is. This is only one of many such chains of epithets in Rabelais' work. It would be interesting to check such epithetic dithyrambs in detail against individual epithet collections and interesting, too, to check John Lyly's, Thomas Nashe's, or by contrast, Thomas Deloney's prose against such collections. So, too, with poetry: a recent study views epithetic poetry as a minor genre under which some of George Herbert's sonnets can be classified (Mollenkott).

In the study of the effects of epithet collections on literature Ravisius Textor's *Epitheta* must be accorded close attention. T. W. Baldwin has shown at great length that this work was one of the most esteemed and most used books for the writing of Latin and English in Shakespeare's day, and that Shakespeare himself might well have used it (1:174; 2:366, 414-16, 455, 508). Ascham's invective against the book itself attests clearly to Textor's popularity, at the grammar school level especially— "Grammar schools have few *epitomes* to hurt them, except *Epithets Textoris*, and such beggarly gatherings as Horman, Wittinton, and other like vulgars for making of Latins" (106-07). It is clear from the context that Ascham is taking "epitome" to refer to any edition of Textor's *Epitheta* or *Officina*, not simply to the abridged editions of the *Epitheta* got up by later editors under the title *Epitome epithetorum*. Indeed "epitome" for Ascham refers pretty much to commonplace collections, in the wide generic sense in which I have been using the term "commonplace collections" here.

In a programmatically repetitive milieu such as that of the commonplace books, one must be careful, of course, in ascribing any given literary production to a particular commonplace book as a source. But sometimes startling instances of correspondences leap to the eye, especially in works or passages that are largely cascades of epithets. Such an instance is one of Shakespeare's best known poems, his Sonnet 129, which suggests how deliberately and directly Textor's *Epitheta* may at times have been used. The sonnet treats of lust and its consummation—but in reverse: first briefly (one and one-half lines) of the consummation of lust ("lust in action") and then retrospectively, in the rest of the poem, of lustful desires ("till action, lust").

> Th'expense of spirit in a waste of shame
> Is lust in action; and till action, lust
> Is perjur'd, murd'rous, bloody, full of blame,
> Savage, extreme, rude, cruel, not to trust;
> Enjoy'd no sooner but despised straight;
> Past reason hunted; and no sooner had,
> Past reason hated, as a swallow'd bait
> On purpose laid to make the taker mad:
> Mad in pursuit, and in possession so;
> Had, having, and in quest to have, extreme;
> A bliss in proof, and prov'd a very woe;
> Before a joy propos'd, behind, a dream.
> All this the world well knows; yet none know well
> To shun the heaven that leads men to this hell.

This poem is almost entirely a piling up of epithets. Other connections of the poem have been pointed out that do not invalidate or contravene the connection with the commonplace tradition examined here and that, indeed, often corroborate or further specify this connection. Peterson notes relationships between the sonnet and rhetorical schemes such as those discussed in Thomas Wilson's *Arts of Rhetorique*. The schemes Peterson treats are admirably suited to the exploitation of epithets, and are themselves from commonplace books.

If we turn in Textor's *Epitheta* to the two key terms with which Shakespeare is concerned, *luxuria* or *luxuries* (both these forms occur in Latin) for "lust in action" and *libido* for lustful desires ("till action, lust"), we find striking equivalents for every epithet in this sonnet, and indeed often two or three Latin terms for one or another English word. Shakespeare's keynote for his sonnet, lust's wastefulness, is sounded loud and clear by the very first epithet supplied by Textor under *luxuria* (luxuries), the epithet *prodiga* (spendthrift, extravagant, wasteful), represented in Shakespeare's first line by "expense" and by "waste."

Some of the correspondence between Textor's Latin and Shakespeare's English can be noted here, with Textor's Latin terms beneath the word (italicized) in Shakespeare's text that they suggest.

> Th'*expense* of spirit in a *waste* of *shame*
>   prodiga   prodigia   prava, nefanda, infamis,
>   turpis, impudens
> Is *lust* in action, and *till action, lust*
>   (LUXURIES)   (LIBIDO)

Is *perjur'd, murd'rous, bloody, full of blame*
    fallax   scelerata   flagitiosa probrosa, vitiosa, nefaria
Savage,   extreme,   rude,   cruel,   not to trust
immoderata, intemperata refrenanda saeva fallax indomita
Enjoyed no sooner but *despised straight*
blanda   odiosa
Past reason hunted, and no sooner had
inconsulta, intemperans, avida
Past reason hated, as a *swallowed bait*
foeda   occulta, personata, astuta
On purpose laid to make the taker *mad*
                           rabida, insane, furens, vecors
Mad in pursuit,   and in *possession so*
praeceps, effrenata,   saeviens, dira
impetuosa
Had, having, and in quest to have, *extreme*
                  infrenata
A *bliss in proof,* and prov'd a *very woe*
blanda, fervens   aerumnosa, intolerabilis, noxia
Before a joy proposed; behind, a dream
illecebrosa   perdita, vana
All this the world well knows, yet none knows well
To shun the *heaven* that leads men to this *hell.*
     carnis arnica   perniciosa, damnosa

This exploitation of epithets, encouraged by Textor and the common-place tradition generally, can strike an age committed to Romantic originality and "creativity" as devastatingly artificial, unrelated to the human world. But to Shakespeare the use of epithets seemed quite the opposite, eminently human and urbane. "All this the world well knows." How? By experience? Yes, certainly. But by direct experience? Hardly. The store of experience with which Shakespeare's sonnet resonates would certainly take a great deal of time to accumulate. Moreover, as Roger Ascham (1515 or 1516-1568) had just reminded readers of *The Schoolmaster* (1570—published posthumously by Ascham's widow), experience is the worst teacher: too many die from it before they learn, or even after they have learned, for the lessons experience teaches can prove fatal.

> Learning teacheth more in one year than experience in twenty, and learning teacheth safely, when experience maketh more miserable than wise. He hazardeth sore that waxeth wise by experience. An

unhappy master he is that is made cunning by many shipwrecks; a
miserable merchant, that is neither rich nor wise but after some bank-
rupts. It is costly wisdom that is brought by experience. (50)

A mature person must have a lot of experience—indeed, more than anyone can have time for directly—but if a person is truly mature, he or she
can, and must, supplement direct experience by vicarious and empathetic
experience. Even direct experience is normally the richer for the vicarious experience brought to it. Shakespeare was hardly so callow as to
believe that all readers of his sonnet would have experienced directly all
the degrees of disillusionment that his sonnet deals with, or that they
needed to have experienced them directly, or even that it would have been
helpful if they had. Experiences of the sort he is concerned with here
would not always leave the sensibility intact enough to appreciate this
sonnet or any other. Many would normally be destructive experiences,
even though not always irreparable.

"All this the world well knows." How then, if not simply from direct
experience? From Ravisius Textor, of course, or from his equivalents and
thus from the total experience of the vast culture that Textor's excerpts
sample. That is to say, from all the literature of classical antiquity—a literature based indeed in one way or another on experience, direct and/or
indirect, matured over hundreds of years of classical and postclassical,
largely Christian, reflection, and by reflection on reflection. The age's
restriction of its references—in principle if not in full actuality—to classical antiquity of course strikes us today as quaint and parochial. There
was, after all, much more to mankind's experience than what
Mediterranean civilization provided. But at least the civilization built
around and in great part out of Mediterranean classical antiquity was
large enough in time and in space to provide a sizable body of experience,
the most sizable and viable body in fact that anyone in Shakespeare's
West had access to. You work with the best you know.

In these perspectives Shakespeare's value becomes once more that of
a skillful conservator and reflector of the amassed wisdom of a sizable
portion of the human race. Like his contemporaries generally,
Shakespeare was not original in the way in which poets since the
Romantic age have often programed themselves to be original. He did not
"create" from nothing. He did not want to, nor did he even consider the
possibility. (There is no such possibility.) He wanted to rework the old
wisdom in an always fresh and meaningful way. Shakespeare is perhaps
our most quotable author in English, or at least the most quoted. It is, or
should be, a commonplace that the reason he is quotable is that his text
consists so much of quotations—not grossly appropriated, but nuanced,

woven into the texture of his work more tightly than is normally possible in any performance, no matter how sophisticated, in the oral tradition, in which the practice of composing out of other compositions is nevertheless grounded, as has been seen. Shakespeare appropriated the oral tradition and exploited it with the condensation and pointedness made possible by writing and even more by print.

And yet the tradition that Shakespeare here exploits in Sonnet 129 and elsewhere in his works—the individual reader can study out for himself where else and how—was moribund at the very time Shakespeare was using it to the maximum. By now it is gone, at least in its Renaissance form. We cannot compose in this way any more. When the heritage of the past is exploited with comparable deliberateness and calculation today, and with comparable effect, it comes out, as in James Joyce's *Ulysses* or *Finnegans Wake*, woven into infinitely more complications than even Shakespeare managed—or wanted to manage—and into different kinds of complications. Shakespeare's world was not what ours is in its relationship to the store of human knowledge—which store itself was different from ours, though not discontinuous with ours. Shakespeare belonged to a world in which typographical culture had not had its full impact, a world in which the accumulation of circumstantial information, vast as it was, could not match that at hand today, and in which information could not be codified so neatly as it can in our superindexed books and supercatalogued libraries and superprogramed electronic computers.

But Shakespeare's world was moving toward ours. With typography and the possibilities it brought of greater codification, the age of intensified information-collecting was beginning to succeed the age more given to utterance-collecting. Soon commonplace collections, which were essentially collections of what persons had said (or, later, written), would be absorbed and superseded by encyclopedias in the modern sense, beginning with the primitive "methodized" works of Johann Heinrich Alsted and terminating in such works as today's *Britannica*, which set before the reader stores of "data" and "information." Encyclopedia users today commonly do not advert to the fact that even today encyclopedia articles, and even dictionary definitions, still represent something that someone "says" (writes) about a subject. There is no way to lay hold of a "fact" without some kind of intervention of voice. But we live in a world that tends to feel that pure "facts," without voice, are there, "contained" in the silent, visible words that are contained in the sentences that are contained in the paragraphs that are contained in the pages that are contained in the volume that is contained in the set that can be located with the help of a trustworthy and convincingly abstract system (Dewey or Library of Congress) upon a specified shelf contained in the library.

Shakespeare lived on the verge of this supercodification or super-localization of the noetic world. But in Shakespeare's day, the codifying, localizing process was in great part still turned primarily not toward purportedly nonvocalized "data" but quite overtly toward sayings, which had been the proper preoccupation of the original oral culture of mankind and which remained a major preoccupation of the residually oral culture of the Renaissance. Without decrying our vast expansion of the poetic world and our need to deal with "facts"—perhaps more gingerly and critically than we usually do—we can ask ourselves whether any poetry or literature can forgo delving into the commonplace world of sayings, of communal memory, from which Shakespeare and Ravisius Textor drew, whether it can bypass the wisdom stored in what men and women out of the past have said about actuality and about their experience, matured by subsequent reflection, and sharpened and driven home. It would appear quite feasible to demonstrate that where modern literature is at its peak it retains a living connection of some sort with the commonplace tradition, and when it is poor its poverty is due to its failure to establish this connection—which is to say to its ignorance of itself, of how it comes to be where it is. The older we get, the more mature our literature deserves to be.

Works Cited

Allen, Don Cameron. *Francis Meres's Treatise 'Poetrie': A Critical Edition.* Urbana, IL: U of Illinois P, 1933. U of Illinois Studies in Language and Literature, 16.3-4.

Ascham, Roger. *The Schoolmaster* (1570). Ed. Lawrence V. Ryan. Ithaca, NY: Cornell UP, 1967.

Baldwin, T. W. *William Shakspere's Small Latine and Lesse Greeke.* 2 vols. Urbana, IL: U of Illinois P, 1944.

Beaurline, L. A. "Ben Jonson and the Illusion of Completeness." *PMLA* 84 (1969): 51-59

Beck, August. "Die 'Studio Humanitatis' and ihre Methode." *Bibliotheque d'Humanisme et Renaissance* 21 (1959): 273-290.

Bolgar, Robert R. *The Classical Heritage and Its Beneficiaries.* Cambridge, UK: Cambridge UP, 1958.

Carlson, Gregory. *Die Verwandlung der homerischen Gleichnisse in Vergils Äneis.* Heidelberg: Ruprecht-Karl-Universität zu Heidelberg, 1972.

Curtius, Ernst Robert. *European Literature and the Latin Middle Ages.* Trans. Willard Trask. New York: Pantheon Books, 1953. Bollingen Series, 36.

"Encyclopaedia," *Encyclopaedia Britannica*. Ed. Warren E. Preece. 24 vols. Chicago: Encyclopaedia Britannica, 1973.

"Florilegia." *New Catholic Encyclopedia*. Ed. William J. McDonald. 15 vols. New York: McGraw-Hill, 1967.

Hajnal, Istvan. *L'Enseignement de l'écriture aux universités médiévales*. Budapest: Academia Scientiarium Hungarica Budapestini, 1954.

Havelock, Eric A. *Preface to Plato*. Cambridge, MA: Belknap P of Harvard UP, 1963.

Höltgen, Karl Josef. "Synoptischen Tabellen in der medizinischen Literatur und die Logik Agricolas and Ramus." *Sudhoffs Archiv für Geschichte der Medizin und der Naturwissenschaften*. Wiesbaden: Franz Sterner Verlag. 79.4 (1965): 371-90.

Hutten, Ulrich de. *Equitis Germani Aula. Dialogus*. Paris: Antonius Aussurdus, 1519.

Johnson, Thomas. *Cornucopiae, or Divers Secrets: wherein is contained the rare secrets in man, beasts . . . plantes, stones, and such like . , , and not before committed to be printed in English, newlie drawen out of divers Latins authors . . .* London: for W. Bailey, 1595.

Karcher, Johannes. *Theodor Zwinger und seine Zeitgenossen: Episode aus dem Ringer der Basler Ärzte um die Grundlehren der Medizin in Zeitalter des Barocks*. Basel: Verlag von Helbling and Lichtenhahn, 1956. Studien zur Geschichte der Wissenschaften in Basel, 3.

Kristeller, Paul Oskar. "The Moral Thought of Renaissance Humanism." *Chapters in Western Civilization*. Ed. The Contemporary Civilization Staff of Columbia College, Columbia University, 3d ed. New York: Columbia UP, 1961.

Lechner, Sister Joan Marie. *Renaissance Concepts of the Commonplaces*. New York: Pageant P, 1962. Reprinted: Westport, CT: Greenwood Press, 1974.

Lindfors, Bernth. "Perverted Proverbs in Nigerian Chapbooks." *Proverbium* 15 (1970): 62 [482]-71 [487].

Maffei, Raffaele. *Commentariorum urbanorum libri octo et triginta*. Rome: Ioannes Besicken Alemanus, 1506. [The British Museum copy—shelf mark 1487. w.3—which I have used here, has no title page, but it does have a colophon.]

Massebieau, L. *De Ravisii Textoris comoediis seu De Comoediis collegiorum in Gallic praesertim ineunto sexto decimo saeculo disquisitionern Facultati Litterarum Parisiensi proponebat L. Masssbieau*. Paris: J. Bonheure, 1878.

McFarlane, I. D. "Reflections on Ravisius Textor's Specimen epithetorum." *Classical influences on European Culture A.D. 1500-1700*. Ed. Robert R. Bolgar. Cambridge, UK and New York: Cambridge UP, 1976. 81-90.

Merleau-Ponty, Maurice. "L'Oeil et l'esprit." *Temps Modernes* 18.184-85 (1961): 193-227.

Mignon, Maurice. *Études do littérature nivernaise: Tixier de Ravisy, Augustin Berthier, Adam Billaut, Cotignon do la Charnaye, Jules Renard*. Gap: Editions Ophrys, 1946.

Mollenkott, Virginia R. "George Herbert's Epithet-Sonnets." *Genre* 5 (1972): 131-37.

Obiechena, Emmanuel. *An African Popular Literature: A Study of Onitsha Market Pamphlets.* Cambridge, UK: Cambridge UP, 1973.

Ong, Walter J. *The Presence of the Word.* New Haven: Yale UP, 1967.

—. *Ramus and Talon Inventory.* Cambridge, MA: Harvard UP, 1958.

—. *Ramus, Method, and the Decay of Dialogue.* Cambridge, MA: Harvard UP, 1958.

—. *Rhetoric, Romance, and Technology.* Ithaca, NY: Cornell UP, 1971.

Peterson, Douglas L. "A Probable Source for Shakespeare's Sonnett CXXIX." *Shakespeare Quarterly* 5 (1954): 381-84.

Pollard, Alfred W. and G. R. Redgrave. *A Short-title Catalogue of Books Printed in England, Scotland, & Ireland and of English Books Printed Abroad 1475-1640.* London: The Bibliographical Society, 1946.

Ramus, Peter. *Petri Rami Basilea ad senatum populumque Basiliensem.* [Lausanne: Ioannes Probus], 1571.

—. *P. Rami Regii Professoris Dialecticae libri duo.* 1st ed. Paris: Andreas Wechel, 1572.

Rollins, Hyder. "Deloney's Sources for Euphuistic Learning." *PMLA,* 51 (1936): 398-406.

Sabellicus, Marc Antony. *Enneades Marci Antonii Sabellici ab urbe condita ad inclinationem Romani Imperii.* Venice, 1498.

Textor, Iacobus Ravisius, ed. *Ioannis Ravisii Textoris Nivernensis Epitheta . . ab authore suo recognita et in novam formam redacta.* Paris: Reginaldus Chauldière, 1524.

—, ed. Prefatory letter to Ludovicus Lassereus. *Ioannis Ravisii Textoris Nivernensis Epitheta . . ab authore suo recognita et in novam formam redacta.* Paris: Reginaldus Chauldière, 1524.

Textor, Ioannes Ravisius. *Specimen epithetorum Ioannis Ravisius Textoris Nivernensis, omnibus artis poeticae studiosis maxime utilium.* Paris: Henricus Stephanus pro Scholis Decretorum, 1518.

Vodoz, J. *Le Théâtre latin de Ravisius Textor 1470-1524.* Winterthur: Imprimerie Geschwister Ziegler, 1898.

Zwinger (Zwingerus), Theodor. *Methodus apodemica in eorum gratiam qui fructu in quocumque tandem vitae genere peregrinari cupiunt, a Theod. Zwinger Basiliense typis delineata et cum aliis tum quatuor praesertim Athenaeum vivis exemplis illustrata, cum indice.* Basel: Eusebii Episcopii opera atque impensis, 1577. [The four "Athens" which Zwinger treats are Basel (the Swiss Athens), Paris (the French Athens), Padua (the Italian Athens), and Athens (the Greek Athens). The book is not unlike a modern travel guide in the miscellaneous information it conveys, although a modern traveler would be put off by Zwinger's procrustean organization (the causes, accidents, and species of travel) and by finding himself presented not with "travel suggestions" but with "rules" (*regulae*) for travelers.]

—. *Theatrum vitae humanae.* Basel: per Ioan. Oporinum, Ambrosium et Aurelium Frobenios fratres, 1565.

—. *Theatrum vitae humanae.* Basel: ex officina Frobeniana, 1571.

—. *Theatrum humanae vitae.* Basel, 1576. [I have never seen a copy of this edition, and the only notice of it I have is its listing in *Antiquariats Katalog* Nr. 159 (1963) of the bookdealer Joseph van Matt, Stans, Switzerland, who had sold the volume by the time I had contacted him but who assured me by letter dated 3 February 1964, that the 1576 imprint is indeed correct.]

—. *Theatrum humanae vitae.* Basel: per Eusebium Episcopium, 1586-87. [The *Biographie universelle*, under Zwinger, lists a 1596 edition, of which I have found no other trace. This work of Zwinger's was widely distributed: in libraries at Cambridge University alone I have found twenty-four complete copies of one or another edition. King's *Intercollegiate* Catalogue at the Bodleian Library lists fourteen copies in libraries at Oxford.]

—. *Theatrum humanae vitae.* Basel: per Sebastianum Henricpetri, 1604.

24

Literacy and Orality in Our Times
(1978)

The English profession has always been concerned with how to create and interpret a written text. The past few years have seen a growth of interest, perhaps more theoretical than practical, in texts as such, in textuality, and a parallel growth of interest in readers as readers. But we know by contrast—an old philosophical principle long antedating modern phonemics and structuralism. Verbalization via texts and readers contrasts obviously with oral verbalization, the ancient and still basic form of verbalization. We have recently learned a great deal about the psychodynamics of orality, how oral verbalization, in pure preliterate form or in residual form within writing cultures, structures both thought processes and expression. But strangely enough, those interested in writing and reading processes, either from a practical or a theoretical point of view, including the many and often brilliant structuralist and phenomenological analysts of textuality, have done little to enlarge understanding of these processes by contrasting writing and reading processes in depth with oral and oral-aural processes. This is what I propose to do here: to review the orality in our long cultural past in order to bring an understanding of it to bear on the present literary and para-literary situation.

I

Many people like to believe that today reading is on the wane. We have all heard the complaint that television is ruining the reading habits of children. This is a contrastive judgment: "ruining" implies that the time spent by today's children before television sets was all spent by yesterday's children with books. The implication appears at the very least naive. It is in fact very difficult to compare the present state of reading and writing skills or activity with those of the past because past student populations do not match those of the present. A few generations ago, there was no academic population with today's mix of family and cultural backgrounds, with the same assortment of entering abilities and disabilities, of skills and lack of skills, of desires and aims. Not long ago, America was largely rural. Now it is overwhelmingly urban or urbanized, even in rural areas, and educational expectations have correspondingly changed. Not long ago, blacks were locked by law—illegal law—into a situation where even the most talented were denied upward mobility. And no one pointed a condemning finger at dropouts in any group because everyone took for granted that most boys and girls undergoing academic education of course dropped out, at least during college if they had not succeeded in dropping out earlier.

Even more importantly, the aims of literacy in the past were not quite the same as now. *McGuffey's Readers*, often cited in "back-to-basics" literature and talk, had objectives quite different from those commonly advanced today. They were in tune with our times in the sense that they were remedial texts—designed to improve the defective elementary and secondary education that William Holmes McGuffey blamed for the poor reading performance of his college students (see Lynn). But "poor performance" meant largely poor oratorical performance: the McGuffey *Eclectic Readers* (so-called because they adroitly incorporated bits of often violently competing theories) introduced their readers to "sound-conscious" literature. "Reading" in McGuffey's world tended to mean training for public speaking and "elocution contests." In the process the McGuffey readers doubtless helped train writers, for as Joseph Collignon has recently pointed out, the ability to write is closely connected with the ability to hear in one's imagination what a written text would sound like when read aloud. But the McGuffey *Readers'* immediate aim was more directly oral.

McGuffey *Readers* touted in rotund periods heroic figures inherited from the old oral world. "Caesar was merciful, Scipio was continent, Hannibal was patient; but it was reserved for Washington to blend them all in one, and, like the lovely masterpiece of the Grecian artist, to exhibit in one glow of associated beauty, the pride of every model, and the perfection of every artist." This typical selection, from Lyman Beecher's "The Memory of Our Fathers" appears in McGuffey's *Rhetorical Guide, or Fifth Reader* (1844, 291).

As in Shakespeare's day and throughout earlier history in the West, literacy was still thought of in nineteenth-century America as somehow serving the needs of oratory, for education in the classical tradition had never been education in the "three R's"—which comes from post-classical, post-Renaissance schools training for commerce and domestic economy—but had been education for the oral performance of the man in public affairs.

Little wonder that Charles Dickens' platform readings from his novels met with such wild success in McGuffey's America. Oratorical power and literary style tended to be somewhat synonymous. (The implications of this fact for the dynamics of Dickens' storytelling are little understood.)

But oratorical literacy was actually on the wane even in Dickens' day. The long-term history of the McGuffey *Readers* in fact registers the gradual demise of the tradition. Regularly revised between 1836 and 1920, the McGuffeys moved more and more away from oratorical to silent reading. Writing was subtly winning out everywhere over the old rhetorical public speaking ethos.

These reflections give some idea of the ways in which the oral and writing traditions have been interacting through not only our distant past but also our rather recent past. Throughout, scholars appear to have been quite unaware of the oral-literacy contrasts and of the gradual inroads of literacy upon orality. No one seems to have noticed as the teaching of rhetoric, which in its Greek original, *technē rhētorikē*, means public speaking, imperceptibly became more and more, over the centuries, the teaching of writing. Earlier generations took their own residual orality for granted, so much so that they really had not even thought of orality explicitly at all as a state of culture or of consciousness.

II

I shall treat orality and literacy in two ways, first examining the ubiquitous and persistent problem of moving from oral expression to writing and then considering briefly some special approaches we might take in teaching writing today because of the new, secondary orality that surrounds us on radio and television. In both instances my remarks are intended to be provocative rather than inclusive. There is no way to treat this protean subject inclusively.

Although its founding fathers were steeped in a still strong oral and oratorical tradition, the United States was founded in literacy, as Denis Brogan liked to point out from his vantage point in England. Written documents—the *Declaration of Independence* and the *Constitution*—are crucial to our feeling for national identity in a way unmatched in any other nation through history, so far as I know. Most Americans, even those who write miserably, are so stubbornly literate in principle as to believe that what makes a word a real word is not its meaningful use in vocal exchange, but rather its presence on the pages of a dictionary. We are so literate in ideology that we think writing comes naturally. We have to remind ourselves from time to time that writing is completely and irremediably artificial and that what you find in a dictionary are not real words but coded marks for voicing real words, exteriorly or in imagination.

To point out that writing is artificial is not to deny that it is essential for the realization of fuller human potential and for the evolution of consciousness itself. Writing is an absolute necessity for the analytically sequential, linear organization of thought such as goes, for example, into an encyclopedia article. Without writing, as I have undertaken to explain in *The Presence of the Word* and in *Interfaces of the Word*, the mind simply cannot engage in this sort of thinking, which is unknown to primary oral cultures, where thought is exquisitely elaborated, not in analytic linearity, but in formulary fashion, through "rhapsodizing," that is, stitching together proverbs, antitheses, epithets, and other "commonplaces" or *loci* (*topoi*). Without writing, the mind cannot even generate concepts such as "history" or "analysis," just as without print, and the massive accumulation of detailed documented knowledge that print makes possible, the mind cannot generate portmanteau concepts such as "culture" or "civilization," not to mention "macroeconomics" or "polyethylene." The *New English Dictionary* entry for "civilization" notes Boswell's report of March 23, 1772, that Dr. Samuel Johnson would not permit the word "civilization" in his first *Dictionary*—it was too much of a neologism. Probably most of the words in our English lexicon today represent concepts that could not even be formed without writing and, often, without print.

In the world of the creative imagination, writing appears necessary to produce accounts of human life, that is, of what Aristotle calls "action," which are closely plotted in the sense in which Greek drama is closely plotted, with a steady rise of complex action to climax, peripeteia or reversal, and subsequent falling action and denouement. Oral genres of much length treating human "action" are typically not tightly organized in this fashion but are loose-knit and episodic. Greek drama, which first provides such tight plotting in the West, is the first verbal genre in the West to be controlled entirely by writing: staged plays were oral renditions of written compositions. Similarly, print, an extension and intensification of the visualized word produced by writing, appears absolutely, and somewhat mysteriously, necessary to produce tightly plotted narrative about the in-close human lifeworld that we find in novels, which are the products of the deep interiorization of print achieved in the Romantic Age.

All this is to say that writing, and to a degree print, are absolutely essential not just for distributing knowledge but for performing the central noetic operations that a high-technology culture takes for granted.

But however crucial for man to arrive at his present state of consciousness, writing is still totally artificial, a technology consciously and reflectively contrived. In this it contrasts with oral speech. In any and all cultures, every human being who is not physiologically or psychologically impaired, inevitably learns to speak. Speech wells up out of the unconscious, supported by unconsciously organized grammatical structures that even the most ardent structural and transformational grammarians now admit can never all be surfaced entirely into consciousness. Speech is structured through the entire fabric of the human person. Writing depends on consciously contrived rules.

Moreover, it depends on absences—which amount to the same thing as artificiality. I want to write a book that will be read by hundreds of thousands of people. So, please, everyone leave the room. I have to be alone to communicate. Let us face the utter factitiousness and fictitiousness of such a situation, which can in no way be considered natural or even normal.

To move from the entirely natural oral world into this artificial world of writing is bewildering and terrifying. How do I deal with persons who are not present to me and who never will be? For except in the case of personal letters or their equivalents, writers commonly know almost none of their putative readers.

A recent article by a friend and former student of mine, Thomas J. Farrell, isolates nicely two of the basic problems a person has to face in moving from orality into the world of writing. Everyone who teaches writing knows the common symptoms of the problems: students make assertions that are totally unsupported by reasons, or they make a series of statements that lack connections. Farrell notes that such performance is not necessarily an intellectual deficiency but only a chirographic deficiency. It is quite consistent with oral conversational situations. In conversation, if you omit reasons backing a statement and your hearer wants them, the normal response is to ask you for them, to challenge you. If the connections between the statements you make are not supplied by the concrete situation—which can supply connections of the most complex, multileveled sort, as students of enthnomethodology well know—your interlocutor can be expected to ask you to specify the connections. Generally speaking, in live oral communication the hearer will not need many "logical" connections, again because the concrete situation supplies a full context that makes articulation, and thus abstraction, at many points, superfluous.

For the writer, the situation is totally different. No one is there to supply a real communicational context, to ask anything. There is no full context other than that which the writer can project. The writer has to provide all the back-up or fill-in. In the case of creative writing, the writer has to anticipate how much detail readers are willing and able to settle for. For there is no absolute measure of how much detail you have to supply in writing about anything. In the case of expository writing, the writer must anticipate all the different senses in which any statement can be interpreted and correspondingly clarify meaning, making sure to anticipate every objection that might be made and to cover it suitably. Every objection? Well, not quite. The situation is even worse than that. Select objections. The objections that the readers being addressed might think of. How is the writer to know what a particular group of imagined readers might think of? How do you imagine a group of readers anyway? For one thing, you have to read, read, read. There is no way to write unless you read, and read a lot. The writer's audience is always a fiction, and you have no way of fictionalizing your audience unless you know what some of the options for imagining audiences are—how audiences have been and are fictionalized.

The writer has also to anticipate all the connections that are needed by a particular audience of readers. In fictional or other narrative writing, this is an exceedingly intricate and elusive business. In expository writing it is difficult, too. The writer has to learn to be "logical," to put matters together in a sequential, linear pattern so that anyone who comes along—or anyone of the group of readers being projected by the writer—can make complete sense of what is being written. There are no live persons facing the writer to clarify his thinking by their reactions. There is no feedback. There are no auditors to look pleased or puzzled. This is a desperate world, a terrifying world, a lonely, unpeopled world, not at all the world of natural oral-aural exchange.

III

Everyone who writes must move at some point or points in his or her life from the world of oral exchange and thought processes into the curiously estranged and yet fantastically productive world of absent audiences that the writer deals with. Today, however, the orality away from which the writer moves is of two sorts. One kind, to use a terminology that I have developed in *Rhetoric, Romance, and Technology*, is "primary orality," the pristine orality of mankind untouched by writing or print that remains still more or less operative in areas sheltered to a greater or lesser degree from the full impact of literacy and that is vestigial to some degree in us all. The noetic processes of primary orality, as we have seen, are formulaic and rhapsodic rather than analytic. As in Homeric epic and to a great extent in classical oratory, particularly of the more orotund variety, this orality operates with the sort of commonplaces, formulary expressions, and clichés ordinarily despised by fully literate folk, for without writing, an oral culture must maintain its knowledge by repeating it. Writing and even more effectively, print store what is known outside the mind and downgrade repetitive styles. In lieu of more elaborate analytic categories, primary oral culture also tends to break down issues in simple polarities in terms of good and evil, "good guys" and "bad guys."

The other kind of orality we now live with I have called "secondary orality." This is the orality induced by radio and television, and it is by no means independent of writing and print, but totally dependent on them. Without writing and print, electronic equipment cannot be manufactured, and radio and television programming cannot be managed. (It should be noted here that despite its name, television is in a fundamental way an oral-aural medium. It must have sound and, so far as I know, never uses purely visual devices: the weather map that you read without difficulty in the newspaper becomes a talk show on television, presided over by an articulate and attractive woman or an equally articulate and handsome man.)

The highly oral culture of our black urban ghettos as well as of certain isolated black and white rural areas is basically a primary oral culture in many ways, although it is more or less modified by contact with secondary orality today. The orality of nonghetto urban populations generally and of suburbia generally, white and black, is basically secondary orality. As Farrell has made clear in the article cited earlier, the problems of moving students out of the two kinds of orality are not the same.

A real incident will illustrate the way in which primary orality can manifest itself. It was reported to me a few years ago by a graduate student in a seminar of mine at Saint Louis University who was at the time teaching a class composed almost entirely of black inner-city students in a community college. It was the time of the Cambodia crisis in the Nixon administration. "What do you think of Nixon's action in Cambodia?" the instructor asked. A hand was raised. "Well?" "I wouldn't vote for that turkey. He raised his own salary."

Such an answer will raise the hackles of many teachers, who can find no sense in it at all. They find it purely emotional, not at all "logical," irrelevant to the question, and, in general, a blatant example of non-thought. However, some kind of basic understanding of thought processes in primary oral culture shows how this sort of response, in such a culture, is perfectly fitting as well as thoroughly intelligent and human.

The question put by the instructor called for some kind of intensive political analysis. In a primary oral culture, intensive analysis is not practiced, and not even thought of. The student was from a culture preserving much of primary orality. He was unconcerned with analysis, yet he recognized that the question was a question. The instructor was getting at something. What could it be? That is to say, into what commonplaces or *loci* or *topoi* could the issue be resolved? How could it be found to reinforce what everybody knew about the deeper issues of life? Selfishness and my reaction to selfishness might be what was at stake. So let's give that a try. "I wouldn't vote for that turkey. He raised his own salary." The reply had the added advantage for a primary oral culture of couching the issue in clearly polarized terms of good and evil. Was Nixon a good guy or a bad guy? Clearly, a bad guy.

Before we write off—and note the term "write off"—this response as naive at our present state of chirographic and typographic culture, let us reflect that sensed in depth, the question, "Is Nixon a good guy or a bad guy?" was very likely what the instructor was really getting at anyway. Cambodia was just an example illustrating the instructor's real concern. Aristotle has said—or written? the exact mix of orality and chirography in Aristotle's works remains uncertain—that in rhetoric, which is fundamentally the art of public speaking or oratory, the example is the equivalent of induction in formal logical operations. Rhetorical examples and logical induction both move from individual instances to generalizations. The highly oral student handled the instructor's query as a rhetorical example, as a concrete instance referring to something at a higher, more generalized level of abstraction. It is rather unlikely that he had read Aristotle, but he was experientially familiar with the terrain of rhetoric. Orality sometimes provides nonanalytic shortcuts into the depths of human issues.

Let us take a second example. A couple of years ago, as a senior member of our Department of English, I was visiting the class of a graduate teaching assistant who was teaching writing. In one of the chairs sat a young man who, as I found subsequently, was from the highly oral inner-city black ghetto. He was very attentive, trying hard. But he had no textbook with him, and it was immediately apparent that he did not feel at all disadvantaged by this fact—even though the class was engaged in an analytic discussion of a text in the textbook with a view to a coming writing assignment. The student did not even try to look at the textbooks of any of the students near him. But he was clearly earnest, trying. Trying what? To be "with it"—just as, in his *Preface to Plato*, Eric A. Havelock has shown that the Greek boys in Plato's time had been trying to be "with it" as they got their Homer by heart. In a primary oral culture, education consists in identification, participation, getting into the act, feeling affinity with a culture's heroes, getting "with it"—not in analysis at all. This is what this freshman student thought the class was all about.

Plato's remedy for an educational tradition that operated simply to enable students to "get with it," to empathize with key figures in a given culture, rather than to analyze, was drastic, as Havelock has shown: Plato simply prescribed excluding all poets from his ideal republic so that genuine analytic thinking could get under way. He saw no other means of achieving what he felt was needed: a noetic *metanoia* or conversion, a complete turning around, a reversal of field—which we now know meant in effect a conversion from oral to chirographic thought. Forget empathy and face up to genuinely abstract questions: What makes a couch a couch? What is couchness?

In our literate culture, you can go too far with analysis, too. Reacting to the classroom situation I had observed, I was not at all inclined to throw out all the poets. But after class, I did try to bring home to the graduate teaching assistant the terrible injustice being done to this student of his if someone did not understand what the student's problem was and try to help him work through it. In my own experience, this is not an impossible thing at all. But you have to know where you are coming from.

Let us take a third example. Father Patrick Essien, an African diocesan priest of the Diocese of Ikot-Ekpene, in South-East State in Nigeria, who has just finished a doctorate in educational administration at Saint Louis University, comes from a primary oral culture of a small village of the Annang, a tribe of some half million persons or more. In the curriculum vitae in his dissertation, which is about the present educational serviceability of proverbs, he proudly displays his oral credentials by noting explicitly that no one is sure of the date of his birth, and then produces complementary credentials as an experienced literate by carefully calculating what the most likely date is. Father Essien's father, now deceased, was a chief. Among the Annang, as among other peoples, this meant that he was also a judge. He used to sit in judgment over such things as property disputes: charges, for example, by a plaintiff that another was pasturing his cattle or planting his yams on the plaintiff's property. The judge-chief would listen to both sides of the case, take the matter under advisement for a while, then cite a saying or proverb, another proverb, perhaps a third and a fourth, and then deliver the verdict. Plaintiff and defendant would leave satisfied.

"But," Father Essien smiles, "you had better give voice to the proper proverbs or other sayings. Otherwise, you are in deep trouble, for if you do not cite the ones that apply to the given case no one who hears the judgment is satisfied." The law is lodged in the proverbs or sayings of Annang culture—or the law was, for Father Essien remarks sadly that it is getting harder and harder to find anyone with the skills that his father practiced so well. The law has become something written and does not work that way any more. Inevitably, Father Essien's feelings are mixed, and agonizing. The Annang must move into writing, for its advantages are incontestable. But writing entails losses of much that was good and true and beautiful in the old primary oral culture. You do what you can: Father Essien's dissertation will preserve some of the orality, but alas! only in writing.

A few months ago I was telling this story to another friend. "Sayings still work that way in the oral world of young children," he said. "Sayings settle disputes." He had had some young children in a car with him for a rather long drive a few days before, and there was a dispute when one wanted to preempt a window seat for the whole ride. "Turn about is fair play," my friend had said. And the dispute evaporated; the boy at the window yielded his seat to one of the others. My friend noted the psychodynamics of the episode: the saying saved the youngster's face. He was moved out of place not because he was weaker or less worthy or unloved—considerations always urgent in the agonistically structured lifeworld of primary orality—but because "Turn about is fair play." This was something everybody knew, or should know, part of the common store of knowledge that a culture consists in. There is a deep humanity in the noetic processes of primary orality.

Settling a property dispute among adults, however, is a quite different matter from settling children's disputes. Not all have recognized this fact. Literates have had trouble understanding oral cultures precisely because in a highly literate culture experience of primary orality—or something close to primary orality—is likely to be limited to experience of the child's world. Hence persons from highly literate cultures have commonly been unable to react understandingly to adult, sophisticated levels of behavior in oral cultures, but have tended to view the whole of "native"—that is, oral—populations as "child-like," including admirably adult men and women, middle-aged and older, who often have coped with life more adroitly and more successfully than their literate critics.

This defensive depreciatory interpretation of another culture by literates is itself curiously childlike. It has forced literary scholars consciously or unconsciously espousing it to go through incredible intellectual contortions to make out the *Iliad* and *Odyssey* to be basically texts composed in writing instead of transcriptions of essentially oral performance, because of the supposition that oral performance is not capable of the sophistication these works manifest. Thanks to the work of Parry and Lord and Havelock and their now numerous epigoni, we should be beyond this today. We should know something of the psychodynamics of primary oral cultures, of primary oral noetics—how the mind works when it cannot rely directly or indirectly on writing and on the thought patterns that writing alone can initiate.

Once we know something about the psychodynamics of the oral mind, we can recognize that primary orality, at least in residual form, is still a factor in the thought habits of many of those to whom we are called upon to teach writing. Such recognition does not automatically solve our problems, but it at least enables us better to identify them. Our students from oral or residually oral cultures come not from an unorganized world, but from a world that is differently organized, in ways that can now be at least partly understood.

IV

What of those students who come from the world of secondary oral culture? Does the oral world of radio and television drive all its denizens back from literate culture to the primary oral noetic economy? Of course not. If it did, that would be the end of radio and television. There is nothing on radio or television, however oral, not subject to some—and most often to utterly massive—chirographic and typographic control, which enters into program design, scripts, advertising, contractual agreements, diction, sentence structure, and countless other details. Primary orality cannot cope with electronic media. I recall talking to radio and television producers in Dakar a few years ago and speculating with them about how it would be to have a television series run by a *griot*, the West African singer of tales, oral purveyor of genealogies, crier of praises and taunts, custodian of the *loci* of the culture. An individual performance by a *griot* could prove interesting, the Senegalese media people knew, but would have to be carefully supervised, for the new kind of orality had made a world utterly different from the *griot's* world, using different techniques. There was no way for a *griot* to program a radio or television series.

But how about the audience? Does the oral world of radio and television reintroduce its viewers, as against its programmers or performers, to primary oral noetics? It appears not in any sophisticated way at all. Television viewers show no tendency, so far as I can discern, to organize their knowledge and express themselves the way the Nigerian villagers do in Chinua Achebe's novels. They have no such oral mastery of proverbial thinking at all. As I have noted in *Rhetoric, Romance, and Technology*, even relatively unsophisticated audiences in a high-technology culture feel they should scorn formulas or clichés as such, although they might not always succeed in avoiding them. Consequently, clichés addressed to audiences in a high-technology milieu tend to be accompanied by signals, verbal or other, that downgrade the clichés themselves. Archie Bunker's clichés are systematically debased by his malapropisms. The audience is encouraged and assisted to reject them and laugh at them. This is only some of the abundant evidence that popular culture is discernibly under the influence of literacy today—and at many levels, even in its relatively unsophisticated members.

Secondary orality, in other words, is to varying degrees literate. In fact, a residual primary orality, literacy, and secondary orality are interacting vigorously with one another in confusing complex patterns in our secondarily oral world.

This situation does not automatically create sensitivity to literature or equip everyone with the ability to write well, but it can be made to work toward such goals. The world of secondary orality is a media-conscious world. In fact, this is the world that effectively brought about the discovery of the contrast between primary orality and literacy, and ultimately the contrast between both and secondary orality. Milman Parry and Albert Lord discovered the orality of ancient Homeric Greece not simply by studying texts but largely through sound recordings of twentieth-century Yugoslavian epic singers.

Because we live in a media-conscious world, we can make students aware of what this paper has attempted to sketch: what oral speech is and what writing is by contrast. This awareness can increase sensitivity to literature and to the problems of writing.

I am not suggesting here more courses in "the media." But I am suggesting that both those who teach writing and those who teach literature can in their teaching make a productive issue of the contrasts between the noetic and psychological milieu of primary orality, that of writing and of print, and that of secondary orality. Understanding these differences not in terms merely of slogans, but circumstantially and in depth is itself a liberal education.

Perhaps I will be permitted to use another and final example from close to home. Last year, in a program at Saint Louis University on Man, Technology, and Society, funded by the National Endowment for the Humanities, we managed to give a course on "Technology and the Creation of Literature," which had to do with writing as a technology and its effects in producing literature in the full sense of the word: verbal communication actually composed in writing. This is what we are teaching when we teach writing. We are not teaching how to transcribe oral performance—as someone, we don't know who and we don't know how, transcribed the Homeric tales from the oral world and made them artificially for the first time into fixed texts, that henceforward had to be not retold but interpreted. We are teaching composing in writing, putting words together not with the help of a live and vocal interlocutor, but with the help of an imagined audience and of something mute outside us. Like it or not, we are teaching a technology, for not only print, but also writing itself is a technology—a matter of tools outside us and seemingly foreign to us, which we nevertheless can interiorize and make human, transforming them and enhancing our own thinking and verbalizing activities in the process, much as a musician interiorizes the machine in the crook of his arm and shoulder that we call a violin.

I had treated this sort of subject earlier in graduate courses, but the course on "Technology and the Creation of Literature" had to be an undergraduate course by stipulation of the NEH grant. Somewhat to my surprise, it worked magnificently for undergraduate students. Their reception of the course showed conclusively that media-sensitive students today are fascinated by carefully worked out contrasts between primary oral performance and writing, and between both these and secondary orality, and that they are liberated by understanding what these contrasts are. The course was a demanding one. Readings included, besides secondary sources, books of the *Iliad* and the *Odyssey*, *The Mwindo Epic* of the Nyanga people in eastern Zaire, parts of Genesis, some Old Testament wisdom literature, Plato's *Crito*, *Everyman*, selections from *The Faerie Queene* and *Paradise Lost*, O. Henry's *The Gift of the Magi*, Poe's *The Gold Bug*, and James' *The Aspern Papers*—the whole gamut from complete primary orality (totally episodic—before the taping of *The Mwindo Epic* no one of the Banyanga had ever put together all the Mwindo stories in sequence) to all-pervasive literacy (the key to Poe's plotting in *The Gold Bug* is the reconstitution of a text and in *The Aspern Papers* the whole character of James's always absent protagonist lodges in his hidden writings, which finally go up in flames).

If undergraduate students can be sensitive to the differences between literacy and orality that this course explored, I am suggesting that it would help our understanding and our teaching of the writing craft for us to be sensitive to them, too.

Works Cited

Brogan, Denis W. *Government of the People: A Study in the America Political System*. New York: Harper, 1944.

Coles, Jr., William E. "Freshman Composition: The Circle of Unbelief." *College English* 31 (November, 1969): 134-42.

Collignon, Joseph. "Why Leroy Can't Write." *College English* 39 (1978): 852-59.

Correll, Robert M. "Freshman Composition." *The College Teaching of English.* Ed. John C. Gerber. New York: Appleton-Century-Crofts, 1965. 91-114.

Douglas, Wallace. "Rhetoric for the Meritocracy: The Creation of Composition at Harvard." *English in America: A Radical View of the Profession.* Ed. Richard Ohmann. New York: Oxford UP, 1976. 97-132.

Essien, Patrick Paul. The Use of Annang Proverbs as Tools of Education in Nigeria. Diss. Saint Louis U, 1978. Ann Arbor: UMI, 1978. Order No. 7814554.

Farrell, Thomas J. "Literacy, Basics, and All That Jazz." *College English* 38 (1977): 443-59.

Greenbaum, Leonard. "The Tradition of Complaint." *College English* 31 (November, 1969): 174-87.

Havelock, Eric A. *Preface to Plato.* Cambridge, MA: Belknap P of Harvard UP, 1963.

Lord, Albert B. *The Singer of Tales,* Harvard Studies in Comparative Literature, 24. Cambridge, MA: Harvard UP, 1960.

Lynn, Robert Wood. "Civil Catechetics in Mid-Victorian America: Some Notes about American Civil Religion, Past and Present." *Religious Education* 68 (1973): 5-27.

Ohmann, Richard. "Freshman Composition and Administered Thought." *English in America: A Radical View of the Profession.* Ed. Richard Ohmann. New York: Oxford UP, 1976. 133-71.

Ong, Walter J. *Interfaces of the Word: Studies in the Evolution of Consciousness and Culture.* Ithaca, NY: Cornell UP, 1977.

—. *The Presence of the Word.* New Haven and London: Yale UP, 1967.

—. *Rhetoric, Romance, and Technology.* Ithaca, NY: Cornell UP, 1971.

Parry, Milman. *The Making of Homeric Verse: The Collected Papers of Milman Parry.* Ed. Adam Parry. Oxford: Clarendon P of Oxford UP, 1971.

Reid, Ronald F. "The Boylston Professorship of Rhetoric and Oratory, 1806-1904: A Case Study of Changing Concepts of Rhetoric and Pedagogy." *Quarterly Journal of Speech* 45 (1959): 239-57.

25

The Agonistic Base of Scientifically Abstract Thought: Issues in *Fighting for Life: Contest, Sexuality, and Consciousness* (1982)

I

These reflections, like the book from which they derive, have grown from work in intellectual history concerned largely with the academic and para-academic milieu in the West. Intellectual activity in this milieu has in the past exhibited pervasive agonistic patterns, clearly integral to the development of philosophical thought, as we know and exercise it. These patterns today appear puzzling, and even bizarre. Strangely, scholarship has mostly left them entirely unexplained and indeed has almost totally ignored them. To help explain these patterns, one must consider human noetic history in a more total context, attending to the larger cultural, psychological, and finally psychobiological settings that have framed organized intellectual activity, at least in the West, and that have apparently been a precondition for the kind of thinking we have learned to do.

Ceremonial or ritual agonistic procedures, that is, procedures built on contest, on trying to get the upper hand, have characterized academic intellectual life in the West from antiquity until very recent times. The 1960s marked the final collapse of these procedures and of the state of consciousness they derived from. I recall a remark made to me in 1967 by a middle-aged Jesuit, German by birth, teaching in an all-boys high school in New York City: "Ach! These boys expect you in the classroom to be their friend. When I was a boy everybody knew that the teacher was the enemy." This teacher's eyes twinkled because he knew, and knew that I knew, that the enmity he referred to, however intense, was on the whole basically a ritual or ceremonial one, accepted as more or less part of the centuries-old game of boys' schooling. Sparring with the enemy was the stuff of intellectual life.

We can notice the agonistic style of thinking in Greek antiquity, when Socrates taught by attacking, relentlessly, like a bull in a bull ring. But Socrates was only adapting an antique, even archaic, intellectual style to the new stage of consciousness to which the Greeks were rising. As we now know, all oral cultures have a deeply agonistic base for their language and thought and, often enough, for their lifestyle. Oral modes of storing and retrieving knowledge are formulaic in design and tend to be agonistic in operation.

Oral noetic processes are formulaic in design because we know only what we can recall. If I say that I "know geometry," I do not mean that I am I thinking of all its proofs here and now, but that I can recall them as need may be. Knowing requires memory. But an oral culture cannot verbalize a lengthy concatenation of thought first and then memorize it afterwards. Without writing, there is nothing to return to for memorizing. Once the words are said, they are gone for good—unless they are said in a way that is in itself memorable. Hence effective thought in oral cultures is thought structured mnemonically. An oral culture does not *put* its knowledge *into* mnemonic patterns: it *thinks* its knowledge in mnemonic patterns. There is no other way for it to proceed effectively. It must use as integral constituents of its thought balance, antithesis, epithetic (that is, standardized) qualifiers, proverbs or other memorable sayings, clichés of any and all arts. It does not add formulaic patterns to its thinking. Its thinking consists in such patterns. Clichés constitute its thought.

Eric A. Havelock has made clear in his *Preface to Plato* that this was the reason why Plato excluded poets from his Republic: they stood for the old cliché-based knowledge forms that Plato wanted to displace with analytic thinking, thereby raising consciousness to a new level above its unconscious base and detaching the individual more from the community. We know now from the work of Havelock and others after him that Plato's kind of thinking and all the philosophical thinking that has succeeded it has been totally dependent upon a deeply interiorized writing that built into the mind resources it had never known before. In the *Phaedrus* and the Seventh Letter, Plato put his jealous denunciation of writing into writing.

Largely because they deal in formulas, in what is already known, all oral cultures that we know—and by implication all early human cultures, for writing of any sort is only about 6000 years old—foster agonistic performance, or virtuosity, in their management of their store of knowledge, and do so with a single-minded intensity that deeply affected early formal schooling when it finally began. In a culture that lives on clichés, almost everything that is said for purposes of deliberation or reflection or speculation is known to almost everyone already. The same is generally true of stories that are told. If the narrative that the storyteller is going to present is familiar to the audience, if it is public property, as it typically is in oral cultures, the narrator's warrant for performance is likely to be simply his or her superior skill. We have heard it before, but no one can tell it so well to this particular audience as this person can now. In its use of thought and expression, an oral culture is performance-oriented, not result-oriented. The results are all on hand in the clichés and other formulas. The eternal truths are known to all. The question is, Who can best make them live? Alexander Pope was the last voice of a residually oral culture when he proclaimed in his *Essay on Criticism* that the poet deals with "What oft was thought, but ne'er so well expressed."

Highly oral cultures, across the globe, often cultivate combative lifestyles, particularly in verbal performance. We find this in "the dozens," the formalized exchange of insulting remarks between male opponents found throughout New World black cultures and in Africa as well. But we find it also throughout the Homeric epics, in *Beowulf*, in the Bible, as in the case of David and Goliath (Samuel 17: 42-47). A principle function of proverbs in an oral culture is formalized polemic: one uses proverbs for intellectual dueling, and of course for settling litigation. Riddles, which are anti-proverbs, formulaically creating confusion rather than clarification, are fundamentally aggressive not only in their use, but in design as well.

Since oral cultures cannot develop elaborate abstract analytic categories, they tend to store most of their knowledge in narrative, even what we would consider quite neutral knowledge, such as the names of the Greek leaders, which we find in the famous catalogue of the ships in the *Iliad*. Since narrative is normally based on agonistic, antipathetic situations, this procedure throws even neutral material into an agonistic frame. The catalogue of the leaders of the Greeks is not a neutral national directory, but a list of essentially "good guys." Oral cultures around the world commonly feature similar catalogues in their narratives.

Socrates' agonistic procedures thus have archaic sources. G.E.R. Lloyd in his *Polarity and Analogy* has studied the way selected cultures across the world attend to oppositions or contrasts and to likenesses. All the cultures he studied attended to both, but he found that the Greeks were unique in that they institutionalized "polarity," that is, opposition or agonistic relationships, made opposition a central intellectual concern, as apparently no other culture has done. This, we now know, was connected with their development and interiorization of the first vocalically complete version of the alphabet.

Formal logic stands as the great monument to the Greek cultivation of oppositions. Formal logic grew out of the formally organized art of rhetoric. Rhetoric arose when the analytic, reflective mental activity implemented by writing attended to oral procedures themselves, organizing public speaking scientifically. Logic appears when these same analytic procedures are directed back on themselves to analyze thought as such. Why does what you say demolish what I say? The seemingly neutral subject of logic derives historically from analysis of dispute, of non-neutral, agonistic thinking. No other culture in the world, not the great chirographic cultures of East Asia, which had incredibly elaborate, elitist forms of writing but no ruthlessly analytic, democratizing alphabet, ever developed the formalized study of rhetoric, nor did they develop any formal logic at all. (The much later and less eventful formal logic developed in India, perhaps independently of the Greeks, also grew out of the analysis of dispute, as Bochenski notes.)

II

The ancient Greeks and Romans knew and used alphabetic writing, but they felt it to be at the service of oral speech. Greek culture as a whole has as its ideal not the philosopher in Socrates' and Plato's sense, but the *rhetor*, the public speaker. The Romans adopted the same ideal. The Middle Ages were far more literate than classical antiquity, but remained almost unbelievably more oral than we are. Although teachers depended upon texts for their learning and even lectured on texts—in this differing paradigmatically from teachers in classical antiquity—medieval universities remained basically oral and deeply agonistic in lifestyle and intellectual style. They never used writing at all to test intellectual achievements, but only disputation or disputation-like *viva voce* examinations. From Abelard through St. Thomas Aquinas and on through the Renaissance and beyond, material that we would today organize in textbooks or treatises was organized typically in disputatious form, apparently because no one had thought of any effective alternative. St. Thomas Aquinas' *Summa Theologiae* proceeds, question after question, from opposition (objections) to his own position, and back to the opposition or objections again. In other works, what we would style "special questions" were called "disputed questions," *quaestiones disputatae*.

Renaissance humanists reinforced, weakened, and endlessly complicated the orality and the accompanying agonistic style that they had inherited. They revived the rhetorical, which is to say oral, ideals of antiquity, but they also invented textual scholarship, since they had the new technology of print to make this feasible as it had never before been. The Enlightenment and strangely enough Romanticism ate away at the old orality, which nevertheless remained in more or less heavy residue to the nineteenth century and, as we shall see, in some places even until the 1960s. Even textuality was strongly oral until very recent times. *McGuffey's Readers*, of which has been estimated at least 120 million copies were printed between 1836 and 1920, were basically oratorical in conception. They were not concerned with reading for comprehension as we are today, but rather with declamatory reading from a podium, orienting school children to what Daniel Boorstin has called "sound-conscious literature" (307).

III

Until the past few generations virtually all academic education had been only for males, with so few exceptions that they are really entirely negligible for most purposes. The male cast of academia correlated very exactly with its agonistic style, and it is at this point that biological matters must be examined in connection with intellectual history.

Since I shall be speaking from now on of the male academic world as such, it is important to say something briefly about the education of women. Often one hears that until recent years women were not educated. This generalization is not true. Or in the limited sense in which it is true, most males were not educated either. What is true is that women, and most males, were not *academically* educated. But in the social milieu more or less comparable to that of boys who were given academic education, girls were often provided with an education that could be formidable by any standards, including present-day standards. This can be illustrated for our purposes very simply by the title of a book by Gervase Markham, a seventeenth-century hack writer. In 1675 one of Markham's books was published in London under the following title: *The English House-Wife, containing the inward and outward Vertues* [that is, skills or competencies] *which ought to be in a Compleat Woman. As Her Skill in Physick* [this means medicine], *Chirurgery* [this means surgery], *Cookery, Extraction of Oyls, Banquetting stuff, Ordering of great Feasts, Preserving all sorts of Wines, conceited Secrets, Distillations, Perfumes, Ordering of Wool, Hemp, Flax: Making Cloth and Dying* [this means in effect, "Here is a handful of wool or flax from which you may make yourself some thread and cloth, and out of it some clothes for your family"]; *the knowledge of Dayries; Office of Malting; of Oats, their excellent uses in Families; of Brewing, Baking and all other things belonging to the*

Household. A Work generally approved and now the Eighth Time much Augmented . . . . This title shows that an intensive education need not have been an academic education. Nonacademic education for women often included also administrative training. Many young women upon their marriage seem to have been quite capable of managing a household of fifty or sixty persons or more, including, very likely, more than a few disgruntled servants.

These observations about women's education clear the way for our return to the male academic tradition in the West. The agonistic cast of the academic tradition related to the 1500-year history of Learned Latin. Latin, we must remember here, was not distinctively ecclesiastical or theological. Because the Latin Rite of the Roman Catholic Church kept Latin longer than did the physicians, the physicists, the grammarians, the mathematicians, the lawyers, and other academically educated persons, Latin has in latter days acquired a distinctively ecclesiastical identity. But in Shakespeare's day, Latin was functional well outside the church. Without Latin there was no way even to know medicine or grammar. These things could not be explained in English or other vernaculars, which had no vocabulary and probably no adequately tuned grammatical structures to handle complex academic specialties. Latin had been kept in the schools for a very practical reason: it had never been feasible to translate academic material into the hundreds of dialects and languages in Europe, most of which have never been written to this day, until one or another dialect became so dominant that it acquired large numbers of speakers and thereby made translation worthwhile. Until this condition began to be realized in at least some places toward the late Middle Ages, by far the simplest thing to do was to teach Latin to the small number of boys who went to school.

When between A.D. 500 and 700 the romance vernaculars had moved so far from Latin that the latter was no longer of a piece with the vernaculars, no longer comprehensible to vernacular speakers as such, Latin became a sex-linked male language (with exceptions so few as to be virtually negligible), spoken over the centuries by millions, but with no direct oral roots. It was an extrafamilial language, no longer a mother tongue—there are no father tongues—a chirographically controlled language, that is, a language ruled fundamentally by writing, not by oral speech, used, even orally, only by persons who knew how to write it, the first language of none of its users, with no baby-talk, lacking direct access to the unconscious and hence eminently useful for thought struggling to be abstract and especially for budding scientific thought endeavoring to maintain a contact with the physical world that worked from immediate, continuous, but unemotional involvement with objects toward full abstraction.

Under these conditions, learning the Latin language became a male puberty rite for the group of males who went to school. First, as in other puberty rites, Latin moved boys out of their families into the tribe where they were inducted into the extrafamilial tribal secrets, in this case the academic subjects. Second, learning Latin took place in the induced physical hardship setting, the deliberately designed stress situations, typical for puberty rites. It normally entailed physical punishment, often very severe. In Renaissance iconography, a schoolmaster is recognized by his bundle of switches. George Orwell thought that it was impossible to teach Latin without physical punishment (4:338). He seems to have been right. For the fact is that wherever Learned Latin was not just the subject of instruction but the language of instruction, as it was in schools in Shakespeare's and Milton's day, and even wherever Learned Latin was, if not the language of instruction, at least the central school subject, as in the British public schools until recently, physical punishment was virtually always its accompaniment. Third, the very contents of the course for Latin learners were often of a cut with the puberty rite hardship setting and with the agonistic style of instruction. In 1531 Sir Thomas Elyot insisted, following Plato's *Republic*, that the boy must be given stories of military and other physical violence to "inflame" his "courage." In the nineteenth century this doctrine was modulated into the idea the Latin "toughens the mind." Fourth, as in other puberty rites, those who underwent the ordeal of learning Latin emerged with a tremendous *esprit de corps*. The recent British movie *If . . .* (Lindsay Anderson, 1969) faithfully portrays the merciless total stress situations and violent punishment characteristic of British public schools and in its second half transmutes the ceremonial violence into outright physical, brutal, and fatal warfare between students and masters, in a way mirroring the events of the 1960s, as will be seen below.

IV

The old academic world of contest and deliberately engineered stress situations was structured by masculine needs. The entrance of girls into the schools, which significantly began at the prepubertal grades, where the sexes are least differentiated, and moved upward, marked the beginning of the end of the old agonistic structures.

What happened all over the academic world earlier can be seen in the microcosm of Roman Catholic seminaries or schools of divinity after World War II, where the old agonistic structures, once common to all subjects, still survived in the teaching of philosophy and theology. When I was studying theology at the Saint Louis University School of Divinity in the mid-1940s, the basic or mainline courses such as moral theology and dogmatic or systematic theology, which formed the core of the curriculum, were all given in Latin, the language in which our earlier basic philosophy courses also had been taught. Textbooks were in Latin for these courses in theology, as in philosophy. Courses consisted of conglomerates of theses that were defended against all conceivable attacks and that were taught by oral lectures. For despite the textbooks, orality still ruled. Everything you had to know, the instructor said out loud. In the mainline courses extracurricular readings were normally never required.

In this still live twentieth-century tradition, education was performance-oriented, and the major performances were oral contests. Students argued about the theses informally and formally in large-scale public disputations or smaller disputations known as "circles." Once in a while a theological student of outstanding competence would perform the "grand act," the greatest oral agonistic performance of all, as did Father Joaquin Villalonga, S.J., on April 29, 1903, when in impeccable logical form and equally impeccable Latin, without the aid of any notes whatsoever, he defended orally his 212 theses from theology and philosophy in open forum against the world. For, in principle, anyone from anywhere in the world could attack the protagonist at the grand act. In fact, President Theodore Roosevelt in this case had the opportunity to do so. He was visiting St. Louis to inspect the site of the coming World's Fair, and, apparently sparring for an additional diversion, came to Father Villalonga's performance. We have a report about the event in the *St. Louis Post-Dispatch*. As a visiting dignitary with a university degree (from Harvard), Roosevelt was greeted by the *preces*, or presiding officer for the grand act, and was asked (in Latin, immediately translated for him by Cardinal Gibbons) if he had any objections to urge against any of the 212 theses. The *Post-Dispatch* reported that for the first, and possibly only time in his life, T. R. was nonplused. He said he had no objections to anything.

By the late 1960s, following the Second Vatican Council, all this had changed. Roman Catholic theology virtually everywhere in the West was loosening its connections with the Latin language, as the other academic subjects had somewhat earlier. As it did so, certain correlative changes occurred. Within two years, 1967-1968, the School of Divinity at Saint Louis University (1) ceased using Latin as a language for instruction, (2) dropped the thesis method as a method of instruction, (3) dropped disputations and "circles" together with oral course examinations as integral parts of its program, supplanting these with written examinations, and (4) admitted women students. So far as I know, no one involved in these four changes adverted to what appears to be the fact from the evidence I have adduced here: these were hardly four changes at all but in effect one. Each change, in its own way, moved theological instruction out of the age-old rhetorical, oral-agonistic world of male ceremonial combat. Seminary instruction in philosophy in various ways made the same changes at about the same time or, often, somewhat earlier.

V

It should be apparent by now that the agonistic elements in academia, including the history of rhetoric and its offspring formal logic, are entangled with the dialectic of masculine and feminine, the history of which makes the evolution of consciousness at least partly intelligible. I refer you to *Fighting for Life: Contest, Sexuality, and Consciousness* for the telling detailed particulars, but shall just briefly outline some connections here.

What are some of the features of the alliance between the old oral-agonistic structures and masculinity? First, the alliance is fostered in all pre-electronic cultures by a grossly physical state of affairs: until electronic amplification the typical male voice could articulate words understandably at a far greater volume than could the typical female voice, so that males had a physical advantage in an oral world. In a setting paradigmatic for our purposes, a little over a hundred years ago Abraham Lincoln and Stephen A. Douglas were debating in the open fields of Illinois in August before audiences of as many as 15,000 persons. The first speaker was allowed an hour, the second an hour and a half, and the first an additional half hour for rebuttal. They strode the platform, lashing out at one another, inviting massive audience involvement, all the while of necessity shouting at the top of their voices. They were not reading from scripts: the newspapers were often accused of reporting inaccurately what the debaters actually said, and no one could prove what was accurate and what not. Compare this with the Kennedy-Nixon debates, as a brilliant young undergraduate did for me recently in her term paper, and you will sense what has changed. Booths to domesticate the speakers. Scripts. Microphones. A two-and-one-half-minute limit. Proscription of any personal attack. Always a quiet voice. In the electronic world, no orator qualifies as stentorian anymore. Most persons alive in the United States today have no experience of what oratory has meant for most of the history of the human race.

A second connection between masculinity and the old orally based agonistic thought processes is psychological or psychophysiological. This is the connection via what we have styled ritual or ceremonial combat. In extending this term, which refers originally to human behavior, to analogous infrahuman animal behavior, we must be careful not to anthropomorphize the latter, attributing human motives and states of consciousness to infrahuman animals that manifest behavior patterns that have their own complex but quite identifiable evolutionary sources. But there are infrahuman analogues to what we have styled ritual or ceremonial combat in the sense of protracted, often elaborately patterned combat that is vigorous and often exhausting, but normally not lethal at all. The human and the infrahuman manifestations of such combat, while different, are also closely related, as will be seen.

Such combat, not only among human beings but pretty well throughout the whole animal kingdom, particularly in its higher reaches, is significantly, and often spectacularly, more the business of males than of females. As the vast literature now makes clear, among infrahuman species such combat is lethal normally only by accident or by artificial human arrangement (such as confinement of fighting males in a small arena). It is often a dispersal mechanism, developed in the evolutionary process to space out breeding pairs in order to assure sufficient food for the young. This is the common pattern among song birds, where the males of the same species never fight one another to kill. Neither do stags or bighorn rams or other males commonly. Whether evolved to assure food supplies or for other effects, intraspecific male combat is a distancing mechanism, making males into loners, often loners preoccupied with territory that they defend against any and all of their conspecific males. Even at the infrahuman level male-with-male combat is a separating mechanism. It has a curiously formal or "abstract" aura. It distances individuals and isolates issues. When two males are fighting for territorial rights, which are often their direct concern rather than access to females, no other issue counts except sheer dominance.

Why is it that by and large throughout the animal kingdom conspecific males are under a compulsion to fight one another far more than females fight one another? The compulsion of males for conspecific fighting suggests that males are more insecure in some profound sense—though certainly not in every sense—that they are somehow basically restless, under certain kinds of greater strain. On biological grounds the insecurity can readily be pinpointed at least in the case of the highest animals, mammals. Among mammals, a male embryo must in very short order start excreting its own testosterone or its masculinity will be destroyed by its mother's female hormones. In fact, even outside an ambiance of female hormones, the male embryo without testosterone would fail to develop as a male. "Nature's first intent is to make a female." The female embryo has no such problem. With its mother's hormones, or even without them, it develops straightforwardly as a female. In this setting, masculinity can be seen as, from the beginning, existence within an environment that is totally necessary, nourishing, and indeed for humans loving, and nevertheless at the same time a threat. This might be called ontogenetic biological insecurity, the insecurity of each individual male of a species regarding his biological maleness.

There is a phylogenetic male insecurity too: as a group, males are expendable. In many species the males are the larger and stronger fighters, who principally protect the species against other hostile species. This means they are killed more often than females. The biological heritage lives in our subconscious. The male marked for death, the "fay" male, is well known in folklore and in literature. Death of a male generally makes little difference philogenetically, since a group of fewer males and many females can normally propagate itself with an efficiency impossible to a group of a few females and many males. Indeed in some species, such as certain aphids and, all the way up to the vertebrates, in certain species of lizards, a totally female population can propagate itself for generations without any fertilization by males at all. The unfertilized eggs simply hatch. No totally male population can reproduce itself at all. Unisex is female.

To ontogenetic and phylogenetic insecurity can be added, for human males, psychological insecurity. All infants' early lives are bound to a feminine environment whether the infants are male or female, totally before birth and all but totally for several years after birth. The male infant needs this feminine environment as much as does a female infant. If in an individual case a mother substitute can be found, this is exactly what has to be found, a *mother* substitute. Because even his extrauterine life must at first be shaped in a feminine environment, a young boy is faced with the problem of proving himself not simply by being what he is but by doing something to show that he is not what he came from—that is, that he is not feminine. If he does not do something that girls cannot do, he is, not without grounds, taken to be feminine, a sissy. Typically, he fights with another boy, a surrogate for himself, to prove that he can stand up to the male insecurity he must carry within himself all his life. It is common in literature and in life for human males who have fought each other to become fast friends. No wonder: the conspecific male enemy is essentially a ceremonial enemy, subconsciously known to be in the same plight as the one who fights him, ultimately a brother.

Feminine insecurity can be very real, but it is not of this sort. Feminine sexual identity, more than male sexual identity, is a matter of self-realization, or self-appropriation, of accepting what one is, not a matter of constructing one's identity within an alien, but needed and nourishing environment. This is true in human beings and, *mutatis mutandis*, in higher infrahuman species generally. Fighting among females is characteristically less ceremonial, more "common sense" or directly related to evident goals, such as securing of food or defense of young. Although through much of the animal kingdom females do fight among themselves to establish a dominance order, often with tactics somewhat paralleling the ceremonial combat of the conspecific males, and although in a few species certain patterns of aggressiveness are more marked in females than in males, across the board the females' fighting for rank is utterly perfunctory compared with the elaborate, grandiose, and, to human onlookers, often ridiculously foolhardy performance of males—the headcracking of bighorn rams charging at full speed into one another, the elaborate display-and-tear scrapping of male Siamese fighting fish, or the hours-long combat of certain tom turkeys that leave the antagonists utterly exhausted, almost unable to move. If the testes of males are removed, they cease behaving this way, as animal breeders have known for centuries.

The striking sexual differences among animals in combat behavior that have been reported by behavioral biologists and behavioral psychologists, have also been earlier registered in folklore and literature form from the remotest times. The vocal but in reality nonlethal *miles gloriosus*, or boastful soldier, has no feminine counterpart. Although we encounter aggressive women such as Chaucer's Wife of Bath or Judy in *Punch and Judy Shows*, we find no female equivalent of Falstaff or Bobby Riggs or Mohammad Ali nor indeed of Don Quixote, anymore than there is any male equivalent of the feminine courage and strength in Michelangelo's Pietà.

VI

What are some of the implications of these agonistic and related phenomena in academia for our understanding of the development of abstract thought in the West?

First, it is to be noted that what we are dealing with here is not by any means biological determinism. What we are dealing with is a biological setting. Recent meticulously detailed studies of biological organisms and of ecological systems in all their evolutionary complexity have given us to understand how deeply structured the biological world is. These studies have provided background for human behavior, including intellectual behavior, far richer and deeper than earlier human beings were ever able to know. But to know a background in detail is not to reduce everything to the background. Intellectual activity is not the same as biological activity, and intellectual history is not the same as biological history. But these activities are interrelated. We are beginning to understand at depths previously inaccessible the old philosophical logion, *nil in intellectu quod non prius in sensibus*, nothing is in the intellect that was not antecedently in the senses. Sociobiology, which Edward O. Wilson defines as the systematic study of the biological basis of all social behavior, has been used to generate some quite indefensible, and indeed, naive, philosophical speculation, but this does not mean that the details sociobiology deals with are irrelevant to philosophy, which, I believe, should be concerned in its own way with everything. What I have done in *Fighting for Life* has, however, gone beyond sociobiology, so that I have coined the term "noobiology" to refer to my concerns. By analogy with such terms as noosphere and noogenesis, noobiology is the study of the biological setting of mental activity and intellectual history. But it does not reduce intellect to biology, though, through the investigation of biological behavioral backgrounds, it undertakes to improve our understanding of what specifically human intelligence is and of certain patterns in intellectual history.

Second, the human intellect and the human power of free choice can and do affect the biological setting in which intellect and will operate. We breed many animals independently of natural selection. But it is important to remember that intellect and will cannot remove the biological setting or remove themselves from the biological setting. Cultures can maximize or minimize male-female differences and/or likenesses, but they can never get rid of them. They can only deal with them. Attempts to get rid of biological differences I would regard as schizoid. In order to be free, we need to know what we are doing, and this includes knowing the grounds on which we must operate. Far from implying biological determinism, noobiology, by helping us attend to the integral human being, should implement human freedom.

Third, as *Fighting for Life* undertakes to explain in perhaps boring detail, contest, with which we have been concerned here, is not the same as war and is not synonymous with aggression. Contest can, in fact, serve the cause of peace. Essentially, it is not lethal or permanently damaging.

With these premises, we can speculate about some of the implications of the phenomena here reviewed. First, it appears evident that the conspicuously agonistic stage of consciousness, closely associated with typically male behavior and with the rise of masculinity in the consciousness both of men and of women, achieved something of unique value, though not without cost. We can speculate that outside an agonistic context, the analytic thinking typical of the West, based on formal logic and entering constituently into all of philosophy (in the common older sense of philosophy, ranging from the physical and biological sciences through ethics and metaphysics) would never have come into existence. In a culture as highly developed intellectually as the Chinese, which did not merely neglect agonistic procedures but positively proscribed them, nothing like the Western analytic enterprise ever really got under way.

We could also ask questions such as these. Is logic essentially a tool for dominance? If it is—and even if it is not—what does dominance entail? In the biological setting we have been examining, dominance is not marked by a master-slave dialectic so much as by distancing. Is distancing a form of enslavement? If it is, the enslaved—the distanced—do not eventually win, as they would in a Hegelian master-slave dialectic. Rather typically, they have no offspring. How does the Hegelian master-slave dialectic relate to the antithetical structures of knowledge? In the noetic arena, agonistic activity leads outside itself, not simply to the disabling of an opponent, but to the generation of formal abstractions, to clarity and distinctness—though perhaps these can mean enslavement, too.

Western analytic thought developed not only through use of the agonistic structures and procedures we have been considering here, but also through the related deep interiorization of the technology of writing in its alphabetic form. This interiorization is too complex to go into here—I have treated it in a variety of ways in three books, which others now refer to as a trilogy, *The Presence of the Word* (1967), *Rhetoric, Romance, and Technology* (1971), and *Interfaces of the Word* (1977). But the intellectual and properly philosophical implications of this interiorization are suggested if we recall that philosophy is impossible to the unaided human mind. We know that no oral peoples can provide lengthy, linear, properly philosophical explanation of anything. They can be, and often are, deeply intelligent and profoundly wise, and can be highly articulate with the proverbs and other sayings in which their thought dwells. But lengthy, abstract, categorical explanation eludes the human mind until the mind has made writing its own and thereby capacitated itself for types of intellectual activity otherwise utterly beyond its powers.

A useful analogy for what happens to the mind that has interiorized writing is found in instrumental music. A musical instrument is a musical tool, a dead thing, a technological creation, that human beings can make so much a part of themselves, can so interiorize, that the violinist or flutist, for example, or the organist, with his or her huge machine, can make inhuman sounds express what is properly and intimately human in a way impossible without the musical tool or instrument. This interiorization of a technological invention—a musical instrument—and the new and properly human freedom that results throws light on what is meant by the origins of philosophical thinking in the Greek interiorization of the fully vocalic alphabet. As earlier noted, the origins of philosophy out of interiorized literacy have been made abundantly clear by Havelock in his *Preface to Plato* and in the host of other studies that have followed on this seminal work of two decades ago.

What the future holds it is hard to say. But attention to the immediate past might throw some concluding light on the present state of affairs and hint at the future. It appears that ceremonial combat no longer operates and no longer can operate in the intellectual and academic world of the West in the way it did in the past. Only the dissertation defense in some places survives, in a moribund state, as the last conspicuous vestige of the old orally-based agonistic culture. The watershed was located in the 1960s, with the drastic shift in faculty-student relationships and the quite irresistible drive toward intervisitation and coeducational residence halls that, among other things it did, conspicuously tamed the male students. But coeducation had not been the first beginning of the liquidation of the old ceremonial academia agonia. It had concluded what the Renaissance began and what the Romantic Age furthered, a movement away from the old male distancing agonistic that worked by maximizing stress to an academia more concerned with self-fulfillment (an objective that an old army sergeant to whom I recently talked found both repulsive and terrifying: he felt that you had to find yourself by standing off others in combat before you had any self worth fulfilling or even any self you could call your own).

We can end by calling to mind some developments in the 1960s relevant to our present considerations. In the 1960s the old agonistic structure collapsed, and combat assumed non-ceremonial, confrontational forms. Several developments illuminate the scenario. First, the conflict of the '60s tended to be between students and administrators, rather than between students and teachers: the principal area for academic ceremonial combat was thereby vacated. Second, attacks made on faculty members in the '60s tended to be because of their personal beliefs, not because of their academic behavior. Again, the academic arena was avoided. Third, there was a feeling that if one argued with a teacher about the teacher's own subject one risked losing: risk, the very rationale of the older agonistic world, was downgraded. Fourth, the academic world itself was often attacked not on academic grounds, but on grounds of social justice as such: the combative academic arena was bypassed again. Fifth, whereas the old agonistic educational methods had prepared for the often ceremonial combat of politics and diplomacy (the British Latin public school), the new agonistic of the '60s worked for revolutionary guerilla combat.

All this suggests that among the paraphenomena of the '60s one finds not only a female identity crisis, but, I strongly suspect, an even more intense male identity crisis. Strangely, perhaps, this male identity crisis to some degree shows itself today in the widespread male addiction to sports on television. Televised spectator sports, especially a territorial sport such as football, appeal almost exclusively to males, as does the greatest loner's territorial game of all, chess, and as do our newest loner's territorial video games. Spectator sports in a stadium are largely social as well as combative events. On television combat is all. Here the male is in an ideal situation, safe at home, fighting, but only vicariously, passionately identified with one or the other side, well nourished with a can of beer, with a comforting female figure, his wife, to lean on, but in a totally male psychic environment that effectively reduces women to outsiders, if we believe the hundreds upon hundreds of cartoons about irate television sports widows. One such widow is reputed to have said that the only way she could attract her husband's attention during one of the seventy-two hour television football orgies was to dress in astroturf. The cartoonist's unconscious was registering awareness of the way in which in the distant biological past the male's concern with territory could take precedence over his concern with his mate.

The implications of the present situation are not all clear, but they are massive, if we are at all aware that the intellectual life of the West and the philosophy we profess developed on an analogous intellectual turf. In our day consciousness has risen to a new level. This is not to say that human life has essentially improved. But it does raise the question: What will be the long-term effects of our new intellectual style?

Works Cited

Bochenski, Joseph M. *A History of Formal Logic*. Trans. Ivo Thomas. Notre Dame, IN: U of Notre Dame P, 1961.

Boorstin, Daniel J. *The Americans: The National Experience*. New York: Random House, 1965.

Havelock, Eric A. *Preface to Plato*. Cambridge, MA: Belknap P of Harvard UP, 1963.

Lloyd, G.E.R. *Polarity and Analogy: Two Types of Argumentation in Early Greek Thought*. Cambridge UK: Cambridge UP, 1966.

Ong, Walter J. *Fighting for Life: Context, Sexuality, and Consciousness*. Ithaca and London: Cornell UP, 1981.

—. *Interfaces of the Word: Studies in the Evolution of Consciousness and Culture*. Ithaca, NY: Cornell UP, 1977.

—. *The Presence of the Word*. New Haven and London: Yale UP, 1967.

—. *Rhetoric, Romance, and Technology*. Ithaca, NY: Cornell UP, 1971.

Orwell, George. "Such, Such Were the Joys." *The Collected Essays, Journalism, and Letters of George Orwell*. Ed. Sonia Orwell and Ian Angus. 4 vols. New York: Harcourt, Brace & World, 1968. 4: 330-69.

Wilson, Edward O. *Sociobiology: The New Synthesis*. Cambridge, MA: Belknap P of Harvard UP, 1975.

26

Technological Development and Writer-Subject-Reader Immediacies (1990)

Research examining oral and written communication over the last twenty-five years has not only revealed an interest from scholars across a number of disciplines (Havelock), but demonstrated that relationships between thought and expression—long considered to be elementary and stable—are much more complex and interactive than previously thought. Notions long fixed in the minds of researchers, and hence rather intolerant of alteration, are now under re-examination. In this instance, the notion of *text,* and its plasticity when subject to various forms of mediated communication, is one such concept in need of more sensitive examination. Since we have burrowed further and further into questions of textuality, we have become increasingly aware (mostly in backhanded ways) that an inscription is not fully a text until someone reads it, that is, until someone produces from the writer's text something nontextual, a sequence of sounds—exterior and audible, or in the imagination—or as in the case of congenitally deaf persons, some kind of sensory temporal sequence related, however indirectly, to sound. To do this requires a code that the text itself does not provide. Texts, as texts, are dependent on something nontextual. All text is pretext. Unless someone has this extra-textual code that makes reading possible and applies the code, the physical inscription remains forever no more than a visible pattern on a surface. The one who has the code and uses it is a reader. (This is not at all to say that everything in writing is merely a transcription of actual speech, but only that writing is ultimately based, if in a variety of ways, on speech.)

The fact that a text is a text because it can be read means, in short, that a text as text is part of discourse. Physically, the text appears *not* to be. Discourse moves. The text is immobile. But by putting words into a text, we do not freeze them, remove them from dialogue. We only suspend the

dialogue with the writer until a reader chances along. The impression a
text creates, that words are fixed because the visible signs are fixed, has
wrought havoc in philosophy, theology, jurisprudence, literary and critical
theory, and who knows where else. No word can be present all at once, as
words seem to be on a visible surface. The word *nevertheless,* for example, is not a thing, but an event: By the time I get to -*theless,* the *never-* is
gone, and has to be gone or I cannot make out the word. Thus, while written texts have a stable quality, they only appear to have whole, fixed meaning and actually lack features of momentary communication that would
provide additional, more complete understanding.

But discourse calls for the presence of two or more persons to one
another. (Here lies the basic sense of presence: person-to-person relationship, not thought-to-word-to-thing relationship.) Such direct personal relationship, texts do interfere with, for normally the writer and reader are not
present to one another. Often, and indeed more often than not in the case
of the book texts on our library shelves, when the reader engages the text,
the writer has long been dead. This absence calls for fictionalizing.
Someone has to play a role: writer or reader or both. And since the reader
has to be alive to read, his or her roles are more proximate to us, and in
some ways easier to discuss, more urgent. They call for special attention.

Out of such considerations has grown, in the words of George L.
Dillon, the "literary theorizing extending from Wayne Booth and Walker
Gibson through Walter J. Ong, Wolfgang Iser, Walter Slatoff, and
Umberto Eco to the recent work of Peter Rabinowitz, all of whom speak
of the reader as playing a role" (139). The roles that readers play can be
categorized in an almost limitless number of ways. Dillon reviews various
"ideal, implied, model, or intended" readers, pretending readers, submis-
sive readers and resisting readers, suspicious readers, innocent readers,
congruent and incongruent readers, mistreated readers, precisional and
wishy-washy readers, and so on and on and on (138-43).

Umberto Eco has deliberately mixed readers' roles in his lengthy narrative *The Name of the Rose,* which has had an extraordinarily wide
appeal for so recondite a work, an appeal suggesting that sensitivity to
reader-writer relationships has roots deep in the psyche at our present
stage in the evolution of consciousness, roots deeper than the explicit,
exfoliated theories that *litterateurs* play with. These deep, unarticulated,
subconscious or unconscious roots help give *The Name of the Rose* its
surprisingly strong appeal even to those who have never heard
reader-writer relationships discussed. Deliberately weaving an
arabesqued intertextuality at all sorts of levels, Eco's remarkable work
creates a new kind of narrative density, supported in part by the author's

earlier theorizing about semiotics, which posits interpretive codes used by his "model reader" as against generative codes used by writers (Sallis). Eco distinguishes two kinds of texts generated by authors, *closed* texts (calculated to elicit a specific response from readers) and open texts (designed in a maze-like structure for readers to labor through), although he wisely notes that the "closed" text is open to more than one interpretation and that the "open" text is not open to random interpretation.

The fictionalizing of readers is a coefficient of the relationship of the writer to his or her own lifeworld. This relationship develops or shifts for many reasons. Today we are hyperconscious of the ways in which the electronic media, notably television, have altered the way persons relate to one another and to the world around them (Gumpert and Cathcart). Now consider briefly a change in relationship in a work on the technological border of the coming electronic age. The work is, perhaps surprisingly, Gerard Manley Hopkins' *The Wreck of the Deutschland*, which has been treated in somewhat different perspective in my *Hopkins, the Self, and God*. Through such a poem we have the opportunity to examine the introduction of a new medium to the communication of thoughts and sentiment, as well as how such a form shapes the text, the relationship between author and audience, and the technology for inducing a presence of mediated immediacy.

Hopkins was not yet in the world of electronics in the strict sense of electronics, which has to do not simply with the use of electricity, but with the emission of electrons as in electronic tubes and transistors. But Hopkins lived in a world of electrically implemented communication. The American Samuel F. B. Morse had exhibited a genuine telegraph instrument in 1837, and his famous message "What hath God wrought" was sent by telegraph from Baltimore to Washington in 1844, the year of Hopkins's birth. A telegraph company was formed in the United States in 1845, and in the same year the Electric Telegraph company was organized in England. The first transatlantic cable, running between Newfoundland and Ireland, was completed in 1866.

Moreover, Hopkins grew up in a family milieu concerned with rapid transmission of information and of information about disasters. His father, Manley Hopkins, was a marine insurance average adjuster (or as we would say today, a marine insurance actuary) keeping account of shipwrecks, among other things, to adjust marine insurance rates—just as modern insurance companies adjust automobile insurance rates according to the number of accidents one has or, we hope, does not have. The Hopkins household was certainly more sensitive than most households to recent—even ongoing—shipping disasters. Hopkins knew the communications milieu on which marine insurance companies relied: In a letter of May 21, 1878, to Bridges, he brands insensitive readings of *The Loss of the Eurydice* as "mere Lloyd's Shipping Intelligence." His family background is hardly irrelevant to the fact that his two long poems are about shipwrecks.

In *The Wreck of the Deutschland*, Hopkins was relying for details on the current *Times* reports, many of which are explicitly identified by the *Times* itself as coming by telegraph (Weyand). The result is a poem not simply about a disaster and suffering, but about *ongoing* disaster and suffering, evoking new kinds of writer and reader responses. Hopkins' relationship to his subject matter differs strikingly from that of Milton's in *Lycidas*, the only other poem in English about a ship foundered off the coast of England to have generated a corpus of commentary comparable to the corpus concerned with Hopkins' poem. The difference reflects the differing states of the communications media in the mid-seventeenth century and the late nineteenth century. The difference is particularly interesting because Hopkins had read and reread Milton, rating him the best of all poets in English, and perhaps in any language. It appears, as John J. Glavin has circumstantially argued, that in his composition of *The Wreck of the Deutschland* Hopkins was reckoning, consciously or unconsciously, with Milton's achievement in *Lycidas* (Ong, *Hopkins*).

Edward King's death was an event well past, and felt as past, when Milton wrote about it, and an event about which Milton had rather scant details. The scantiness of detail in pre-electric and pre-electronic cultures, not to mention oral cultures, as compared to the avalanche of details in such electronic-age displays as the Watergate case, deserves more attention than it has been given. Scant details foster commonplace treatment— for want of specificities one has to fall back on tried and true generalities, whether in poetry or in law court rhetoric. Setting Edward King in a pastoral elegy (to the annoyance of Dr. Johnson), Milton involves him in the classical world of the past (laurels, myrtles, nymphs, watery bier, remorseless deep, Tempe, the Muses, and so forth), even while assigning him current relevance to seventeenth-century ecclesiastical disputes. Milton's concluding line is "Tomorrow to fresh Woods, and Pastures new." The line is a kind of foreclosure. The past is past. King is dead and gone.

For Hopkins, the German nun's death he celebrated—there is no more apt word—in *The Wreck of the Deutschland* was a distant but far more immediate experience. Far from detached and past, the sense of presence, immediacy and (consequently) reader interaction is not merely "captured" but entwined as part of its meaning. In short, those concepts of intimacy that one associates with momentary communication are features of the text and facilitated by new technological advances. The *Deutschland* struck on the sands of the Kentish Knock on Monday, December 6, and the *Times* accounts run from Tuesday, December 7, through Saturday, December 11 (when the German nun's cry "O Christ, come quickly" was reported among other details), on through the following Monday, December 13 (Weyand). The British people, Hopkins among them, were aware of the wreck and its sequels as ongoing events, distant but pressing on them. Among the *Times* stories, as just noted, are telegraphed news reports, identified by the *Times* as such. Hopkins' sense of immediacy is indirectly reflected in his reference to the storm as "electrical horror" (in *The Loss of the Eurydice*, Hopkins also refers explicitly to electricity: "deadly electric"). The near-synchronicity effected by the telegraph, abetted by the railroad tying together the east coast of England, off which the ship foundered, and the west coast near which Hopkins was living in Wales, leads Hopkins to reflect on exactly what he was doing at the very time the *Deutschland* was breaking up and some 78 of her 213 (or 223) passengers and crew were being cast to their deaths in the North Sea.

> Away in the lovable west,
> On a pastoral forehead of Wales,
> I was under a roof here, I was at rest,
> And they the prey of the gales.

With Hopkins, the reader shares the press of the events with which the poem is involved. The reader, who of course is typically not reading the text while the writer is writing it—most certainly not in Hopkins' case here—is nevertheless caught up in the immediacy of the writer's experience when he or she later enters into the text. The synchronic sense with which he experienced the *Deutschland* disaster was not strange to the world Hopkins lived in: Other persons read the *Times* and profited from telegraphed news. Yet the rapidity of communication relative to the normative standards of conventional technology provided a response so rapid that it presented for readers a proximity to the event that approached the spontaneity, and hence degree of imminence, associated with speech. Electric technology, facilitating the rapidity of print, provided an immediacy readers today take for granted. A few generations before Hopkins, readers knew nothing of this pressure within the present.

We are concerned not only with writers, but also with readers. Does Hopkins' electrically implemented relationship with his subject establish any special relationship with his readers? It does establish a new kind of directness in the relationship, a new intimacy, a participatory intimacy. This is not an intimacy of the sort that Hemingway readers are often made to feel, a kind of buddy-buddy relationship, so that the reader is made to feel like the writer's boon companion, and a very understanding companion (see Chapter 22 in the present collection). Rather, it is a kind of immediate personal involvement.

A paradox is at work here, as always when we are dealing with the application of technologies to the word, from writing onward. Electricity means generators, machinery, and mechanical equipment. It interposed a great deal that is not directly human between the written verbalization of the events by reporters (whom the *Times* still identifies as "correspondents"; Weyand 355) off the east coast of England and the reception of this verbalization on the west coast of the island in Wales. The interposition is not so massive as in the case of the technologies at work in the more nearly instantaneous electronic communication, but it is massive enough. Sending a telegram is not the same as sending a messenger. Yet its rapidity itself brings closeness, dissolving distance.

With Hopkins' close attention to the self and to the relations of one self to another, this immediacy is particularly significant and effective. John Robinson astutely observes that in some of Hopkins' poems, including the early *Nondum* (1886), "It was not his own fate that caused such a shudder of loneliness but a feeling of the ultimate inaccessibility of others' lives and deaths" (124). Hopkins' poetry and, much more, his prose writings show how intensely he was aware that one person cannot enter into the consciousness of another directly, that the "taste" of one's self as such is incommunicable. But he was also aware that love can bridge the gap. And at the center of *The Wreck of the Deutschland*, his intent is to enter into the mind of the German sister at her moment of crisis when she calls out, "O Christ, Christ, come quickly" ("The Majesty! What did she mean?"). He discerns her meaning as the welcoming of her death, where Christ was coming to her. The drive to immediacy and to intimacy of interpretation here appears as great as it can well be for human beings. Unlike Milton's classical closing of King's case in the last line of *Lycidas* ("Tomorrow to fresh Woods, and Pastures new"), Hopkins' last lines abide in the present: "Dame, at our door/Drowned, and among our shoals/ Remember us." This is not classical apostrophe, but prayer to a real person, still accessible after death to Hopkins' Catholic faith, which here abets the media development to enhance a sense of personal presence.

The reader is caught up into this immediacy-effected-at-a-distance, which is of a new intensity in the history of literature. The reader's role is to penetrate maximally with Hopkins into the interior of another human being's consciousness, physically but not temporally distanced. Earlier literature does not achieve or attempt such intensity in quite this way.

Hopkins' closeness is a deep union of self-consciousness. Granted that in Hopkins' day the use of new technologies of communication could paradoxically foster in the reader the sense of immediacy as just explained, what can be said about the effect of still more sophisticated electronic technologies? Do they foster among readers any new roles of intimacy with the writer and his or her subject matter? This is a large and almost impossibly complicated question, and only a few suggestions shall be offered that may move toward answers.

From Hopkins' age on, and with increasing intensity in the age of electronic communication, the old oratorical expectations that for two thousand years and more so largely governed writer and reader, and held writer and reader commonly at a formal distance, have virtually disappeared. Electronic communication on radio, television, and now the computer has done away with the old declamatory tone of the ancient rhetorical tradition and the distances this tone implied. Readers trained by the *McGuffey's Readers* were still very much caught up in rhetorical declamation and distancing; readers were still thought of as reading aloud and their roles were tailored accordingly. Here is a sample of what readers of *McGuffey's Readers* read, taken from McGuffey's *Rhetorical Guide, or Fifth Reader*. The passage is from Lyman Beecher's "The Memory of Our Fathers," "Caesar was merciful, Scipio was continent, Hannibal was patient; but it was reserved for Washington to blend them all in one, and, like the lovely masterpiece of the Grecian artist, to exhibit in one glow of associated beauty, the pride of every model, and the perfection of every artist" (1844, 291). This sounds like an oration, but it was presented by McGuffey as something to read—which meant to declaim, for the *Readers* were largely intended to be used for declamatory voiced reading. The reader's role in this age was still largely associated with oratory. One was likely to read even alone somewhat as though one were declaiming.

People still read on the radio and on television from teleprompters, but they do not declaim when they do. They conceal the fact that they are reading, and often pretend to be informal and extemporaneous. A new line of intimacy—or of pseudo-intimacy—has been established in the close conversational verbalization normal on radio and in the pseudo-face-to-face relationship of speaker and audience on television (Gumpert and Cathcart). Now oral presentation to millions of persons has been tailored by electronics to appear to break down all artificial borders, although it separates sender and receiver from one another by technologies of Byzantine complexities that reach to outer space and back.

For Hopkins, the innovations of technology provided the opportunity for written communication to increase in the rapidity of expression.

Diminishing the temporal distance of the printed word decreased the impersonal distance between reader and writer. Eventually other forms of mediated communication will provide greater, more direct interaction beyond the immediacy of the event and increase the interactive nature of the discourse in ways that artificially simulate (but nonetheless approach) direct verbal communication. Just as the electronic technology of Hopkins' era altered the rapidity and immediacy of the "text," so also will new forms of mediated communication compel us to adopt a more malleable notion of the text than our current predispositions allow. We need continued investigation of the ways in which these new uses of the technologies of the word affect the way we write when we write fiction or essays or scholarly works, and how they affect the roles of readers when readers read such things today.

Works Cited

Dillon, George L. *Rhetoric as Social Imagination: Explorations in the Interpersonal Function of Language.* Bloomington: Indiana UP, 1986.

Eco, Umberto. *The Name of the Rose.* Trans. William Weaver. New York: Harcourt Brace Jovanovich, 1983.

Glavin, John J. "'The Wreck of the *Deutschland*' and 'Lycidas': Ubique naufragium est." *Texas Studies in Litterature and Language* 22 (1980): 522-46.

Gumpert, Gary and Robert Cathcart, eds. *Inter/media: Interpersonal Communication in a Media World.* 3rd ed. New York: Oxford UP, 1986.

Havelock, Eric A. *The Muse Learns to Write: Reflections on Orality and Literacy from Antiquity to the Present.* New Haven: Yale UP, 1986.

Hopkins, Gerard Manley. *The Letters of Gerard Manley Hopkins to Robert Bridges.* Ed. Claude Colleer Abbott. London: Oxford UP, 1935.

—. *Poems of Gerard Manley Hopkins.* Ed. with Notes Robert Bridges. 2nd ed. London: Oxford UP, 1930.

Ong, Walter J. *Hopkins, the Self, and God.* Toronto: Toronto UP, 1986.

—. *Interfaces of the Word: Studies in the Evolution of Consciousness and Culture.* Ithaca, NY: Cornell UP, 1977.

Robinson, John. *In Extremity: A Study of Gerard Manley Hopkins.* Cambridge, UK: Cambridge UP, 1978.

Sallis, S. "Naming the Rose: Readers and Codes in Umberto Eco's Novel." *Journal of the Midwest Modern Language Association* 19 (1986): 3-12.

Weyand, Norman, ed. *Immortal Diamond: Studies in Gerard Manley Hopkins.* New York: Sheed & Ward, 1949.

27

Information and/or Communication: Interactions (1996)

I. Information and Communication

The present age of humanity is often styled an "information age" and often a "communication age." Frequently these two descriptions are taken as roughly synonymous. But they can also be distinguished, and often are. The implications of this distinction are vast and often intertwined. This is an attempt to enter into some of their intertwining that marks our age and to relate the two, information and communication, to two other phenomena that mark our age, namely, preoccupation with digitization and preoccupation with hermeneutics.

The common distinction between information and communication is well known. Information is generally understood as a message transmitted by a code over a channel through a receiving (decoding) device to a particular destination (*Britannica* 6:312) and communication is commonly understood as "the exchange of meanings between individuals through a common system of symbols" (3:496).

Thus understood, information (for example, a genetic code in living cells) does not of itself involve meaning. It does not involve human consciousness, or consciousness of any kind, including that of subhuman species. Of course, it should be noted, since we are treating here two rival characterizations of the present age of *humanity*, neither the consciousness of subhuman species nor their modes of communication enter directly into our present concerns. There is a huge body of published material on information and on human communication, but the foregoing understandings of the two terms are well in line with widespread usage and will serve our purposes here. These definitions, like all definitions, of course can call for further interpretation. Indeed such interpretation will be the business of much of this present treatment. No definition ever brings matters to a permanent standstill.

The communication to be attended to here directly is specifically human verbal communication as such, although, of course, human verbal communication is associated with many other sorts of human communication, such as pictorial, gestural, or tactile. Communication by means other than verbal will be attended to here only as occasion demands.

Communication Is Interaction

"Communication," as just suggested, consists of interactions between conscious human beings (paradigmatically, "I" and "You"). By contrast, "information" is something transmitted by a mechanical operation—no consciousness as such involved, but only various signals or indicators moved spatially over "channels" from place to place. In this sense of information, familiar in information processing and information theory, the "message" has "nothing to do with any inherent meaning," but "is rather a degree of order, or non-randomness, that can be measured and treated mathematically" (*Britannica* 6:312). Thus in information as such, as here understood, and in the transmission of information as such, there is nothing distinctively human, and nothing involving even subhuman animal awareness.

For example, a genetic code—such as an organic chemical pattern in DNA or RNA making for specifiable results in an organism—is "information" only, of itself not transmitting thoughts or symbols, but simply bringing about physical results. Although millions of such codes are operating all the time in the bodies of living beings, such as our own, to keep these bodies alive and functioning, the codes have of themselves no place directly in human consciousness. If by painstaking research human beings have been able to become consciously aware of such information codes in other organisms and in themselves and to work with the codes in the world of human communication, such an information code and physical transmission of the encoded information nevertheless existed first, with no direct reference at all to human consciousness or to communication as here understood.

Compared to communication, information as such is thus clearly an earlier, more primitive, prehuman phenomenon. Information systems such as genetic codes have been essential to the organization and evolution of all earlier life, subhuman as well as human, all the way back to the time when DNA (or possibly RNA, followed by DNA) first appeared on earth around three and a half billion years ago, when the now approximately four billion-year-old planet earth was around a half billion years old (Stringer). However, until quite recent scientific thought and technology opened to inspection the organic world's all but infinite complexity, human beings have known virtually nothing of such natural information systems, despite their tremendous antiquity.

Knowledge of such systems first effectively surfaced only in 1865-1866, when the Austrian monk Gregor Mendel (1822-1884), reported on a series of experiments with the breeding of garden peas that he had begun in 1856. These experiments established the existence of "particulate heredity," that is, of heredity passed on to offspring by designable particular organic codes or genes in parent organisms. Once the human mind could encompass this information, the information could enter the realm of communication in human consciousness. The information system had been operating for hundreds of millions of years, but first figured in communication less than a century and a half ago.

Communication Is Not Transportation

Human verbal communication is sometimes carelessly conceived of according to an information model, as simply the movement of an item from one point to another. But human communication involves much more than simple diffusion of units of information. Contrary to common assumptions, there is no way for me to transport a concept from my mind or consciousness into yours, no "channel" carrying my thought from me to you. In communicating with you in oral words, for example, I make certain sounds that are carried over physical media such as the air and the nervous system and to which, if you know the language (symbol system) that I am using, you can react to form a concept of your own in your own mind or consciousness. In this activity, both I and you use a code, but my thoughts are not "sent" to you by the code over or through a "channel," transported from my mind to you as an electric impulse is transported from a sending telegraphic instrument to a receiving telegraphic instrument. A human communications "medium," so-called, such as speech, is more than just a "medium," more than a "channel." I cannot place my thoughts in your mind. I can perhaps influence the way you think, but you always have to produce your own thoughts. I. A. Richards put it well in 1928:

> Communication takes place when one mind so acts upon its environment that another mind is influenced, and in that other mind an experience occurs that is like the experience in the first mind, and is caused in part by that experience. (quoted in *Britannica* 16:623)

Richards' "occurs" here is a bit noncommittal: What happens is that the second mind out of its own resources produces an experience like that in the first mind.

Marshall McLuhan's famous dictum, "The medium is the message," like its programmatically reconstituted formulation in the title of his book, *The Medium Is the Massage*, coauthored by Quentin Fiore, is warranted because what happens in human communication is more than transmission through a medium in the usual sense of this word. In communication (between conscious persons) the medium is more than what the medium is in information processing.

II. Information Codes and Verbal Communication

Although information systems are not of themselves communication systems, they relate intimately to human verbal communication in at least three ways. First, communication, verbal and other, between self-conscious human beings necessarily involves in each human being physiological processes consisting of the operation of many massive, highly evolved biological information systems in our bodies implementing and supporting communication processes, and, indeed, life itself, without any necessary conscious awareness on the part of the person communicating as to what the information codes are or how they work or even of their existence. Such information systems have only begun to be understood, but they have been working in *Homo sapiens* for some 150,000 years (Stringer) and, in simpler form, in the ancestors of *Homo sapiens* for millions of years. Human communication entails far more nonconscious operations than had earlier been known.

Second, verbal communication, besides depending on the operation of physiological information systems, can make such information systems themselves the subject of study and of communication. Communication can consciously envelop information systems. For example, the now well-known human-genome project is undertaking, with massive collaborative research, to establish and make immediately available to conscious knowledge the entire information system constituted by all the extant genes in the chromosomes of the cells of any and all human bodies. That is to say, human beings are making this enormous code, previously entirely unconscious, subject to conscious communication and control. Communication systems—conscious, and thus involving an "I" and a corresponding "you" (singular or plural)—unlike information systems, are omnivorous. In principle, verbal communication can bring all natural information systems of the physical world into its conscious ambit. Whether anyone could live long enough even to begin to familiarize himself or herself with such a glut of information is another question.

Third, besides creating in itself conscious knowledge of such natural unconscious information systems, human verbal communication can and does also consciously construct and, in the process, build into itself and its activities any number of artificial information systems, such as those consciously designed for writing and now the almost unbelievably more massive systems designed for computers. These linguistic and computerized information systems are brought into being by conscious communication: They are information systems, such as the complex systems in computers, built up consciously by persons communicating with one another.

The Social Foundation of Computerized Information

But if communication can generate information systems, it can never generate information systems that do not retain some connection with communication. Philip Leith has shown, for example, that the foundation or the ground of a computerized information system is not fully formalized, not mathematical or "scientific" (as all "information" is *inside* a computer system), but is necessarily sociological, which means generated by communication beyond the realm of simple information. In designing this computer system, why did you start with this particular question or set of questions and not another question or set? A computer cannot tell, but sociology and the ethnography of verbalization perhaps can. Thus an information system devised by human beings cannot result simply from other information, but needs also previous communication, motivation tied in with discourse between conscious human beings. Computers have their ultimate origins in people, not in another computer or in a concatenation of other computers *ad infinitum.*

Thus, in sum, information systems are older than verbal communication by billions of years, but have been known and studied as such, that is, incorporated into communication activity, for only some 130 years (beginning with Mendel). But despite the immensely greater antiquity of information systems, the far more recent verbal communication systems have been the much older subject of human attention and reflection. They have, in various ways, commanded widespread and acute conscious attention long before writing was developed around 6000 B.C. Among the ancient Greeks, for example, written works on communication (rhetoric) are abundant from the time of the Sophists, Plato, and Aristotle in the fourth century B.C. The study of tremendously old information systems is brand new, while the study of communication, a phenomenon younger than information systems by billions of years, is relatively old.

III. Speech and Power

Communication in the broad sense (not restricted to verbal communication) is essential to the development of each human individual from earliest life: it begins for each individual with the vagaries of infant nonverbal interpersonal communication and reaches a significant climax in the process of moving a child gradually out of infancy (Latin *infans*, non-speaker—*in*, non+ *fari*, to speak) into the world of speech. All parents or others engaged in child care must attend in one way or another to the development of communication, and at a certain peak to verbal communication. Communication is empowerment, and, most especially, speech is empowerment. Power is not of itself exploitative: it can be at the service of love for others. But speech is still power. Even in texts words are powerful, but we can restrict the present discussion to oral speech, which (except for the congenitally deaf) is the usual entry of a human infant into the world of verbal communication.

It is an anthropological and linguistic commonplace that in oral cultures, innocent of all writing, commonly the "man (or woman) of words" is a consummately powerful social and/or political figure because such persons preserve much of a culture's heritage (the epic poet or storyteller) or dominate its political life (the orator, politician, political leader), knowing, as they do, so many names or words, and being skilled in using them.

Naming and Power

The power that communication involves is exemplified in naming, an operation essential to full communication. To know any subject, one has to master a nomenclature, a battery of names or nouns (the English terms *name* and *noun* come from the same Indo-European root; in Latin the single word *nomen*, from the same Indo-Germanic root, is the term for both *name* and *noun*). A self-proclaimed pharmacist who does not know any names of any pharmaceutical products is powerless, quite unable to operate as a pharmacist. In ordinary life, naming, in the case of proper names as well as of common names or common nouns, such as *tree, bird, fence*, is conspicuously empowerment. This is one reason why children find learning names so much fun. It gives them power and freedom.

Nothing in the world comes equipped with a name. Names are all given by intelligent beings, applied from outside the person or object or action to which they are attached. The proper names of individuals deserve attention here. The individual does not find his or her name within. Someone else outside, operating in a (quite necessary) power role, enveloped in parental love (mother and/or father, typically) gave me "Walter" as a name, which I soon appropriated as my own. But however passionately a person may feel that his or her own name is a deeply personal possession, a name as such is exterior to the person—a "handle," as a name is sometimes appropriately called, for a name is indeed like a handle in both establishing contact and in distancing what it is attached to—what it names.

The power inherent in names is indicated by the fact that on occasion an individual will also give himself or herself a name, if he or she feels and/or wants to establish extraordinary personal power—as Josip Broz named himself "Tito" and Iosif Vissarionovich Dzhugashvili named himself "Stalin," which means "steel." This is the ultimate in assertion of power: naming oneself, asserting what all others are to call you, proclaiming fundamental and total independence of domination by others. But such a self-given name comes also from the outside: it is given, applied, to himself or herself as to a kind of exterior object by the very person it names.

"I" Is Not a Name

However, if human beings are all normally given names from without, each human being finds something else within that is too interior to be expressed by a name given from outside. Each of us at one point in learning to speak (somewhere around the age of three or four years) discovers within himself or herself an "I" (or its equivalent in whatever language a child first acquires). This "I" is not a name, for it is precisely not given from outside by another or by the individual attaching it to himself or herself. The sound "I" in an English-speaking environment, or its equivalent in any other language environment, is picked up of course from outside, by hearing others use the word, each this same word for himself or herself. But the sense it expressed comes not from without, but is felt from within. The meaning of my "I" is different from that of every "I" that I hear others utter. To me, every other person's "I" is "you." The meaning of my "I" simply presents itself from within as applying from within my own consciousness (after much work in talking and otherwise interacting with others), and then, far from being applied from the outside, is "outered" or "uttered" from the inside of the person whose "I" it is (etymologically, "uttered" is simply a by-form of "outered"). "I" is not a name or a noun (as earlier noted, the etymological roots of these latter two words are the same in English).

The Uniqueness of "I"

"I" is not a noun but a *pronoun* (Latin *pro* means *in place of*—a pronoun is something "in place of" a name). A child learns from others to form and utter the sound "I," but the "I" means for the child something it means to none of the others whom the child imitates in uttering the sound of his or her "I." No other human being *gave* me the "I" that I alone can "outer" or utter, discover in and project out of *my own* interior. If I were named Tom,

Dick, or Harry, instead of Walter, the "I" that I now utter would be entirely the same. In sum, a name comes from outside, but the "I" is always discovered from within—of course with help from outside in discourse with others (other "I's," other interiors known from the interior of the discovering "I" as "you"). By discourse with others using the pronoun "I," the child finally manages to sense how her or his own use of "I" can work. Earlier, before learning how the "I" works, the child refers to himself or herself by a name (noun, not pronoun)—Johnny or Mary or as a kind of object, not as the person the "I" expresses.

IV. Greeks and the Study of Communication

Writing and the Birth of Analysis

After the development of writing, which made formal analytic "study" possible (Ong, *Orality* 78-115), communication became and has remained the object of intensive, reflective analysis. With the rest of the human race, from time immemorial, long before writing existed anywhere, the ancestors of the ancient Greeks, like peoples in other human cultures, had made at least unreflective use of rhetoric, understood widely as the practice of persuasion. In this broad sense, rhetoric pertained to and governed communication in its nonverbal as well as verbal contexts, operating not simply through words but through gesture, facial expression, and in countless other nonverbal ways. Indeed, understanding rhetoric in this comprehensive way, as "general rhetoric," a means for one individual to induce another individual to a desired action, George A. Kennedy has argued that as a nonreflective activity, "general rhetoric" antedates humanity, being found pretty well through the animal kingdom in the signals animals give to one another to elicit varying responses.

However, once the ancient Greeks had developed the first complete (vowelized) alphabet in the world, they formed rhetoric, as other activities, into an "art" (Greek, *techne*), an analytically rationalized procedure dealing largely with words, but also reflectively with *ethos*, the perceived character of the speaker as registering with his hearers, and with *pathos*, the nonverbalized dispositions of the hearers, such as emotions.

Before rhetoric was thus formed into an "art," Greeks and other human beings had of course practiced persuasion from time immemorial, learning by a kind of imitative apprenticeship. The emergence of formal rhetoric was a complex development, and one with roots antecedent to writing. In fifth-century and fourth-century ancient Greece, its primary models were not what they have often been imagined to be, that is, uses of pragmatic discourse or demonstrative reasoning, but were, rather, the epideictic or poetic performances long familiar in earlier epic singers, as a recent study by Jeffrey Walker has shown.

The Centrality of Rhetoric

Since ancient Greek times, formal rhetoric has been one of the most central and intensive preoccupations of Western academia and the academic subject most immediately and widely operative in the Western human lifeworld through the Enlightenment. Rhetorical activities have been guides to much of actual human behavior, intellectual, political, and other (see the texts in Bizzell and Herzberg). In skilled, reflective study of rhetoric, study of communication systems takes formal shape as a reflective art. Greek civilization and those civilizations that have opted to follow its intellectual lead in the West were all decidedly self-consciously communication cultures. But they were far from being information cultures in any sense at all comparable to our modern information age.

From what has thus far been surveyed here, it is evident that identifying the present age in the West and/or elsewhere as distinctively the age of communications can be seriously misleading. Because of the longstanding and intensive focus on communication from classical antiquity in the West, and because of comparable attention to communication in all other known human societies, styling our present age a communications age does not differentiate it so readily from past ages so much as styling it an information age does. The age of the ancient Greeks was conspicuously an age in effect at least as concerned with communications as we are. And later on, as is well known, the Western European Middle Ages, the Renaissance, and later centuries were obsessed with the study of communication under the banner of rhetoric.

Our own age's tremendous growth in the design and use of communications media and thus its growth in the use of communications derives not from a new enthusiasm for communications as such but from the vast increment of information that the technologies of writing, print, and electronics have made available to us, with today's resulting explosive electronic enlargement. The glut of information today is available for use in communications as well as in virtually all other human activities. In sum, human beings in the West had been attending reflectively and analytically to communication for more than two millennia. They have not been studying information systems, which have existed for billions of years, for more than a few generations. Now they know very well what information systems are. They are exceedingly useful. Can they be threatening as well?

V. Information Overload

Where are we in our evolving universe when information in the quantities we know today is being loaded into human consciousness? When this loading gives no signs of ever decreasing but of becoming exponentially greater and greater for the foreseeable future?

Richard A. Lanham's *The Electronic Word: Democracy, Technology, and the Arts* is one of the very best of several recent books suggesting how the noetic world is changing and how the neat worldview rooted in ancient Greece and notably dominant worldwide since the time of Newton is being supplanted by a world in which rhetoric is attaining a new dominance. For, as Lanham shows, rhetoric was dominant through the Western European Renaissance, which can be earmarked as the restoration of rhetorical culture after the relative ascendance of logic in the High Middle Ages—relative ascendancy, for the Middle Ages remained far more basically rhetorical in their cast of mind than many have commonly allowed.

A Role for Rhetoric Today

Rhetorical thinking serves some purpose in our present communication chaos. Rhetoric is more comprehensive than logic. Rhetoric is not contained in logic, since logic has no use for rhetoric and from its beginnings has fought to keep itself free of rhetorical "contamination." But logic is contained in rhetoric, since it can be used and is used within rhetorical thinking and expression for rhetorical purposes. In this age of an information explosion and information chaos, rhetoric is coming to the fore again. From the study of well over twenty significant Western thinkers, a recent two-volume work edited by Chip Sills and George H. Jensen, generates its telling title, *The Philosophy of Discourse: The Rhetorical Turn in Twentieth-Century Thought*. Rhetoric has to do with human communication as such, not with merely information, although it of course now includes the use and study of information systems.

Information Buildup

As preoccupation explicitly with information systems as such has recently overwhelmed our human lifeworld, entering in depth into our communications revolution itself, we are today flooded with processed information to an extent quite unimaginable only a few generations ago. Human beings have never had to cope with information even remotely so abundant as that with which we now live. Of course, the present state of affairs shaped up in stages. The information buildup in oral cultures that accelerated with the development of writing and was intensified with the development of the alphabet increased exponentially with the development of printing from movable alphabetic type in the mid-1400s and has now increased even more exponentially following on the development of the first modern computers some five decades ago.

With the proliferation of computers, the quantity of information on hand or accessible to human consciousness is already billions upon billions of times what it was even a hundred years ago and is increasing by the hour beyond any readily assignable limits. Inevitably, information theory in the past few generations has deeply affected the study of communications itself, for as just noted, communications can include any and all information, and increasingly will do so in one way or another.

Computer Frustration and the Quest for Intimacy

To understand even in a preliminary fashion what has happened as a result of our present flooding of information into communications activity calls for a comprehensive historical and philosophical view of all human existence of a scope that we are only beginning distantly to imagine. In computerized communication (e-mail, bulletin boards, and the rest) the overwhelming preoccupation with achieving intimacy is indicative of haunting frustration: the more information we flood in to facilitate intimacy, the more virtual everything is. How do I know that the one I am electronically communicating with is the one I think he or she is?

The modern communication age, swollen by its enveloping of the information explosion, can be viewed as having begun with the telegraph and telephone and moving pictures. These were all initially electric in the sense that they used electricity, but they were not, strictly, electronic—that is, they did not operate by the emission of and control of electrons as such. But these electrically operating media were soon transmuted into electronic media proper, such as vacuum-tube radio, television, and computerized media of countless sorts, digital recording discs, and so on, increasing their ambiance exponentially into the future.

Moreover, communication in recent times was immeasurably enhanced not only by electric and electronic inventions, but also by the development of rapid transportation media, which enlarge the range and amount of person-to-person communication across the world. Thus in a very real sense our age is an age beyond a doubt distinguished by immeasurably expanded communication between human brings across the globe and out into space and back. Developments in transportation of human beings directly foster the development of communication between persons, although they can also be used for the physical distribution of mere information as such.

If our expanded media can be put to uses that increase genuine human communicative interaction, they need not thereby improve true communication between human persons at all, and can, in fact, numb and decrease it. This does not deny that our new and growing communication devices are not admirable human creations, much less make them evil, but it does advertise their extrahuman, mechanical nature and the need to inject into them massive intelligent and moral management (which in this electronic age must, paradoxically, be carried on with the aid of the new information media themselves).

Expanding Communication Studies

We have noted that because it has been enlarged by incorporating within itself the vast spread of information now available to us, the study and use of communication is immeasurably more comprehensive than it was when it was limited to the older study of rhetoric. The study of communication has been deepened by many other new developments. First, the modern growth in the "human sciences," such as psychology and anthropology and cultural studies generally, has enlarged and deepened modern understanding of communication far beyond what was available in earlier ages. And, of course, this growth has been implemented vastly by putting to work more and more information systems within the network of truly human communication.

The "Information Age"

In sum then, even though communication today is more widespread and varied than ever before, our age is nevertheless more distinctively an age of information than an age of communication in the sense that it is the vast increase of information accessible to us that had made the growth in communication both possible and imperative. The widely expanded and varied use of communication today is itself often aimed not so much at simply improving human interaction, but also at laying hold of more and more information systems operating independently of human consciousness in the world around us generally—where "laying hold of" information systems means introducing them into conscious communication systems. The end result of what is going on in the study of information systems is the amplification of communication systems as well as information systems, with no end in sight at all.

VI. Digitization and Hermeneutics

How can we assess the introduction into the human lifeworld of billions upon billions of new information systems (some natural, as the human genome and other genomes, some of human origin, as new humanly devised and humanly managed information systems, such as those being generated daily on Internet and the World Wide Web)? This vast load in human communication is new and growing so fast as to be in fact immeasurable. It is making of human consciousness something other than what consciousness used to be. What does this overload of information, or as it is now commonly referred to, this information chaos, call for in the human being of today and tomorrow? We are moving into, or are already in, a situation where, in principle, everything that is known or has been known can be made accessible to everyone everywhere anytime. Even though this accessibility cannot ever be realized in fact, the question of where we are and where we are going in our information-saturated world of communication is of concern not simply to the designers of computer software, but also to the shared human consciousness of the world.

Writing in the Information Age

David Bolter's fascinating *Writing Space: The Computer, Hypertext, and the History of Writing* addresses itself to the state of writing in our present information age and holds out the hope that the development of hypertext will give us some way of coping in our present situation, when the age of print has clearly been in some way superseded (although more is being printed today by far than ever before, including more and more books). In principle, though never even remotely in fact, hypertext can make available here and now everything ever inscribed about every subject under the sun. Fully implemented hypertext would function by means of a computerized index to everything ever printed. If hypertext could ever be fully activated, it would provide computer users with immediate access to every printed document in the world—a condition that of course can never be realized or, in fact, even approximated. But hypertext has no fixed boundaries, only those determined by human exhaustion. Bolter finds that the hierarchic organization of thought enabled by print (and, earlier, to a less intensive degree, by writing) is superseded today by networking, as on Internet and, most explicitly, in the use of hypertext.

Overload: The Need for Hermeneutics

When a communications system, which works between persons through symbols, is overloaded with great masses of information, you create an urgent need for interpretation or hermeneutics. Symbols, unlike sheer information, are of themselves multivalent and have long fascinated and hyperactivated human consciousness. Total verbal explicitness is impossible: any statement can call for further interpretation that makes its meaning (apprehended not only explicitly, but also implicitly by its unuttered but really apprehended context in a given utterance). Once the accessible information load becomes heavy, as it has become in recent years, and is interwoven into the symbolic human communication world—which is always open to being made more and more explicit—human beings are driven inexorably to study more intensively than ever both communication as such and information itself as such. Human consciousness wants to relate everything to everything else and to do so consciously, so far as this is possible. This situation is one that underlies (although it does not entirely account for) the explosion of hermeneutics, which is to say interpretation, in recent years. How are we to understand the vast network of knowledge available in the world of consciousness today?

Digitization and Hermeneutics

Elsewhere I have examined the twin phenomena of the current growth of digitized information systems and the current burgeoning fascination with hermeneutics, attempting to show how digitization and hermeneutics are complementary (Ong, "Hermeneutic"). Digitization proceeds by division of what it deals with into numerically distinct binary units. Hermeneutics drives ultimately not to divide (although it may make tactical use of division), but to form wholes, ultimately to relate everything that is known to everything else that is known.

As particulate information has grown, we find in databases countless kinds and ranges of hermeneutics, under headings such as "literary hermeneutics" through "hermeneutics and analysis," "science, hermeneutics, and praxis," "Buddhist hermeneutics," "hermeneutics as method, tradition, and critique," "context and hermeneutics," "hermeneutics, tradition, and reason," "hermeneutics and deconstruction." "hermeneutics and social science," "hermeneutics as politics," "hermeneutics of modernity," "hermeneutics versus science," (sometimes hermeneutics is allied with science, sometimes opposed to science, sometimes demanded by science), "the hermeneutics of the subject," "postmodern literary hermeneutics," "religion, literature, and hermeneutics," "feminist hermeneutics," "philosophical hermeneutics," "transcendence and hermeneutics," "T. S. Eliot and hermeneutics," "Yeats' autobiography and hermeneutics," "energetics and hermeneutics," "hermeneutics and critical theory," "Jung's challenge to biblical hermeneutics," "hermeneutics and the social structure of language," and so on and on and on (Ong, "Hermeneutic").

VII. The Technologizing of Verbalization

With the technologizing of verbalization, beginning with writing (the commitment of evanescent sound, which is not a thing but an event, to a manufactured visual object), the use of words to an extent takes on special qualities associated with information systems rather than communication systems as such (Ong "Writing"). Oral communication is not a technology: it uses no tools and produces no product, leaves no residue. Spoken words exist only when they are going out of existence. Spoken words are not things: they are events (Ong, *Presence*). When I pronounce *existence*, the *exis-* has to be gone by the time I get to the *-tence*, or I am simply incomprehensible.

The movement of spoken words is allied to the movement of thought itself, which is also an event, although thought is not simply a parallel to words. We cannot possibly describe in its entirety all that goes on in us, unconsciously and consciously (through information systems built into our physiology, through our human reflectiveness, etc.) when we think. But even when thinking comes to a head in such cardinal actions as the juncture of subject and predicate in propositional statement, thought moves in time. *The kangaroo is a marsupial* proceeds in time from the subject to the predicate: the term *marsupial* comes along after the *kangaroo* is gone. Sounds and the thoughts they register are not abiding products at all. They can be recalled an infinite number of times successively: They cannot be stabilized, immobilized in time.

Text and Sound

Writing is a technology. It uses tools (Clanchy 88-115) and produces a material product, which we call a text. A text is a physical object, which can be moved around in ways suggesting moving information over a "channel." But text is also related by code to always evanescent sound (DeFrancis), to which, if it is to convey meaning, the text has to be reduced once more by being read (that is, reconstituted as sound either interiorly in the imagination or exteriorly). Read, the text functions as communication. Restoring a physically quiescent text to sound runs it through time, syllable after syllable, word after word, for as just noted, sound itself always runs through time.

Text as Information

Although its aim is communication, the inscribed text itself, as the *object* that it is—written, printed, or computerized—can be viewed as belonging in a way to the world of information rather than the world of communication, as these terms have been distinguished here. Once a text is inscribed, it enjoys existence as a physical object, and this existence is independent of human communication, of an active sender or receiver. The physical text exists independently of its originator (who may well be dead) and, until it is read (sounded), exists independently of any recipient or recipients. It is not of itself an exchange between living human beings, as are spoken words, which are in themselves not simply information but communication. Because the technologizing of the words in texts assimilates words to things, which can be accumulated and kept in place, text encourages compilation in the sense of convenient spatial juxtaposition of written verbal materials for visual retrieval. With texts record-keeping comes into its own—as against tallying by notches or strokes (one notch or stroke equals one of whatever is being tallied—see Schmandt-Besserat). The greater part of the earliest writing we have, in Mesopotamian cuneiform, is especially thing-like in that it registers economic transactions (Ong, *Orality* 48). Early writing is not "literature" in the sense of belles lettres. The use of writing for aesthetic verbal effects came later, and its use for highly interiorized, personalized communication between living individuals much later still.

Text as Pretext

Yet all text is pretext. It is pretext in the sense that the words and thoughts that go into it have an antecedent oral existence at least in the imagination—a pretextual existence. It is pretext also in the sense that a text does to a degree pretend to be what it is not: spoken words. For—and this paradox is absolutely ineradicable from the textual situation—text, as has been indicated, functions precisely as text, and not simply as one more inert visual and tactile object that we encounter, only when it is lifted from the visual field to the auditory field, either in the imagination or in external, oral speech, and made to move in the reconstituted, nonvisual world of sound—only when it is no longer simply visible text.

If writing encouraged the engagement of sounded words with marks in space, print did so even more, for once type had been set, an indefinite number of copies could be produced from it mechanically. Handwritten texts belonged to a less mechanical world: The words in the text to be copied normally passed through the vocalized consciousness of the scribe. Printed pages were simply produced mechanically on a press. Until read—that is, until converted into something more than just print—they belonged to the world of information. By the mid-1700s print had reached the point where it was flooding the commercial market with what in our present perspectives can be seen as huge information banks—such as Samuel Johnson's *English Dictionary* (1755) and Diderot's and d'Alembert's *Enclopédie ou dictionnaire raisonné des arts, des sciences, and des métiers* (1751-1772).

The age of dictionaries and encyclopedias and other materials processing words coded in writing for convenient visual retrieval immediately preceded the time when hermeneutics, labeled as such, became a major preoccupation of European scholars, largely in the nineteenth century (Gadamer 146-47). Compilations of information continued to grow apace until the advent of the computer, when information storage entered a new phase in which information compilation and manipulation had prospects it could never have had before in cultures which, by eighteenth-century and subsequent standards, we can see were information-poor.

The ages of writing and print moved verbalization into the age of "secondary orality," that is, orality produced by machines devised through the use of reading and writing and print—radio, television, and associated mechanical creations (Ong, *Interfaces* 298-99). In this age, sound itself is produced technologically and the resulting manufactured spoken words become like things. Spoken words (and other sounds) can be retrieved at will, as spoken words in primary oral cultures—cultures without writing—cannot be.

VIII. The Presence of Presence

Attention to the ultimately "I"-"you" ground of all communication brings awareness that the "presence" that fills communication is a "presence" not of names or of things, but of persons, who figure in communication not as named items, but simply as self and other, as "I" and "you." "I" and "you" and their equivalents in languages other than English are unique among words. They advertise a person-to-person relationship with which even the proper names of the interlocutors interfere. In a conversation, when one interlocutor uses the other's name, the reference of the name is in a way oblique to the fundamental relationships in the dialogue. The name is set off by a pause before and after—indicated in a text by commas: "Would you, Margaret, help us out?" The full "presence" in communication is the conscious personal presence to one another of those in a dialogic, speaking situation, the presence of an "I" to a "you," and of a "you" to an "I."

My name can *re*present me. The "I" that I utter does not *re*present me as a name does, but simply presents me to you, as your "I" presents you to me. One conscious person can be present to another in a way no mere object can be present. Consciousnesses are interpenetrative: In the given context of a given speech act, I can tell that you know that I am present to you and you to me. And you can tell that I know that you know that I am present to you. And so on *ad infinitum*. Without such reflectiveness, there is no full "presence." The "presence" of things, even directly to the senses, is a weak analogy for this personal, interpenetrative presence.

Of course, personal presence in a text is not the same as the presence of two persons to one another in spoken dialogue. And indeed in some texts—such as lists, certain perfunctory reports, and the like—the presence of the text's author can be minimized. But, however remotely, it is there, although it lies in the background. Someone had to make this list, or program this computer. As Leith insists (208-11), the base of computer activity is sociological. Why was the computer program begun this way and not another way? The answer will have to be found in human society, not in a computer.

In "literary" texts (as against such relatively impersonal discourse as a list), the presence of the person of the author of a text and the person of the reader is insistent, directly or indirectly. In the course of literary history, this presence may be exquisitely derivative and complex, as we have been made well aware by the flood of printed works—and talk—on intertextuality with which we are surrounded. Bakhtin has insisted that such derivative and complex relations between the person of the author and the person of the reader are to be found par excellence, and in their greatest complexity, in the novel, but that, however complexly realized, a personal and somehow interactive presence remains even there.

I - You, and Discourse

All discourse, that is to say, every speech act, spoken, written, printed, or computerized, rests somewhere, however remotely, in I-you dialogue. In our reader-response milieu, we need no longer be told that different readers—each of whom is a different "I"—react to the same text with different responses that call up different potentials within the text itself. Although "the writer's audience is always a fiction" (see Chapter 22), it is still a personalized fiction and involves personal presence, at whatever distance and with whatever variety. In the reading of any text, there is an "I" (or "we") at one end, however obscurely or self-effacingly or disguisedly or fugitively, and a "you" at the other. Words ultimately do not generate themselves: They derive from persons. No computer can say "I."

"I" is not a marker, such as deconstructionists refer to. It is self-referential. It comes from within personal consciousness, and no one else can say "I" and make it mean what I mean when I say "I." You will say, "Yes, I can. I mean 'I' in the sense you mean it when you say 'I.'" But here it is the "you" that carries the burden. No matter how great the number of individuals in the universe is, one feels no real danger that one of them will be a duplicate me, saying an "I" that means what I mean when I say "I."

IX. Conclusion

The present age is referred to sometimes as the information age and sometimes as the communication age. We have seen here that there is warrant for both because of the interrelation between communication (among conscious, reflective human persons) and information (impersonal and not necessarily conscious at all). Conscious communication can build into itself an indefinite amount of information and today is exponentially increasing the amount of information it is accessing. Recorded and retrievable as communication in countless manuscripts, books, and in computerized storage, this information-within-communication is doubtless billions of times as great as it was, let us say, a century ago. In this sense, our age is distinctively a communication age. Communication has laid hold of information in quantities and to degrees unimaginable to earlier generations.

The reason why the field of communication is so enlarged today is less developments within the interpersonal field of communication, with its always present symbol system, than it is developments enlarging immeasurably the information systems available for possession and/or retrieval by human consciousness. But much of the information incorporated or capable of being incorporated into human consciousness cannot as yet be integrated into other information accessible to consciousness so that most of the information accessible to the mind remains in a deep sense unprocessed. Such is the state of most of the huge quantities of information now available through the computerized "information highway."

For this reason it appears more warranted to style ours an information age rather than a communication age. Even as communicators, we are captives of information, for uninterpreted information can create an information chaos and, indeed, has done so, and quite clearly will always do so. Information-wise, we don't know which end is up. Hermeneutics (interpretation) remains a major concern, and will so remain for the foreseeable future, because of the felt need to interpret in depth what the information is around and in us and to realize what it all does or can mean.

Our evident inability to create a hermeneutic adequate to interpret the information flooded into human consciousness shows the plight we are permanently in. Human life must be ultimately managed humanly by more than information-plus-hermeneutic, which is to say by what it has always been managed by when it has been humanly managed, that is, by interpersonal and intergroup personal interaction and the love of human beings for one another that has held human society together, when it has been humanly held together, from the start of humankind. Information and also hermeneutic are, so far as accessible, helpful and necessary, but in the last analysis they are inadequate to the world lying ahead. The ultimate solution to human existence cannot be found in anything humanly accessible. Yet we hope for a solution. So long as we hope, we must be reaching for a solution that lies beyond mere information—in the human lifeworld, and, believers will be convinced, in access to a personal God.

Works Cited

Bakhtin, M. M. 1981. *The Dialogic Imagination: Four Essays.* Trans. C. Emerson and M. Holquist. Ed. M. Holquist. Austin: U. of Texas P, 1981. (Original 1975).

Bizzell, P. and B. Herzberg, eds. *The Rhetorical Tradition: Readings from Classical Times to the Present.* Boston: Bedford Books of St. Martin's P, 1990.

Bolter, J. David. *Writing Space: The Computer, Hypertext, and the History of Writing.* Hillsdale, NJ: Lawrence Erlbaum Associates, 1991.

Clanchy, M. T. *From Memory to Written Record: England 1066-1307.* Cambridge, MA: Harvard UP, 1979.

DeFrancis, John. *Visible Speech: The Diverse Oneness of Writing Systems.* Honolulu: U of Hawaii P, 1989..

Gadamer, Hans-Georg. *Truth and Method.* Eds. G. Barrett and J. Cumming. New York: Crossroad, 1975. (Original 1960).

Kennedy, George A. "A Hoot in the Dark: The Evolution of General Rhetoric." *Philosophy and Rhetoric* 25 (1992): 1-22.

Lanham, Richard A. *The Electronic Word: Democracy, Technology, and the Arts.* Chicago: U of Chicago P, 1993.

Leith, Philip. *Formalism in AI and Computer Science.* New York: Ellis Horwood, 1990.

McLuhan, Marshall and Quentin Fiore. *The Medium Is the Massage.* New York: Bantam, 1967.

New Encyclopedia Britannica. 15th ed. 29 vols. Chicago: Encyclopedia Britannica, Inc., 1998.

Ong, Walter J. "Hermeneutic Forever: Voice, Text, Digitization, and the 'I.'" *Oral Tradition* 10 (1995): 3-26.

—. *Interfaces of the Word: Studies in the Evolution of Consciousness and Culture.* Ithaca, NY: Cornell UP, 1977.

—. *Orality and Literacy: The Technologizing of the Word.* London: Methuen, 1982.

—. *The Presence of the Word: Some Prolegomena for Cultural and Religious History.* New Haven: Yale UP, 1967.

—. "Writing and the Evolution of Consciousness." *Mosaic: A Journal for the Comparative Study of Literature and Ideas* 18 (1985): 1-10.

Schmandt-Besserat, Denise. *Before Writing.* 2 vols. Austin: U of Texas P, 1992.

Sills, Chip and George H. Jensen. *The Philosophy of Discourse: The Rhetorical Turn in Twentieth-Century Thought.* 2 vols. Portsmouth, NH: Boynton/ Cook, 1992.

Stringer, C. B. "The emergence of modern humans." *Scientific American* 263.6 (1990): 98-104.

Walker, Jeffrey. "Before the Beginnings of 'Poetry' and 'Rhetoric': Hesiod on eloquence." *Rhetoric: A Journal of the History of Rhetoric* 14.3 (1996): 243-64.

28

Digitization, Ancient and Modern: Beginnings of Writing and Today's Computers (1998)

A review essay on Schmandt-Besserat, Denise. *Before Writing*. 2 vols.. Austin: U of Texas P, 1992. Pp. xviii + 269; xxxvi + 416.

Prelude

Recent findings have made it possible to see an intriguing relationship between developments leading into writing in its very earliest form and our only recently devised writing with the digital computer.

Historians of writing have noted that the three major early systems of writing in the world, the Sumerian (c. 3000 B.C.), the Chinese (c. 1500 B.C.), and the Mayan (c. A.D. 300), each developed, independently it appears, from a pictographic stage through a rebus stage to the final stage, which, more or less comprehensively, represents sound itself as such by visual symbols (DeFrancis 50, 122). These sequential stages are incontestable, but, it now appears, pictography was not the earliest development leading into full writing. The recent exhaustively documented two-volume work of Denise Schmandt-Besserat, *Before Writing,* has now shown conclusively how the Sumerian pictographic stage was preceded by a still earlier stage using three-dimensional tokens that were initially not pictographic or iconographic at all, but were normally handmade abstract clay figures (cones, spheres, disks, cylinders) constituting numerically discrete units used to process data for reckoning purposes. These are reflections on some deeper implications of Schmandt-Besserat's noteworthy discoveries.

Processing data in terms of numerically distinct units is what is meant by digitization, and digitization thus appears as the earliest crucial development leading directly into Sumerian writing. A curious affinity would seem to exist here between the digitization enforced by today's computers

527

and the first beginnings of the earliest known full writing, Sumerian cuneiform. What this might mean is not a simple question, but one perhaps opening on a deeper understanding both of earlier human culture and of our postmodern age. "Basically," as Florian Coulmas has observed in *The Writing Systems of the World* (9), "microchips are merely a technical improvement on clay tokens." How is our most super-sophisticated modern technology of communication related to the most primitive roots of information processing? Has it returned us somehow to those roots? Or is it perhaps reminding us that we have never left them—at least in the case of alphabetic writing, which initially appeared in the Near East among Semitic peoples in the ambiance of Sumerian cuneiform? Does digitization as such belong fundamentally somehow to the development of writing? Such questions will be raised rather than answered here. Answering them in depth will take some time. Today, we need not be reminded of how tangled the roots of writing have been in the history of the human psyche.

I. Some Digitization in Antiquity

Today we think of digitization commonly, though of course not exclusively, with reference to the binary digitization of the computer and computerized information processing. It must be noted here that digitization is not necessarily binary, as it is in the digital computer, which performs all operations with two digits only, 0 and 1. Division of a mile into 5280 feet is digitization calculating in discrete units within a decimal number system, running 0-1-2-3-4-5-6-7-8-9, rather than within a binary number system, running 0-1. In a binary number system, the counting of four discrete units would be written 1 for one, 10 for two, 11 for three, 100 for four, etc. Here we are considering digitization as concerned with discrete units independently of the way they are expressed in any number system.

Although she had no reason to advert to digitization as such, Schmandt-Besserat's rich discoveries, which are sure to be mined with great profit through coming decades, show how the first cuneiform writing grew out of what we might style conspicuous digitization, that is, a digitization implemented by the use of three-dimensional tokens, rather than out of a digitization operating on a two-dimensional writing surface, the digitization today typically carried out in writing. The tokens were more conspicuously digitizing than two-dimensional digitization on a writing surface in that they were not only discretely numerable, but also so discrete that they were individually manipulable, manually separable from one another. The three-dimensionality and physical manipulability of the tokens makes them and their use a particularly forceful example of digitization. This early digitization gives a new resonance to Jay David Bolter's account of the evolving interrelationships between space and writing in his book *Writing Space*. Space becomes even more spacious when we find three-dimensional digitization leading into the first writing known.

II. A Route Toward Full Writing

It has often been noted that writing as such was not an "invention" in the sense that it was not "a conscious search for the solution to a clearly conceived problem" (DeFrancis 215). What is often called "full writing," in the sense of "a system of graphic symbols that can be used to convey any and all thought" (5), was gradually stumbled upon by persons working over centuries to perfect what were initially clumsy and incomplete visual codes. "Full writing" could not be effectively projected in the imagination until after it had been realized. It was at first not easy to imagine a comprehensive set of silent visual marks that could somehow substitute for the bewildering flow of sounds that users of a given language had for ages employed without reflection. The complete transition from sound to sight was arduous.

I recall seeing a videotape at the University of Dayton in January of 1989 in which a Methodist mission worker was explaining how she had devised a way of writing the previously altogether unwritten language of a native people in one of the South Sea islands where she was living and working. The people were not receptive to the idea. "Our language cannot be written," they insisted. "English and French and other languages can be written, but not ours. We speak it and we know that it cannot." Presumably, they believed that in written languages the spoken language was itself derived from writing—an idea that some purist teachers of English and, correspondingly, of other modern written languages find sympathetic enough. But, even so, despite their misconceptions, the response of these South Sea islanders shows how far apart written language and spoken language can be, how difficult imagining the bridge between what is purely sound and representation of sound exclusively in sight.

Verbal communication had come into existence in human societies initially as sound and to this day is rooted in sound in the sense that sound has been the ultimate foundation, direct or indirect, of all known languages everywhere (DeFrancis 3-19, 47-49, 217), including sign languages, although these latter develop their own special life independent of sound (Wolkomir). No known language has developed out of script alone, independently of oral antecedents direct or indirect. Articulate thought is initially tied directly into sound as into no other sensory field, despite the massive advantages of tying it subsequently into vision in incalculably numerous and complex ways.

The stages leading from sound into full writing, as earlier indicated here, have been commonly studied as beginning with pictographs. A pictograph is a visual illustration, such as a drawing or a painting, used to "stand for" a visualizable object, as a tree or a dog or a tent, and thus used to represent words for such objects in human speech. (Clues concerning precisely how to relate strings of pictographs to one another, how to structure a group of them grammatically, are commonly ambiguous at best.) The next step, the rebus, is crucial. For a rebus is the drawing of a thing that is used not simply to stand for the thing pictured, but rather to call forth the sound of the word suggested by the thing the rebus pictures, as when a picture of a bee is used by English-speakers to call forth the sound *be*. Rebuses signal a major breakthrough: visual designs that stand not for objects but for sounds.

Pictographic systems are numerous across the world, but by far most have died without developing into even the rebus stage or, a fortiori, into full writing. Pictographic systems are all exceedingly limited in what they can express (DeFrancis 47)—none can express, for example, what this present paragraph says. Rebuses as such are more expressive but, as such, are still of very limited serviceability—again, none can express what this paragraph says. Rebus systems have often been deadends, perishing without developing into full writing.

The basic difference between an oral utterance and a text reproducing the utterance should be noted here. An oral utterance is not an object but an event. It leaves no physical residue. Sound exists only when it is going out of existence. Written texts are objects. They can be stored or moved around from one place to another, as sounds cannot be. Today, in addition, texts can of course be put through all sorts of internal as well as external visible movements on an electronic screen, where bits of text can chase one another, absorb one another, turn upside down, shrink, swell up, or simply explode into smithereens. Yet for all their new active intrusion into present time through physical movement, and for all the exterior sound effects in which they may be immersed, texts as texts never take themselves out of their abiding silence, which is to say, they never read themselves. A text in front of you is in itself totally mute. Living persons read, calling forth from within themselves the sounds that the visual marks encode. In computerized sound readings of an inscribed text, the text is not reading itself. The voice the listener hears is not produced by the text, but by a machine, a computer in which an originally live human voice has been electronically tied to the text's visual signals—or to most of them, for perhaps no computerized sound reader encodes all textual visual signals in any given writing system.

The discontinuity between sounded words and sight is what a full writing system bridges. It provides a visual code for the oral sounds in which human verbal expression initially comes into existence. The massive and diversified data showing that all full writing, in any form of inscription at all, does just this in however various ways have been assembled and painstakingly analyzed by DeFrancis in his *Visible Speech: The Diversified Oneness of Writing Systems*. DeFrancis notes that when it had finally evolved to its mature form, Sumerian cuneiform writing "has the distinction of being the earliest system of full writing ever created" (71). Its historical primacy here gives Sumerian cuneiform particular relevance as the primary focus of this present study.

III. Prehistory of Cuneiform Writing

The prehistory of Sumerian cuneiform writing, we now know, begins with the use of the three-dimensional movable tokens earlier referred to. These are deployed and manipulated for accounting purposes. The tokens at first are basically not pictographic or otherwise iconographic, not images of a particular object or commodity, but are simply "small clay counters of many shapes, such as cones, spheres, disks, and cylinders, that served for accounting in prehistory" (Schmandt-Besserat 1:6). They are mostly 1-2 centimeters across, with larger subtypes 3-5 centimeters across (1:17). The tokens are not originally iconographic. Initially a sheep, for example, will not be represented by a token shaped to resemble a sheep, but by a geometrical shape to which the meaning "sheep" has been assigned.

After having labored for nearly two decades with a data bank now consisting of over 10,000 such Near East tokens and their sequels, dating from c. 8000 to c. 3100 B.C. (1:13, 18, 198), Schmandt-Besserat has described in painstaking detail the stages leading from the one-to-one token-based tallying system initially developed for keeping count of agricultural produce and livestock to the development of cuneiform writing. Her work ties in with earlier archaeological and interpretive work by many others whom she cites (1:8-9), notably A. Leo Oppenheim, Pierre Amiet, and Maurice Lambert. But *Before Writing* claims to be and is uniquely inclusive, "the first systematic study of tokens, based on the analysis and interpretation of a selection of eight thousand specimens from 116 sites in Iran, Iraq, the Levant, and Turkey," stored in museums of the Near East, North Africa, Europe, and North America (1:7). The specimens have been excavated over the years by numbers of archaeologists and carefully dated individually.

Near Eastern archaeological sites actually provide information of even earlier primitive reckoning devices consisting of simple notches or other incisions on bones, dating from as early as c. 15,000 B.C. (Schmandt-Besserat 1:118 and *passim*). These notches or incisions are also digital, for they reckon in terms of discrete numerical units (one notch equals one commodity unit), but notches or other incisions on bones serving as reckoning units are not individually maneuverable and could not be so useful for calculating operations as the individual separate, movable, three-dimensional tokens, each token representing a commodity unit, could be.

The development of the use of tokens in the Near East is crucial to the subsequent development of writing, but as Schmandt-Besserat explains,

> Because they were minuscule, colorless, innocuous-looking artifacts, tokens have been mostly ignored, though they are a unique source of information on major aspects of culture during five thousand years of Near Eastern prehistory, including two critical periods: the beginnings of agriculture and cities. They were the precursor of writing and document communication in prehistory. They were the precursors of numerals and shed light on the origin of mathematics. (1:195)

It is noteworthy that the earliest tokens, which have just been referred to here and which Schmandt-Besserat describes as "plain" tokens, are objects of human manufacture, not naturally occurring objects such as pebbles, twigs, or grains, which have been used by many earlier cultures for reckoning in tallying systems—one pebble the equivalent of one coconut, another pebble the equivalent of another coconut, etc. (1:161). The tokens she later describes as "complex" tokens, as will be later explained here, were a fortiori objects of human manufacture. As humanly manufactured objects, the tokens are like writing, which also is made up not of natural units, but is a product of human manufacturing.

Beginning around 8000 B.C. (Schmandt-Besserat 1:198) and continuing through five millennia (1:44), the tokens were hand-molded out of clay, sometimes afterwards baked in an oven or fired in a kiln. In later periods a relatively small number were cut out of stone (1:20-31).

Usually occurring in geometric forms, as earlier noted, the plain tokens are shaped very infrequently into rough "naturalistic shapes such as vessels and animals" (1:27). But most early tokens were abstract geometric shapes. To each different geometric shape a specific meaning was assigned: one shape representing a sheep, another shape a measure of grain, and so on. The tokens were employed initially (1:39, 187, 197, and passim) in a system of simple tallying, using one-to-one correspondence.

In a one-to-one correspondence system, four sheep were represented by four clay tokens each of the shape assigned to a sheep. This one-to-one correspondence system did not entail the notion of "fourness" as such at all, that is, any notion such as ours of a "set" of "four sheep" or of "four" of anything else. You had one sheep and one sheep and one sheep and one sheep, each represented by an individual token, until you came to the last of the tokens being used in a given tally, with no attention to "four" of anything. A tally, in the strict sense of this term, does not use counting at all. That is, it works only by one-to-one correspondence, with no twos or threes or fours, etc.

IV. From Tallying to Cardinal Numbers

Citing numerous works by others as well as earlier work of her own, Schmandt-Besserat reviews the evidence showing how widespread such tallying by tokens in one-to-one correspondence with commodity units (sheep, cattle, measures of grain, etc.) has been in the ultimate development of counting within many cultures. She notes that historians of mathematics find that our present way of counting by the use of cardinal numbers (1, 2, 3, 4, . . . 27, 28 . . .) that are applicable to any sort of object or concept— walnuts or years or clouds or sunsets or smells or flavors or feelings, or imaginative images, or whatever—is the term of a very long evolution.

After simple tallying and before the exploitation of cardinal numbers, one finds what Schmandt-Besserat styles "complex tokens," beginning around 4400 B.C. (1:24-25, 198). These complex tokens were more diversified and marked by greater use of "naturalistic forms." For example, as has earlier been noted, while some few plain tokens were only occasionally given forms related to objects they "stood for" (a plain token might at times be modeled to resemble crudely a dog's head if it was to "stand for" a dog), the complex tokens quite often were shaped as more conspicuously recognizable objects or parts of objects they represented—for example, a particular animal head for a given animal. This was in keeping with the otherwise more complex organization of complex tokens, which often bore also a profusion of markings such as parallel lines and/or crosses and/or "punctuations," that is, depressions punched in various patterns on a token's surface (1:14, 82). Such markings on "complex tokens" could serve to differentiate otherwise similar tokens, for example, by sex so as to distinguish ewes from rams. Thus complex tokens exploited a repertoire of forms far greater than that of the "plain tokens."

The advent of complex tokens was connected with the beginning of the redistributive economy that marks urban life, when certain urban dwellers (merchants) received animals and agricultural produce from farmers and redistributed the animals and produce as demanded and paid for by city dwellers (1:176-77). The latter, in turn, could again redistribute what they got from the farmers to the temple bureaucracy or elsewhere. Within the city, other urban dwellers became manufacturers of new products for distribution to other persons by barter or otherwise.

In the varied urban settings, the complex tokens could readily differentiate the growing variety of commodities being dealt with, as the plain tokens could not. However, the use of complex tokens (Schmandt-Besserat 1:49-92) did not signal the total abandonment of the plain tokens, although it did open the way for many further developments in the history of information processing—for information processing was exactly what the use of tokens was all about. The markings on the complex tokens are not all decipherable, but some are, for they continue after the development of cuneiform writing, which at times notes explicitly the meaning of certain otherwise undecipherable token markings (1:151).

With the advent of complex tokens, earlier types of counting were not immediately displaced by cardinal numbers, even when operations did not all continue in the one-to-one correspondence stage of tallying (1:185-87). Intermediate between the use of tallying and the use of cardinal numbers, came the use of "concrete" counting. Concrete counting uses not just one-to-one correspondence, but also "sets." One complex token alone was now at times used to symbolize three sheep, in place of the original three separate tokens representing one sheep and one sheep and one sheep. Here we find operative the notion of a numerical set, a number of things of the same kind lumped together. Simple one-for-one tallying is transcended. But the number symbols are not applicable to anything at all, as in the case with cardinal numbers. The numbers are "concrete," in the sense that there are different sets of numbers representing different commodities. Three sheep are symbolized by one token, but this token is specialized in that it can represent only three sheep. Three jars of oil can be represented by one symbol alone, but it can represent only three jars of oil.

Cardinal numbers appear at a later stage and, as noted earlier, represent a major advance in thought. The "sets" in concrete counting are not abstract, but are all sets of one or another kind of thing: a set of sheep or a set of cattle, and so on. Cardinal numbers are different: they are pure abstractions, human constructions. Cardinal numbers are empty sets. They are more difficult to conceive of than "concrete" numbers attached to named items. Outside the mind, in nature, there can be no such thing as free-floating numbers of nothing at all, applicable to anything. Outside the mind, in nature, there are simply individual existents. The "empty" sets that we style cardinal numbers, can be filled with any kind of item: the number 2 or 6 or 365 can "contain" indifferently trees or rocks or days or colors or thoughts or clouds or carnivorous animals or pixels, and on *ad infinitum*. "Sets" of things of the same kind—a "set" or group of six trees or six dogs or seven days such as occurs in concrete counting—can be conceived of more readily than purely cardinal numbers.

V. Simplicity to Complexity: Urban Life

Schmandt-Besserat notes field work and studies that show that many cultures, some still extant, count only to two or three and after that designate all quantities simply as "many." Until the past century, the Weddas of Sri Lanka had "no specific word for numbers beyond expressions such as "a single," "a pair," "one more," and "many" (1:184). Wishing to indicate how many coconuts he had, a Wedda resorted to one-to-one tallying, without any count at all. He gathered a bundle of sticks and "to each coconut assigned one stick: one nut = one stick. When he had matched each individual coconut with an individual stick, he merely pointed to his pile of sticks and said, 'that many'" (1:185). Later, the pile of sticks enabled him to verify directly that all his coconuts were there—which might be all he wanted to know. If he found that there were one or two more sticks with no corresponding coconuts, something was wrong. He might have been robbed. The use of abstract cardinal numbers could be initially inconvenient not only because such numbers do not occur in nature, but also because simple tallying by matching stick-to-coconut could be quite serviceable with no counting at all.

It is noteworthy also that tokens as such were useful for multilingual data processing since they did not represent words as such, but like the Weddas' sticks, were simply one-for-one coordinates for commodities, and thus could be understood by persons speaking languages other than that spoken by the originator of the tokens (Schmandt-Besserat 1:161, 164). In scrupulous detail, Schmandt-Besserat carefully traces the sequence of changes whereby further stages of tallying, of "concrete counting," and eventually of counting by cardinal numbers followed one another in the Near East in the use of clay tokens. These stages were not clear-cut. As has been noted earlier, they often overlapped: a given place might be calculating at some places in one stage and at other places in another or even using earlier and later forms of calculating simultaneously in the same place. One can observe that the propensity of tokens to generate cardinal-number counting is striking evidence of their affiliation to digitization in its common meaning of conversion of data to numerical form or calculation by numerical methods or discrete units.

With cardinal numbers, the mind could focus on numbers as such, pure and simple, in themselves not referring to anything other than themselves. Mathematics became possible, and with mathematics, it would appear, so did Platonic "ideas" and their attendant philosophy.

Schmandt-Besserat points out that tokens were major developments in societies in which they are found, central enough to Near Eastern cultures to be used for ceremonial purposes such as funerary offerings (1:41, 103-04, etc.). Throughout (e.g., 1:11), she expresses her awareness that her work, for all its thoroughness, will of course have to be supplemented by further work. But it is safe to say that she has shown in great particularity and with great success the overall pattern of the developments growing out of the use of clay tokens in prechirographic and protochirographic cultures of the Near East (1:195-99). She is careful to relate tokens and their evolution and sequels to the larger human context, social, economic, technological, and other.

VI. Concrete to Abstract

Use of "concrete counting" such as is found in many early cultures exists residually today even in high-tech cultures, which regularly use cardinal numbers for counting anything and everything and which are otherwise hospitable to all sorts of abstractions. Many languages today, including English, still retain some few instances of "concrete counting." Thus, in English, the term trio, for example, merges the number 3 with the item counted—you can have a trio of musicians, but not of rivers or planets or thunderstorms (Schmandt-Besserat 1:186). Or again, we speak of a "brace" of quail, but a "pair" of dice, or a "couple" of hours or of people or of acres. You never have a brace of hours or a pair of miles. Developmental psychologists report that toddlers asked to count a number of pencils find something like concrete counting more congenial. They find it easier to count more homogeneous elements, such as blue pencils or red pencils, but have to be coaxed into counting the total of both blue and red pencils together (1:186). The complex concrete ways of counting from one to ten still imperative in modern Japanese are well known (see Ogawa and Sato 58-69): one series of numbers is used for thin, flat objects such as paper; another for machines and vehicles; another for smaller things such as nuts, candy, cakes, boxes, watches (but not pills or grain); another series for stick-like or linear things such as pencils, trees, lines, hairs, rails, belts; another for bound sheets of paper such as books or notebooks; another for insects, worms, fish, cats and smaller dogs; another for larger animals such as horses and elephants and larger dogs; another for birds (with which are included here rabbits!); another for people; another for days, and so on. This object-discriminatory counting remains in a sense basically "concrete."

Counting by cardinal numbers, as suggested earlier, is by contrast quite definitely abstract in that cardinal numbers are not of themselves linked to anything but other cardinal numbers. Although they may have been generated by dealing at first with fixed kinds of things, when they become cardinal numbers, they are separated or "abstracted" from everything else.

In the evolution of the use of tokens, one can recognize signs of the underlying movement from the more totalizing or aggregative mentality marking oral cultures generally, a mentality at times represented by numbers bound to a certain kind of commodity, to the more analytic or disjunctive thinking marked by distinctions or separations. Cardinal numbers are in themselves "empty," as has been seen, and thus in themselves distinct from everything they encompass. (See Ong, *Orality* 38-39, with references to Claude Lévy-Strauss and others). With the developments in handcrafted tokens toward the more abstract, writing is in the offing among the ancient Sumerians. Of course, it should be noted that all human thinking is to some degree abstract. Abstraction does not by any means originate with writing, but writing—abetted today by its sequel, computerization—encourages the development of abstraction to an extent so great as to be by today quite incalculable.

VII. Cumbrous Clay Envelopes to the Stylus

At one point in the development of the tokens, it became a practice to store plain tokens in pod-like envelopes made of hollow clay, often closed with a cylinder seal (Schmandt-Besserat 1:68-69) for more or less permanent records or archives (1:68-69, 198), or, alternatively, to perforate and string numbers of tokens together on a cord, with its two ends sealed to each other by a lump of clay embedding both ends and thereby both "identifying the account and preventing any tampering" (1:109), and also serving for more or less permanent recording. In a subsequent development, beginning c. 3500 B.C. some envelopes bear on the outside marks corresponding to the number of tokens inside: thus, five enclosed tokens (each representing, for example, one sheep) were indicated by five corresponding outside marks, and so on. These marks were sometimes made as simple lines, or sometimes made by impressing a given kind of token (e.g., the token for a sheep) the requisite number of times on the outside of the clay envelope when the clay was still wet (1:198-99 and passim). With these stable collections of individual tokens, some sort of representation of a "set" (5 in the instance here; or 7, 10, etc.) had been accomplished, but the number for the set was not fully abstract but still "concrete" in the sense just mentioned: each token represented by the individual mark referred to one unit of only the specific type of commodity that the token represented. But a container inevitably grouped the individual marks into a set of 5 or whatever number of units the container held and thus doubtless furthered thinking in sets in place of single-unit tallies. This use of clay pod-like containers or envelopes is found in the period c. 3700-1200 B.C. (1:198).

With their enclosed set of tokens, the pod-like clay containers or envelopes were serviceable to prevent cheating that might be carried on by changing the marks on the outside: if you added to an original five marks another sixth one, breaking open the container would detect the fraud. But this created a problem: to verify the number of marks of a given commodity made on the outside of the container, the container had to be broken open. At this point, the tokens that had been inside could themselves be added to or subtracted from or dispersed—so that, in effect, verification by resort to the inside tokens was a one-time verification, and thus of relatively little worth. Strings of a given number of tokens, with the ends of the string tied and sealed in a lump of hardened clay, were more useful than tokens in a pod—the number of tokens was stabilized and always visible: they could be counted over and over again as discrete units for recording or verification purposes.

But the strings of tokens were cumbersome to store and manipulate. A new step was taken when in the period 3500-3100 B.C. the pods or envelopes with their enclosed tokens were superseded by simple clay tablets with impressed markings on their surfaces like those that had been made on the clay containers, but of course, with no enclosures, that is, with no tokens inside since the flat clay tablets had no inside in which to store tokens or anything else. They were much thicker than a sheet of paper today, but no more than a sheet of paper did they have a hollow interior. On the early containers "the markings only repeated the information encoded in tokens for the convenience of accountants" (Schmandt-Besserat 1:154).

With the tablet stage, a new technology came into play: reed styluses altogether replaced the tokens (1:137-39). Impressing a plain token into the surface of a clay envelope-pod produced only an imprint of that kind of token. Tokens produced only signs of themselves. Reed styluses were truly instruments, designed not to reproduce their own shapes as reeds, but to produce any number of differing signs. Once it became the practice to incise signs by designing them with a reed stylus instead of simply impressing fixed-design tokens into the clay surface of containers or of early tablets, a way to full writing was opened, for the stylus was a versatile writing instrument suited to forming designs of limitless sorts, including stylized pictographs of commodities and objects for which there had never been any equivalent in tokens (1:199, 159, and *passim*). Thus used "abstractly," that is, not for their own concrete shapes but for other designs that they could create, styluses belonged to the more abstract world encouraged by writing. Cuneiform (that is, "wedge-shaped") writing was the product of using styluses to form various and limitless designs out of wedge-shaped gouges on a wet clay surface, subsequently dried or baked or fired for permanency.

For all this, the evolution of writing as such moved at a snail's pace. As noted earlier above, the stages of development in the use of the plain tokens and their various sequels overlapped, and after the development of clay tablets and even of clay tablets marked with a stylus, some use of tokens still lingered, although it dwindled (1:198).

VIII. Numeracy Before Literacy

The succession from token impressions to stylus-created markings is clear from massive diggings at Uruk, well known as "the first and foremost Sumerian city" and located in southern Mesopotamia (now modern Iraq). Uruk has yielded "the largest and most varied collection of complex tokens ever recovered in a fourth-millennium site" (Schmandt-Besserat 1:49). Here archaeological soundings at the deepest levels have surfaced complex tokens marked on the outside by impressing various plain tokens into the complex tokens' surfaces, while soundings at higher archaeological levels (representing more recent deposits) have surfaced "the first precursors of the Sumerian incised signs, traced with a stylus" (1:68).

Pictographs, which the stylus made possible and encouraged, show a relative abstractness. Even though each pictograph more or less resembled what it "stood for" and in that sense was "concrete," pictographs also reveal a relative abstractness in that they have never been found repeated in one-to-one correspondence as tokens and token imprints had been—that is, pictographs never occur, for example, with one pictograph to represent one sheep, another pictograph to represent a second sheep, etc. Instead, at the pictograph stage multiples of pictographs were indicated by a mark for one of the cardinal numbers (2, 3, 4, 6, 10, and so on), which as has been seen are significantly abstract concepts, no longer entailing the "concrete counting" that had separate kinds of numbers for different kinds of items being counted.

Cardinal numbers could of course possibly have been much earlier known and used orally in Sumerian culture and other cultures independently of any inscriptions. But, in fact, as the foregoing account here indicates, they came into use in the inscriptions themselves in a quite indirect way, as a late spinoff from a millennia-old technology, the technology of manufacturing three-dimensional clay tokens for reckoning items present within the ambiance of the user's lifeworld.

This circumstantial prehistory of writing worked out in painstaking detail by Schmandt-Besserat shows the tortuous complexity of the road to writing among the Sumerians (who, we recall again, developed the first full writing in the world). Their writing clearly does not begin with two-dimensional pictographic designs, as chirographic folk of today might imagine. The history is psychologically and even physiologically far more complicated and introverted. The road to writing was worked out of a three-dimensional representational world. We think of early writing as typically using two-dimensional designs to represent things or concepts. In reality here, the first steps toward writing among the Sumerians used three-dimensional things to represent other three-dimensional things. There writing emerged from a kind of prototypic objectocentrism in a way that might have serious implications for theories of logocentrism.

In any event, the prototypical three-dimensional world of the Sumerians record-keeping was initially a world of digitization, always processing data of various sorts in discrete numerical units. In Sumerian history, numeracy is antecedent to literacy, Schmandt-Besserat has made clear. Other writing systems may have other prehistories. However, the Sumerian system was temporally antecedent to the development of all other writing systems, though discontinuous from other systems except perhaps to some degree the alphabet.

IX. Technologizing the Evanescent Oral Word

Oral speech, the only form of verbalization known to Homo sapiens since the species first appeared some 150,000 years ago until only some 6000 years ago, is not a technology and involves no technology at all. The spoken word consists of sound produced in present time from living organisms. Oral speech needs no tools and, in itself, leaves no residue. Sounds are not things but events, as has earlier been seen. Sound is evanescent, not of itself enduring. Sound exists only when it is going out of existence.

As sounds, spoken words are also events, sound events in time, existing only when they are going out of existence. Sound always signals the present use of power. I can see a buffalo, smell a buffalo, touch a buffalo, and taste a buffalo when the buffalo is inert or dead. But if I hear a buffalo, I had better watch out. Something is going on. Sound is always "alive," indicating that some physical action is going on. Although we tend to, or learn to, disregard the fact, writing inevitably and always misrepresents each and every word it records in the sense that writing makes the word seem somehow present as a whole all at once. No word, of however short duration, can be present all at once. In reading a fixed text, the reader must introduce the coded marks constituting the visible text into the temporal and evanescent sound world, either exteriorly in vocal sound or in his or her imagination. This is what reading consists in: sounding in a moving time sequence what is signaled by an immobile visual code. When I read the word "existence" from a fixed text, either by audible vocalizing or in my auditory imagination, I project into moving time the motionless textual codification: when I get to the "-tence," the "exis-" is gone. Otherwise, if the syllables were all sounded simultaneously, the sound, and thus of course the text itself, would be unintelligible, even though in the text the word from beginning to end, and whole pages of words, exist all at once, as they cannot when vocalized by a speaker or reader.

This is not at all to say that the written word is no more than a stand-in for the oral word. When words are written, they undergo all sorts of changes that can affect human thought and the entire human lifeworld. About these changes, there is now a huge literature, being added to daily (see Ong, *Orality* passim, with the hundreds of references there, and consult the plethora of current databases).

At the root of the changes from sound to visual text is the fact that unlike oral speech, writing is a technology, just as much as Sumerian token production was. Writing is a physical product manufactured by working with materials and with tools. Over the centuries, writing would become more and more technological, which is to say more and more artificial. This does not make it inhuman, but eminently more human. For there is nothing more natural for a human being than to be artificial. The technology of writing is subject to many non-technological human activities.

To make inscriptions, of which handwriting is the earliest form, a better and better product, writing would become more and more technological. Artisans would develop better and better prepared surfaces of papyrus, parchment, and eventually paper, specially manufactured pens or brushes and ink, inkhorns of hollow cattle horns (ink must be mordant, biting into the surface to which it is applied, and, when stored, its corrosive effects are resisted by horns in earlier ages when glass was expensive). To sharpen the goose-quill writing pens, small knives would be made (we still speak of and use "pen knives," though seldom any more to sharpen pens).

Writing not only uses tools, but does so in order to create a physical object distinct from the person producing the object. That is, it manufactures a text. Any text is a technological product, a physical object distinct from the person producing it. Most of the books in the world today have been written by people now dead, often long dead. The author's absence makes no difference: without him or her, the text still "holds" the same words.

Technologies of writing have varied in different cultures. For example, in East Asia writing was for centuries done with carefully manufactured brushes rather than with pens, and ink for the brushes was not liquid but supplied by a solid ink block. Here we cannot attend to all the diverse writing technologies developed over the ages (see Clanchy, DeFrancis) but will remain with some of the developments following the Sumerian and related Near East developments, particularly those involving the alphabet.

X. The Alphabet: Orality-Friendly and Computer-Friendly

The alphabet was "invented" only once, among the Semitic peoples of the Near East, following on the development of cuneiform writing by the Sumerians (who were neighbors but, as earlier noted, apparently were not a Semitic people). All alphabets in the world—from the Greek and Roman to the Korean and later alphabets—trace, directly or indirectly, to the Semitic alphabet (Ong, *Orality* 85-93). This suggests that the alphabet was desperately difficult to come upon. Like the first writing of the Sumerians, it was stumbled into by persons not making "a conscious search for the solution to a clearly conceived problem" (DeFrancis 215), but working for better ways of bridging the orality-writing gap, which they were only gradually managing to deal with effectively and expertly.

No other writing system has been accommodated to so many different languages and cultures as has the alphabet (DeFrancis 174-208). The designs of the various letters of the alphabet can vary from one alphabet to another. A given alphabet may represent the phoneme *m* by a design not visually resembling the *m* of the Roman (and English) alphabet, and so with all letters. Alphabets also may and do vary somewhat in the number of letters they use to accommodate the varying number of phonemes in various languages. But whatever the design and number of the letters, the basic alphabetic principle can accommodate to any and all spoken languages. The reason is that this basic principle operates in the visual field in the basic way oral speech operates in all languages: oral speech combines meaningless units of sounds to make meaningful words. In the word *dog*, the sound *d* means nothing, the sound *o* means nothing, and the sound *g* means nothing. But put together in the proper order, in English they mean dog. Ideally, an alphabet for a given language works this same way in the field of vision, where it has a separate meaningless letter for each individual phoneme in the language—phonemes being sounds that in a given language distinguish one meaning from another: in English the sound *p* in pit and the sound *f* in fit are two different phonemes yielding two different meanings although each is followed by the same sound, *-it*. All alphabets have this basic principle, but all at times compromise to a degree. To represent all its phonemes, English, for example, would need some forty letters. In fact, English uses the letter *a* for three different phonemes in *ape, at, all*. English also uses different letters or combinations of letters for the same phoneme, as the *f, ph*, and *gh*, in *fish, phone, cough*. But the principle remains generally applicable: one letter for each phoneme, one meaningless visual mark (letter) for each meaningless differentiating sound (phoneme).

The alphabet is unique among writing systems in that it is distinctively orality-friendly and computer-friendly. It is orality-friendly because, as has just been noted, it operates visually the way all speech in any language operates orally: oral words are made up of meaningless sounded phonemes, and alphabetically spelt words are made up of corresponding meaningless visible letters, one for each phoneme as a general principle (with some exceptions, as noted, that must be learned individually).

The alphabet is computer-friendly for reasons allied to those that make it orality-friendly: the English alphabet provides the computer with twenty-six meaningless letters out of which an absolutely unlimited number of meaningful words can be constructed. The editor's Preface states that *Webster's Third New International Dictionary* lists over 350,000 words and that "it would have been easy to make the vocabulary larger," but that would have called for a multivolume work. The multivolume *Oxford English Dictionary* contains only 290,500 "main entries," but provides more information on its entries. No one knows, or can know, how many words there are in English—or any other living language—made out of the repertoire of phonemes in a given language. Words can be added in indefinite numbers and are being added to English annually and daily and hourly. The English alphabet, like other alphabets, opens into a computer hacker's unbounded paradise.

Nonalphabetic writing systems, notably the Chinese, which can have advantages of various sorts over the alphabet, are severely handicapped for computer use (DeFrancis 266-67, etc.), chiefly because they lack a system of "clean" characters divested of all meaning. Chinese today can be written in an alphabetic text known as Pinyin, but cultural resistance to Pinyin is massive, and Pinyin would indeed make impossible the retention and conveyance of the rich layers of multiplex meanings with which individual Chinese characters are visually loaded. But to try to manage efficiently on a computer over 40,000 different characters, each loaded with often multiple nondetachable meanings, is a challenge that computer programmers simply cannot meet directly.

XI. Digitization, Alphabetization, and Print

The various alphabets have generally a fixed order in which the individual letters are situated when the alphabet is recited. In English, the order a, b, c, d, . . . z is as fixed as that of the numerical digits 0, 1, 2, 3, . . . 9. Our word alphabet derives from the first two letters of the Hebrew alphabet, fixed in order with the rest of the alphabet: aleph (a) and beth (b). An individual who does not "know the alphabet"—which is to say, cannot repeat its letters automatically in their accepted fixed order—is impossibly handicapped in an alphabetic literate culture. Alphanumeric systems are forms of digitization. Merging the order of the letters of the alphabet with the order of cardinal numbers, alphanumeric systems can of course be used in handwritten script as well as its sequels, printing from movable alphabetic type and, most intensively, in computer operations.

From its beginning in the mid-1400s, letterpress printing from movable alphabetic type created and used a huge number of separate, discrete, countable, cast type metal units each bearing on its face an individual letter of the alphabet or a cardinal number or one of various other symbols—punctuation marks, %, #, and so on, all presorted in regular sequence into a case of type for use in composing text. Each individual type or numerical or other symbol is quite discrete, physically movable as a unit. These discrete units were assembled and locked into position by the tens of thousands and more in a printer's form (also spelt forme). The form was then locked into a printing press for the production of printed text.

(With the invention of the Linotype in 1884, separate letters could be cast together on one "slug" of type metal the required length of each line, so that a page of type was made up of prefabricated lines of letters and other writing units combined into text.)

The maneuvers in alphabetic letterpress printing involved digitization in that they called for operations with discrete units in carefully calculated fashion and with measurements galore for the line, the form, the size of the bed of the press, etc. More recent developments in print, beginning with offset printing and now running through the preparation of press-ready copy on computer disks, have drastically reorganized printing procedures and in doing so have only advertised more and more spectacularly the connection of print with digitization. The binary digitization of the computer governs the present-day equivalents of the earlier and grosser forms of digitization, speeding them up astronomically.

But before our more recent and far more complicated digitizing developments, the world opened by print had shown its digitizing tendencies in ways still not all accounted for. The very existence of print soon favored the production in great quantity of dichotomized or binary outlines structured as today's binary computer flowcharts. Such outlines were known but rare in previous manuscript cultures because hand-copying of detailed branched dichotomized outlines was arduous and sure to result in many errors. Once such binary outlines had been set up and locked into place in type, hammering out perfect copies by the hundreds was easy.

Probably the most spectacular binary representations produced by print can be found in the hundreds of editions of printed books featuring dichotomized (that is, binary) outlines of human knowledge produced by the sixteenth-century educational reformer Peter Ramus (Pierre de la Ramée, 1515-1572) and his thousands of followers (Ong, *Ramus*). In these binary outlines, found in hundreds of editions of books by Ramus and his followers, they constructed by the dozens what are in effect binary flowcharts suitable for computer programs without having as yet any idea at all of what a computer might be (see Ong, *Ramus*, paperback vii-viii; Freedman, "Philosophical," "Diffusion"; and the discussion in Leith 73-91). Ramism, supported by the digitizing bent of print, is a major span in the bridge between print and the computer.

XII. Some Digitizing Associations of Human Thought

The full history of digitization is certainly more complex than are the developments followed here, however central these may be. Aware of their limited scope, as well as their importance as leading into and on beyond the first full writing system known, what are we to make of these developments?

The movement of verbalization from its initial oral field of speech into the visual field of writing and its sequels of print and electronics was momentous and has by now been the subject of a vast number of studies. The development of digitization, more and more dominant in information and communication systems today, is tied to this movement from sound to sight.

Vision presents its objects as extended in space. Texts, written or printed or electronic, exist in visual space, and hence are extended and divisible objects (see Bolter). As visual, texts invite, at least in the imagination, division into discrete numerical units, which is to say, digitization.

Although the development of writing and print and more recently of electronics moved the dominating economy of verbal communication from the oral-aural world to the visual world of the text, it by no means eliminated the oral, for after the invention of writing, people kept talking as much as ever or, even more. If a text functions truly as a text, it must be read—that is, moved in one way or another, directly or indirectly, from the silent world of the stable visual surface into the always moving, "alive" world of sound. It is thus bound to time, for all sound is an event in time, existing, as has been seen, only when it is going out of existence. Texts can seem to de-emphasize sound, but they can never eliminate it.

The complementary ally of vision is touch, for both vision and touch have to do with the extension of objects in space. The intimate relationship of vision and touch can be seen in the development of Braille texts for the blind. Here touch, not sight, transforms the oral into the spatial.

But vision and touch contrast in their separate relationships to space. Where touch demands maximum proximity—physical contact between the sensory apparatus and its object—vision demands always at least some distance, and in this sense encourages abstraction, in the sense of the distancing of the knower and the known. Physical contact between eyeball and its object makes vision impossible. The eye must be at some distance from its object in order to see, and it negotiates immense distances with ease. We not only see mountain ranges a hundred miles away or more, but we also see stars which are billions of light years away (and thus no longer in the place to which direct eyesight assigns them).

For distancing, sight is more serviceable than touch, for touch always involves immediate awareness of the sensing being as well as awareness of the object sensed. I do not see myself seeing, hear myself hearing, smell myself smelling, or taste myself tasting, but I do feel myself feeling. We tell hardness from softness or the hot from the cold, or the rough from the smooth, etc.—for touch is not one sense, but a bundle of many senses—by feeling self and object simultaneously and experiencing the interaction between the two. Still, despite its involvement with the knowing subject, touch more irrefutably than sight provides evidence of the discreteness of objects that digitization demands. Feeling the space or distance between two objects is often surer evidence that the space is there than observation by sight.

Human understanding of anything profits from its affiliation with both touch and sight in the sense that human knowledge is maximized when it commands both proximity and distance. To know something as fully as possible, we need to be close to it (physically or experientially, intellectually, emotionally, and in every other possible way), and we need at the same time to be distanced from it, to have it "in perspective," an object notably distinct from ourselves. Sound is more distancing than touch (as well as more distancing than the other senses of smell and taste), but never at all so distancing as is sight. Eric A. Havelock, with many others since, has made the point that one of the principal advantages of (visually perceived) writing is the distancing of the knower from the known. Writing represents the object of knowledge as "out there," in the text. The hearers listened to Homeric oral epic songs not to be able to analyze Achilles' and others' characters or motives, not to stand back at a psychological distance and assess the characters and motives "objectively," but to identify with the characters and their motives. The same nonanalytic, appropriative sensibility is found in hearers of other oral epics across the world to this day (Foley *passim*). The auditors listen not to achieve abstract understanding of their culture and its heroes, but precisely to be "with it" (close to it, merged with it). With writing, merging of oneself with the thing known could be and often was downplayed: unlike oral speech, a written text was something "out there," separate from the reader, and knowing came to be felt more and more as a matter of dealing with "objects," separate from the self and analyzable, that is, admitting of intellectual "dissection."

Given that writing is a technological product storing knowledge outside the human individual and thus encouraging a sense of the known as separate from the knower, it appears to be no accident that the prehistory of writing begins with enumeration of visible, material commodities, object-things seen and/or felt as distinct from human thinkers and verbalizers, such as Schmandt-Besserat finds in the commodities with which the Near East tokens deal. This is to say that the object-world in oral mythopoetic cultures innocent of writing tends to be psychologically merged with the subjective world more intimately than is usual in chirographic, or, even more, in print cultures. Plato, who wanted to do away with mythology in favor of hard-nosed logos, although he professed to despise the textualized word, nevertheless produced large numbers of texts and evinces deep textual-visualist alliances in his insistence that the philosopher was not to identify himself with the object of his thought, but ideally to distance himself maximally from all physical objects by betaking himself to the purportedly pure, immaterial, immobile world of "ideas" (the Greek root of which refers to vision and is allied to this English term) (Ong, *Orality* 78-83). This Platonic ideal of distantiation we know was connected with the currency of written texts, unknown in Homer's milieu.

Writing, as has been seen, had been historically exceedingly hard to achieve. The first full writing in human history, as several studies reviewed here have shown, was arrived at only circuitously. Schmandt-Besserat's work shows that the route was more circuitous and complex than had been thought. The earliest known immediate antecedent of writing was not a system of marks on a two-dimensional surface apprehended by vision such as matured texts would be, but rather a three-dimensional system of accounting (Ong, *Orality* 78-83) was both visual and highly tactile in operation, and was in fact a system of digitization in the ordinary sense of this term, calculation by discrete units—as three-dimensional moveable objects, very discrete—even grossly so. Originally, writing was not so much a "communication" device (involving interchange between two conscious persons)—although it was this to some extent—as it was a simple "information" system (a coding system), although it was not entirely this either. The way into writing remains, psychologically and sociologically, somewhat mysterious. At the heart of the mystery is the role that digitization, now matured in the computer, played in the ways human beings stumbled into writing in the first place.

Works Cited

Bolter, Jay David. *Writing Space: The Computer, Hypertext, and the History of Writing*. Hillsdale, NJ: Lawrence Erlbaum Associates, 1991.

Clanchy, M. T. *From Memory to Written Record: England, 1066-1307*. Cambridge, MA: Harvard UP, 1979.

Coulmas, Florian. *The Writing Systems of the World*. Oxford: Basil Blackwell, 1989.

DeFrancis, John. *Visible Speech: The Diverse Oneness of Writing Systems*. Honolulu: U of Hawaii P, 1989. [DeFrancis's work is impressively comprehensive and up-to-date. The literature with which his work interlocks is massive and dizzying, and, for the most part, I make reference to his work alone when dealing with matters where his positions are relevant and are notably well-founded, referring to his ample notes and bibliography the reader who may want to examine other authors perhaps contesting or qualifying DeFrancis's positions. The alternative would be impossible clutter].

Foley, John Miles, ed. *Comparative Research in Oral Traditions: A Memorial for Milman Parry*. Columbus, OH: Slavica Publishers, 1987.

—, ed. *Oral Traditional Literature: A Festschrift for Albert Bates Lord*. Columbus, OH: Slavica Publishers, 1981.

Freedman, Joseph S. "The Diffusion of the Writings of Petrus Ramus in Central Europe, c.1570-c.1630." *Renaissance Quarterly* 46.1 (Spring 1993): 98-153. [Reproduces scores of printed outlines, mostly binary or dichotomized, showing the intrinsic relationship of individual subjects in academic curricula to one another. The binary outlines here are the equivalent of binary computer flow-charts (see Ong *Ramus*, paperback, vii-viii). The science of discovering these relationships was known as *technologia* or, in English, technology (the logos or science of the interrelationship of each *techne* or art to the others—the original meaning of the term "technology").]

—. "Philosophical Instruction within the Institutional Framework of Central European Schools and Universities during the Reformation Era." *History of Universities*, Vol. 5. Oxford: Oxford UP, 1985. 117-66. [Reproduces many outlines continuous with those in Freedman's work here above.]

Havelock, Eric A. *Preface to Plato*. Cambridge, MA: Belknap P of Harvard UP, 1963.

Leith, Philip. *Formalism in AI and Computer Science*. New York and London: Ellis Horwood Division of Simon and Schuster, 1990.

Ogawa, Yoshio and Jun'ichi Sato. *Colloquial Japanese in Four Weeks*. Tokyo: Daigakusyorin, 1963.

Ong, Walter J. *Orality and Literacy: The Technologizing of the Word*. London and New York: Methuen, 1982.

—. *Ramus, Method, and the Decay of Dialogue*. Cambridge, MA: Harvard UP, 1983 (paperback edition with its added Author's Preface to the Paperback Edition). Originally: Cambridge, MA: Harvard UP, 1958.

Schmandt-Besserat, Denise. *Before Writing*. 2 vols. 1. *From Counting to Cuneiform*. 2. *A Catalogue of Near Eastern Tokens*. Austin: U of Texas P, 1992.

—. "Reckoning before Writing." *Archaeology* 32 (1979): 23-31. [All references in the text to Schmandt-Besserat are to the preceding comprehensive work listed here, which subsumes material in this present work.]

Webster's Third New International Dictionary (1961).

Wolkomir, Richard. "American Sign Language: 'It's Not Mouth Stuff—It's Brain Stuff.'" *Linguistics at Work: A Reader of Applications*. Ed. Dallin D. Oaks. Fort Worth, New York, Toronto: Harcourt Brace College Publishers, 1998. 311-21.

Index